SKELETAL TRAUMA

IDENTIFICATION OF INJURIES RESULTING FROM HUMAN RIGHTS ABUSE AND ARMED CONFLICT

SKELETAL TRAUMA

IDENTIFICATION OF INJURIES RESULTING FROM HUMAN RIGHTS ABUSE AND ARMED CONFLICT

Erin H. Kimmerle
José Pablo Baraybar

CRC Press
Taylor & Francis Group
Boca Raton London New York

CRC Press is an imprint of the
Taylor & Francis Group, an **informa** business

CRC Press
Taylor & Francis Group
6000 Broken Sound Parkway NW, Suite 300
Boca Raton, FL 33487-2742

Printed in the United States of America on acid-free paper
10 9 8 7 6 5 4 3

International Standard Book Number-13: 978-0-8493-9269-6 (Hardcover)

Library of Congress Cataloging-in-Publication Data

Kimmerle, Erin H.
Skeletal trauma : identification of injuries resulting from human rights abuse and armed conflict / Erin H. Kimmerle and Jose Pablo Baraybar.
p. ; cm.
"A CRC title."
Includes bibliographical references and index.
ISBN 978-0-8493-9269-6 (alk. paper)
1. Forensic osteology. 2. Musculoskeletal system--Wounds and injuries. 3. Human rights--Health aspects. 4. War victims--Yugoslavia. 5. Torture victims--Yugoslavia. I. Baraybar, Jose Pablo. II. Title.
[DNLM: 1. Forensic Anthropology. 2. Bone and Bones--injuries. 3. Human Rights Abuses. 4. Violence. 5. War Crimes. W 750 K49s 2008]

RA1059.K56 2008
614'.17--dc22 2007034506

Visit the Taylor & Francis Web site at
http://www.taylorandfrancis.com

and the CRC Press Web site at
http://www.crcpress.com

I dedicate this book to my family, Mike, and Sean.

E.H.K.

I dedicate this book to Maite and Sofia

J.P.B.

Contents

A Foreword by Andrew T. Cayley, Esq. ix
A Foreword by Morris Tidball-Binz, M.D. xi
Preface xiii
Acknowledgments xv
Abbreviations xxv

1 An Epidemiological Approach to Forensic Investigations of Violations to International Humanitarian and Human Rights Law 1

Case Study 1.1: Firefight in Lima: Wounded/Killed Ratio Analysis of MRTA Casualties in the 1997 Hostage Rescue Operation at the Japanese Embassy
By C.C. Snow, J.P. Baraybar, and H. Spirer 14

2 Differential Diagnosis of Skeletal Injuries 21

Case Study 2.1: Finite Element Models of the Human Head in the Field of Forensic Science
By J.S. Raul, B. Ludes, and R. Willinger 87

3 Blast Injuries 95

Case Study 3.1: Skeletal and Soft Tissue Injuries Resulting from a Grenade *By A.B. Seneviratne* 117

Case Study 3.2: A Case of Blasting Injury from Colombia
By J.M. Pachón 124

Case Study 3.3: "Human Bomb" and Body Trauma
By A. Samarasekera 128

4 Blunt Force Trauma 151

Case Study 4.1: The Interpretation of Skeletal Trauma Resulting from Injuries Sustained Prior to, and as a Direct Result of, Freefall *By O. Finegan* 181

Case Study 4.2: A Khmer Rouge Execution Method: Evidence from Choeung Ek *By S.C. Ta'ala, G.E. Berg, and K. Haden* **196**

5 Skeletal Evidence of Torture **201**

Case Study 5.1: Torture Sequels to the Skeleton *By H.P. Hougen* **234**

Case Study 5.2: Multiple Healed Rib Fractures: Timing of Injuries with Regard to Death *By T. Delabarde* **236**

Case Study 5.3: Dating of Fractures in Human Dry Bone Tissue. The Berisha Case *By G.J.R. Maat* **245**

Case Study 5.4: Torture and Extra-Judicial Execution in the Peruvian Highlands: Forensic Investigation in a Military Base *By J.P. Baraybar, C.R. Cardoza, and V. Parodi* **255**

6 Sharp Force Trauma **263**

Case Study 6.1: Disappearance, Torture and Murder of Nine Individuals in a Community of Nebaj, Guatemala *By S. Chacón, F.A. Peccerelli, L. Paiz Diez, and C. Rivera Fernández* **300**

Case Study 6.2: Probable Machete Trauma from the Cambodian Killing Fields *By G.E. Berg* **314**

7 Gunfire Injuries **321**

Case Study 7.1: Firearm Basics *By C.J. Waters* **385**

8 Variation in Gunfire Wounds by Skeletal Region **401**

Case Study 8.1: Tyranny and Torture in the Republic of Panama *By A.H. Ross and L. Suarez S.* **438**

Case Study 8.2: The Pacific War: A Chilean Soldier Found in Cerro Zig Zag, Peru *By E. Tomasto Cagigao and M. Lund* **441**

References **449**

Index **477**

A Foreword by Andrew T. Cayley, Esq.

SENIOR PROSECUTING COUNSEL AT THE INTERNATIONAL CRIMINAL COURT AND FORMER SENIOR TRIAL ATTORNEY OF THE INTERNATIONAL CRIMINAL TRIBUNAL FOR THE FORMER YUGOSLAVIA

On a warm September evening in 1999, in northeast Bosnia-Herzegovina, we were visiting the most recently discovered mass grave linked to the events in Srebrenica of July 1995. We were at Glogovac. José Pablo Baraybar was stripped to the waist and working in the excavated site. We watched him as he gently recovered the mortal remains of one of the thousands of victims of the genocide that had taken place in and around Srebrenica 4 years before. From these human remains and the other items found in the mass graves evidence would be recovered that became incontrovertible at the subsequent trial.

We led a substantial part of the forensic evidence at the trial of General Krstic, who was charged with crimes in and around Srebrenica in July 1995. The revelations of the human remains from Srebrenica left us all with a profound sense of shock and horror but also the satisfaction that nobody could deny that these catastrophic events had really taken place. Victims had been shot in the back of the head, victims had disabling injuries at the time of death, and bodies had been robbed from the primary sites and reburied in much more remote secondary locations in order to prevent discovery. Truth and condemnation poured forth from the Bosnian soil and into the trial chamber.

As the Krstic trial judgment made clear, "The extensive forensic evidence presented by the Prosecution strongly corroborates important aspects of the testimony of survivors from the various execution sites .... Overall, the Trial Chamber finds that the forensic evidence presented by the Prosecution provides corroboration of survivor testimony that, following the take-over of Srebrenica in July 1995, thousands of Bosnian Muslim men from Srebrenica were killed in careful and methodical mass executions."

As this timely book demonstrates, skeletal remains reveal not just the causes of death but also much about human suffering prior to death. The book is based on forensic analysis carried out in the former Yugoslavia, South America, and Cambodia. It is written by two experts in the field. Its future use by forensic practitioners, and prosecution and defense lawyers, will ensure the maximum exploitation of human remains for the purposes of proof in both domestic and international criminal prosecutions.

> We owe respect to the living, to the dead we owe only the truth.
>
> **Francois Marie Arouet Voltaire**

A Foreword by Morris Tidball-Binz, M.D.

FORENSIC COORDINATOR

INTERNATIONAL COMMITTEE OF THE RED CROSS,
GENEVA, SWITZERLAND

Just three decades ago, the suggestion of a causal link between the forensic identification of skeletal trauma and human rights advocacy and humanitarian action would have triggered a compassionate sneer from most forensic practitioners, human rights activists, and humanitarian workers alike. Not any longer: the need for proper interpretation of skeletal trauma in investigations into atrocities and disappearances is nowadays an obvious fact for all those concerned. Since the mid-eighties, a bulk of experience and knowledge has been acquired and a series of innovative human rights and forensic standards have been developed by practitioners worldwide to assist and guide investigations of extra-judicial killings, mass graves, and torture. These include, for example, the *UN Manual on the Effective Prevention and Investigation of Extra-legal, Arbitrary and Summary Executions* ("Minnesota Protocol") and the *UN Manual on the Effective Investigation and Documentation of Torture and Other Cruel, Inhuman or Degrading Treatment or Punishment* ("Istanbul Protocol"). The United Nations has also adopted resolutions on human rights and forensic sciences and has prepared a standing list of forensic practitioners from around the world available for human rights investigations. Scientific literature increasingly includes articles on the forensic documentation of human rights violations. As a result of such remarkable developments—which the second author and some of the contributors of this book helped pioneer—forensic scientists are increasingly called on the world over to help investigations into war crimes, crimes against humanity, and genocide. Additionally, the use of forensic sciences in helping clarify the fate of the missing, including the identification of the living and of the dead, has also evolved remarkably over the past twenty years.

Nevertheless, in parallel to these developments, a false dichotomy has emerged regarding the purpose of using forensic sciences, including the analysis of trauma, for human rights and humanitarian investigations: On one hand, the need to document trauma, including torture, and establish the cause, manner and circumstances of death of victims, for ensuring the accountability of perpetrators (human rights' purpose); and on the other, the forensic identification of victims of abuse, to fulfill the needs of bereaved families (humanitarian purpose). In effect, some large-scale forensic investigations into mass graves carried out during the nineties to prosecute the perpetrators of massacres overlooked the need to identify the remains of victims, something which compounded the suffering of bereaved families and led to understandable criticism from concerned stakeholders. Much debate followed about the role and duties of forensic practitioners involved in human rights and humanitarian investigations, to help ensure that the identification of victims also be part of their investigations into massacres, genocide, and other crimes against humanity. In 2003, the International Committee of the Red Cross (ICRC) organized an international conference on The Missing, which stressed the need and importance of proper recovery and identification of human remains to help fulfill the right to know for bereaved families. Recommendations from that conference on the use of forensic sciences focus on the proper recovery, management and identification of human remains, with the understanding that this is as important as establishing the cause, manner, and circumstances of death of the deceased.

The analysis of trauma is essential for both purposes. In effect, the diagnosis of pre-mortem, peri-mortem and, on occasions, even post-mortem trauma in human remains is often central to their identification. The debate and dichotomy on the purpose of forensic investigations into violations of human rights and Humanitarian Law is now over. But forensic scientists involved in human rights and humanitarian investigations still face the difficult challenge of identifying complex patterns of trauma, often in human skeletal remains and on a scale rarely encountered in domestic criminal investigations, to help establish their identity and how they died.

Forensic practitioners and other concerned investigators of gross violations of human rights and Humanitarian Law are therefore in greater need than ever of sound guidance for interpreting evidence from skeletal trauma suffered by the victims of such violations. The publication of this book, which is borne from solid research and extensive practice in the field, is as timely as it is necessary. It is set to become a guiding tool for forensic scientists, human rights activists, and humanitarian workers committed to giving a truthful voice to the dead.

Preface

The creation of the International Tribunal for the Prosecution of Persons Responsible for Serious Violations of International Humanitarian Law Committed in the Territory of the Former Yugoslavia since 1991 (ICTY) resulted in multinational, multidisciplinary forensic investigations that recovered, analyzed, and presented a range of physical evidence on cases involving thousands of individual victims. In the course of these investigations, search and recovery methods evolved to meet the particular circumstances of each new case. Likewise, mortuary analysis of physical evidence and the postmortem examinations of human remains grew into a sophisticated system capable of processing thousands of individual cases in a single field season. The forensic protocols and case law that have resulted from the ICTY have set a precedence for future investigations into international humanitarian and human rights law.

Crucial evidence for the successful prosecution of alleged war criminals includes the determination of the cause and manner of death among victims. Interpreting the circumstances surrounding a death begins with a reconstruction the person's injuries, as this evidence provides information as to crimes committed and establishes a record of what events occurred. Recovering skeletal remains and other evidence, such as bullet fragments or shrapnel from a grave, correctly and efficiently using clothing and radiography to aid in the recovery process, and analysis of complex skeletal injuries all lead to the correct identification of skeletal trauma.

Many victims of human rights atrocities and armed conflicts suffer multiple injuries, including high velocity gunfire and blasting injuries. It is not uncommon for victims to have suffered multiple gunfire injuries throughout the body from a variety of trajectories resulting from multiple attackers or complex fatal environments. In addition, extreme efforts have been made by the perpetrators of violence in some cases to hide evidence. Deceased bodies are blown up, burned, thrown off bridges or cliffs, altered in cursory attempts to hide the truth, buried in clandestine graves and sometimes re-interred multiple times to hide their locations. Each of these processes leaves its mark on the skeleton. Sorting through injuries, taphonomic alterations, and postmortem fractures for each victim is a routine part of the postmortem examination and paramount for accurately diagnosing the mechanism of injury.

Increasingly, the use of emerging judicial systems such as international tribunals and domestic truth commissions sets the stage for future forensic investigation in the pursuit of documenting, analyzing, and prosecuting these cases. This book is written to aid in the process of skeletal trauma identification in the context of large-scale human rights violations or armed conflict. It is our objective that this book will facilitate an understanding of mechanisms of injuries interpreted from skeletal remains, provide a synthesis of the variation in wounding patterns, and construct an epidemiological framework for interpreting physical evidence for use at trial.

The examples used throughout this text are taken from human rights violations, ethnic and armed conflict, extrajudicial executions, and acts of terrorism from numerous regions throughout the Americas, Europe, and Asia. Evidence is interpreted through an epidemiological model and set in a legal framework. Methods of differential diagnosis are used to describe and analyze wound characteristics to classify skeletal trauma and interpret the mechanisms of injury. It should be noted that the cases presented here were immediately fatal or without medical intervention. Therefore, the similarities or differences as compared to the large body of clinical literature and medical research, particularly related to war surgery may vary. The examples from the Balkans and many of the other examples discussed in this book have already been presented as evidence in criminal trials, such as those held by ICTY. In numerous examples, physical evidence of injuries and maltreatment, the mechanisms of trauma, and the manners of death are corroborated by witness testimony or other physical evidence and are discussed. Twenty-six leading scholars and practitioners from anthropology, pathology, and forensics have contributed their research, cases, and photographs comprising 16 contributed case studies throughout the book. There is a wide international spectrum of contributors, many of whom have extensive fieldwork investigating human rights cases internationally such as the armed conflicts in Guatemala, Peru, Sri Lanka, Panama, Cambodia, Rwanda, Haiti, and the Balkans.

Chapter 1 discusses contextual information about international forensic investigations and criminal proceedings into violations of international humanitarian law through international tribunals and other emerging judicial systems, and outlines an epidemiological framework for collecting and analyzing physical evidence. Chapter 2 discusses methodology for differential diagnosis of wounds during postmortem analysis and protocols for systematic data collection. The specific mechanisms of injuries, associated weaponry, and legal framework are discussed in the following chapters 3–8, organized topically: Blasting Injuries, Blunt Force Trauma, Skeletal Evidence of Torture, Sharp Force Trauma, and Gunfire Injuries. Within each chapter, there is a discussion of the wounding mechanisms, the pathophysiology of wounds, relevant legal examples for the type of evidence presented, and contributed case studies from leading experts in medicine, anthropology, and ballistics.

Readers will benefit from this book by using it in the course of postmortem analysis as well as for teaching the next generation of investigators. The practical applications of this resource extend beyond international forensic investigations and are relevant for general forensic casework, medicolegal death investigations, mass disaster incidents, skeletal biology, bioarchaeology, and emergency war surgery. This book is intended to share our research, cases, and experience working with the skeletal remains of victims of war and terror, of extrajudicial execution, and enforced disappearances. *In these cases, the most basic human right was denied—life!*

Erin H. Kimmerle and José Pablo Baraybar

Acknowledgments

We would like to take this opportunity to say thank you to those friends and colleagues who worked with us, contributed to the research and writing of this text in numerous ways, and provided support and friendship. First, we would like to thank Michael Boland, Daniela O. Bercovitch, our parents and immediate family and friends for their encouragement and support during the preparation of this book and the many years of research and service leading up to its development. Dr. Sue Black for providing insightful and supportive comments when this book was first proposed. David Tolbert, Esq., Peter McCloskey, Esq., Eamonn Smyth, and Gerold Siller of The ICTY; for permission to use photographs and their support and assistance in the field, courtroom and throughout the writing of this book. Andrew Cayley, Esq. and Dr. Morris Tidball-Binz for writing forewords and their continued friendship. Becky McEldowney-Masterman, Pat Roberson, and Jim McGovern from the Taylor & Francis Group for their hard work and continued support throughout the writing of this text.

We are sincerely thankful to our colleagues who shared their cases, research, photographs, and experience through contributed case studies—these contributions are invaluable to this project. We thank team members of the Peruvian Forensic Anthropology Team (EPAF), the Guatemalan Forensic Anthropology Foundation (FAFG), Fredy Armando Peccerelli, Claudia Rivera, and countless former International ICTY Forensic Team Members, anthropologists, pathologists, radiographers, autopsy technicians, scene of crime officers—all of the enthusiastic people that applied their skills and knowledge to a noble cause. We thank Dr. Lisa Leppo for her service and contributions to the cases. We thank Elayne Pope for sharing her research and photographs on burned bone. We also thank Carlos Jacinto, Juan Carlos Tello, Jorge M. Pachón, Max Popenker, Dr. Matthias Okoye, Dr. David Kiple and Jane Beck for contributing photographs. Special thanks to Alain Wittmann who contributed so many of the photographs.

We are very grateful for the time and thoughtfulness of our colleagues who reviewed drafts of the manuscript and provided meaningful commentary—all of whom helped to refine and improve this book. We thank Dr. Martin Fackler for his review and insightful comments on wound ballistics. We appreciate the time, reviews, and editorial comments provided by Dr. Kathy Haden, Dr. Wesley Johnson, Dr. Doug Ubelaker, Sgt. Jack Waters, and Greg Berg. We also thank the USF graduate students who provided valuable research assistance to this project. In particular we thank Cristina Echazabal for her assistance.

Finally, José Pablo Baraybar would like to thank his former staff at the Office on Missing Persons and Forensics (OMPF), in particular all forensic doctors, anthropologists, archaeologists, forensic scientists, laboratory technicians and assistants with whom he carried out so many autopsies including those too many to name here: Dr. Marek Gasior, Dr. Ananda Samaresekera, Dr. Maria Dolores Morcillo, Dr. Arsim Gerxhaliu, Dr. Asoka Seneviratne, Dr. Prijanith Perera, Dr. John Clark, Dr. Duarte Nuno Vieira, Dr. Maria Cristina de Mendonca, Dr. Joao Pinheiro, Dr. Annie Geraut, Dr. Maryelle Kolopp,

Dr. Carlo Campobasso, Dr. Bernhard Olbert, Peter Hoff-Olsen, Hans Petter Hougen, Thierry Marin, George Szilagyi, Patrick Reynolds, Rosmarie Hardmeier, Tom Grange, Hroar Frydenlund, Tania Delabarde, Oran Finegan, Ximena Novoa, Israel Hershkovitz, Edixon Quinones, Jennifer Randolph, Shuala Drawdy (Martin), Dr. Steve Symes, Carmen Rosa Cardoza, Juan Carlos Tello, Claudia Rivera, Catherine Cannet, Luc Tetrault, Susan Salazar, Klaire Kasibayo, Driton Spahiu ("Tony"), Izedin Durguti ("Dino"), Armend Haxhimustafa, Driton Shabani.

We believe that first and foremost this book belongs to the victims, their families and all survivors—from whom we learn the truth in the pursuit of justice.

Authors

Erin H. Kimmerle is an Assistant Professor in the Department of Anthropology at the University of South Florida (Tampa, Florida USA). She received her degrees in Anthropology from The University of Tennessee (Ph.D.), the University of Nebraska (M.A.), and Hamline University (B.A.). She served as Chief Forensic Anthropologist for the United Nations, International Criminal Tribunal for the Former Yugoslavia in 2001 and has worked on numerous missions in Kosova, Bosnia and Herzegovina, Bermuda, and Croatia. Dr. Kimmerle also worked as an osteologist for the National Museum of Natural History, Smithsonian Institution, in Washington, D.C., and the Osteology Laboratory at Hamline University in St. Paul, Minnesota. She continues to serve as a consultant for casework and law enforcement training in the United States and Internationally. Dr. Kimmerle has conducted extensive research in the areas of trauma, pathology, growth and development, and aging. She has published numerous scientific journal articles and book chapters and serves on the Advisory Board of the Nebraska Institute of Forensic Science, Inc.; the Executive Board of the Human Development Center, Tampa, FL; Adjunct Senior Lecturer, College of Medicine, Lagos State University, Nigeria; and is a member of the Florida Emergency Mortuary Operations Response System (FEMORS).

José Pablo Baraybar is President of the Peruvian Forensic Anthropology Team (EPAF). He obtained a M.Sc. at the University of London; a B.A. in archaeology at the University of San Marcos in Lima, Peru; and is currently a doctoral candidate at the University of Strasbourg, France. From the beginning of his career Mr. Baraybar worked on the recovery and analysis of human remains in archaeological contexts. He later applied his professional background to the forensic investigation of human rights abuses working as a consultant in forensic anthropology in various countries including: Peru, Guatemala, Ethiopia, Congo and Sierra Leone. He joined the United Nations in 1995 working for the International Civilian Mission to Haiti (MICIVIH), after which he joined the International Criminal Tribunal in Rwanda and later that for the former Yugoslavia. He has worked as resident forensic expert for the Office of the Prosecutor of the International Criminal Tribunal for Rwanda and Chief forensic anthropologist/archaeologist for the Office of the Prosecutor of the International Criminal Tribunal for the former Yugoslavia in Bosnia-Herzegovina, Croatia and Kosovo testifying and submitting expert reports in multiple cases. In June 2002 he was appointed Head of the Office on Missing Persons and Forensics (OMPF) in the Department of Justice of the United Nations Interim Administration in Kosovo, post he held until April 2007; in November 2006 OMPF was awarded the UN-21 Award.

Contributor Biographies

Gregory E. Berg earned his B.A. in anthropology from the University of Arizona in 1993 and his M.A. from the bioarchaeology program from Arizona State University in 1999. He is completing a Ph.D. at the University of Tennessee. He is currently a forensic anthropologist at the JPAC-Central Identification Laboratory in Hawaii where he works on the recovery and identification of missing U.S. service personnel. He has over fifteen years of field experience in archaeology and physical anthropology and has presented or published numerous articles and papers in the Journal of Forensic Sciences, Journal of Archaeological Science, and at various annual meetings. His recent research has concentrated on trauma analysis, aging techniques, human identification and eyewear, and intra- and inter-observer error studies, which have been particularly focused on aging and population determination methods used in human identification.

Shirley Chacón, studied Archaeology in Universidad San Carlos de Guatemala, she joined the Guatemalan Forensic Anthropology Foundation in 1997. She has led many Forensic Anthropology Investigations. She has also worked as an expert in Bosnia & Herzegovina and Honduras. Currently holds the position of Coordinator of the FAFG Osteology Laboratory.

Tania Delabarde, Ph.D., is a physical anthropologist with a subspecialty in bioarchaeology. She graduated from the University of Talence and Paris I La Sorbonne, France. Dr. Delabarde worked as consultant forensic anthropologist for the International Criminal Tribunal for the former Yugoslavia (ICTY) in Bosnia in 2001 and for the Office of Missing Persons and Forensic in Kosovo between 2002 and 2006. Dr. Delabarde collaborates with the Institute of Legal Medicine of Nancy and is a consultant for the French Police International Cooperation. Her actual research focus is on experimental studies of sharp force trauma linked to dismemberment activities. She is currently affiliated with the French Institute of Andean Studies (IFEA) where she also assists the Office of The Prosecutor of Ecuador in forensic cases where she now resides.

Oran Finegan M.Sc., M.A., is currently working for the United Nations Committee on Missing Persons in Cyprus under contract with the Argentine Forensic Anthropology Team (EAAF). Mr. Finegan earned his B.Sc. in Anatomy at Queen's University Belfast (1994–1997), a M.Sc. in Forensic Anthropology in the University of Bradford, England (1997–1998) and an M.A. in Theory and Practice of Human Rights in the University of Essex (2003–2004). Mr. Finegan has worked as a consultant forensic anthropologist for the International Criminal Tribunal for the former Yugoslavia in Bosnia, Croatia and Kosovo (1998, 2000, 2001) and for the Office on Missing Persons and Forensics (OMPF) in Kosovo (2002–2003, 2004–2006).

Kathryn Haden-Pinneri earned her M.D. degree from the University of Texas Southwestern Medical School at Dallas in 1997. She completed a residency in Anatomic and Clinical Pathology at the University of Tennessee Medical Center at Knoxville in 2002 and a fellowship in Forensic Pathology at the Dallas County Medical Examiner's Office in 2003. She is currently an Assistant Medical Examiner at the Harris County Medical Examiner's Office in Houston, Texas where she performs autopsies and medicolegal death investigations. She is also a member of the Disaster Mortuary Operational Response Team (DMORT). She is board certified in Anatomic and Forensic Pathology and is a member of the American Academy of Forensic Sciences and the National Association of Medical Examiners.

Professor Hans Petter Hougen earned his M.D. and Ph.D. from the University of Copenhagen as well as an MPA from the Copenhagen Business School. Dr. Hougen carried out post-Doctoral training in Forensic Pathology in the United States. Dr. Hougen is currently Professor of Forensic Medicine at the University of Copenhagen and Chief Forensic Pathologist for East Denmark. Dr. Hougen's areas of expertise and interest are sudden cardiac death, the epidemiology of suicides and homicides, the forensic aspects of Human Rights violations and the Pathology of gunshot and explosion injuries.

Mellisa Lund is a member of the Peruvian Forensic Anthropology Team (EPAF). She earned her B.A. in Archaeology at the University of San Marcos in Lima and is currently working on a Masters degree in Forensic Anthropology and Bioarchaeology at the Catholic University in Lima (PUCP). Ms. Lund has a long experience in the analysis of human remains both from archaeological and forensic contexts and has worked as forensic anthropology consultant for the International Criminal Tribunal for the former Yugoslavia (ICTY) in Bosnia, Croatia and Kosovo in 2001 and 2003.

Professor Bertrand Ludes, M.D., Ph.D., teaches legal medicine at the Louis Pasteur University of Strasbourg (France) medical school. Professor Ludes holds a specialization in forensic pathology and DNA identification namely in disaster victim identifications. He is the director of the Institute of Legal Medicine of Strasbourg (France). Professor Ludes participated as consultant pathologist for the International Criminal Tribunal for the former Yugoslavia in Bosnia.

Professor George Maat earned his M.D. and Ph.D. at the University of Leiden, Holland in 1973 and 1974 respectively. Dr. Maat taught at Surinam University (1974–1976), Leiden University (1977–1986), Kuwait University (1986–1990), Utrecht University (1991–1993) and again at Leiden University Medical Center since 1993. In addition to teaching human anatomy, embryology and histology he teaches physical anthropology since 1977 and forensic anthropology since 2004 at the Forensic Human Identification Course at the University College London. Dr. Maat's fields of research are paleopathology and forensic anthropology. He currently is co-editor of the International Journal of Osteoarchaeology. He is affiliated with the Netherlands Forensic Institute at The Hague and is Honorary Professor at the University of Pretoria. As permanent member of the Dutch Disaster Identification Team and as a temporary member of the British Forensic Team, he has been deployed in Kosovo (ICTY; 1999, 2000, 2003), Enschede (fireworks disaster; 2000), Thailand (tsunami; 2004–2005) and in Afghanistan (military helicopter crash; 2006).

Jorge M. Pachón, B.A., is a Criminalist (Administrative Department of Security (Departamento Administrativo de Seguridad-DAS) and Professional Technician in Forensic Ballistics (Judicial School of Technical Police) in Colombia. Mr. Pachón has 17 years experience working at the National Institute of Legal Medicine and Forensic Sciences in Bogota. His area of expertise during the last ten years is the examination of projectile injuries and blunt force trauma in cadavers as well as skeletal remains. Mr. Pachón has been trained in Administration and Operations of the Integrated Ballistic Identification System (IBIS) for the DAS and DAS stations in Colombia. He also worked as a Scene of Crime Officer in Kosovo for the International Criminal Tribunal for the former Yugoslavia and in 2003 for the Office on Missing Persons and Forensics.

Leonel Paiz Diez, B.A., has worked in mass grave investigations since 1997, as an Archeologist, Forensic Anthropologist, and Coordinator of the Laboratory. Currently he is the Director of Forensic Archaeology Direction of the Guatemalan Forensic Anthropology Foundation (FAFG). He has performed as an advisor for the Guatemalan Truth Commission, instructor for the Chief Examiner's Office in Honduras and Prosecutors in Perú, as an expert consultant in forensic investigations in Bosnia & Herzegovina, Croatia and Kosovo for ICTY. He has participated in lectures for the American Association of Forensic Sciences. He is also a founder and member of the Latin American Association of Forensic Anthropology.

Vanessa Parodi, B.Sc., joined the Peruvian Forensic Anthropology Team (EPAF) in 2005. She earned her B.Sc. in Psychology and Physical Anthropology at the University of Toronto, Canada, and has worked for almost 10 years in the analysis of human remains of different archaeological and historical sites. She worked as consultant forensic anthropologist in Kosovo for the Office on Missing Persons and Forensics in 2005.

Carmen Rosa Cardoza, B.A., is a founding member of the Peruvian Forensic Anthropology Team (EPAF). She earned her B.A. in Archaeology at the University of San Marcos in Lima, Peru and is currently working on a Master in Forensic Anthropology and Forensic Genetics at the University of Granada, Spain. For the last 10 years Ms. Cardoza has participated as consultant forensic anthropologist for the International Criminal Tribunal for the former Yugoslavia (ICTY) in Bosnia, Croatia and Kosovo between 1997 and 2000 and for the Office on Missing Persons and Forensics (OMPF) in Kosovo between 2004 and 2005. Ms. Cardoza has also participated as expert in a number of cases or the Office of the Prosecutor, the Judiciary or the Defense in Peru.

Fredy Armando Peccerelli, B.A., began his career in forensics when he joined the Guatemalan Forensic Anthropology Team in 1995; later in 1997 he became a founding member of the Guatemalan Forensic Anthropology Foundation. He studied Physical Anthropology and Osteology in Brooklyn College, New York City University and from 2003 to 2004 he studied an MSc in Forensic & Biological Anthropology in Bournemouth University, England. During 1997, 1998 and 2001 he participated in forensic investigations conducted by the United Nations International Tribunal for the Prosecution of Persons Responsible for Serious Violations of the International Humanitarian Law Committed in the territory of the former Yugoslavia, since 1991. On May 1999, he was selected by Time Magazine and

CNN as one of the 50 Latin American Leaders for the New Millennium and on September 1999, he was selected by the Guatemalan National Youth Council as an icon for the youth of Guatemala. On May 2006 he received the Washington Office of Latin America's (WOLA) Human Rights Award. Currently Mr. Peccerelli is the Executive Director of the Guatemalan Forensic Anthropology Foundation.

Jean-Sébastien Raul, M.D., Ph.D., is an Associate Professor of Legal Medicine in Strasbourg University. He is a neurosurgeon, forensic scientist, and medical expert in legal medicine and toxicology. His research includes developing the use of finite element models in forensic sciences with a special focus on adult and child head injury with Remy Willinger's team working on Impact Biomechanics at University Louis Pasteur in Strasbourg, France.

Claudia Rivera, B.A., is an Archeologist graduated from Universidad San Carlos de Guatemala. She worked in Mayan traditional archaeology, and in 1997 she started working for the Guatemalan Forensic Anthropology Foundation (FAFG) finding human remains from Guatemalan citizens that were killed during the Internal Armed Conflict. Since then she has participated in international missions in Bosnia & Herzegovina and Kosovo. Currently she holds the position of Director of Operations at the FAFG.

Ann H. Ross, Ph.D., is an Associate Professor of Anthropology at NC State University. She is a physical anthropologist with a subspecialty in forensic anthropology and bioarchaeology. She received her education from the University of Tennessee. Her research focus includes developing population specific identification standards using traditional measurement techniques and modern three-dimensional methods. Dr. Ross has participated in Human Rights missions in Bosnia, the Republic of Panama and Chile. She also consults on a regular basis for the Republic of Panama Institute of Legal Medicine and occasionally consults on local cases in North Carolina.

Ananda Samarasekera, M.D., M.B.B.S., D.L.M., D.M.J. (London), Dip. F. M. (Glasgow). Dr. Samarasekera is Chief Forensic Medical Examiner in the Office on Missing Persons and Forensics (OMPF), Department of Justice, United Nations Mission in Kosovo (UNMIK) since 2004. Dr. Samarasekera received his Medical Degrees as well as a Diploma in Legal Medicine in Sri Lanka and a Diploma in Medical Jurisprudence and one in Forensic Medicine in the United Kingdom (London and Glasgow respectively). Dr. Samarasekera was Chief Judicial Medical Officer in Colombo North, Sri Lanka (1991–2004). Dr. Samarasekera worked as consultant pathologist for the International Criminal Tribunal for the former Yugoslavia between 1999 and 2001 and is currently President of the College of Forensic Pathologists of Sri Lanka and treasurer of the Indo Pacific Association of Law, Medicine and Sciences. During his tenure in Sri Lanka Dr. Samarasekera has been involved with many forensic investigations of many bomb explosions.

Asoka B. Seneviratne, M.D., M.B.B.S. and D.L.M. (Sri Lanka), D.M.J. (Pathology, London) is Consultant Judicial Medical Officer in the General (Teaching) Hospital in Kandy, Sri Lanka. Dr. Seneviratne received his Medical Degrees as well as a Diploma in Legal Medicine in Sri Lanka and a Diploma in Medical Jurisprudence in Pathology in London, UK. Dr. Seneviratne worked as a consultant pathologist for the International Criminal Tribunal for the former Yugoslavia (ICTY) in Bosnia and for the Office on Missing Persons and Forensics

(OMPF) in Kosovo. Dr. Seneviratne is member of the Board of Studies in Forensic Medicine and examiner, Post-graduate Institute of Medicine, University of Colombo, Founder member of College of Forensic Pathologists of Sri Lanka and Life member, Medico-Legal Society of Sri Lanka and of the Kandy Society of Forensic Medicine.

Clyde Collins Snow, Ph.D., D.A.B.F.A., is a board certified forensic anthropology consultant. His notable cases include the John Wayne Gacy serial murders, the 273-victim DC10 accident (Chicago 1979), the identification of the notorious Nazi war criminal Dr. Josef Mengele and the 1995 Oklahoma City bombing. Beginning in 1984, he extended his investigative efforts to the identification of victims of human rights violations and war crimes. Since then, he has participated in investigative missions in over twenty countries, ranging from Argentina to Zimbabwe. He has testified as an expert witness in many U.S. states, foreign countries and international tribunals. In 2006, he gave expert testimony in Baghdad at the trial of Saddam Hussein and his co-defendents for their genocidal campaign against the Kurds. His testimony was based on evidence of mass executions and chemical warfare from mass graves he and his team exhumed in Iraqi Kurdistan in 1992. However, his proudest achievement has been in helping recruit and train the forensic anthropology teams of Argentina (EAAF), Guatemala (FAFG) and Peru (EPAF) who are recognized throughout the world as the pioneers in the application of the forensic sciences to the investigation of human rights violations.

Herbert F. Spirer, Ph.D., is Adjunct Professor of International Affairs, Columbia University, New York, a Professor Emeritus of Information Management at the University of Connecticut at Stamford, as well as a consultant on statistical science for numerous corporations and organizations. He received his Ph.D. from the University of Columbia in 1970. He has been a statistical science consultant for the UN's International Tribunals on the Former Yugoslavia and Rwanda (1994–1997), and Chair of the American Statistical Association Committee on Scientific Freedom and Human Rights (1990–1993). He is further a Fellow of the American Statistical Association (1996), and elected member of the International Statistical Association (2000) in recognition of achievements in applying statistics to human rights.

Loreto Suarez S., B.A., received her training in archaeology at the Universidad de Chile and served as Director of Anthropology for the Panamanian Truth Commission.

Sabrina C. Ta'ala, B.A., earned her B.A. in Anthropology from the University of Colorado at Boulder, and M.A. in Anthropology from East Carolina University. She is currently a forensic anthropologist working to recover and identify missing U.S. service members with the Joint POW/MIA Accounting Command, Central Identification Laboratory (JPAC-CIL) in Hawaii. Ms. Ta'ala has excavated a variety of historic and prehistoric archaeological sites throughout the world. Recent research has focused on geophysical techniques for detection of clandestine graves, trauma analysis, determination of ancestry from skeletal remains, and the use of eye wear to predict identity. Her work has been published in the *Journal of Forensic Sciences* and presented at regional and national archaeological and forensic meetings.

Elsa Tomasto Cagigao, Lic., is Lecturer of Physical Anthropology at the Pontificia Universidad Catolica del Peru (PUCP) and former Curator of Human Remains at the National Museum of Archaeology, Anthropology and History of Perú. She earned her B.A. in archaeology at the PUCP where she is currently working on a Masters degree in Forensic Anthropology and Bioarchaeology. Ms. Tomasto has a long experience in the analysis of human remains from archaeological contexts and has worked in multiple projects on the subject. Ms. Tomasto also worked with the Truth and Reconciliation Commission in Peru.

Sgt. C. J. Waters is a retired police sergeant who is currently the Forensic Investigation Unit Supervisor in the Criminal Investigation Division, Tampa Police Department. Sgt. Waters has more than 40 years of experience in law enforcement with special emphasis on crime scene investigation and ballistics. He obtained his B.A. at the University of Tampa where he studied History, Criminology, and Political Science. He formerly worked for the United States Army Security Agency and holds a teaching license in Police Science. He is also on the Board of Directors for the Human Development Center and is active in other community NGOs.

Professor Rémy Willinger, Ph.D., has managed a research team since 1972 working on Impact Biomechanics at University Louis Pasteur, Strasbourg, France. His background is mechanical engineering applied to biomechanics. The activity ranges from biological tissues identification and modelling to human body characterization followed by lumped and distributed mathematical modelling. Once validated the numerical and physical models are used for theoretical and experimental accident reconstruction in order to derive tolerance limits relative to specific injury mechanisms. Human models are also coupled to protective systems in order to optimise them in respect to biomechanical criteria. Most of his work addressed the cranio-cerebral and cervical complex. Main result of this research is the development of an improved head finite element model and the proposal of new tolerance limits to specific head injury mechanisms.

Abbreviations

AAAS	American Association for the Advancement of Science
AIS	Abbreviated injury scale
BFT	Blunt force trauma
BiH	Bosnia-Herzegovina
CCIU	Central Investigation Unit
CEH	Guatemalan Historical Clarification Commission
CSF	Cerebro-spinal fluid
CTS	Cracked tooth syndrome
CWF	Conventional warfare
EAAF	Argentine Forensic Anthropology Team
EOD	Explosive ordinance device
EQUITAS	Colombian Interdisciplinary Team on Forensic Work and Psychosocial Services
EPAF	Peruvian Forensic Anthropology Team
FAFG	Guatemalan Forensic Anthropology Foundation
FEM	Finite element modeling
FMJ	Full metal jacket
FRY	Federal Republic of Yugoslavia
FW	Fatal wounds
GAMBIT	General acceleration model for brain injury threshold
GSW	Gunshot wounds
HE	High order
HHRR	Human rights
HIC	Head injury criterion
ICC	International Criminal Court
ICTJ	International Center for Transitional Justice
ICTR	International Criminal Tribunal for Rwanda

ICTY	International Tribunal for the Prosecution of Persons Responsible for Serious Violations of International Humanitarian Law Committed in the Territory of the Former Yugoslavia since 1991 (also referred to the International Criminal Tribunal for the Former Yugoslavia)
ICRC	International Committee of the Red Cross
ID	Identification
IED	Impoverished ordinance device
IHL	International Humanitarian Law
IHRL	International Human Rights Law
ITF	Incomplete tooth fracture
JNA	Yugoslav National Army
KLA	Kosovo Liberation Army (UÇK, Oslobodilacka Vojska Kosova)
LE	Low order
LTTE	Liberation Tigers of Tamil Eelam
MRTA	Movimiento Revolucionario Tupac Amaru
NHTSA	National Highway Traffic Safety Administration
NRW	Non-fatal wounds
OMPF	Office of Missing Persons and Forensics
PHR	Physicians for Human Rights
PDW	Personal defense weapon
RPG	Rocket propelled grenade
RTA	Road traffic Accident
SFT	Sharp force trauma
SDH	Subdural haematoma
SIMON	Simulated injury monitor
WSU	Wayne State University
W/K	Wounded to killed ratio
ULP	Universitė Louis Pasteur
UNCHR	United Nations Committee of the Red Cross
UNMIK	United Nations Mission in Kosovo
UN	United Nations
USF	University of South Florida

1

An Epidemiological Approach to Forensic Investigations of Violations to International Humanitarian and Human Rights Law

> It was never the people who complained of the universality of human rights, nor did the people consider human rights as a Western or Northern imposition. It was often their leaders who did so.
>
> **Kofi Annan***

Contents

International Law and Forensics 2
An Epidemiological Framework for Trauma Analysis 5
- Demography 5
- Context 7
- Intent 8
- Scientific Protocol 8
- Weaponry 9
- Cause and Manner of Death 10

Summary Guidelines for Best Practice 13
- Case Study 1.1: Firefight in Lima: Wounded/Killed Ratio Analysis of MRTA Casualties in the 1997 Hostage Rescue Operation at the Japanese Embassy *By C.C. Snow, J.P. Baraybar, and H. Spirer* 14

The identification of skeletal trauma is based on the recovery of remains and physical evidence such as bullet fragments or shrapnel from a grave, correctly and efficiently using clothing and radiography to aid in the recovery process, and analysis of complex skeletal wounds. Many victims of human rights (HHRR) atrocities and armed conflict suffer multiple injuries, including high velocity gunfire and blasting trauma. Further, these cases are typically investigated years later, once bodies have decomposed and been exposed to natural elements that may also alter the physical remains. Sorting through injuries, taphonomic alterations, and postmortem fractures for each victim is a routine part of the postmortem examination and is essential to accurately diagnose the mechanism of injury that may have contributed to the death.

This book was written to aid in the process of skeletal trauma identification in the context of large-scale human rights violations, extrajudicial executions, terrorism, and armed conflict. The purpose of this book is to offer a point of reference that synthesizes the variation of wounding patterns through the use of photographs and illustrations, and an

* Kofi Annan was the seventh UN Secretary-General. Quote cited in Singh 2001.

analytical discussion of the pathophysiology of wounds and the biomechanics of skeletal trauma. The primary objectives are to facilitate an understanding of the mechanisms of injuries interpreted from skeletal remains, provide an overview of variation in wounding patterns, and construct an epidemiological framework for the interpretation of physical evidence for use at trial. This chapter outlines background information about international forensic investigations and criminal proceedings in violation of international humanitarian and human rights (IHL and IHRL) laws through international tribunals and provides an epidemiological framework for collecting and analyzing trauma evidence.

International Law and Forensics

Anthropological and medicolegal investigations can uncover potential violations to international humanitarian (IHL), human rights (IHRL) and domestic laws, such as genocide and crimes against humanity or peace (i.e., Gray 1986; Benomar 1993; Geiger and Cook-Deegan 1993; Best 1994; Edelenbosch 1994; Binford 1996; Grodin and Annas 1996; Stover and Shigekane 2002; Coupland 1997; Leaning 2003; Bosnar et al. 2005; Blau et al. 2006; Tidball-Binz 2006; Warren 2007). Conventions promote enforcement of human rights through judicial accountability, for those who commit "grave breaches" against them and are aimed at distinguishing between civilians and combatants, protecting civilians or unarmed persons, the wounded, and captured soldiers (refer to the Geneva Conventions 1949 and 1977). IHRL differs from IHL in that this body is designed to protect people both in times of armed conflict and in peace. The sources for these laws are also diverse, but they have generally developed on a common theme—to protect individuals or groups from government actions—and are applicable to cases in which armed insurgents or militia groups are fighting each other or the state (Tidball-Binz 2006).

Increasingly, the application of forensic sciences to HHRR investigations falls within a variety of legal contexts, subject to variation within legal rules of evidence, admissibility, and scientific witness testimony (Goldstone 1997; Wilson 2005). Anthropologists, pathologists, and other forensic investigators working within the IHL or IHRL framework may function under a number of different judicial or investigative contexts based on culture and are guided by the various international bodies involved. During the course of operation, these frameworks may even change as cases are transferred from international tribunals to domestic courts. To understand this variation, one only needs to look at the range of emerging court systems and the transformation of existing systems (Hayner 1994; Hinton 2002). For example, during the 1990s genocides occurring in Europe and Africa caught the world's attention with the disappearance, torture, murder, and forced evacuations of millions of people; the need of judicial accountability for serious war crimes led to the formation of two international ad hoc tribunals. The United Nations Security Council established the International Criminal Tribunal for Rwanda (ICTR)* and the International

* ICTR was established by the Security Council, acting under Chapter VII of the Charter of the United Nations, titled, *The International Criminal Tribunal for the Prosecution of Persons Responsible for Genocide and Other Serious Violations of International Humanitarian Law Committed in the Territory of Rwanda and Rwandan Citizens Responsible for Genocide and Other Such Violations Committed in the Territory of Neighboring States, between January 1, 1994, and December 31, 1994.* The resolution states, "hereinafter [the Tribunal is] referred to as the International Tribunal for Rwanda." UN Security Council *Resolution 1994/995* provides a mandate to investigate crimes committed in Rwanda in 1994.

Tribunal for the Prosecution of Persons Responsible for Serious Violations of International Humanitarian Law Committed in the Territory of the Former Yugoslavia since 1991* (ICTY). These courts have been referred to as the "second-generation" of criminal courts (Romano et al. 2004)†. More recently, the International Criminal Court (ICC)‡ has also begun to investigate cases in various regions of Africa and South Asia. A growing body of jurisprudence and international "hybrid" legal systems have also emerged in recent years in the form of "third-generation" courts, such as regional human rights courts and truth commissions, i.e., the War and Ethnic Crimes Court in Kosovo, the Special Court for Sierra Leone, the Serious Crimes Panels in the District Court of Dili in East Timor, and the Extraordinary Chambers in the Courts of Cambodia (Romano et al. 2004). These ad hoc judicial bodies seek justice for war crimes or other violations of human rights and humanitarian laws. In contrast, many of the well-known examples of international forensic and anthropological investigations are examples of domestic truth commissions that in some cases have relied on international investigative teams (e.g., Argentina) but occur in domestic courts who have jurisdiction over domestic or customary law (e.g., Guatemala, Peru, or South Africa) (Romano et al. 2004).

The relevance of these courts and medicolegal investigations is noteworthy. They offer more than legal accountability; they provide a platform for education, law enforcement, and a foundation for emerging democratic and judicial reform (www.ictj.org) (UN, *ICTR Tribunal at a Glance*). For example, in prosecuting cases the ICTY has taken the testimony of more than 4500 witnesses who were able to give their name, document their story, and in most cases testify in court (UN, *ICTY Tribunal at a Glance*). Increasingly, forensic investigations into HHRR violations and war crimes pursue accountability and reconciliation through a framework of *transitional justice*. The emerging concept of transitional justice is supported by many organizations who seek to rebuild postconflict societies. In their mission statement, the ICTJ (International Center for Transitional Justice) wrote that their organization was " … founded on the concept of a new direction in human rights advocacy: helping societies to heal by accounting for and addressing past crimes after a period of repressive rule or armed conflict." Increasingly, forensic science under the purview of transitional justice has much to offer in the areas of missing persons, human identification (for both victims and perpetrators of offenses), the documentation of historical events and crimes committed, and is playing a significant role in the enforcement of IHL through judicial process (e.g., Skinner 1987; Snow et al. 1984; Lollar 1992; Skolnick 1991; Kirschner 1984; Tedeschi 1984; Kirschner and Hannibal 1994; Koff 1996; Scott and Conner 1997; Burns 1998; Ferllini 1999; Campobasso et al. 2003; Haglund et al. 2000; Haglund 2001; Hunter et al. 2001; Schmitt 2001; Skinner et al. 2001; Arnold 2002; Cordner and McKelvie 2002; Fondebrider 2002; Komar 2003; Koff 2004; Juhl 2005; Wilson 2005; Okoye et al. 2006; Brinkley et al. 2007).

* The ICTY mission was "to prosecute persons responsible for serious violations of international humanitarian law committed in the territory of Yugoslavia since 1991" (UN Security Council *Resolution 1993/827*).

† *First-generation* courts refer to the Tokyo and Nuremberg Trials, whereas *second-generation* refers to the ICTY, ICTR, and ICC (Romano et al. 2004).

‡ The ICC was established (1998) by United Nations members participating in the "United Nations Diplomatic Conference of Plenipotentiaries on the Establishment of an International Criminal Court." Members established the treaty and currently 104 states have become party to the statute (UN, *ICC Tribunal at a Glance*).

Over the past 20 years, a variety of organizations[*] have employed forensic anthropologists, pathologists, or other forensic experts and scientists to monitor, collect, document, and analyze evidence of HHRR violations (e.g., Gibbons 1992, Stover and Eisner 1982, Joyce and Stover 1991, Snow and Bihurriet 1992, Welsh and Van Es 2003). Physical evidence provides tangible proof that is more challenging to refute than testimony alone; ICTY Deputy Prosecutor Graham Blewitt writes: "[physical evidence] provides unequivocal corroboration of what could otherwise be suspect or dubious evidence" (Blewitt in Cordner and McKelvie 2002, 284). For example, recent international proceedings have relied on large-scale forensic evidence, specifically forensic anthropological evidence of violations of IHL in Rwanda and the former Yugoslavia, including such cases as *The Prosecutor v. Kayishema and Ruxindana* (ICTR-95-1), *The Prosecutor v. Rutaganda* (ICTR-96-3), *The Prosecutor v. Mrksic, Radic, Sljivancanin, Dokmanovic* (IT-95-13a), *The Prosecutor v. Jelisic* (IT-95-10), *The Prosecutor v. Cesic* (IT-95-10-1/a), *The Prosecutor v. Krstić* (IT-98-33), *The Prosecutor v. Brdjanin and Zupljanin* (IT-99-36), *The Prosecutor v. Blagojevic and Jokic* (IT-02-60), *The Prosecutor v. Nikolic* (IT-02-60/1), *The Prosecutor v. Obrenovic* (IT-02-60/2), *The Prosecutor v. Mejakic* et al. (IT-02-65), and *The Prosecutor v. Banovic* (IT-02-65), *The Prosecutor v. Limaj* et al. (IT-03-66), *The Prosecutor v. Milutinovic* et al. (IT-05-87), and *The Prosecutor v. Popovic* et al. (IT-05-88).

Forensic investigations play a crucial role in the successful prosecution of high-ranking officials as listed in the criminal cases prosecuted by the ICTR and ICTY. Moreover, such investigations provide public education and discourse about HHRR and contribute to the corpus of IHL and IHRL jurisprudence. In addition to witness and survivor testimony about human rights abuses, forensic science provides essential physical proof of crimes committed though new sources of information (Kirschner and Hannibal 1994). Eriksson and Wallensteen (2004) report:

> A total of 229 armed conflicts in 148 countries have been recorded for the period after World War II (1946–2003). Of these, 116 conflicts in 78 countries were active in the period after the end of the Cold War (1989–2003). Most conflicts are internal: only seven interstate armed conflicts were recorded in the period 1989–2003, of which two were still active in 2003. The measurement of armed conflict is mainly based on news reporting, and it suffers from national and cultural biases. But the scrutiny of armed conflict is becoming more intense, and new sources of information are emerging.

The investigation and excavation of graves for victim identification has itself been viewed as an act of justice and is well articulated in a report by the Commission for Historical Clarification in Guatemala (in Cordner and McKelvie 2002, 870): "The Commission believes that exhumation of the remains of the victims ... is in itself an act of justice and reparation and an important step of the path to reconciliation ... because it constitutes part of the right to know the truth and it contributes to the knowledge of the whereabouts of the disappeared ... ." The effect of

[*] For example, some of the most active organizations include the United Nations, the American Association for the Advancement of Science (AAAS), Physicians for Human Rights (PHR), Amnesty International, and various regional forensic teams (the Argentine Forensic Anthropology Team EAAF, the Guatemalan Forensic Anthropology Foundation FAFG, the Peruvian Forensic Anthropology Team EPAF, and the Colombian Interdisciplinary Team on Forensic Work and Psychosocial Services EQUITAS). Additionally, many forensic scientists from various fields have directly worked for governments, human rights organizations, and other nongovernmental organizations.

international criminal investigations on influencing the behavior of some perpetrators in their attempts to conceal crimes or avoid prosecution is well documented (*The Prosecutor v. Krstić,* IT-98-33). However, the range of effects from these criminal proceedings have yet to be fully realized.

An Epidemiological Framework for Trauma Analysis

Medicolegal death investigations provide critical evidence as to the manner and cause of death, the demography of victims, and the nature of crimes committed. The main objective of postmortem analysis is to diagnose skeletal wounds and accurately interpret the mechanism of injury, from which the diagnosis of the cause of death may be derived, as this evidence demonstrates whether a crime was committed. An epidemiological framework provides an accurate and meaningful approach to the differential diagnosis of wounds and their mechanism of injuries in the context of IHL and IHRL (Coupland 1994; Coupland 2001; Reza et al. 2001; Taback and Coupland 2005). Coupland (2001, 35) wrote, "An epidemiological approach to armed violence is an essential component in promoting and strengthening all laws, including international laws, pertaining to weapons and armed violence." Constructing an epidemiological paradigm for analysis of scientific evidence involves answering a number of questions. Building from Coupland's model (2001), we add components of differential diagnosis for skeletal wounds, evidence from the grave or fatal environment, weaponry, and ballistic science, as presented in Table 1.1. Epidemiological methods have been applied to paleopathology (e.g., refer to Cook and Powell [2006] for a general overview, or to Barrett et al. [1998] and Walker [2001] for specific examples). For various examples of demographic and other epidemiological variables' influence on wounding and skeletal trauma, refer to Ormstad et al. (1986), Missliwerz and Wieser (1989), and Leibovici et al. (1996). Applying this framework for forensic evidence provides context and new lines of data for a robust interpretation.

Demography

Demography is such an important topic for armed conflict and forensic science that it is an "emerging new field" within the auspice of IHL (Brunborg 2000; Brunborg and Tabeau 2005).

Table 1.1 Epidemiological Framework for Trauma Analysis

- Demography of victims
- Vulnerability of victims
- Wound to killed ratio
- Context
- Fatal environment
- Intention of perpetrators
- Scientific protocols
- Methods for differential diagnosis
- Weaponry and ballistics science
- Estimation of cause of death
- Manner of death

Coupland (2001, 33) wrote, "... weapons differ considerably both in the way they are used to execute violence and in their potential to do so; and the type and number of weapons available influence not only how, when, and why the violent act is committed, but also who the victims are and how they are affected." For example, gunfire and landmine injuries are more common among military fatalities in combat, whereas fragmenting explosive ordinance devices (EOD) are more common among civilians caught in an armed conflict (Meddings and O'Connor 1999). The age and sex distribution of victims, the ratio of wounded to killed, patterns among civilians versus soldiers, and the risk to victims provides evidence of the type of crime committed (Missliwerz and Wieser 1989; Leibovici et al. 1996; Salama et al. 1999). Former Under-Secretary-General for Humanitarian Affairs of the United Nations Jan Egeland* wrote:

> In Iraq, Sudan, Uganda, Somalia, Afghanistan and the Democratic Republic of the Congo ... civilians continued to bear the full brunt of armed conflict and terror. Despite all efforts, women were still raped and violated as a matter of course; children were still forcibly recruited; and defenseless civilians continued to be killed—in violation of the most basic principles enshrined in centuries of international lawmaking.

For example, the El Mozote Massacre in El Salvador (1981) resulted in the recovery and analysis of 143 skeletons, 136 of whom where children, whose mean age at death was 6 years (Amnesty International 1990). The children and adults were put into a church where they were murdered, and the church burned (Kirschner and Hannibal 1994). In another example, 420 patients in the Vukovar Hospital, Croatia (1992), were taken out of the hospital, bused to a nearby farm, and executed (Kirschner and Hannibal 1994). The remains of more than 200 individuals were recovered in a mass grave. The intentional targeting of a hospital in this example is not an isolated incident. The OSCE Verification Mission HHRR reports (1999a, 1999b) on violations in Kosovo in 1998–1999 discuss numerous incidents where children, the elderly, and the wounded were held for ransom, murdered in front of others to instill fear, raped, burned alive, or beaten. These examples illustrate the demographic trends of victims of mass atrocities, namely society's most vulnerable, noncombatants, small children, and the wounded who were specifically targeted (refer also to Dean [1992]). Refer to Case Study 6.1 in Chapter 6, "Disappearance, Torture and Murder of Nine Individuals in a Community of Nebaj, Guatemala," by Chacón and coworkers, for a further example of differential violence targeted at a 14-year-old boy.

Demography also has implications for wounding patterns and the identification of skeletal trauma based on differential morphological or physiological responses (Lee et al. 2006). For example, the immature skeletal remains of a child or the osteoporotic skeleton of an elderly female can substantially affect the morphology of skeletal wounds and influence fracture patterns or wound severity. A comprehensive study of 1155 injuries due to gunfire and blast injuries resulting from terrorist activity reports that gunfire victims were on average older than blast victims because of the specific public areas targeted for attack, such as buses and cafes (Peleg et al. 2004).

The unique contribution of anthropologists to medicolegal death investigations is their biocultural framework built on an understanding and study of human variation.

* UN, Security Council SC/8763, 5476th Meeting, 28 June 2006 http://www.un.org/News/Press/docs/2006/sc8763.doc.htm.

How does who you are or how healthy you are affect bone injuries? In other words, what does human variation have to do with biological differences in wounding? Bone composition depends on genetics, growth, health, age, the type of applied stress, and the underlying bony architecture (Gorman 1981). Therefore, individual characteristics such as who is injured or targeted, who survives, and what are the wounding features, i.e., differential fracture patterns may be significant in interpreting skeletal evidence in HHRR investigations (Gorman 1981a, 1981b, 1981c; Salama et al. 1999; Coupland 2001; Reza et al. 2001; Peleg et al. 2004; Taback and Coupland 2005; Stawicki et al. 2002; Ryan et al. 2006).

Context

Taback and Coupland (2005) report the most significant factors of mortality among civilian victims in armed conflicts are not only the number and type of weaponry but also the victim's vulnerability and the context. Context accounts for the intention of those perpetrating crimes and the fatal environment (i.e., where the incident took place). Were the victims fighting, detained, bound, crowded into a small concrete room, or lying in a field at the time of their deaths? Coupland (2001, 33–34) wrote:

> The extent of tissue damage is determined by the mass, velocity, construction, and stability in flight of the bullet as well as by the rapidity with which the weapon can fire multiple bullets. These are the "design-determined" effects of the weapon. The potential to use a weapon, however, is influenced by the weapon itself, the user's perception of the design-determined effect, and the number of other people armed. The users perception of the vulnerability of the intended victim or victims also comes into play.

The examples throughout this book demonstrate that the specific context of the victim at the time of death is not only informative about the manner of death but also has important implications in wounding variation. This is discussed in greater detail in subsequent chapters. For example, when dealing with HHRR violations or armed conflict, it is important to understand that the use of high-velocity assault rifles against civilians or detained persons will generate patterns of injury and mortality different then what is expected in traditional warfare (Meddings 1997; Michael et al. 1999).

Patterns vary when victims are intentionally targeted or medical treatment is not available, or not allowed. What implication does the context have for the interpretation and presentation of injuries? Coupland and Meddings (1999) demonstrate the ratio of the number of people injured to killed ranges from 2:1 to 13:1, depending on context. In situations in which people killed had been "immobilized, in a confined space, or unable to defend themselves," the ratio of wounded to killed may be zero and indicative of war crimes (Coupland and Meddings 1999, 407). Further, Coupland and Meddings (1999, 409) discuss the psychology of perpetrators, who at closer range aim for the head or chest, which results in a higher fatality rate:

> The My Lai massacre has been examined in depth. In the mass shootings in which the wounded-to-killed ratio was less than 1, the civilians were unarmed or could not take cover. The implication of this is that when the victims are military, an equally low wounded-to-killed ratio could be a strong indicator of death by execution rather than in battle.

Finally, cases in which victims were intentionally targeted may include evidence multiple shooters, multiple injuries, multiple mechanisms of injuries or other evidence of maltreatment. Refer to Case Study 1.1, by Snow and co-workers, presented at the end of this chapter, for a practical demographic example of possible war crimes.

Intent

Evidence of executions, such as blindfolds, ligatures, wounds to the back of the head, or those inflicted when the individual was in a kneeling or lying position and witness testimony or other investigative/documentary forms of evidence are all indicative of murder. The location, number, and severity of wounds also demonstrate this intention. For example, the frequency of injuries caused by firearms may provide an indication of intent because firearms require an "act of volition" (Meddings and O'Connor 1999). Moreover, the distribution of injuries in areas such as the head or trunk in civilian populations, devoid of body armor, provides additional evidence of the intention to kill (Baraybar 2006).

Moving human remains after *primary* interment results in commingled body parts and incomplete recovery of bodies. In the 2001 verdict against General Radislav Krstić (*The Prosecutor v. Krstić,* IT-98-33: 596, p. 212), evidence of *secondary* burials was accepted by the trial judges:

> ... a strong indication of the intent to destroy the group as such in the concealment of the bodies in mass graves, which were later dug up, the bodies mutilated and reburied in other mass graves located in even more remote areas, thereby preventing any decent burial in accord with religious and ethnic customs and causing terrible distress to the mourning survivors, many of whom have been unable to come to a closure until the death of their men is finally verified.

Consequently, the way in which bodies are disposed of and the specific burial environment may influence what data are present for analysis and show clear evidence of the intention to conceal crimes.

Scientific Protocol

The various exhumation, autopsy, anthropological, and investigative protocols for medicolegal death and missing persons investigations must be integrated in a way that provides a functional, consistent, and reliable model and at the same time remains flexible to adapt to varying contexts. International protocols for medicolegal death investigations, postmortem analysis, and forensic science are flexible and adaptable by design to fit the context and goals of each mission. International work in a multiplicity of cross-cultural settings requires protocols that can be adapted due to biological, cultural, and legal variation of each setting. At the same time, these protocols must be consistent in the collection, preservation, analysis, and presentation of data, built on scientific rigor and forensic standards such as chain of custody, to ensure the findings are reliable and admissible in court. Some examples of the guidelines commonly referenced for general standards of best practice include the Interpol's *Disaster Victim Identification Guide* (2005; first publication 1984), Protocol for Preventing Arbitrary Killings through Adequate Death Investigation and Autopsy ("Minnesota Protocol" 1988), *UN Manual on the Effective Prevention and Investigation of Extra-Legal, Arbitrary, and Summary Executions* (1991), *Guidelines for the Conduct of United Nations Inquiries into Allegations of Massacres* (1997), *Istanbul Protocol:*

Manual on the Effective Investigation and Documentation of Torture and Other Cruel, Inhuman or Degrading Treatment or Punishment (2001), and the Human Remains and Forensic Sciences Electronic Workshop (2002).

Anthropologists and pathologists are scientists, and as such serve as expert witnesses. Each discipline has a set of standard protocols and methodology for the documentation and analysis of trauma (Moritz 1954; Ortner and Putschar 1981; Spitz 1993; Buikstra and Ubelaker 1994; Mason and Purdue 2000). These methods are scientifically verified and peer-accepted to be admissible in most courts. Refer to Chapter 2 for an in-depth discussion of the anthropological protocol for trauma analysis, as used throughout this text and also to Snow (1982), Orentlicher (1990), and Olmbe and Yakub (2002).

The indictment against Pavle Strugar, retired Lieutenant general of the JNA (*The Prosecutor v. Pavle Strugar*, IT-01-42-T), included six counts of violation of the laws or customs of war (Article 3 of the Statute of the Tribunal) for the murder and maltreatment of four civilians during an artillery attack against Dubrovnik, Croatia. In this case, the defense attorney questioned the prosecution's witness, a forensic pathologist, as to whether the forensic protocol was followed. The defense claimed that the pathology report presented by the prosecution:

> ... was not compiled in conformity with the rules of forensic medicine. According to these forensic rules he contended, in a report, among other things, all wounds must be described, the exact amount of fluid must be measured, and consistency and colour of the blood must be recorded. [The pathologist] on the other hand did not use the required parameters [performed only an external examination, not a full autopsy, and] in his report and made liberal remarks, such as, "There is a lot of blood." (*The Prosecutor v. Pavle Strugar*, IT-01-42-T, Trial Judgment, 31 January 2005, para. 247: 116)

Although the defense attempted to demonstrate that the prosecution's witness (a pathologist) did not fulfill all of the legal requirements of an autopsy by following the protocol, the argument was not persuasive to the Trial Chamber:

> ... [autopsies] conducted under remarkable circumstances which explain entirely, in the Chamber's view, his nonobservance of more normal procedures. He had to examine the bodies of 19 deceased people on 7 December 1991. There was no power for refrigeration or lighting and there was no running water. Despite these restraints, in the Chamber's finding, he was able to draw on his clear expertise to reach entirely satisfactory and persuasive findings which the Chamber accepts. (*The Prosecutor v. Pavle Strugar*, IT-01-42-T, Trial Judgment, 31 January 2005, para. 257: 119)

Importantly, the Chamber recognized that the extenuating circumstance surrounding the postmortem examinations of the victims in a war zone, as carried out by the forensic pathologist, does not preclude the use of such evidence collected outside the boundaries of postmortem protocols.

Weaponry

In today's conflicts, most civilian deaths are caused by *small arms* (Aboutanos and Baker 1997), which by definition are light-weight and designed to be used by a single person (i.e., revolvers, pistols, rifles, shotguns, submachine guns, assault rifles, grenades, landmines, or mortars).

In many regions, even farming or utilitarian tools have been used to systematically commit HHRR abuses or war crimes, such as the use of machetes in the Rwandan Genocide (refer to Chapter 6 of this volume for a thorough discussion of these types of weapons and the resultant injuries).

Small arms are generally classified based on the materials used to construct the weapon and the intended purpose of the weapon, i.e., antipersonnel, antiaircraft, antitank, or hunting weapons (refer to Bellamy [1992], Boutwell et al. [1995], Bowen and Bellamy [2002], Ben-Ya'acov et al. [2005], and Celiköz et al. [2005] for wounds and weapons related to modern war). *Antipersonnel weapons* are those designed to attack people. Firearms include handguns (pistols and revolvers), rifles, and shotguns for which a chemical charge launches a projectile down a riffled or smooth-bored barrel. The term *missile* is generally used to describe projectile weapons but also refer to rockets that are guided after launch (Bellamy 1992). Explosive weapons are designed to be destructive either through a blast or by spreading shrapnel, which act as small projectiles.

Aboutanos and Baker (1997) point out that civilians account for the greatest number of casualties in modern wars with an increasing number of deaths resulting from explosive devices such as artillery and mines. According to Coupland (2001, 36), "small arms were transferred following the Cold War to many untrained, undisciplined, or nonmilitary users." This point is further illustrated in the Human Security Report, which states (2005, 5):

> Today most wars are fought in poor countries with armies that lack heavy conventional weapons or superpowers patrons. In a typical low-intensity conflict weak government forces confront small, ill-trained rebel forces equipped with small arms and light weapons. Skirmishes and attacks on civilians are preferred to major engagements.

The Conventional Arms Branch of the UN Department for Disarmament* reports:

> There are over 600 million small arms and light weapons (SALW) in circulation worldwide. Of 49 major conflicts in the 1990s, 47 were waged with small arms as the weapons of choice. Small arms are responsible for over half a million deaths per year, including 300,000 in armed conflict and 200,000 more from homicides and suicides.

Consequently, the high lethality of small arms and a lack of medical treatment in many conflicts, contributes to the high number of civilian casualties (Champion et al. 2003).

Cause and Manner of Death

T.D. Stewart (1979, 76) wrote, "When a forensic anthropologist has finished his examination of a skeleton, he is likely to be asked: 'Did you learn the cause of death?'" For Judicial accountability, the number, case, and manner of death must be considered. Can the cause and manner of death be ascertained from skeletonized or even fragmented remains? Can the cause of death be determined for the majority of individuals from a given site, considering that many mass atrocities often result in mass burials or *commingled* remains? Further, can the systematic and widespread distribution of crimes be demonstrated over a given time range or wide geographic distribution?

* Peace and Security through Disarmament. Conventional Arms Branch of the UN Department for Disarmament Affairs. http://disarmament.un.org/cab/index.html.

The cases presented throughout this book demonstrate that the answer to these questions is most often yes, cause and manner of death can be determined from skeletal injuries.

Anthropologists play leading roles in medicolegal death investigations into war crimes and HHRR abuses, from interviewing witnesses or family members about antemortem (or missing person's) information, to locating and excavating clandestine burials to the laboratory analysis of skeletal remains, in which they document skeletal trauma and biological parameters useful for victim identification. Although ascertaining the cause and manner of death falls within the expertise and legal responsibility of forensic pathologists, investigations into cases of war crimes, human rights abuses, extrajudicial executions, or armed conflicts most often occur years after the deaths occurred. Therefore, postmortem examinations in the course of these investigations occur after remains have become skeletonized. Clues about who the victims were and the circumstances surrounding their deaths lie in the bones themselves. Anthropologists and pathologists are tasked with piecing together the fragments of remaining skeletal tissue and associated physical evidence to elicit a mechanism of trauma that is factually based, methodologically scripted, and scientifically interpreted.

The *manner of death* explains how death occurred and assigns responsibility to nature, a random mishap, the decedent, or someone else. The classification system used in the medicolegal system includes five manners of death: natural, homicide, suicide, accidental, and indeterminate or unknown. The *cause of death* refers to the "medical condition which *initiates* the lethal chain of events culminating in death" (Adams and Hirsch 1993, 178). This is known as the proximate (or direct) cause and should not be confused with associated complications that may arise as a result. Numerous provisions of IHL and customary law provide guidelines for dealing with the deceased, including protocols for death investigations and diagnosing the cause of death (Tidball-Binz 2006). A few examples include guidelines on:

- How the dates and places of capture, death, and burial are to be recorded (Geneva Convention, Protocols I–IV)
- How the identity of victims, their personal effects, and the cause and manner of death are to be determined (Geneva Convention, Protocols I–IV)
- How the remains should be identified and repatriated to family members (Geneva Convention, Protocol I, Article 34[2][c])

How does the manner and cause of death contribute to the investigation and prosecution of violations of IHL? Stated simply, they establish whether a crime has been committed and, if so, what crime. In prosecuting violations of IHL, the individual and collective identities of victims and the circumstances surrounding the victim's death attests largely to whether a crime was committed. For example, during the trial of General Radislav Krstić (*The Prosecutor v. Krstić*, IT-98-33; para. 3769), the defense lawyer questioned the cause and nature of deaths as presented in court, which were largely attributed to gunfire. Specifically, the defense questioned whether the deaths resulted from combat or were in fact the result of suicides, to which the anthropological witness replied (*The Prosecutor v. Krstić*, IT-98-33; 3769): "Well, I just would like again to point out that I have investigated many suicides. I have never seen an individual with their hands bound behind their back shoot themselves multiple times."

The scientist as an expert witness provides a level or degree of certainty. Opinions and estimations of fact, drawn from physical evidence, are presented with varying levels of certainty such as a "reasonable degree of certainty," or a "preponderance of evidence" (Adams and Hirsch 1993, 191). Interpretations presented as "probable" are based on statistical levels of probability based on quantifiable likelihood estimates but are not applicable to trauma analysis. The documentation and interpretation of injuries are based on experience and professional opinion. The scientist who is called as a witness to provide testimony on trauma in a criminal trial provides an expert opinion. Adams and Hirsch (1993, 192) wrote:

> Medical opinions are conclusions based on facts. Some facts, such as gross autopsy findings generally do not change. Other facts, especially those derived from witness accounts, do change. Opinions are based on the facts and findings as they are known at the time the opinion is formulated. If the facts which form the foundation of the opinion changes, the opinion can and often will change.

The military shelling of civilian populations as already discussed in the case of *The Prosecutor v. Pavle Strugar* (IT-01-42-T) highlights a number of important issues of which anthropologists and pathologists need to be aware in their analysis of skeletal injuries, their reporting, as well as testimony (refer also to Kravetz [2004]). In this case, the defense attorney questioned the prosecution's forensic pathologist and claimed that the time and cause of death could not be determined from postmortem examination because the standard forensic protocol was not followed when only an external examination was performed:

> The Chamber has received, and accepts, evidence of the physical circumstances in which [the victim] was suddenly injured at the time of the explosion of a shell during the bombardment of the Old Town by JNA forces. [The victim] died a relatively short time thereafter. A skilled and experienced pathologist ... discovered that a fragment of shrapnel had torn his right lung from which death resulted. In the experienced opinion of [the pathologist] the injury bore all the characteristics of an injury caused by an explosive device ... There was an explosion of a military shell in the vicinity of [the victim]. He was obviously wounded when this occurred. Not long after he died. Examination revealed a shrapnel wound characteristic of such an explosion which caused injuries which would normally cause death if intervention could not prevent death. Given these circumstances the Chamber is entirely satisfied that the fact of death and the cause of death are established. (*The Prosecutor v. Pavle Strugar,* IT-01-42-T, Trial Judgment, 31 January 2005, para. 248: 116)

Importantly, this case demonstrates that even when the specific cause of death cannot be ascertained, as in many instances in which only skeletal evidence is present, the *fact of death* may be established by the nature of the injuries and the lack of medical intervention.

In a prior case prosecuted by the ICTY, the same issue was addressed and shown to apply also to cases in which there may not be a body but death can be inferred from other evidence. According to the trial judgment in *The Prosecutor v. Krnojelac* (IT-97-25; Trial Chamber II Judgment, 15 March 2002, para. 326):

> The fact of a victim's death can be inferred circumstantially from all of the evidence presented to the Trial Chamber. All that is required to be established from that evidence is that the only reasonable inference from the evidence is that the victim is dead ...

In this and similar cases,* the prosecution has been able to demonstrate that the nature of injuries, without medical intervention would have been inevitably fatal. A similar concept,

* Refer also to *The Prosecutor v. Kvocka* et al., IT-98-30/1, Appeals Judgment, para. 260, *The Prosecutor v. Tadic,* IT-94-1, Trial Judgment, para. 240, and *The Prosecutor v. Strugar,* IT-01-42, Trial Chamber, para. 236.

fatal if untreated, has been used as a category for the documentation of injuries and provides a framework for determing the *most likely cause of death* (Baraybar and Gasior 2006).

Summary Guidelines for Best Practice

Two decades after the application of forensic sciences to human rights reporting and enforcement, the potential of the field are just beginning to be realized. As anthropologists, pathologists, and forensic investigators work in postconflict societies within the framework of transitional justice, they are challenged as scientists to work within an epidemiological framework—cognizant of culture, context, and varying legal systems. Interpreting trauma to estimate the cause and manner of death helps families and communities. Work in this area over the past 20 years has raised the bar for standards of serving both families and the judicial system. New technology and innovations such as DNA analysis add promise for victim identification; at the same time, practical constraints to funding and access remind investigators that the process must move along a path toward justice, in keeping with the practical functional needs of the communities and judicial entities being served.

Technological advances are widening and strengthening the use of forensics in the pursuit of justice. Future applications will require interdisciplinary teams for investigative and analytical purposes, the creation of specialized teams to ascertain the fate of the missing after internal conflicts, a need for training local practitioners in conflict areas, and innovative solutions to bring new lines of evidence to light. There is also a need for creative solutions to make the results accessible and understandable to members of the communities being served, refinement of protocols and methods for increased reliability and broad applicability, and cooperation between States regarding the fate of missing persons after international conflicts. Above all, science and technology must become accessible and applicable in the countries where armed conflicts occur and where financial support is not always available. The need for multidisciplinary research in anthropology, medicine, forensics, and international law cannot be postponed. Building from the model and jurisprudence of international tribunals, future investigations will find an appropriate epidemiological model useful for enforcing human rights through forensics.

Case 1.1: Firefight in Lima: Wounded/Killed Ratio Analysis of MRTA Casualties in the 1997 Hostage Rescue Operation at the Japanese Embassy

Clyde Collins Snow
Norman, Oklahoma

José Pablo Baraybar
Peruvian Forensic Anthropology Team

Herbert Spirer
Columbia University, New York
Professor Emeritus of Information Management
University of Connecticut at Stamford

Investigators of alleged human rights violations resulting in many deaths are often confronted with conflicting stories. On one hand, the accused perpetrators—usually military or police—stoutly maintain the victims were killed in armed confrontations. On the other hand, survivors and their sympathizers adamantly claim the dead were victims of extrajudicial execution. Forensic scientists investigating such events must put aside the claims of both sides and, instead, objectively follow the evidence wherever it leads. Stated simply, they must let the dead tell their own stories.

In a 1999 review article, Coupland and Meddings (1999) compared the proportion of combatants wounded to those killed (W/K ratio) in ordinary combat with instances in which defenseless people are killed in mass murders. In conventional warfare, they found that, normally, the wounded outnumber fatalities by at least two to one (W/K $\geq$ 2). In mass murders, on the other hand, the number killed is usually greater than the number wounded (W/K $\leq$ 1). The authors conclude that the W/K ratio has implications for recognizing violations of the internationally accepted rules of warfare. Thus, in incidents in which the killed outnumber the wounded, the "threshold of suspicion" that such a violation may have occurred is lowered. They suggest the W/K ratio may be helpful in developing a preliminary evaluation of the nature of mass casualty incidents reported in the media or other sources and therefore might be a useful rule of thumb for journalists, human rights investigators, and others who monitor compliance with the laws of war.

To illustrate, suppose "Force Red" attacks a town defended by "Force Blue." After a battle lasting a couple of days, Force Red prevails and occupies the town and their commander announces that 500 Force Blue soldiers were killed but does not allow journalists to verify his claim by visiting the battlefield. However, an enterprising reporter visits the local hospital and finds that only 50 Force Blue wounded were brought there for treatment. If it is assumed that the Force Red commander was telling the truth, the W/K ratio would be 50/500 or 0.1, suspiciously low, suggesting that many of the Force Blue defenders were killed while trying to surrender or after being wounded. On the other hand, it is also possible that he was simply attempting to bolster his military reputation by exaggerating the extent of his victory. In either case, the low W/K ratio triggers doubts that would justify further investigation. If this led to the exhumation of the mass grave where the Force Blue fatalities were buried and only ten bodies were found (W/K ratio = 5.0), the Force Red commander would simply be exposed as a liar. However, if it indeed revealed 500 bodies, the low ratio of wounded to dead might suggest a war crime and justify further investigation.

As forensic scientists who frequently serve as expert witnesses are fully aware, testimony based on a "rule of thumb" is not likely to carry much weight with an aggressive cross-examiner or a skeptical judge. On the other hand, opinions that can be soundly defended with good science and statistics are usually well received in court. We feel that the data on which the authors based their findings are sufficient to lend some statistical rigor to their approach and, therefore, might prove a valuable evidentiary tool.

In the present study, we will explore this possibility by applying the Coupland–Meddings approach to the 1997 operation conducted by Peruvian special forces to rescue hostages held by 14 *Movimiento Revolucionario Tupac Amaru (MRTA)* terrorists in the Japanese embassy in Lima. Although exemplary in planning and execution in that 71 of 72* hostages were rescued, essentially unscathed, all 14 of the *MRTA* terrorists were killed. Soon after the attack, stories began to circulate that some of the guerillas had been extrajudicially executed. For example,

> One of the hostages said that he saw a member of the *Tupac Amaru* … shot to death despite the fact that he was holding up his hands in surrender …. Another said that he saw an *MRTA* rebel captured alive and taken out by soldiers, "I realized that the arrested rebel was killed when I heard a report that all 14 rebel members died in the raid," he said. (*Asahi Evening News*, April 24, 1997)
>
> A CNN report on April 25 cited a Lima newspaper (*La Republica*) as stating that the two female rebels were not killed in the initial assault and that listening devices picked up their pleas not to shoot as they huddled in a doorway but that the soldiers open fire. An unidentified intelligence officer was given as the source of this information.
>
> Shortly after the incident, Hidetaka Ogura, an embassy political officer, stated that he saw three of the guerillas—two men and one woman—alive and held as prisoners. The woman and one of the men, who was handcuffed, were standing on the second floor, surrounded by soldiers. On the first floor, he saw the third man, whom he recognized as "Tito" (Eduardo Nicolas Cruz Sanchez), lying on the floor, handcuffed with his feet trussed. Mr. Ogura's steadfastness in this claim apparently cost him his diplomatic career, and he has been accused of being a victim of the "Stockholm syndrome." He has since written a book recounting his hostage experience (Caretas 2001, 1661).

Peruvian authorities staunchly denied these claims:

> "All of them died in combat," Peruvian Interior Minister General Cesar Saucedo said … Peruvian President Alberto Fujimori … vehemently denies any executions took place (CNN, April 27, 1997).

Methods

This study is based on military casualty figures reported in the medical literature and other official sources. The casualties were incurred in conflicts in which the internationally accepted rules of war have generally been observed and in which both sides have employed conventional weapons. The latter, as defined by Coupland and Meddings (1999, 407), "legitimate weapons … that utilize projectiles or nonnuclear explosions." They thus include firearms as

* An elderly male hostage died of an apparent heart attack a few hours after being rescued.

Table 1.2 Nonfatal (NFW) and Fatal Wounds (FW) in Conventional Warfare (CWF) Conflicts

No.	Conflict	Nonfatal Wounds	Fatal Wounds	Total Casualties	FrqF	Reference
1	U.S. Army, New Georgia 1943	3873	1094	4967	0.220	Hopkins 1962
2	U.S. Army, Burma 1944	156	56	212	0.264	Hopkins 1962
3	U.S. Army, Bougainville 1944	1393	395	1788	0.221	Oughterson et al. 1962
4	U.S. Army, Italy 1944	52386	15642	68028	0.230	Snyder and Culbertson 1962
5	U.S. Army, Europe 1945	148816	42401	191217	0.222	Bzik and Bellamy 1984
6	U.S. Army, Korea 1950–53	77788	21310	99098	0.215	Bzik and Bellamy 1984
7	U.S. Marine Corps, Korea 1950–53	23744	4267	28011	0.152	Bellamy 2000
8	British Army, Malaya 1950–53	386	204	590	0.346	Clyne 1955
9	U.S. Army, Dominican Republic 1965–66	172	27	199	0.136	Pike 2005
10	U.S. Navy, *USS Liberty* attack 1967	170	33	203	0.163	Pike 2005
11	U.S. Army, Korean DMZ 1966–69	111	43	154	0.279	Pike 2005
12	U.S. Army, Vietnam 1964–73	96811	28862	125673	0.230	Bzik and Bellamy 1984
13	U.S. Marine Corps, Vietnam 1964–73	51399	12944	64343	0.201	Bzik and Bellamy 1984
14	Omani Forces, Oman 1972–73	71	9	80	0.113	Melsom et al. 1975
15	British Army, North Ireland 1970–80	1700	300	2000	0.150	Smith 1981
16	British Army North Ireland 1974–84 (bombs)	612	216	828	0.261	Mellor and Cooper 1989
17	U.S. Army, *Mayaguez* rescue 1975	50	18	68	0.265	Pike 2005
18	Israeli Army, Lebanon 1982	1599	351	1950	0.180	Gofrit et al. 1997
19	U.S. Army, Grenada 1983	119	19	138	0.138	Pike 2005
20	U.S. Army, Panama 1989	292	25	317	0.079	Dice 1991
21	U.S. Army, Persian Gulf War 1991	458	147	605	0.243	Pike 2005
22	Croatian Army 1991–92	78	15	93	0.161	Butkovic-Soldo et al. 1995
23	U.S. Army, Somalia 1993	125	18	143	0.126	Mabry et al. 2000
24	Israeli Army, Palestine 2001–2	73	23	96	0.240	Lakstein and Blumenfeld 2005
25	U.S. Marine Corps, Iraq 2003	337	56	393	0.142	Chambers et al. 2005

well as fragment-producing explosive devices ranging from hand grenades to artillery shells, missiles, and aerial bombs. It is also understood that they are nonchemical/biological.

Coupland and Meddings cited eleven studies dealing with casualties sustained in combat between ground forces. In reviewing the literature, we have found 14 additional reports, including one of a naval action, bringing the total series to 25. Chronologically, the conflicts range from World War II to U.S. marine casualties in Iraq in 2003. Eighteen (72.0%) are reports on casualties sustained by U.S. forces. The remaining seven treat casualties of other armed forces: British (n = 3), Israeli (n = 2), Omani (n = 1), Croatia (n = 1). Most of these reports were compiled by military physicians and statisticians whose objectives were to evaluate the effects of weapons, improve treatment of the wounded, and assess the protection offered by body armor. They are confined to the study of battlefield casualties caused by hostile action and do not include illness and death from disease or from injuries in "behind-the-lines" incidents such as vehicular or aircraft accidents. The studies from which we have drawn the data used in the analysis are shown in Table 1.2.

In the data tabulated in Table 1.2, the first category, *nonfatal wounds* (NFW), refers to hospitalized casualties; it does not include lightly wounded combatants returned to duty after treatment in the field. The second category, *fatal wounds* (FW), includes both those killed in action (KIA) and those who died of wounds (DOW) after hospitalization.

For statistical convenience, we use the *frequency* of fatal wounds among all casualties rather than the ratio of killed to wounded employed by Coupland and Meddings. Thus,

$$\textit{Frequency of fatal wounds (frqF)} = FW/(NFW + FW) \tag{1.1}$$

Results

The distribution of *frqF* values in the surveyed conventional warfare series is shown in Figure 1.1. Despite the wide variation in the type and size of conventional warfare (CWF) conflicts, the frequency of fatal wounds has remained close to about one in five over the six decades of this survey. Although the series is small, it meets the criterion of a Gaussian (normal) distribution (*Kolmogorov–Smirnov distance* = *0.121*, $p > 0.10$, *ns*). The 95% *prediction interval* (P.I.) defines the limits beyond which values are statistically significant at the 0.05 probability level.

Thus, an incident in which fatally wounded combatants comprise more than a third of total casualties, (*frq*F > 0.33) falls above the limit expected in conflicts where legitimate weapons are used and the laws of conventional warfare observed. Such a statistically unusual incident might prove worthy of further investigation to determine, if possible, what factors were at work to produce such a high fatality rate.

An Example: The *MRTA* Incident

As noted previously, soon after the embassy hostages had been rescued, controversy arose over allegations that at least some of the *MRTA* combatants had been extrajudicially executed after being wounded, or having surrendered. This suspicion was fueled in part by allegations of witnesses among the hostages themselves. However, as many studies have shown, eyewitness statements often prove fallible, especially in tense and life-threatening situations. Forensic scientists investigating such incidents must confine their analysis to objectively observable facts. In the case of the embassy firefight, it begins with the stark mathematical

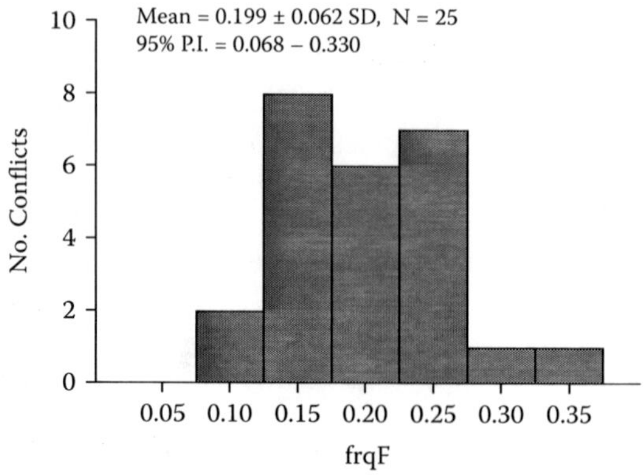

Figure 1.1 Distribution of frequencies of fatal wounds (*frqF*) in conventional warfare conflicts (1943–2003).

fact that there were no survivors among the 14 *MRTA* combatants. In this case, the *frqF* is 14/14 or 1.0, the highest possible value and one that far exceeds the CWF series mean of 0.199.

However, a further factor must be considered: the relatively small number of *MRTA* combatants. Even when the laws of war are observed, such a small force might all receive lethal wounds just by chance. In other words, sometimes the "fortunes of war" transmute into "bad luck." It is therefore fair to ask how often, through chance alone, might we expect to encounter a 100% mortality rate in a group of 14 wounded in a CWF situation? The binomial probability of such an outcome is calculated from the equation:*

$$P_{N:F} = \left(\frac{N!}{F!(N-F)!} \right) frqF^{F}(1-frqF)^{N-F} \tag{1.2}$$

where
N = Number of seriously wounded (NWF + FW)
F = Number of fatally wounded (FW)
*frq*F = Mean frequency of fatal wounds in CWF combat
$P_{N:F}$ = Probability of F fatal wounds in N wounded

In the embassy case, N = 14, F = 14, and *frq*F = 0.199, so substituting the values in the preceding equation yields:

$$P_{14:14} = \left(\frac{14!}{14!(14-13)!} \right)(0.199)^{14}(1-0.199)^{14-1}$$

$$P_{14:14} = 0.00000000015 \tag{1.3}$$

* The tedious calculations involved can be avoided by using a spreadsheet function such as "BINOMDIST" in Microsoft Excel, which returns the binomial probability of observing a specified number of "successes" in a fixed number of independent "trials."

Discussion

From the preceding account, it is apparent that the chances of all 14 *MRTA* combatants being killed in an ordinary CWF are extremely remote. The finding allows the case to be pinpointed as one worth further investigation to determine, if possible, what factors were at work to produce the observed results. Ideally, such an effort would be multifaceted. The investigation would begin, of course, with a detailed examination of the scene itself, using accepted forensic methods such as blood-splatter and trajectory analysis in relation to body locations. It would also include detailed medicolegal autopsies of the victims to determine the number, location, and range of their wounds. A third investigatory component would consist of detailed and independent, after-action interviews of combat participants and other witnesses to see to what extent they corroborate or contradict the material evidence collected through the crime scene and autopsy investigations. Any available documentary evidence, such as orders specifying the roles of combatants and rules of engagement would also be collected and reviewed. Finally, meta-analysis of the scene, medicolegal testimonial, and documentary evidence would be conducted.

In the *MRTA* case, it might be found that certain factors of the combat environment contributed to the higher-than-expected mortality. For example, one factor might be *range*—the distance between the shooter and the targeted opponent. Shots fired at closer range result in larger wounds and increase the chance of multiple wounds—especially when automatic weapons are employed. Also, at closer ranges, shooters are more likely to direct their fire at the head or chest (Grossman 1995). Average ranges would have been shorter within the confined space in which the *MRTA* casualties occurred. Another environmental factor that may have influenced the outcome was *target density*—a function of the number of shooters to the number of targets. The 14 (n = 14) *MRTA* were outnumbered by a factor of about 10:1 (ten to one); therefore, the probability of their receiving multiple wounds was correspondingly increased. Finally, autopsy findings of close-range gunshot wounds of the head, corroborated with eyewitness testimony of the hostages, might confirm the allegations of extrajudicial executions.

Conclusion

The MRTA mortality rate observed during the hostage rescue mission at the Japanese Embassy in Lima is significantly higher than the range observed in modern military conflicts in which conventional arms are employed. While this finding is not evidence *per se* of a war crime, it lowers the threshold of suspicion that at least some wounded or captured MRTA combatants may have been executed. As wounded combatants are protected by the first Geneva Convention and prisoners of war by the third, the further investigation of this case as a possible war crime is justified.*

* The remains of all fourteen MRTA victims were disinterred in March 2001 and brought to the *Instituto Medicolegal de Lima (IML)*. There they were examined jointly by two authors of this report (CC Snow & JP Barybar), assisted by members of the *Equipo Peruano de Anthropologia Forense (EPAF)* and *IML* pathologists. Examination of cranial gunshot wounds indicate that, indeed, several of the victims had been extra-judicially executed. These findings will be published elsewhere (Snow and Baraybar, *manuscript in preparation*).

Differential Diagnosis of Skeletal Injuries

2

What are all the possible causes of a pathological condition and which one is the most likely cause?

Don Ortner*

Contents

Reconstructing Skeletal Fractures to Identify Trauma 22
Skeletal Reconstruction: A Practical Example of Associating Remains from Multiple Sites 27
The Anthroposcopic Examination of Skeletal Injuries 30
Ruling Out Normal Skeletal Variation and Skeletal Pathology 32
Classification of Fractures and Mechanisms of Injury 44
The Microscopic Examination of Skeletal Tissue 54
The Timing of Fracture Based on Gross Inspection 54
Antemortem Fractures 55
Peri- versus Postmortem Fractures 57
Peri- versus Postmortem Burning 65
Diagnosis of Injuries without Evidence of a Defect 70
Radiography and Three-Dimensional Imaging 71
The Usefulness of Clothing as Evidence 80
Photography 85
Summary Guidelines for Best Practice 86
Case Study 2.1: Finite Element Models of the Human Head in the Field of Forensic Science *By J.S. Raul, B. Ludes, and R. Willinger* 87

Accuracy in the skeletal diagnosis of injuries around the time of an individual's death relies on the integration of as many lines of evidence as possible. Data from a variety of sources should be used in combination—the anthropologist's examination of the skeletal tissues, microscopic analysis of the affected bone surfaces, radiographic data, the assessment of the individual's clothing, the evaluation of the physical evidence of weaponry, etc. After all the evidence is considered, deduction is used to classify each injury category, identify the mechanism of the injury, and determine the most likely cause of death.

The objectives of this chapter are to demonstrate the techniques for reconstructing fragmented skeletal remains and outline the methodology for identifying skeletal trauma. First, fractures resulting from possible injuries are differentiated from normal skeletal variation and nontraumatic skeletal pathology. Second, a brief overview of fracture classification and mechanisms of injury provide a framework for interpreting trauma data. Third, the timing of fractures is established to differentiate antemortem injuries, perimortem

* Ortner 2003, 4.

trauma, and postmortem modification or taphonomic processes. Fourth, supporting evidence for trauma identification from radiographic data and clothing analysis are presented. Additionally, the characteristics of burned bone and features used to differentiate peri- from postmortem burning and microscopic techniques for interpreting fracture evidence are discussed. (Refer to case study 2.1.)

Reconstructing Skeletal Fractures to Identify Trauma

A postmortem examination of skeletal remains begins with radiography or fluoroscopy,* followed by detailed examination of each bone and associated clothing, to ensure that all evidence, even the smallest skeletal fragments, are recovered. The skeletal remains are washed and laid out in anatomical order. Adherent tissues are removed either through washing or boiling. The anthropologist then reconstructs fractured bones so that the fracture type, pattern, and overall distribution of wounds are evident. Adhesive material is used to bind fractured skeletal remains.† The strongest and easiest adhesives to use are "instant adhesives" or commercial grade cyanoacrylates composed of methyl methacrylate, which are activated with a catalyst or accelerator. This type of adhesive is instantly binding and creates a very strong bond that allows reconstructed skeletal elements to be handled, photographed, and if necessary, radiographed without the need of external support structures. In our experience, this type of glue often remains bonded even after reconstructed skeletal elements are placed in body bags, transported, and later reexamined.

Skeletal reconstructions of fractured remains, depends on the amount and type of fracturing, subsequent warping or deformation due to burial, or other postmortem damage. Experience has shown that creating two units, the face and vault, and then uniting the two segments create an accurate and stable reconstruction. When reconstructing fragmented cranial remains, each bone is put together as completely as possible before uniting different structures to one another. Once each bone is reconstructed, then aspects of the vault should be articulated, beginning with the left and right parietals. The occipital should then be added to the parietals followed in order by the frontal, temporals, and sphenoid. We recommend reconstructing the facial bones by first attaching the nasals and zygomatics to the maxilla. Depending on the location and nature of the fractures, it is sometimes necessary to first attach the zygomatics to the frontal and temporal bones and then add the maxilla. Approaching the cranium anatomically as two units, the vault and the face, and uniting them with the sphenoid create an accurate and strong reconstruction. Figures 2.1–2.2 depicts a cranial reconstruction following a gunshot wound to the skull. Extreme fragmentation is consistent with high-velocity trauma, particularly when multiple injuries are present. Through the reconstruction, the fracture patterns are elucidated and enough information about the injuries is available to accurately interpret the mechanism and number of injuries.

* Although scanning the remains with an x-ray machine or a fluoroscope is recommended, it is not always possible in cases where such equipment is not available. Close examination of remains and clothing will recover metal fragments and is recommended (Baraybar and Gasior 2006).

† It is recommended that samples for DNA or histology are taken prior to the use of adhesives or any chemical agent for processing. The protocol described here for skeletal reconstruction is based on practical experience; varying contexts may require modification to laboratory methods. It may not always be possible to reconstruct skeletal remains due to deformation from burial or incomplete recovery (Refer to Steadman et al. 2006 for discussion of lab methods.)

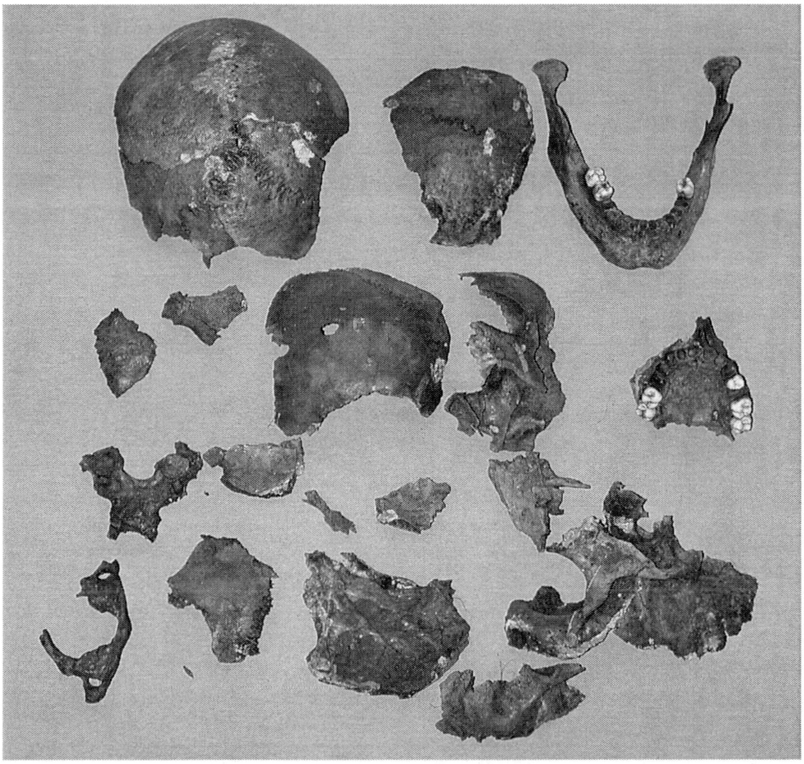

Figure 2.1 Fractured cranial remains are washed and laid out in anatomical order. Two circular entry wounds are present on the right parietal. The first cervical vertebra is fractured and the left maxilla exhibits a circular defect indicating additional injuries. Extreme fragmentation is consistent with high-velocity trauma. (Printed with permission from International Criminal Tribunal for the former Yugoslavia.)

Figure 2.2a Reconstruction begins with each bone individually. Bones of the vault are joined followed by the face. Fragments are joined posteriorly to anteriorly. The lateral fragments are then added to the vault and face. Pictured here is Edixon Quinones, OMPF (ICTY).

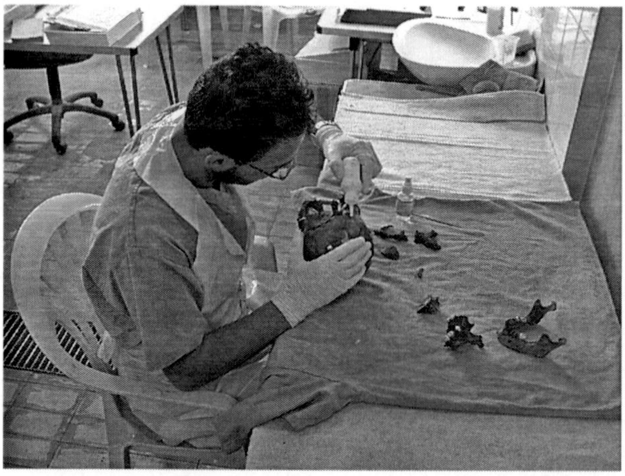

Figure 2.2b The vault is reconstructed and the smaller fragments are added to the vault (ICTY).

Figure 2.2c "Hot glue" adhesive material is used to reconstruct fractured elements together (ICTY).

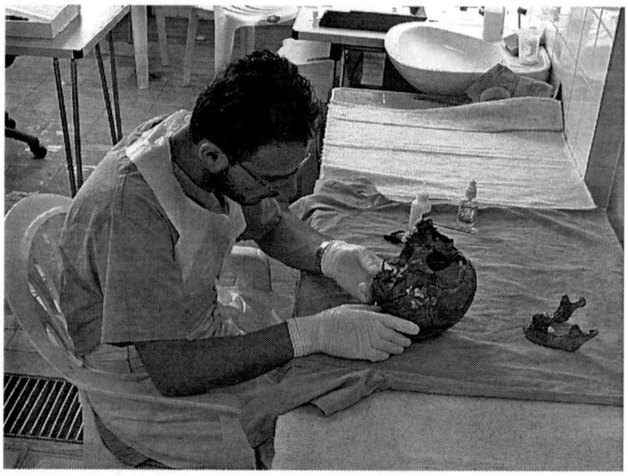

Figure 2.2d The base of the skull is reconstructed once the calotte is in place. (Printed with permission from International Criminal Tribunal for the former Yugoslavia.)

Reconstruction of the mandible and most postcranial elements tends to be simpler than that of the cranium, although extreme damage in the form of crushing and comminuted fractures may shatter structures, such as areas of spongy bone in the distal femur or lower vertebra. Fractures through thick areas of trabecular bone from crushing mechanisms may be more difficult to reconstruct. Nevertheless, attention to the outer cortex of the remaining bone will often reveal typical wound characteristics that allow the mechanism of the injury to be estimated.

The largest fragments should be reconstructed first, followed by smaller sections of bone added to the primary or larger piece. To begin, investigators work through the fragments, uniting segments into units and then combining the units together. These units may then be combined to whatever extent possible and added to the bone from which it fractured. Figure 2.3 illustrates the reconstruction of a comminuted fracture to the femoral shaft fragmented by a gunshot wound in an autopsy case.

Successful reconstructions are dependent on expert knowledge of osteology and the ability to recognize and position small fragments of bone. Of equal importance is good

Figure 2.3a The projectile penetrated from the lateral aspect of the left thigh and exited through its medial wall, creating a keyhole defect on the anterior wall of the proximal one-third of the femoral shaft. Trajectory of the bullet demonstrates piercing of the femoral artery. (Reprinted with permission from Baraybar, J.P. and Gasior, M. 2006. Forensic anthropology and the determination of the most probable cause of death: an example from Bosnia and Herzegovina. *J Forensic Sci* 51(1): 103–108.)

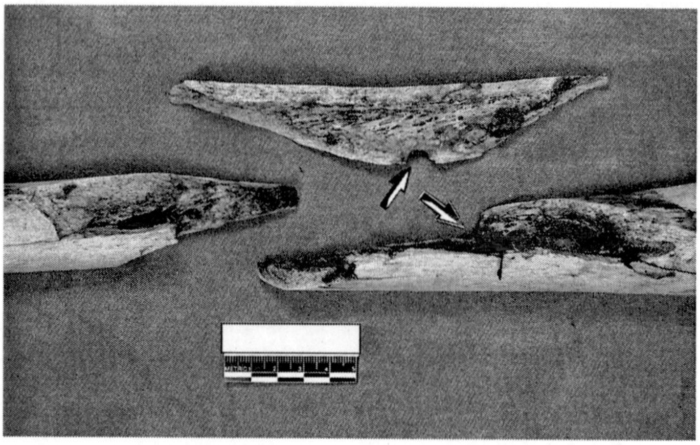

Figure 2.3b Comminute femoral shaft before reconstruction. (Reprinted with permission from Baraybar, J.P. and Gasior, M. 2006. Forensic anthropology and the determination of the most probable cause of death: an example from Bosnia and Herzegovina. *J Forensic Sci* 51(1): 103–108.)

archaeological recovery of all fragments. Therefore, careful excavation and assessment of clothing is crucial, as small fragments may be embedded in clothing or become disarticulated following decomposition of the soft tissues. The type of weaponry or blasting material used to create the injury may also compromise the recovery of fragments. Bone and tissue may be expelled at the time of injury or pass through the body as secondary projectiles and therefore not even be present at the time of burial. The use of *secondary burials*, in which graves are dug up and moved to new and different sites also results in a loss of materials as bone becomes exposed and small fragments disarticulated. Ultimately, complete recovery of all skeletal elements depends on the context and archaeological excavation of the grave. Despite great efforts in some cases to hide burials (Schmitt 2001; Skinner et al. 2001), skeletal fragments resulting from gunfire wounds to the head have been recovered from multiple sites and rearticulated in the laboratory.

Figure 2.3c Reconstruction of a femur exhibiting a through-and-through single gunshot to the left thigh with high-velocity ammunition, 7.62 × 39 mm. (Reprinted with permission from Baraybar, J.P. and Gasior, M. 2006. Forensic anthropology and the determination of the most probable cause of death: an example from Bosnia and Herzegovina. *J Forensic Sci* 51(1): 103–108.)

Skeletal Reconstruction: A Practical Example of Associating Remains from Multiple Sites

This example demonstrates how skeletal materials from multiple locations were reconstructed based on skeletal morphology and later confirmed through DNA testing (Figures 2.4–2.8). In July 1998, the Kosovo Liberation Army (UÇK, Ushtria Clirimatre e Kosovoës) detained 85 Kosovo-Serb civilians in the vicinity of the Orahovac/Rahovec village. After the subsequent release of 45 of the victims, approximately 40 males were still unaccounted for (HRW 1998).

In October 2004, the police undertook an investigation into a case of 16 unidentified bodies that had been exhumed and autopsied by the ICTY in 1999. The remains were reburied on the eastern side of the Peja/Pec cemetery. These bodies, apparently due to their condition, could not be identified at the time of the autopsies. According to the information from various human rights organizations in Kosovo, seven other corpses were found in different locations in the Peja/Pec region between 2000 and 2001 and were brought to the morgue of Peja/Pec hospital. Following autopsies, they were also buried in the Peja/Pec cemetery. It was not clear at the time whether the remains were associated, due to their incompleteness. In November 2004, one of the graves in Peja/Pec cemetery, marked with a wooden marker but without an inscription, was exhumed and given a site code. This grave contained eleven plastic bags and body bags containing multiple skeletal remains.

In April 2001, the Regional Investigation Unit responded to three separate calls about the existence of bones, allegedly human, found by people searching in a cave between the Volljak/Volujak and Sverska villages, in the Kline/Klina municipality of Kosovo. The police were given a number of bones and pieces of clothing, allegedly exposed by rainwater and light excavation. The skeletal remains were transported to the Rahovec/Orahovac mortuary where they were kept. A brief examination of the remains concluded that more than one individual was represented and that it was possible further remains were still to be found at the location from which they were originally collected.

The Volljak/Volujak site consists of a large crater (20 × 10 m), at the bottom of which is the entrance of a cave that spans more than 245 m. The depth of the crater is approximately 25 m

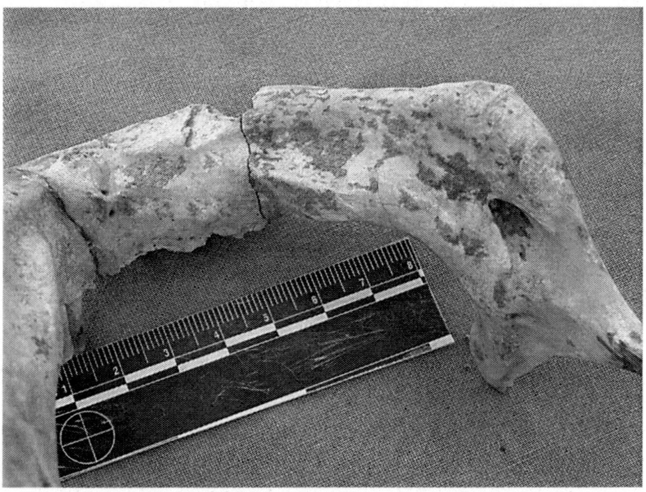

Figure 2.4 Two reassociated fragments of mandible found in different locations: a cave (left ramus) and in buried in a cemetery (symphysis) (Alain Wittmann).

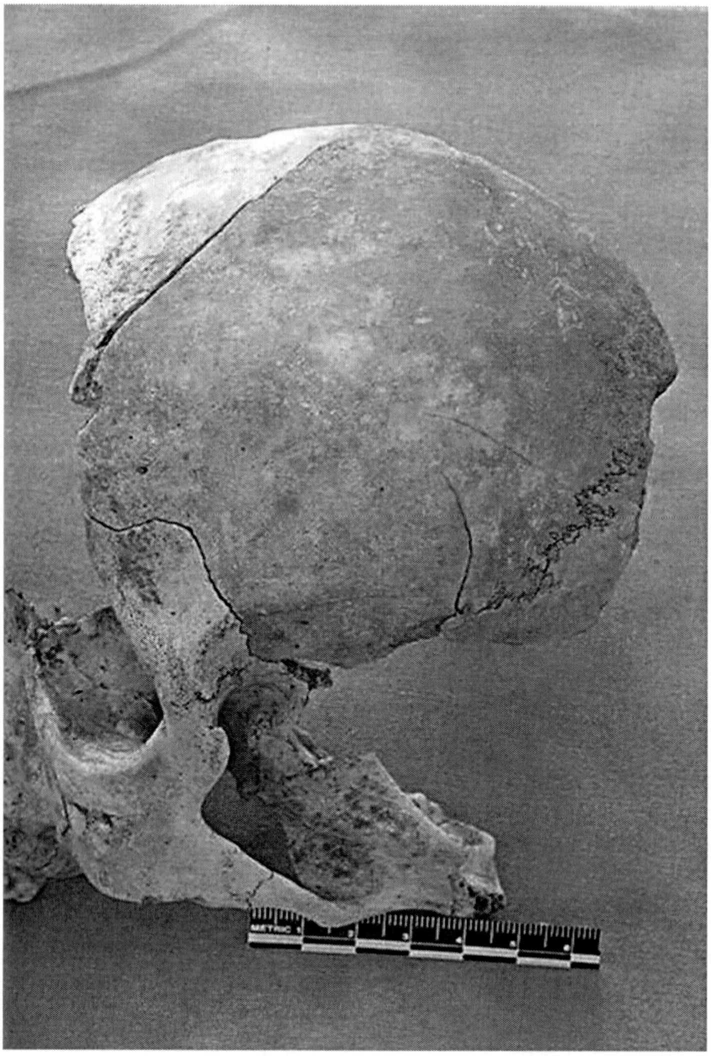

Figure 2.5 Reassociated fragments. The left side of the face of this individual was found in the cave, whereas a fragment of the frontal bone was found in the cemetery (Alain Wittmann).

and is part of a geological formation characterized by volcanic rock. A narrow ravine connects the cave complex to a nearby plain from which floodwaters and melting snow follow their course into the cave. The cave is characterized by a succession of chambers of different sizes; in general terms, the entrance is tall and wide and becomes narrower as it progresses. The surface of the cave is irregular, ascending and descending in different sections, with a total of 13.7 m from the entrance of the cave down to its end, vertically.

Human remains, shell cases, clothing, and other items such as car keys were found on the ground surface, both outside and inside the cave. The excavation and reconnaissance of items began in the interior of the cave from the sections farthest from the entrance. Some of the sectors had areas with water that had to be pumped out. In certain areas, a ladder was installed to reach the bottom of the underground reservoirs into which the remains had washed.

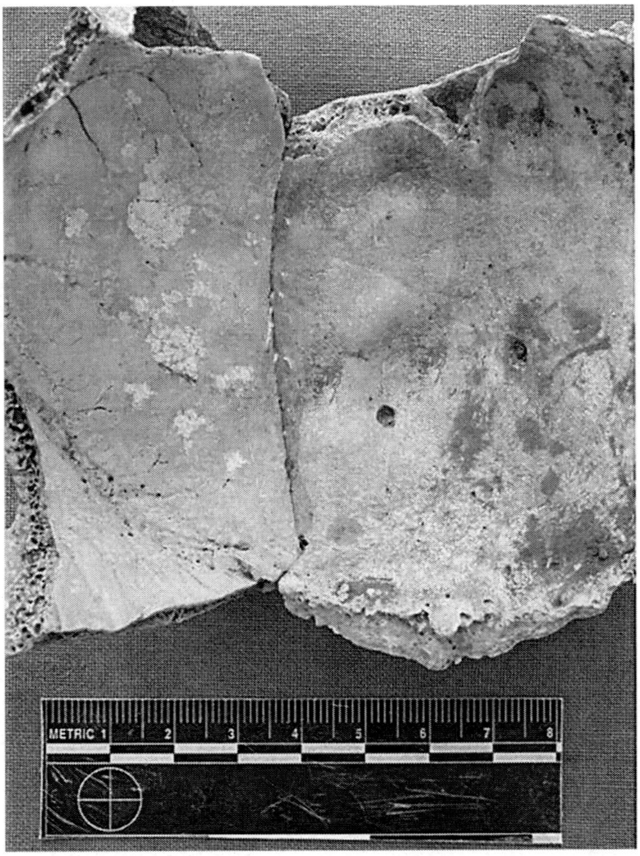

Figure 2.6 Reassociated fragments. Two fragments of frontal bone found in different locations (cave and cemetery) (Alain Wittmann).

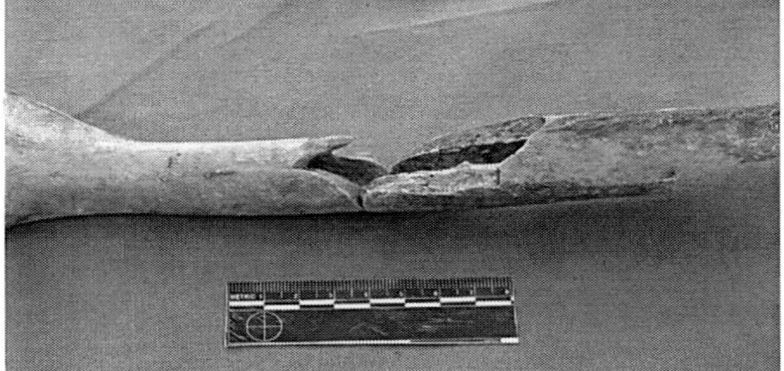

Figure 2.7 Reassociated fragments. Right humerus; each half was found in a different location (cave and cemetery) (Alain Wittmann).

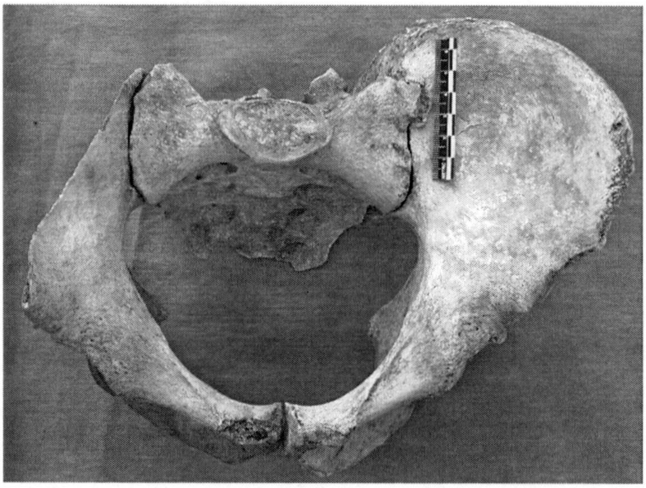

Figure 2.8 Reassociated fragments. Complete articulation of sacrum (found in the cemetery) and pelvic bones (found in the cave) (Alain Wittmann).

Surface searches inside the cave recovered human remains that were commingled and disarticulated, as well as shell casings. Outside the cave, the remnants of a pyre were found. The pyre had been prepared by filling the rocky bottom of the ravine with clay and rocks and by placing some wood branches over it, measuring 4.10 × 1.30 m. In addition, shell casings, coins, burned clothing, a "plate and screws," commingled burned bones, and ashes were also found. The pyre contained the remains of two almost complete skeletons mixed with fragments of a rubber tire. The search at the top of the hill, overlooking the pyre was carried out using a metal detector. Shell casings, one live round, and bullets representing four different calibers of ammunition were recovered. A field experiment was performed to evaluate the possibility that the bodies could have been at the top of the hill and fallen into the cave. Through this, it was observed that the bodies could have fallen in close proximity to the area where the pyre was found.

Shortly after commencing the exhumation of the cave, an ID card was found on the site. Additionally, three DNA results linked bone samples from the cemetery to the bones found years before and to the name on the ID card. In addition to DNA tests, further empirical links were established between the remains recovered from the cemetery and those found in the cave, including physical reassociation of body parts burried in the bags in the cemetery and the cave. These two lines of evidence demonstrated that the remains buried in the cemetery originated from the cave. Therefore, after combining the bones found in the cemetery with those in the cave, a minimal number of 28 (n = 28) individuals were established.

The Anthroposcopic Examination of Skeletal Injuries

The marriage of anthropology and pathology in forensic investigations blends different areas of expertise that may provide a very detailed and comprehensive reconstruction of what events occurred and at the same time, highlights differences in the methodology or terminology of the various disciplines. This book relies on several standard texts for definitions of anatomical, medical, and anthropological terms and methodology (Spitz 1993; Ortner and Putschar 1981; Buikstra and Ubelaker 1994; Ortner 2003).

The classification of skeletal wounds begins with a description of the location, type, and number of fractures or abnormal changes for bone, as well as for the specific aspects of each bone affected. The overall distribution of fractures throughout a particular region or the entire skeleton is examined. An estimation of the number of injuries present is possible based on the pattern or distribution of wounds and intersecting fractures. If more than one injury is noted, then these same lines of data will enable the investigator to sequence the injuries. Consequently, the first question an investigator must ask is whether the observation is normal; if it is determined to be abnormal, the methodological approach should include a differential diagnosis (Table 2.1). Consideration should be given to all lines of data, including radiography and examination of weaponry, if available or associated, so that a possible diagnosis is deduced and the most probable cause and manner of death may be interpreted.

In cases where there is one injury, several bones or different aspects of the skeleton may be affected. For example, a single gunshot wound to the skull may enter anteriorly through the frontal bone and exit the skull posteriorly through the occipital bone. In this scenario, different areas of the skull are affected with multiple fracture lines. Determination of a single gunshot wound is evident after documenting the type and location of each fracture, then analyzing the overall distribution of fractures in relation to one another. It is also common to have different regions of the body affected by a single gunshot wound. For example, in a study of terrorist-related gunfire and blast injuries, Peleg et al. (2004) report that the majority of trauma was from blast injuries and that the ratio of wounds (gunfire:blast) was

Table 2.1 Differential Diagnosis of Skeletal Trauma

1. Inventory all affected bones.
2. List the location of specific affected areas on bone, including the side/region/aspect.
3. Provide a description of:
   - The number and types of fractures or defects
   - The presence of any abnormal bone shape, growth, or loss
   - The severity, state, and distribution of abnormal bone changes
4. Documentation of any radiographic evidence (fractures or weaponry).
5. Analysis of clothing (defects, tears, burning, or weaponry).
6. Estimation of the timing of fractures based on:
   - Presence of bone reaction (remodeling)
   - Color of fractured edges
   - Shape of defect or cut mark
   - Size of affected area, defect, or cut mark
   - Appearance of tissue bending
   - Location of affected area
   - Number of fractures or cut marks
7. Classification of skeletal pathology by disease category (i.e., infectious, nutritional) and the specific mechanism (i.e., periostitis versus osteomylitis or scurvy versus anemia).
8. Estimation of the mechanism of injury, class of weapon, distance of fire or blast, and victim's position relevant to the direction of the force in relation to the point of impact.

the following: gunfire injuries had a higher number of open wounds (63:53) and fractures (42:31) but fewer cases with multiregions of the body affected (47:62).

Ruling Out Normal Skeletal Variation and Skeletal Pathology

A differential diagnosis requires a careful description of each defect, lesion, fracture, or abnormally shaped bone, which is then compared with the characteristics defined for each possible known condition (Ortner and Putschar 1981; Buikstra and Ubelaker 1994; Goodman 1993). The investigator must have a clear understanding of the range of variation normally likely to occur. This includes knowledge of normal skeletal variation due to epigenetic traits, such as accessory foramina or vessels in bone and vertebral fractures, or skeletal nonunion such as spondylosis, cleft neural arches, or spina bifida. Many examples of skeletal epigenetic traits may be confused with traumatic injuries, even to experienced practitioners. Therefore, a clear understanding and evaluation of normal skeletal variation is necessary to avoid the misdiagnosis of variation verses inflicted trauma or skeletal disease.

Table 2.2 provides a summary list of commonly observed epigenetic or congenital traits observed throughout the skeleton (complied from Barnes 1994). This is only a partial list of the traits exhibiting variation or congenital anomalies, but it does provide a summary of the traits typically observed during osteological analysis that may be easily confused with wounds resulting from inflicted trauma. Variants can be grouped into categories:

Table 2.2 Common Epigenetic or Congenital Traits of the Skeleton that May be Confused with Skeletal Trauma

Congenital Disorders	Skeletal Region Commonly Affected
Transitional vertebra	Occipitalization of cervical (C1)
	Thoracization of cervical (C7)
	Lumbarization of thoracic (T12)
	Lumbarized first sacral (S1)
	Sacralized fifth lumbar (L5)
	Lumbar-sacral undetermined
	Fused coccyx
Bone fusion	Multiple vertebrae
	Sternum/manubrium/xiphoid process
	Sternum/ribs/costal cartilage
	Ilium/sacrum
	Tibia/fibula
	Hand or toe phalanges
	Carpals or tarsals
Bone nonunion	Sternal body segments
	Bifurcated neural arches
	Acromion process unfused (*Os acrominale*)
	Spina bifida/occulta
Abnormal shape	Hemivertebra
	Talus *Os trigonon*
	Abnormally small nasal bones
Accessory foramina	Septal apature (humerus)
	Sternal foramen (sternal body)

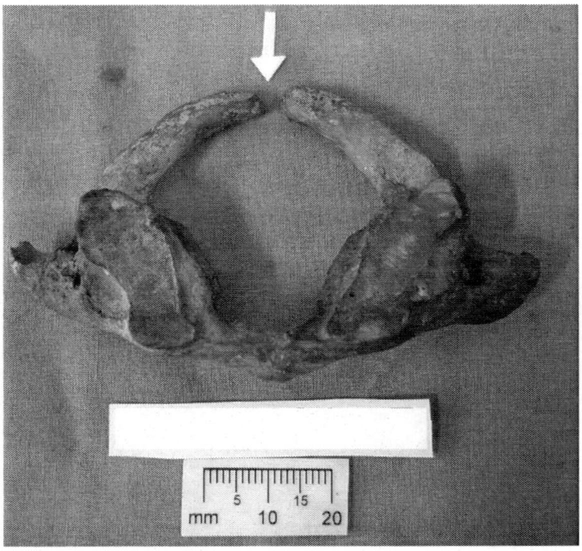

Figure 2.9 First cervical vertebra, superior view. Posterior cleft neural arch, congenital defect. (Printed with permission from International Criminal Tribunal for the former Yugoslavia [ICTY].)

(1) transitional vertebra, (2) abnormal but nontraumatic bone fusions, (3) abnormal but nontraumatic nonunion of skeletal segments, (4) abnormally shaped bones, and (5) accessory foramina. Barnes (1994) provides a detailed and comprehensive text for identifying epigenetic traits and a thorough review of their etiology and frequency. Figures 2.9–2.16 illustrate examples of normal skeletal variation.

Figure 2.10 Adult thoracic vertebrae, posterior view. Bifurcated neural arches, congenital defect (Courtesy of Jane Beck).

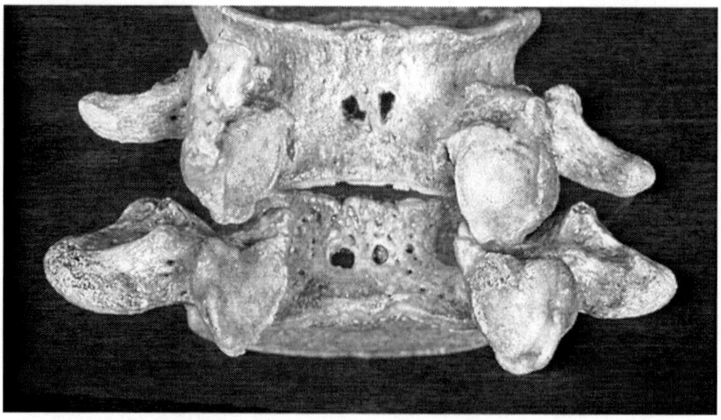

Figure 2.11a Adult fourth and fifth lumbar vertebrae, posterior view. Neural arches never fused to vertebral bodies. Complete spondylolysis. Common congenital defect. Note the smooth, rounded edges of the laminae visible along the top border of the inferior articular facets (Courtesy of Jane Beck).

Although not all disease processes manifest in the skeleton, there are a large number of skeletal indicators of malnutrition, growth disruptions, physiological stress, infectious disease, and antemortem wounds that commonly result from neglect and poverty associated with human rights (HHRR) abuse and armed conflict. The health consequences associated

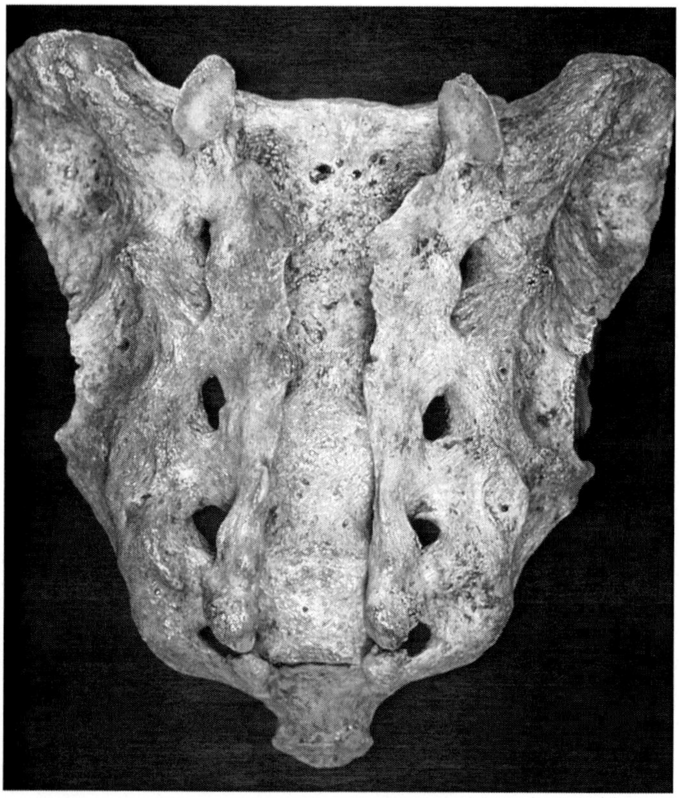

Figure 2.11b Adult sacrum, posterior view. Complete spina bifida. Nonunion of the sacral neural arches, segments 1–5. Congenital defect (Courtesy of Jane Beck).

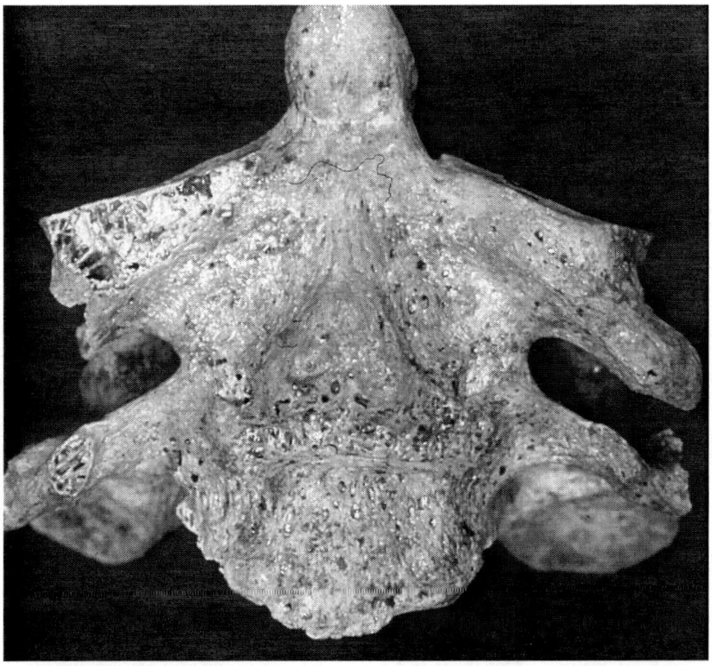

Figure 2.12 Adult cervical (C) vertebrae, anterior view. Vertebral bodies of C2 and C3 congenitally fused (Type II, Klippel-Feil syndrome) (Courtesy of Jane Beck).

with armed conflict are well documented. Some examples include inadequate nutrition, a lack of or denial of medicine and medical intervention, poor sanitation, debilitating injuries, and increased prevalence of infectious diseases (Levy and Sidel 1997; Henderson and Biellik 1983; Garfield and Neugot 1991; Toole et al. 1993; Weinberg and Simmonds 1995; Zaidi et al. 1995; Goldson 1996; Salama et al. 1999; Spiegel and Salama 2000; Murray et al. 2002; Van Herp et al. 2003; Holdstock 2004; Morley 1994; Taipale et al. 2002). In an editorial to the *Medicine Conflict and Survival*, Holdstock wrote (2004, 291):

> Estimates of war-related deaths and illness among civilians are even less precise; when does the death of a malnourished child become war-related? In Iraq, the combined effect of infrastructure damage from the 1991 Gulf War and subsequent sanctions may have caused the premature death of half a million children. The contributing disruption of health care in Iraq today will add many more to the total and is surely a consequence of war.

People may be intentionally or unintentionally affected as access to supplies or aid may be lacking due to embargoes, roadblocks, or the destruction of social infrastructure. The Human Security Report (2005, 7) states:

> The biggest death tolls do not come from the actual fighting, however, but from war-exacerbated disease and malnutrition. These "indirect" deaths can account for as much as 90% of the total war-related death toll. Currently, there are insufficient data to make even rough estimations of global or regional "indirect" death toll trends.

Basic human securities may be intentionally compromised as a form of control or with the intention to commit genocide. Thereby, basic human securities may be manipulated and

Figure 2.13 Adult manubrium and sternal body, anterior view. Nonfusion of segments. Segment 1 is not fused to the second and third segments. Note that the left and right sides of the distal segment did not fuse. Further, the presence of a sternal aperture (foramen) is present in the distal segment of the sternal body. These traits are congenital anomalies of the skeleton (Courtesy of Jane Beck).

used as *weapons* against civilian populations. According to the Human Security Report (2005, 7), "disease and hunger result in more deaths than trauma from actual war wounds, with a ratio of indirect to direct as high as 10:1." The particular health consequences resulting from war atrocities and armed conflict will further depend on whether people were detained prior to death and the overall context and duration of the situation.

Observable skeletal pathology should be systematically documented through postmortem examinations not only to enable differential diagnosis of perimortem trauma related

Figure 2.14 Adult individual. First (S1) and second sacral (S2) elements congenitally never fused (vertebral shifting, lumbarization of S1). Postmortem damage also present in the anterior surface. (Courtesy of Jane Beck.)

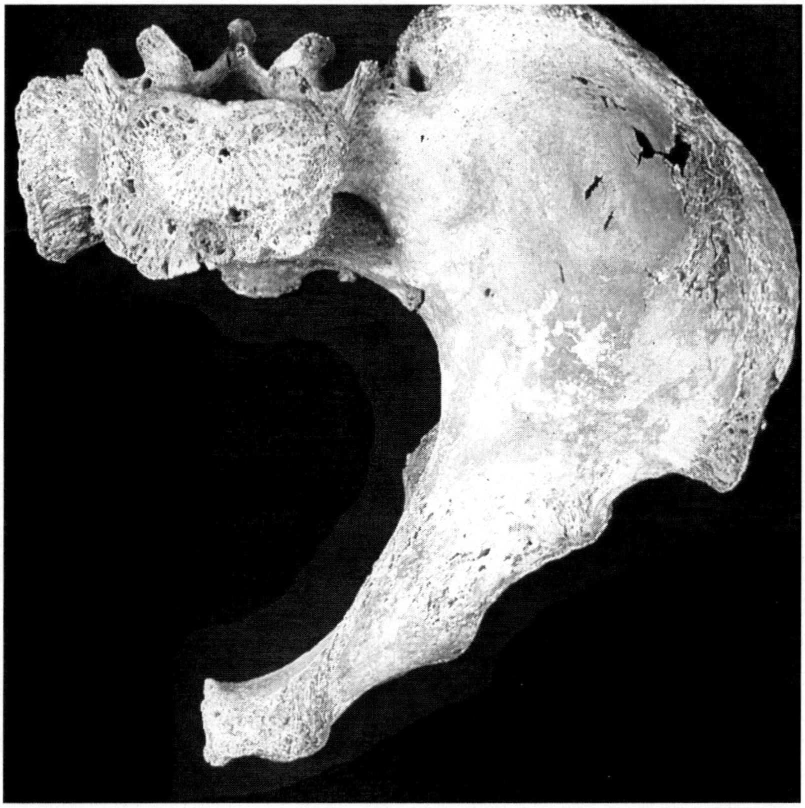

Figure 2.15 Adult pelvis, superior view. Fusion of the left sacroiliac joint. Right sacroiliac joint has accessory facets, where the two bones articulate, posterior to the articular surface (Printed with permission from International Criminal Tribunal for the former Yugoslavia [ICTY]).

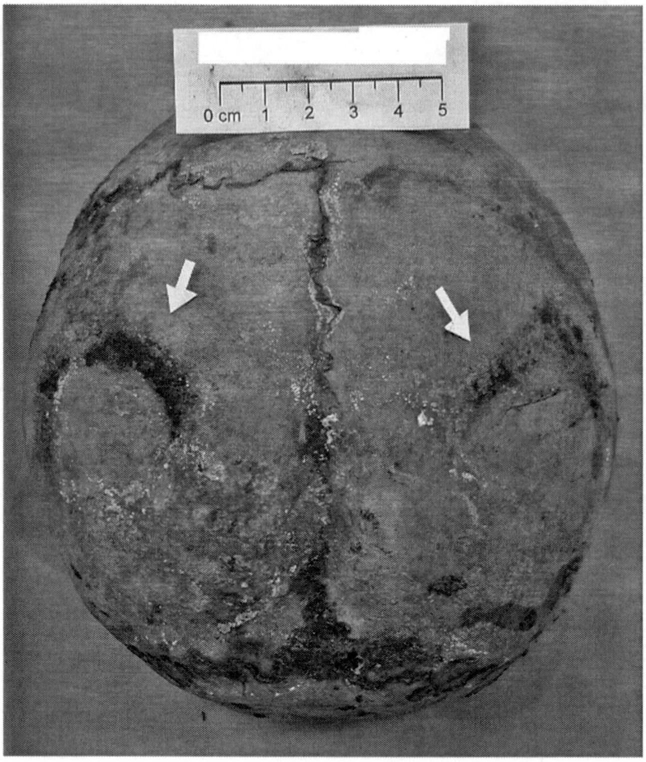

Figure 2.16 Superior view of the adult cranium. Congenital bilateral parietal thinning (Printed with permission from International Criminal Tribunal for the former Yugoslavia [ICTY]).

to the individual's death but also as a matter of historical record, to provide possible evidence of maltreatment, to obtain information that may assist with victim identification, and to understand wounding patterns that may be altered by age or disease (Buchsbaum and Caruso 1969; Evans 1973; Schmidt 1979; Morse 1983; Berryman and Symes 1998; Catanese and Gilmore 2002; Hart 2005). Schmidt (1979, 103) wrote: "Experience shows that with advancing age the resistance of adults against deformation shrinks. Even a fall on flat ground may cause a series of rib fractures in an old person. Experiment confirms that, whole body or single rib alike, the difference in breaking strength with differences in age are considerable."

The paleopathological literature is full of similar examples from archaeological populations throughout the world where diseases manifest in bone without the benefit of modern medical intervention. The examples discussed here are a few of the more common conditions we have encountered. For comprehensive texts on skeletal pathology, readers are referred to Steinbock (1976), Brothwell (1981), Ortner and Putschar (1981), Aufderheide and Rodriguez-Martin (1998), Roberts and Manchester (1995), Ortner (2003), and Mann and Hunt (2005). Forensic anthropologists in the United States are often trained as bioarchaeologists and skeletal biologists and may have extensive experience working with archaeological populations whose skeletal pathologies may resemble populations today, if victims have not had access to modern health care, antibiotics or other medicine, or adequate nutrition.

Similarly, the diagnosis of *battered child syndrome* based on fracture patterns and other evidence of neglect or maltreatment also has implications for ill-treatment or torture cases

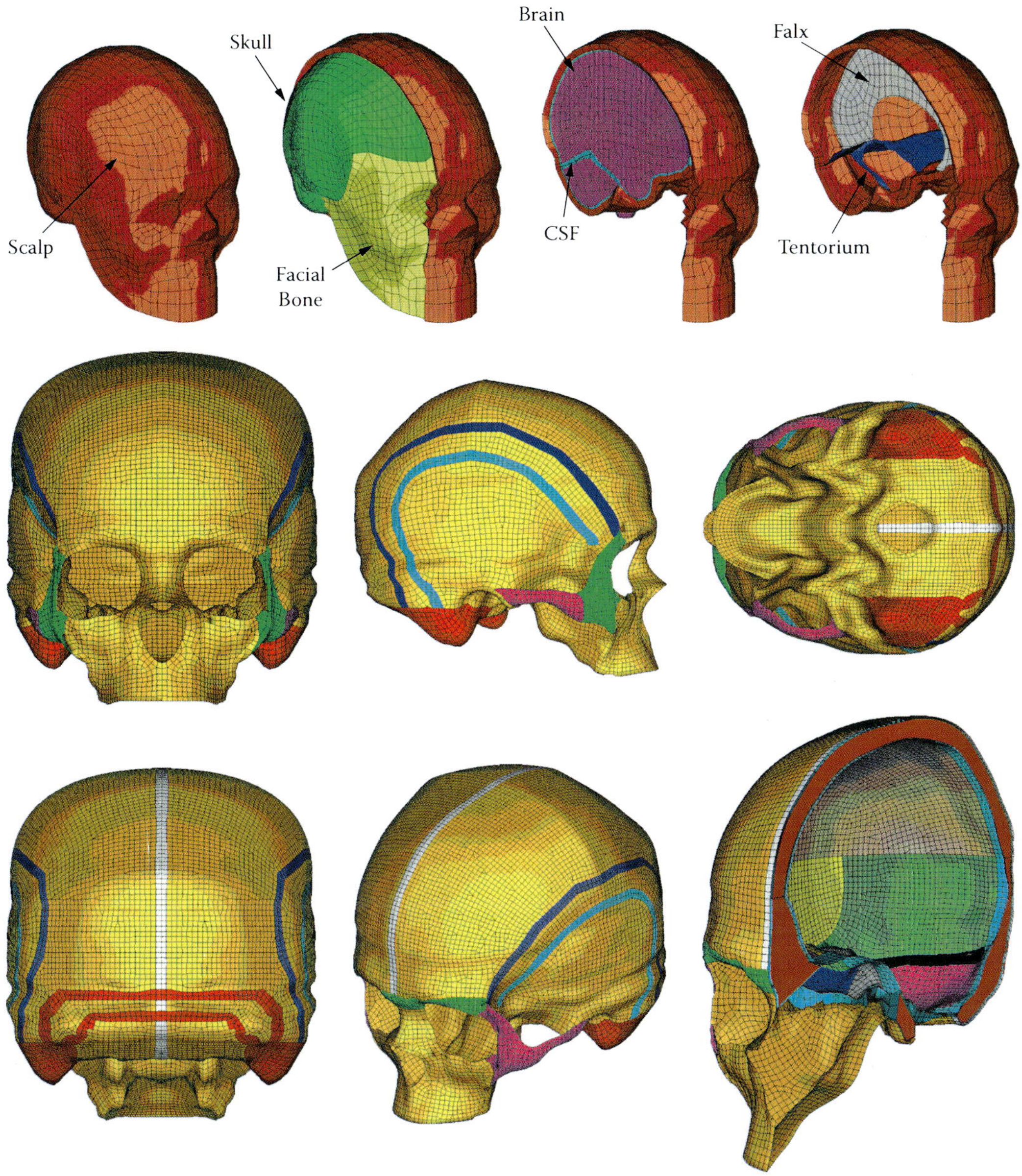

Color Figure 1 Finite element models of human head.

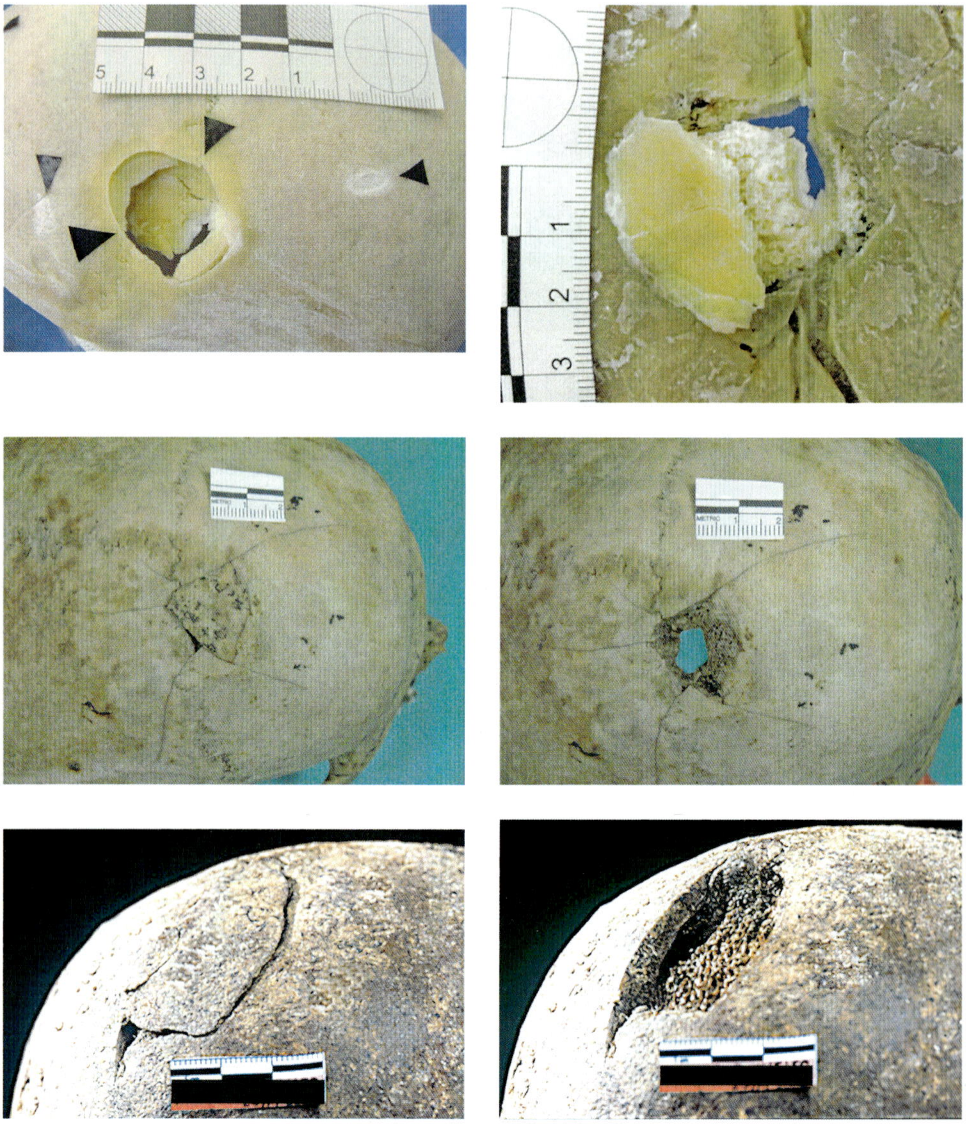

Color Figure 2 Here are three examples of different mechanisms of injury to the skulls of different individuals resulting from BFT, GSW, and SFT. Note that the defects produced similar but distinct wounds.

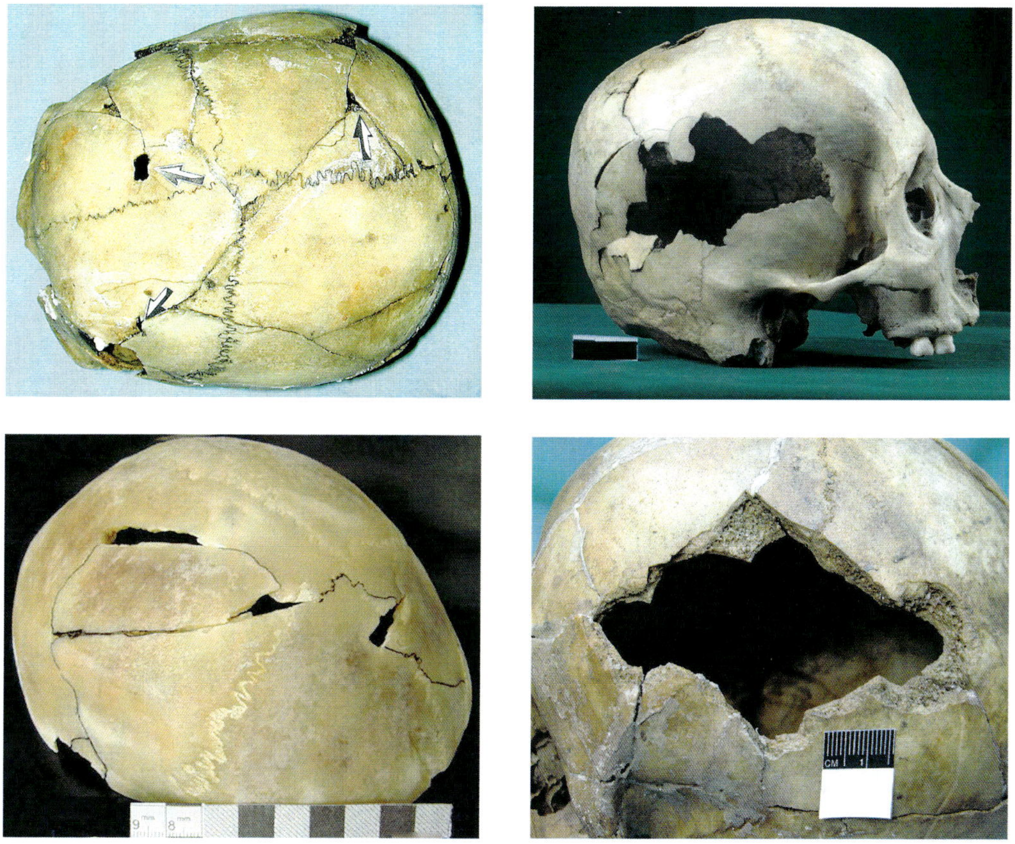

Color Figure 3 Variation in cranial wounds resulting from Shrapnel-Blast, BFT, SFT, and GSW trauma (right to left).

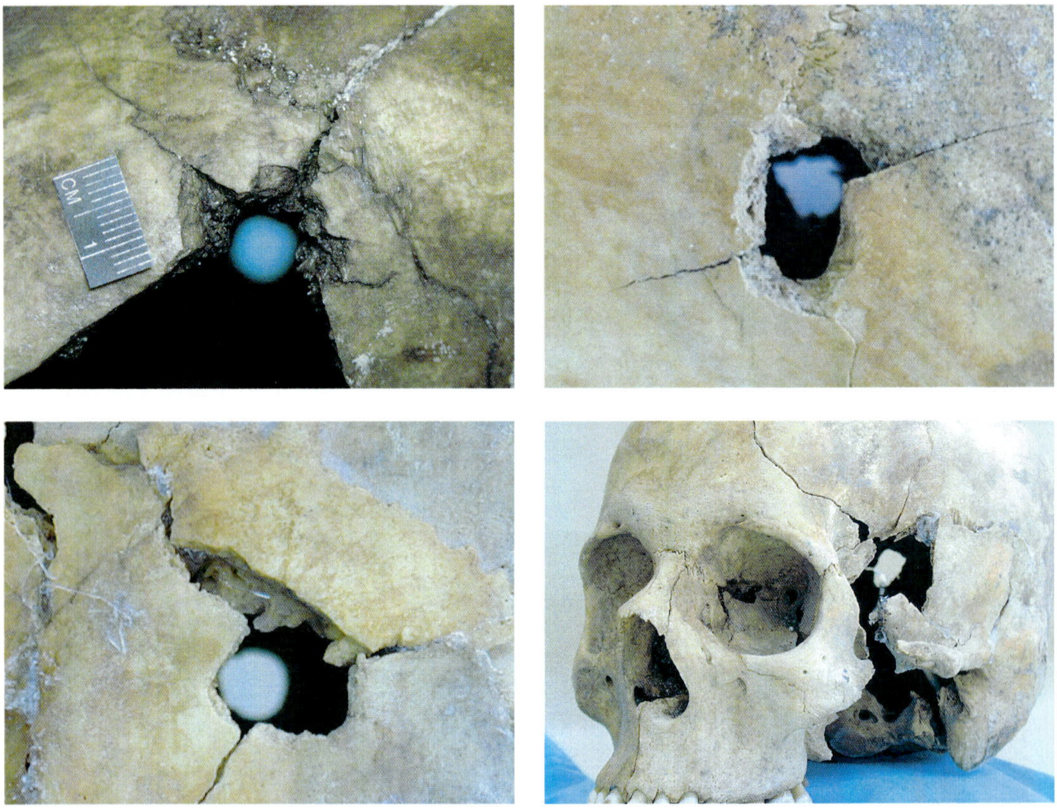

Color Figure 4 Variation in cranial wounds resulting from gunfire. Note these are exit wounds and the entrance wounds can be seen through the defects in the skull. The entrance defects reflect the shape and angle of impact such as the bullet entering sideways or perpendicular.

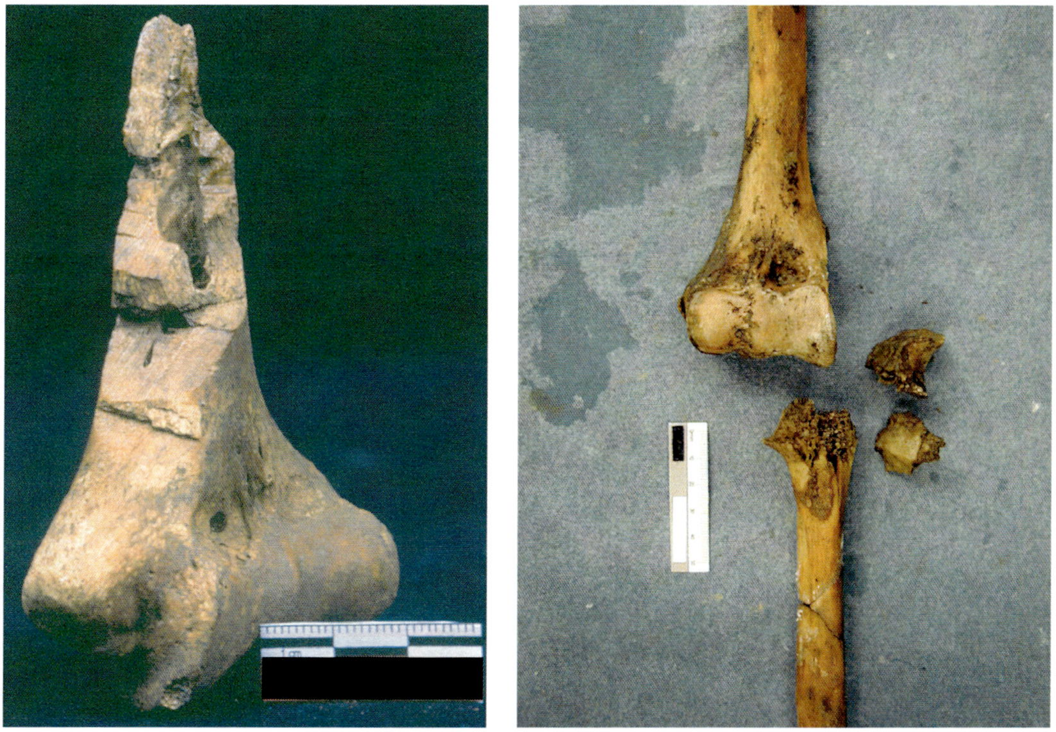

Color Figure 5 Comparison of sharp-blunt injury to the distal humerus from a machete to a GSW to the elbow region of a second individual.

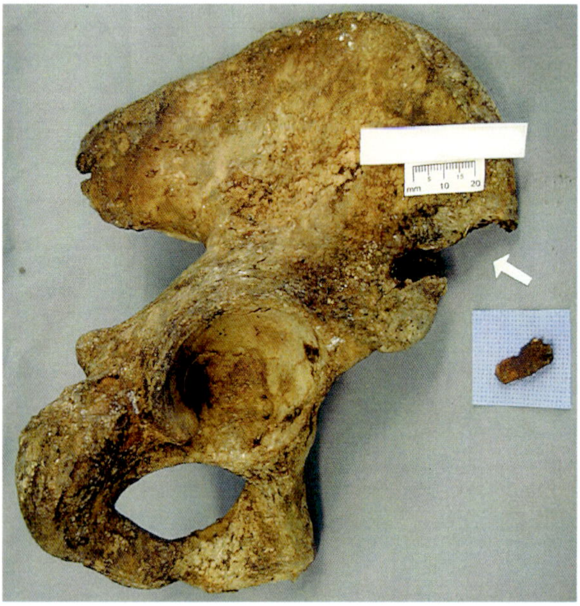

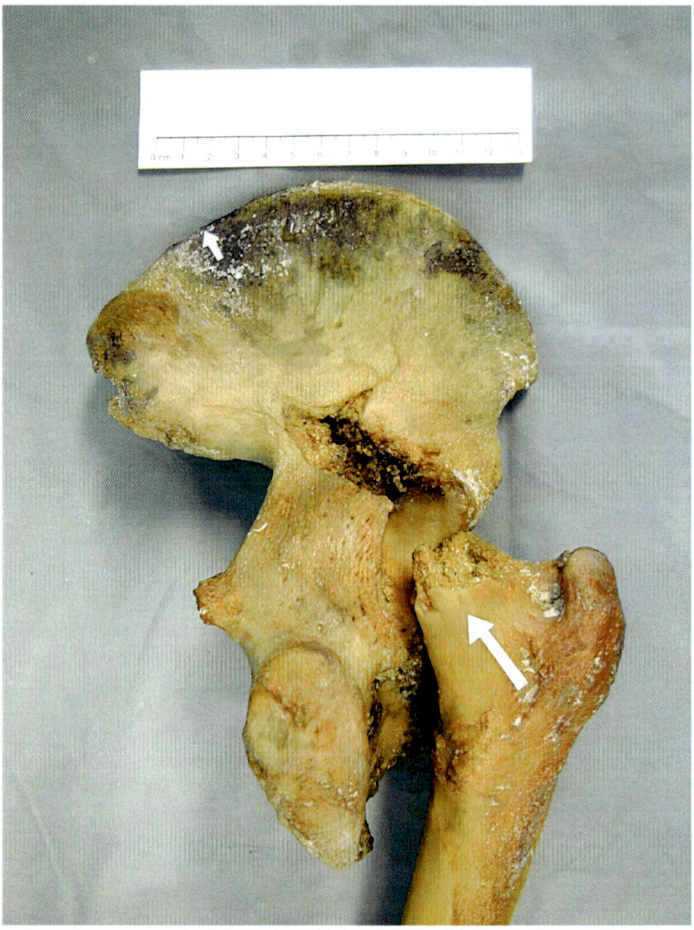

Color Figure 6 Comparison of skeletal defects, shaped as gutter wounds, in the posterior ilia of two different individuals, resulting from shrapnel (blast injury) and a gunfire injury (AK-47).

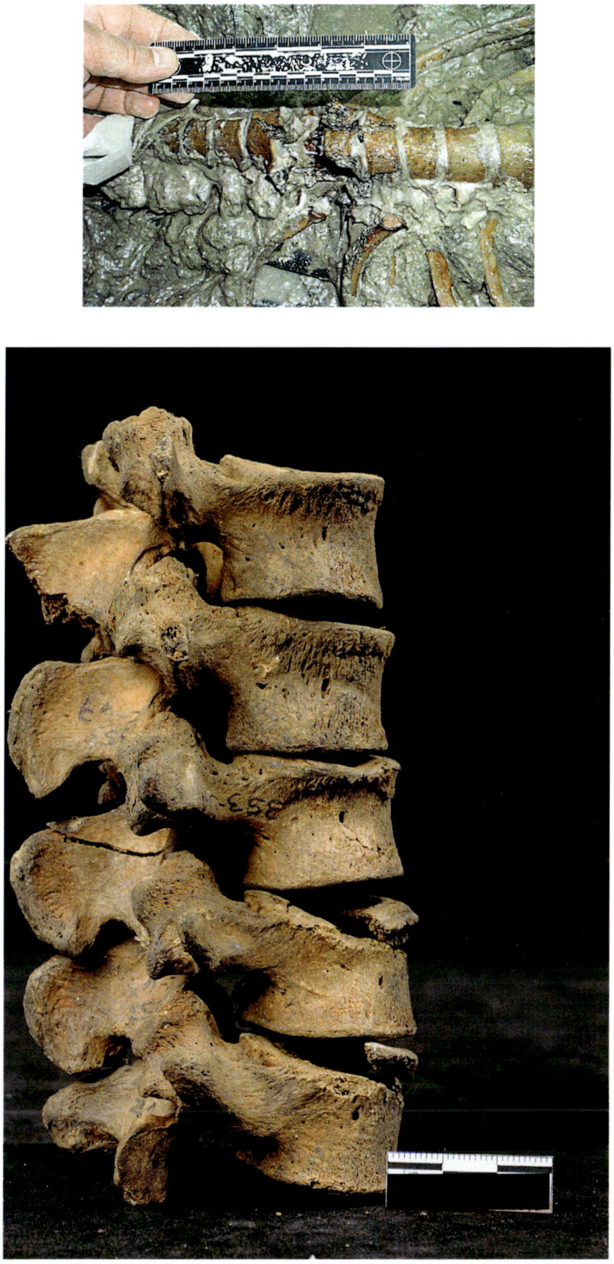

Color Figure 7 Comparison of injuries to the spine resulting from a gunshot wound and blunt force trauma. Note the *crumbing* appearance of the trabecular bone and the extent of vertebrae affected in the gunfire example.

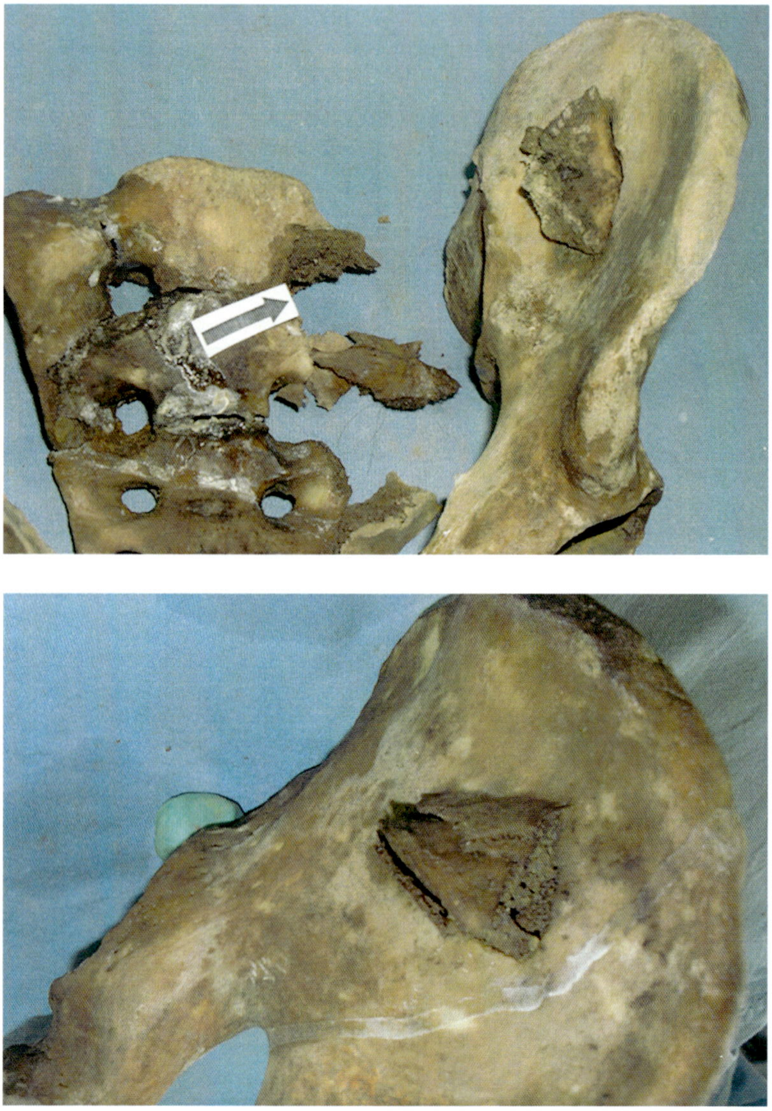

Color Figure 8 Sacral fragment completely fractured following gunfire injury (AK-47) and became embedded in the left iliac fossa, secondary projectile. (with permission from ICTY.)

in HHRR investigations (Rae 1969; Betz and Leibhardt 1994; Reynolds 1998; Cheung 1999; Brogdon and Vogel 2003a; Altun et al. 2004; Cattaneo et al. 2006). For example, skeletal manifestations of battered child syndrome can include nutritional deficiencies and infectious diseases (Rae 1969, Krogman and Iscan 1986). Issues of malnutrition and starvation raised in several of these examples highlight an important point about skeletal evidence of nutritional deficiencies, which may cause a variety of skeletal or dental reactions (Figures 2.17 and 2.18). For example:

- Vitamin D deficiency may result in rickets, osteomalacia, or marked bowing of the tibia.

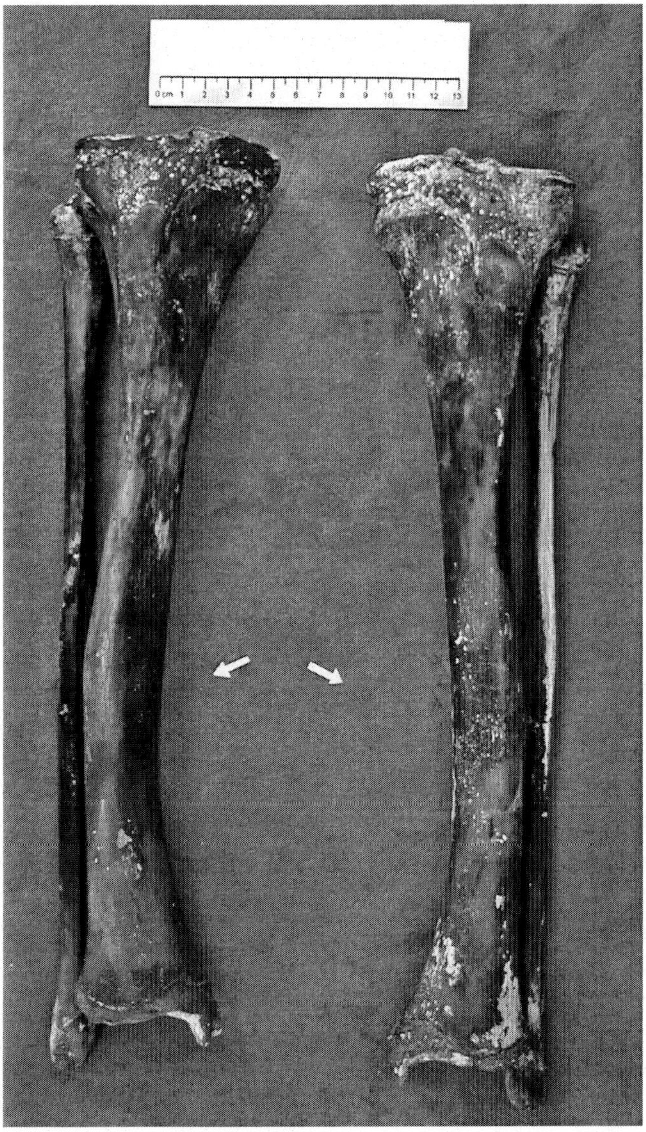

Figure 2.17 Bilateral tibiae and fibulae exhibit bowing, likely resulting from childhood nutritional deficiency, possibly rickets. (Printed with permission from International Criminal Tribunal for the former Yugoslavia [ICTY].)

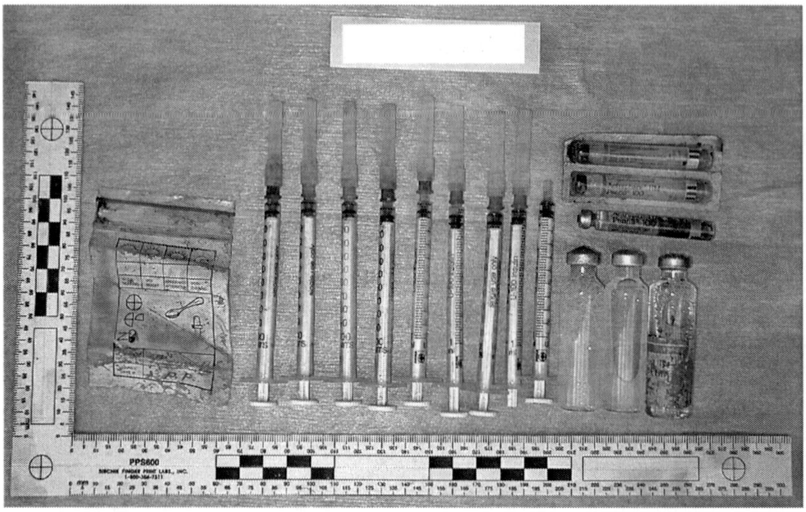

Figure 2.18 Insulin bottles and the hypodermic needles. These objects were recovered from the pockets of a victim exhumed from a mass grave. The presence of insulin is suggestive of the victim having had diabetes. The victim died of a gunshot wound following detainment. (Printed with permission from International Criminal Tribunal for the former Yugoslavia.)

- Vitamin C deficiency may be evident skeletally in the form of scurvy, including skeletal lesions, cribra orbitalia, ectocranial porosis, and lytic lesions of the sphenoid, zygomatic, maxillary, and temporal bones.
- Malnutrition and starvation may result in severe osteoporosis, delayed skeletal development, or abnormal growth.
- Various forms of physical skeletal evidence may be indicative of neglect or abuse. This may illuminate patterns of human insecurities among populations in crisis.

Figures 2.19 and 2.20 depict severe dental disease, abscesses, and large caries in an individual excavated on a mass grave in Bosnia-Herzegovina (BiH). From the extent of pathology (n = 11 abscesses), there was no dental treatment. This raises an important issue for human identification, because even in cases in which antemortem dental or health records may be available, victims who are detained or are in a conflict area for a long period of time may develop new pathological conditions, or preexisting conditions may worsen to a point at which the postmortem record will be sufficiently different from the antemortem record. Table 2.3 lists commonly observed dental conditions. Understanding dental variation and pathology can be important for interpreting injuries (Salis et al. 1987; Pollak and Wieser 1988).

Generalized infections affecting bone are very evident in the form of abnormal bone growth or loss, skeletal disruptions to growth, Harris lines, enamel defects or hypoplasias, and skeletal asymmetries. Generally, infectious processes in bone may be classified as either periostitis or osteomyelitis. Many infectious agents affect skeletal tissue, some of which are easily distributed by the morphological characteristics present. Some examples include streptococcicosis, mastoiditis, osteomyelitis, sinusitis, peritonitis, smallpox, tuberculosis, treponematosis, and syphilis. Infections to bone commonly are the result of streptococci and may be associated with an injury such as a fracture.

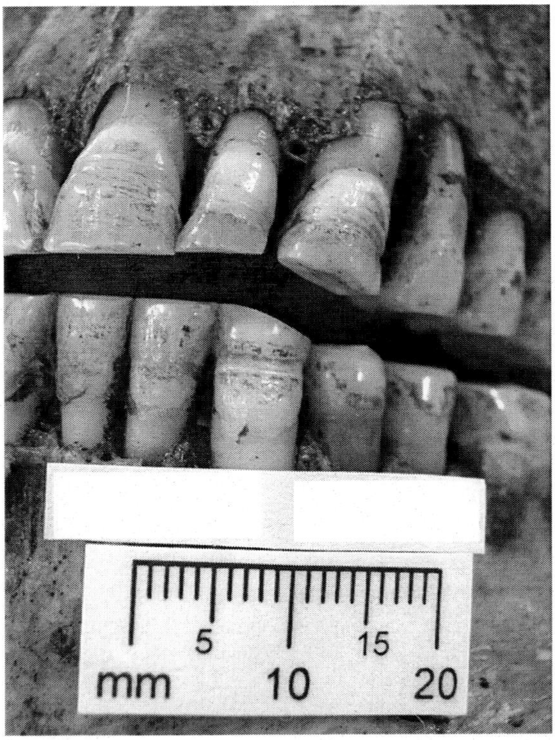

Figure 2.19 Dental hypoplasia in the form of linear bands. Indicative of nutritional stress, possibly associated with infectious disease during early childhood. (Printed with permission from International Criminal Tribunal for the former Yugoslavia [ICTY].)

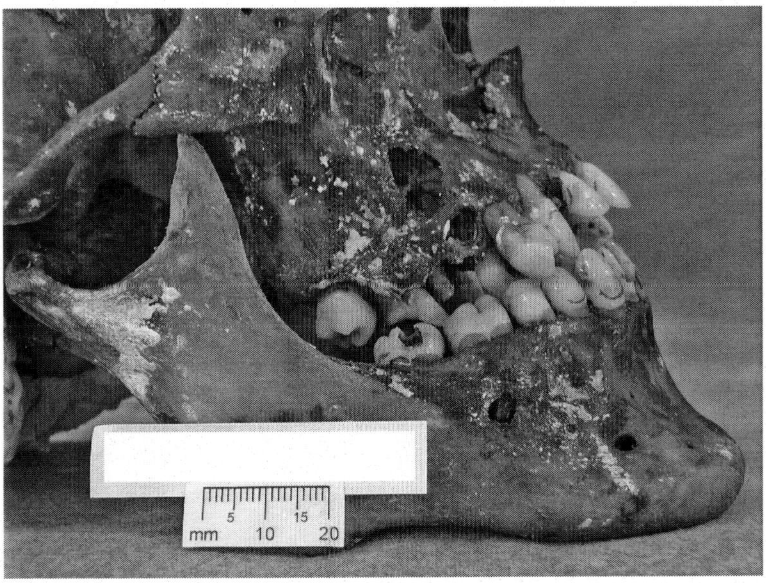

Figure 2.20 Right lateral view of craniofacial region and mandible, adult skull. Large caries present in second mandibular molar (M_2). Multiple abscesses of varying sizes (n = 11) present throughout maxillary and mandibular alveolar processes. (Printed with permission from International Criminal Tribunal for the former Yugoslavia [ICTY].)

Table 2.3 List of Dental Abnormalities

Condition	Etiology
Enamel hypo/hyperplasia	Malnutrition, infectious disease, antibiotics
Caries	Infectious disease
Maxillary and mandibular abscess	Infectious
Antemortem tooth loss	Infectious, age related, traumatic, therapeutic
Congenitally absent or unerupted tooth	Congenital
Periodontal disease	Infectious disease
Fractures	Accidental or inflicted trauma, age related

Figures 2.21–2.23 depict various examples of osteomyelitis with severe abnormal bone growth, the formation of bone remodeling with cloaca.* The left tibia with ankylosed fibula in Figure 2.21 is a case of acute osteomyelitis. The remains of this adult male individual were recovered from a grave in Croatia. Note that the two elements are almost entirely encased in abnormal bone. The mode of infection may be hematogenous, or direct to the bone following a traumatic injury. Figures 2.24 and 2.25 also illustrate examples of infectious disease manifest skeletally.

In addition to nutritional and infectious disease processes affecting skeletal tissue, various forms of neoplastic disorders are evident, quite commonly. Lytic lesions such as those depicted in the adult ilium and ribs (Figure 2.26) are extensive circular, smooth-walled defects resulting from a neoplasm.

Figure 2.21 Adult left tibia with ankylosed fibula, anterior view. Both bones exhibit acute osteomyelitis. The two elements are almost entirely encased in abnormal bone. Mode of infection may be either hematogenous or direct infection of the bone, following a traumatic injury. (Printed with permission from International Criminal Tribunal for the former Yugoslavia [ICTY].)

* The examples in the pathology section have been observed for modern populations in conflict areas. The figures primarily come from these cases but in several incidents were supplemented by museum examples, when a photograph was not available for illustration (refer to figure descriptions).

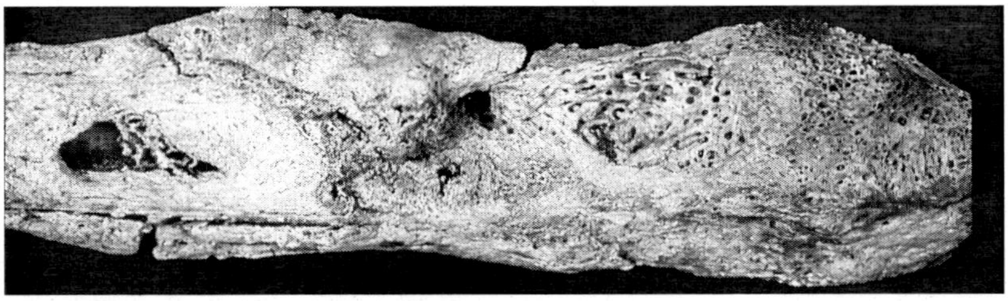

Figure 2.22 The shaft of a lone bone presented with extensive bony growth, cloaca on the left aspect. Severe osteomyelitis, indicative of bone infection, likely resulting from a traumatic injury (Courtesy of Jane Beck).

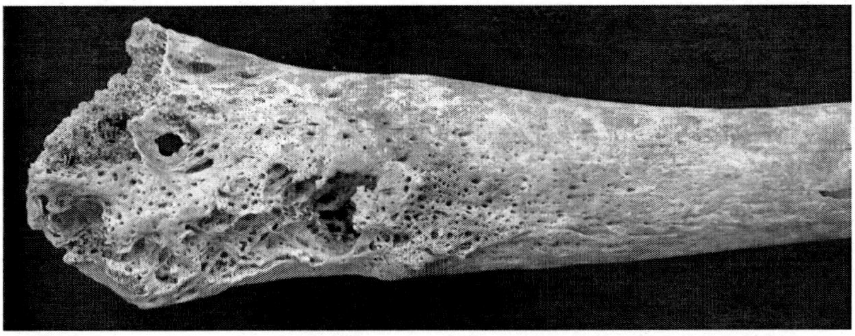

Figure 2.23 Juvenile, right humerus, anterior/distal view. Infectious bone remodeling with cloaca. Postmortem damage is also present along later margin (Rafael Guerra, USF).

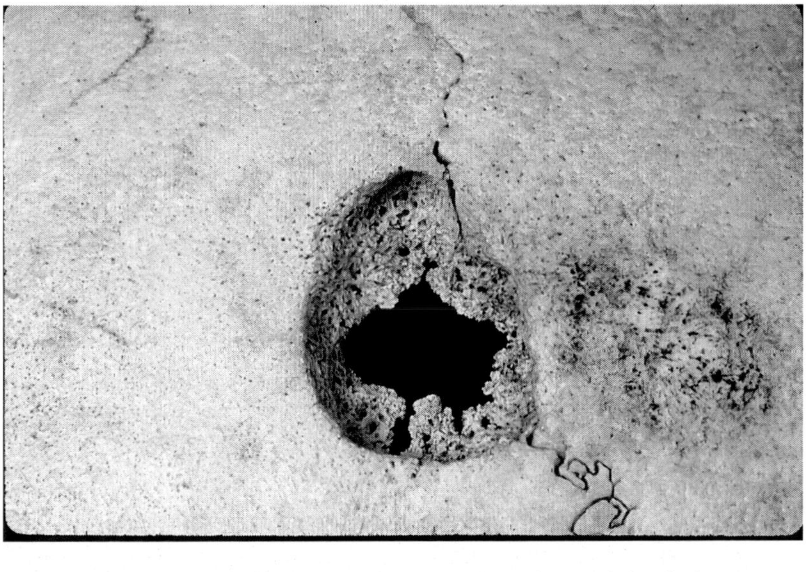

Figure 2.24 Close-up view. Lytic lesion on the cranial vault; note the diplöe is exposed around the circumference of the irregularly shaped defect. Adult. Infectious lesion. Not to be confused with external beveling of a GSW. Lesion is circumscribed with smooth edges. Margins along inner table are irregular. To the right of the defect on the ectocranial surface is abnormal bone loss, caries sicca. Lesions consistent with syphilis (Courtesy of Jane Beck).

Figure 2.25 Superior view of the cranial vault showing extensive lesions. Defects perforate the cranial vault. Extensive porosity is present. Skeletal evidence is consistent with infectious disease, most likely syphilis (Courtesy of Jane Beck).

Classification of Fractures and Mechanisms of Injury

In part, the biomechanical properties of bone account for variation in wound morphology observed for all mechanisms of trauma. Extrapolating the cause or manner of death from skeletal injuries requires interpretation of the mechanism of injury based on the available evidence. The production of fractures depends on the strain rate which is the rate at which deformation in response to force is applied (refer to Gurdjian *et al.* 1950, Evans 1973, Gurdjian 1975, Rogers 1992, Harkess 1984, Nahum and Melvin 1985). The factors guiding boney responses to applied force include the strength, stiffness, elasticity, and composition of the affected tissue as well as the surrounding soft tissues that may provide a barrier or cushion (Rogers 1992, Catanese and Gilmore 2002). Therefore, interpretations of the mechanism of injury from skeletal characteristics must consider the anatomical location and biomechanical properties of the bony tissue affected. Variation in the weapon or mechanism that is applying external force, such as the velocity, weight and distance further influence the skeletal reaction. Refer to the case study at the end of this chapter by Raul and co-workers for a discussion on the application of finite element modeling in forensic medicine.

Yield has a specific meaning in mechanics referring to an applied stress point past which the material will not return to its original dimensions. A material in its 'elastic range' is flexible and will return to its original dimension. Depending on the force applied, the elasticity allows for some yield in the bone. A slow load will make the bone yield into the elastic phase, deforming it before failing, whereas higher force mechanisms will result in a fracture (Gorman 1981). Generally, compression or torsion results in a dislocation rather than a fracture, unless shearing or bending is also applied, which occurs more commonly

Figure 2.26a Circular, lytic lesions on the right ilium. Three of the four defects do not perforate the bone. Note the symmetrical, round, smooth edges of the defects. These lesions are the result of osteomyeoloma (Alain Wittmann).

(Gorman 1981). Several comprehensive texts and published case studies provide information on the biomechanics of tissue response to abnormal stress and recommendations for differentiating mechanisms of injuries or classes of weapons based on fractures (for example, refer to Lefort 1901, Gurdjian *et al.* 1950, Moritz 1954, Gorman 1981, Ortner and

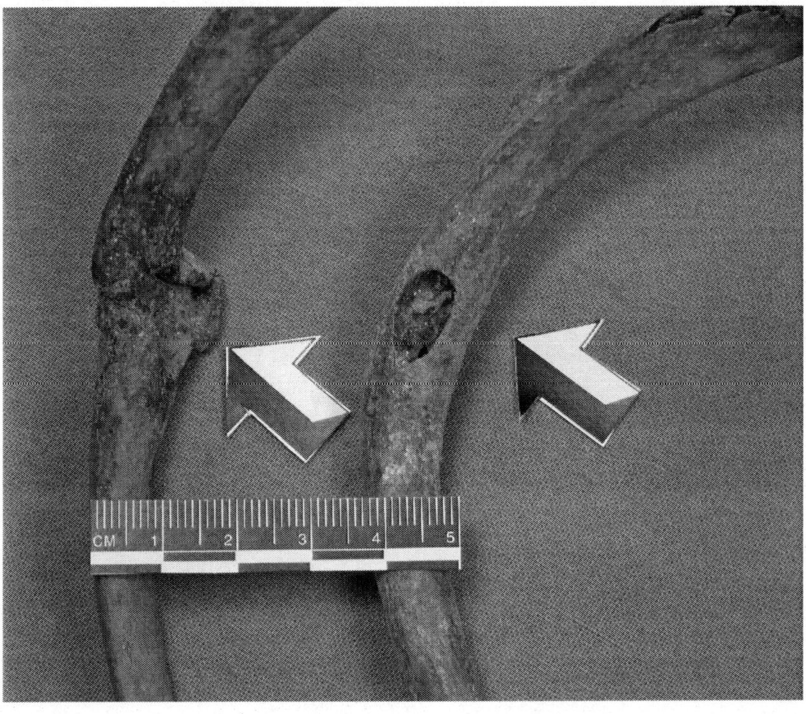

Figure 2.26b Right ribs from the same case with circular lytic lesions (Alain Wittmann).

Putschar 1981, Rogers 1992, Berryman *et al.* 1995, Ross 1996, Lovell 1997, Berryman and Haun 1998, Berryman and Symes 1998, Quatrehomme and Ĭscan 1998, Galloway 1999, Cowin 2001, Browner 2003, Ortner 2003, Byers 2005, Hart 2005).

There are several classification systems for skeletal fractures (Figures 2.27–2.34). Generally, fractures are characterized as *simple* or *multi-fragmented* and further classified by geometric properties (i.e. spiral or linear), the position or location of the fracture, the completeness of the break and the orientation of the fracture relative on the bone. A break that is complete and separates the bone tissue into two pieces is called a *simple fracture.* A break that is complete but results in three or more bone fragments is a *multi-fragment* or *comminuted fracture.* In contrast, a break that does not completely separate is called an *infarction.* Radiating fractures typically originate from the point of stress and extend as force dissipates though bone. Linear fractures may also occur peripheral to the point of impact, extending away from the force, but not actually originating from that point (Gurdjian *et. al.* 1950, Gurdjian 1975, Berryman and Symes 1998) – though this finding is debated by some. *Linear fractures* run parallel to the axis of the bone, whereas *transverse fractures* runs across this axis. *Concentric* or "*hoop*" *fractures* occur circumferentially around the point of impact. *Radiating* and *concentric* fractures are common in high stress

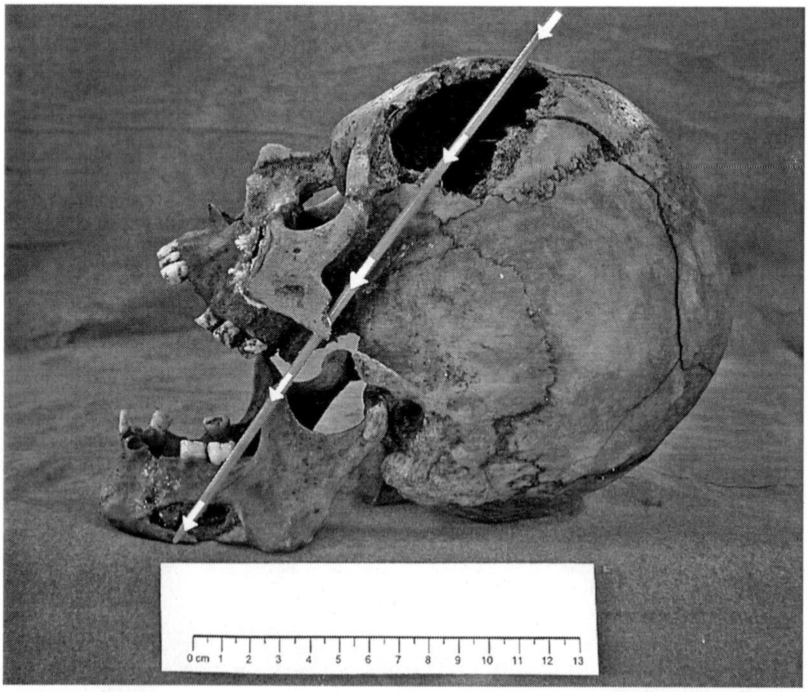

Figure 2.27 Multiple regions of the skull and mandible are fractured resulting from a single gunshot wound from a high-velocity rifle. The shot enters the skull at the top of the forehead (anterior frontal bone), creates a gutter wound as it runs along the frontal bone on the left side, enters into the left cheek (posterior to the zygomatic), and impacts the left mandible, creating a single gutter defect. Radiating fractures from the left frontal to parietal bones, along the left maxilla, and left zygomatic arch are present. (Printed with permission from International Criminal Tribunal for the former Yugoslavia [ICTY].)

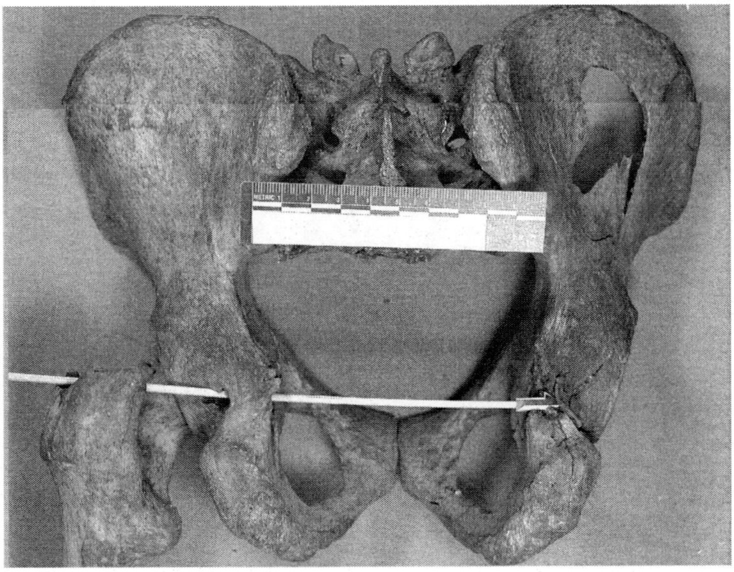

Figure 2.28 Multiple regions of the body are affected by a single gunshot wound, a left to right shot from a high velocity rifle. The projectile enters through the left hip (greater trochanter of the femur) and passes through the left femur. The projectile enters the left ishium, passes through the pelvic region, and enters the right ishium where it becomes embedded in bone (Alain Wittmann).

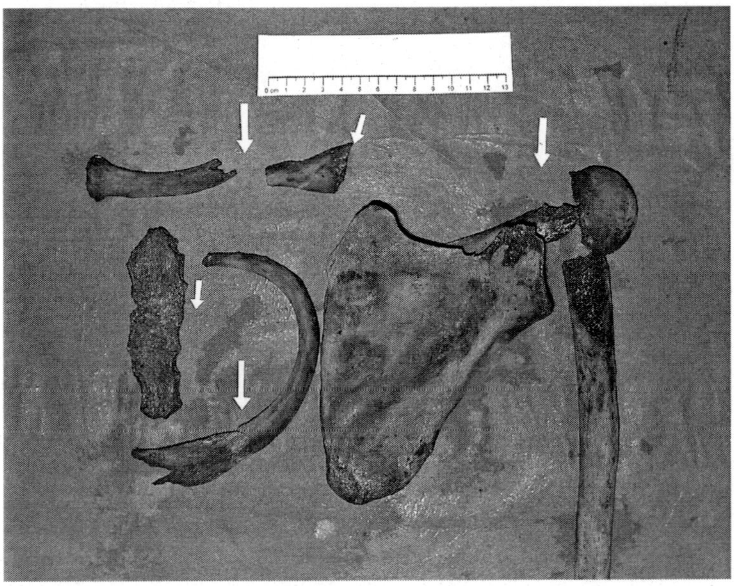

Figure 2.29 Pectoral girdle demonstrating multiple fractures of the left clavicle, sternal body, left scapula, and left proximal humerus. This is an example of a single GSW from an AK-47. The projectile entered from behind the left shoulder with a downward trajectory, and exited through the chest. The humerus, scapula, and rib exhibit beveled defects consistent with back-to-front shot. Note the clavicle was struck left to right and fractured on the acromial end and distal 1/3 shaft. (Printed with permission from International Criminal Tribunal for the former Yugoslavia [ICTY].)

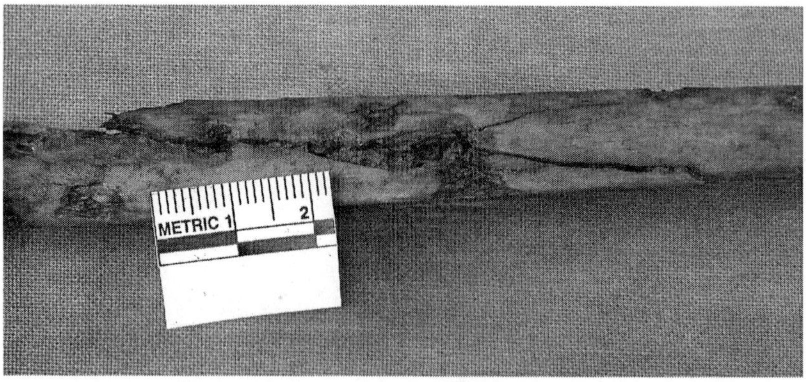

Figure 2.30 Reconstructed comminuted fractures resulting from a shotgun injury to the left tibia, adult (Alain Wittmann).

trauma (Harkess *et al.* 1984, Symes *et al.* 1991), although concentric fractures can occur without radiating fractures (Gurdjian 1975).

Fractures result when abnormal stress is placed against the bone and is characterized by its direction and focus (Ortner and Puschar 1981). The *direction of force* includes tension, compression, torsion, bending, or shearing, and, typically, force is applied from several directions in combination. *Focus* refers to the size of the surface area affected on impact and is categorized as narrow or wide. To some degree, the mechanism of injury may be categorized by its focus and the load of the force, specifically the amount of energy that is displaced from the weapon to the soft and bony tissues.

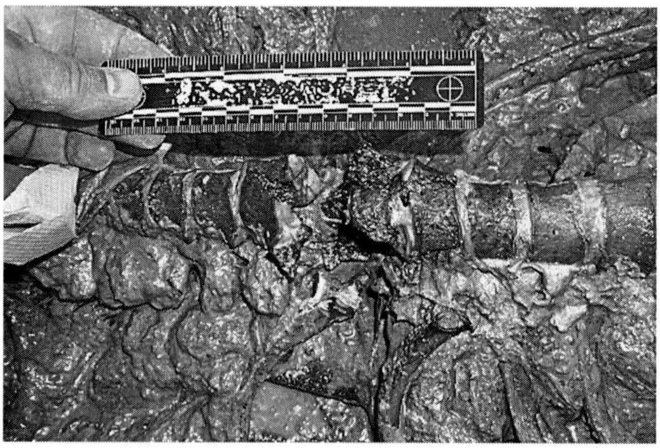

Figure 2.31 (See color insert following page 38) Single gunfire wound with a shotgun at close range to thoracic vertebrae, front-to-back shot. Vertebral bodies fractured and almost completely destroyed. Fractures extend from T5 to T8. The point of impact was on T6. T7 exhibits slightly less damage than T6, yet a significant portion of the body is destroyed. Note that T5 and T8 exhibit fractures that split the body into two or more fragments. (Printed with permission from International Criminal Tribunal for the former Yugoslavia [ICTY].)

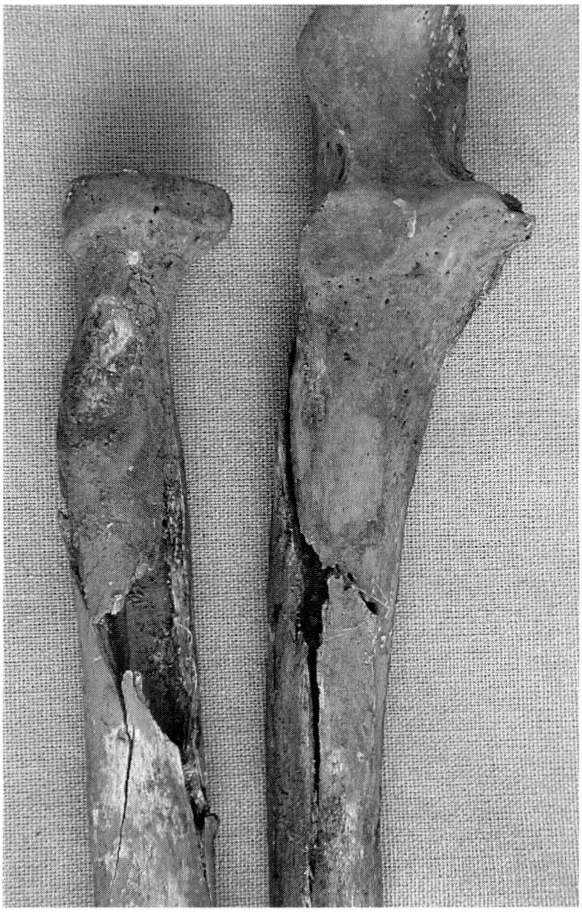

Figure 2.32 Anterior view, adult remains. Incomplete radiating fractures of the right radius and ulna as a result of single gunfire injury (Alain Wittmann).

Blunt force injuries usually have a wide focus, whereas projectile and deeply penetrating wounds have a narrow focus. Shrapnel injuries from explosions or blasting mechanisms are characterized by narrow-focus projectile wounds dispersed over a wide region of the body. The range of the explosion, location of blast, and the type of explosive device and materials used in the construction of the device will vary the dispersion of wounds in blasting injuries and the degree to which fracturing results from the blast wave. Blunt force injuries, compared to gunfire injuries, result from slow load force. However, actually within each mechanizing category, there is a range of slow/low to fast/high load. Fackler (1994), in regard to gunfire injuries, points out that wounding ballistics is not a matter of velocity, but of the bullet–tissue interaction, and the amount of tissue disruption is due to the fragmentation of projectiles and number of injuries.

Fractures may be further characterized by their anatomical location. Skull fractures tend to be depressed, radiating, linear, comminuted, blowout, or basilar. Fractures to long bones are differentiated into intra- and extra-articular aspects according to Lovell (1997); refer to Table 2.4. Intra-articular fractures involve the joint and the metaphysis. These may

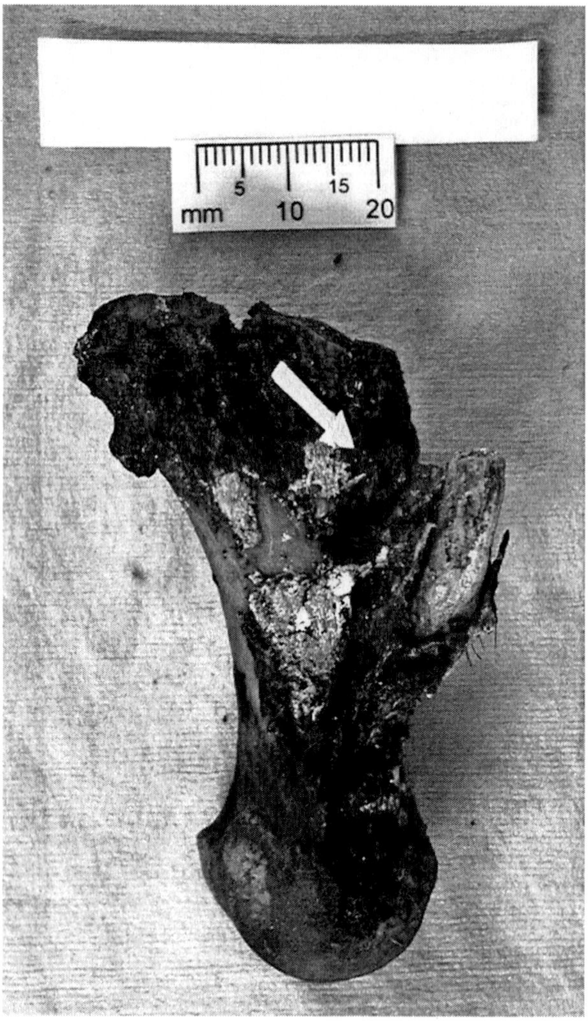

Figure 2.33 Left inferior view of adult 1st metatarsal with embedded projectile. Incomplete fracture with a projectile embedded along the medial surface. The projectile is a full metal jacketed bullet that was fired from an AK-47. The projectile likely stopped when passing through the bone when it hit the floor. Bullet tip points superior. (Printed with permission from International Criminal Tribunal for the former Yugoslavia [ICTY].)

be linear, comminuted, or impacted (Lovell 1997). Extra-articular fractures occur along the shafts of long bones or nonarticulating surfaces of *flat* and *irregular* bones and are classified as linear, comminuted, or segmental (Lovell 1997). Linear fractures may be further subdivided to include information about the direction of force, such as transverse, oblique, or spiral fractures. Comminuted fractures, characterized by multiple fragments, are also referred to as *butterfly* fractures.

Tension occurs from pulling on a bone and usually results in dislocations (Byers 2005). Vogel (2003a) reports examples of "positional torture" in which victims were hung from their knees while their wrists and ankles were bound or suspended by their fingers. "Positional" injuries, likely result in joint dislocation, particularly to the shoulder

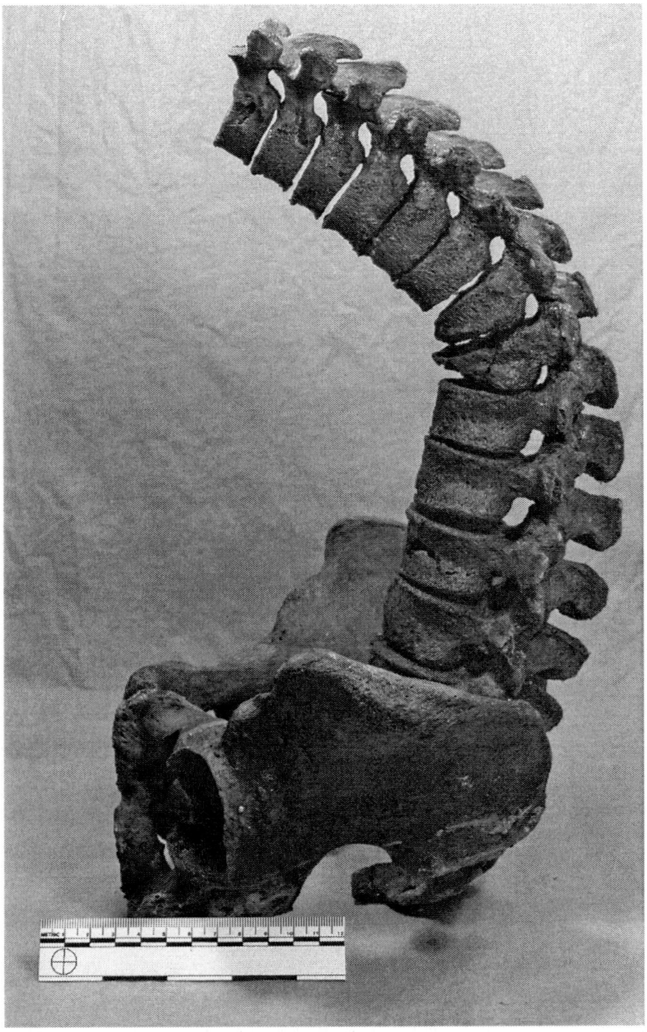

Figure 2.34 Vertebral column and pelvis, left lateral view. Severe anterior compression fracture of 11th and 12th thoracic vertebra with spinal kyphosis (Alain Wittmann).

Table 2.4 General Bone and Fracture Classification

Bone Class	Examples of Skeletal Elements	Classification of Fractures Commonly Observed
Flat	Cranial vault, scapula, ilium, ribs	• Depressed, radiating, linear, comminuted, blowout, basilar
Long/Short	Humerus, radius, ulna, femur, tibia, fibula, metacarpals, metatarsals	• Extra-articular: linear, comminuted, segmental • Intra-articular: linear, comminuted, impacted
Irregular	Sacrum, vertebrae, facial bones	• Extra-articular: linear, comminuted, segmental, radiating, linear, comminuted, depressed, crushing

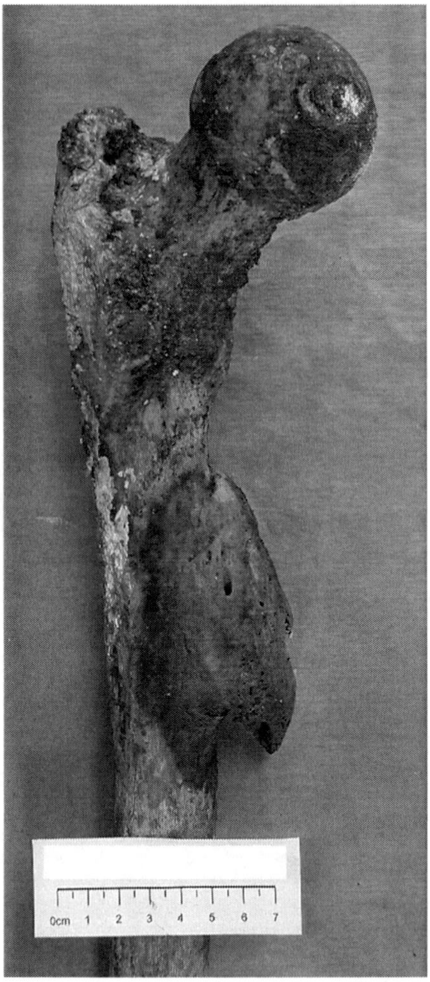

Figure 2.35 Right femur, anterior view. *Miositis ossificans traumatica.* (Printed with permission from International Criminal Tribunal for the former Yugoslavia [ICTY].)

(Vogel 2003a, 131). For example, reported cases of torture from Africa and Latin America include injuries resulting from joints that were bent and rotated to maximum flexion that produced pressure lesions and atrophy (Vogel 2003a). Figure 2.35 depicts an example of *myositis ossificans traumatica.*

Compression forces result from pushing on bone. Blunt force trauma from compression results in crushing injuries, depressed fractures, and penetrating defects with or without radiating fractures, Projectile injuries are also a form of crushing injury and variably result in radiating fractures or penetrating defects of various shapes, depending in part on the shape of the projectile, the angle of entry, and the amount of force.

Overall, the anatomical structure and composition of the particular bone due to the biomechanical properties of bone (i.e., strength, elastic modulus, hardness, and conductivity) will affect the type and pattern of fracture that results. Gorman (1981) notes that trabecular bone crisscrosses for maximum strength to allow for normal loading of body weight and physical activities, such as walking or running. As many researchers have discussed, bone is generally more resistant to compressive forces than to tension; therefore, failure usually occurs first on the side of tension (Gorman 1981, 1981b, 1981c; Harkess et al. 1984; Berryman and Symes 1998). According to Berryman and Symes (1998), bone fractures first on the side of tension, which is on the external table in blunt force mechanisms when the force does not perforate the bone and on the internal table in gunfire or shrapnel injuries when the projectile does perforate the bone. Hart (2005) differentiated injury mechanisms by the location of beveling and illustrated significant differences that can be used to predict the mechanism of injury by isolated fragments.

In most cases of compression injuries, force is also applied through bending or shearing (Gorman 1981a). Vogel (2003b) reports on compression fractures to hands and feet in cases of torture. In these examples, force is applied to the sole's of feet or to the fingers and hands. Other common examples of crushing injuries or *depressed fractures*, result from blunt trauma to the head and ribs (Fenton et al. 2003). Shearing force is essentially a bending force that is applied when the bone is immobilized. However, this type of injury often occurs in deeply penetrating or sharp force injuries. Torsion occurs as a result of twisting bone and is often seen in cases of beatings and torture that use some type of a weapon to strike the victim.

Ortner and Putschar (1981) report that fractures resulting from bending forces are the most ubiquitous but that they rarely occur without other types of force also applied. Force applied to bone will cause the bone to bend until it reaches maximum threshold, at which point it will fail and fracture. Byers (2005, 285) points out that bending force rarely results in linear fractures at either the point of impact or on the opposite side of tension. Rather, injuries resulting from bending force typically occur in cross section as the force is applied at a 90° angle. This may result in a *butterfly* fracture in which the fracture lines extend away from the point of impact and create a triangular wedge of bone (Figure 2.36). This is frequently observed in cases of blunt force and projectile injuries to the long bones or ribs.

Detailed descriptions of the location and geometric properties of skeletal fractures provide the necessary information from which interpretations may be drawn about the mechanizing force. The mechanisms most relevant to skeletal trauma in cases of HHRR abuses, extrajudicial executions, and armed conflict include blasting and gunfire injuries, deeply penetrating wounds or sharp force trauma, and blunt force injuries. Numerous mechanizing forces occur in blasting injuries, producing crushing blunt force trauma, acceleration/

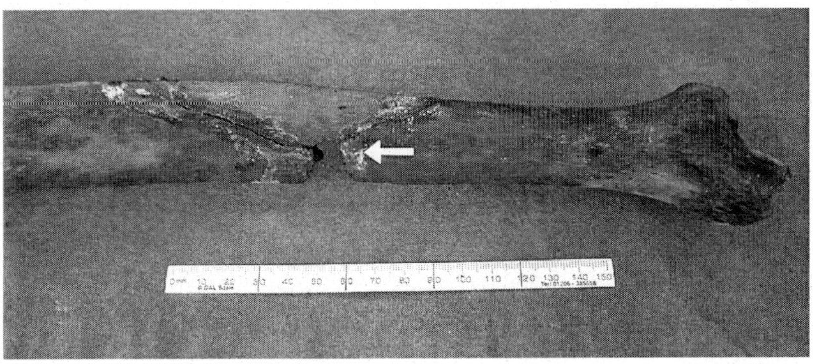

Figure 2.36 Gunshot wound to the left tibia, right to left. Circular defect indicates where the projectile entered the bone is evident. Note two fractures radiating from the defect to the anterior margin, creating a butterfly fracture. (Printed with permission from International Criminal Tribunal for the former Yugoslavia [ICTY].)

deceleration wounds, and penetrating shrapnel injuries. Blunt force trauma occurs when a victim is struck with an object, thrown in a blast, and may be associated with gunfire, torture, or explosive injuries. Sharp force trauma includes penetrating wounds that cut, chop, or stab with a sharp edge that slices or cuts tissues. Chopping wounds from axes or machetes are associated also with blunt force trauma as high-energy blows from such heavy objects are swung at a victim, both cutting and crushing tissues. Gunfire wounds are penetrating wounds that crush tissues. Both shrapnel/blasting and gunfire injuries produce projectile trauma. However, they can be differentially diagnosed based on characteristics of skeletal wounds, the distribution of injuries to the skeleton, and fracture patterns.

Generally, projectile injuries result in penetrating or grazing defects, complete, linear, radiating, and multifragmented fractures that displace bone fragments. By nature, they create patterned wounds reflecting the diameter or cross section of a bullet and impart a lot of force to tissues in a relatively narrow area. Shrapnel behaves similarly to gunfire projectiles in that it creates penetrating defects. However, shrapnel generally produces irregular-shaped defects (reflecting irregularly shaped metal fragments), is commonly embedded in bone, and rarely perforates the body. In contrast, blunt force injuries have a wide impact site with compression, shearing, and bending forces applied, resulting in either simple or comminuted fractures. In addition to projectile trauma, blasting mechanisms also produce a multitude of these forces from the blast wave that results in traumatic amputations of body parts or skeletal fractures. Sharp force injuries from knives have a narrow focus, whereas chopping instruments may have a wide focus.

The Microscopic Examination of Skeletal Tissue

The microscopic examination of skeletal tissues is a useful tool for distinguishing ante-, peri-, or postmortem changes in bone (Shipman 1981). It is also a useful tool for timing antemortem healing among fractures that occurred prior to death (Feik et al. 1997; Islam et al. 2000; Glencross and Stuart-Macadam 2000; Walsh-Haney 1999). Due to the specialized equipment and training needed for histological analysis, as well as time and financial constraints coupled with the high volume of cases, it has rarely been applied in the contexts of HHRR investigations, with a few notable exceptions (refer to Case Study 5.3 in Chapter 5). For example, microscopic techniques have been used to investigate cases of torture in which individuals were detained, beaten, and later killed. The timing of antemortem fractures in various stages of healing can demonstrate chronic abuse. It is useful for investigators to understand the biomechanical and physiological changes that occur microscopically and will likely manifest more broadly in the future.

The Timing of Fracture Based on Gross Inspection

Victims of HHRR abuses or extrajudicial executions are rarely killed and buried in the same place. More often, efforts are made to hide the crimes committed. Concealment or efforts to hide the cause of death or actual physical remains may take several forms; the body of the deceased may be hidden, graves may be moved or disguised for concealment, and death or autopsy records may be falsified. Victims may be killed in one location, then transported, and buried. Sometimes these graves are dug up and subsequently reburied in *secondary sites* (*The Prosecutor v. Krstic,* IT-98-33-T: 596, p. 212). Through this process, carnivores and rodents may have access to the remains. Burial and excavation tools may also leave marks on bones. Further attempts to hide or destroy evidence include dismemberment, burning, or bombing the remains—sometimes multiple strategies are used in combination. Having been buried in clandestine graves or within known cemetery plots, during the process of legal investigations, the remains are excavated, transported, stored in refrigerated coolers, and autopsied. Therefore, evidence of perimortem injuries, postmortem modification, and taphonomic processes that naturally occur during the decompositional process may all be visible on the remains and must be differentiated. To ascertain that the fracture is perimortem and possibly a contributing factor to the cause of death, the location, size, color, morphology, and number of modifications are documented and carefully interpreted. These variables have been widely documented in the bioarchaeological and paleoanthropological literature (Behrensmeyer and Hill 1980; Shipman 1981; Willey and Snyder 1989; Micozzi 1991). The timing of antemortem (before death) fractures, perimortem (at or around the time of death) trauma, and postmortem modifications (occurring after death) is discernable.

It is important to point out that the timing of these injuries is standard in anthropology but may vary slightly from pathology, where antemortem and perimortem categories may be combined or used interchangeably. Anthropologists refer to antemortem as a classification for events that occurred prior to and apart from the death event itself. Injuries related in time with the death, are classified as perimortem.

Antemortem Fractures

Antemortem injuries are easily distinguished because of evidence of healing (bone remodeling) such as abnormal bone growth, callus formation, abnormal bone shape, necrotic tissue, or characteristics associated with an infection (Ortner and Putschar 1981). By 1 to 3 weeks after the injury, the edges of the break become rounded (Sauer 1998) as the two elements reunite. After approximately 6 weeks, a bony callus begins to form (Sauer 1998). New (woven) bone growth is structurally different in form and may be best described as *disorganized.* Brickley (2005) demonstrated that rib fractures healing at the time of death were an important tool for demonstrating the history in child abuse cases. Over a long period of time, evidence of the break may only be visible radiologically if sclerotic bone is formed. A similar approach has been taken to document patterns of abuse and torture. Figures 2.37–2.42 illustrate examples of antemortem factures in various stages of healing.

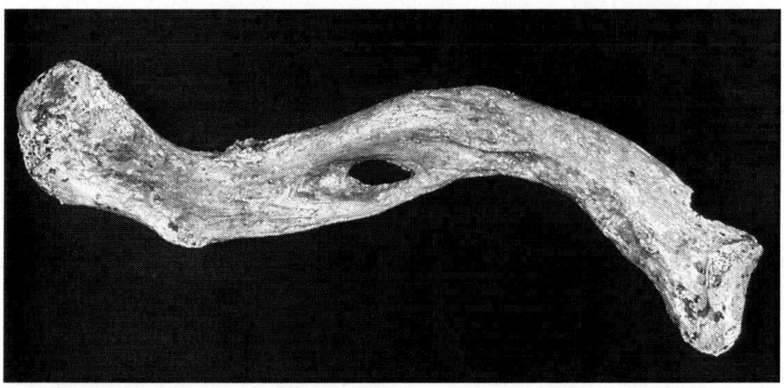

Figure 2.37a Right clavicle (inferior view). Healed antemortem fracture with partial non-union in midshaft in the shape of a circular defect, giving the impression of a foramen (ICTY).

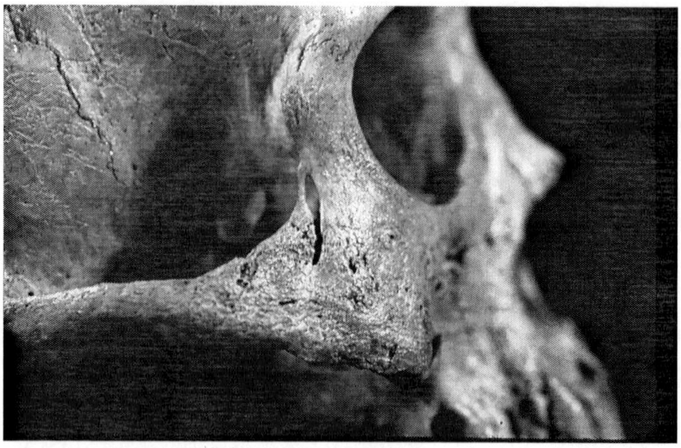

Figure 2.37b Right lateral adult skull. Healed SFT to right zygoma, defect still evident. Note round smooth edges of defects (ICTY).

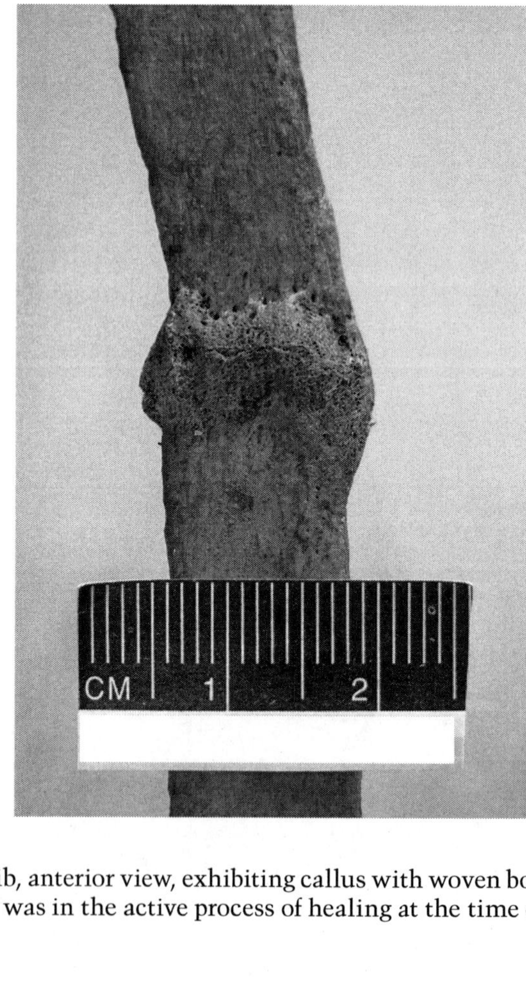

Figure 2.38 Right rib, anterior view, exhibiting callus with woven bone resulting from antemortem fracture. The rib was in the active process of healing at the time of death (Alain Wittmann).

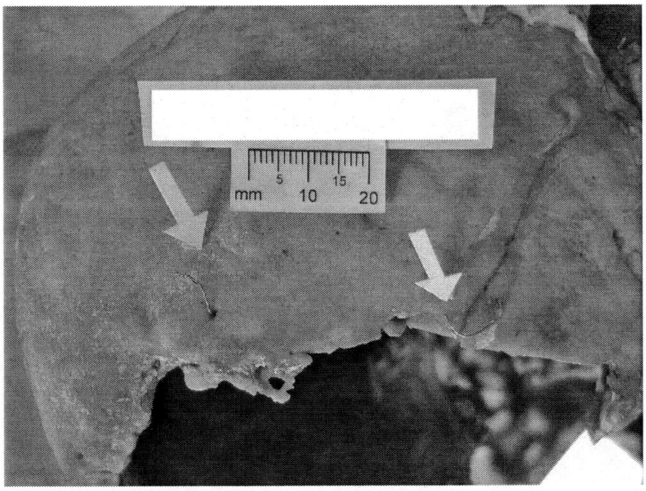

Figure 2.39 Evidence of craniotomy with healed bone tissue. Note the edges of the cranial fracture are smooth and blunt or rounded. There is also evidence of surgical wire present, indicating old injury with previous medical intervention. The individual died of a gunshot wound to the skull that resulted in extensive fracturing of the facial bones and mandible. (Printed with permission from International Criminal Tribunal for the former Yugoslavia [ICTY].)

Peri- versus Postmortem Fractures

Perimortem fractures, in contrast to antemortem injuries, exhibit no evidence of healing. Further, perimortem fractures, unlike postmortem fractures, occurred while the bone was wet and encased in muscle, periostium, skin, and other soft tissues. Therefore, the skeletal remains exhibit characteristics unique to the timing of these injuries, including uneven

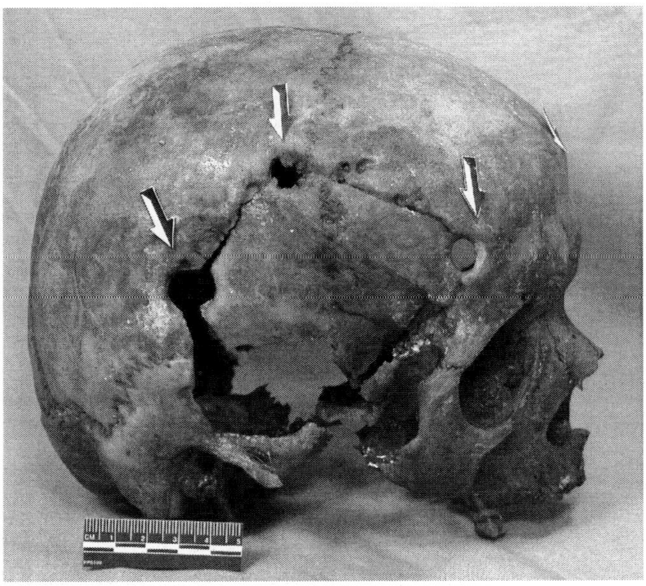

Figure 2.40a Evidence of craniotomy with remodeled bone tissue. Note the edges of the cranial fracture are smooth and blunt or rounded. Also, perimortem lateral through and through GSW, to the skull evident in the temporal region (ICTY).

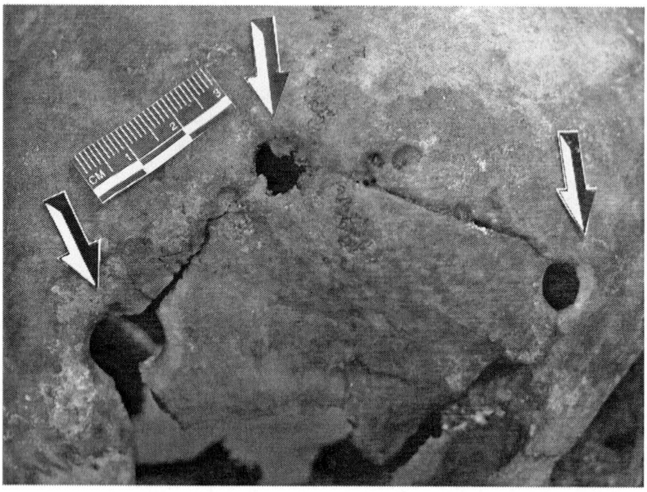

Figure 2.40b Numerous small, circular defects in cranial vault are present, as indicated by arrows. These defects were created as part of surgical intervention and healed with extensive bone remodeling (ICTY).

edges that may also be irregular, hoop fractures (the bone may be bent or warped), radiating or concentric fracture lines, and an angled or jagged fracture edge (Maples 1986; Sauer 1998). Figures 2.43–2.48 illustrate examples of postmortem damage.

Distinguishing peri- and postmortem fractures may be the most challenging but also extremely important for accurately reconstructing the circumstances around and after death. Postmortem fractures occur during or following the decomposition process and,

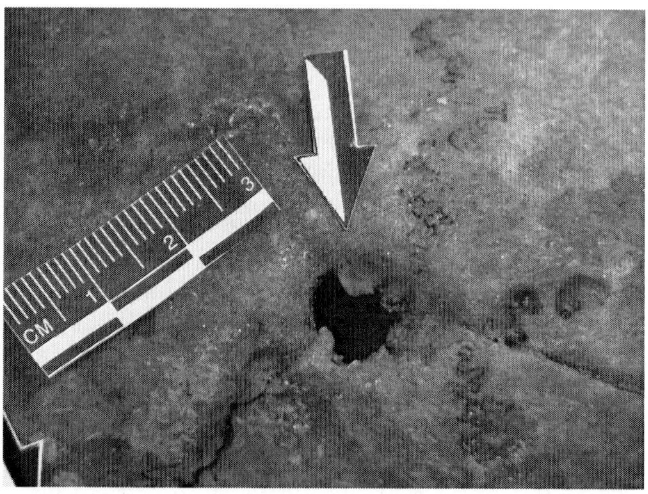

Figure 2.40c Lateral view of the cranium with trephination. Note the edges of the circular defect have a slight margin. The fractures between the defects were part of the surgical intervention. The bones show clear signs of healing. (Printed with permission from International Criminal Tribunal for the former Yugoslavia [ICTY].)

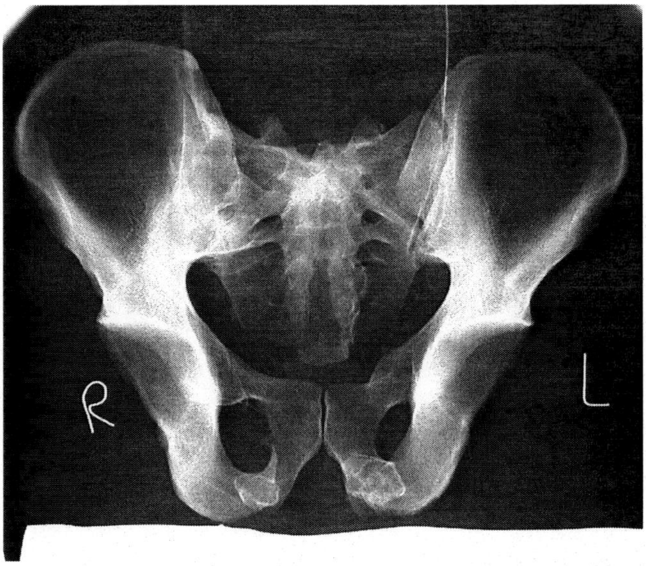

Figure 2.41 Radiography can be useful to correctly diagnose and document antemortem trauma. Healed fracture of left pubic bone with sclerotic bone is indicative of old fracture. (Printed with permission from International Criminal Tribunal for the former Yugoslavia [ICTY].)

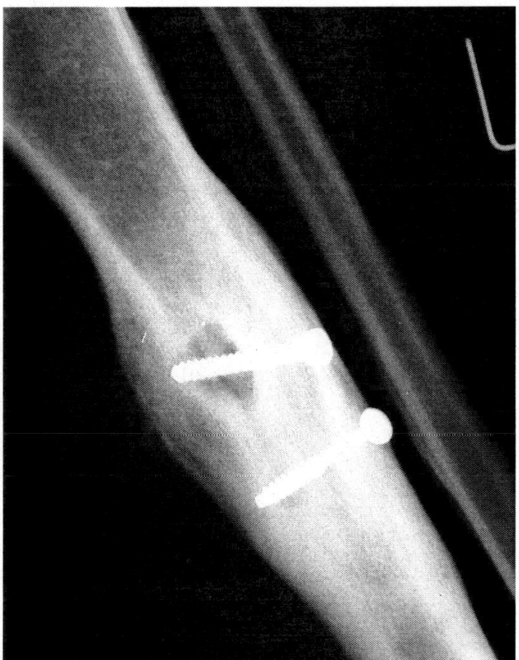

Figure 2.42 Radiographic image. Two screws used to set antemortem fracture to the tibia and fibula. (Printed with permission from International Criminal Tribunal for the former Yugoslavia [ICTY].)

Figure 2.43a Postmortem skull fractures resulting from burial compression (ICTY).

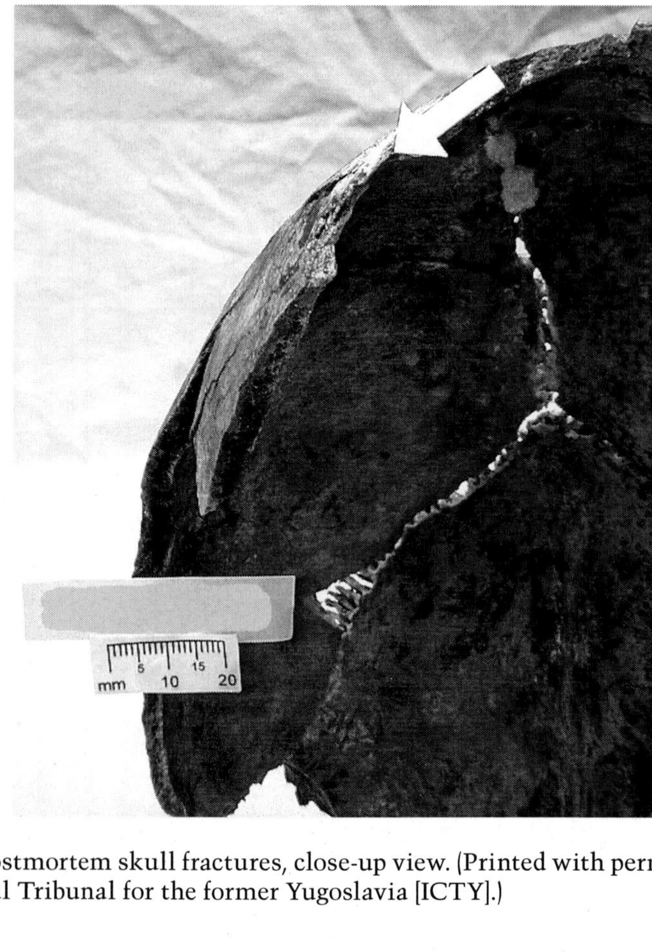

Figure 2.43b Postmortem skull fractures, close-up view. (Printed with permission from International Criminal Tribunal for the former Yugoslavia [ICTY].)

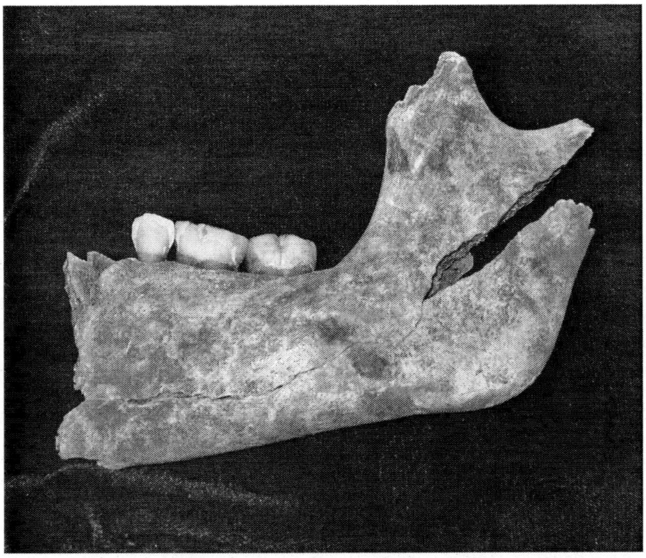

Figure 2.44a Right lateral mandibular fragment, adult. Breakage postmortem (Rafael Guerra, USF).

therefore, may occur before the bone has become dry. The time for it to dry varies, depending on the burial environment. Generally, when bone is dry, fractures tend to have straight and sharp edges with no evidence of bending (Villa and Mahieu 1991; Ubelaker and Adams 1995). The broken surface may differ in color from the rest of the bone, and there will be an absence of fractures, such as radiating fractures.

Puskas and Rummey (2003) illustrate how postmortem scavenger marks may be distinguished from perimortem gunfire injuries. In cases in which heavy equipment, such as

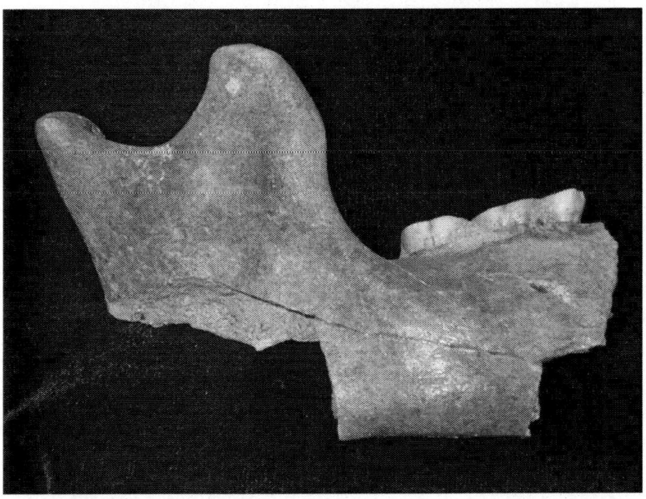

Figure 2.44b Left lateral mandibular fragment from a second adult individual. Breakage also occurred postmortem (Rafael Guerra, USF).

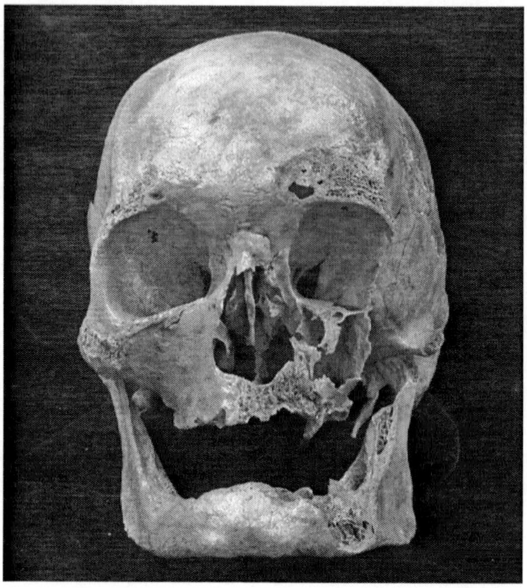

Figure 2.45 Adult male skull. Frontal bone, maxilla and mandible exhibit postmortem damage. The fractures are associated and appear linear, likely the result of excavator or shovel damage. When the fractures are aligned, notice that the mandible is not in anatomical order. Commonly following decomposition, the mandible will disarticulate from the cranium. This misalignment is also indicative of damage occurring postmortem (Rafael Guerra, USF).

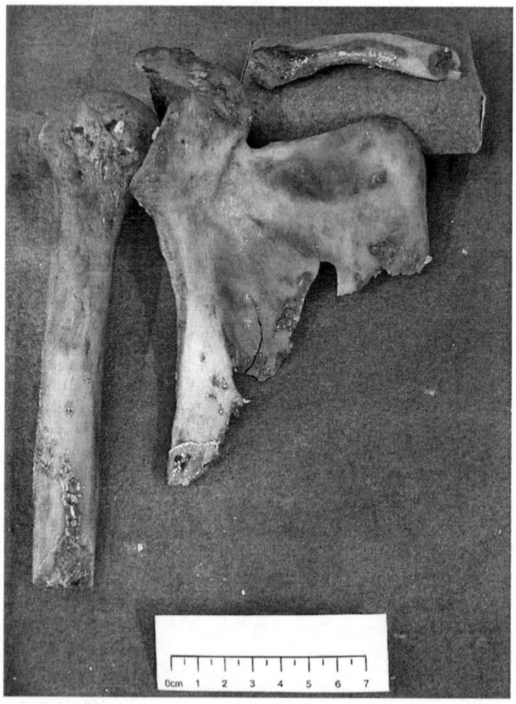

Figure 2.46 Postmortem fracture of the right shoulder. The clavicle, scapula, and humerus exhibit characteristics consistent with damage from heavy equipment. Remains recovered from a secondary mass grave. Note the straight, transverse cut across the shaft of the humerus and the linear cut across multiple bones. (Printed with permission from International Criminal Tribunal for the former Yugoslavia [ICTY].)

Figure 2.47 Adult right femur, anterior view. Postmortem damage, likely excavator damage. Outer cortex of bone poorly preserved, taphonomic change due to weathering (Rafael Guerra, USF).

bulldozers and backhoes, were used to create or move graves, bilateral transverse fractures of long bones and crushing fractures to other skeletal elements have been observed (Baraybar and Gasior 2006; Tuller and Djuric 2006). Transverse fractures resulted in the loss of limbs or body parts, often breaking through the shafts of long bones, with only the fragments of the fractured elements recovered in the grave. In these cases, the missing body parts were rarely recovered. The edges of the fractured segments were irregular and occurred primarily as linear fractures in the transverse plane of the shaft. Crushing fractures were also noted in the ribs, vertebrae, and pelvic girdle. The fractured edges exhibited bone spicules and "peeling" of the outer surface of the bone with some plastic deformation to the surrounding tissue. Segments of ribs or cranial remains may also exhibit severe deformation due to warping from ground pressure.

Finally, postmortem fractures tend to be lighter in color than the rest of the bone. Generally, incisions to bone will not cause deformation, but a trowel or other tools used for excavation or burial may cut or deform the bone. Cutting or chopping mechanisms will generally produce striation marks in bone that may have characteristics useful for differentiating postmortem modification from sharp force injuries (Greenfield 1999):

- Metal knives produce either a narrow V-shaped groove with a distinct apex at the bottom or a broader U-shaped groove with a flat bottom.
- Metal knives make more uniform patterns on the bone.
- In general, metal knives produce a clean and more even slicing cut (except for scalloped-edge knives and sawlike blades).

(a)

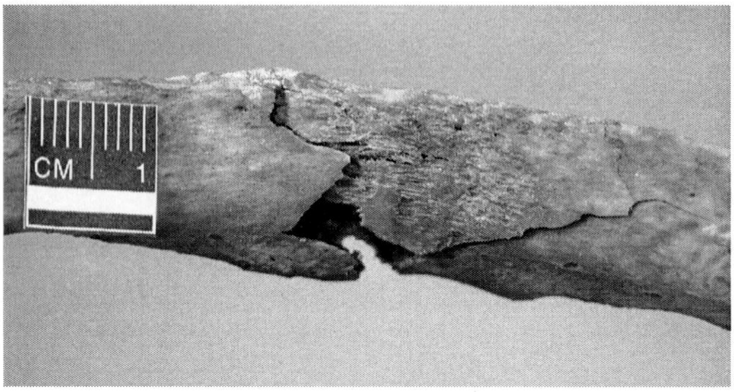

(b)

(c)

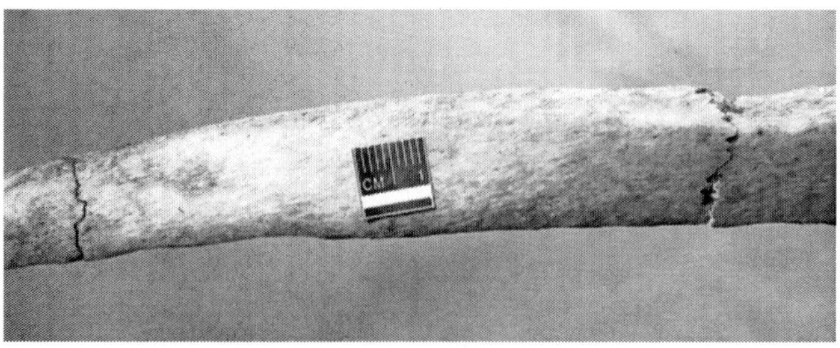

(d)

Figure 2.48(a–d) Adult ribs, various views. Postmortem breakage and fracturing (Alain Wittmann).

For more discussion on how to distinguish perimortem cut marks from postmortem modification (i.e., taphonomic factors or animal damage), refer to Haynes (1983), Willey and Snyder (1989), Berryman et al. (2001), and Symes et al. (2001).

Peri- versus Postmortem Burning

Just as with fractures it is important to distinguish perimortem from postmortem burning. Skeletal evidence of burning is fairly easily recognized, but, interpreting the timing of the burning may be challenging as burned bone has also been observed in cases in which perpetrators attempted to conceal evidence of victims or crimes committed. Burned bone will discolor, fracture in a variety of different ways, crack, and shrink (Mayne 1997). Burning characteristics are influenced by the use of an accelerant, clothing or associated materials burned with the remains and the location of the event in an open or closed space, the temperature of the fire, and time of exposure, as well as the presence of soft tissues (Shipman et al. 1984; Reinhard and Fink 1994; Mayne 1997). Numerous authors (Bradtmiller and Buikstra 1984; de Gruchy and Rogers 2002) have pointed out that understanding the morphological features of burned bone can be vital for differentiating perimortem trauma. Van Vark (1970), in controlled experiments cremating bone, reported:

- There is no bone shrinkage under temperatures of 600°C; however, the bones become more brittle as the temperature increased.
- There was up to 5–10% bone shrinkage at 700°C.
- There was up to 20% bone shrinkage at 800°C. Interestingly, at temperatures of 900–1500°C no more shrinkage occurred.

Illegal attempts to destroy evidence through burning rarely result in the complete destruction of skeletal tissue. Reconstructions of the biological profile (Bass 1984; Thompson 2004) and trauma analysis (Dirkmaat 2001; de Gruchy and Rogers 2002) have been possible following cremation attempts. de Gruchy and Rogers (2002) demonstrated that it was possible to identify knife and chopping wounds that had been burned. They reported that hacking trauma weakened the bony tissue, and therefore areas with trauma were more likely to fragment when burned, but most importantly the burning had little effect on trauma identification as they report that chop and cut marks were easily recognizable following cremation (de Gruchy and Rogers 2002). Further, the volume and weight of cremated remains may be useful in estimating how complete the body of the victim was prior to burning or the number of victims (Murad 1998; Bass and Jantz 2004). In a series of images provided by Elayne Pope based on controlled experimental studies, examples of bone burned peri- and postmortem, including cases with preexisting perimortem trauma are illustrated (Figures 2.49–2.57). Based on color, location of burn patterns, and the morphology of the fractures, peri- and postmortem burning is distinguishable. Further, identification of preexisting fractures may be detected from cremated remains and are discussed in Chapter 6.

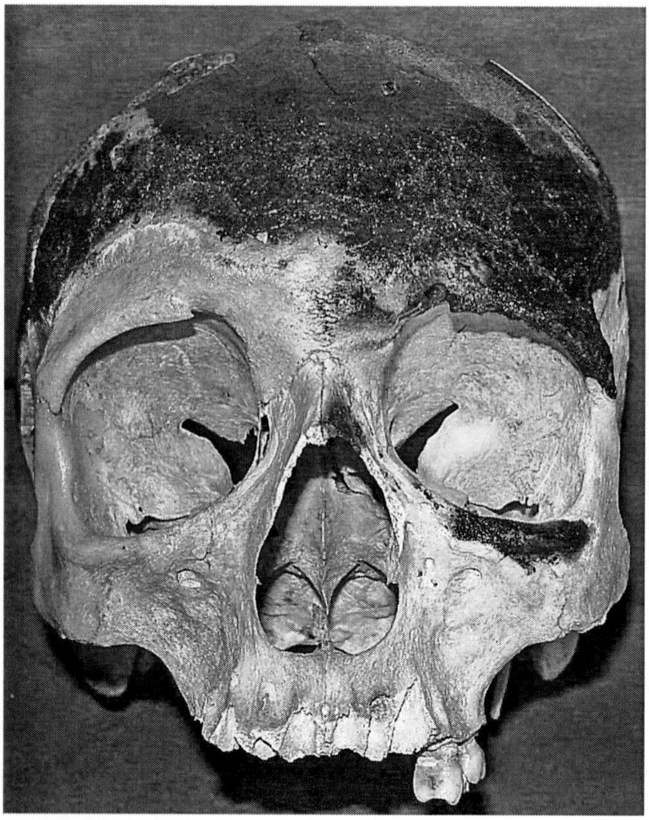

Figure 2.49a Adult crania, anterior view. Burn patterns, fleshed head burned to mimic perimortem event (Elayne Pope).

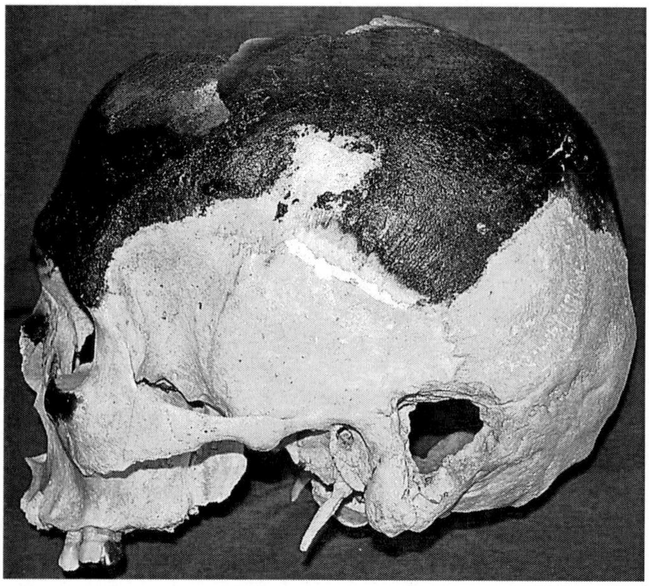

Figure 2.49b Adult crania, left lateral view. Burn patterns, fleshed head (Elayne Pope).

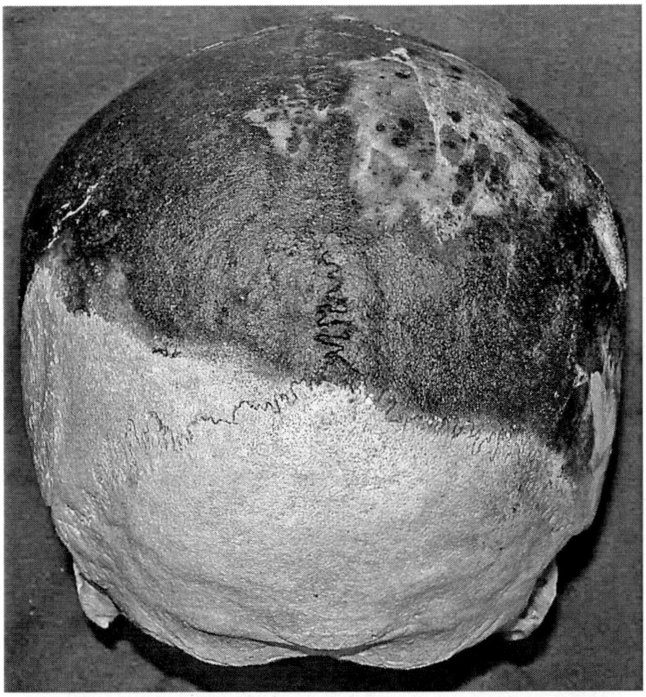

Figure 2.49c Adult crania, posterior view. Burn patterns, fleshed head (Elayne Pope).

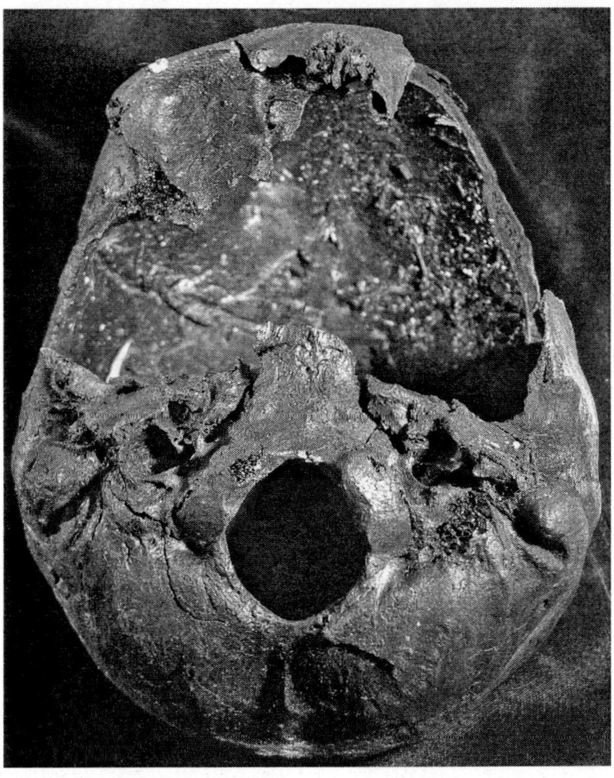

Figure 2.50a Adult crania, basiliar view. Patterns of postmortem burning without flesh present (Elayne Pope).

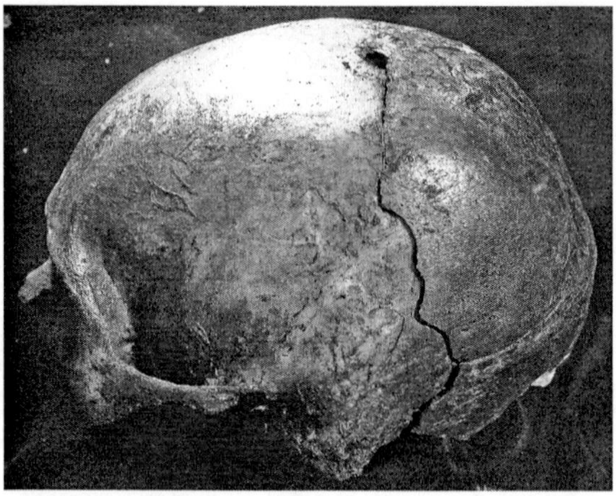

Figure 2.50b Adult crania, left lateral view (Elayne Pope).

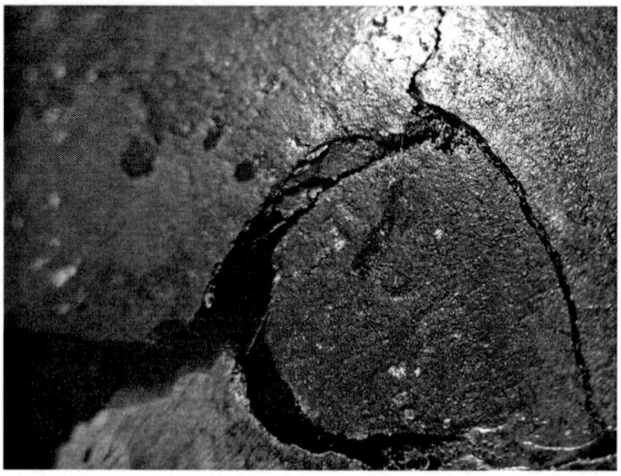

Figure 2.51 Adult crania, right lateral view. Crania burned with pre-burning fracture present (Elayne Pope).

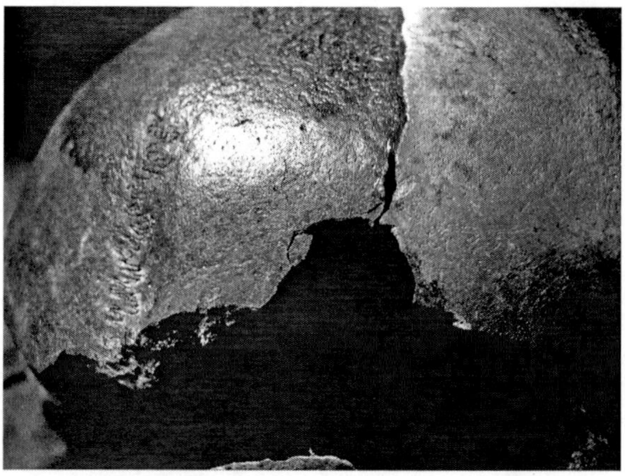

Figure 2.52 Adult crania, right lateral view. Differential coloring of the cranial fragments resulting from preexisting fracture to the skull. Cranial fragments separated during burning resulting in differential color patterns among associated cranial fragments. Color pattern is useful to determine if the fracture was present before burning (Elayne Pope).

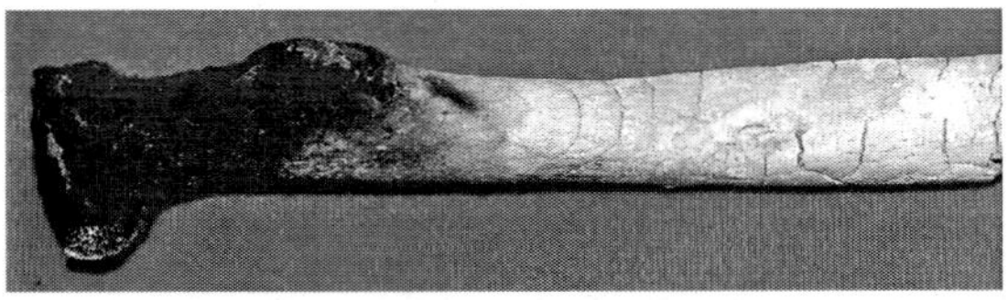

Figure 2.53 The color and curved fractures on this bone fragment are indicative of a bone that was fleshed when burned (Elayne Pope).

Figure 2.54 The curved lines indicate the bone was fleshed when burned and the direction of the fire, as tissues pull away from the heat (Elayne Pope).

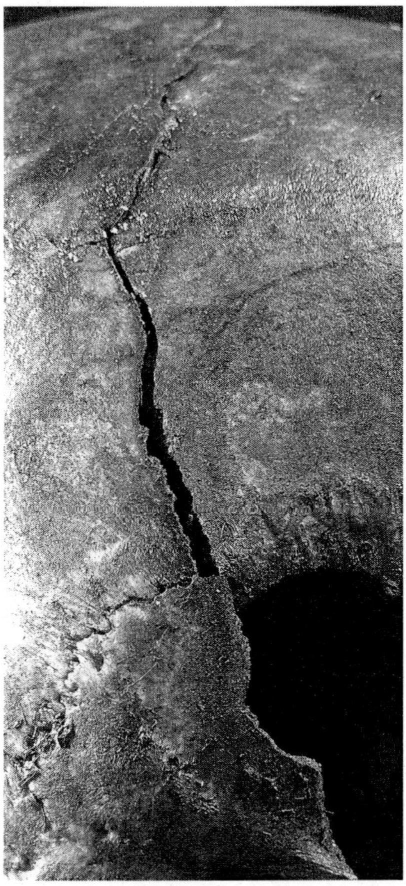

Figure 2.55 Fracture present before the skull was burned. However, the deformation and shrinkage are the results of the fire (Elayne Pope).

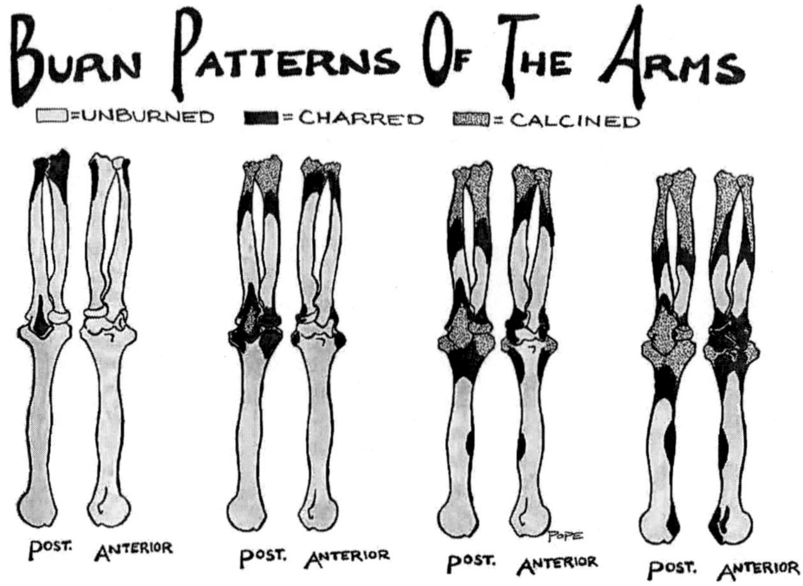

Figure 2.56 Burn patterns of fleshed upper limbs (Elayne Pope).

Diagnosis of Injuries without Evidence of a Defect

A skull may be so extensively fractured that even after reconstruction, it may not be possible to identify a defect or point of impact that clearly allows estimation of the mechanism of injury. So what can be deduced from a fragmented bone without any defects? First, the

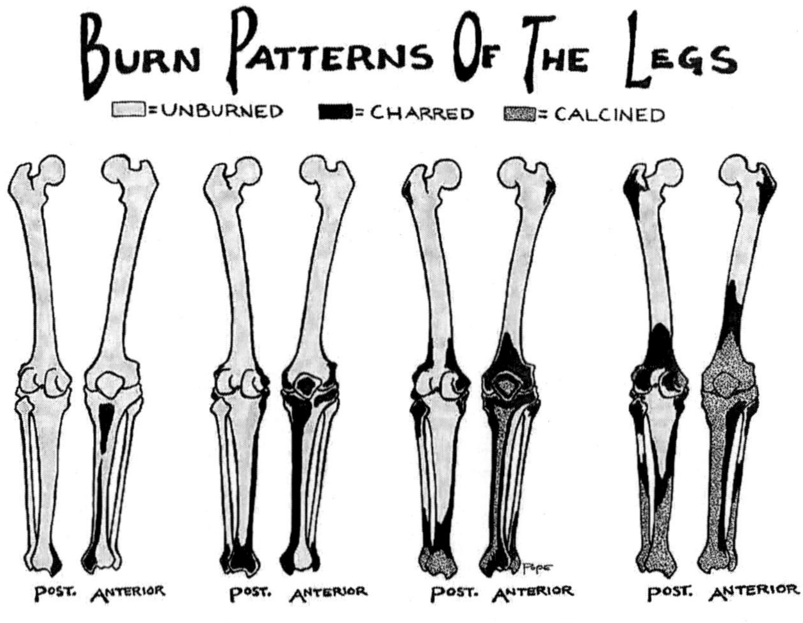

Figure 2.57 Burn patterns of fleshed lower limbs (Elayne Pope).

timing of fractures must be established. In other words, did the fractures occur during the peri- or postmortem interval? Postmortem fracturing of the skull is usually accompanied by plastic deformation of the vault and may or may not have soil staining along the broken edges of bone. Fractures also tend to be isolated or without a clear origin. Postmortem fractures, if not caused during the excavation (in which case they may show patterned injuries with tool markings caused by a pick, shovel, or the "teeth" of a backhoe) may be caused by compression of the head during burial, generally in an anterior–posterior or lateral direction. For example, compression may cause "sinking" of the face into the neurocranium. The facial structures retain their integrity and appear "pushed into" the vault without any possibility to restore them to their original position. Cranial remains may be difficult to reconstruct in these cases because of warping.

Perimortem fractures, without evidence of a ballistic defect may still be consistent with gunfire injuries and indicative of low- or high-velocity forces. Fracturing due to high-velocity forces generally cause extensive comminuted fractures of significant regions of bone; generally, this is associated to multiple generations of radiating and concentric fractures. In the skull, more extensive fracturing occurs at the exit point. In long bones, extensive fracturing will occur at the entry and exit points. In high-velocity cases, radiating fractures sometimes cut across or circumvent areas of buttresses that would not typically break with a low/slow load force. As a general principle, radiating fractures do not show plastic deformation. Comminuted skull fractures can be easily reconstructed with negligible deformation. As explained earlier, however, a fractured skull can be subsequently deformed due to taphonomic factors, such as ground pressure from burial, postmortem.

Second, the type of trauma (i.e., gunfire or blunt force) may be estimated based on fracture patterns, even in the absence of specific defects. For example, on reconstruction of a severely fractured skull, a combination of radiating and concentric fractures becomes evident. It is highly likely that the fractures result from a gunfire injury because of the type, location, and association of fracture lines that are consistent with a gunfire injury, not postmortem damage. In cases in which the defect is not observable, there may still be metal fragments present evidence by inspection or through radiography.

Radiography and Three-Dimensional Imaging

There are several radiographic references that provide specific and useful guidelines for radiographic methodology for interpretation in postmortem examinations (Ortner and Putschar 1981; Knight 1991; Brogdon et al. 2003). Radiographic techniques specifically in cases of HHRR or political abuse have also been a focus of recent discussion (Farkash et al. 2000; Brogdon et al. 2003; Fitzpatrick 1984). For most cases involving excavated human skeletal remains, the primary objective for radiographic analysis is to locate physical evidence of weaponry such as lead wipe from a projectile or shrapnel fragments (Figures 2.58 and 2.59). A further benefit is the safety of the investigators as live munitions such as hand grenades present in clothing should be identified prior to the examination (Figure 2.60).

In skeletonized cases, radiography can be used for understanding fracture patterns, assessing the number of injuries, or sequencing multiple injuries. Injuries involving high-velocity gunfire or explosions result in significant fracturing that will appear on x-ray as a pile of bone fragments. For the investigator who reconstructs a fractured skull or long bone, radiography has little diagnostic value in interpreting fracture patterns. Rather,

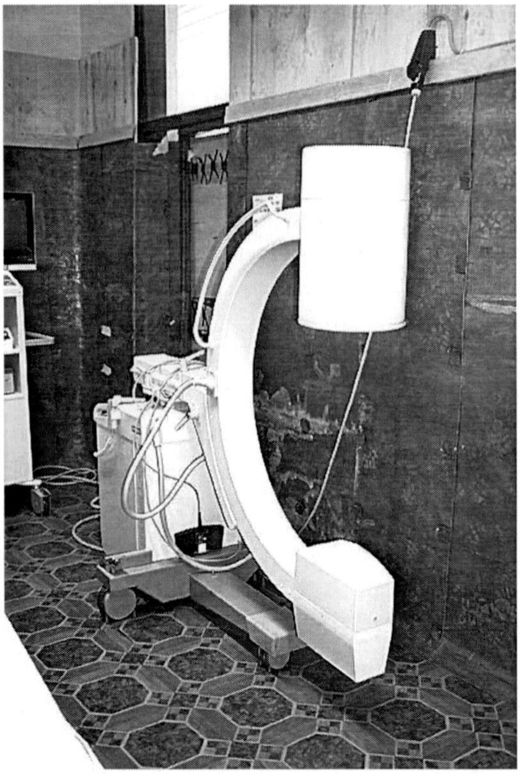

Figure 2.58 Portable Fluoroscope. (Printed with permission from International Criminal Tribunal for the former Yugoslavia [ICTY].)

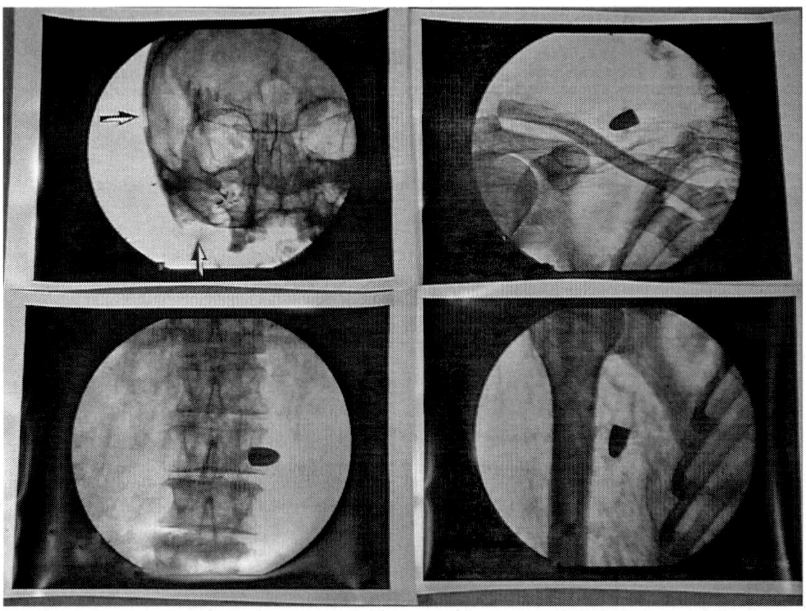

Figure 2.59 Series of images displaying projectiles embedded within body cavities. Images are from a fluoroscope. (Printed with permission from International Criminal Tribunal for the former Yugoslavia [ICTY].)

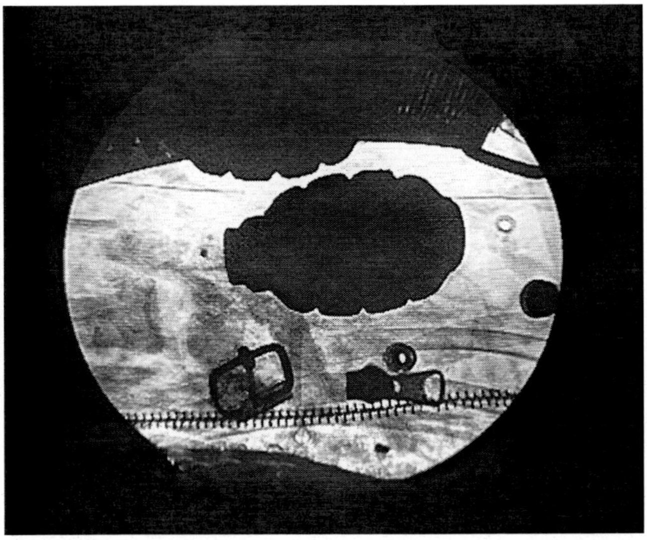

Figure 2.60a Radiography is also useful for identifying weapons, ammunitions, or unused explosives within pockets or layers of clothing. Pictured here are two grenades stuffed into a pocket. These grenades were not found in the field at the time of excavation, but later after being transported to the morgue and scanned with a fluoroscope (ICTY).

radiography as a diagnostic tool involves cases in which soft tissue is present, holding the skeletal elements in anatomical position. However, these do not make up the majority of cases for the anthropologist, as demonstrated by material presented in this book. Data may be obtained on fracture type or fragment location that are not visible or recognizable by gross inspection of the body alone. Typically, these *fresh* cases have not yet decomposed and the data yielded through radiographic techniques may prove useful in the identification of skeletal trauma (i.e., Cattaneo et al. 2006). In fresh cases, imaging is used to differentiate

Figure 2.60b The actual grenades recovered in clothing. (Printed with permission from International Criminal Tribunal for the former Yugoslavia [ICTY].)

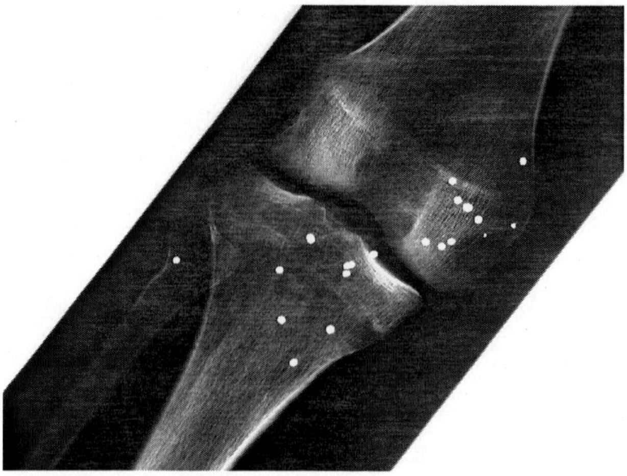

Figure 2.61 Gunshot pellets embedded in the left knee. Shot was fired right to left at an intermediate distance based on the spread of the pellets. Note also the skeletal defect on the right lateral margin, indicating an entry wound. (Printed with permission from International Criminal Tribunal for the former Yugoslavia [ICTY].)

different types of trauma (Oliver et al. 1997), elucidate complex fractures (Salvolini 2002; Oehmichen et al. 2003), or identify fragments from weaponry (Figures 2.61–2.69).

Radiography is very useful in cases in which trauma or skeletal pathology occurred antemortem and for diagnosing the timing of antemortem injuries or the type of skeletal reaction due to a pathogen. Radiography also serves important functions in assessing the amount of epiphyseal union among juveniles or diagnosis of skeletal pathology. In diagnosing skeletal pathology, radiography illustrates skeletal reaction on the surface of a bone or within the tissue structures and the location and distribution of bony responses. Further, radiology provides useful imaging for ante-and postmortem comparisons for

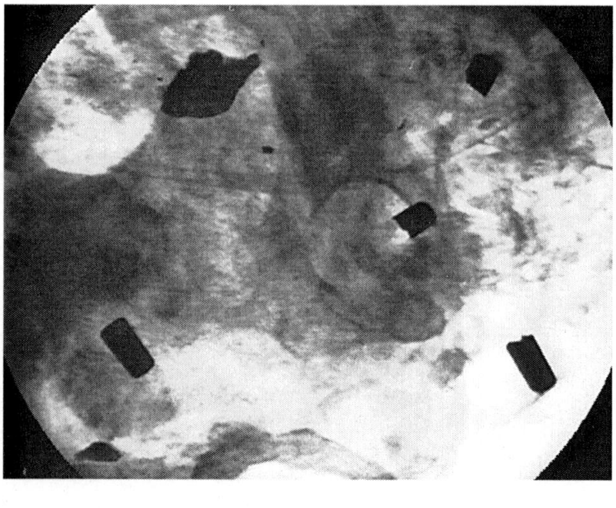

Figure 2.62 Metal shrapnel fragments resulting from a blasting injury. Note the symmetrical, rectangular-shaped pieces of metal. (Printed with permission from International Criminal Tribunal for the former Yugoslavia [ICTY].)

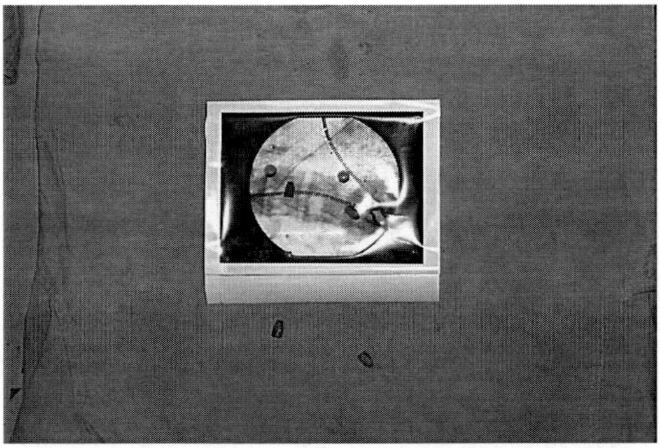

Figure 2.63 Two projectiles visible on fluoroscope image along lower vertebrae. The metal artifacts from clothing, such as zippers, are also evident. The same projectiles recovered from within the tissues are pictured. (Printed with permission from International Criminal Tribunal for the former Yugoslavia [ICTY].)

victim identification, such as dental x-rays, orthopedic hardware, or unique skeletal structures such as sinuses or trabelcular bone patterning in the pelvis or hip regions.

Radiography has another important function as a visualization tool for the courtroom presentation of injuries and illustration of circumstances around death for a panel of judges or a jury (Meyers et al. 1999; Thali et al. 2002a, 2002b). In this context, radiography is not used as a diagnostic tool, but it provides imaging, even three-dimensional (3D) imaging of reconstructed bones, that is understandable to non-experts (Figures 2.70 and 2.71).

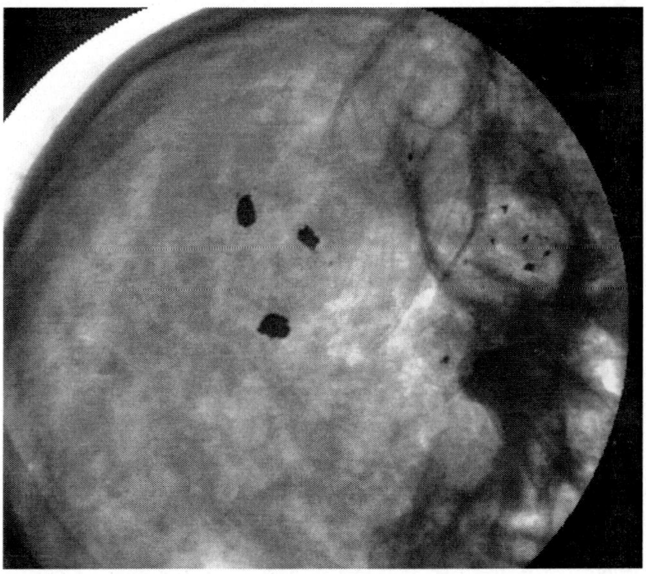

Figure 2.64 Fluoroscope image. Metal fragments from a gunfire projectile are evident in this skull. (Printed with permission from International Criminal Tribunal for the former Yugoslavia [ICTY].)

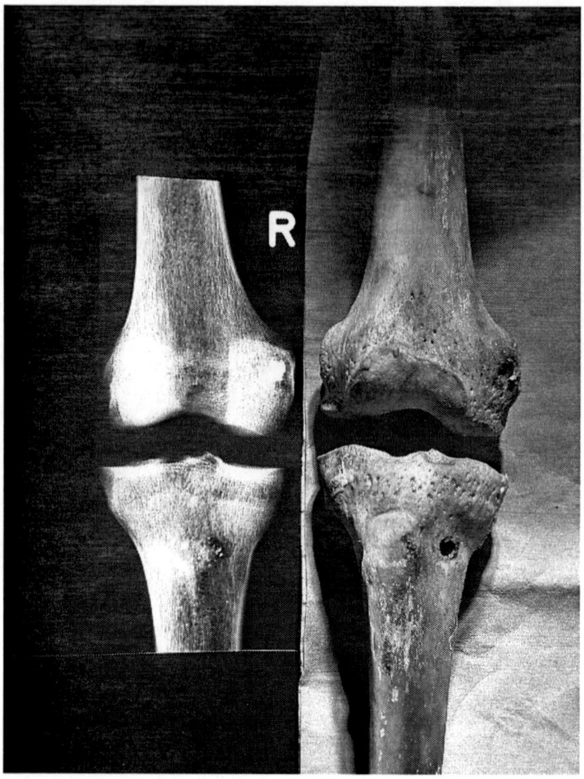

Figure 2.65 The right knee (distal femur and proximal tibia) are pictured. Two gunfire injuries are present. The projectiles did not exit either bone. The fragmented metal pieces from the projectiles are evident on the x-ray image. (Printed with permission from International Criminal Tribunal for the former Yugoslavia [ICTY].)

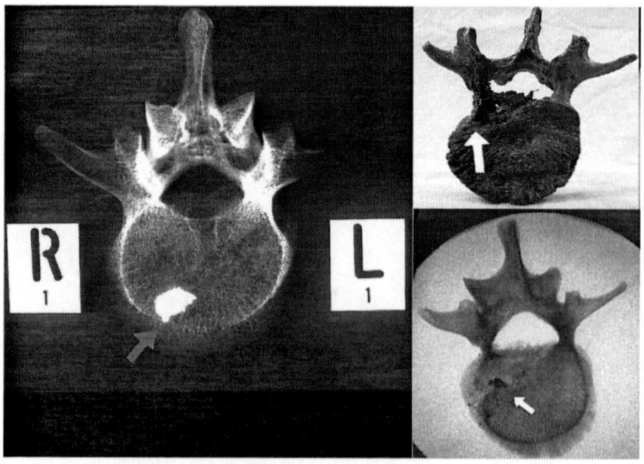

Figure 2.66 The image on the right: projectile fragment from a gunfire injury. Fragment is embedded in the body of a lumbar vertebra. The depth of the fragment and fracture line is evident in the fluoroscope image. The images on the right illustrates a lumbar vertebra from a different case that also has a fragmented metal piece of a projectile from a gunfire injury. The actual bone and an image taken with a standard x-ray are shown. The differences in visualization between fluoroscope and standard x-ray images are apparent. (Printed with permission from International Criminal Tribunal for the former Yugoslavia [ICTY].)

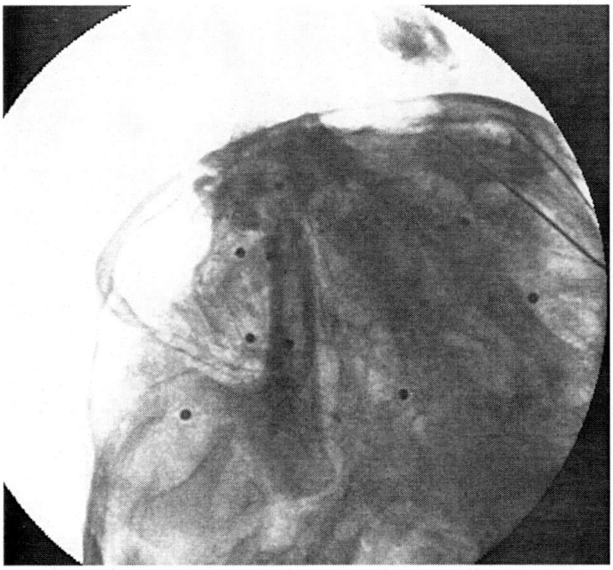

Figure 2.67 Shotgun pellets in the skull, evident in fluoroscope image. Distance among pellets consistent with shot fired from a distance. (Printed with permission from International Criminal Tribunal for the former Yugoslavia [ICTY].)

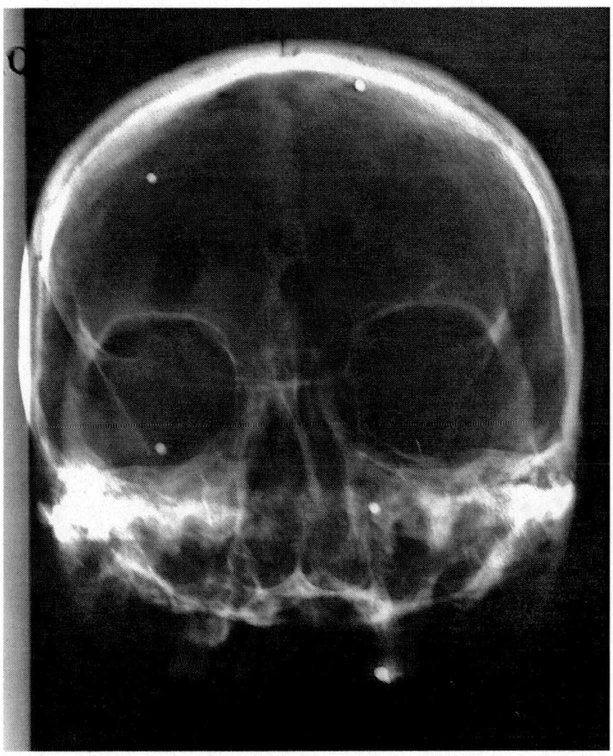

Figure 2.68 Shotgun pellets in the skull shown in the frontal view, taken by a standard x-ray. The distance between the pellets indicate the shot was fired from a distance. (Printed with permission from International Criminal Tribunal for the former Yugoslavia [ICTY].)

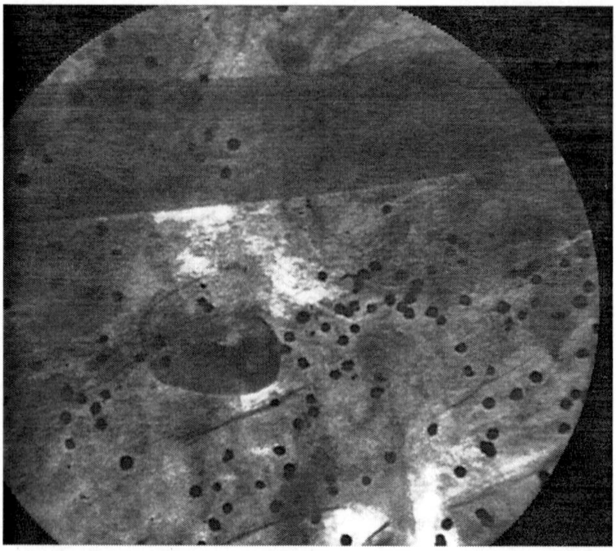

Figure 2.69 Numerous shotgun pellets present in decomposing soft tissue, disarticulated femur also evident in fluoroscope image. The pellets are close to one another, which is indicative of a shot fired from an intermediate distance. (Printed with permission from International Criminal Tribunal for the former Yugoslavia [ICTY].)

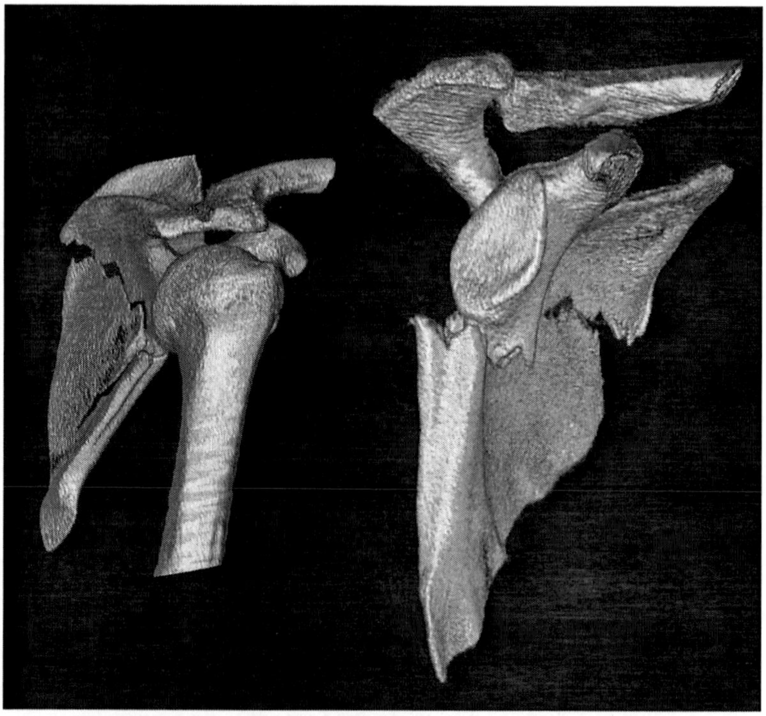

Figure 2.70 3D-CT image. Blunt force trauma to the left scapula. A compression fracture is present on the acromion process and a linear fracture extends across the scapular body (right side). The humerus was digitally removed in the image on the right to allow better visualization of the scapula and glenoid process. (Image reprinted with permission from Dr. Matthias Okoye and Dr. David Kiple.)

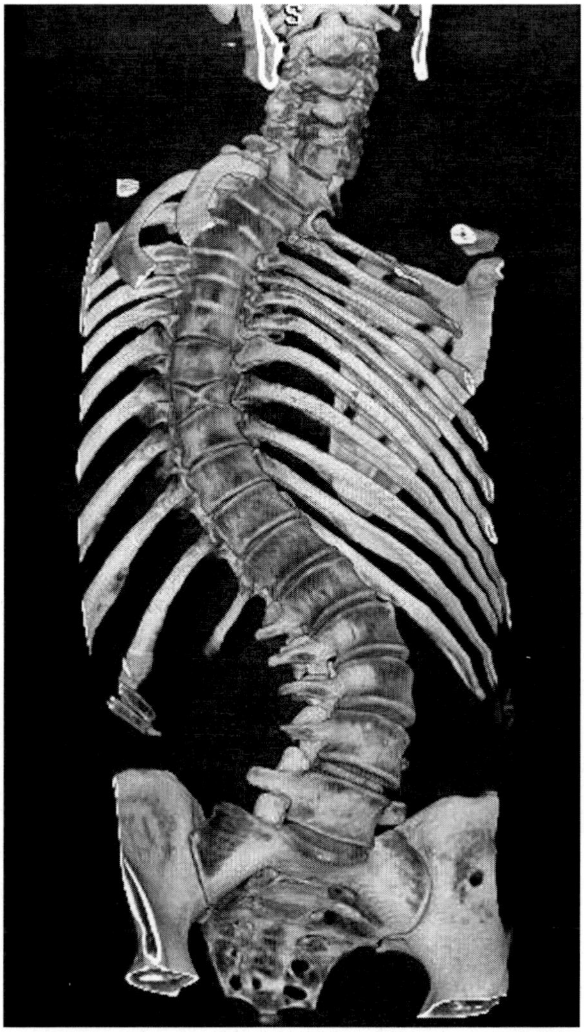

Figure 2.71 3D-CT image. Spine and thorax recreated digitally to demonstrate scoliosis and hemivertebra in thoracic region. Congenital defects. (Image reprinted with permission from Dr. Matthias Okoye and Dr. David Kiple.)

Any image produced from a radiograph, fluoroscope, MRI, or CT scan may be useful in this way. In particular, images reconstructed from CT scans or taken with 3D scanners present the bone in three-dimensional space that can be rotated or viewed from different angles. This is useful for illustrating the trajectory of an injury or describing how one projectile may affect different regions of the body (Donchin et al. 1994). Radiographic images such as 3D reconstructions also allow data files to be shared electronically, which is valuable for obtaining a second opinion, regardless of where investigators are located throughout the world and are being used in real-time applications such as virtual autopsies (Thali 2003a, 2003b; Thali et al. 2002a, 2002b; Thali et al. 2003a, 2003b).

The Usefulness of Clothing as Evidence

Clothing in human rights investigations is an important line of evidence in the initial phase of the identification process. Clothing is also an important tool for understanding the mechanism and number of injuries, and the trajectory path and range of fire in ballistic and shrapnel wounds (Figures 2.72–2.76). The interpretation of injuries and victim identification from clothing is relevant to the context of the situation, the nature of the armed conflict, and the victim's age, sex, and identity (i.e., military or civilian). For example, the types of clothing that are present, the amount of clothing a person may have been wearing at the time of disappearance, whether the clothing was owned by the person wearing it (or issued something to wear), and what items were contained within pockets or layers reveal important attributes about the nature and intention of crimes committed.

Protocols for postmortem examinations must always include a strategy for handling clothing and guidelines to recover all associated evidence obtained within and preserve and curate the items for future reference or use at trial. The component of a projectile, shell casings, shrapnel from blasting injuries, and small bone fragments may become embedded in clothing. Clothing should not be cut at the site to collect the bones from a clothed

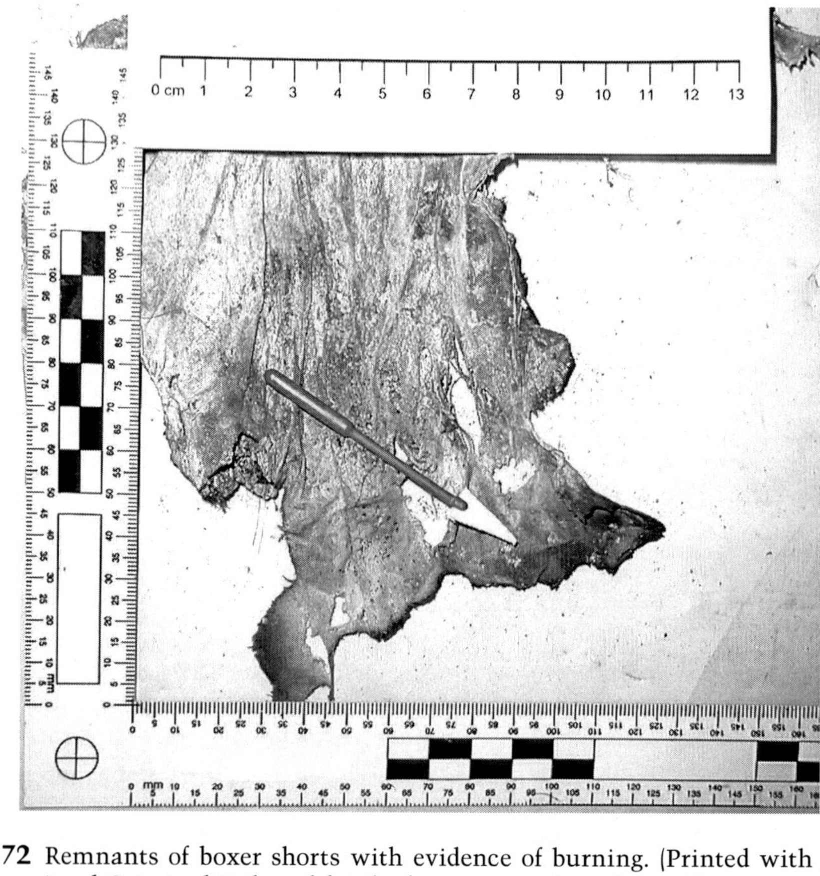

Figure 2.72 Remnants of boxer shorts with evidence of burning. (Printed with permission from International Criminal Tribunal for the former Yugoslavia [ICTY].)

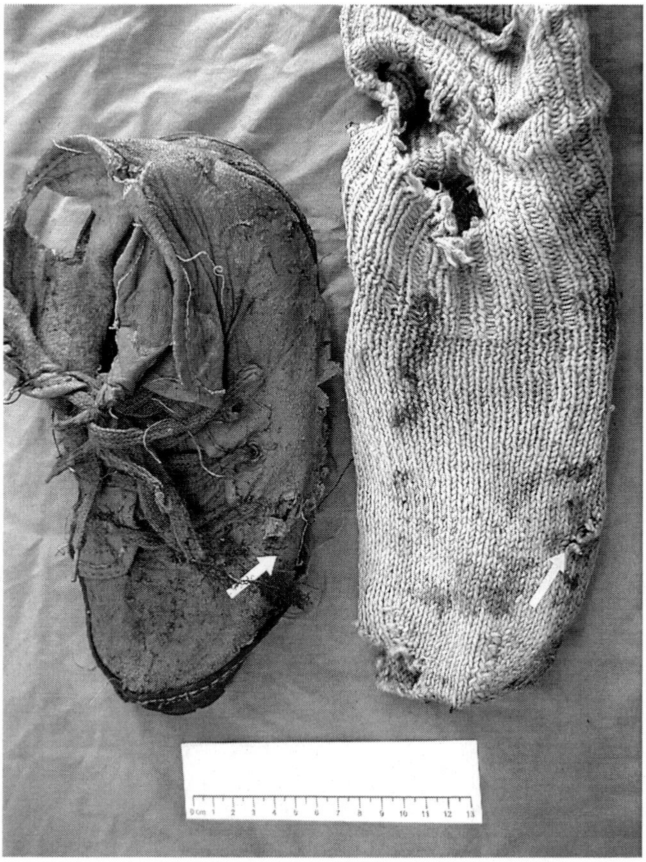

Figure 2.73 Gunfire injury to the left foot. Entrance evident on left side of shoe and a corresponding injury is noted on the left sock. No burning, soot, or gunpowder is present, indicating an intermediate or distant shot. (Printed with permission from International Criminal Tribunal for the former Yugoslavia [ICTY].)

skeleton, nor during the postmortem examination. Further, clothing should always be x-rayed separately from the body, prior to its being washed. Clothing should be thoroughly inspected and photographed both prior to and after washing for later use in the identification process, and to review defects indicative of injuries. The clothing, by evidence of soot or burning, provides information that assists with understanding the circumstances around death such as mechanism of injury, the range of fire, and postmortem taphonomic processes that affected the remains (Maples and Browning 1994).

Clothing is also a meaningful tool to link an unidentified person to a particular family or village thereby establishing group identity. For example, textiles proved to be very useful for personal identification (Schmitt 2001; Doretti and Snow 2003) during investigations into mass atrocities against the Kurdish people in Iraq (1987–1989) and the Maya in the highlands of Guatemala (1980–1984). In both of these examples, textile patterns and colors play a significant cultural role and uniquely represent each village. In either of these cases, no attempts were made by the perpetrators of the crimes to hide the victim's

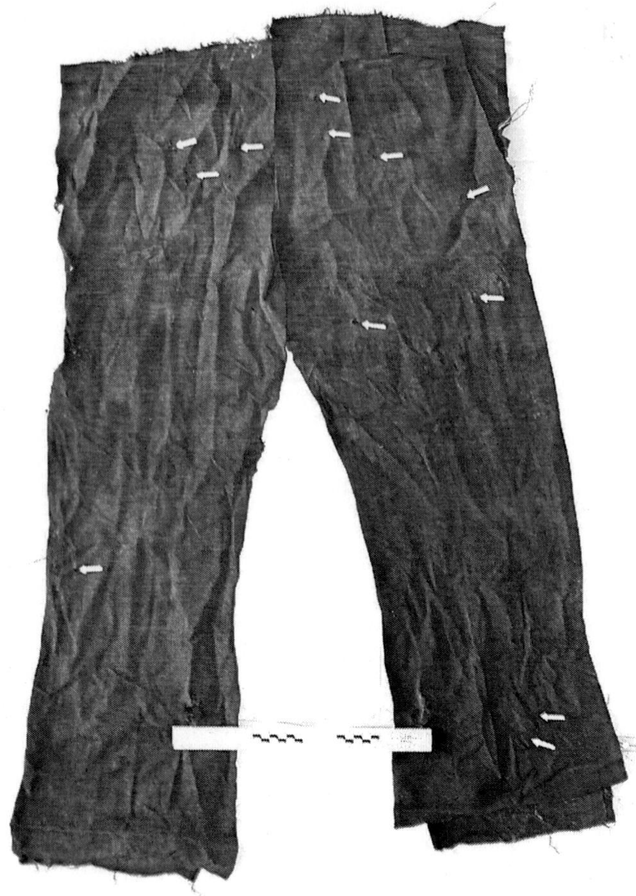

Figure 2.74 Pellets from a shotgun injury pattern consistent with pellets fired from a distance. (Printed with permission from International Criminal Tribunal for the former Yugoslavia [ICTY].)

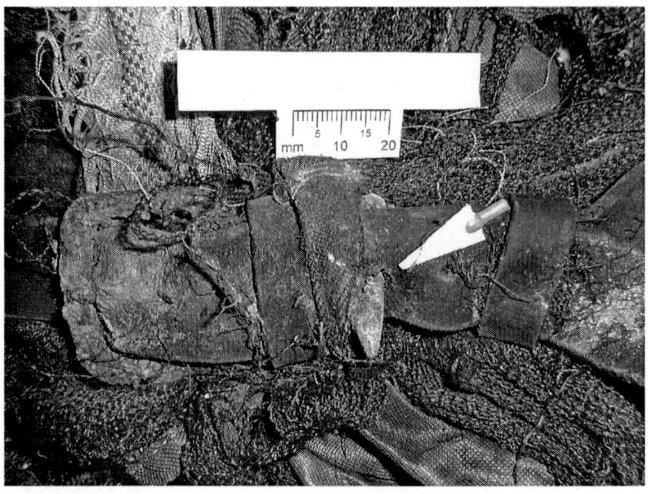

Figure 2.75 A 7.62 × 39 mm full metal-jacketed bullet, fired from an AK-47, is embedded in a leather belt buckle. (Printed with permission from International Criminal Tribunal for the former Yugoslavia [ICTY].)

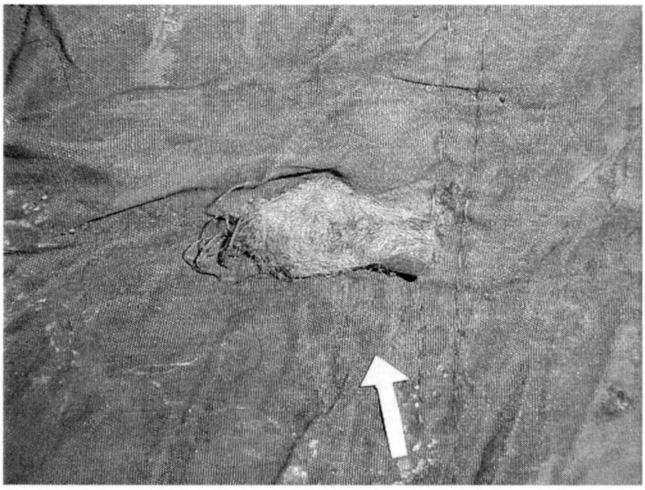

Figure 2.76 A 7.62 × 39 mm full metal-jacketed bullet, likely fired from an AK-47, is embedded in the fibers of a jacket. (Printed with permission from International Criminal Tribunal for the former Yugoslavia [ICTY].)

identity, such as taking their clothing, nor were the victims generally held captive prior to their executions. Therefore, *group identity* was established based on textiles.

In some cases in which victims are detained, concealing identity may not be an issue. Doretti and Snow (2003) report on the Kotebe case from Ethiopia, where 30 men disappeared after being held in custody. During detainment, family members were allowed to visit and bring clean clothing (Doretti and Snow 2003). Therefore, even though the men were held captive, clothing was useful for personal identification. Throughout the Balkan conflict (1991–1999), there was considerable variation in the events surrounding the murder of thousands of people. In cases associated with Srebrenica, as discussed in Chapter 1, men were told to leave their personal items such as suitcases and identification papers outside as they entered into buildings. Many of the bodies of those who were killed were then disposed of into mass graves and later exhumed and moved to *secondary* sites by the perpetrators in an attempt to hide the location of the graves. Ultimately, these graves were exhumed and used as evidence of violations of international humanitarian law (IHL), including war crimes and genocide. Although significant efforts were made to hide graves, clothing was not generally taken away prior to the killings. Not only the clothing that the victims were wearing but also piles of folded clothing were recovered in graves, providing evidence that civilians were intentionally killed (refer to *The Prosecutor v. Kristic IT-98-33-T*, particularly the transcripts related to the testimony of Baraybar on Nova Kasaba sites).

Later, in 1999 Kosovan Muslims were fleeing their homes as the Serbian authorities attempted to expel them from the region. Many of the victims were recovered wearing numerous layers of shirts, sweaters, trousers, and socks. Wearing so much clothing was one way to stay warm as they were fleeing to the mountains during the cold months of the year, and it provided a means to carry more items (both clothing and personal items) as they left their homes. Identification papers, money, medicine, photographs, personal papers, jewelry, and ammunition have been recovered from pockets or within the socks

Figure 2.77 Clothing folded in a grave. Luggage taken from civilian men killed in Srebreniča in July 1995 and buried in mass graves. (Printed with permission from International Criminal Tribunal for the former Yugoslavia [ICTY].)

that people were wearing at the time of their deaths. In Kosovo, many people were also killed in or around their homes. In most cases, no attempts were made to hide the identity of victims or their murders. Most victims were left in their homes, and the bodies were not even moved or disposed of by those who committed the atrocities.

Throughout the Balkans, as elsewhere, such clothing and personal items have been useful tools for presumptive victim identifications as families identify these personal items (Figures 2.77 and 2.78) (OMPF 2004; OSCE Report 1999a, 1999b).

The cultural context in which the conflict occurs is an important consideration when interpreting cultural objects as evidence, such as clothing. Clothing is a good example of this, as it cannot always be used for identification as in the cases of Argentina and Peru (refer to Case Study 5.4 in Chapter 5).

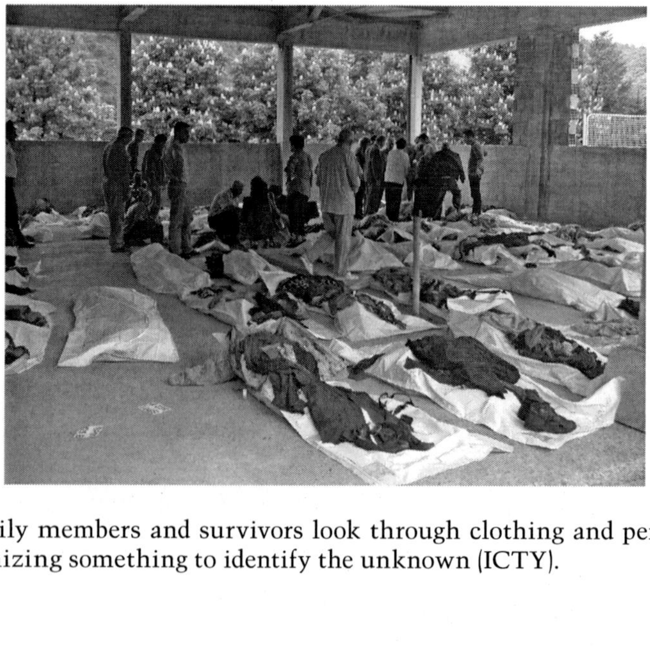

Figure 2.78 Family members and survivors look through clothing and personal artifacts in the hope of recognizing something to identify the unknown (ICTY).

For example, in Argentina ("The Dirty War," 1976–1983), clothing was taken from individuals who were imprisoned prior to execution for the explicit purpose of taking away their identity (Doretti and Snow 2003). This was done to degrade and dehumanize victims as they were imprisoned and was one of the many forms of psychological and physical torture inflicted on detainees. Consequently, exhumations and postmortem examinations of victims, during criminal investigations many years later, has meant that clothing worn by them cannot be used for identification (Doretti and Snow 2003). In cases such as Argentina or Peru, clothing is still an important evidentiary tool for trauma analysis and for the possible inclusion/exclusion of individuals in the initial stages of collective identification.

Photography

Photography of skeletal wounds and associated artifacts is important for documenting what happened and for presenting a visual image of what is observed. Ideally, when the resources and time permit, a photography protocol should specify that both standard and special shots be taken. A photo log is kept, documenting all of the photographs taken. The log should include information on the case number, date, name of photographer, number of the shot, description of what appears in the photo, and comments on the distance of the camera to the specimen and its orientation. Traditionally, photographs were taken in black/white and in color; however, digital photography has cut costs substantially, allowing large numbers of high-quality photographs to be easily recorded and digitally stored. The photographic record of the hundreds of cases examined by the Office on Missing Persons and Forensics (OMPF) in Kosovo has primarily been based on digital photography.

Generally, the camera should be mounted on a tripod and placed perpendicular to the object being photographed. Black-colored cloth such as velvet or green medical scrubs provide strong contrasts as backdrops to bone. Standard photographs are taken of views of all every skull and innominate aging surface depicting each surface of the specimen. The shots should be in anatomical position, requiring strict guidelines for the position and angles of the skeletal materials to the camera. Standard shots of the skull include eight views (frontal, left lateral, right lateral, posterior, superior, inferior, maxillary occlusal, and mandibular occlusal). Two standard views are taken of the *Os coxa* (that illustrate the auricular surface and pubic symphyseal face for age estimation). "Special shots" should also be taken of all fractures, injuries, skeletal and dental pathology, or cultural and medical modifications. These cases require standard shots and special angles, close-up views, and multiple views from oblique angles. Experience shows that articulating anatomical parts such as the skull to the cervical spine, the mandible to the cranium, or the forearm to the humerus and gluing them together assist in depicting the extent and complexity of injuries. In addition, it is a more didactic tool to present the most visually interesting and clear image in court than the photograph of an isolated bone with an injury. Records of the site/burial/case numbers indicate where the subject is from. This label and a scale should appear in at least one photograph for reference per case. When shooting film outside the morgue or without control over the amount and direction of light, images should be bracketed with the exposure set higher and lower. Several shots with varying light will ensure the right exposure and a good result.

Summary Guidelines for Best Practice

Methods, organization, and clear terminology are needed for reliable and consistent analyses of skeletal trauma to be useful in medicolegal death investigations. Furthermore, careful and consistent recovery is needed to ensure the collection of all evidence. Radiography and the analysis of clothing are also important lines of evidence adding to information about injuries. This chapter provides a comprehensive step-by-step guide on how to reconstruct skeletal injuries. The utility of three-dimensional imaging in the assessment of trauma and the visual presentation of injuries in court are discussed. Finally, a correct diagnosis of skeletal fractures is necessary to differentiate peri- and postmortem trauma. Various examples and a list of criteria for differentiating postmortem damage from perimortem skeletal injuries are provided.

Accuracy in the skeletal diagnosis of injuries around the time of an individual's death relies on the integration of as many lines of evidence as possible. Data from a variety of sources should be used in combination; these include the anthropologist's examination of the skeletal tissues, microscopic analysis of the affected bone surfaces, radiographic data, the assessment of the individual's clothing, and the evaluation of the physical evidence of weaponry. After all of the evidence is considered, deduction is used to classify each injury category, identify the mechanism of the injury, and determine the most likely cause of death.

Some of the unusual skeletal pathologies that occur during conflicts and the implications for the process of victim identification are discussed. During wartime and human rights conflicts, individuals often do not have adequate health, nor dental care or proper nutrition, because of imposed embargoes, military seizures, the dissolution of the social infrastructure, or forced refugee status. Consequently, a number of health-related issues arise as medical problems are untreated or child growth and development are inhibited. As a result, the postmortem record of skeletal and dental pathology may not match potential antemortem records of the affected individuals. Moreover, juvenile age estimation may be skewed as a result of growth delays from malnutrition. Documenting this at autopsy may illuminate HHRR atrocities or critical human insecurities.

Case Study 2.1: Finite Element Models of the Human Head in the Field of Forensic Science

Jean-Sebastien Raul
Institut de médecine légale, Strasbourg, France

Bertrand Ludes
Institut de médecine légale, Strasbourg, France

Rémy Willinger
Institut de mécanique des fluides et des solides, Strasbourg, France

Until recently, the legal system relied on the testimony of medical experts to determine whether the force imparted to the human head in a given scenario was consistent with the resulting human head injury. Finite element models (FEMs) can provide interesting tools to the forensic scientist when different human head injury mechanisms need to be evaluated (e.g., adult and child head injuries, and ballistic human head injuries). Human head FEM are not in common use in forensic science and are mainly used for car crash safety evaluations. Technological progress has resulted in creating more simple tools that can be used in forensic cases. The last 40 years have seen biomechanical studies emerging in forensic research. Many of these aimed at establishing whether a head injury of an infant was the result of accident or abuse and, if it was abuse, what were the possible mechanisms leading to certain injuries such as subdural hematomas (Cory et al. 2003; Jones et al. 2003). Other works such as multibody dynamics reconstruction of adult head injury accidents and biomechanical studies of falls have recently been published (Bandak and Chan 1999; Vock 2001; Zhang et al. 2001; Ruan et al. 2003).

FEMs are considered a promising tool to investigate the dynamic response of the human head under impact conditions. Moreover, by reconstructing well-documented real-world accident cases it has been possible with these models to derive tolerance limits for skull fracture, subdural hematoma, and neurological injuries. Recent work has been published using the Université Louis Pasteur FEM for the evaluation of human head injuries in forensic cases (Raul et al. 2005; Raul et al. 2006; Roth et al. 2006).

Standards for car safety and head protection systems rely on criteria for human tolerance, which are based on biomedical research performed more than 30 years ago. Measures designed to improve human head protection are typically evaluated against the measurement of a rigid mass acceleration and the calculation of the head injury criterion (HIC). The predictive capability of this criterion has been widely criticized because of its limited ability to predict the wide range of head injury mechanisms. It has been suggested that specific deformation or stress of the skull and brain tissue, as well as a measure of the relative motion of the brain and skull, would be much better injury mechanisms to assess human head protection.

To date, more than ten different three-dimensional human head FEMs have been described and validated against skull deformation, as well as brain pressure data from experimental impact tests onto the front of the head of cadavers, and against brain skull relative motion, with data obtained from high-speed x-ray experiments. Most advanced approaches were proposed by Ruan et al. (1993), besides NHTSA (National Highway Traffic Safety Administration) by Bandak et al. (2001), Wayne State University (WSU) model by Zhou et al. (1996) and Yang and King (2003), and ULP-Strasbourg (Université Louis Pasteur) by Kang et al. (1997).

To derive tolerance limits from these models, Zhou et al. (1996) simulated a fully documented road accident with the WSU model; the shear stresses predicted by his model agreed approximately with the location of axonal injury described by the medical report. More recently, Newman et al. (2000) presented a detailed methodology for the assessment of mild traumatic brain injury based on the reconstruction of accidents of the American National Football League, using the human head FEM in Zhou et al. (1996) and the ULP head model in Willinger and Baumgartner (2003).

The WSU brain injury model was also used to correlate brain Von Mises shearing stresses with angular head acceleration on the one hand and brain pressure with the head linear acceleration on the other hand. Correlation coefficients of 0.86 and 0.82, respectively, were found in the study by Yang and King (2003). In 2001, Bandak et al. (2001) presented a first version of a human head injury assessment tool based on a very simplified human head FEM called Simulated Injury Monitor (SIMON). In this approach, tolerance limits were established for subdural hematoma, diffuse axonal injuries, and brain contusions by scaling up animal test results from the literature. In other studies, SDH (Subdural hematoma), the parasagittal elongation of bridging veins, or their elongation rate, are computed with the FEM by Bandak et al. (2001). For contusion and diffuse injuries dilatation and brain strain are computed respectively.

Currently, real-world accident analysis is used in an attempt to correlate a known human head injury parameter with the AIS (Abbreviate Injury Scale) value sustained. An attempt by Chinn et al. (1999) to correlate initial human head impact velocity, maximum linear and rotational acceleration, HIC value and General Acceleration Model for Brain Injury Threshold (GAMBIT) value (which takes into account not only linear acceleration but also rotational acceleration of the human head) versus AIS gave correlation coefficients of 0.3 to 0.6, which is not satisfactory. The main reason for the poor correlation between a given parameter and AIS was that the same AIS levels can be reached from very different injury mechanisms. A much better approach is to take into account the likelihood of the human head injury mechanism.

When the type of lesion, rather than the AIS, is used for comparison, Willinger *et al.* (2003) showed by simulating sixty-six (n = 66) head trauma with the ULP-Strasbourg head model, that brain Von Mises stress is a good indicator for brain neurological lesions, whether they are moderate or severe. Moreover, this mechanical parameter allows distinguishing these lesions into two categories: moderate or severe. The tolerance limits for neurological moderate or severe injuries with a 50.0% risk are established for brain Von Mises stress of 18 kPa and 38 kPa, respectively. These values can be compared to previous reported data such as 11 kPa by Zhou *et al.* (1996), 15 kPa proposed by Kang *et al.* (1997), or 27 kPa suggested by Anderson (2000) on single cases. The reconstruction of this high number of head trauma with a ULP model also shows that global strain energy in the cerebro-spinal fluid (CSF) layer and in the skull structure is a reasonable indicator for subdural hematoma and skull fracture respectively. Brain pressure has been shown by Ward et al. (1980) to be correlated with brain hemorrhages resulting in brain contusions, edema and hematoma when reaching values above 200 kPa.

The global strain energy of the subarachnoid space has been shown to be correlated with hemorrhages resulting in subdural and subarachnoid hemorrhage when reaching values above 5.5 J with a 50% risk of occurrence. For skull fracture a 50% risk was established by a skull strain energy of 2.2 J. This later limit is well confirmed by tolerance limits for skull fracture reported from experimental data in terms of impact force (4 to 14 kN) by

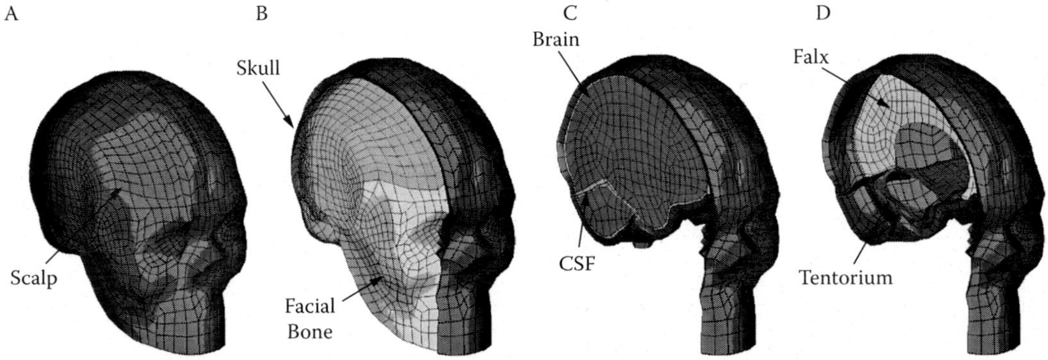

Figure 2.79 ULP-Strasbourg finite element model of the human head.

Yoganandan and Pintar (1994) as well as in terms of strain energy (around 2 J) by Gurdjian and Webster (1958). More recently, Marjoux et al. (2006) reconsidered the previous head trauma database and computed the injury prediction capability of HIC, SIMON, and ULP criteria and concluded that the ULP criteria are the most accurate, especially for moderate neurological injuries.

FEMs also give a good cinematic image of ballistic wound cases studied and can be a complementary tool when discussing the effect of ballistic impact wounds to the head (at the present time, the effect of penetrating gunshot wounds to the head by FEMs is still in a research stage). In the framework for the analysis of the rear effect of military helmets Deck et al. (2004) developed an improved version of the ULP model by considering the skull thickness variation and by integrating the reinforcement beams. It was possible then to reproduce not only linear fractures but also local depressive fractures of the skull. Using injury criteria calculated by simulation, some injuries sustained by the victim may be discussed—such as brain hemorrhage, subdural hematomas, or a loss of consciousness.

The human head FEMs presented in Figures 2.79–2.85 consider the head segment only without any boundary conditions at neck level. Therefore, impacts to the human head can be discussed with only minor uncertainty. The possible effects of impacts to the trunk or to the arms and legs preceding the impact to the human head can be taken

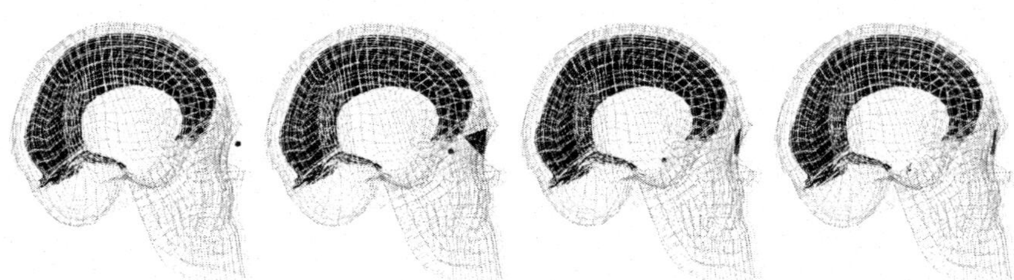

Figure 2.80 FEM cinematic illustration of a .22 caliber bullet shot between the eyes and ending its course in the dorsum sellae in a case of multiple gunshot to the head suicide.

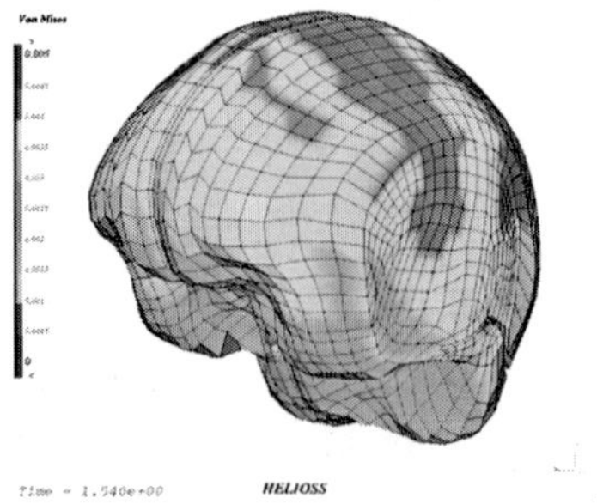

Figure 2.81 Von Mises Stress distribution after 1.5 4ms (same case as Figure 2.81).

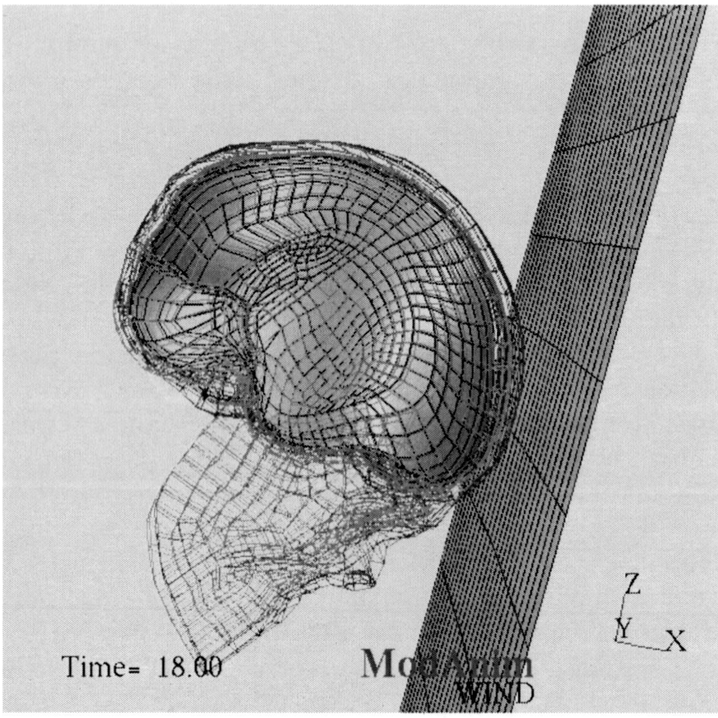

Figure 2.82 Blunt force trauma: impact simulation configuration: frontal impact.

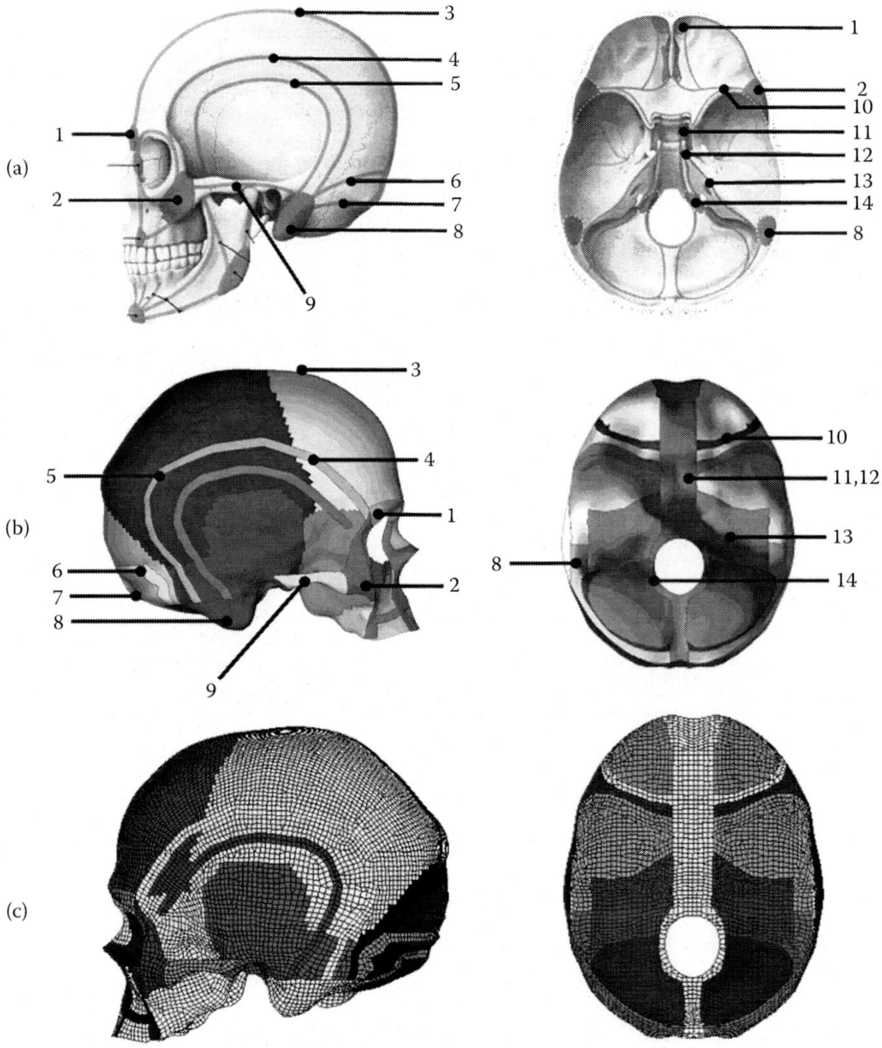

Figure 2.83 Location of the reinforced beams (a), outer and inner surfaces (b), the meshing (c). 1. Frontal beam, 2. Zigomatic arch, 3. Spheno-frontal beam, 4.5. Lateral superior and inferior arches, 6.7. Semi-circular occipital arch, 8. Mastoïdian pilar, 9. Zigomatic arch, 10. Spheno-frontal beam, 11. Sphenoïdal arch, 12. Occipital beam, 13. Petrouse beam, 14. Occipital beam.

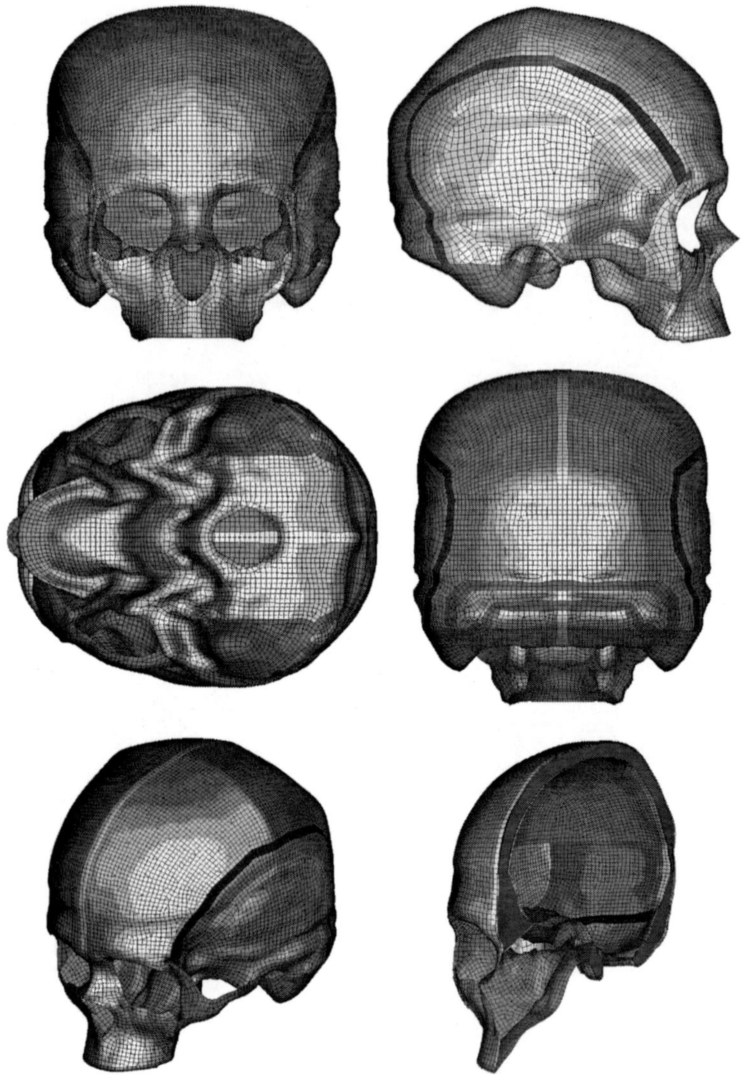

Figure 2.84(a–f) Reinforcement beams on the new ULP head model.

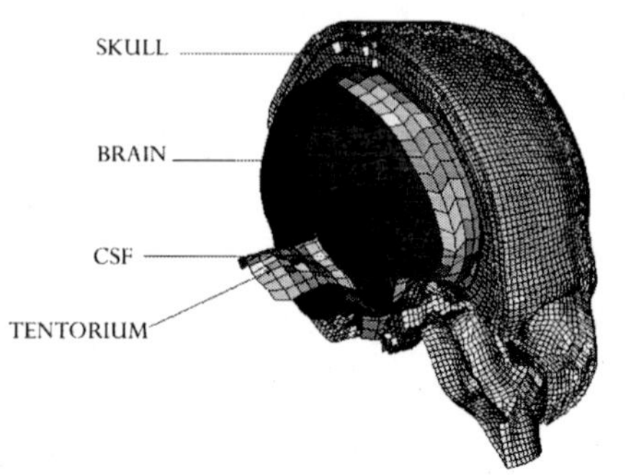

Figure 2.85 New ULP Head model: global view.

into account but may raise many questions concerning the energy of the impact to the human head. Therefore, the biomechanical study can be completed by the use of multibody dynamics.

A biomechanical approach can be very helpful to investigate forensic cases, and there is a need for collaboration between forensic sciences and biomechanics to objectively and scientifically evaluate adult and infant head injuries using well-documented cases.

Blast Injuries

3

> The explosions were terrible. One followed another. The buildings were shaking as if there was an earthquake going on. There was smoke everywhere. There was dust everywhere. There were these blazing lights coming in through the window. To put it quite simply, it was hell.
>
> **Witness A***

Contents

Explosive Ordnance Devices 97
Pathophysiology of Blast Injuries 100
The Context: Fatal Environment and Intent 102
Differential Diagnosis of Fragmented Blast from Gunfire Injuries 107
Summary Guidelines for Best Practice 116
Case Study 3.1: Skeletal and Soft Tissue Injuries Resulting from A Grenade *By A.B. Seneviratne* 117
Case Study 3.2: A Case of Blast Injury from Colombia *By J.M. Pachón* 124
Case Study 3.3: "Human Bomb" and Body Trauma *By A. Samarasekera* 128

Explosive ordnance devices (EOD) are used to destroy civilian populations, cities, homes, or farmland, invoke fear and terror into a community, and to control the movement of populations, for example, deter refugees from returning to an area or crossing borders. The use of EODs is so prevalent in armed conflicts and war crimes that they are a crucial aspect of any discussion of injuries or medicolegal death investigations. In fact, the indiscriminate bombing and shelling resulting in death and maltreatment of civilian populations has been successfully prosecuted by the International Criminal Tribunal for the former Yugoslavia (ICTY) for violation of International Humanitarian Law (IHL) (*The Prosecutor v. Stanislv Galič*, IT-98-29-T; *The Prosecutor v. Pavle Strugar*, IT-01-42-T). Kluger (2003, 235) wrote: "Bombing and explosions directed against innocent civilians have become the primary instrument of global terror and induce death, injury, fear, and chaos." These incidents often result in a high number of fatalities, a higher number of wounded victims, and, depending on the context and type of explosive ordnance, may lead to significant tissue damage and commingling of remains.

Explosive ordnances are highly variable, serving different functions depending on how they were manufactured and their intended purpose (Hayda et al. 2004). It has been reported that blast injuries are more common in war, human rights (HHRR) abuse, and terrorism than gunfire injuries (Aboutanos and Baker 1997; Coupland and Meddings 1999;

* Witness A, T 3627, *Prosecutor v. Pavle Strugar*, Case No. IT-01-42-T, Judgment, para. 1 http://www.un.org/icty/strugar/trialc1/judgment/index2.htm.

Covey 2002; Kluger 2003; Hadden et al. 1978). Covey (2002) reports that blast injuries are the most prevalent wounds in modern warfare and that secondary blast injuries resulting from shrapnel comprise the majority of these cases. According to Covey (2002, 1222), "Injuries of the musculoskeletal system are the most common type of wounds seen in modern warfare, accounting for 60 to 70% of all wounds. In recent wars, most penetrating musculoskeletal injuries were not caused by bullets but by exploding ordnance such as bombs, artillery shells, mortar rounds, grenades, or land mines." The high number of civilian deaths is the result of civilians being directly targeted, particularly in populated areas, such as hospitals or hotels, and the high lethality of EOD (Aboutanos and Baker 1997).

Unlike gunfire that ends when the violence ends, EODs may be present and lethal in communities years after a conflict in the form of landmines or unexploded ordnances (Coupland and Korver 1991). In 2000, following the NATO airstrike in Kosovo, demining the region involved clearing more than 8 million square meters of mines and collecting over 8000 antipersonnel and antitank mines, 4591 cluster bomblets, and 9412 other unexploded ordnances (Landmine Monitor Report 2000). At that same time, there were 492 documented victims of mines or unexploded ordnances in Kosovo (Landmine Monitor Report 2000).

The presence of EOD and landmines as a continued threat of injury and death is not limited to recent conflicts. Bun Heng and Key (1995, 435) report, "The history of violence has left a legacy unique to Cambodia: large numbers of disabled people and about 13 million landmines in a land of 9 million people. There are about 20,000 people with amputations in the country; each month between 100 and 200 people have a limb amputated and a further 200 or so die of injuries caused by landmines." Therefore, it is important to understand the mechanisms of blast injuries, when and how they are likely to occur, and how the skeletal evidence of blast injuries may have judicial significance.

Forensic anthropologists involved in EOD cases have traditionally been called into investigations of large-scale, high-order explosions. In these incidents, there was massive destruction, resulting in large numbers of casualties, with limited body recovery. Forensic investigations immediately following the incidents have led to successful convictions of those responsible for such attacks and served families and survivors through victim identification. Here are a few examples:

- A car bomb explosion in the Murrah Federal Building in Oklahoma City, OK (April 19, 1995) resulted in more than 500 injured and 168 fatalities. Timothy McVeigh and Terry Nichols, sympathizers of an antigovernment militia, were convicted of conspiracy and murder (*United States v. Timothy James McVeigh* [D.C. No. 96-CR-89-M]. United States Court of Appeals Tenth Circuit, Case No. 01-1273, June 7, 2001. http://fl1.findlaw.com/news.findlaw.com/cnn/docs/mcveigh/10thorderjud60701.pdf; *United States v. Terry Lynn Nichols* [D.C. No. 96-CR-89-M]. United States Court of Appeals Tenth Circuit, Case No. 98-1231, Feb. 26, 1999. http://www.kscourts.org/ca10/cases/1999/02/98-1231.htm). Michael Fortier testified for the prosecution and was convicted on lesser charges for failing to inform authorities (*United States v. Michael J. Fortier* [D.C. No. 95-CR-111-VB]. United States Court of Appeals Tenth Circuit, Case No. 99-6381, March 16, 2001. http://www.kscourts.org/ca10/cases/2001/03/99-6381.htm). The bomb used contained 5000 lb (2300 kg) of mixed fertilizer and fuel oil (Giordano 2003).
- In the World Trade Center bombing on February 23, 1993 more than 1000 people were injured and 6 were killed. The bomb was an improvised explosive device (IED), consisting of approximately 1500 lb (544–680 kg) of urea nitrate, a homemade

fertilizer-based explosive, placed in a Ryder rental van in the parking garage below the building. Hundreds of investigators sorted through more than seven tons of debris for victims and forensic evidence, which resulted in the convictions of ten conspirators (Gillespie 1999).

- On September 11, 2001, four hijacked airplanes were turned into weapons by crashing into various targets (2,974 fatalities): (a) American Airlines flights 11 and 175 were hijacked and flown into the World Trade Center, (b) United Airlines flight 93 crashed in a field in Pennsylvania, and (c) American Airlines flight 77 crashed into the Pentagon (Smith 2002). These incidents have resulted in massive forensic investigations, ongoing judicial action, and foreign military action by U.S. Armed Forces in Afghanistan, since 2001, and in Iraq, since 2003 (Smith 2002).

In these and similar examples, anthropologists have been involved in medicolegal death and forensic investigations. The human remains recovered in cases such as these consist of fragmented body parts rather than complete bodies and a high degree of commingling of the remains. Anthropological expertise in these situations is often directed toward recovery and identification, rather than cause of death or trauma analysis. In the literature, such investigations typically fall under the heading *mass disasters*; or acts of terrorism. Recent scientific research has been directed toward improving mass disaster response protocols, recovery techniques, explosive identification, advances in human identification methods, and innovative radiological methods for victim identification (Nye 1996; Kahana et al. 1997; Glass 1998; Jordan 1999; Fixott et al. 2001; Glass 2001; Budimlija et al. 2003; Campobasso et al. 2003; Pryor 2003, Kapur et al. 2005; Koppl 2005).

In HHRR investigations, injuries from EOD may be highly prevalent in the form of military shelling into civilian populations or smaller-scale explosions such as grenades or bombs used against civilian targets. Therefore, unlike incidents of major terrorist bombings, these cases tend to be investigated years later. EODs are designed to cause injury from the blast and from fragmenting shrapnel. Shrapnel injuries may be similar in appearance to gunshot wounds, particularly in cases of shotguns or fragmenting bullets, but as the following discussion demonstrates, these mechanisms of injury can be differentiated from skeletal wounds.

The purpose of this chapter is to review cases of blast injuries among civilian targets that resulted during armed conflicts investigated by the United Nations, ICTY, in Kosovo (1998) and Bosnia-Herzegovina (1991–1995). A brief overview of EOD weaponry and the pathophysiology of blast wounds are presented. Documented cases of grenades and mortar injuries are discussed. The methodology for differential diagnosis of penetrating wounds resulting from shrapnel injuries caused by grenades and mortars from gunfire projectile wounds is outlined. Further, specific case studies involving grenades and improvised explosives used by "human" bombers are presented from Kosovo, Colombia, and Sri Lanka at the end of the chapter (refer to Case Studies 3.1 by A. Senevirante, 3.2 by J. Pachón, and 3.3 by A. Samarasekera).

Explosive Ordnance Devices

Accurately identifying skeletal trauma that results from blast injuries requires a basic understanding of explosive weapons and possible injury patterns that may occur, based on wound ballistics (Kluger 2003; Cernak et al. 1999). Explosive weapons are designed to be destructive either through the sudden pressure changes of the blast or by spreading shrapnel, which act as small projectiles and cause deeply penetrating high-energy wounds. Shrapnel includes

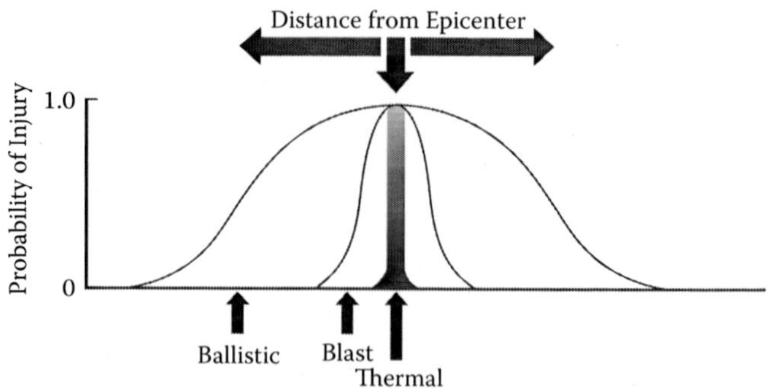

Figure 3.1 Diagram of probable injury based on distance from blast. (Reprinted from *Emergency War Surgery,* 2nd United States revision, NATO Handbook. U.S. Government Printing Office, Washington, D.C., 1988.)

metal objects that are expelled through the explosion and may consist of the container used to hold the explosive materials (i.e., the outer shell of a grenade), metal fragments placed within the bomb or grenade (i.e., nails), and metal objects in the vicinity of the blast that are expelled at the time of the explosion, further contributing to crushing injuries.

Explosive weapons are characterized as high-order explosives or low-order explosives (refer to the CDC Primer 2003). High-order explosives (HEs) tend to be military-issued or "manufactured" and are characterized by a rapid detonation resulting in injuries from the overpressurization *blast wave* force (CDC Primer for Clinicians). As the explosive material is converted to a gas, the sudden pressure change results in a blast wave that radiates from the point of origin (Kluger 2003). HEs produce a significant amount of energy producing a blast front that radiates from the point of the explosion in the form of a supersonic heat wave (Figure 3.1). Kluger (2003, 237) states:

> A charge of 25 kg TNT will induce a 150 psi peak overpressure for 2 ms that transverses at 3000–8000 m/s, and more explosive will prolong the duration of the blast front, adding to the wounding potential. The blast wind movement induced by the explosion depends on the air density and the blast wind velocity: the higher the velocity, the greater the generation of casualties.

Weapons that fall into the HE category are classified as primary, secondary, tertiary, and quaternary explosives based on their sensitivity to shock, friction, and heat. In contrast, Low-order explosives (LEs) are rapidly burning mixtures of propellants such as gun powder, which creates a subsonic wave, or "blast wind." They differ from HEs in that they do not produce a supersonic blast wave.

Conventional bombs release energy through a shock wave and are fueled by chemical explosives. The term *bomb* generally refers to military-issued weapons but may also refer to IEDs (improvised explosive ordinance) which are modified military EODs, or "homemade" bombs, such as pipe or car bombs. It has been pointed out that disabled explosive ordnances are more easily obtained than activated military ammunition (Chowdhury and Mohan 2004; Shah 2006). Such weapons can not only be reactivated but also further modified to increase its wounding power through added explosive material or shrapnel. Shah (2006, 5) reports on the transfer and reactivation of EOD for use in armed conflicts, "Thus arms transfers involve all countries, whether they suffer the effects of arms or transfer of weapons—not only newly manufactured arms, but reexported, secondhand, surplus, or collected weapons, and weapons in transit." Injuries (61%) occur more often from improvised weapons, such as modified grenades, and artillery shelling, as reported by Chowdhury and Mohan (2004). Some common examples of IEDs include pipe or car bombs, TNT nail bombs, and shrapnel added to military-issued EODs. The type of shrapnel added to manufactured EODs has included essentially any available metal cut down to size, such as household utensils or utilitarian metalware such as street signs.

Generally, bombs create a significant amount of damage and have a high number of victims, including people both injured and killed. Hiss and Kahana (2000, 94) wrote, "The objective of the bomb defines its design. Bombs that are used primarily against personnel have warheads designed to injure by fragmentation; antimaterial bombs have most of the weight devoted to the explosive and most of the damage done is due to the blast produced." Consequently, there may also be significant body mutilation, poor recovery of victims, and commingling of body parts (refer also to Cooper et al. [1983], Coupland [1993], Cukier and Chapdelaine [2002], and De Palma et al. [2005]).

An epidemiological approach to interpreting skeletal injuries is particularly useful for blast and shrapnel mechanisms because the fatal environment is a critical part of the lethality and pattern of injury, thereby affecting interpretation of the mechanism of injury. The number of fatalities will depend on the amount and type of explosive materials used as well as the context and location of the blast. For example, as reported by Scott et al. (1986), the terrorist bombing of the U.S. marine barracks in Beirut in 1983 consisted of more than 12 tons of TNT, resulting in 234 immediate deaths and 122 injured victims. Bombs also create a large amount of damage to property and buildings in the vicinity of the blast. The building materials and objects within the enclosed structure (i.e., a home, a bus, or a tractor factory) are the objects that cause injuries to victims from crushing, blunt force, or shrapnel.

The types of investigations covered in this chapter differ from those relating to large-scale terrorist or manufactured HE bombs in that they occur on a much smaller scale and are investigated years after the incident. The following discussion includes examples of commonly encountered weapons (i.e., grenades and mortars) in investigations of civilian targets (Figure 3.2), although there are many more conventional EODs and IEDs than

Figure 3.2 Examples of EODs commonly found in the Balkan conflict: mortars, artillery, landmines, and grenades. (Printed with permission from International Criminal Tribunal for the former Yugoslavia [ICTY].)

Table 3.1 Variables Affecting Wounding Potential and Morphology in Blast Injuries

- The type of explosive used
- The type and amount of materials used to construct the weapon and amount of shrapnel
- The location of the explosion—within or outside a structure
- The composition of the structure
- The location of the victim relative to the blast
- The presence of an intermediate target between the victim and the blast
- The age, health, and weight of the victim

described here (refer to Aboutanos and Baker 1997; Covey 2002; Taipale et al. 2002; CDC Primer 2003; Kluger 2003).

Pathophysiology of Blast Injuries

Explosive ordnances are widespread and highly variable; consequently, there is a wide range of variation observed among blast wounds. The range of factors that affect the pathophysiology and morphology of blast wounds are presented in Table 3.1 (adapted from Frykberg 2002). Patterns of variation in wound morphology are evident between manufactured and improvised explosive devices, particularly due to the specific materials present or amount of explosive used. Likewise, shrapnel from military EOD is distinguishable from gunfire projectiles and is typically recovered, enabling further ballistics analyses.

The mechanisms of HE injuries affecting the skeletal system, following the weaponry classification, are categorized as primary, secondary, tertiary, or quaternary injuries (Table 3.2). Covey (2002, 1224) writes, "The sudden pressure change caused by the blast wave can damage living tissue by four putative mechanisms: spalling, implosion, acceleration–deceleration, and pressure differentials." The blast wave, shrapnel, and debris may result in

Table 3.2 Classification of Injury Mechanisms in Explosion

Explosive and Injury Mechanisms	Injury Patterns	Skeletal Wound Characteristics
Primary	Skeletal fractures from supersonic blast wave	• Traumatic amputation, decapitation, skeletal fractures
Secondary	Shrapnel or container fragmentation, projectile trauma	• Projectile defects, radiating, concentric, or comminuted fractures • Distribution of injuries has a narrow or wide focus depending on location of victim to the blast
Tertiary	Blunt force trauma, acceleration/deceleration injury, crushing injury	• Depressed or linear fractures, contracoup skull fractures
Quaternary	Flash burns	• Skeletal burn marks such as discoloration and cracks or fractures

Note: Injury mechanisms and wound attributes adopted and modified from the *CDC Primer* for blast injuries.

a number of skeletal responses such as fractures, blunt force trauma, and deeply penetrating sharp or projectile trauma. Primary wounds are caused by the blast; spalling or implosion may cause skeletal fractures (Covey 2002, 1224). The sudden pressure change results in significant tissue damage and skeletal fracturing. Kluger (2003, 237) states:

> Spalling, implosion, inertia and, pressure differences are the putative mechanisms by which blasts induce damage in the tissue. Overpressure of 1.8 psi generates glass shards capable of penetrating the abdominal wall, and 3 psi overpressure can throw the human body, causing 1% fatality. Lung injury with 1% fatality is observed at 35 psi overpressure, but at 65 psi it results in 99% fatality.

Primary injuries also include disruption to body tissues, decapitation, or traumatic amputations (Tsokos et al. 2003). According to Covey (2002), stepping on a landmine results in the "traumatic amputation of the foot or leg." By stepping on the mine, the victim is at the epicenter of the blast.

LE ordnances do not produce primary wounds. Rather, LE explosions produce a blast wind, which results in injuries that are consistent with projectile, deeply penetrating, and blunt force trauma and burns (the secondary to quaternary mechanisms of explosion injuries). Secondary wounds result from penetrating shrapnel or fragmented bomb components. Projectiles consist of a variety of materials that tend to vary in size and are often irregularly shaped. As a result, these wounds tend to vary in size, be irregular in shape, and create a great amount of tissue damage, particularly at lower velocities. The internal damage will often be quite extensive and widespread through various systems or regions of the body. Covey (2002) points out that slow projectiles cause significant tissue damage that may exceed low-velocity bullet wounds.

Shrapnel ballistics are similar to low-velocity gunfire projectiles, but because they are not expelled from a rifled barrel they lack *streamlining* (Covey 2002, 1225). In other words, projectiles tend to tumble through flight or upon penetration into body tissues and do not have a straight flight trajectory. Therefore, the location of the blast relative to the victim is determined through the distribution of wounds in the skeleton (Hiss and Kahana 2000). The distance or radius of projectile fragments, wound morphology, and the pattern of wounds throughout the skeleton indicate the general direction and distance of the blast. Unlike bullets fired, shrapnel tend to perforate the body only in particular circumstances and more often become embedded in skeletal tissue.

Tertiary wounds consist of acceleration–deceleration injuries, blunt force compression, blunt–sharp penetrating wounds, or crushing injuries from flying debris (Covey 2002), including bone fractures throughout the skeleton, blunt force trauma to the head, and traumatic amputation of the limbs (Hull et al. 1994; Hiss and Kahana 2000). Both HE and LE mechanisms may create tertiary wounds. Blunt force trauma may also be associated with penetrating injuries from sharp objects (Tsokos et al. 2003). Most commonly, individuals are thrown through the air by the blast wave (rapid acceleration) and then hit a hard surface such as a wall or the floor (rapid deceleration). Hall et al. (2006, 1070) wrote, "Tertiary blast injuries are caused when victims are forced into stationary objects by the explosion."

Quaternary wounds affecting bone consists of burning and may result from either HE or LE devices. Flames are produced by materials ignited by the blast wind (Hiss and Kahana 2000). Generally, burn injuries, called *flash burns*, are superficial and affect those areas of skin that are not protected by clothing (Rajs et al. 1987; Tsokos et al. 2003). However, depending on the type and location of the blast, more significant burns may be evident.

The Context: Fatal Environment and Intent

The intention of the persons initiating an attack is inextricably linked to the fatal environment. Likewise, demographic factors may also be important for determining the lethality of the EOD and show a directional trend depending on the specific target, such as a hospital or bus. Kluger and coworkers (2006) report the Netanyas Park Hotel Bombing had a 22% mortality rate, with the mean age of victims killed being 82.0 ± 16.8 years. Interestingly, head injuries were the most common among fatal cases. Hall and coworkers report (2006, 1070), "The elderly are at greater risk for secondary complications from head trauma due to cortical atrophy and shearing of the bridging veins." Overall, mortality rates in enclosed spaces are reportedly higher than that in open areas (Hill 1979; Born 2005). Kluger (2003) reports a 29% fatality rate in enclosed spaces, as reported by the Israel Center for Disease Control. Differences in fatality rates based on the location of the explosion are more significant for blast or primary wounds than other mechanisms of injury associated with the explosion. The smaller the space, the less the distance for the blast wave to travel before victims are struck and the energy dissipates. Katz and coworkers (1989) also point out that explosions within closed structures result in crushing injuries from falling building materials. This also depends on the context of violence, the intention of those perpetrating the attack, and its duration.

A promising method investigates the distribution of injuries between combat and noncombat contexts for demonstrating war crimes. Many authors have reported that shrapnel and fragmenting ammunition wounds account for most of the casualties in combat situations, whereas gunfire injuries are the second most frequent type of injury (Rautio and Paavolainen 1988; Biocina et al. 1997; Hinsley et al. 2005; Korzinek 1993; Situm et al. 2004; Ropac and Milas 1999; Soldo and Puntavic 1998; Rukavina 1998; Petricevic et al. 1998; Hodalic et al. 1999). In contrast, the reverse pattern is observed in noncombat situations when civilians are the direct target of violence (Michael et al. 1999). In addition to the frequency, the distribution of wounds is reported different, based on the context. Most shrapnel injuries in combat contexts tend to affect the extremities (Rukavina 1998 and Hodalic et al. 1999), whereas the location of injuries by firearms (a weapon of volition) tends to vary according to the situation in which they are used. In combat situations, injuries tend be located primarily in unprotected areas where there is no body armor whereas in noncombat situations, the injuries are primarily located in the head and chest (Baraybar and Gasior 2006; Baraybar 2006). Using frequency and distribution data of shrapnel versus gunfire injuries in noncombat situations may be an important tool in demonstrating the occurrence of HHRR violations.

For example, in the Srebreniča massacre in BiH in 1995, more than 7500 men, including children and the elderly, were killed over several days (*The Prosecutor v. Krstić*, IT-98-33). In the village of Protocari, men and women were separated, women were bused away, luggage was burned, and thousands of men were killed. The Kraviča warehouse was one location where several hundred unarmed civilian men were detained and intentionally killed. Soldiers from the Bosnian Serb army stood in the doorways to the building and fired into the crowd. Additionally, mortars were fired into the building at the men, and grenades were thrown through the windows. Only two men were able to survive the attack by hiding under the bodies of the deceased and later escaping into the nearby woods. The bodies of the men were dumped with bulldozers into large mass graves nearby, created by backhoes. It had become known that U.S. planes had photographed the events (men detained in fields, buses taking women from the area, and the creation of mass graves). So, several weeks later many of the graves were opened and moved to secondary locations to

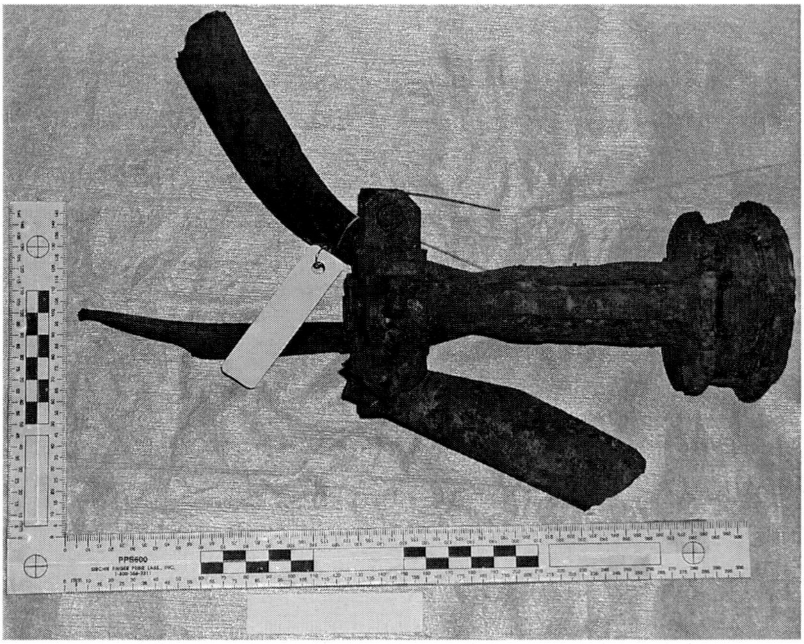

Figure 3.3 Fin-stabilizer from the tail of a mortar recovered from a mass grave. (Printed with permission from International Criminal Tribunal for the former Yugoslavia [ICTY].)

hide the evidence and conceal their locations. Many of the mass graves have been opened by the ICTY in association with the Srebreniča massacre, and the physical evidence collected has been used in war crimes trials (*The Prosecutor v. Krstić,* IT-98-33).

The skeletal remains of victims associated with Srebrenica and other regions in BiH, showed evidence of extensive wounds and fractures from gunfire, shrapnel, and blasting injuries (Figures 3.3 and 3.4). Examples of some of the larger pieces of shrapnel recovered

Figure 3.4 Fin-stabilizer from the tail of mortars recovered from a mass grave after being washed. (Printed with permission from International Criminal Tribunal for the former Yugoslavia [ICTY].)

Figure 3.5 Shrapnel from an M26 fragmentation grenade in the body tissues of a victim recovered from a mass grave. These consist of irregular metal fragments from the outer shell of the grenade case, round ball bearings, and oval-shaped shrapnel. (Printed with permission from International Criminal Tribunal for the former Yugoslavia [ICTY].)

from body tissues are illustrated in the radiographic images in Figures 3.5–3.10. Note the variation of size and shape of the metal fragments. Figure 3.11 depicts the ectocranial view of the superior aspect of an adult cranium; the arrows point to irregular defects caused by shrapnel from a grenade. Note the radiating fractures from each point of impact. Due to the multiple points of impact and numerous radiating fractures that resulted, the cranium fragmented and had to be reconstructed. The large defect on the right frontal bone is circular along the lateral margin and square along the medial edge, reflecting the shape of the

Figure 3.6 Close-up view of shrapnel fragments of the outer shell of a grenade recovered from body tissues. (Printed with permission from International Criminal Tribunal for the former Yugoslavia [ICTY].)

Figure 3.7 Close-up view of oval-shaped shrapnel recovered with grenade. (Printed with permission from International Criminal Tribunal for the former Yugoslavia [ICTY].)

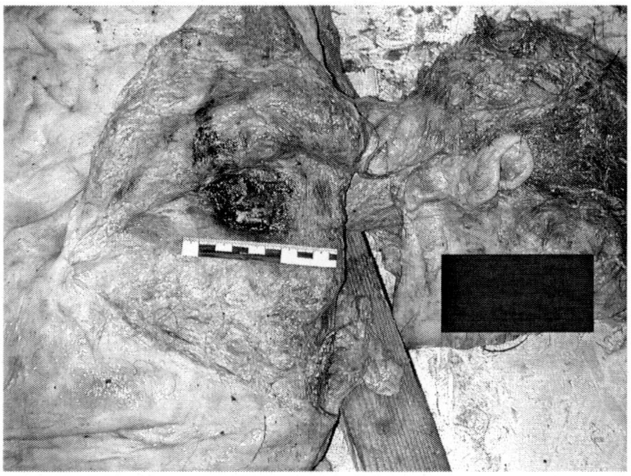

Figure 3.8 Posterior view of the upper back region of an adult male, depicting embedded shrapnel in vertebral column. The shrapnel came from front to back and consisted of a piece of metal from a tractor that exploded from the blast. (Printed with permission from International Criminal Tribunal for the former Yugoslavia [ICTY].)

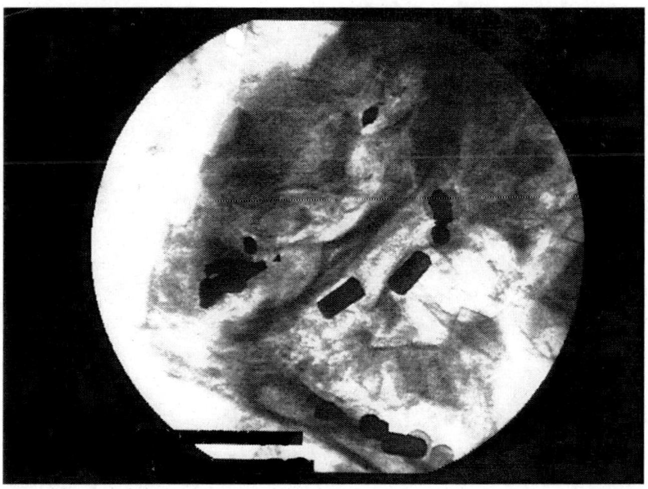

Figure 3.9 Large pieces of shrapnel as viewed in a fluoroscope image of decomposing tissues. Note the number and variation of size and shape of metal fragments. (Printed with permission from International Criminal Tribunal for the former Yugoslavia [ICTY].)

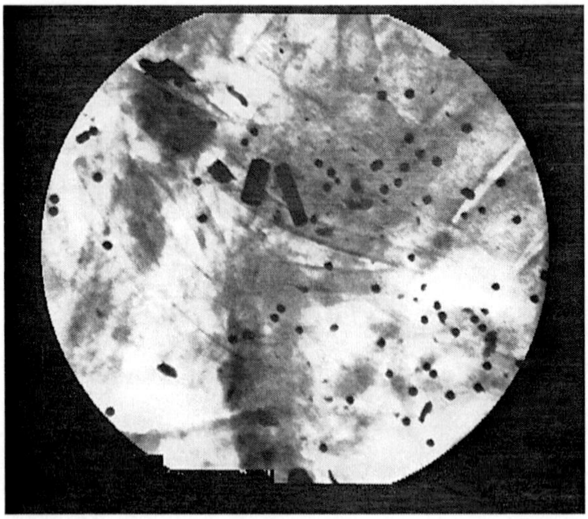

Figure 3.10 Shrapnel of various sizes, including round ball bearings and irregularly shaped shrapnel fragments embedded in the thorax of victim. (Printed with permission from International Criminal Tribunal for the former Yugoslavia [ICTY].)

shrapnel and angle of impact (the same types of metal objects are visible in Figures 3.12–3.17). The patterned defect is indicative of shrapnel other than the fragmented grenade casing itself—probably metal objects that were in the vicinity at the time of the explosion. Endocranially, the defects exhibit "internal beveling" around the margins (Figure 3.18).

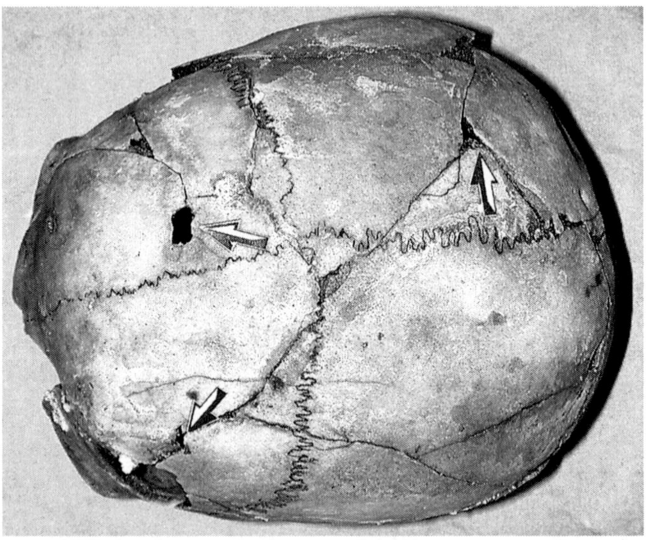

Figure 3.11a (See color insert following page 38) Ectocranial view of superior aspect of adult cranium that retained metopic suture in the frontal bone. Arrows point to irregular defects caused by shrapnel. Note the radiating fractures from each point of impact. Due to the multiple points of impact and numerous radiating fractures that resulted, the cranium completely fragmented and had to be reconstructed. The large defect on the right frontal bone is circular along the lateral margin and square along the medial edge, reflecting the shape of the projectile and angle of impact. (Printed with permission from International Criminal Tribunal for the former Yugoslavia [ICTY].)

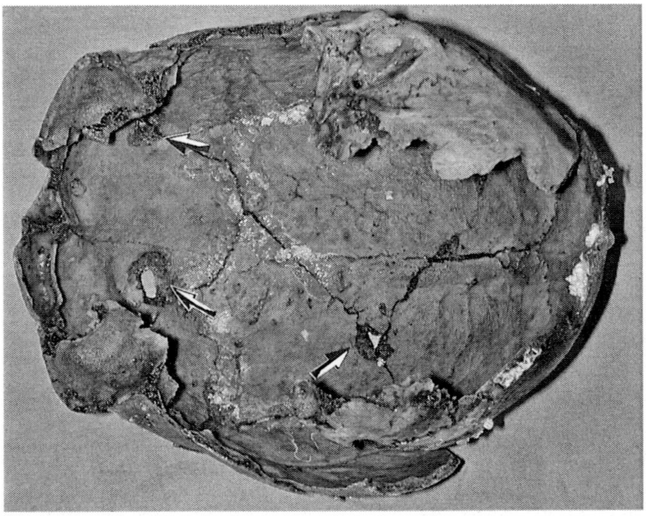

Figure 3.11b Endocranial view of calvarium (Figure 3.11a). Arrows point to irregular-shaped defects. Note the internal beveling around penetrating shrapnel defects. (Printed with permission from International Criminal Tribunal for the former Yugoslavia [ICTY].)

Penetrating shrapnel such as this typically penetrates the body but rarely perforates or exits the head or body. Table 3.3 outlines general patterns of injuries from grenades (Protocol modified from Covey 2002).

Differential Diagnosis of Fragmented Blast from Gunfire Injuries

The advantage of skeletal analysis over fresh cases is that the entire skeleton can be thoroughly examined for injury. Wounds present externally on soft tissues may be small but the internal damage is often more significant than what the external examination would indicate. Moreover, direct inspection of skeletal tissue is preferable to radiographic images of bone. When the skeletal remains are viewed directly, the actual extent of damage is not

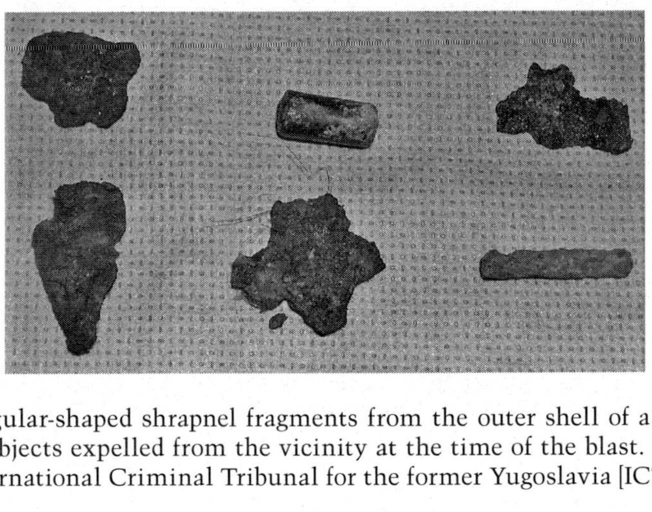

Figure 3.12 Irregular-shaped shrapnel fragments from the outer shell of a grenade case and patterned metal objects expelled from the vicinity at the time of the blast. (Printed with permission from International Criminal Tribunal for the former Yugoslavia [ICTY].)

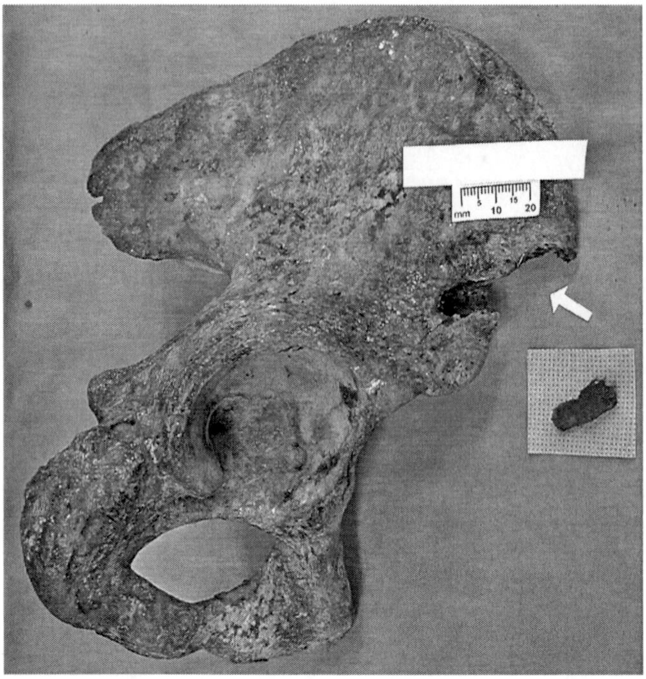

Figure 3.13 (See color insert following page 38) Large defect in the posterior right ilium from oval-shaped metal shrapnel that had been embedded in bone. Note that the shape of the wound generally reflects the shape and size of the projectile. The shrapnel was embedded in the bone. There is only one small radiating fracture, extending anteriorly from the defect. (Printed with permission from International Criminal Tribunal for the former Yugoslavia [ICTY].)

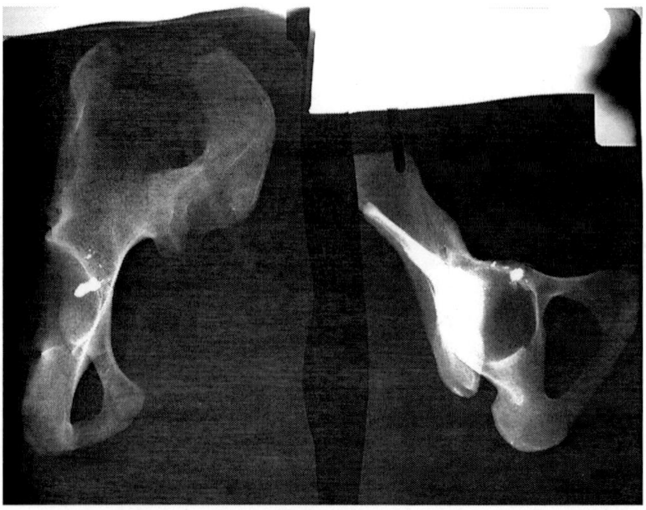

Figure 3.14 Fluoroscope image of the right innominate illustrates embedded shrapnel in bone. Note the variation in size and shape of fragments in close proximity to one another. (Printed with permission from International Criminal Tribunal for the former Yugoslavia [ICTY].)

Figure 3.15 Embedded shrapnel fragment in posterior aspect of proximal tibia of juvenile. The proximal epiphysis is not yet fused due to age. Also, note there are no radiating fractures. (Printed with permission from International Criminal Tribunal for the former Yugoslavia [ICTY].)

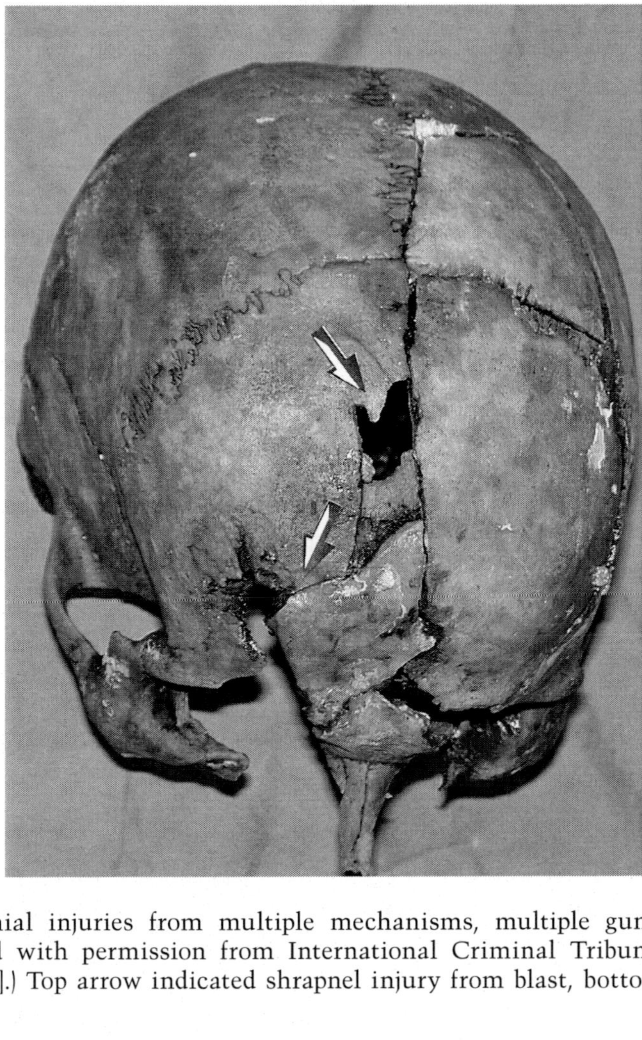

Figure 3.16 Cranial injuries from multiple mechanisms, multiple gunfire wounds, and shrapnel. (Printed with permission from International Criminal Tribunal for the former Yugoslavia [ICTY].) Top arrow indicated shrapnel injury from blast, bottom arrow points to gunshot wound.

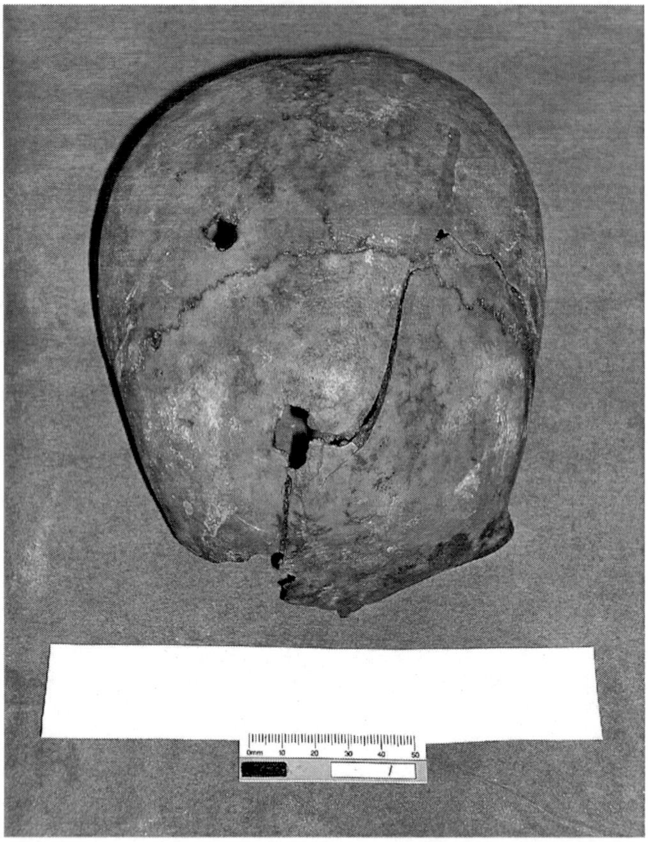

Figure 3.17 Two defects present on the frontal and right parietal bones. Large radiating fractures extend from the defect on the frontal bone and across the coronal suture onto the left parietal bone. Note the irregular shape of the defects caused by penetrating shrapnel. (Printed with permission from International Criminal Tribunal for the former Yugoslavia [ICTY].)

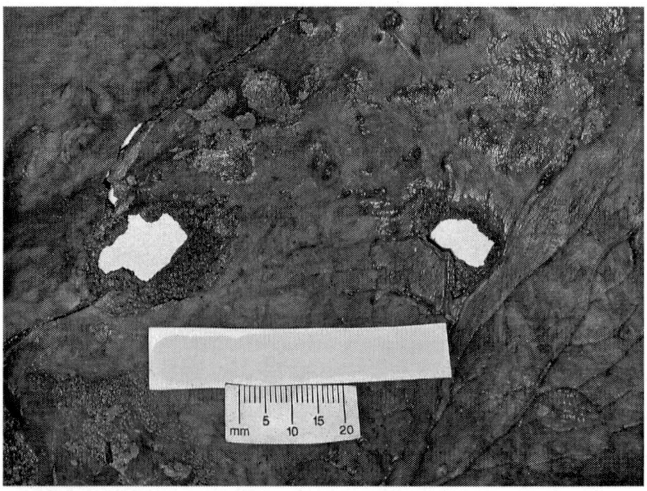

Figure 3.18 Endocranial view of irregular penetrating wounds from shrapnel. Note beveling around the defects, along the inner table. (Printed with permission from International Criminal Tribunal for the former Yugoslavia [ICTY].)

Table 3.3 Description of Explosive Injuries Related to Grenades*

Injury Pattern	Location of Explosive Relevant to Victim	Skeletal Wounds Characteristics
Pattern 1	Grenade explodes within close range of victim	• Random pattern of wounds, concentration greatest in an area near the blast • Deeply penetrating projectile trauma, comminuted skeletal fractures, projectiles embedded in tissue or bone • Skeletal fractures resulting from the shock wave, in an anatomical region near the epicenter of the blast
Pattern 2	Grenade explodes within an intermediate to distant range of victim	• Random pattern of deeply penetrating shrapnel injuries, distribution of wounds varied but generally greater with increased distance from the blast
Pattern 3	Victim holding exploding grenade	• Patterned wounds to hands and face, including deeply penetrating shrapnel and projectile injuries, and traumatic amputation

*Modified from Covey 2002.

masked by soft or decomposing tissues. The mechanisms of injury from EOD as observed skeletally can be very similar to other mechanisms of trauma, i.e., gunfire projectiles or blunt force trauma (e.g., Haung et al. 1996). Therefore, differential diagnosis of blast injuries in skeletal remains requires close inspection of each wound, careful interpretation of the distribution of wounds or injury patterns throughout the entire skeleton, examination of evidence of weaponry (i.e., shrapnel fragments), shrapnel ballistic evidence, and investigative evidence pertaining to the circumstances of the incident.

Differentiating projectile wounds from blast or gunfire injuries is based on the tendency of projectiles to become embedded in bone and the differences in the size, shape, number, association, and distribution of wounds. Shrapnel wounds are highly variable and have a tendency to be irregular or asymmetrical in shape (Figures 3.19). The large defect in the posterior right ilium from oval-shaped metal shrapnel is a common finding. The shrapnel was embedded in bone. The wound reflects the shape and size of the projectiles/shrapnel. Figure 3.20 shows an adult humeral head and a fluoroscope image of the bone fragment with an embedded shrapnel fragment. The fluoroscope image in Figure 3.21 illustrates a small circular pellet embedded in the bone, not to be confused with a shotgun pellet. Also, note the extensive fractured areas of the sacrum, which had to be reconstructed during the postmortem examination and is being held together with glue in the photograph.

Shrapnel enter into the body or cranial vault and exit only in particular circumstances. As a result, there tends to be a large number of shrapnel fragments that are recovered and a significant number of wounds per individual. Overall, blast injuries have high wounding power, due to the amount of shrapnel fragmenting as projectiles, but generally low impact force, except for those situations in which HE materials are used or the victims were close to the epicenter of the blast, as with a landmine or in a confined space. In addition to shrapnel wounds, explosive injuries also have a combination of different injury mechanisms, such as blunt force fractures and traumatic amputations. Therefore, it can be challenging to track the path of shrapnel projectiles through the body based on skeletal wounds alone.

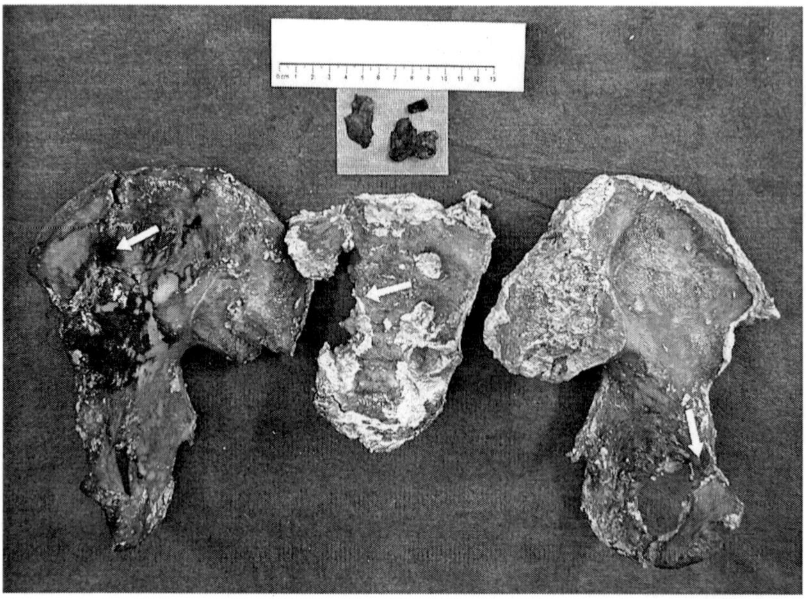

Figure 3.19 Shrapnel wounds. The arrows point to large defects and radiating fractures in the right ilium, right sacrum, and left iliopubic area. Irregular and oval-shaped shrapnel were recovered from decomposing soft tissue and bone. The irregular fragments are from the outer shell of a grenade. The oval objects come from metal in the area expelled at the time of the blast. (Printed with permission from International Criminal Tribunal for the former Yugoslavia [ICTY].)

Two examples associated with the Kosovo conflict in 1999 demonstrate this point. First, refer again to Figure 3.11 depicts an adult male cranium with multiple gunfire and shrapnel injuries. One exit wound is located above the right eye orbit, resulting from a through-and-through gunshot wound from back to front. The large defect in the center of

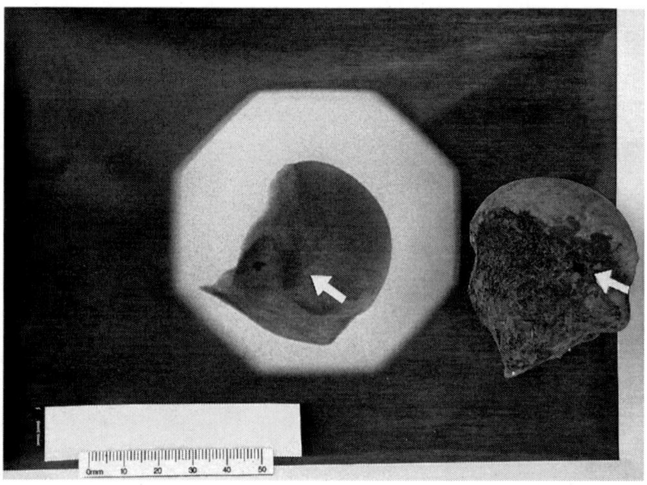

Figure 3.20 Humeral head radiograph and bone fragment. Arrows point to shrapnel embedded in the humeral head made visible through the radiograph and fractured outer margin of bone. (Printed with permission from International Criminal Tribunal for the former Yugoslavia [ICTY].)

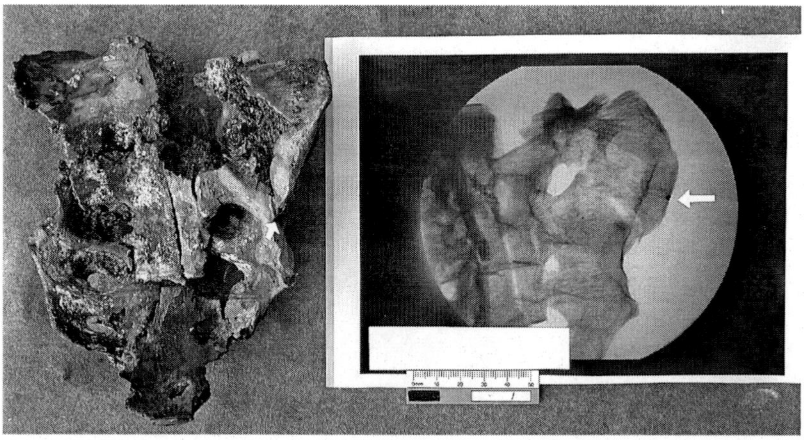

Figure 3.21 Shrapnel wounds from blast injury to sacrum. Fluoroscope image illustrates small circular ball bearings embedded in bone. Note also the large fractured areas of the sacrum. The bone was reconstructed and is held together with glue due to severe fragmentation. (Printed with permission from International Criminal Tribunal for the former Yugoslavia [ICTY].)

the superior cranium is a shrapnel injury. Based on intersecting fracture lines, it is evident that the shrapnel injuries occurred before sustaining gunshot injuries. Second, refer again to Figure 3.17 illustrates two defects present on the frontal and right parietal bones. Note the large radiating fractures that extend from the defect on the frontal bone across the coronal suture onto the left parietal bone and the irregular shape of the defects. Endocranially, the wounds exhibit beveling. Despite the irregular nature of the defect, the diplöe is exposed circumferentially (Figure 3.18).

In contrast to shrapnel wounds, the size and shape of gunfire wounds tend to be consistent with the size and shape of the projectile. Variation in the shape of the defect may also reflect the angle at which the projectile strikes the bone and the shape of the bullet. Defects from the bullets that strike perpendicular to the bone tend to be round in shape and similar in size to the diameter of the bullet. Generally, the shape is symmetrical or patterned.

Perforating wounds are common in gunfire injuries, though not always present. Tracking the trajectory of the bullet through the bone is fairly straightforward even in cases where the bullet ricochets internally and changes direction (refer to Chapter 7 for more discussion of bullet trajectory). The number of wounds, most often, is one or two per shot, although transecting multiple regions of the body may increase this number. As with shrapnel injuries, projectiles may be embedded in bone or clothing and therefore available for analysis. In radiographic images, grenade and mine shrapnel can appear nearly identical to gunshot pellets (Figures 3.22 and 3.23). On gross examination of the skeletal trauma and recovered ballistic evidence, differences between shotgun pellets and steel bearings from a grenade are evident:

- Grenade and mine shrapnel will often contain ball bearings in association with other irregularly shaped metal fragments.
- Grenade and mine shrapnel become irregularly shaped and deformed upon exploding.
- Shotgun pellets are typically made of lead, whereas grenades and mine shrapnel are made of different metals, including steel.

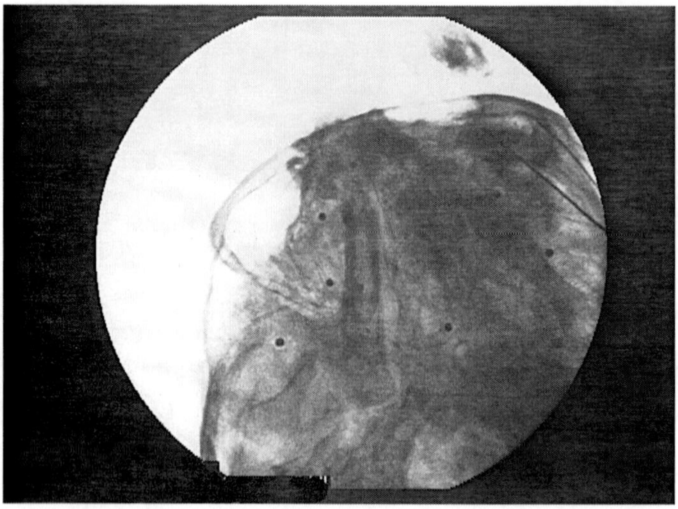

Figure 3.22 Small, round ball bearings embedded in the cranium visible in the fluoroscope image; shrapnel from an M26 fragmentation grenade. (Printed with permission from International Criminal Tribunal for the former Yugoslavia [ICTY].)

Figure 3.23 Posterior cranium. Defects resulting from shotgun pellets. (Printed with permission from International Criminal Tribunal for the former Yugoslavia [ICTY].)

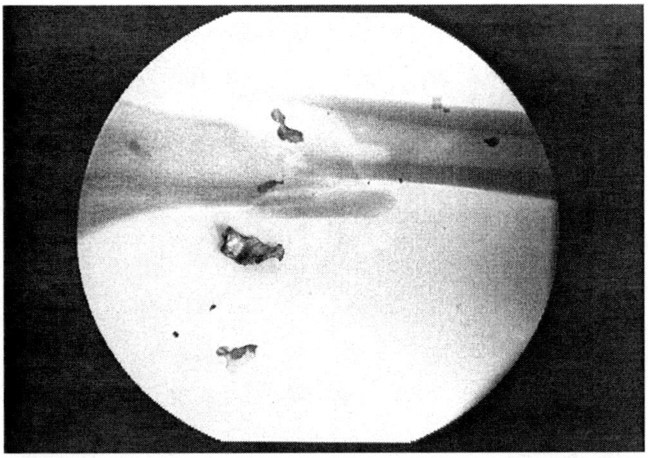

Figure 3.24 Fluoroscope image of humeral shaft that sustained a gunshot wound with a 7.62 × 39 mm round. Observe the fragmentation of the round upon impact. Shown here are the expended layers of copper from the jacket. (Printed with permission from International Criminal Tribunal for the former Yugoslavia [ICTY].)

Gunfire projectiles may also fragment, thereby creating several wound tracks or irregular-shaped defects in bone. A fragmented high-velocity, 7.62 × 39 mm round fired from an AK-47 was recovered from bone and soft tissues. Figure 3.24 illustrates the expended layers of copper from the steel core of the bullet. Multiple wound tracks may result as fragments penetrate through soft tissue or bone along separate tracks. Fragmented gunfire projectiles are quite distinguishable from EOD shrapnel by the type of metal or composition of the shrapnel, the number of wounds, the tendency of the projectile to perforate the head or body, and the distribution of wounds; wounds that are oblong or irregular in shape result when the object strikes the bone at an angle.

Shrapnel from blast injuries and gunfire projectiles have the potential to create radiating fractures at the point of impact. This depends on the force of impact, skeletal morphology, and composition of the anatomical feature affected. Fracture patterns for the types of injuries tend to follow the same predictable patterns of fractures due to biomechanical properties such as shape and thickness of bone, circumventing areas that are thick, buttresses, or sinus cavities. Moreover, the characteristics of wounds depend largely on the specific anatomy of skeletal tissues impacted, i.e., compact or trabecular bone. The variation in wound morphology occurs due to a number of variables and the range of modifiers affecting those variables. Therefore, although the parameters vary, these general findings should serve to help investigators with standards of best practice. The general observations listed in Table 3.4 outline a general comparison between the two mechanisms of injuries.

Table 3.4 Differential Patterns of Explosive Shrapnel from Gunfire Projectile Trauma

Variable	Modifier	Shrapnel/Blast	GSW
Size	• Ranges from small to large defect	Highly variable	Patterned, generally consistent with diameter or cross section of bullet
Shape	• Defect mimics shape of projectile	Shrapnel tends to be irregular or asymmetrical	Projectiles tend to be symmetrical or regularly patterned
	• Trajectory	Generally lacks streamlining	Streamlined
Entrance wound	• Present or absent	Generally present	Generally present
Exit wound	• Present or absent	Rarely present	More often present than shrapnel
Tendency of projectile to embed in bone[a]	• Weak-to-strong association	Varied	Varied
	• Presence of intermediate target		
	• Material construction of bullet or shrapnel		
Number of wounds	• Total number of wounds	High	Low
	• Number of wounds per projectile	Single	Single or double
Distribution of wounds	• Wide or narrow	Wide	Narrow

[a] Tendency of metal fragments or projectiles to embed in bone depends largely on the specific bone impacted. Trabecular areas such as vertebra are more likely to have embedded fragments or bullets than the skull; therefore, this is largely dependent on the region affected.

Summary Guidelines for Best Practice

Through an epidemiological model, projectile trauma from blasting mechanisms can be differentiated from gunfire. Overall, the context, location, and type of explosives are essential factors influencing trauma variation. Shrapnel injuries can appear similar to gunshot injuries, in cases were small pellets or ball bearings are present. Note that there was only one small radiating fracture extending anteriorly from the defect. In other cases, shrapnel injuries are unique in that the shrapnel may consist of the shells of the explosive or surrounding materials. In such cases, the penetrating fragments are highly irregular, and thus the skeletal defects vary considerably. Careful consideration should be given to skeletal evidence of blast injuries, as it has been significant in the prosecution of violations to IHL and will likely appear in human rights investigations in the future.

Case Study 3.1: Skeletal and Soft Tissue Injuries Resulting from a Grenade

Asoka B. Seneviratne
Consultant Judicial Medical Officer
General (Teaching) Hospital, Kandy, Sri Lanka

According to the information provided by the police, a 50-year-old male had sustained injury due to a blast inside a house. He had died within a short period after the blast. An autopsy of the remains revealed the following: blackening in the front aspect of the clothes, mainly in the lower half of the jacket and the trousers with multiple circular tears, and multiple small circular puncture lacerations with underlying skeletal defects and fractures (Figures 3.25). A grenade explosion has taken place in front of the victim. Note the high concentration of wounds on the left leg, midregion, which was the area closest to the blast. The left femur exhibits a spiral fracture in the distal 1/3 of the shaft (Figures 3.26 and 3.27). The explanation for this injury is a fall subsequent to the blast. The uncommon site (distal 1/3 of the femur) can be explained by weakening of the bone prior to the fall due to shrapnel injuries of the same area of the bone. These shrapnel injuries are clearly seen at the margin of the fracture in Figure 3.27.

There were multiple puncture lacerations, diameters varying from 0.3 to 2.0 cm. Almost all of these puncture lacerations were in the front aspect of the body, mainly toward the left side of the deceased. The circular punctures in the right upper arm were on the posterior aspect, probably due to the orientation of the body at the time of the incident (Figure 3.28). Puncture lacerations were concentrated in the lower part of the body and mainly in the lower legs (Figure 3.29). Circular metal balls were recovered from most of these puncture sites—including some embedded within the bones. Bleeding due to visceral injuries resulting from penetrating shrapnel in the front aspect of the chest, abdomen, and pelvis was sufficient to cause death.

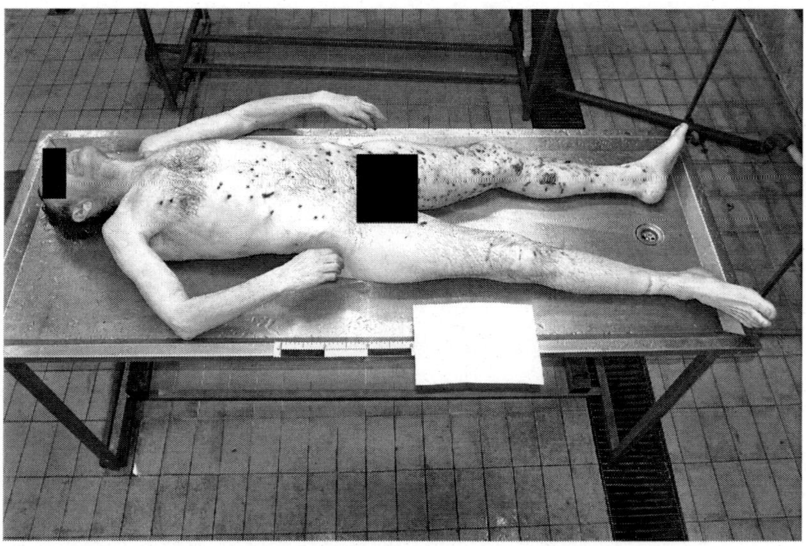

Figure 3.25 Victim died of blast injuries from a grenade. Note the high concentration of wounds on the left leg, midregion (Alain Wittmann).

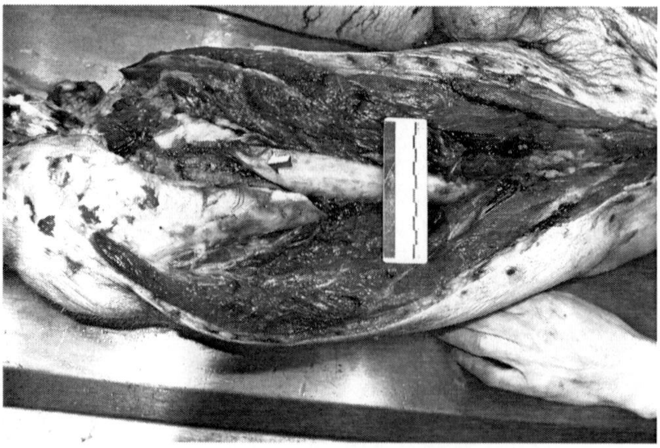

Figure 3.26 Spiral fracture sustained to the distal 1/3 of the femur (Alain Wittmann).

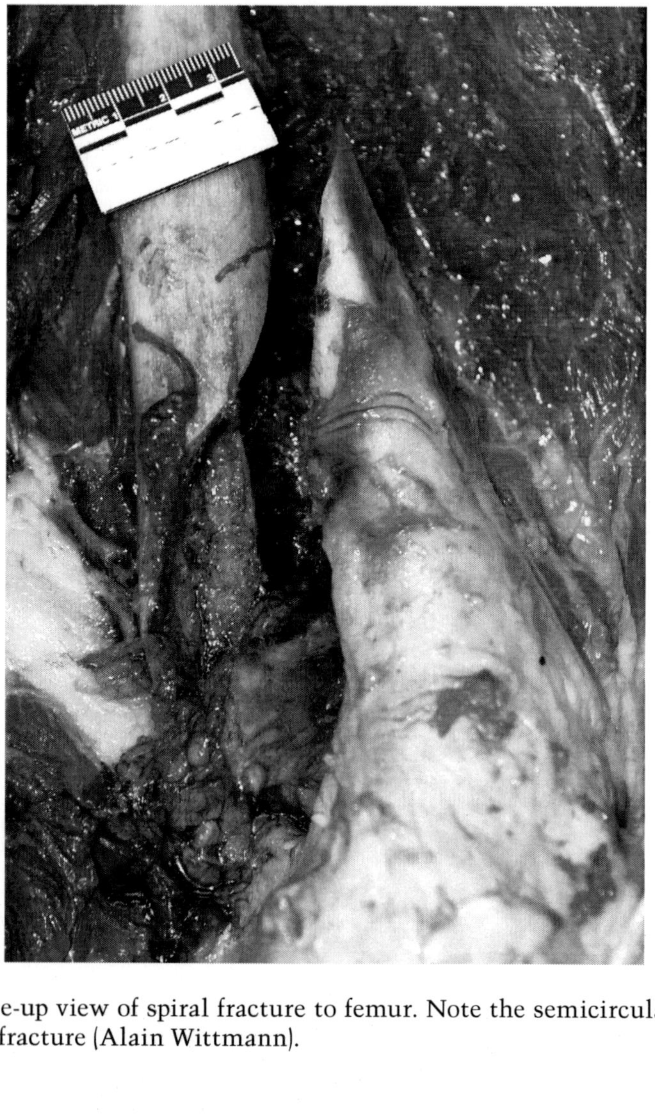

Figure 3.27 Close-up view of spiral fracture to femur. Note the semicircular bone defects at the margin of the fracture (Alain Wittmann).

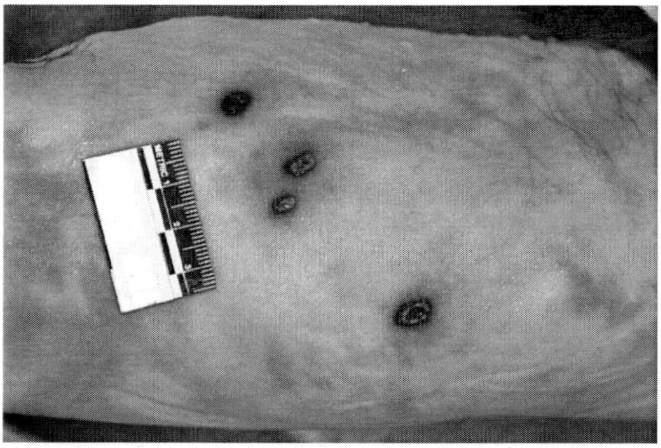

Figure 3.28 Four circular defects on the skin of the leg due to shrapnel injuries (Alain Wittmann).

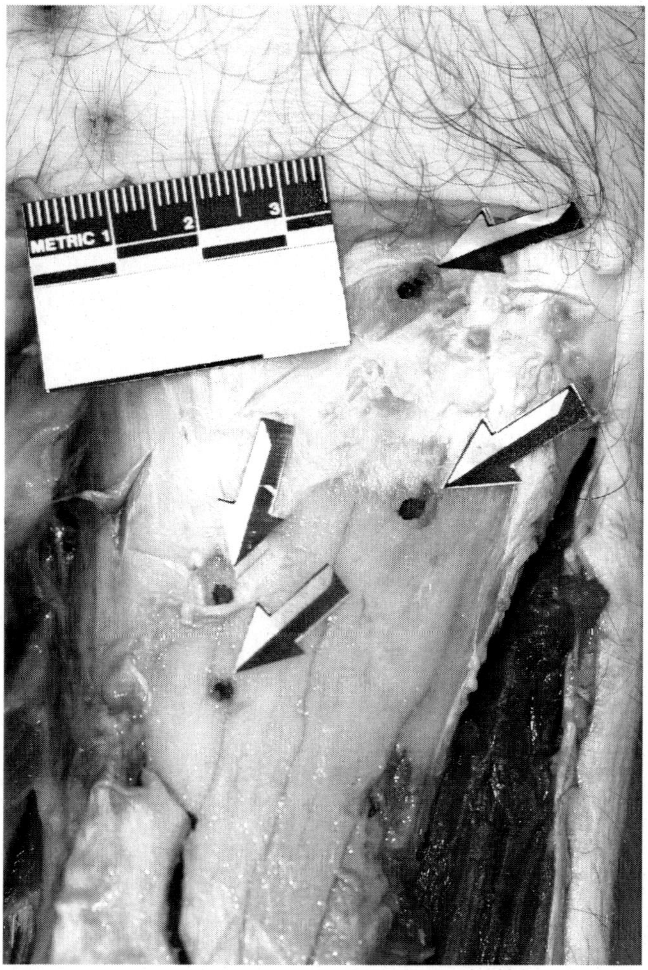

Figure 3.29 Close-up view of circular defect from shrapnel on underlying bone. Small circular defects on the skin were found corresponding to the sites seen in the picture (Alain Wittmann).

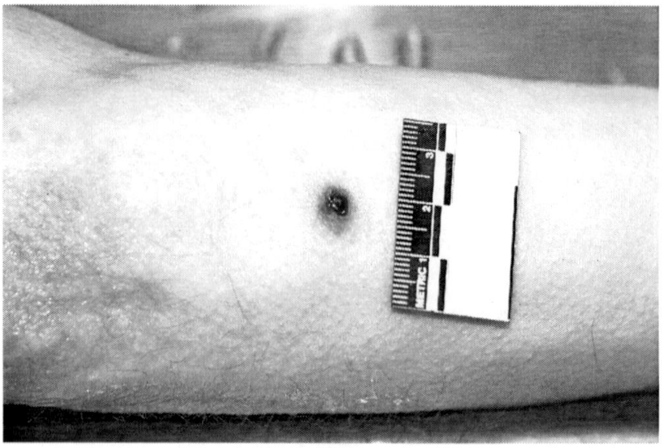

Figure 3.30 A circular defect on skin of leg from shrapnel (Alain Wittmann).

The injuries to the left lower leg are of particular significance. There are multiple circular punctures in the left tibia associated with soft tissue injuries. There is a 4.5 × 4.6 cm laceration with a metal fragment within it in the front aspect midthird of the left lower leg. There is a comminuted fracture in the left tibia. Comminution was more extensive around the metal fragment. Other fracture lines connected the circular punctures. External wounds may not always be indicative of extensive internal trauma or the amount of skeletal fracture resulting from the injury. Examination of the proximal tibia reveals several small round wounds from shrapnel with thin radiating fractures extending below the defects (Figure 3.30). The radiating fractures extending downward from the defects suggest that the pellets penetrated the body from down to top, which is consistent with what is known about the location of the victim relative to the blast (Figure 3.31). Further, note the distribution of defects, near one another, suggesting that the blast occurred at close range to the victim. The defects are small, circular, and symmetrical.

An irregular-shaped metal fragment is embedded in the lower leg (Figures 3.32–3.35). It was extracted from the skeletal wound and comes from the cap of a grenade. The resulting

Figure 3.31 Small, round defects from shrapnel. Note the distribution of defects, near one another, suggesting the blast occurred at close range (Alain Wittmann).

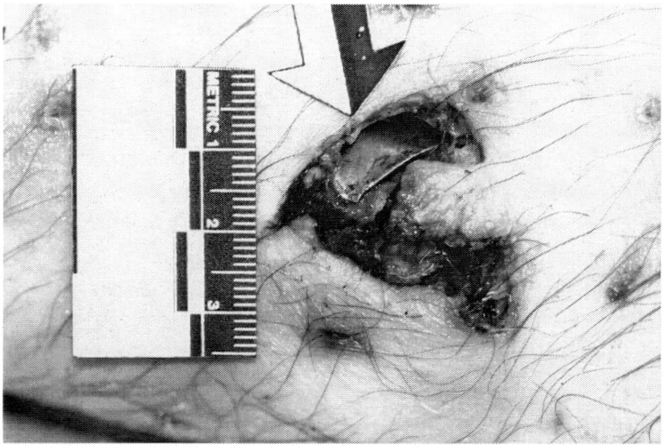

Figure 3.32 Irregular-shaped metal fragment embedded in soft tissues of leg from blast injury (Alain Wittmann).

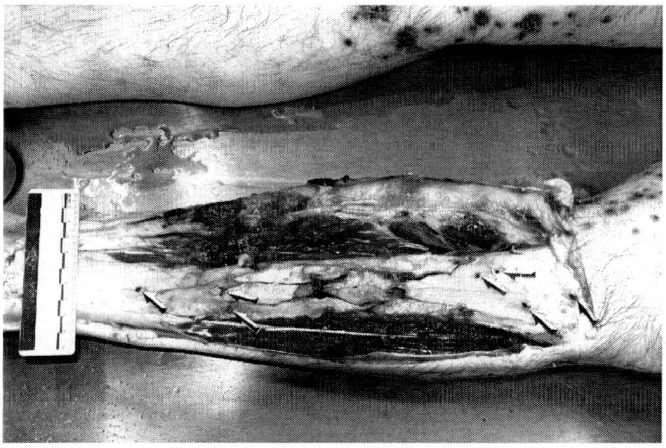

Figure 3.33 Soft tissues of leg reflected in areas of the wounds. Circular defects are present in the anterior midshaft of the left tibia with associated comminuted fractures (Alain Wittmann).

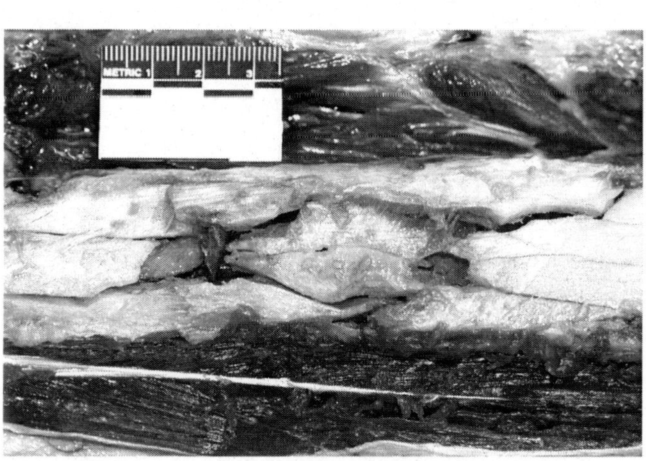

Figure 3.34 Close-up view of tibial fractures from embedded shrapnel defects (Alain Wittmann).

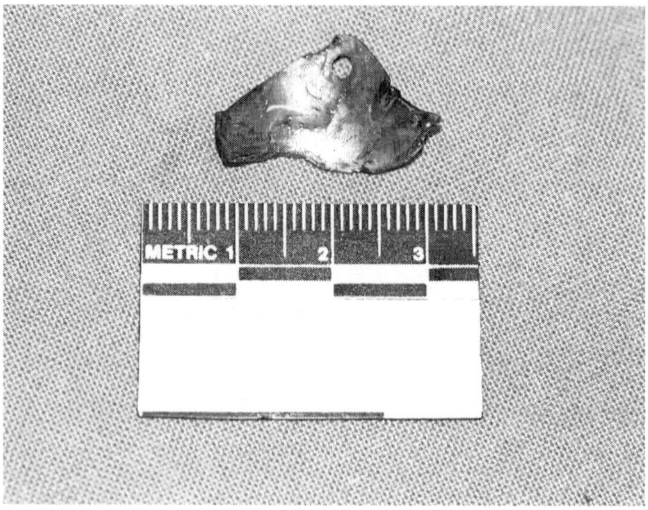

Figure 3.35 Metal fragment extracted from skeletal wound. Metal projectile comes from the cap of a grenade (Alain Wittmann).

extensive comminuted fractures from the projectile are evident. Figure 3.36 shows the lighter that had been in the pocket of the victim. Circular defects in the plastic reflect the general size and shape of the steel balls from the grenade. Steel ball bearings from an M26 fragmentation grenade were recovered from soft and bone tissue pictured in Figure 3.37.

The blackening on the front aspect of the clothes indicates that the epicenter of the blast was in close proximity to the victim. Two possible mechanisms of injury can be considered:

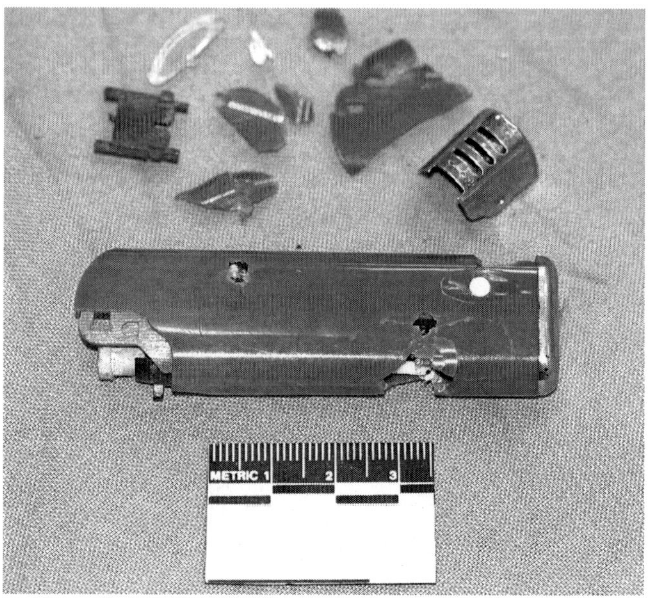

Figure 3.36 A plastic lighter from the pocket of the victim at the time of the blast. Note the circular defects in the plastic, reflecting the shape and size of the pellets (Alain Wittmann).

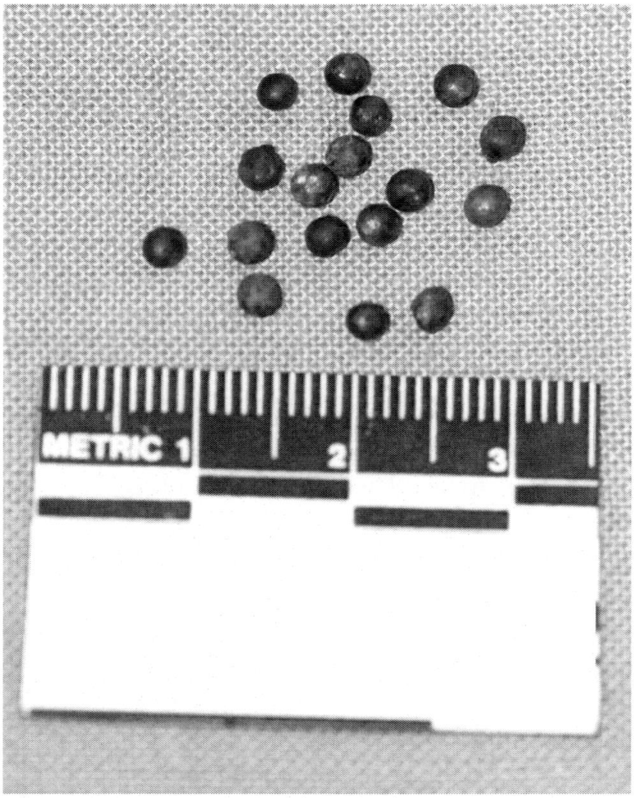

Figure 3.37 Small pellets from an M26 fragmentation grenade. Shrapnel were recovered from bone and tissues (Alain Wittmann).

(1) a smooth-bore firearm injury using a cartridge containing bird pellets, or (2) a small bomb blast, similar to a grenade. The possibility of a firearm injury can be ruled out without difficulty due to the following reasons:

1. There was blackening in the clothes, including the jacket, indicating a short distance between the explosion and the victim.
2. Wide distribution of pellet injuries in the front aspect of the body, which cannot be expected in a close-range firearm injury.
3. Large metal fragment found embedded in the left tibia. If this is a result of a ricochet of a firearm discharge, it is unlikely to see blackening in the clothes.
4. Pellets without deformities were recovered. This is also a reasonable cause to exclude a ricochet.

This case study demonstrates the wound morphology shrapnel from a grenade. This is useful as small ball bearings could be mistaken for shotgun pellets. It further demonstrates how to recognize blast injuries skeletally so that a correct estimation of the mechanism of injury may be obtained in cases in which only fragmented skeletal tissue is present, as in the following case study.

Case Study 3.2: A Case of Blast Injury from Colombia

Jorge M. Pachón
Criminalist and Professional Technician in Ballistics
Bogota, Columbia

A set of incomplete and skeletonized remains representing cranial, mandibular, and maxillary fragments of an adult male individual were analyzed to determine the mechanism of injury. According to the original autopsy report, only the head was affected; therefore, the rest of the body was not autopsied. The autopsy report did not describe any fractures or visible injuries to either the pectoral girdle or the cervical spine. The remains belonged to a man who according to the official investigation, died in an armed confrontation between the Colombian Army and insurgent groups.

Upon examining the remains, it became apparent that facial bones were absent, and multiple fractures made it difficult to associate the corresponding fragments. Both the maxilla and mandible lacked a number of dental pieces and were also fragmented with loss of bone material. It was determined that the latter would have been caused by a fast-load, high-energy force (Figures 3.38–3.45 illustrate cranial fractures, defects, and radiographic images of embedded shrapnel).

A radiograph of the fragments show radiopaque elements consistent with metallic particles; two fragments are of rectangular shape, whereas one is round. The fragments seem to be embedded on the left side of the skull and in the left side of the mandible. Examination of the skull showed multiple rectangular defects with approximate dimension of 2 × 5 mm on the right mastoid and occipital regions. The defects showed clear external beveling. Incomplete defects, identified only through remnants of internal beveling, were found on the left parietal and occipital.

Skeletal trauma was restricted to the head only. The loss of bones of the face, vault, maxilla, and mandible were caused by a high-energy mechanism that left patterned defects and extensive fracturing. The injuries observed are therefore consistent with the explanation of having been caused by a blast, and the presence of regularly shaped metallic particles point toward an explosive device. The absence of bones from the facial area and the existence of externally beveled area located on the left side of the head (parietal and occipital) suggest that the explosion and subsequent fragmentation took place on the right side of the head.

Two metallic fragments previously seen on the radiograph were examined under a stereomicroscope and identified as the prefragmented metal sheet covering of a grenade. In addition, a ball bearing also recovered from the skull was identified as being part of the same structure. Both prefragmented metal and ball bearings are typical of the M26 fragmentation grenade. This grenade consists of prefragmented sheet of metal and ball bearings folded as a spiral around HEs (TNT). The latter is kept together in a high-resistance plastic cover. When the explosion takes place, it spreads the metal particles and ball bearings at high velocity over a large area. The findings were not consistent with the official version of the event, namely, that the victim died in combat operations. Witness testimony supported the former and indicated that a fragmentation grenade was placed close to the head of the victim while he slept. After the blast, his body was thrown in an open field to give the impression that he died in a confrontation.

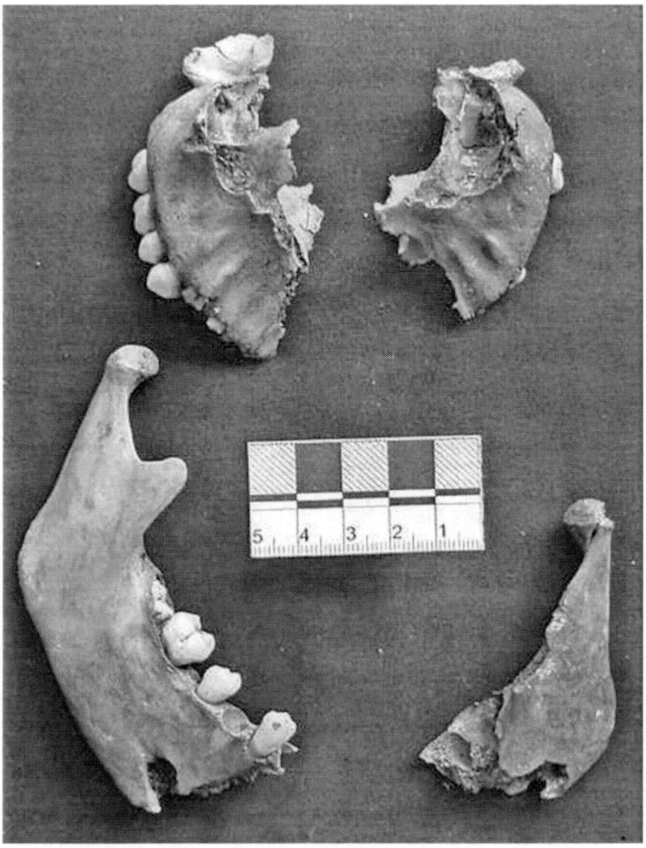

Figure 3.38 Overview of the maxilla and mandible in four fragments (Jorge Pachón).

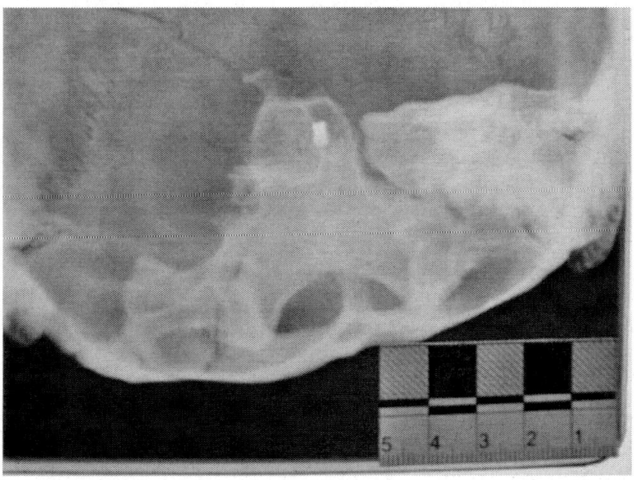

Figure 3.39 X-ray of a skull showing rectangle-shaped metal particle in the *pars basilaris* (Jorge Pachón).

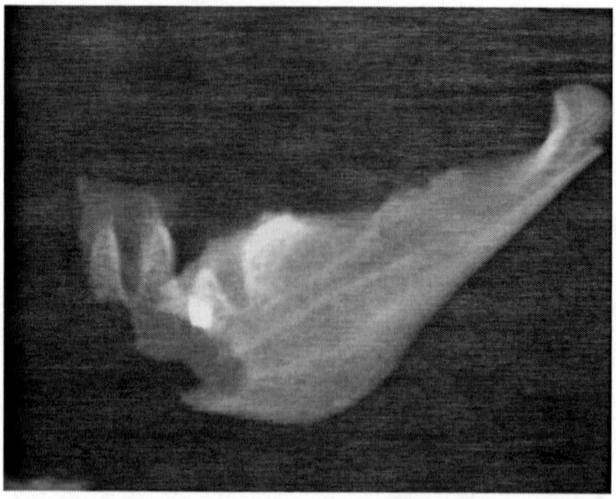

Figure 3.40 X-ray of the mandible showing a rectangle-shaped metal fragment embedded in the body (Jorge Pachón).

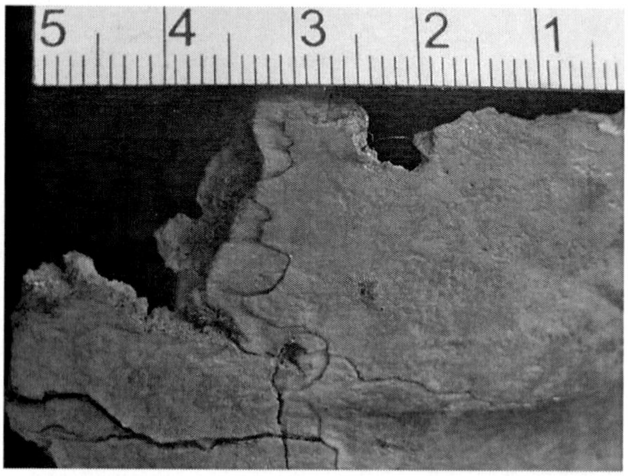

Figure 3.41 Detail of the outer table of the skull, right occipitomastoid area with three irregular defects, probably caused by the grenade fragments (Jorge Pachón).

Figure 3.42 Detail of the inner table of the skull, right occipitomastoid area with three irregular defects, probably caused by the grenade fragments. White arrows show internal beveling caused by grenade fragments penetrating the skull (Jorge Pachón).

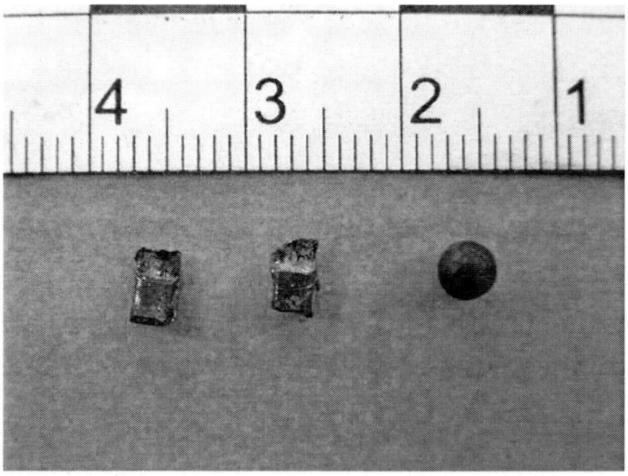

Figure 3.43 Metal fragments recovered from the bones: two rectangle-shaped metal fragments and ball bearing, all elements of a fragmentation grenade (Jorge Pachón).

Figure 3.44 Overview of different components of an M26 fragmentation grenade, made in Colombia (Jorge Pachón).

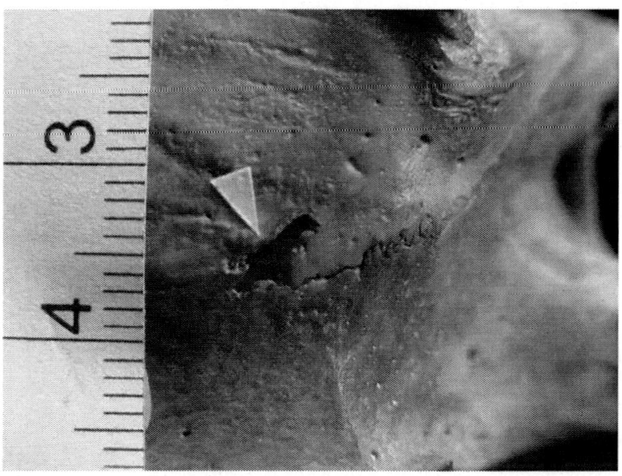

Figure 3.45 Detail of the entrance wound of a grenade fragment. Observe the rectangular shape mimicking the shape of the fragment (Jorge Pachón).

Case Study 3.3: "Human Bomb" and Body Trauma

Ananda Samarasekera
Chief Forensic Medical Examiner, Office on Missing Persons and Forensics, UNMIK
Chief Judicial Medical Officer, Colombo North
Teaching Hospital, Ragama, Sri Lanka

A *human bomb* may be defined as a modality of suicide attack where the perpetrator carries the explosive device strapped to his or her body, using a garment specially designed for that purpose with the intention of killing others along with him- or herself in the process. This is a kind of suicide attack on foot, or a "living bomb"; the target is primarily other people, and the attacker is killed upon detonation. The two types of kits commonly used are explosive belts and explosive vests or jackets. A pair of shorts with an explosive device also has been used, though it is uncommon. Explosive belts were commonly used by Palestinian suicide bombers (Figure 3.46), and explosive vests/jackets, by the Liberation Tigers of Tamil Eelam (LTTE) suicide attackers.

Although the first human bomb explosion was seen in the war in Lebanon, the tactic has been perfected by the LTTE in Sri Lanka since 1987.[*] The first human bomb that exploded in October 1993 in Sri Lanka was carried in a pair of shorts (Figure 3.47). Since 1987 until the end of 2006, there have been between 76 and 168 (estimates vary) suicide bombings using more than 240 attackers throughout South Asia.[†] According to the Sri Lanka database, there were 78 suicide attacks since 5th July 1985 till 1st December 2006.[‡] Among these, about 28% (n = 22) cases have been forensically confirmed in Sri Lanka as human bombs; perpetrated by 24 persons (11 males and 13 females) of which two attacks done by two persons in all except one case where the jacket-type device was used[§] (Figure 3.48), and most of the explosions had taken place in the open air.[¶]

Figure 3.46 Palestinian suicide bomber in a parade. (Ananda Samarasekera, Image courtesy of http://www.waronline.org/en/terror/sucide.htm.)

[*] http://en.wikepedia. org/wiki/Suicide_attack.
[†] http://en.wikepedia.org/wiki/Suicide_attack.
[‡] http://www.satp.org/satporgtp/countries/shrilanka/database/data_sucide_killings.htm.
[§] Personal communication with WGDS Gunathilake, Deputy government Analyst, Sri Lanka.
[¶] http:// www.spur.as.au/chronology_of_suicide_bomb_attacks_by_Tamil_Tigers_in_Sri Lanka, pp. 1–17.

Figure 3.47 Explosive device in a pair of shorts, the type of a kit used by the LTTE in Sri Lanka at the beginning (Ananda Samarasekera).

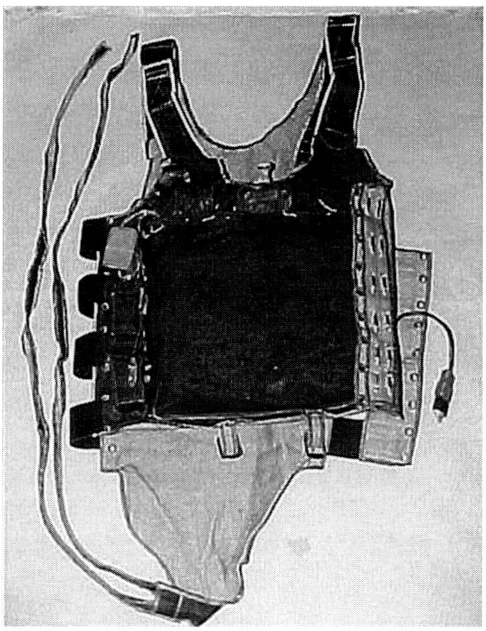

Figure 3.48 Jacket- or vest-type kit commonly used by the LTTE in Sri Lanka. (Ananda Samarasekera, image courtesy of WGDS Gunathilaka, Deputy Government Analyst of Sri Lanka.)

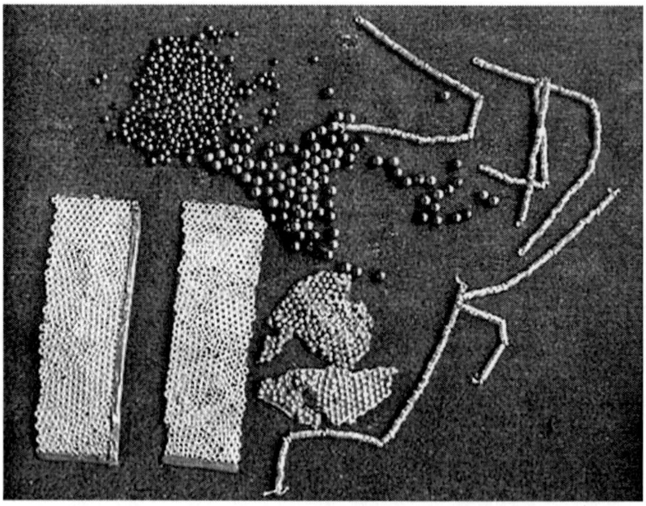

Figure 3.49 Steel balls (shrapnel) of two different sizes and a plate of high-explosive material. Note: This is used after being embedded on the plate in an explosive device in a human bomb (Ananda Samarasekera).

The explosive device of the vest- or jacket-type kit consists of two parts. An inner plate of high-explosive chemical charge of 1–2 kg, mainly Tetryl or C-4, with its outer surface impregnated with a layer of steel balls, 3–4 mm diameter each, amounting to 1.5 to 2.5 kg of shrapnel (Figure 3.49). This device is enclosed in a vest or a jacket made of cloth, usually denim material, to fit onto the torso, usually in the front. Although other types of shrapnel of suitable size, such as nails, screws, nuts, or thick wire could be impregnated, they have not been identified forensically in Sri Lanka.* The explosive belt usually consists of several cylinders filled with HE chemical charge (*de facto* pipe bombs) or more sophisticated versions with plates of explosive surrounded by a fragmentation jacket/vest that produces shrapnel, making the jacket/vest a crude body-worn claymore mine.† A loaded vest may weigh 5–20 kg and may be hidden under thick clothes, usually a jacket or a snow coat (Figure 3.50). Such a vest covers the entire abdomen, usually has shoulder straps, and can be worn both by males and females. Palestinians terrorists mainly use two types of chemical explosive charges: homemade TATP (triacetone triperoxide), known as *Mother of Satan* for its instability, and TNT, which is industrially made. Sometimes they use C4 or other plastic explosives‡ (Figure 3.51). The shock wave of a human bomb is rather small due to the relatively small quantity of explosive chemical used. The main killing power of this type of bomb is neither the explosion proper nor the shock wave. Most of its lethality is due to shrapnel, and the explosion resembles multidirectional shotgun blasts§ (Figure 3.52). Shrapnel is responsible for about 90% of all casualties caused by this kind of device.¶ In an explosion, the shrapnel is launched at high velocity, with kinetic energy close to that

* Personal communication with WGDS Gunathilake, Deputy government Analyst, Sri Lanka.

† http://en.wikipedia.org/wiki/Explosive_belt, p. 1.

‡ http://www.waronline.org/en/terror/suicide.htm, p. 2.

§ http://en.wikipedia.org/wiki/Explosive_belt, p. 1.

¶ http://en.wikipedia.org/wiki/Explosive_belt

Figure 3.50a Jacket- or vest-type kit on a dummy. (Ananda Samarasekera, image courtesy of WGDS Gunathilaka, Deputy Government Analyst of Sri Lanka.)

Figure 3.50b Belt-type kit on a dummy. (Ananda Samarasekera, http://www.waronline.org/en/terror/sucide.htm.)

Figure 3.51 C-4 high-explosive chemical under manufacture (Ananda Samarasekera).

of a bullet.* The most widely used and most dangerous shrapnel are ball bearings of 3–7 mm† (Figure 3.53). With explosives, a suicide attack does not require remote or delayed detonation.‡ The trigger, or the "red button" is usually located in the pocket or on the chest itself and operated by the individual.

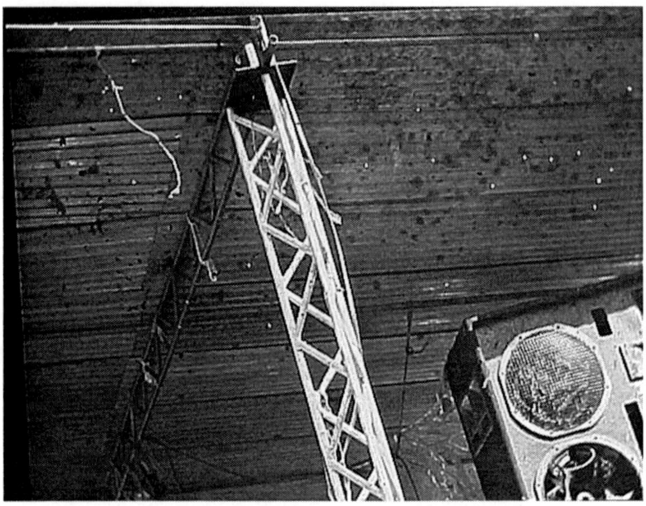

Figure 3.52 Multiple circular holes in the corrugated roof sheets of the shed at the site of an explosion of a human bomb due to piercing by shrapnel (Ananda Samarasekera).

* http://www.waronline.org/en/terror/sucide.htm, p. 6.
† http://www.waronline.org/en/terror/sucide.htm, p. 5.
‡ http://en.wikipedia.org/wiki/Sucide_attack, p. 3.

Figure 3.53 Shrapnel embedded in internal soft tissues of a dead victim in a human bomb blast. (Ananda Samarasekera, image courtesy of S.M. Colombage, Judicial Medical Officer, Colombo South, Sri Lanka.)

Mechanisms of Causation of Injuries

Several different factors cause injury following an explosion, and the relative importance of each varies considerably with the type of detonation, e.g., pure blast effects are more important with high-explosive projectiles designed purely for military use than with the homemade terrorist bombs, the lethality of which may be primarily caused by flying fragments (Knight 1991).

The mechanisms of causation of injures in a human bomb explosion could be divided as primary and secondary.

Primary mechanisms are due to the blast itself and its direct effects:

- The blast itself
- Shock wave
- Heat
- Flash and flame
- Flying missiles

Secondary mechanisms are due to causes other than the blast and its direct effects:

- Falling masonry, furnishings, and similar objects dislodged by the explosion striking the victims
- Debris being scoured away, including dust and dirt due to the explosion
- Secondary impact on the body or body parts due to falling after dispersion

When triggered, the explosive charge detonates, and the explosion occurs disintegrating the torso or the part of the body to which the explosive device is strapped. As in any other HE blast, a unidirectional conical-shape shock wave is discharged, though relatively small, and a small amount of heat is generated with a relatively mild flash and flame. Shrapnel is

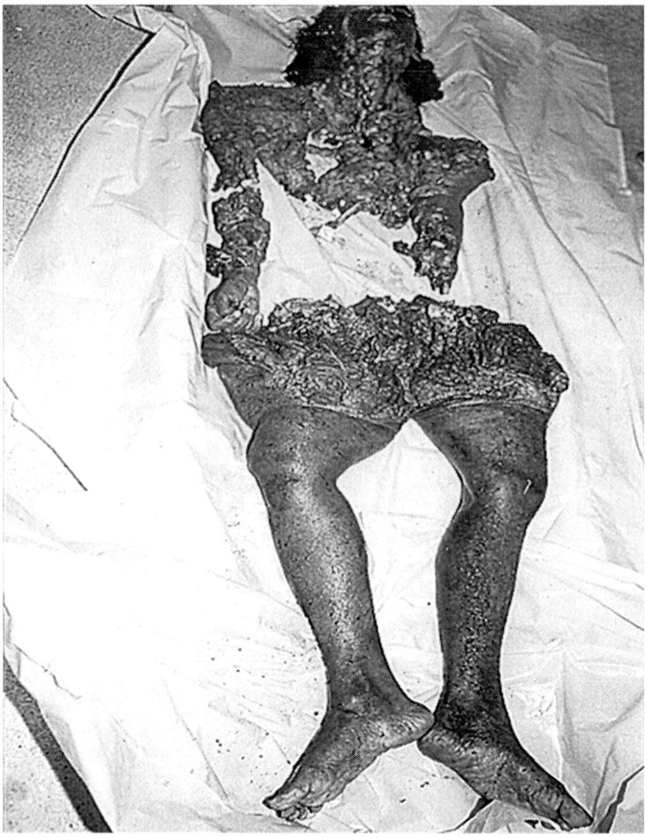

Figure 3.54 Reconstituted remaining parts of a dismembered body of a human bomb, a female (Ananda Samarasekera).

dispersed in almost all directions, but due to their relative location in the explosive plate most shrapnel travels in the opposite direction of the plate, away from the body of the bomber. Primary damage to the "carrier" and animate and inanimate objects in the immediate vicinity are due to the blast itself, shock wave, heat, flame, flash, and the shrapnel. There could be damage due to subsequent effects, such as secondary impact and falling masonry, furniture, and similar objects dislodged by the explosion.

Most extensive injuries are suffered by the carrier and are due to the blast itself (Figure 3.54). Complete disruption of the body is unusual in a bomb blast; it occurs essentially only when a person is in contact with the bomb when it explodes, either carrying it or sitting with it. Hence, it is to be expected in the small group of suicide bombers who deliberately hold the bomb or, in some instances, strap it to themselves. The body is literally blown into bits, and its parts are distributed over an area of perhaps 200 m radius (Crane 2000).

The human bomb explosion cases investigated in Sri Lanka, however, revealed that the average area of distribution was only about 15 to 25 m radius, probably due to the small quantity of explosive material used. Usually, the head is severed at the level of the upper cervical vertebrae and flies up to several meters before it falls back on its resting place. In Sri Lanka, dismembered heads have been recovered from places such as the top of a tree, roof of a building, or a shed in the near vicinity of the explosions (Figure 3.55).

Figure 3.55 The decapitated head of a bomber lying on the roof of a shed at the site of an explosion, 5 m high (Ananda Samarasekera).

Dismembered limbs fly several meters away in different directions and come to rest on the ground or some intervening place (Figures 3.56 and 3.57). The torso is grossly disintegrated and mangled, and the remains are hard to recover, except for some small parts of the torso of opposite to the side to which the bomb was strapped (Figure 3.58). For example, if the bomb is carried on the front of the chest, parts of fractured lumbar vertebrae may be found at the scene. The extent of damage to the torso or to any other part of the body to which the explosive device is strapped depends mainly on (1) the quantity and power of the explosive used and (2) its contact surface, i.e., the area and side of the body.

The extent of primary damage to the target and other animates and inanimates at the site of the explosion varies mainly with the distance. The rule is, closer the blast, the more

Figure 3.56 A dismembered hand and some flesh found at the scene of an explosion of a human bomb (Ananda Samarasekera).

Figure 3.57 A dismembered upper limb found at the scene of an explosion of a human bomb. Note: fractured end of a long bone jutting out from the mangled soft tissues (Ananda Samarasekera).

the damage (Marshall 1978). Most people close to the site of explosion remain largely in one piece (Crane 2000). The main element in the human bomb responsible for causing injuries to the animate target is the shrapnel, but the shock wave also may contribute to a lesser extent. Dismemberment of a limb or a part other than those of the carrier is sometimes found among the dead victims at the scene (Figure 3.59). A detailed study of the mechanisms of traumatic dismemberment of limbs by bomb blasts confirmed that flailing of the limb is not the cause; instead, direct coupling of the shock wave of the explosion causes fractures and preferential traumatic amputation through the shaft rather than the joints of long bones (Hull et al. 1994).

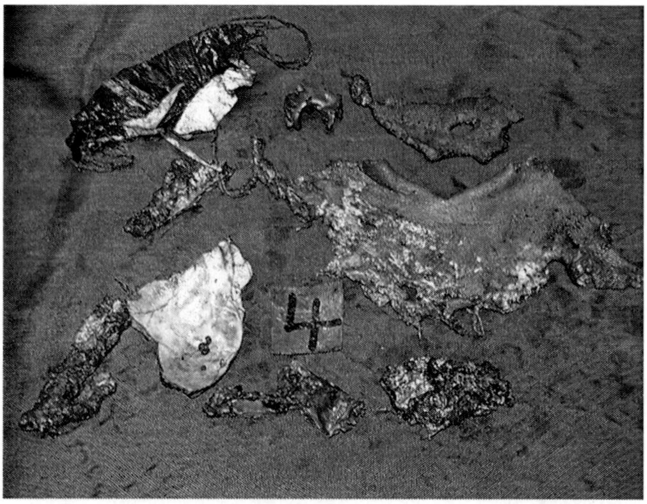

Figure 3.58 Some remains from the missing body parts of the bomber, after cleaning. (Ananda Samarasekera, image courtesy of S.M. Colombage, Judicial Medical Officer, Colombo South, Sri Lanka.)

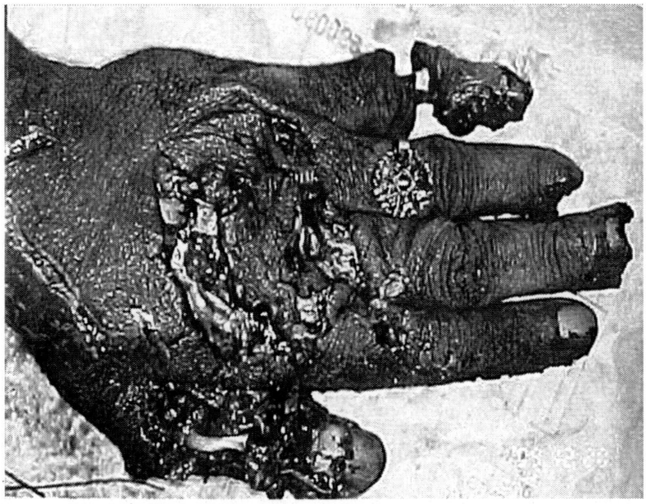

Figure 3.59 Dismembered hand of the targeted victim. Note: This was identified from the ring by the wife of the deceased (Ananda Samarasekera).

Injuries

Exposure of a body to a high explosion produces a well-defined pattern of injury (Hull et al. 1994). The spectrum of injuries in a human-bomb blast is somewhat similar to any other high-explosive blast, but not to the same extent and degree. The injuries are as follows:

- Almost complete disruption of a large part of the body to which the bomb is strapped and also any other body part, usually a part of a upper limb, that directly comes in contact with the device (Figure 3.60)
- Severed limbs and the head of the carrier, with mangling at the severed end

Figure 3.60 Torso of carrier absent. This is the distinguishable feature of the carrier in a human bomb explosion (Ananda Samarasekera).

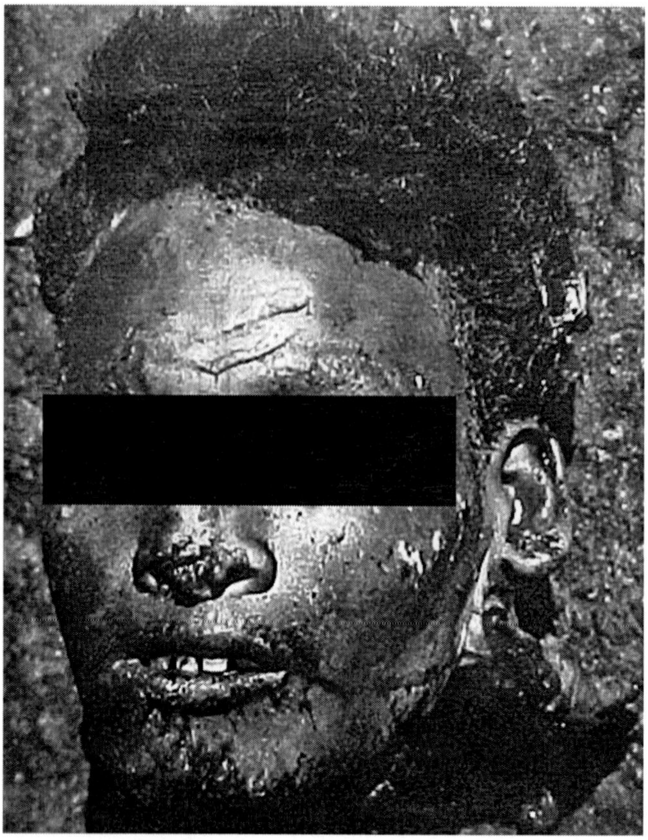

Figure 3.61 Dismembered head of the carrier. Note: Singeing of hair at the front hair margin and eyelashes, flash and flame burns on the forehead and nose, and some dust tattooing together with "peppering" appearance associated with larger lacerations and abrasions (Ananda Samarasekera).

- Explosive injuries; blown-off part of a body, usually a limb, and characteristic "peppering" appearance on the exposed areas of the skin due to a triad of small contusions, punctuate abrasions, and puncture lacerations (Marshall 1976) caused by numerous small missiles (other than the primary missiles) of the explosive device (Figure 3.61)
- Blast (shock) wave injuries
- Flash and flame burns
- Penetrating injuries from the flying missiles (Figure 3.62)
- Mechanical injuries (lacerations, contusions, abrasions, incised injuries, and fractures) due to falling masonry, furnishings, and similar objects dislodged by the explosion, and secondary impact due to falling

The injuries sustained and their pattern on the carrier are distinctly different from those on the victims. The distinguishable feature of the carrier is the almost complete disruption of torso, and blown-off limbs (which is mangled) and the head in dispersion. Except for small torn parts of skin, lumps of soft tissue such as muscles, small pieces of spine, and a major limb joint, the entire torso, including internal organs, is absent (Crane 2000).

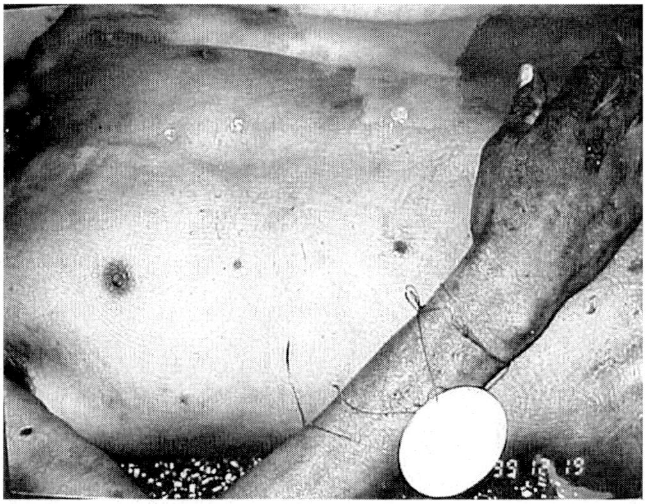

Figure 3.62 Penetrating injuries on the chest caused by shrapnel (Ananda Samarasekera).

Dismemberment of the upper limbs usually occurs at mid-upper arm, and mid-thigh level in the lower limb (Figures 3.63–3.65). The skin and soft tissues at the dismembered ends of the limbs are extensively torn and mangled, and the muscles are crushed. The long bones of the proximal part of the limbs are fractured, usually at their midshafts. The distal parts of the limbs are more or less intact, particularly the bones. In some cases, extensive injury or absence or dismemberment of a hand could be seen. This happens due to the blowing off of the hand that was used to trigger the bomb by placing it on the torso, which is strapped with the bomb. On the skin of the uncovered parts of the remaining limbs, characteristic patterns of small contusions, punctuate abrasions, and puncture lacerations associated with dust tattooing and purplish discoloration of the skin due to the heat effect (Crane 2000) may be present, but to a much lesser extent. The head is usually severed at

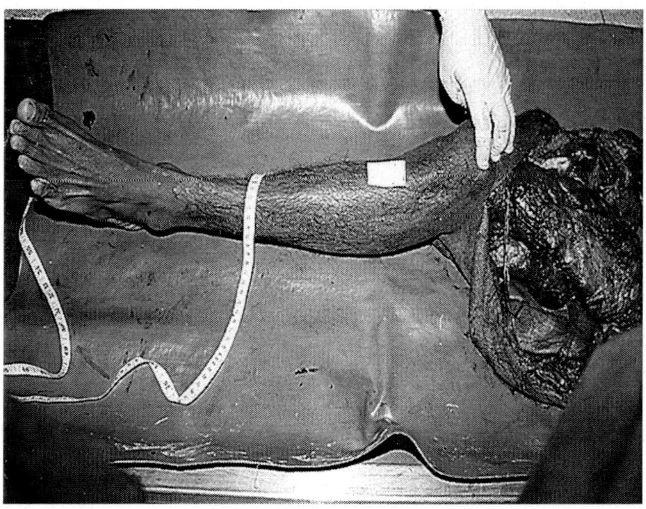

Figure 3.63 Dismembered right leg of the carrier, at midthigh level, mangling only at the amputated end. (Ananda Samarasekera, image courtesy of S.M. Colombage, Judicial Medical Officer, Colombo South, Sri Lanka.)

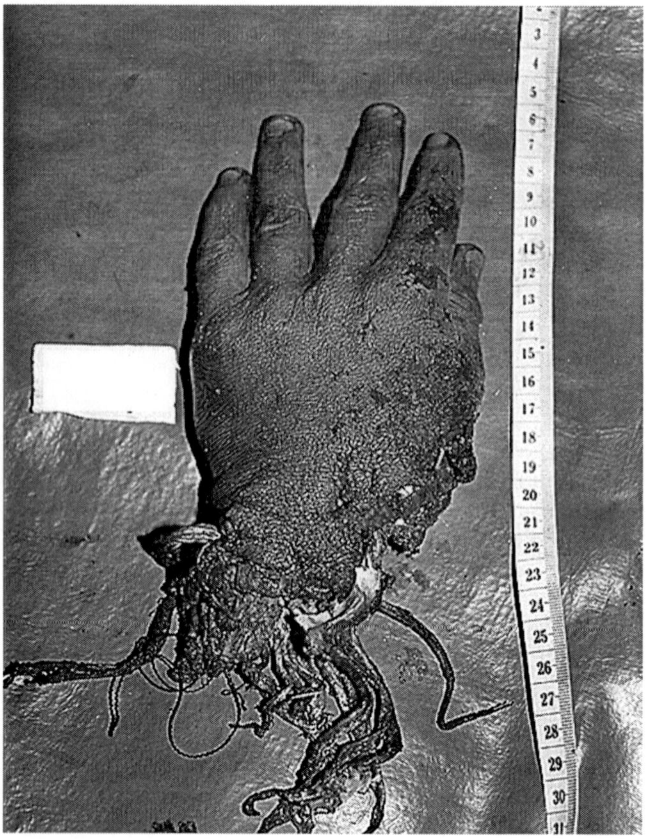

Figure 3.64 Dismembered left hand of the carrier. More or less intact hand severed close to the wrist, with the rest of the arm absent. This is an unusual site for dismemberment and probably occurred due to the missing part coming into close contact with the explosive device. (Ananda Samarasekera, image courtesy of S.M. Colombage, Judicial Medical Officer, and Colombo South, Sri Lanka.)

the upper cervical level, and a few fractured vertebrae may still be attached. Flash and flame burns, including singed head hair, eyebrows and eyelids, and small superficial burns on the face, are caused by the explosion. Usually, the dismembered head is intact, but the mandible is commonly fractured with or without fracturing of the cranium; most of the teeth may be found in their sockets, but some may be fractured along with the corresponding alveolar bone with or without subluxation or avulsion of the corresponding teeth (Figure 3.66). Despite the presence of injuries, the head is more often reconstructible even for the purpose of identification by visual recognition (Figures 3.67 and 3.68). The skin and underlying soft tissues at the dismembered end of the neck are extensively torn and flaring upward (Figure 3.69). A few small penetrating injuries could be present when flying missiles penetrate the head. These missiles may be lodged in the cranial cavity and could be detected radiographically (Figure 3.70).

As opposed to the carrier, the bodies of dead victims are more or less intact with penetrating injuries due to shrapnel and flying missiles that emanated from the explosive device (Figure 3.71). The amount of penetrating injuries and mangling mainly depends on the distance between the explosion and the victim in the absence of intervening objects

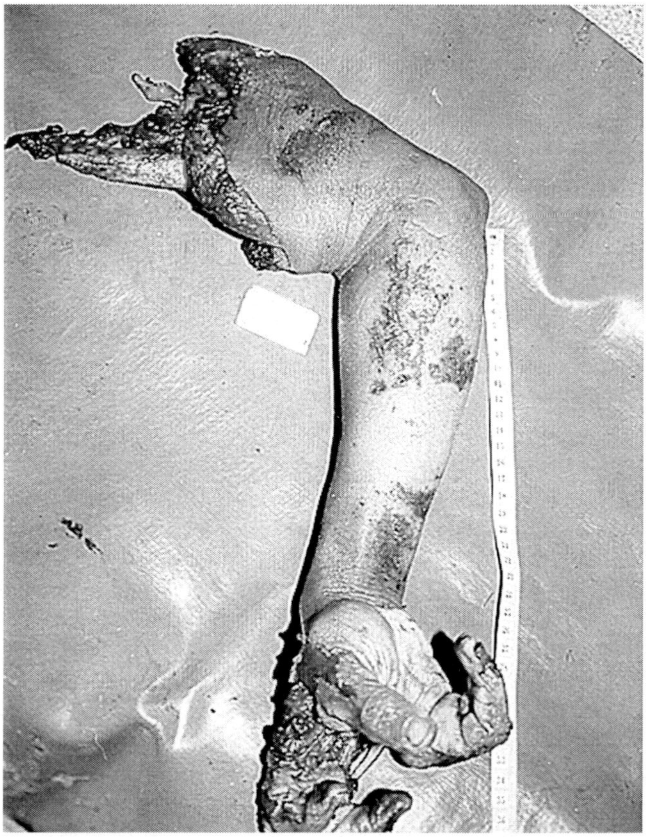

Figure 3.65 Dismembered right upper limb of the carrier. Transversely fractured humerus at midshaft together with mangled tissues at the amputated end and in the hand. The area in between is intact, except for minor superficial injury. (Ananda Samarasekera, image courtesy of S.M. Colombage, Judicial Medical Officer, Colombo South, Sri Lanka.)

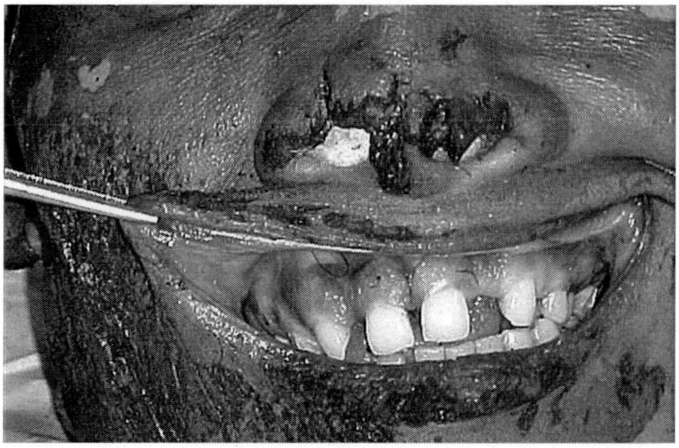

Figure 3.66 Intact front teeth of the carrier. Congenital absence of both upper lateral incisors was used to establish the identity of the deceased (Ananda Samarasekera).

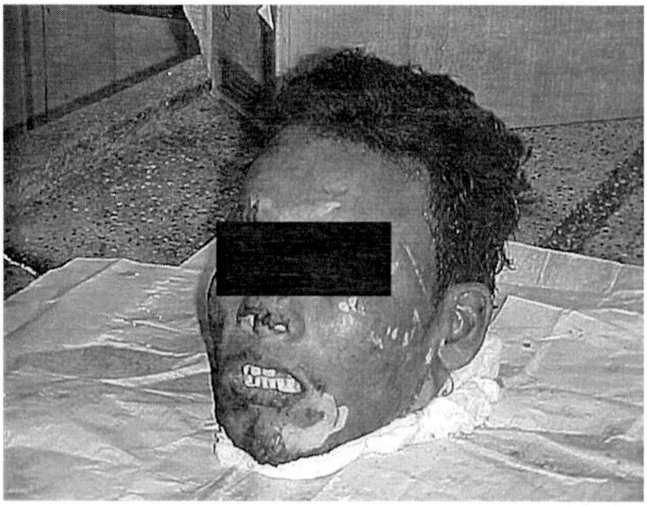

Figure 3.67 Reconstructed head of a human bomb, a male. The deceased was identified by the mother after reconstruction and later confirmed by DNA profiles (Ananda Samarasekera).

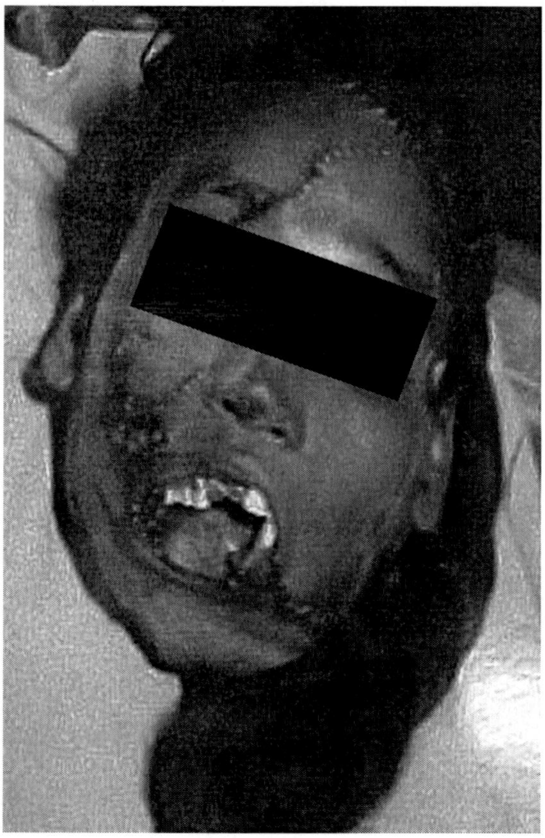

Figure 3.68 Reconstructed head of a female human bomb (Ananda Samarasekera).

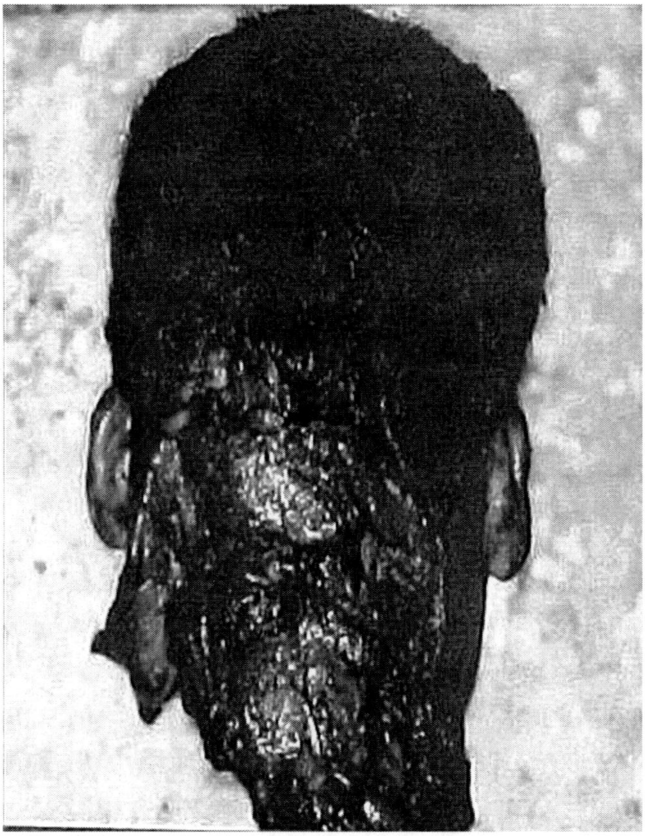

Figure 3.69 Back of the dismembered head of a carrier. Upward flaring of skin and subcutaneous tissues (Ananda Samarasekera).

(Figures 3.72 and 3.73). Injuries are largely seen on the side of the body of the victim facing the explosion. Most mangling and the highest number of penetrating injuries are seen on the exposed area on the body surface of the victim closest to the explosion (Figure 3.74). The side of the body opposite to the explosion and other areas not stricken by missiles are usually spared of direct injuries, except for some due to the exit of penetrating missiles (Figures 3.75–3.77). A victim may lose a limb if hit by a shock wave, though small, and this in turn is dependent on the amount and the strength of the explosive charge and the distance (Figure 3.78). The characteristic peppering appearance due to the triad of blast injuries may be infrequently seen on the skin of some victims who were close to the blast. Burns and heat effects are usually uncommon on the victims. Skeletal injuries include penetrating fractures of different shapes and sizes (depending on the shrapnel used) in the skull, ribs, and long bones, sometimes associated with linear fractures. A transverse fracture of the long bone at the amputated site, together with multiple fractures associated with larger mechanical injuries such as lacerations, contusions, and abrasions in the distal part, is the common pattern of injury in dismembered limbs.

Mechanical injuries caused by indirect effects of the explosion, such as impact on falling, being struck by masonry, furnishing, and other similar objects, and the piercing of

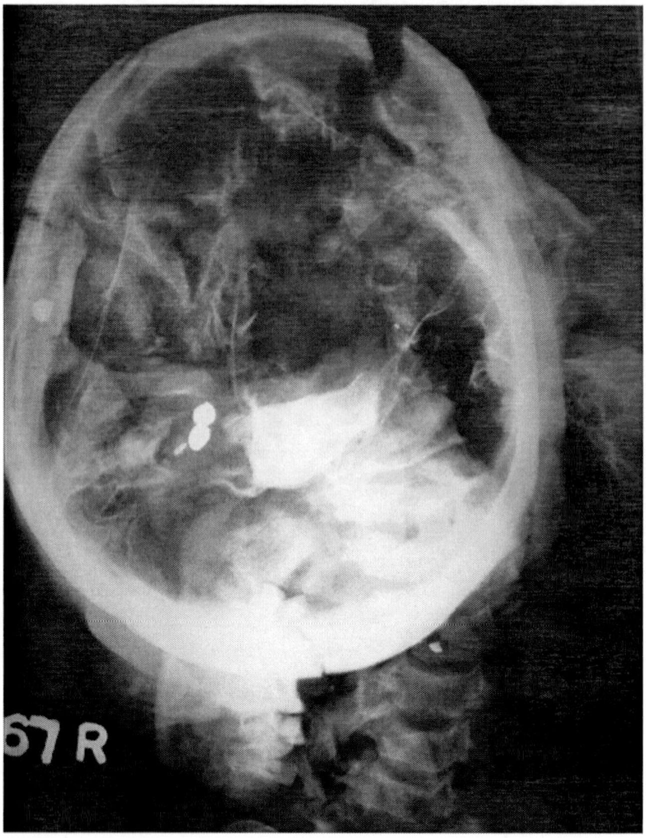

Figure 3.70 X-ray of the dismembered head of a carrier. Two penetrating fractures of the skull on both sides and the presence of high-density, somewhat circular opaque areas due to penetrated shrapnel. (Ananda Samarasekera, image courtesy of S.M Colombage, Judicial Medical Officer, Colombo South, Sri Lanka.)

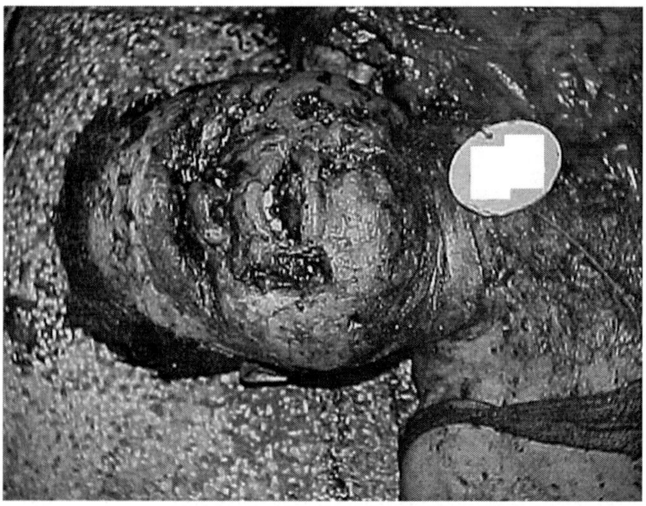

Figure 3.71 Upper part of the body of the targeted victim. Characteristic triad of injuries on the face together with large lacerations, contusions, and abrasions (Ananda Samarasekera).

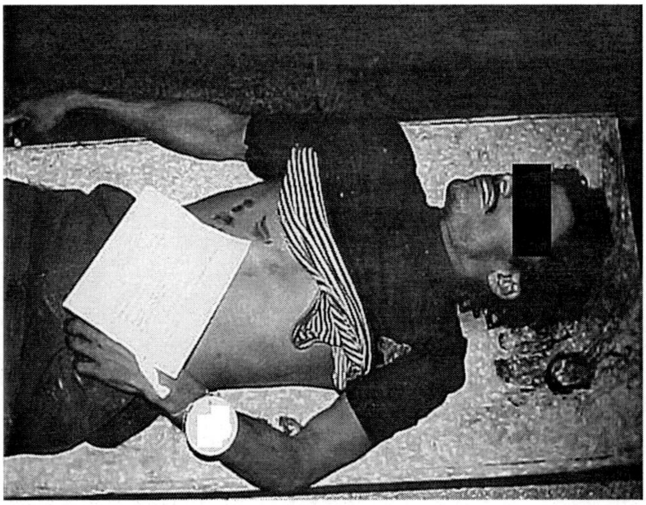

Figure 3.72 A dead victim of a human bomb blast. No damage, except for a few penetrating injuries to the front chest. The body was recovered at a distance of about 35 m (Ananda Samarasekera).

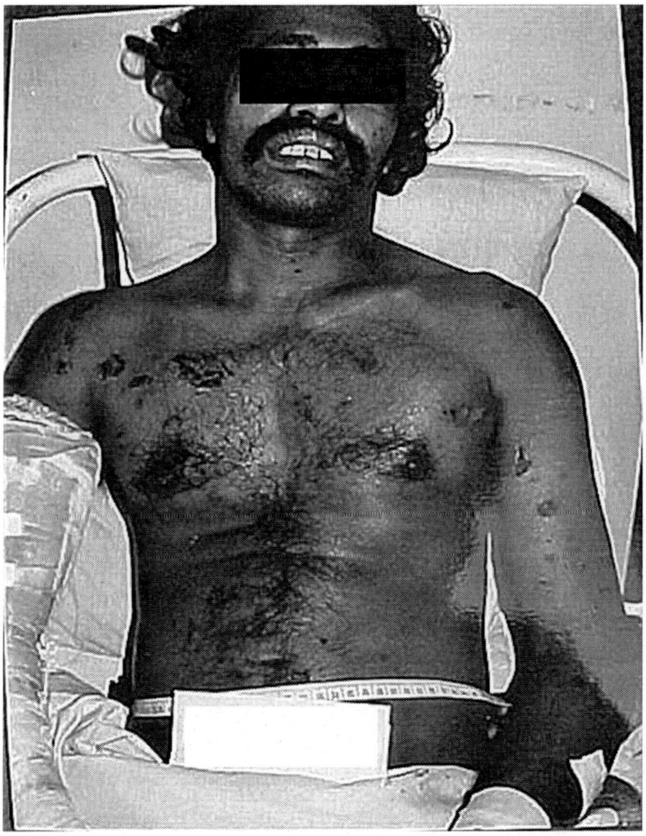

Figure 3.73 Survived victim of a human bomb blast. Only a few minor superficial injuries are present. He was standing at a distance of about 50 m (Ananda Samarasekera).

Figure 3.74 The front view of the lower part of the body of the victim shown in Figure 3.71. The body is more or less intact despite mangling on the front aspect due to multiple penetrating injuries (Ananda Samarasekera).

soft tissues and skin by fractured margins of bones, are not uncommon. Large perimortem injuries such as abrasions, contusions, lacerations, incised wounds, and even fractures could occur as a result of these effects. Such bodily damages could also occur during retrieval of bodies. These injuries and damages could be sustained both by the carrier and the victims making it difficult at times to distinguish them from those caused by direct effects of the explosion when both occur together or overlap (Figure 3.79).

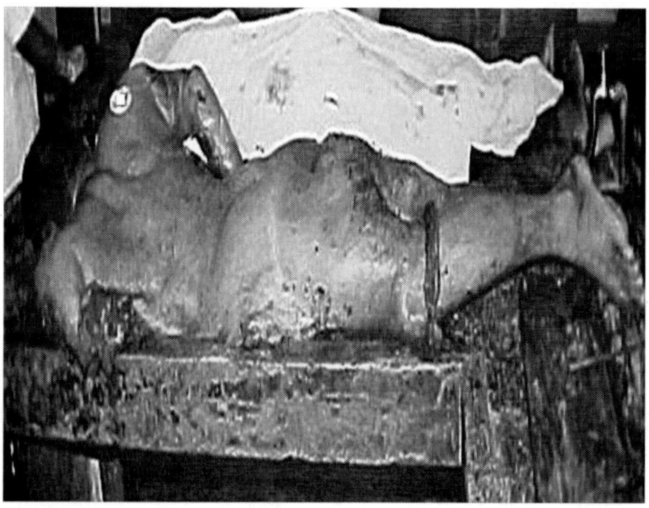

Figure 3.75 Back of the body shown in Figure 3.74. Except for a few penetrating injuries, the skin is almost undamaged and intact (Ananda Samarasekera).

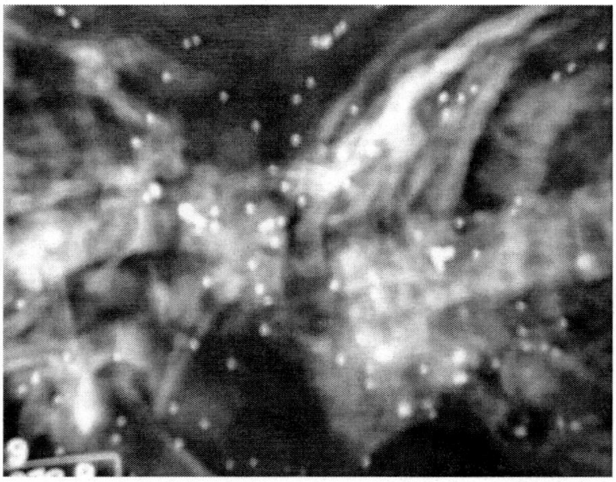

Figure 3.76 Preautopsy x-ray of the victim shown in Figure 3.71. Several circular high-density opacities due to presence of shrapnel (Ananda Samarasekera).

Apart from the primary and secondary effects of the explosion, some panic-stricken persons may sustain mechanical injuries due to falling, trampling, etc., when trying to run away. In most instances, there is *prima facie* inference of a bomb explosion, but at the outset, there may be very little confirmatory evidence of a human-bomb explosion. On contrary, there may be much speculation of a human bomb, but forensic evidence may show otherwise.

There have been a few instances of other suicide bomb attacks mimicking a human-bomb explosion at the outset, e.g., a motor cycle crashed onto the motor vehicle in which deputy chief of staff of the Sri Lankan Army was traveling on a public road on June 26, 2006,

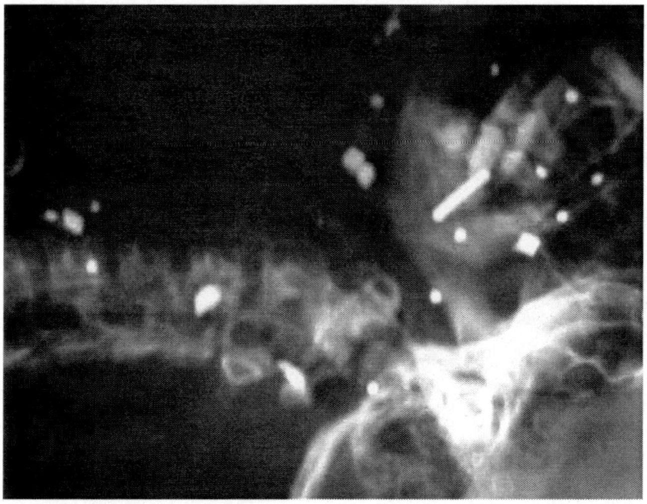

Figure 3.77 Preautopsy x-ray of a dead victim. Several high-density opacities of different sizes and shapes due to the presence of missiles (Ananda Samarasekera).

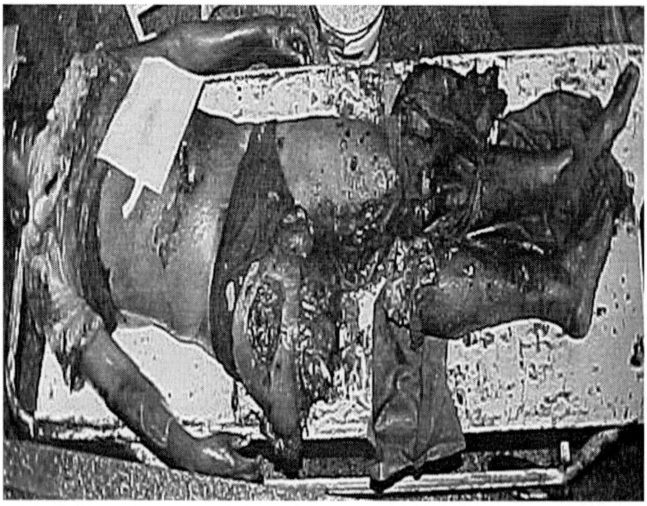

Figure 3.78 A dead victim of a human bomb blast. Amputation of the right lower limb at midthigh level (Ananda Samarasekera).

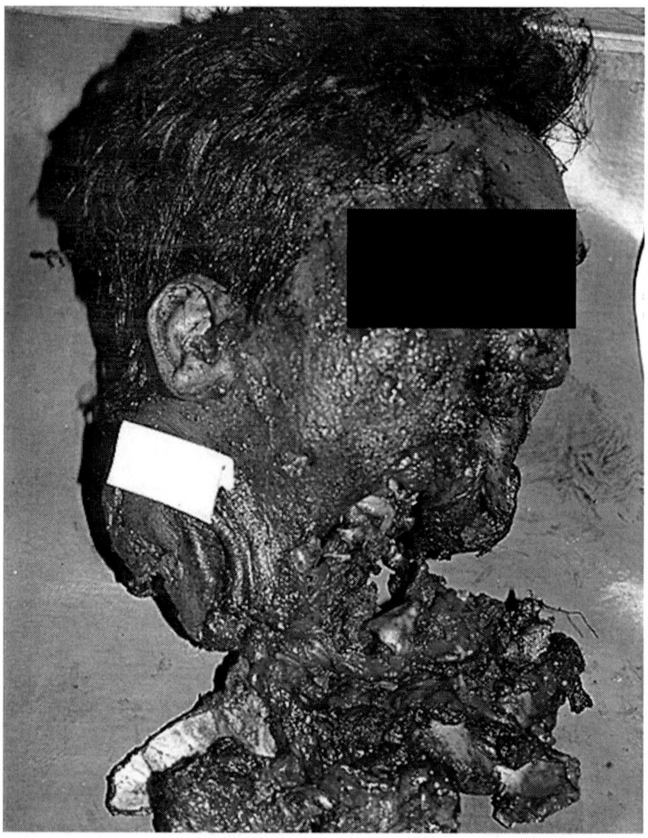

Figure 3.79 Decapitated head of a human bomber. Extensive injuries to the lower part of the head, which are difficult to distinguish from those due to secondary effects and other damages (Ananda Samarasekera).

killing him and few others.* The injury pattern on the remains of the bomber had some similarities to and differences from the usual injury pattern of a human bomb explosion. There was severing of all four limbs as in a case of a human bomb, but the burns were more extensive at the severed ends of the remaining parts; the entire neck was missing, and the head was extensively damaged with evidence of burning. There was a significantly high number of penetrating injuries in the remaining body parts, including the head. Forensic analysis of the wreck of the motorcycle concluded that the site of explosion was the upper surface of its petrol tank, which had burst. The reconstruction inferred that the rider detonated the bomb which was on the petrol tank while bending over it and the handle of the motor bicycle.† This case illustrates the importance of careful analysis of the injuries and their pattern and corroboration of the autopsy findings with other forensic evidence before arriving at final conclusions in an apparent case of a human bomb explosion.

Cause of Death

The carrier and some victims of human bombs may succumb to body trauma caused by the explosion, whereas others who were present at the site of the explosion may survive with or without injuries. The fatality and the survival period depend mainly on the lethality of the trauma, but both may be altered by timely retrieval and medical intervention.

The carrier is the first person to die, and the death is inevitable and instantaneous due to blasting and disintegrating of the body part, usually the torso, in which many vital organs essential for maintaining life are located. Some victims die due to injuries to vital organs or as a consequence of their effects such as hemorrhage. Necessarily fatal injuries to vital organs are usually caused by penetration of missiles, and most victims die of them. Victims who sustain such single or multiple, necessarily fatal penetrating injuries to the chest or head involving vital organs such as the heart, brain, or both could die instantaneously or immediately, whereas those who sustain a few penetrating injuries to nonvital organs or nonlethal injuries to vital organs may survive longer or recover. Some victims may sustain injuries that are not necessarily fatal but may die due to lack of medical intervention in time or delay in retrieval; e.g., hemorrhage due to penetrating injury of a kidney or severing of a limb. Those who are retrieved with nonfatal injuries and given medical treatment also could die due to subsequent complications such as infections, crush syndrome, or "neurogenic shock" syndrome. As the effect of the shock wave fall off very rapidly with the distance (Marshall 1978), which is very small in a human-bomb explosion, only those in the immediate vicinity could suffer some damage. Even when there is internal trauma caused by a small shock wave in some victims, death is invariably caused by penetrating injuries sustained as a result of their close proximity to the explosion; there is hardly any autopsy evidence of shock wave trauma as injuries due to penetrated missiles mask them. Burns due to flame and flash are not sufficient to cause deaths in human bomb explosions. Those who sustain mechanical injuries due to secondary mechanisms may die depending on the severity and the lethality of such injuries. Death due to traumatic or crush asphyxia caused by falling masonry or systemic air embolism described in other types of bomb blasts (Crane 2000) is not yet recorded in human bomb explosions in Sri Lanka.

* http://www.defence.lk.

† Personal communication with Dr. S. M. Colombage, Judicial Medical Officer, Colombo South. Sri Lanka. (The forensic pathologist investigated this case.)

Blunt Force Trauma

4

Crimes are committed by people. They are not committed by abstract entities like nationalities. The victims are not abstractions, although they are often perceived as such when their numbers accumulate by the thousands.

Louise Arbour*

Contents

The Pathophysiology of Blunt Force Injury 152
Establishing the Number and Sequence of Injuries 157
Cranial versus Postcranial Variation 158
  Cranial Fractures 158
  Atypical Wounds of Cranial Vault 164
  Mandibular Fractures 167
  Postcranial Injuries 170
Blunt Force Trauma Associated with Gunfire Injury 174
Summary Guidelines for Best Practice 176
  Case Study 4.1: The Interpretation of Skeletal Trauma Resulting from Injuries Sustained Prior to, and as a Direct Result of, Freefall *By O. Finegan* 181
  Case Study 4.2: A Khmer Rouge Execution Method—Evidence from Choeung Ek. *By S.C. Ta'ala, G.E. Berg, and K. Haden* 196

Blunt force trauma (BFT) is injury resulting from a broad instrument. The classification of BFT is dependent on the mechanism that caused the injury and is evident by the characteristics of the wound, particularly in light of the specific bone affected. Spitz (1993, 199) wrote, "A sharp object, such as a knife or a broken piece of glass, cuts and divides the tissues as it penetrates. A wound produced by blunt impact tears, shears and crushes, falls or blows with a blunt instrument, such as a hammer, brick, mat, fist or pipe, typically result in blunt injury."

BFT may result from a variety of objects used as weapons as evident in this definition, and most commonly in human rights (HHRR) investigations it occurs in cases of beatings, torture, and explosions.

The purpose of this chapter is to provide a brief overview of blunt force injuries, guidelines for establishing the number and sequence of injuries, and common patterns observed for the skull and various postcranial elements. Importantly, interpreting BFT in combination with gunfire injuries is also discussed. For example, BFT trauma may occur in gunfire cases when the projectile strikes the bone, creating a crushing injury but does not penetrate the bone, as discussed later in this chapter. In addition, two interesting contributed case

* Louise Arbour (former chief prosecutor, ICTY) cited in Stover and Peress (1998, 314).

studies are presented at the end of this chapter. Case study 4.1, by Finegan, discusses extensive BFT injuries resulting from a forced fall into a deep cave, and Case study 4.2, by Ta'ala and coworkers, discusses cranial BFT resulting from extrajudicial executions in Cambodia.

The category BFT includes a variety of mechanizing forces such as direct impact, crushing, acceleration–deceleration, or sharp–blunt impact. Consequently, examples appear throughout many of the chapters of this book. Refer to chapters 3, 5, and 6 for more examples of BFT.

The Pathophysiology of Blunt Force Injury

The circumstance surrounding the mechanizing force is an important variable to consider when interpreting BFT. For example, did the object hit an individual (i.e., the object may be a club, the butt of a gun, or a fist)? Conversely, was the individual thrown through the air following an explosion? BFT is characterized by a low or high load; low-force injuries result from an object hitting a person, such as a club or hammer, whereas high-force injuries result from an object hitting a person during an explosion or when the person is pushed from the force of a blast and hits a stationary object. Blunt force injury to bone results in a variety of different types of fractures, depending on the biomechanical properties of bone, as previously discussed in Chapter 2, and external factors such as the class of weapon. For more discussion of the biomechanical properties affected bone, particularly with regard to BFT, refer to the literature cited (Moritz 1954; Gurdjian et al. 1950; Curry 1970; Rogers 1992; Harkess et al. 1984; Berryman et al. 1995; Symes et al. 1991; Berryman and Symes 1998; and Galloway 1999).

The mechanical properties of blunt force affect skeletal elements differently, depending on the shape or composition of the bone, the size and shape of the impacting instrument, the age of the victim, and the amount of applied force. For example, thick or dense areas of bone will displace the force, and the fracture will travel around large or thick skeletal features such as an eminence or buttress. Gurdjian et al. (1950) found that the particular anatomy, type of bone, and morphological features of the injured area may affect the presence and appearance of wounds, such as the thickness of the cranial vault or enlarged Pacchionian pits. Osteoporosis or cranial vault thinning due to advanced age has also been shown to result in greater cranial fracturing (Berryman and Symes 1998; Byers 2005). Figure 4.1 depicts a circular defect on the skull. The defect is patterned with a narrow focus that forms a "plug" resulting from the crushing force. The margins of the defect are bent inward; refer to Figures 4.2 and 4.3.

The overall distribution of injuries is useful for interpreting the mechanism of injury (Table 4.1). The high number of variables affecting blunt force wound variation results in part from the number of mechanizing forces that cause injury. In documenting skeletal wounds, the location, length, width, shape, fracture type, and fracture patterns of wounds (Lovell 1997) are recorded. In general terms, the speed (i.e., a blow to the head from a hammer versus flying debris in an explosion) and weight of force are essential aspects in describing blunt force injuries to bone (Stewart 1979). Skeletal wounds may also reflect the size and shape of the object—a *patterned injury*. Most often, patterned injuries will be evident in the cranial vault or other *flat bones*, such as the ilium. For

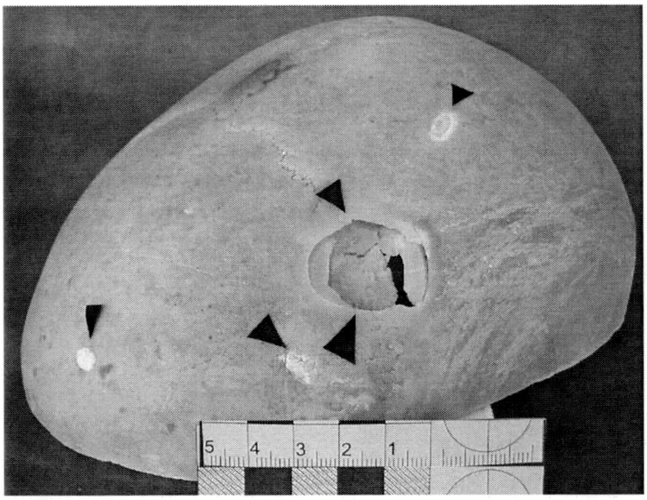

Figure 4.1 Ectocranial view of patterned, crushing injury (Jorge Pachón.)

example, Figures 4.4 and 4.5 exhibit a large irregularly shaped depressed fracture on left frontal bone. There are no fractures radiating from the defect, nor does the defect entirely perforate through the skull. Note the rim along the left edge of the defect where bone reflects inward. This is a patterned injury resulting from a crushing force. Given the range of possible weapons and variables affecting wound morphology, patterned injuries may not always be evident.

It is recommended that focus be given to the class, rather than the specific type, of instrument that caused the injury. A cranial reconstruction derived through 3D-CT imaging, depicts the multiple blunt and sharp force wounds to the skull (Figure 4.6) (refer to Meyers et al. 1999 for full discussion of this case). The left parietal and temporal region

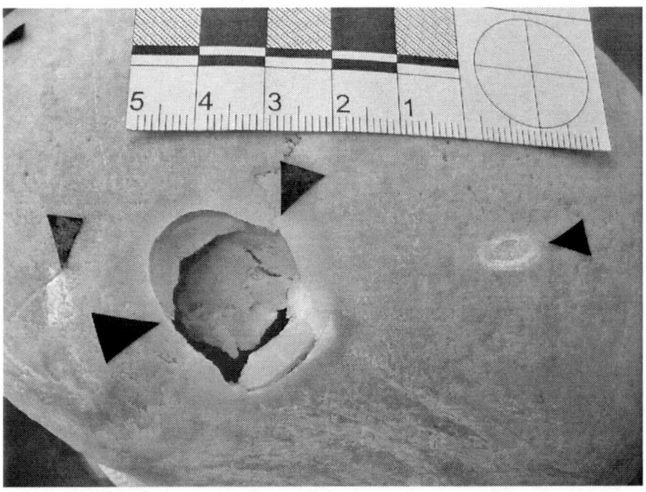

Figure 4.2 (See color insert following page 38) Close-up ectocranial view of skull with patterned injury (Jorge Pachón).

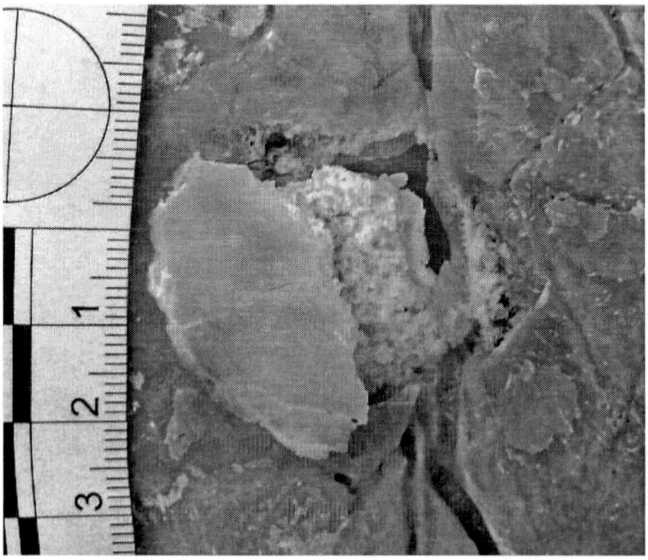

Figure 4.3 (See color insert following page 38) Endocranial view of crater defect with a bone plug displaced internally (Jorge Pachón).

Table 4.1 Variables Affecting Wound Variation in BFT

Intrinsic Factors/Bone	Applied Force	Extrinsic Factors/Weapon	Distribution
• Shape	• High (strong)	• Shape	• Localized
• Density	• Moderate	• Size	• Generalized
• Location	• Low (light)	• Weight	• Whole body affected
		• Speed	

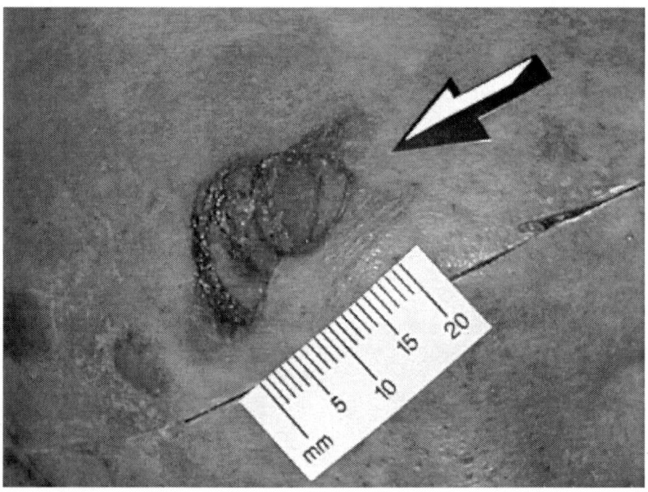

Figure 4.4 Close-up ectocranial view of depressed cranial fracture. The small, comminuted bone fragments within the affected area are clearly visible (Jorge Pachón).

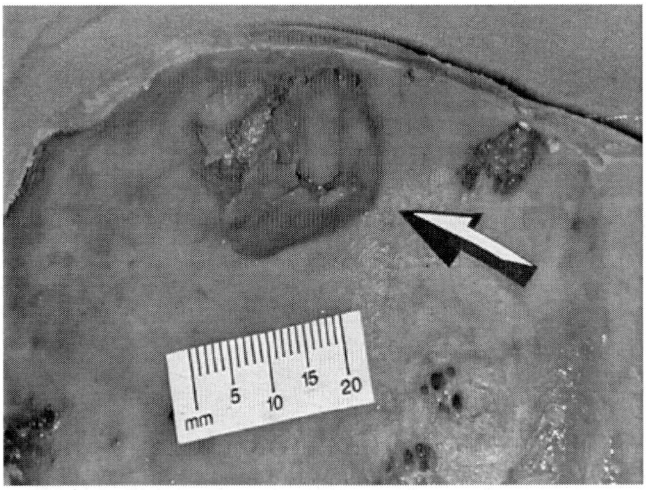

Figure 4.5 Endocranial view of depressed cranial fracture. The incomplete nature of the fracture indicates a slow load force (Jorge Pachón).

exhibits a large, oval-shaped defect with complete and hoop fractures. The posterior view of skull exhibits a patterned circular defect to the left parietal (Figure 4.7). Note that the right aspect of the fracture is incomplete and bent inward, a common occurrence in BFT to the skull. Patterned defects mimic the shape of the weapon. In this case, the defect most closely resembles either a hammer or a crowbar. Molds of each weapon were created to match the characteristics of the weapons to the defect on the back of the skull (Figure 4.8).

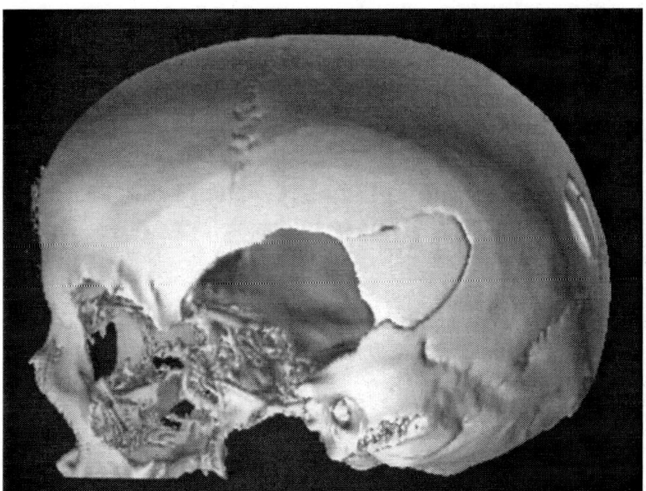

Figure 4.6 3D cranial reconstruction based on CT imaging. This young female received multiple blunt and sharp force wounds to the cranial vault, face, neck, and thorax. Nine distinct fractures are present on the skull. The left parietal and temporal region exhibits a large, oval-shaped defect with complete and hoop fractures. (Image courtesy of Dr. Matthias Okoye and David Kiple)

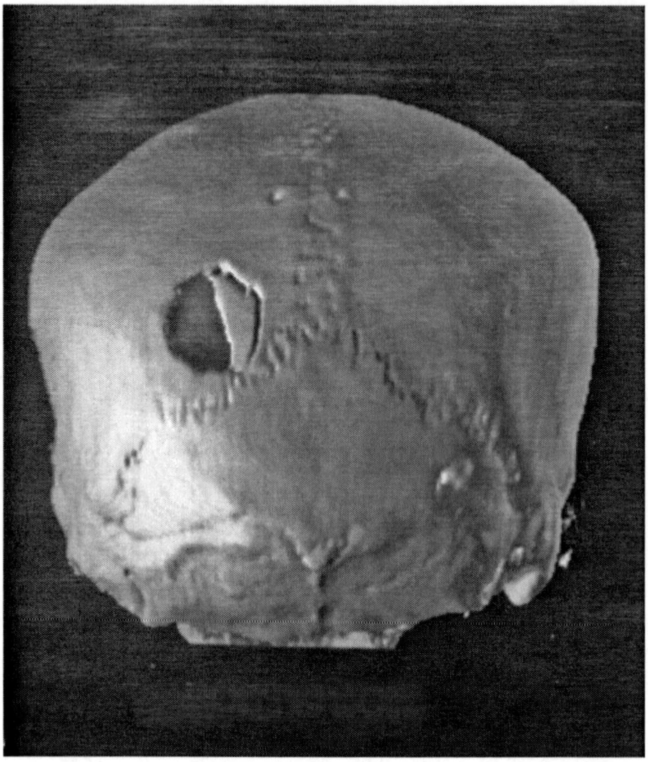

Figure 4.7 Posterior view of the skull exhibits patterned circular defect to left parietal. Note that the right aspect of the fracture is incomplete and bent ("pushed-in"), a common occurrence in BFT to the skull. (Image courtesy of Dr. Matthias Okoye and David Kiple.)

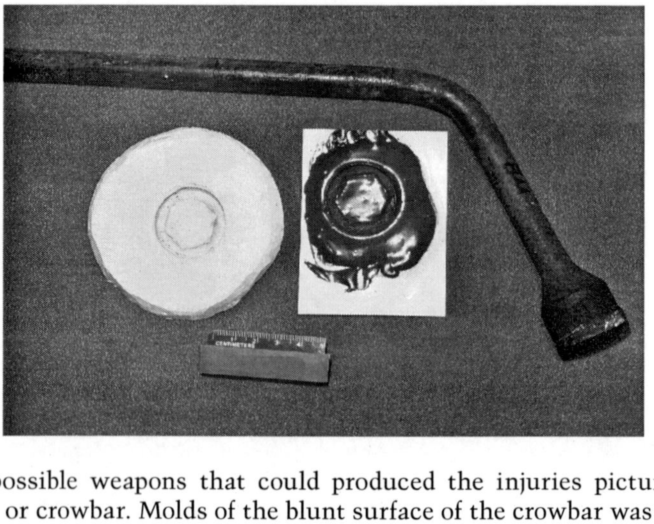

Figure 4.8 The possible weapons that could produced the injuries pictured in Figure 4.7 include a hammer or crowbar. Molds of the blunt surface of the crowbar was made to compare the size, shape, and pattern to that observed on the skull. (Image courtesy of Dr. Matthias Okoye and David Kiple.)

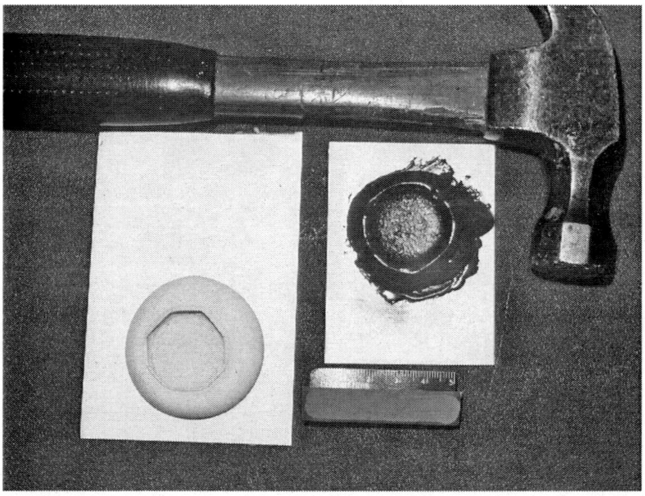

Figure 4.9 The wound characteristics are most consistent with the hammer. Note the outer edges of the cranial defect and the outer edges of the hammer impression (Figure 4.7). Both are patterned with straight edges in octagon shape. In contrast, the crowbar is circular, with patterned straight edges on the internal area. (Image courtesy of Dr. Matthias Okoye and David Kiple.)

Note the internal difference in shape between the crowbar and the hammer. Based on this comparison, the wound characteristics are most consistent with the hammer (Figure 4.9), although the shape of the defect does not indicate which exact hammer was used.

Establishing the Number and Sequence of Injuries

The estimated number of injuries, as always, is the *minimum number*, because evidence of multiple injuries may overlap one another. The number is calculated by the inventory and distribution of wounds. Analysis of fracture lines that are arrested by previously occurring fractures is necessary for estimating the number and sequence of injuries in cases of multiple blows to the same bone or region, particularly in the cranial vault, ilium, or other *flat bones*. The technique used to order multiple injuries based on intersecting fracture lines, referred to as *Puppe's rule* (Madea and Staak 1988; Rhine and Curran 1990), assumes a fracture line will generally be arrested by a preexisting fracture. The sequence of impacts may be estimated by distinguishing which fracture lines intersected preexisting fractures. Although this technique was originally applied to blunt force trauma, it can also be applied to gunfire injuries. Figure 4.10 depicts blunt force injury to left occipitotemporal area of an adult cranium, along inferior lambdoidal suture. Force was applied directly, with a narrow focus. A large radiating fracture extends superiorly along the occipital and left parietal. Note that the fracture on the occipital is larger than the fracture on the parietal that appears as an isolated thin infarction.

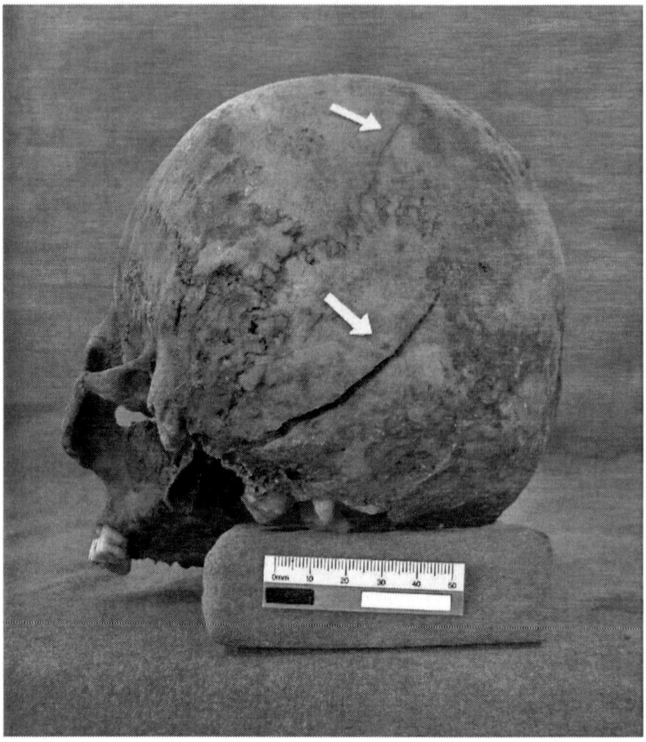

Figure 4.10 Adult cranium, left lateral view. Blunt force injury to left occipitotemporal area. Two fractures present. A large radiating fracture extends superiorly along the occipital, and a second fracture is present on the left parietal. (Image printed with permission from ICTY.)

Cranial versus Postcranial Variation

Cranial Fractures

Cranial fractures resulting from blunt force trauma primarily consist of *depressed, radiating, comminuted, blowout,* or *basilar* fractures (Figure 4.11). The bone around the point of impact bends inward, away from the direction of force, in cases of *depressed fractures.* Depressed fractures may occur up to 1 inch in any direction around the point of impact (Lovell 1997). Gurdjian et al. (1950) describe the biomechanical properties of skeletal wounds such as the inbending that occurs at point of impact, and the outbending of skeletal tissue along the parameter of this area. Fractures may occur in the inner table at of the point of impact, depending on the level of force. According to Gurdjian et al. (1950, 313):

> At impact, the area around the point of application of the blow is inbended. Simultaneously, there is an outbending of the bone peripheral to the inbended area. This outbending is selective and may be localized to a certain part of the skull, where a linear fracture is initiated due to the resultant tearing-apart forces.

Gurdjian et al. (1950) further demonstrated experimentally that, as force is applied to bone and bends inward at that point, the peripheral areas where "outbending" occurs

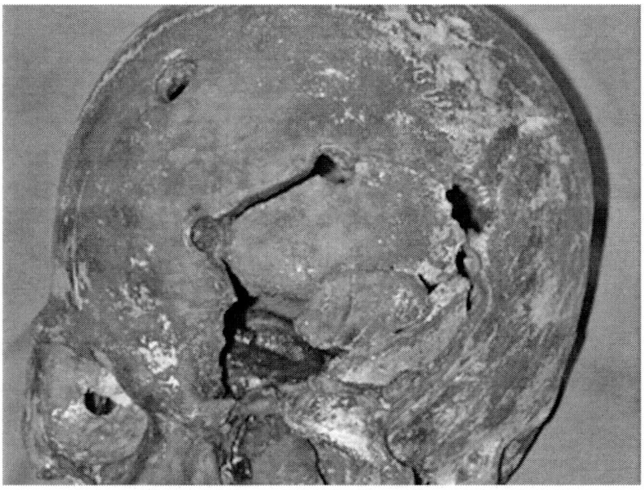

Figure 4.11 Ectocranial surface of blunt force fracture with comminuted fracture to the frontal bone and subsequent craniometry. Note the active bone remodeling on endocrinal surface. Also, note the bone remodeling and growth in the large radiating fractures. (Image printed with permission from ICTY.)

may fracture. More recent experimental research challenges this notion, suggesting that fractures only originate at the point of impact, not in peripheral areas (Kroman 2004).

If the force is great enough, it will penetrate the skull and fractures will radiate from the point of impact. Secondary fractures or concentric fractures may form. The fracture will follow predictable patterns based in curvature or anatomical features, bone thickness, sinus cavities, sutures, or preexisting fracture lines. Often, the fracture follows the path of least resistance (Vance 1927). For example, the region of the supercillary arches, glabella, or the external occipital protuberance provide thick areas, around which fractures tend to form (Moritz 1954; Rogers 1992). The sinus cavities and surrounding soft tissues also play an important role in dissipating force and fracture formation.

In a second example of BFT resulting from a hammer in a case from Guatemala (courtesy of FAFG), patterned defects to the skull with depressed fractures and complete penetration of the bone are depicted (Figures 4.12–4.15). The large "circular" defect is consistent in size and shape with the flat head of a hammer. Many other objects also leave patterned wounds. Figures 4.16–4.20 illustrate multiple views of an adult cranium that had received multiple blunt force injuries to the head with the leg of a chair (courtesy J. Pachón). Note there are two patterned defects, though different from one another in size and shape. The outer edge is roughly ^-shaped. Figure 4.17 depicts the endocranial surface of a patterned injury, with a narrow focus and significant crushing/deformation around the edges. In this example, as with the previous case, there are no radiating fractures.

According to Lovell (1997), penetrating wounds that create a defect occur with a minimal area of the skull affected. Bone in the area of applied force absorbs the energy and either rebounds or forms "a plug" of the same approximate size that is then internally displaced. In cases of a greater amount of force, concentric fractures form around the point of impact, and wedge-shaped bone fragments are displaced inward (Berryman and Symes 1998). This type of fracture is called a hoop or concentric fracture. Blunt force to the ilium, other

Figure 4.12 (See color insert following page 38) Right lateral view, adult cranium (Carlos Jacinto, FAFG). Multiple BFT resulting from assault with hammer.

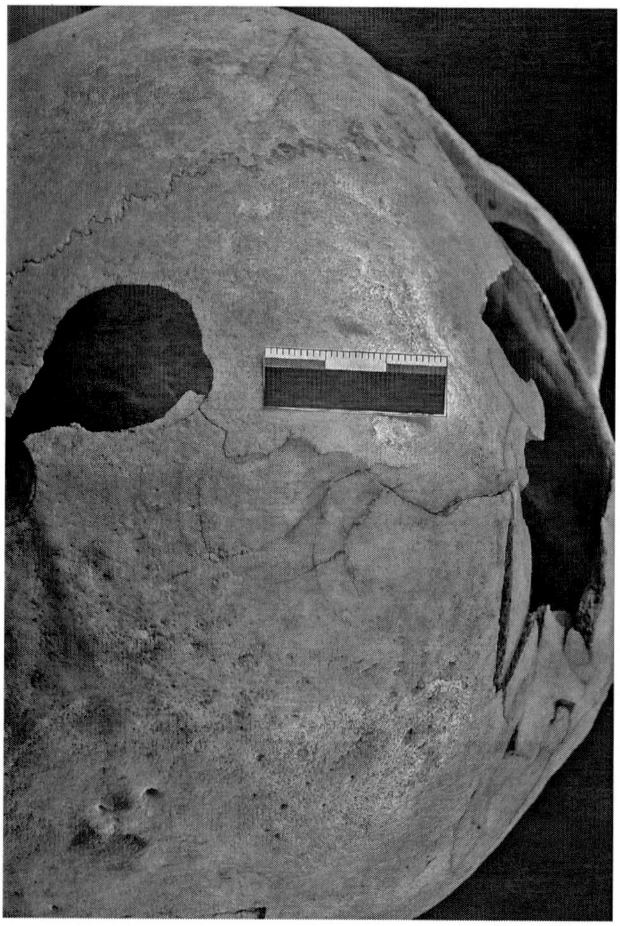

Figure 4.13 Close-up view of superior right side of the skull. Circular patterned injury reflecting shape of hammer (Carlos Jacinto, FAFG).

Figure 4.14 Close-up view of posterior-right side of the skull. BFT resulting from assault with a hammer (Carlos Jacinto, FAFG).

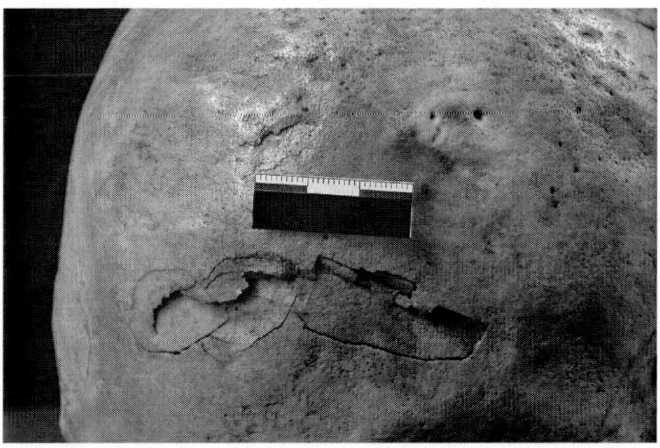

Figure 4.15 Posterior view, adult cranium. Incomplete fracture from hammer (Carlos Jacinto, FAFG).

Figure 4.16 Ectocranial view of the superior view. BFT resulting from assault with wood chair leg (Jorge Pachón).

flat bones, or the ends of long bones (the femur in particular) sometimes results in similar appearing depressed fractures. Depressed fractures typically occur when an object strikes the skeletal tissue. In contrast, in cases in which an individual falls or is thrown against an object, as in an explosion, radiating fractures, away from the point of impact, are common

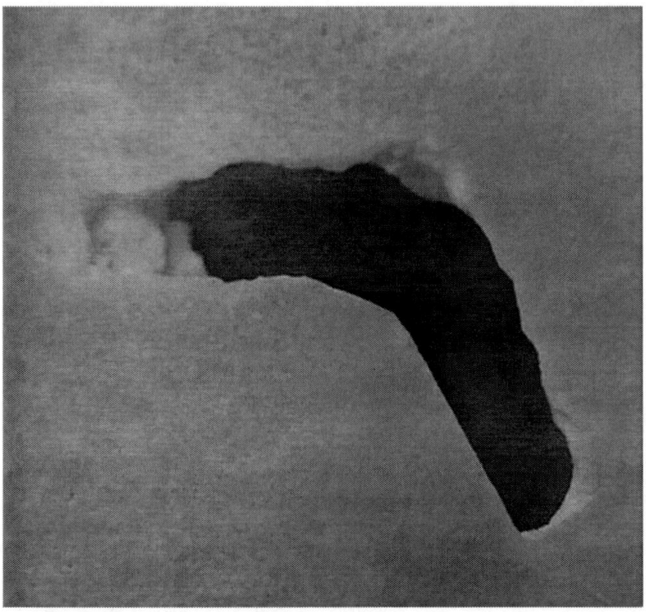

Figure 4.17 Ectocranial view of defect 1. Patterned injury resulting from the leg of a wood chair. Narrow focus without radiating fracture or significant crushing/deformation around the edges (Jorge Pachón).

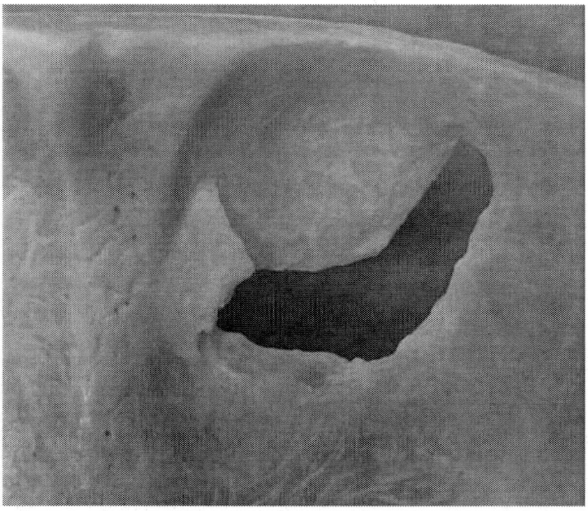

Figure 4.18 Endocranial view of defect 1 (refer to image 4.17). Wedge of bone "peels" inward (Jorge Pachón).

Figure 4.19 Ectocranial view of defect 2. Note the small, well-defined shape of the defect (Jorge Pachón).

Figure 4.20 Endocranial view of defect 2 (refer to Figure 4.19). Bone is displaced inward, but defect does not completely penetrate the bone (Jorge Pachón).

and depression fractures are rare (Spitz 1993). According to Stewart (1979), these fractures are called *countre-coup* because it is believed that the force penetrates through the calvarium, resulting in fractures from what is essentially a "second blow." *Countre-coup* fractures often result from force applied to the superior or posterior regions of the skull and typically result in comminuted fractures of the thin bones of the eye orbits (Spitz 1993, 236). It should be noted that such fractures may result from blunt force or gunfire injuries (Spitz 1993) and are discussed in further detail in Chapters 7 and 8 of this volume.

Atypical Wounds of Cranial Vault

Two unusual cases of blunt force trauma to the skull, with subsequent craniometries are presented. In case I, the skull of an adult male was recovered from a multiple grave in Croatia (Figure 4.21). During the postmortem examination, it was noted that there was a large hoop fracture running across the top of the cranium from side to side. A large oval

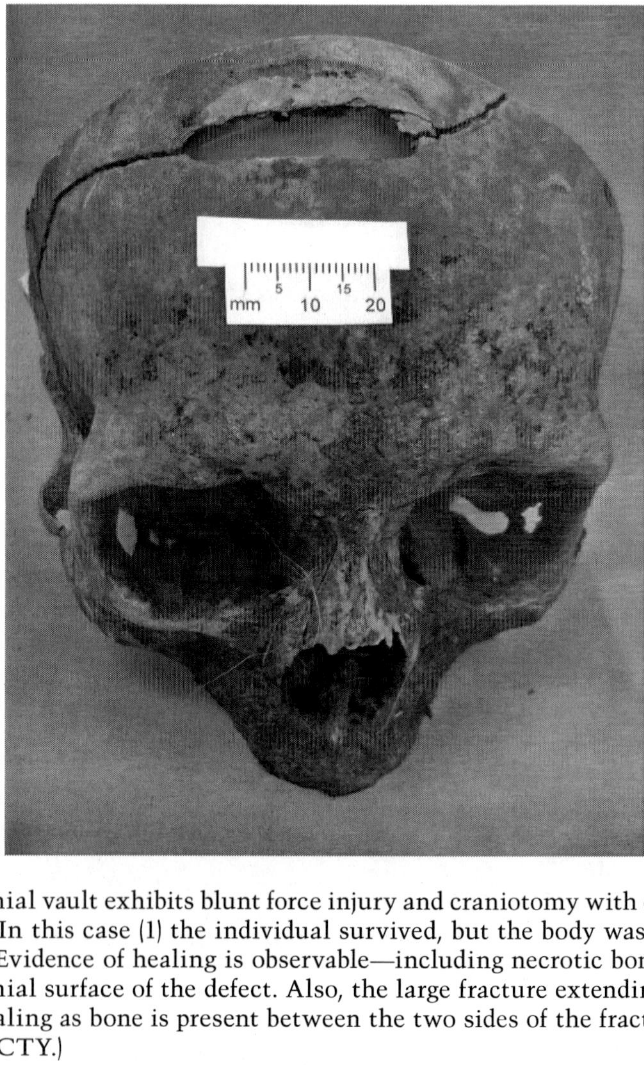

Figure 4.21 Cranial vault exhibits blunt force injury and craniotomy with evidence of moderate bone healing. In this case (1) the individual survived, but the body was later recovered in a multiple grave. Evidence of healing is observable—including necrotic bone tissue along the posterior, ectocranial surface of the defect. Also, the large fracture extending across the skull shows signs of healing as bone is present between the two sides of the fracture. (Printed with permission from ICTY.)

Figure 4.22 Endocranial view of trephinated skull. Note the presence of bone remodeling, indicating the individual survived for a short period of time, case I. (Image printed with permission from ICTY).

defect perforated the frontal bone. Further, there was evidence of bone remodeling around the edges of the defect endocranially, within the margins of the large facture, and necrotic tissue on the ectocranial surface (Figure 4.22). This evidence demonstrated the individual survived for some period of time after sustaining this injury as the fractures were in the process of healing at the time of his death. Following this incident he was later killed and disposed of in a multiple grave as the fractures were in the process of healing.

In case II, a similar hoop fracture due to blunt force trauma is present on the skull of an adult male (Figures 4.23 and 4.24). In this case, the individual sustained massive cranial trauma, and surgical intervention was attempted. The margins of the defect are scalloped

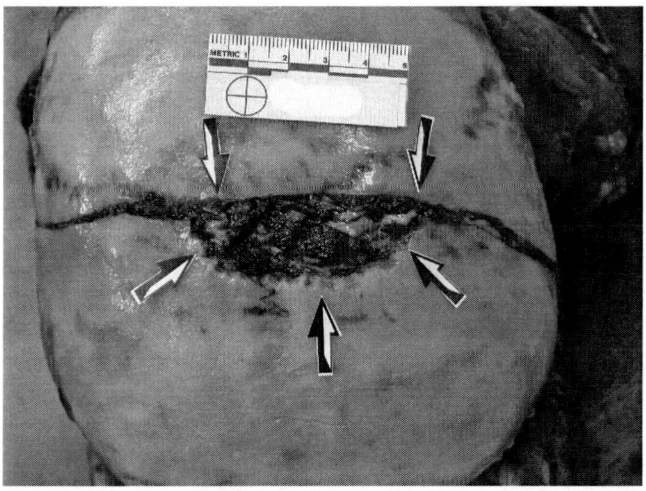

Figure 4.23 A large hoop fracture is evident across the cranial vault. The fracture extends across the coronal section of the cranium. Surgical intervention was attempted, but the victim died. The large defect, with a regular scalloped edge along the posterior rim is a result of the craniotomy, case 2 (Alain Wittmann).

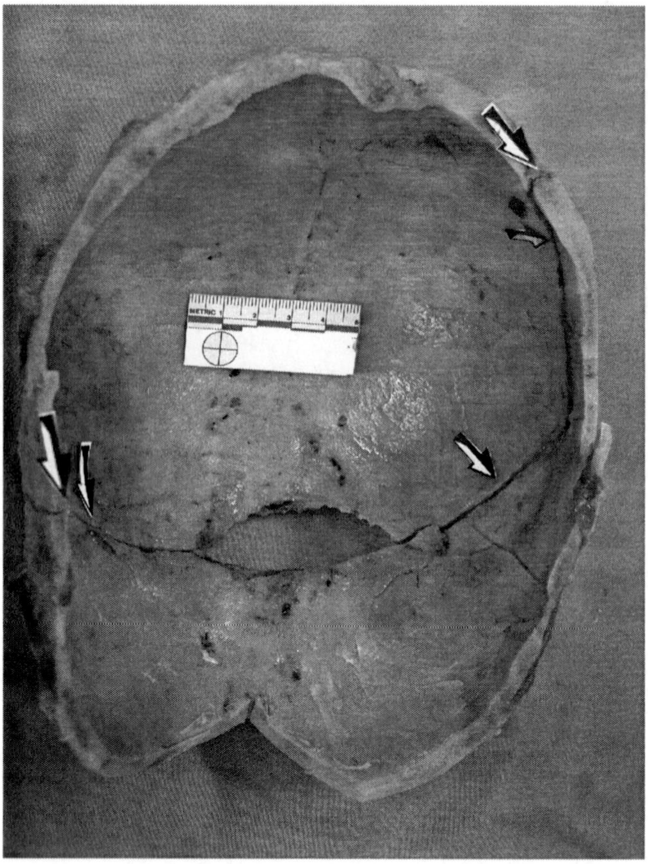

Figure 4.24a Endocranial view of blunt force fracture and craniotomy case 2 (Alain Wittmann).

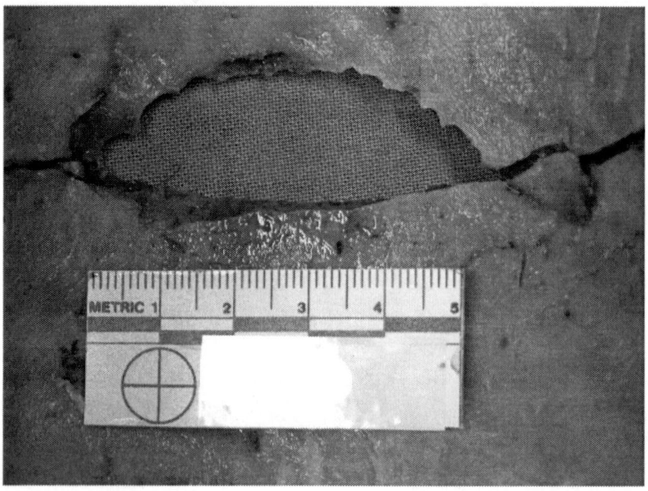

Figure 4.24b Close-up view Figure 4.24a, endocranial view, case 2 (Alain Wittmann).

in a uniform pattern, consistent with trephination. In this instance, the individual did not survive the surgery and was subsequently autopsied.

The postmortem findings of cranial injuries, the timing of the injury in the first case, and evidence of medical intervention in these two cases provide a clear comparison of identical fractures with and without bone remodeling. Further, they demonstrate that once bone remodeling alters the edges of the defect, the scalloped margins are less clear, and the circumstances around the injury are more difficult to interpret. At the time of the initial postmortem examination (case I), the circumstances of this injury, within the given context (i.e., a multiple grave), were open to interpretation. The subsequent documented case provides a clear picture of injury mechanisms and subsequent medical intervention that occurred for both incidents.

Mandibular Fractures

Direct blows to the mandible are generally straightforward. However, cases where more than one mechanism is present or suspected can prove more challenging. Mandibular fractures generally occur as either a consequence of anteroposterior force applied to the chin or lateral force applied against the ascending ramus of the mandible. DuChesne et al. (2003) describes injuries from lateral force correlated to assault and is discussed further in Chapter 5.

The necessary force required to break the lateral aspect of the mandible is lower than force applied from front to back or anteriorly (Figures 4.25 and 4.26). Through an experimental model, Unnewehr et al. (2003) established that a frontal or anterior impact against the chin would make the bone fail at a distance of 150 cm, requiring a force between 2.5 and 3.1 kN. In contrast, force applied laterally may cause a fracture from a distance of 70 cm but with a greater amount of force, between 0.6 and 0.8 kN. The result of these experiments confirmed that force applied to the front of the mandible results in symmetrical fracturing at the angle and/or the posterior margin of the mandibular body, condyles, and coronoid processes. In contrast, lateral force to the mandible typically causes unilateral fracturing, radiating from the point of impact. One important modifying factor is that occlusion plays a significant role in predicting fracture patterns. In other words, a tightly closed mouth creates more resistance to an external blow from any direction.

As the work of Unnewehr et al. (2003) demonstrates, fractures resulting from the front/anterior direction, require a specific amount of force and distance. One possible weapon that could meet these conditions is the butt of a military rifle. In 23 cases of extrajudicial executions in Peru, the cause of death was high-velocity gunfire injuries from military rifles (n = 7) and handguns (n = 15). Two of the seven individuals killed with a military rifle exhibited unilateral mandibular fractures of the body at the level of the second or third molar (Figures 4.27 and 4.28). No mandibular fractures were present for any of the handgun cases. Although this example does not prove whether lateral mandibular impacts resulted from BFT due to being struck with the rifle before being shot, it does demonstrate a possible association between a weapon used to cause death and other mechanisms of injury.

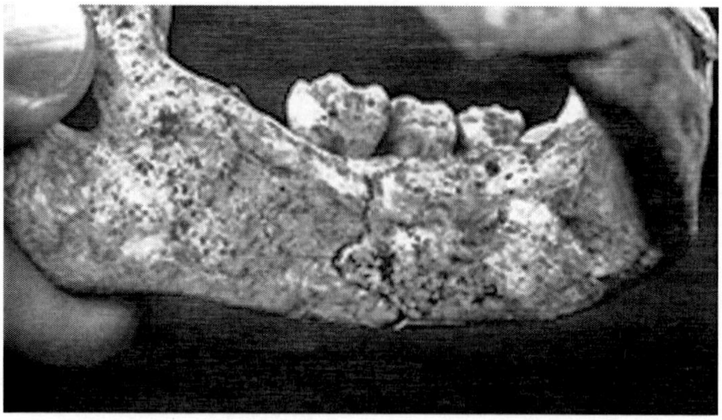

Figure 4.25a Internal view of left side of mandibular body showing breakaway spur indicating that the point of impact was external (Carlos Jacinto, FAFG).

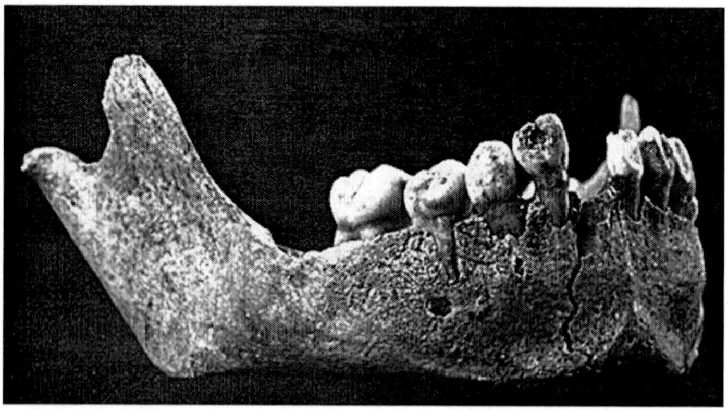

Figure 4.25b Vertical fracture of mandible with formation of wedge in the symphyseal area indicating point of impact (Carlos Jacinto, FAFG).

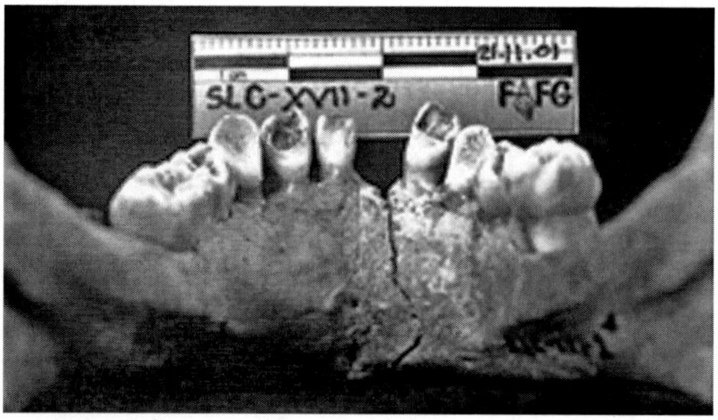

Figure 4.25c Internal view of the same case showing fracture of mandible between central incisors (Carlos Jacinto, FAFG).

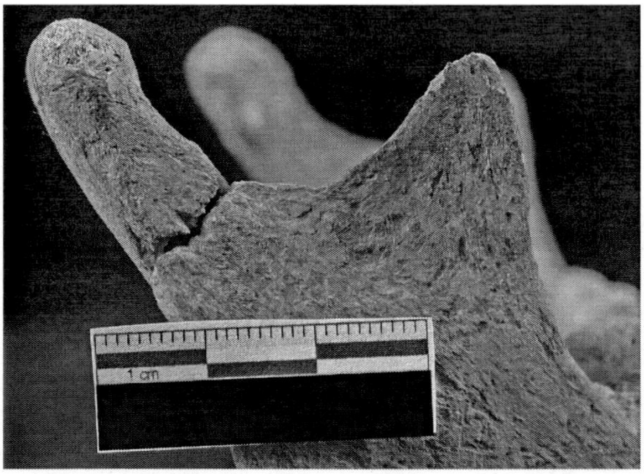

Figure 4.26a Sub-condylar fracture; right side (Carlos Jacinto, FAFG).

Figure 4.26b Oblique fracture across ascending ramus between the condyle and the coronoid process (Carlos Jacinto, FAFG).

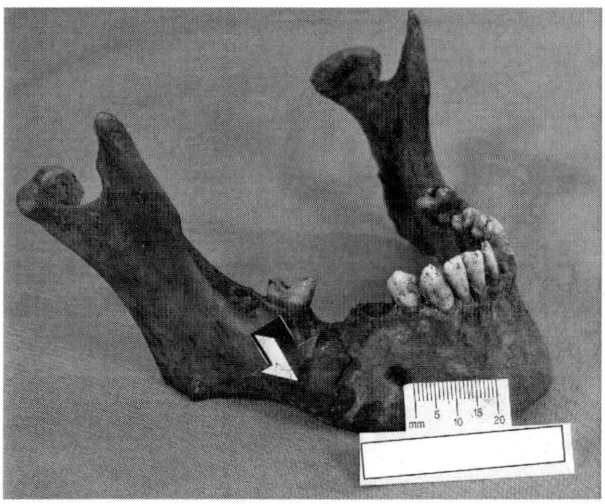

Figure 4.27 Mandibular fracture on right side of the body. The breakaway spur is located externally indicating that compression was applied internally. This would have happened as a result of an intraoral gunshot wound (Alain Wittmann).

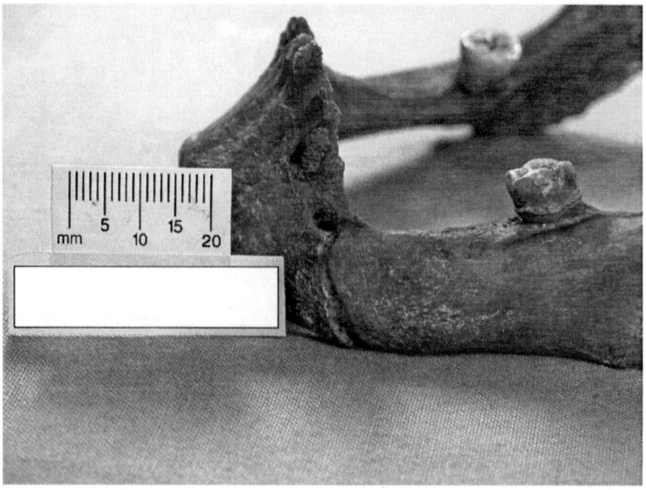

Figure 4.28 Oblique mandibular fracture of left side of the body. The breakaway spur is located internally indicating blunt force was applied externally around the area where the fracture is located (see also 4.25a) (Alain Wittmann).

Postcranial Injuries

Blunt force injuries to the postcranial skeleton are innumerable; for a thorough discussion and classification refer to Galloway (1999). Direct injuries to postcranial elements are described in Chapter 5. In this section, several examples of variation in wounding morphology from direct impact to the ribs (Figure 4.29), sternum, vertebra, and fibula (Figures 4.30–4.32) are illustrated. It should also be noted that blunt force injuries to the hands and arms are commonly observed when a person attempts to shield herself/himself

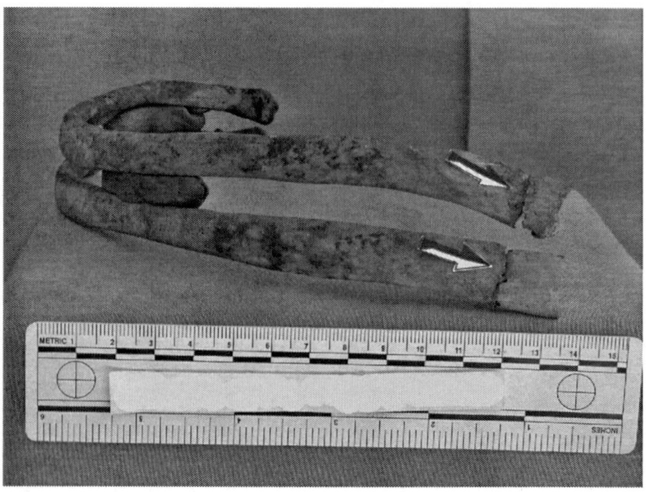

Figure 4.29a Adjacent rib fractures along sternal margin of the ribs. Fractures resulted from compression to the sternal area resulting from a beating (Alain Wittmann).

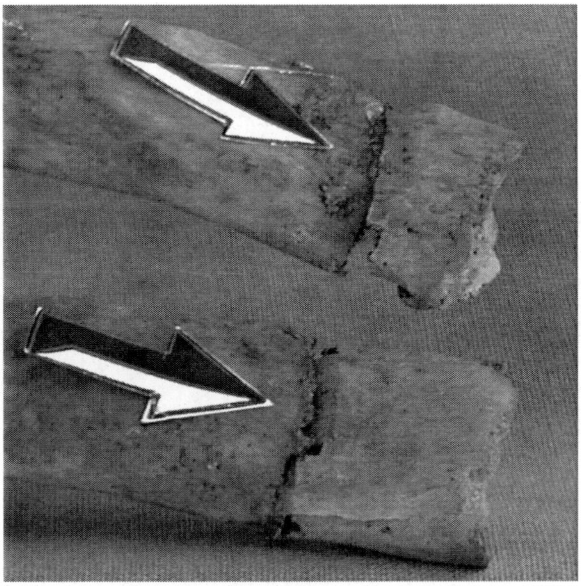

Figure 4.29b Close-up view of rib fractures, anterior surface (Alain Wittmann).

from an attacker or flying debris. This category of wounds are generally referred to as *defensive wounds*. Defensive wounds are observed with all different types of injury mechanisms, BFT, GSW, and SFT, provided the person's hands are not bound, and able to be moved them into that position. In cases of torture, often the victim is bound and unable to defend him or herself, therefore there may be a distinct lack of defensive injuries in some types of

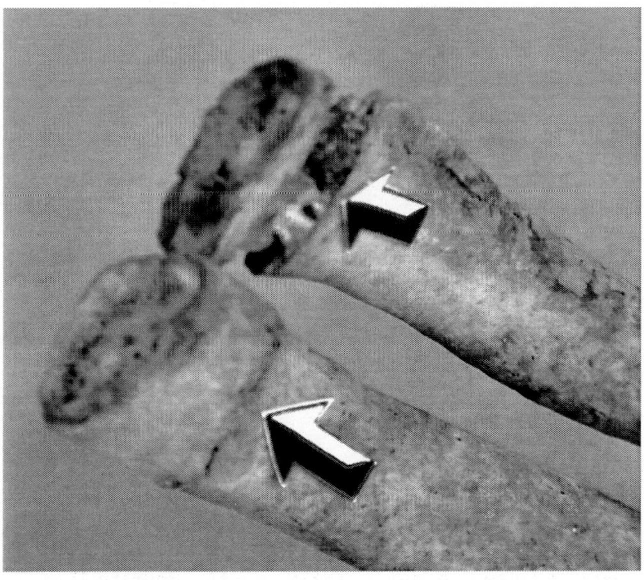

Figure 4.29c Close-up view of rib fractures, posterior surface (Alain Wittmann).

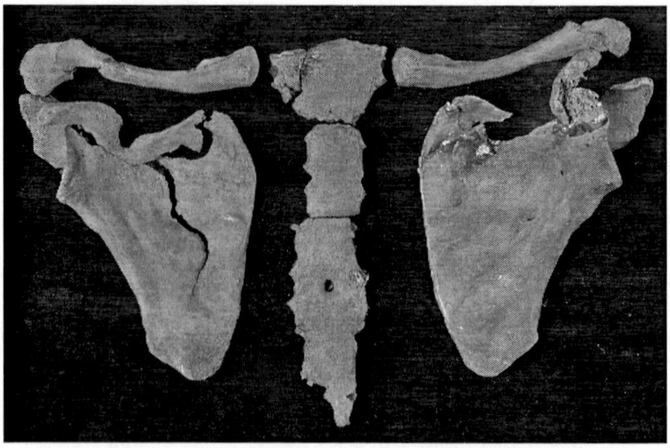

Figure 4.30a Pectoral girdle, anterior surface, left side. Blunt force injuries (Carlos Jacinto).

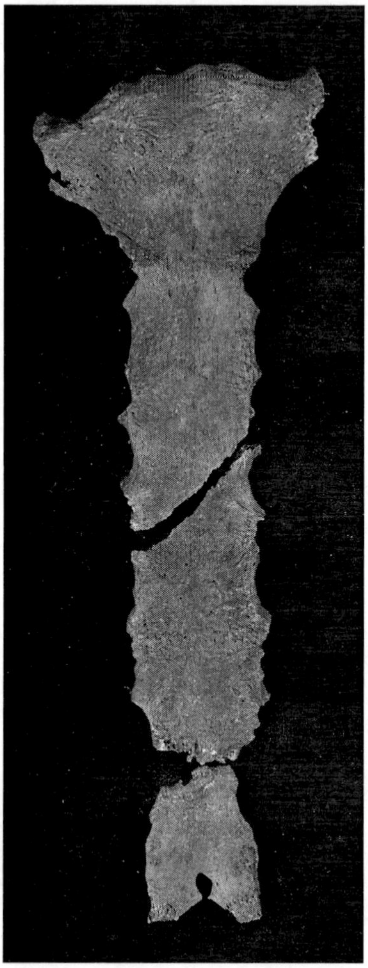

Figure 4.30b Close-up view of sternal body with transverse fracture (Carlos Jacinto, FAFG).

Figure 4.31a Anterior vertebrae, blunt force injury (Carlos Jacinto).

assault cases. A *Parry fracture* is a common fracture associated with defensive wounds and describes a complete, transverse fracture on the mid-to-distal one-third region of the ulnar shaft. The ulna, struck on the medial aspect of the diaphysis as the forearm is in pronation, is held up to shield one's head. In some cases, depending on the severity of the blow, the radius may also be fractured at the same location. This type of fracture should not be confused with gunshot wounds through the ulnar or radial shaft, which may fracture the bones in the same region.

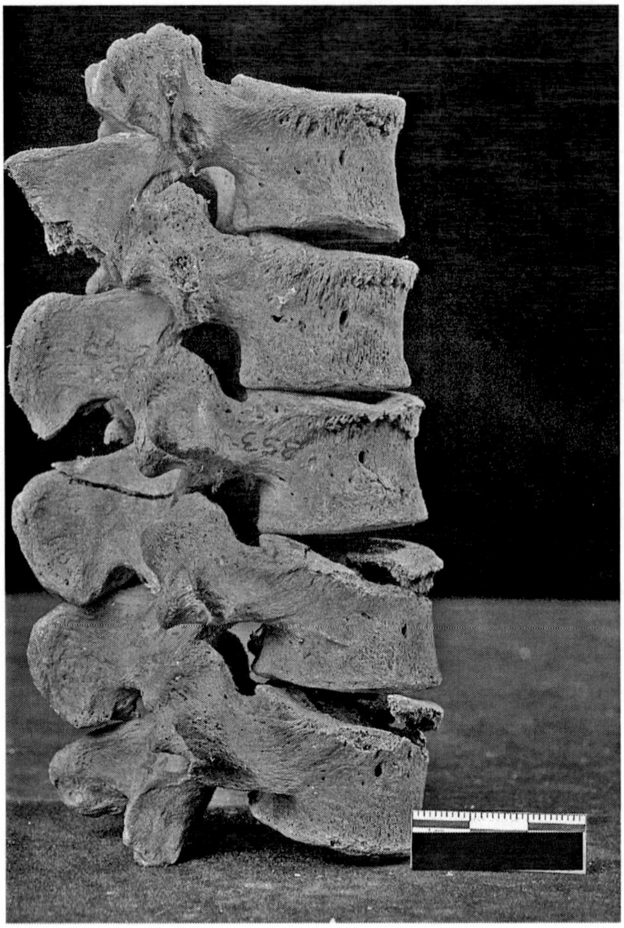

Figure 4.31b (See color insert following page 38) Lateral view of vertebrae, blunt force injury (Carlos Jacinto, FAFG).

Blunt Force Trauma Associated with Gunfire Injury

Atypical wounds from gunfire projectiles may occur if the bullet strikes bone but does not penetrate the skeletal tissue. Similar cases in which projectiles caused blunt trauma to skulls have been reported by Haden and Berg (2007). Such injuries may result in a "dented" or "depressed" wound appearance. A study by Anglin et al. (1998) reports 11.0% (14/154) depressed skull fractures related to tangential GSW to the head. A similar case, of an individual shot and recovered from a mass grave, exhibits a crushing or depressed but nonpenetrating injury, resulting from a projectile (Figure 4.33). The impact site occurred along the anterior, lateral border of the iliac fossa. In this region, the ilium becomes thicker and curves upward in the area adjacent to the fossa, which provided enough resistance to prohibit complete fracturing. The affected region is the thin, flat aspect of the iliac fossa. In the center of the defect, the point of impact is clearly evident by the fracture lines. The radiating and subsequent concentric fractures extend outward, creating a weblike fracture matrix. The projectile was recovered in the pelvic region. Note that the posterior surface of the

Figure 4.32 Fibula, blunt injury. Comminuted fractures (Carlos Jacinto, FAFG).

ilium exhibits no fractures or evidence of trauma. Although the mechanism of injury in this case is still gunfire, examination of the skeletal fractures without the presence of the projectile or knowledge of the context may appear to be have been caused by something other than gunfire. This is a clear example of the range of variation that may occur from very common mechanisms.

Blunt force injuries may also result from a direct blow if the victim is struck before being killed (as discussed earlier in the example of mandibular factures). Isolated linear fractures of the skull generally occur in the parietal, temporal, and occipital bones. These fractures are caused by direct impact to the head, possibly as a consequence of a blow with a rifle butt or similar weapon. When associated with a gunshot wound through the head, the interception of fractures radiating from the bullet entering the cranial vault demonstrates the blow to the head occurred before the gunfire injury. For example, a through and through gunshot wound to the cranium, from back to front and left to right, is present in association with BFT to the head (Figure 4.34). The gunshot entrance wound is located on the occipital bone. The entrance wound exhibits circumferential delamination around the outer borders of the wound, a common finding among full metal jacket ammunition.

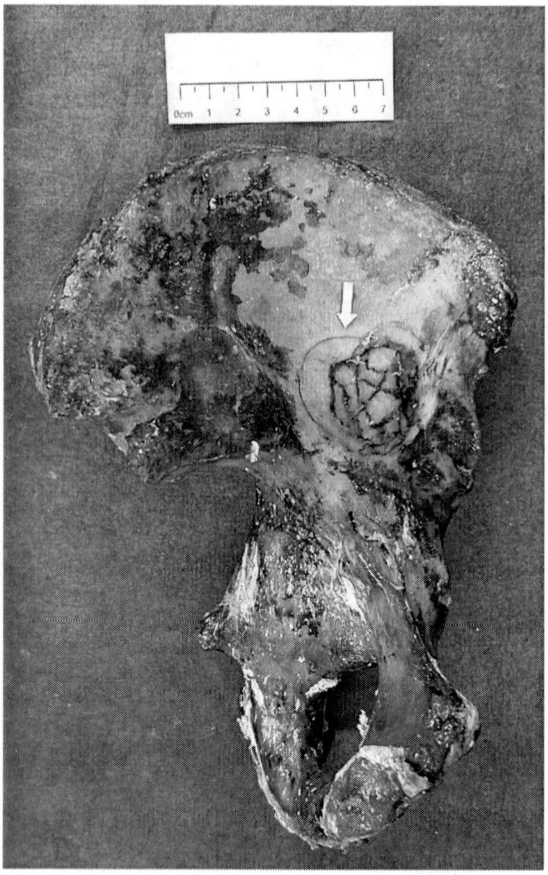

Figure 4.33a Left ilium exhibits "blunt force" injury from gunfire projectile that struck but did not penetrate the bone (ICTY).

A long linear fracture extends from the back to front along the sagittal plane of the skull, extending from the occipital bone to the frontal bone. This linear fracture resulted from a blow to the head before the gunfire injury was shot.

Summary Guidelines for Best Practice

Understanding the mechanisms of BFT is important and highly variable as injury may result from many different objects, for example, common broad instruments, including the flat end of a rifle or pistol, a club, hammer, or fist. Blunt injury mechanisms are also highly variable in that the person may move into a stationary object or a swinging/flying object may strike the individual. Consequently, BFT is observed in cases of blasting injuries, interpersonal violence, torture, and gunfire.

Injury characteristics vary by the speed and weight of force. Low-force impacts often result in skeletal infractions, whereas high-speed impacts more often result in complete

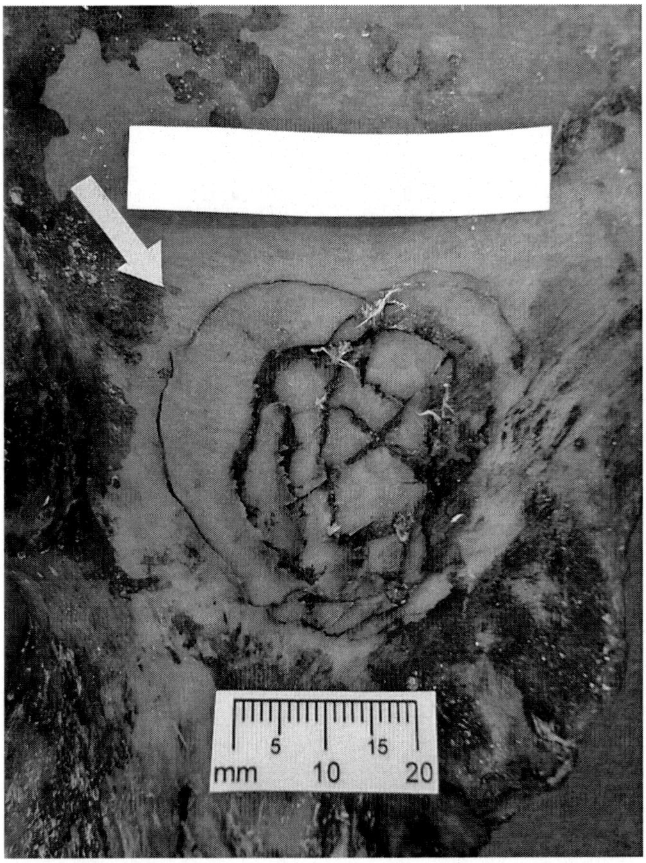

Figure 4.33b The radiating and subsequent concentric fractures extend outward, creating a weblike fracture matrix (ICTY).

fractures. The wound characteristics, fracture patterns, and overall distribution of injuries are essential components for interpreting the mechanism of injury. There may be multiple injuries present, from BFT or from a multitude of mechanisms, and therefore the *minimum number* of injuries are estimated and, typically, easily differentiated, based on overlapping or intersecting fractures. Finally, atypical wounds from a variety of causes should not be overlooked, such as gunfire projectiles that may occur if the bullet strikes bone but does not penetrate the skeletal tissue, thereby resulting in a "dented" or "depressed" defect. The combination of BFT and other mechanisms of injury such as gunshot trauma is useful in characterizing the events surrounding the death of the victim and illustrates whether a crime has been committed.

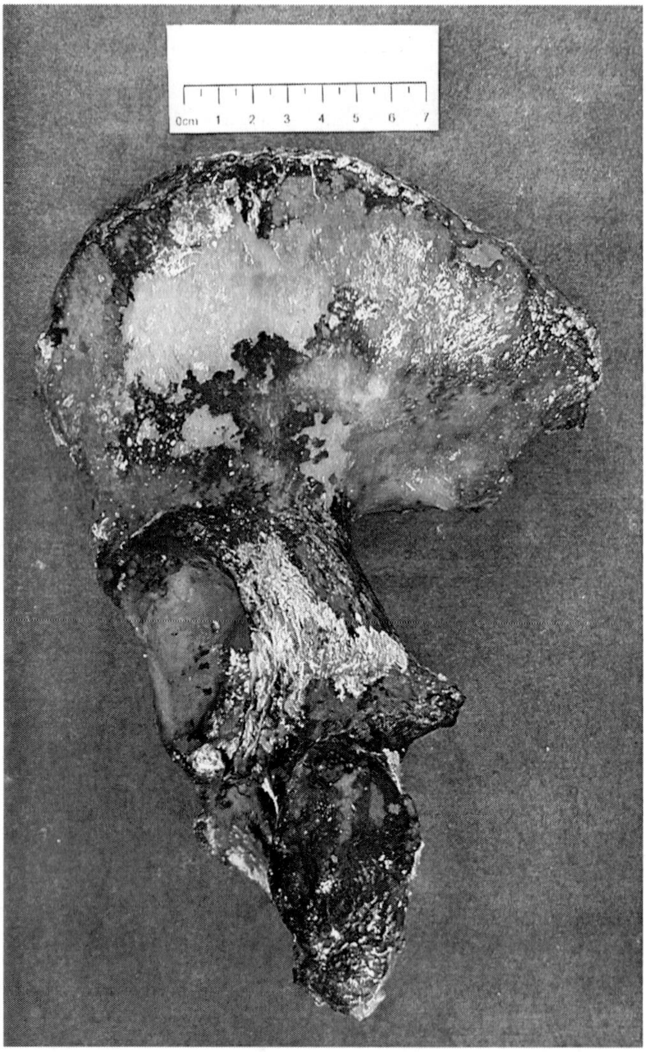

Figure 4.33c The posterior surface of the ilium exhibits no fractures or evidence of trauma. (Image printed with permission from ICTY.)

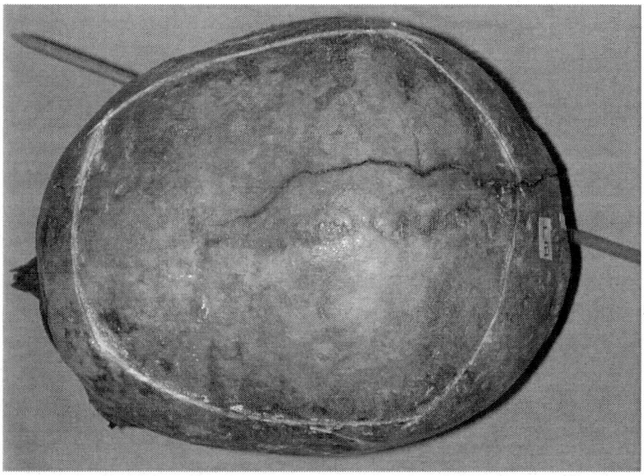

Figure 4.34a A through-and-through gunshot wound to the cranium, from back to front and left to right, is present in association with blunt force trauma to the head (ICTY).

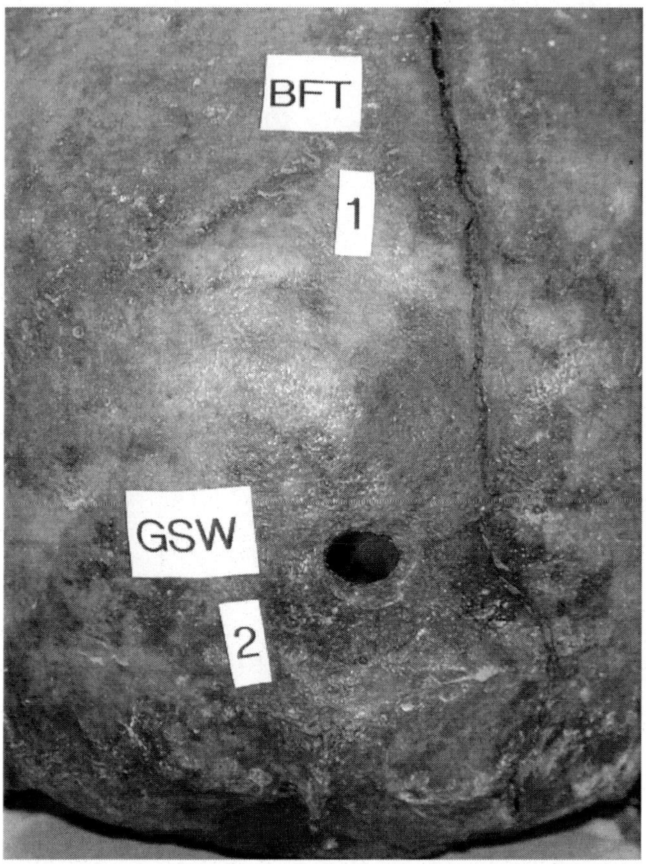

Figure 4.34b Close-up view of gunshot entrance wound and blunt force trauma (BFT) fracture (ICTY).

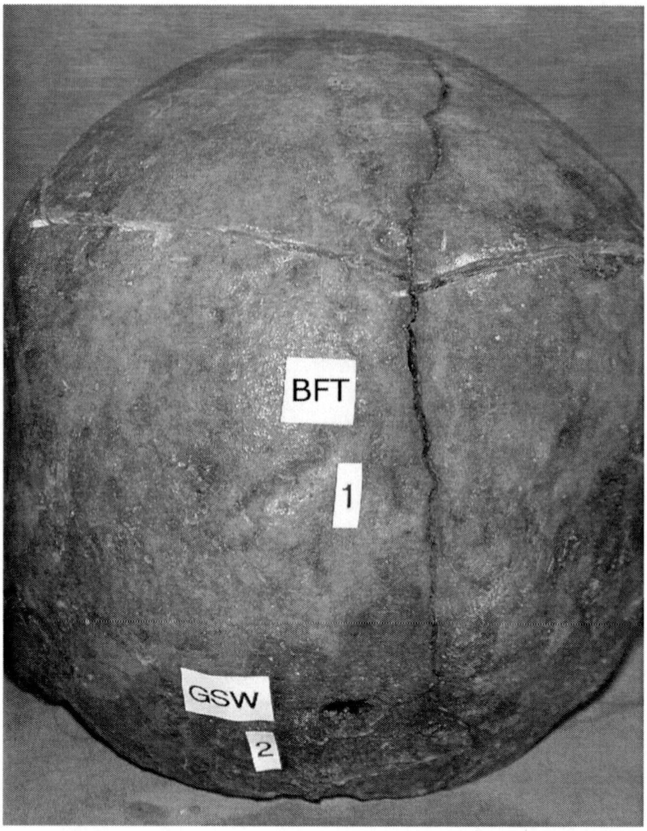

Figure 4.34c A long, linear fracture extends from the back to front along the sagittal plane of the skull, extending from the occipital bone to the frontal bone. (Image printed with permission from ICTY.)

Case Study 4.1: The Interpretation of Skeletal Trauma Resulting from Injuries Sustained Prior to, and as a Direct Result of, Freefall

Oran Finegan
United Nations Committee on Missing Persons
UN mission UNFICYP, Nicosia, Cyprus

In this case study, a homicide victim whose remains were discovered in a cave, more than 60 m below the surface, is discussed. Entry into and exit from the cave could only be accomplished through the use of specialized climbing equipment. Thus, it was concluded that the remains found their final resting place are as a result of a freefall into the cave. Due to the narrow diameter of the entrance, disposal of the body into the cave could only have been effected if the victim was either feet or head first in orientation.

On discovery, the remains were found largely skeletonized except for the presence of a small amount of adherent soft tissue. On examination of the remains in the laboratory, it was clear that there was a diverse range of skeletal trauma. A case of freefall, such as this, affords one the opportunity to see such a diverse range of trauma affecting many elements of the skeleton. The implications of this case for understanding skeletal trauma are discussed here. It is hoped that this case study can shed some light on the, sometimes, very complex nature of skeletal trauma.

Skeletal Injuries from Freefall

Pelvis

There is evidence of crushing involving both pelvic bones. The pattern of injury would lead to the conclusion that a possible lateral impact was sustained to the left or right pelvic region, causing compression of the left auricular surface of the sacrum. The sacrum also displays fracturing along the left sacral foramina (Figure 4.35). The fracture runs directly through the first foramina and just lateral to the second sacral foramina, ending just below the inferior aspect of the left auricular surface of the sacrum. There is a small, centrally

Figure 4.35 Fracture along the left sacral foramina (Alain Wittmann.)

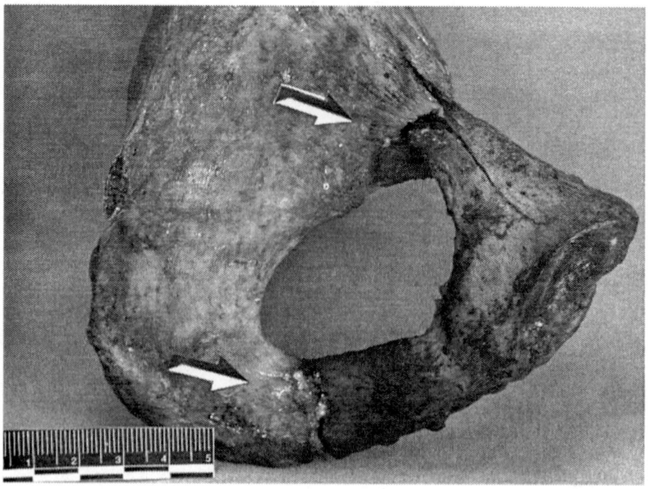

Figure 4.36 Fracturing and compression in the region of the superior ramus of the pubic bone (Alain Wittmann).

located, defect along this fracture line with two radiating fractures. The defect is 4.1 mm in diameter, 35.5 mm from the superior surface of the first sacral segment.

The left pelvic bone is fractured across the ischiopubic ramus, 51.5 mm from the most distal point of the pubic symphysis. There is also fracturing and compression in the region of the superior ramus of the pubic bone (Figures 4.36 and 4.37). The right pelvic bone displays

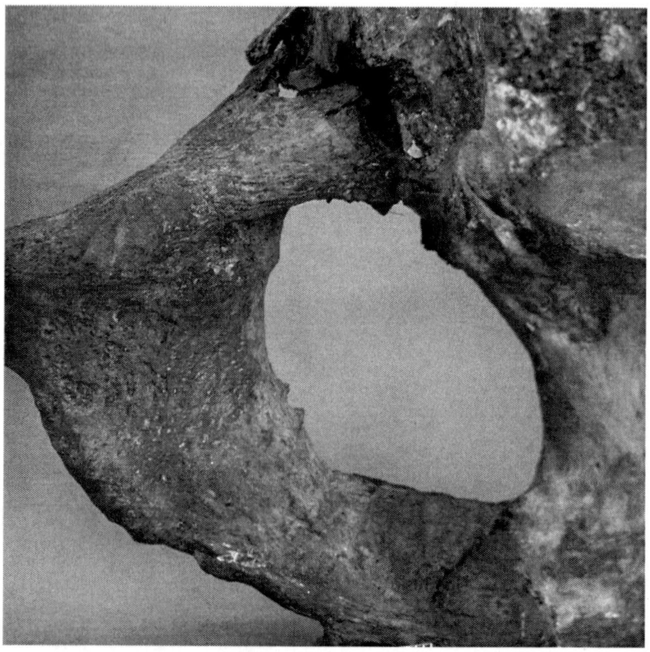

Figure 4.37 Fracturing and compression in the region of the superior ramus of the pubic bone ventral view (Alain Wittmann).

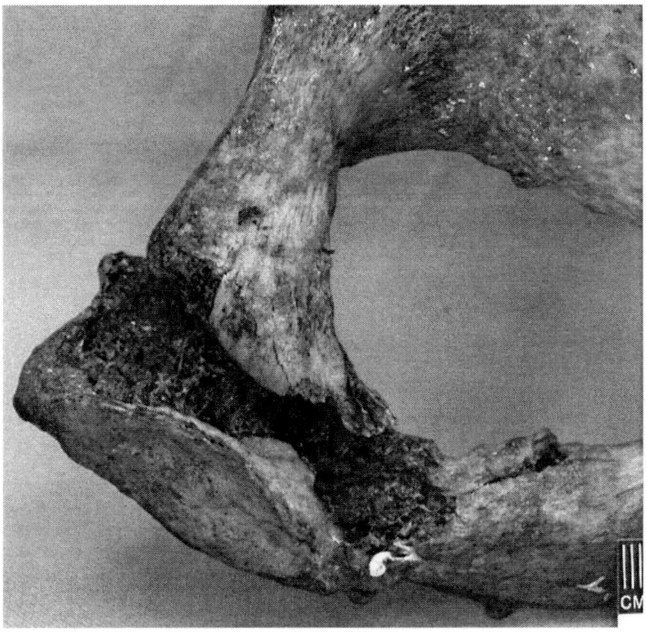

Figure 4.38 Fracture line radiating down the ischiopubic ramus, dorsal surface (Alain Wittmann).

crushing of the pubic symphysis, with a fracture line radiating down the ischiopubic ramus, ventral surface (Figures 4.38 and 4.39). There is also an incident of blunt force trauma evident on the right iliac fossa. It is situated 18.4 mm from the iliac crest and measures 51.7 mm in length and 4.6 mm in width (Figure 4.40). The bone has been pushed out on the exterior surface as a result of the impact (Figure 4.41).

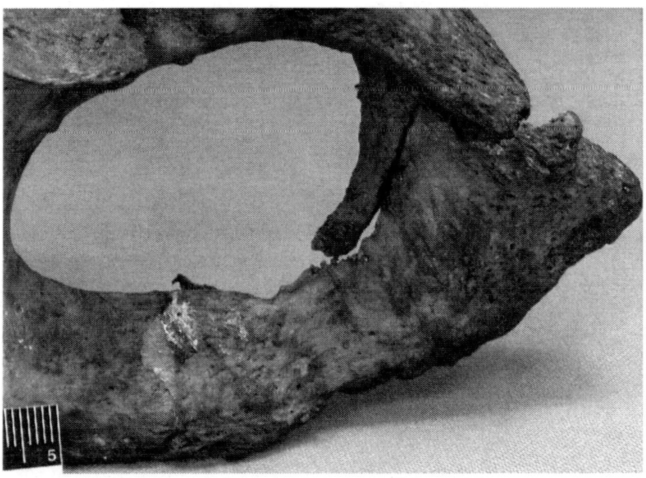

Figure 4.39 Fracture of the ischiopubic ramus, ventral surface (Alain Wittmann).

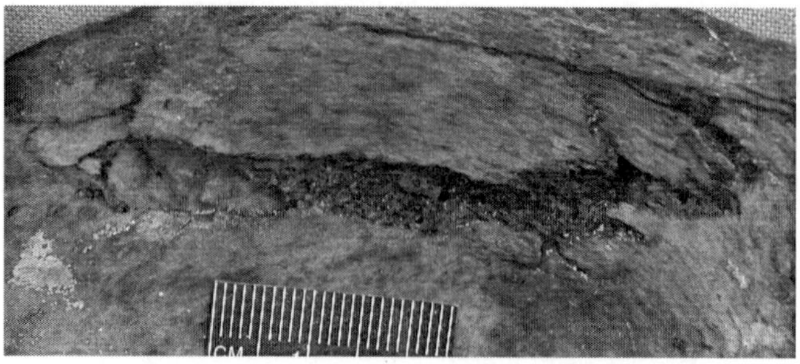

Figure 4.40 Incident of BFT evident on the right iliac fossa (Alain Wittmann).

Vertebrae

The vertebrae display a variety of injury types. The injuries are limited for the most part to the thoracic vertebrae, with only the first lumbar vertebra showing any sign of significant trauma. In regard to the thoracic vertebrae, the following injuries were observed: The spinous processes of the 3rd, 4th, 6th, 7th, and 9th through 12th thoracic vertebrae are fractured off. It is possible the 5th is also involved, but due to postmortem damage it is not possible to accurately confirm this.

Compression of the bodies of the seventh and eighth thoracic vertebrae are also apparent (Figure 4.42). There is also associated fracturing of both vertebrae. The compression observed is consistent with a force being transferred along the vertebral column. The first lumbar vertebra also displays evidence of extensive fracturing, possibly resulting from compression to the spine. These injuries are most likely a result of a fall, considering the force needed for such injuries to occur.

Ribs

There has been massive fracturing of the ribs on both left and right sides (Figure 4.43). On the left side, ribs numbered 1 through 9 have been fractured. The vast majority of fractures are concentrated in the body of the rib, with some fracturing evident toward the sternal

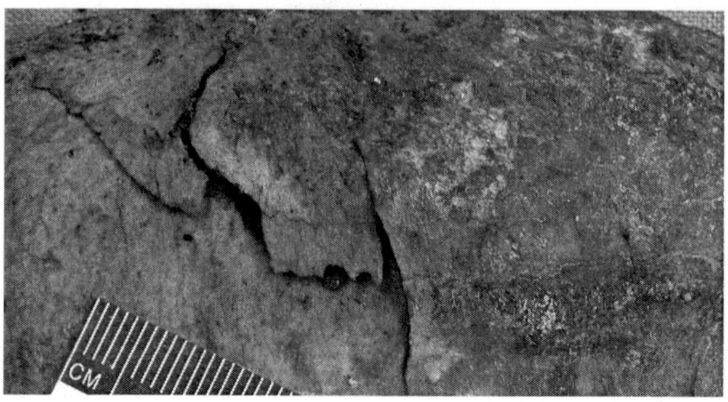

Figure 4.41 Effect of BFT impact on exterior surface of bone (Alain Wittmann).

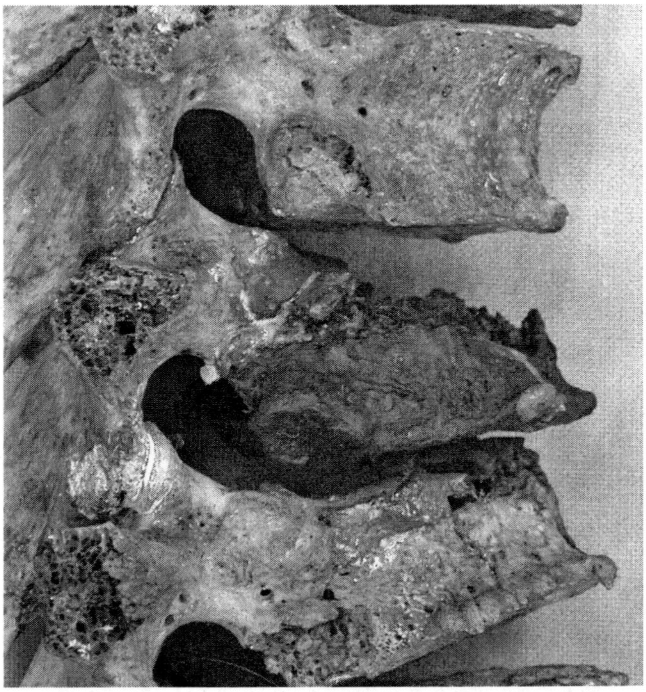

Figure 4.42 Compression of the bodies of the seventh and eighth thoracic vertebrae (Alain Wittmann).

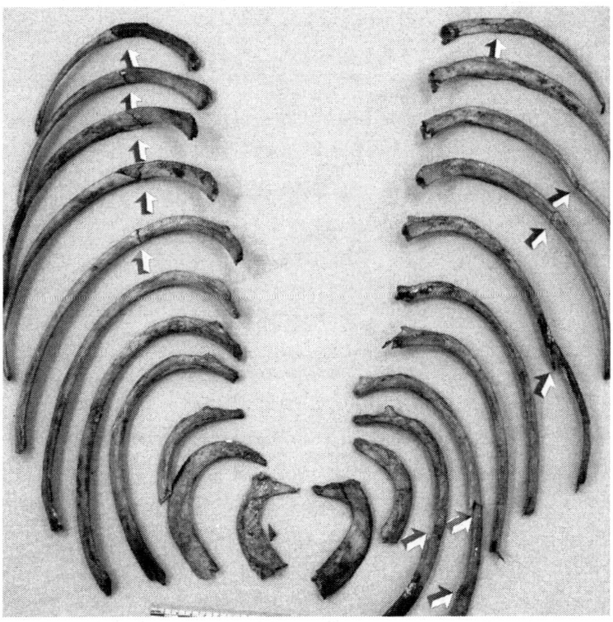

Figure 4.43 Fracturing of the ribs on both the left and right side (Alain Wittmann).

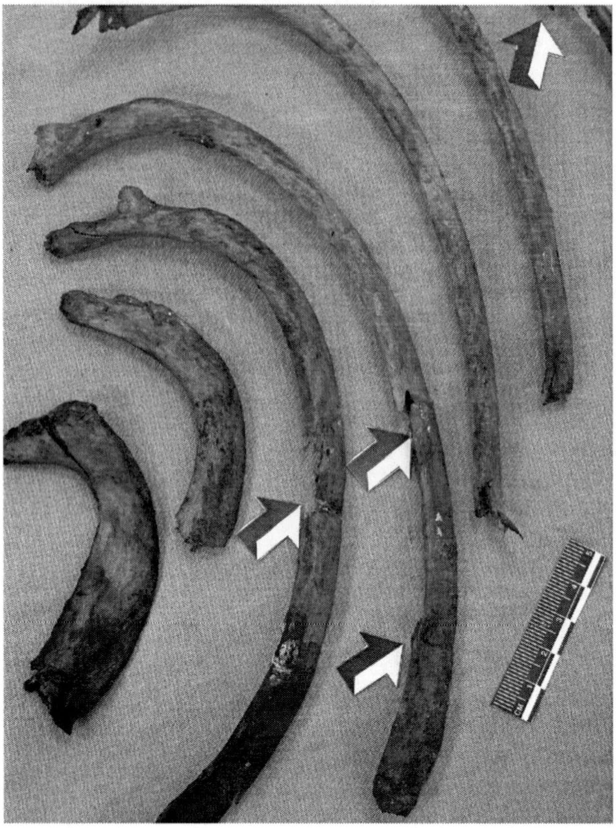

Figure 4.44 Distribution of fracturing on left ribs (Alain Wittmann).

end (Figure 4.44). Only the 12th rib shows signs of fracturing in the neck and head region. In contrast, on the right side, both the type and location of the fracturing are different. Most of the fracturing is concentrated toward the neck and head of the ribs (Figure 4.45). The fracture types displayed on the right side are both butterfly and complete fracturing of the rib body (Figures 4.46 and 4.47). On the left side, the ribs display buckle-type fractures (Figure 4.48). Unlike the right side, the rib heads of all fractured ribs display evidence of damage. Tables 4.1 and 4.2 list the ribs affected on both left and right sides.

Skull

The skull displays evidence of both gunshot trauma and blunt force trauma. The proposed gunshot trauma will be assessed first. There is a small circular defect situated on the left temporal bone. The defect measures 4.5 mm in diameter and displays internal beveling on the inner table. There are three fractures radiating from the point of impact. These findings are consistent with a gunshot wound entrance (Figure 4.49). Due to the size of the defect described, it is more likely that it has resulted from a pellet, not a bullet. Two other defects are situated on the left side of the frontal bone. The first measures 3.3 mm in width and 11.7 mm in length. The second is situated superior to the first and, similar to the first, is

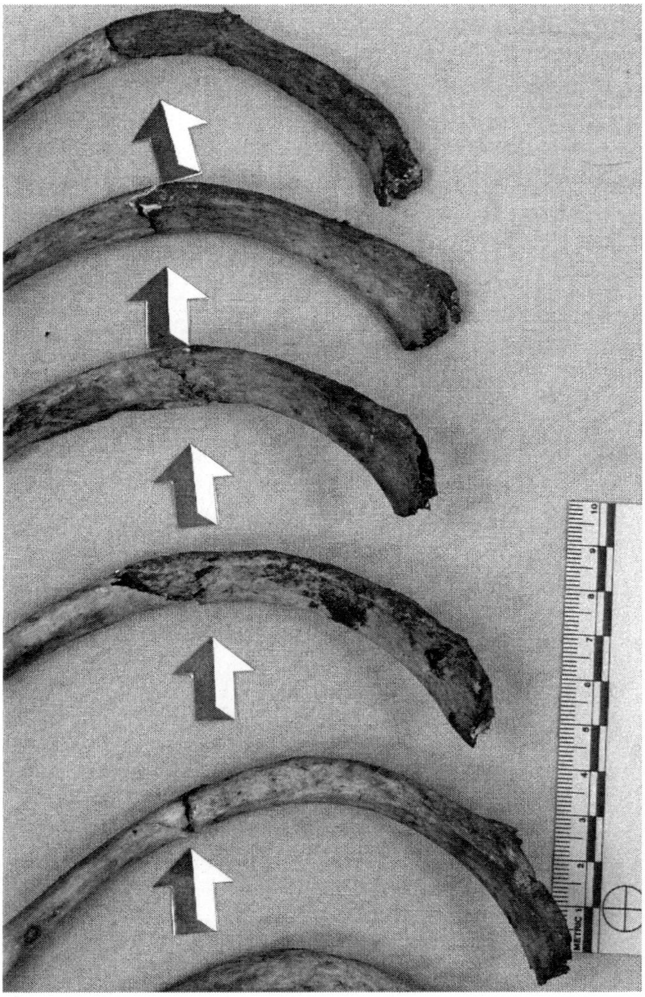

Figure 4.45 Distribution of fracturing on right ribs (Alain Wittmann).

situated on a fracture line. It measures 3.5 mm in width and 11.2 in length (Figure 4.50). Neither projectile has entered the cranium; this conclusion is supported by the absence of a defect on the inner table at either site.

Blunt Force Trauma

There is a large defect situated on the posterior half of the right parietal bone. Its dimensions are 62.8 × 37.6 mm. There are at least four fractures radiating from the defect site (Figure 4.51). On one edge along the posterior aspect of the defect is a depressed fragment of bone, consistent with a slow-loading force. It is worthy to note that no ring fracture at the base of the cranium was observed (Figure 4.52). The forcing of the skull onto the vertebral column, as in the case of falling headlong or feetfirst, has been described by Berryman

Figure 4.46 Close-up view of a fracture on the right rib (Alain Wittmann).

and Symes (1998) as resulting in this type of fracturing (Byers 2005). The implications of this will be covered in more depth in the discussion section of this case study.

Discussion

There are a number of events to be taken into consideration in this case. The actual sequencing of these events will be proposed later, but for the time being they are discussed with no particular order: (1) low- to medium-velocity projectiles that impacted the skeleton at a number of different locations; (2) blunt force trauma to the right parietal bone; (3) extensive rib fracturing on both the left and right sides of the thorax; (4) fractures to the left and right pelvic bones and the sacrum, most likely related to rib fractures; and (5) compression and fracturing of a number of vertebrae.

Low- to Medium-Velocity Projectiles

A number of high-velocity projectiles have impacted the skeleton at a number of different sites. All of the defects described previously are limited to the left side of the skeleton.

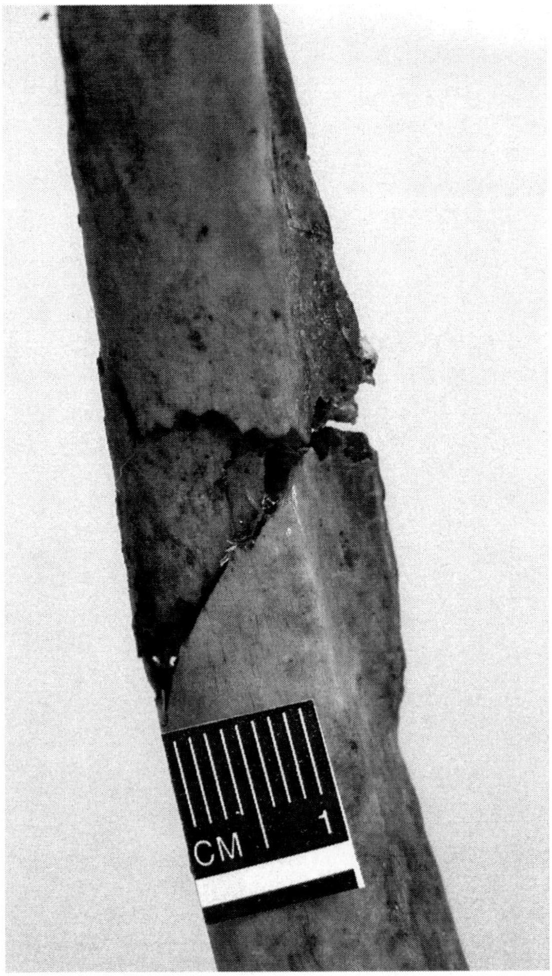

Figure 4.47 Close-up view of a second fracture on the right rib (Alain Wittmann).

As mentioned earlier, these defects are located on the left cranium. The width of defects observed measure between 3.3 and 5.4 mm. It is proposed by the author here that these defects were most likely caused by the same type of projectile, most likely, a pellet.

Blunt Force Trauma to Right Parietal Bone

It is difficult to determine if this injury was inflicted before or as a result of the fall. However, in Figure 4.53 it is possible to see a fracture line from the blunt force injury and a fracture line from the GSW intersecting on the frontal bone. It appears that the BFT fracture line continues further than that from the GSW. This means that the fracture from the GSW has been arrested by the one originating from the BFT, and therefore the GSW occurred subsequent to this particular blunt force injury. Based on these fractures, it appears that the cranial BFT and GSW must have occurred before the fall, because of the inaccessibility of the cave.

This event appears to be isolated in its occurrence. In other words, the blunt force fracture to the skull is unrelated to the BFT affecting the ribs or pelvis. The absence of a ring fracture on

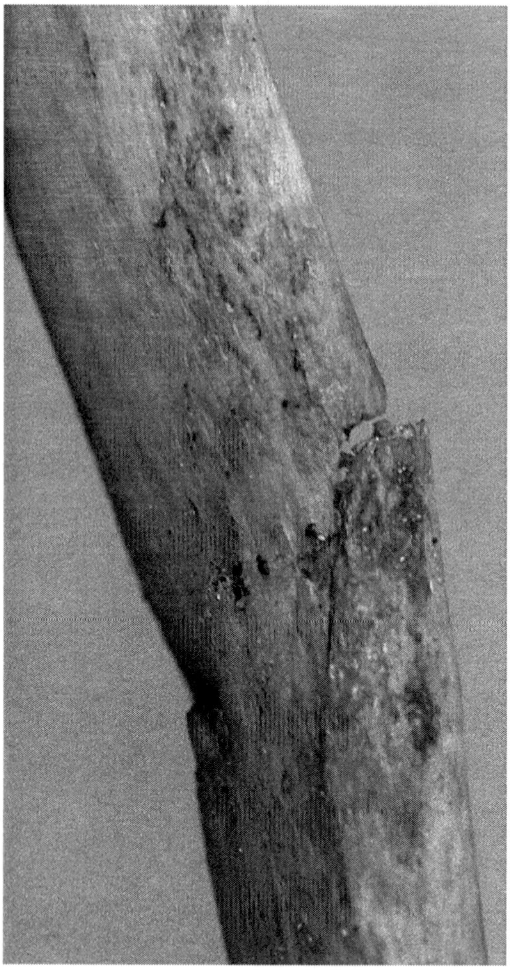

Figure 4.48 Left rib exhibiting a buckle-type fracture (Alain Wittmann).

Table 4.2 Left Rib Fractures

Rib No.	Site of Fracture/Distance from Sternal End (in mm)
1	Along neck of rib
2	26
3	45
4	20; 46
5	44
6	60
7	15; 54
8	In midshaft region
9	In midshaft region
10	—
11	Medial half of rib
12	—

Table 4.3 Right Rib Fractures

Rib No.	Site of Fracture/Distance (in mm)	
	From Sternal End	From Rib Head
1	—	At rib head
2	44.5	—
3	Twice in midthird of rib	—
4	Not possible to measure[a]	—
5	Not possible to measure[a]	—
6	At mid-line	—
7	80	—
8	64	—
9	64	—
10	68	—
11	75	—
12	57	—

[a] Due to condition of bone.

the base of the occipital further supports the opinion that the cranial fracture was not due to the impact of the body from its fall onto the head or feet. Studies have shown that prone bodies tend to position themselves horizontally during a fall (Christensen 2004). It is this author's conclusion that the individual was already dead before he was disposed of in the cave.

Rib Fractures

The left and right rib fractures are of great importance in understanding the series and pattern of events in this case in relation to multiple traumatic events. Due to the

Figure 4.49 Left temporal bone, gunshot wound (Alain Wittmann).

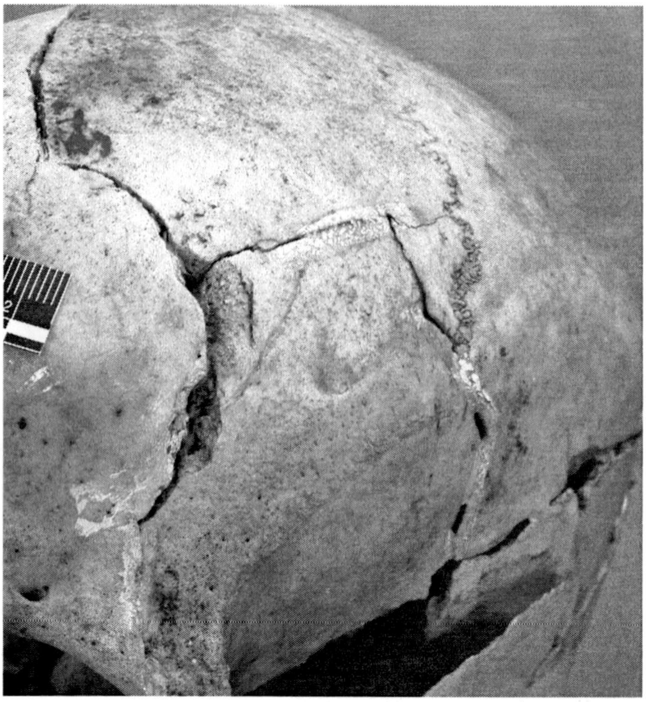

Figure 4.50 Evidence of a small projectile having impacted on frontal bone (Alain Wittmann).

number of fractures, as well as the position and type of fracturing, it is most likely that the cause was a high-energy impact, for example, a fall from a considerable height, i.e., the hypothesis is that the individual came to be found on the base of the cave as a result of a fall.

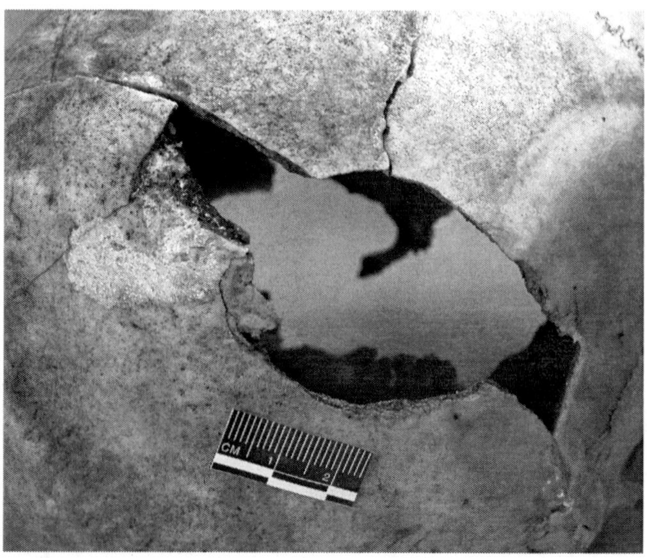

Figure 4.51 Large defect on the right parietal bone resulting from BFT (Alain Wittmann).

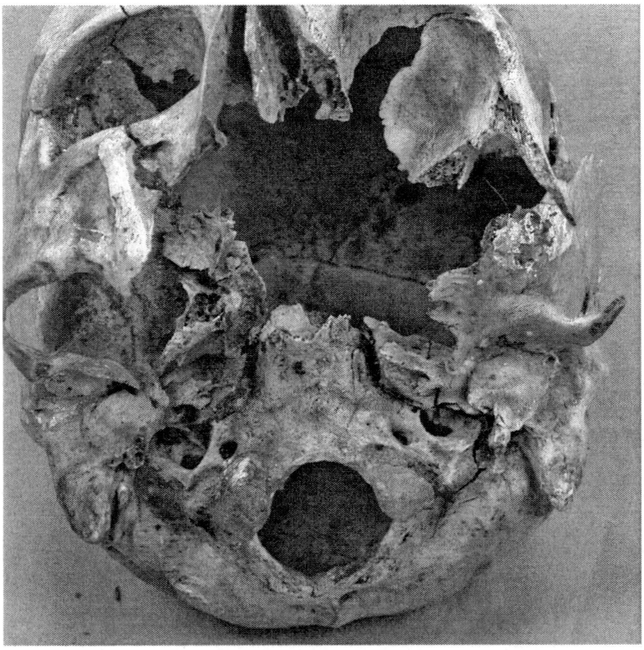

Figure 4.52 Base of cranium displaying absence of ring fracture (Alain Wittmann).

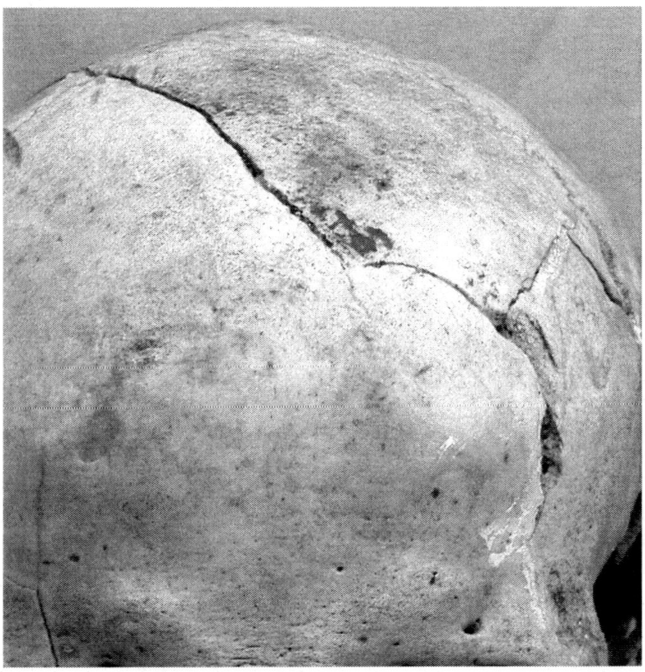

Figure 4.53 Close-up view of fracture lines on the left side of the frontal bone (Alain Wittmann).

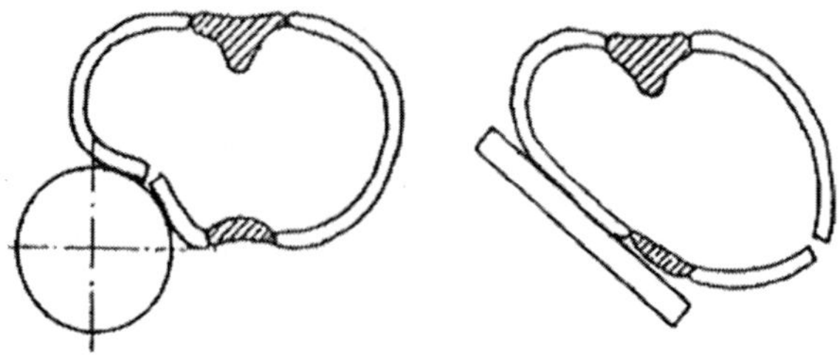

Figure 4.54 Site of rib fracture depending on the point of impact on the body. (Schmitt, K.-U., P. Niederer, F. Walz. (2004). *Trauma Biomechanics: Introduction to Accidental Injury*. Springer, Zurich.)

From the appearance, location, and type of fractures observed, it appears that the impact was sustained on the right side of the rib cage, more specifically in the area of the 7th–11th right ribs. The fractures described for the left ribs have resulted from the compression sustained on the right side of the rib cage and the resulting lateral displacement of the left side. According to Schmitt et al. (2004), lateral impacts to the thorax typically result in multiple rib fractures and greatly influences the exact location of rib fractures (Figure 4.59). The precise locations of rib fractures are useful for estimating the position and orientation of a body during freefall and how it came to be positioned in its final state. What is of interest in this case is the presence of related fractures, resulting from the deceleration injury sustained along the right side of the lower ribs. Christensen (2004, 2005) wrote, "Impact energy refers to the amount of energy transferred to the falling object (here, the fall victim) at impact. At the moment of impact, when the falling body undergoes deceleration, the vast majority of the kinetic energy is converted to mechanical energy, which is absorbed by the fallen object." This mechanism described by Christensen is clearly observable in relation to the injury sustained in the right lower ribs and suggests the impact occurred directly on this region (Figure 4.45). Finally, the presence of buckle fractures on the left ribs also suggests impact from the fall occurred on the right side of the body.

Pelvic Fractures

As described previously, there are a number of fractures present on the left and right pelvic bones and the sacrum. It is proposed that all but one of these fractures resulted from the same traumatic event (note that the fracture on the right iliac crest is considered as a separate event and will be discussed separately). The question is whether the pelvic fractures occurred from the fall or prior to the fall.

Schmitt et al. (2004) proposed that fractures to the public rami and sacrum are common in lateral impact injuries to the pelvis (Figure 4.55). Most frequently, fractures to the sacrum occur in the region of the sacral foramina and result from *extensive* pelvic trauma (Schmitt et al. 2004). Fractures to the sacral foramina are clearly observable in this case. The sacral fractures in conjunction with fractures to the pubic rami strongly support the conclusion that a lateral compression force was applied to the skeleton in this region. When observed together, the trauma observed on both the ribs and pelvis could be related to the same event, in that the body hit the ground on the right side as a result of the fall.

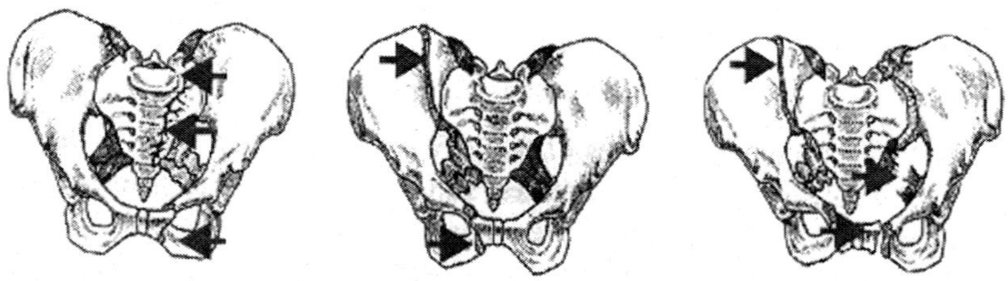

Figure 4.55 Possible locations for fractures arising from lateral compression. (Oran Finegan; Schmitt, K.-U., P. Niederer, F. Walz. (2004). *Trauma Biomechanics: Introduction to Accidental Injury*. Springer, Zurich.)

Conclusion

This case demonstrates a variety of different injury types sustained through a series of events. The task in such a case is to locate the various injuries and estimate the number of incidents of trauma involved and to associate each injury with a traumatic event. When there are a variety of incidents of BFT occurring before and immediately after death, it is important to determine if, and how, they are associated. In the case of a fall where a large amount of BFT may occur, it can make such interpretations considerably more difficult, and thus a careful examination and understanding of the trauma involved is imperative. This case has again brought to the forefront the question of injury patterns resulting from a freefall. From this example, it is the opinion of this author that more research is needed if we are to better understand how trauma manifests itself as a result of a freefall.

Case Study 4.2: A Khmer Rouge Execution Method—Evidence from Choeung Ek

Sabrina C. Ta'ala
Joint POW/MIA Accounting Command—Central Identification Laboratory
Hickam AFB, Hawaii

Gregory E. Berg
Joint POW/MIA Accounting Command—Central Identification Laboratory
Hickam AFB, Hawaii

Kathryn Haden
Harris County Medical Examiners Office
Joseph A. Jachimczyk Forensic Center
Houston, Texas

The Khmer Rouge regime, which ruled Cambodia from 1975 to 1979, is believed to be directly and indirectly responsible for the deaths of approximately 1.5 million Cambodians (Chandler 1999). Khmer Rouge soldiers used a variety of execution methods, including but not limited to stabbing, shooting, drowning, throat cutting, and suffocation (Kiernan 1996; Kamm 1998; Chandler 1999). Victims' remains were often buried in mass graves (or "killing fields") scattered across the country. The mass graves of Choeung Ek, near Phnom Penh, contain the remains of approximately 8000 prisoners from the central Tuol Sleng or "S-21" prison (Chandler 1999). The skeletal remains of approximately half of these individuals were disinterred in the early 1980s, and those remains are currently stored, in a completely disarticulated condition, at a memorial shrine on the site.

A sample of 85 crania from the Choeung Ek memorial shrine was examined. The sample excluded subadults; although sex estimates were recorded, these estimates were necessarily tentative because all crania were disarticulated from their postcranial elements and mandibles. Most of the 85 crania examined (74 of 85, or 87%) were estimated to be male. Of the 85 crania, 10 (12%) displayed a pattern of BFT distinguished by extensive damage to the occipital focused between the external occipital protuberance and the foramen magnum, with radiating fractures extending to the cranial base (Figures 4.56–4.58). Trauma analysis and historical research indicates the likeliest source of the observed trauma was a particular execution method in which kneeling victims were beaten on the back of the head or neck with any one of a variety of blunt weapons. Published literature describes witness accounts of this method of execution (Kiernan 1996; Chandler 1999), and the artwork (Figure 4.59) of one former Tuol Sleng prisoner depicts this particular method of execution; refer also to Nath (1998).

This execution method employed the application of massive force directed at the inferior squamous portion of the occipital, often resulting in an extensively fractured cranial base. Although, structurally, this area is strongly buttressed, sufficiently forceful blows to this area can easily result in death, because of the proximity of the cerebellum, the brainstem, and the spinal cord. In the cases presented, all but one cranium exhibits radiating fractures, and two of the crania exhibit concentric fractures from the point of impact. In one case, a radiating fracture penetrates the external occipital protuberance, splitting a well-developed inion hook. Other observed fractures migrate across the basilar synchondrosis sutures and into the lesser wings of the sphenoid, but in only one case is the petrous portion of either temporal completely fractured. Multiple blows are apparent on

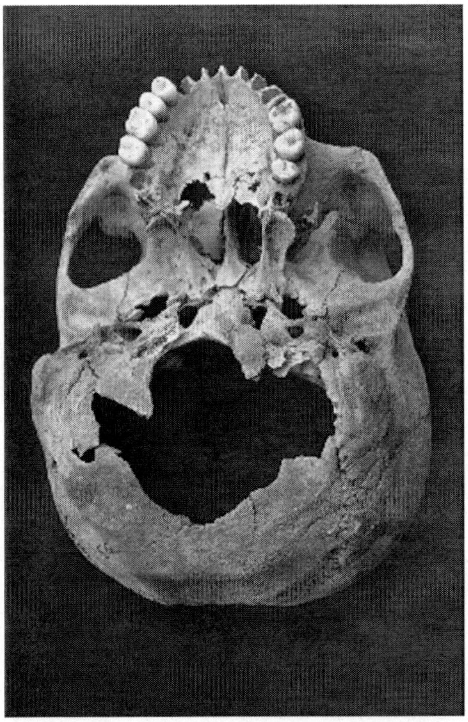

Figure 4.56 An example of blunt force cranial trauma on a Choeung Ek cranium. Note the intact occipital base and radiating fractures (Greg E. Berg).

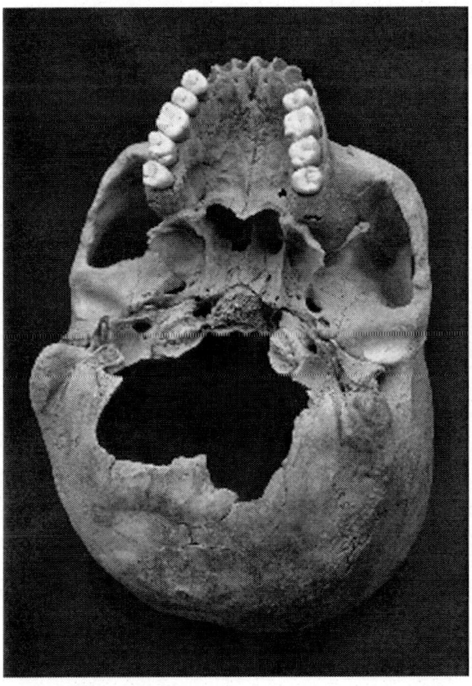

Figure 4.57 Probable multiple blows to the posterior occipital. Note the concentric fractures and the absence of the occipital base (Greg E. Berg).

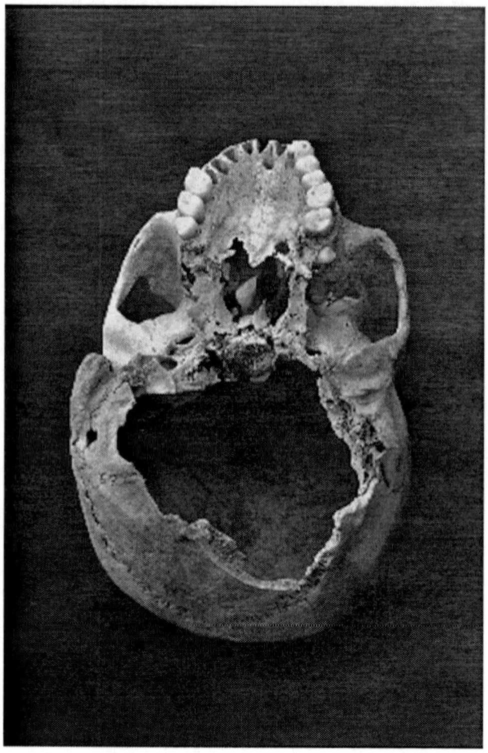

Figure 4.58 Blunt force trauma on the inferior cranium. Note missing petrous portion of the left temporal, missing cranial base, and combination internal/external beveling lateral to the external occipital protuberance (Greg E. Berg).

Figure 4.59 Photograph of a painting by Tuol Sleng survivor Vann Nath depicting the execution of a kneeling victim by blunt force to the back of the head. This painting is currently on display at the Tuol Sleng prison museum in Phnom Penh (Greg E. Berg).

four crania. Internal beveling is present on some fracture margins in all but two of the crania. Internal beveling is particularly marked at the internal/external occipital crests and protuberances in five cases. Two cases display both internal and external beveling in this particular section of the occipital.

In four instances, the generalized appearance of the defects can be described as rounded on at least one margin. The shape of the other defects is essentially oval in two cases, jagged in the three cases, and irregular in the final case. The impact areas are focused centrally on the squamous portion of the occipital in three cases, oriented to the left or right in six cases, and focused on the basilar portion of the occipital in one case. The occipital is fractured posterior to the occipital condyles in four cases; in the other six cases, the entire occipital base is absent. The areas of missing bone range in size from maximum dimensions of 9.7 × 8.5 cm to minimum dimensions of 6.0 × 3.5 cm.

In terms of interpretations about likely weapon size and shape, the dimensions of the defects are somewhat misleading, because the force of the blow typically created radiating fractures that effectively loosened the entire cranial base. In many cases, the cranial base split completely from the cranium due to these radiating fractures. Although it is clear that these individuals were executed by means of a systematic method of blows to the back of the head, the specific implements used cannot be definitively identified on the basis of fracture analysis. The Choeung Ek trauma pattern can be broadly summarized as follows:

1. The squamous portion of the occipital is affected by blunt force trauma.
2. The posterior fracture margins typically display internal beveling, particularly at the internal/external occipital crests and protuberances. Due to the buttressed structure of the cranial vault, fracture margins may display variable internal/external beveling.
3. Radiating fractures may terminate at the foramen magnum, or encircle it, resulting in severe fracturing and, possibly, partial detachment of the cranial base. Radiating fractures may split such strong bony structures as occipital protuberances and the petrous portion of the temporal.

This fracture pattern should not be confused with ring or basilar fractures. Superficially, these two fracture patterns may appear similar to the Choeung Ek pattern, but the former are generally caused by force applied to a disassociated cranial vault zone that forces the spine into or away from the cranium (Berryman and Symes 1998; Spitz 1993), rather than direct blows to the back of the head/neck, with distinct impact points on the occipital bone. This distinction is critical because the resulting injuries to the underlying brain are different. An injury inflicted by a moving object on a stationary head will create cortical contusions at the site of the primary impact (coup-contusion) (Dolinak and Matshes 2002). This is the pattern of injury expected with the identified Choeung Ek pattern. A countre-coup cortical contusion is produced when the head is in motion and strikes a fixed or firm surface, a result more likely to occur in instances of ring and basilar fractures. A more detailed discussion of the Choeung Ek trauma pattern can be found in Ta'ala et al. (2006).

Skeletal Evidence of Torture

5

On one occasion we were called to go down there. We had tea. We sat there. There was an unpleasant situation for me and for my son. We had to watch as … They would beat every one of them for five or ten minutes, slapping them, kicking them, hitting them on their legs. One of them was unable to stand at all. At any rate, they were beaten up.

Prosecution Witness*

Contents

What is Torture? 202
Documented Cases of Torture with Skeletal Remains from Kosovo and Peru 205
- Kosovo/Kosova 205
- Peru 207
- Skeletal Evidence 209
- Fractures of the Cranium and Teeth 212
- Fractures of the Sternum 215
- Fractures of the Ribs 217
- Fractures of the Lumbar Spine 224

Differential Diagnosis of BFT Resulting from Torture, Accidents, and Nonaccidental Mechanisms 226
- Differential Diagnosis: A Practical Example 226

Summary Guidelines for Best Practice 233
- Case Study 5.1: Torture Sequels to the Skeleton *By H.P. Hougen* 234
- Case Study 5.2: Multiple Healed Rib Fractures—Timing of Injuries in Regard to Death *By T. Delabarde* 236
- Case Study 5.3: Dating of Fractures in Human Dry Bone Tissue—The Berisha Case *By G.J.R. Maat* 245
- Case Study 5.4: Torture and Extrajudicial Execution in the Peruvian Highlands: Forensic Investigation in a Military Base *By J.P. Baraybar, C.R. Cardoza, and V. Parodi* 255

Medicolegal death investigations into human rights (HHRR) abuse must focus on the types of trauma that may be inflicted before death, as well as those that contribute to the cause of death. In such cases, blunt force trauma (BFT) to the face, ribs, sternum, and spine may be good indicators of torture or ill-treatment. Supporting witness testimony in combination with physical evidence based on skeletal remains among documented cases of torture indicate possible abuse. An analysis of wounds, the location, morphology, and frequency of injuries enable a differential diagnosis and the estimation of the mechanism

* This testimony was presented in the case *The Prosecutor v. Limaj et al.* (IT-03-66), June 1, 2005, T 1341-1342, refer to Table 5.1 for a longer excerpt.

of injury. Therefore, based on these characteristics, it may be possible to differentiate blunt force injuries resulting from inflicted trauma from accidents or other mechanisms.

The purpose of this chapter is to discuss common injuries to the skeleton resulting from torture, specifically beatings. Interpretations of ill-treatment based on skeletal injuries observed are further supported by witness testimony in documented cases from Peru and Kosovo. The patterns of injuries are discussed. Using this framework, an unknown but alleged case of torture is compared to known cases to assess the possible mechanisms of injury and the manner of death. A differential diagnosis between BFT resulting from abuse and road traffic accidents (RTA) suggests the injuries of the alleged torture case in fact most probably resulted from an RTA.* The location and nature of skeletal trauma resulting from these two mechanisms are clearly differentiated and provide a basis for which skeletal correlates of physical beatings may be interpreted. Four case studies at the end of this chapter provide practical examples of diagnosing ill-treatment from skeletal remains (Hougen) and timing antemortem fractures (Delabarde) that demonstrate chronic abuse over a period of time. Histological methods (Maat) for timing fractures are discussed and demonstrated for the case study presented by Baraybar and coworkers.

What is Torture?

Article 27(1) of the Convention against Torture and Other Cruel, Inhuman or Degrading Treatment or Punishment, which came into force in 1987 according to the United Nations General Assembly Resolution 39/46, states:

> The term "torture" means any act by which severe pain or suffering, whether physical or mental, is intentionally inflicted on a person for such purposes as obtaining from him or a third person information or a confession ... when such pain or suffering is inflicted by or at the instigation of or with the consent or acquiescence of a public official or other person acting in an official capacity.

Implicit in this definition is the fact that torture includes acts designed primarily to inflict harm or maim the victim rather than kill the individual, as well as the perpetrator's motive or intention to inflict harm for the purpose of obtaining a confession or causing suffering. Establishing proof of *torture* for prosecution is well defined in International Humanitarian Law (IHL) (*The Prosecutor v. Limaj et al.* Judgment, para. 235; *The Prosecutor v. Tadic* Jurisdiction Decision, para. 94; *The Prosecutor v. Aleksovski* Appeals Judgment, para. 20; and *The Prosecutor v. Kunarac* Appeals Judgment, para. 66):

> The law on torture is well settled by the jurisprudence of the Tribunal. For the crime of torture to be established, whether as a war crime or as a crime against humanity, the following three elements must be met: (1) There must be an act or omission, inflicting severe pain or suffering, whether physical or mental; (2) the act or omission must be intentional; and (3) the act or omission must have been carried out with a specific purpose such as to obtain

* Road traffic accidents were chosen for comparison and differential diagnosis because in this case it was alleged that the injuries resulted from an RTA. The subsequent investigation was to assess whether this finding was accurate. Moreover, RTAs are common occurrences and often result in BFT; therefore, this example highlights patterns of trauma beyond the scope of this example.

> information or a confession, to punish, intimidate or coerce the victim or a third person, or to discriminate, on any ground, against the victim or a third person.

The term torture tends to conjure images of complex and convoluted techniques or medieval instruments aimed at inflicting pain; however, the most common injuries result from punches, kicks, and beatings. Brogdon and coworkers wrote (2003, 105):

> Those of us who grew up on a diet of American movies circa 1930–1960 are apt to think of torture as a means of forcible extraction of confessions from the bad guys or of information from the good guys—an inexcusable naiveté in today's world. Torture is a global reality employed as a political tool in more than 100 countries to systematically break the spirit and destroy the very identity and personality of its victims.

As Brogdon and colleagues point out, torture may be biological, chemical, or psychological, and physical evidence of torture may not be evident as victims tend to disappear. The criteria they (Brogdon et al. 2003, 106) list as necessary evidence to support claims of torture include comparisons to documented or "known" cases of torture (i.e., the pattern and distribution of injuries); the timing of injuries; pathological findings consistent with detainment (i.e., malnutrition or rampant infections without medical intervention); and corroboration of physical findings with multiple forms of evidence (i.e., witness testimony).

The diagnosis of torture has typically been based on the assessment, treatment, and rehabilitation of living victims and in some cases on the postmortem examination of alleged victims (Leth and Banner 2005; Lie and Skjeie 1996; Pollanen 2002; Perera 2006; Thomsen & Voight 2000; Moisander and Edston 2003; Hougen 1988; Petersen and Wandall 1995; Asirdizer et al. 2004; Pounder 1997; Savnik et al. 2000; Amnesty International 2003; Gaessner et al. 2001). Further, the skeletal correlates of ill-treatment of children and the elderly have been extensively studied and provide a basis for documenting the patterns and timing of such trauma (Kleinman et al 1992, 1996; Kleinman and Schlesinger 1997; Walker et al. 1997). This body of literature is useful, particularly for cases of chronic abuse where injuries have time to heal. Sequencing the timing of multiple antemortem injuries in various stages of healing is indicative of chronic abuse and is common in torture cases. Skeletal evidence consistent with torture or ill-treatment is likely to be more common among victims of enforced disappearances that are followed by extrajudicial executions. Victims in these situations are often beaten, perhaps over a period of time, and therefore fractures at different stages of healing will also be evident.

Excluding accidents of any type, the leading cause of skeletal trauma is interpersonal violence, defined as "the intentional use of physical force or power, threatened or actual, against oneself, another person, or against a group or community, that either results in or has a high likelihood of resulting in injury, death, psychological harm, maldevelopment, or deprivation" (WHO 2004). The distribution of injuries caused by interpersonal violence across cultures is analogous to the beatings that occur in torture cases and tend to show some consistency in decreasing order, to the head/neck region, trunk, and limbs (Kontio et al. 2005). Although the type of assaulting weapon varies, overall, in cases where the same type of weapon is used, the head and neck tend to be the most affected areas (Kontio et al. 2005). Several other studies also suggest that the craniofacial area is by far the most affected region of the body (Brink et al. 1998; Shepherd et al. 1990) followed by the chest region (Danielsen et al. 1989) in cases of beatings. In contrast to accident victims, several researchers report that the limbs may be affected more frequently or equally to the chest, but generally occurs less often than the head/neck region (Kjaerulff et al. 1989; Aalund et al. 1990.

Cultural differences have been observed in the mechanism of injury in cases of assault, primarily in the type of weapon used (Wright and Kariya 1997). Therefore, finding identical injuries in different populations suggests the injuries resulted from a consistent mechanism. For example, homicidal injuries caused by blunt trauma occur more frequently to the head, whereas sharp trauma occurs more commonly to the thorax (Ambade and Godbole 2006; Mohanty et al. 2005). Victims of assault may also show defensive injuries (Ambade and Godbole 2006), whereas victims of torture rarely exhibit defensive injuries as they are typically submitted to conditions of abuse while defenseless (i.e., they are tied or bound in some fashion preventing self-defense). The lack of defensive injuries is further evidence of intention, which in the case of torture is maiming, not killing, the victim (Perera 2006).

The primary mechanism of injury in cases of torture is BFT. Vogel and Brogdon (2003b, 109) point out that beatings may be localized or generalized and often result in fractures of the face, extremities, and thorax. Hematomas and edema result in the soft tissues. Chronic abuse may lead to various infections of the injured areas, such as "prisoner's sinusitis" (Vogel and Brogdon 2003b, 109). Resulting conditions that may arise include infections or malnutrition and commonly leave physical evidence in the form of pathological processes on bone (i.e., osteomyelitis, lytic lesions, and abnormal bone loss or growth).

The differential diagnosis of torture in skeletal remains must consider the fact that the lesions observed are only a fraction of injuries occurring in the body and that there are many ways to cause harm without breaking bones. Alternatively, the intention may be to inflict pain or cause harm by breaking bones. The distribution or patterns of bone fractures must be interpreted in light of the expected patterns of injury caused by known agents, requiring a differential diagnoses based on injury patterns from beatings versus accidents or falls. To illustrate this point, various forms of thoracic trauma are described in this chapter (i.e., the location of BFT and patterns of injuries in the thorax and sternum due to beatings, RTAs, or falls). To accurately attribute skeletal injuries to torture, several lines of evidence are used in combination:

- Mechanism of injury
- Documentation of the location, type, distribution/pattern, and recurrence of wounds
- Estimation of whether or not the wounds present contributed to the cause of death
- Approximate timing of injuries
- Reconstruction of the circumstances surrounding the injuries
- Ruling out accidents and estimating the manner of injuries as intentional, interpersonal violence

Finally, the context in which victims are found is an important factor in assessing trauma related to torture or ill-treatment. Investigations into the disappearance, detainment, or treatment of the victim may provide witness testimony or other evidence of what events transpired.

Documented Cases of Torture with Skeletal Remains from Kosovo and Peru

The skeletal injuries of 19 individuals from Kosovo and Peru are presented. Eleven cases are from Kosovo, nine of which were presented as evidence in *The Prosecutor v. Limaj et al.* (IT-03-66 November 30, 2005). For the Kosovan sample, the testimonial evidence presented by survivors regarding torture and ill-treatment during detention was presented at trial and was available for comparison to the postmortem findings. The skeletal injuries and associated witness testimony to the torture and beatings that occurred are also discussed for the eight individuals from Peru (EPAF 2006). The context, witnesses, and forensic evidence for Kosovo and Peru are presented, followed by a discussion of the skeletal evidence of injuries.

Kosovo/Kosova

The conflict in Kosovo in 1998–99 between the Kosovo Liberation Army (KLA) and Serbian security and paramilitary forces resulted in the disappearance of 5200 people and the deaths of approximately 5000 people (OMPF 2004). NATO troops entered the Province in June 1999, and the Serbian troops departed from the area; thus, Kosovo became a "de facto" protectorate of the international community through the enforcement of UN Security Council Resolution 1999/1244.

Between 1999 and 2000, the International Criminal Tribunal for the former Yugoslavia (ICTY) carried out large-scale operations to gather evidence against Serbian political leaders of whom Slobodan Milosevic, former president of Serbia was the most prominent Head of State indicted *(The Prosecutor v. Slobodan Milosevic,* IT-02-54-T). However, indictments for war crimes and, specifically, allegations of torture were not limited to Serbians (i.e., *The Prosecutor v. Tadic,* IT-94-1; *The Prosecutor v. Aleksovski,* IT-95-14/1, and *The Prosecutor v. Kunarac et al.,* IT-95-23 and 23/1). Two indictments against former KLA commanders were also issued. In this case, *The Prosecutor v. Limaj et al.* (IT-03-66), skeletal evidence of torture was used by the prosecution as evidence in trial along with witness testimony from survivors.

In 2001, nine sets of skeletal remains were excavated from different locations across Kosovo by the Central Investigation Unit (CCIU) of the UNMIK Police (United Nations Mission in Kosovo). The remains showed evidence of animal scavenging by carnivores (most likely dogs). Eight sets of these remains were positively identified. In addition, two sets of human remains excavated by the Office on Missing Persons and Forensics (OMPF) are also described here. Witness testimony was not available for the two OMPF cases, however; the skeletal injuries are consistent with the other nine documented cases. A description of scene and ballistic evidence is provided from the Trial Judgment (*The Prosecutor v. Limaj et al.,* IT-03-66, para. 457):

> … there were no marked graves or holes in the location and that the bodies had been covered with soil which was not soil natural to the location. This and other findings led her to conclude that the victims, while killed in the location where the bodies were found, had been covered at some later time …. [The] autopsy established for all the bodies that death had occurred more than two years earlier, which is consistent with the time of the alleged murders. Two anthropological examinations of the remains were further carried out by a team of experts led by José Pablo Baraybar between November 2002 and December 2003, and by Dr. George Maat in July 2003 … The ballistic analysis of cartridge cases, bullets and fragments, which, as the parties have agreed, were found at the exhumation site, reveals the

> presence of more than 30 cartridge cases of the caliber used in Kalashnikov automatic rifles, most of which were manufactured in Albania, a few in China, and one in East Germany. As discussed previously, the conclusions of the ballistics expert seem to indicate that most of the cartridge cases were fired from two different Kalashnikov-type weapons, but a few cartridge cases of similar caliber could not be positively determined to have been fired from either of those two Kalashnikovs. Another group of five bullets and a jacket stem were also analyzed. However, not surprisingly, it could not be determined whether or not any of the bullets were fired from any of the cartridge cases or whether or not any had been fired from either of the two weapons previously mentioned, or, indeed, from a third weapon of similar caliber.

In total, the partial to fully complete skeletonized remains of 11 adult male individuals showed different types of injuries caused by GSW blunt force applied to the thorax, sternum, tibia, and teeth. In most cases, fractures to the ribs, sternum, and tibia showed evidence of reactive bone formation and areas of resorption around, or adjacent to, the fractured edges, indicating survival for several days following the injuries. The documented skeletal trauma for nine of these individuals was used as evidence of torture and ill-treatment in *The Prosecutor v. Limaj et al.* (IT-03-66), setting a precedent for diagnosing torture from skeletal remains and presenting such evidence at trial. The Trial Summary Judgment (*The Prosecutor v. Limaj et al.*, IT-03-66, November 30, 2005, para. 1) states:

> The three Accused, Fatmir Limaj, Haradin Bala, and Isak Musliu, are indicted for crimes allegedly committed by them, and other members of the Kosovo Liberation Army ("KLA"), from May to around the 26th of July 1998 against Serbian civilians, and Kosovo Albanian civilians who were perceived as Serbian collaborators, in central Kosovo. The Indictment alleges that at least thirty-five civilians were abducted by KLA forces, detained in a prison camp in the village of Llapushnik/Lapusnik for prolonged periods of time under inhumane conditions, and routinely subjected to assaults, beatings, and torture. Fourteen named prisoners are alleged to have been murdered in the course of their detention. Another ten were allegedly executed in the nearby Berishe/Berisa Mountains on or about the 26th of July 1998 when KLA forces were forced to abandon the village of Llapushnik/Lapusnik, and the prison camp, under attack from advancing Serbian forces. All three Accused are charged with eight counts of imprisonment, cruel treatment, inhumane acts, and murder, for their alleged participation in the crimes at the prison camp.

Specifically, Count 6 of the Indictment alleges that the detainees were subjected to cruel ill-treatment (*The Prosecutor v. Limaj et al.*, IT-03-66, November 30, 2005, Summary Judgment):

> … 30 prisoners are alleged to have been detained. The identities of some of these are not known. The identities of some 27 of them have been established. Almost all of these have been proved to have been detained in either a very small basement storage room, or in another very small room normally used as a cowshed. The evidence establishes that the conditions in each of these rooms were absolutely inhumane. There was, at most times, gross overcrowding. There was no provision for washing or toilet, although after an initial period, one bucket was provided for use as a toilet in the storage room. This bucket was not regularly emptied, so that it would overflow. The prisoners slept on the concrete floors or on some straw. Meals were provided at irregular intervals; at times days would pass without food. The food was eaten in the rooms. There was very little light or ventilation in the two rooms. The atmosphere was absolutely oppressive with heat and stench. On rare occasions prisoners in the storage room were allowed fresh air for a short time at night. Many of the prisoners were tied by the hands,

> or feet, or both. Some were tied to other prisoners. In the cowshed, most prisoners were chained to the wall and unable to move from their position in the room. They were forced to soil themselves in their clothes. Many of the prisoners had been badly injured, with broken limbs, bones or internal injuries. Others had been shot. No medical treatment of any kind was provided, even though there was a doctor and a medical clinic in the village which was used by KLA personnel.

Skeletal trauma provided physical evidence that corroborated witness testimony the detainees were routinely beaten, denied medical treatment, and systematically tortured (*The Prosecutor v. Limaj et al.*, IT-03-66, November 30, 2005, Summary Judgment):

> Forensic examination discloses that 6 of the 9 victims died from bullet wounds fired from Kalashnikov rifles, which was the type of weapon used by the KLA guards. The precise cause of death of the other 3 bodies was not identified by the forensic examination. These three bodies, however, had fractures of bones caused at about the time of death. Some bodies had been shot more than once.
>
> … supported there is a significant body of evidence which details individual acts of severe physical violence committed by various KLA members on individual prisoners. The evidence indicates that it was a regular occurrence for a prisoner to be blindfolded, tied, and taken from the room at night by KLA soldiers, who often wore hoods to hide their faces. The prisoners were then severely beaten or subjected to other extreme violence, and later were returned to the detention room, at times unconscious or in severe pain.

Table 5.1 provides an excerpt from the trial transcript of witness testimony on the torture that occurred. Specifically, Haradin Bala was found guilty, pursuant to Article 7(1) of the Statute, of the following offences (*The Prosecutor v. Limaj et al.*, IT-03-66, November 30, 2005, Summary Judgment):

> Count 4: Torture, a violation of the laws or customs of war, under Article 3 of the Statute, for having aided the torture of a prisoner named in the written Disposition:
>
> Count 6: Cruel treatment, a violation of the laws or customs of war, under Article 3 of the Statute, for having personally mistreated 3 prisoners, and aided another episode of mistreatment of one of those prisoners, and for your personal role in the maintenance and enforcement of inhumane conditions of detention in the Llapushnik/Lapusnik prison camp.

Peru

During the years 1980–2000, more than 65,000 Peruvians lost their lives due to the armed conflicts between national security forces and the two insurgent organizations Sendero Luminoso and the Movimiento Revolucionario Tupac Amaru (MRTA). In 1998, Peruvian Law No. 26926 criminalized torture. Since the passing of this law, HHRR organizations have been recording cases of torture in the country (Amnesty International 2003; Fraser 2004). According to the Truth, Justice and Reconciliation Commission (CVR 2003), current estimates point to over 13,500 people missing as a consequence of the armed conflict (EPAF 2006).

Three separate cases representing eight (n = 8) individuals are described from Peru. These cases occurred during separate incidents differing temporally and geographically

Table 5.1 Testimony by the Prosecution from a Witness to Torture in Kosovo

A man is interviewed about torture he witnessed. This excerpt is taken from the trial transcript in *The Prosecutor v. Limaj et al.* (IT-03-66), June 1, 2005, T 1341-1342.

Q. Did you ever go back to the room on the ground floor, the first one that you were taken to when you arrived at the farm?
A. Yes. On one occasion we were called to go down there. We had tea. We sat there.

Q. Did anything else happen besides having tea?
A. Yes. There was an unpleasant situation for me and for my son. We had to watch as other men were beaten.

Q. I know it's unpleasant, but I'm going to ask you to describe that occasion for the Trial Chamber. First, do you remember how many men were there being beaten?
A. They brought four or five of them. I don't know the exact number, but it wasn't more than five. They lined them up and started beating them. They would beat every one of them for five or ten minutes, slapping them, kicking them, hitting them on their legs. One of them was unable to stand at all. At any rate, they were beaten up.

Q. Did you recognize any of the soldiers who participated in the beating?
A. Yes. The same man that beat [the witness] beat these people. I'm referring to the first day when we arrived there, in that facility.

Q. Was this person armed now on this occasion that you're describing right now?
A. He had a pistol.

Q. Did he do anything with that pistol?
A. Yes. I remember that. When they stopped beating them he handed the pistol to one of these men and he told him to kill the others. The man lifted the pistol up and put him next to a person's forehead. They were crying, begging for mercy. Then this first man took the pistol, put it next to the other man's forehead and fired it, but it was empty. I think it was some kind of psychological torture.

throughout the country. All three incidents involved unarmed civilians and the security forces. The cases are the following:

1. Peru case I (n = 1): An elderly individual was detained by the Peruvian Army. According to witnesses, he was severely beaten at the time of the arrest and during his detention. It was suspected that he was subsequently shot; the body was buried by his family.

2. Peru case II (n = 2): A group of five people were arrested by the police. According to the testimony of one of the survivors of this incident, they were severely beaten and ill-treated during their arrest, and four members of the group were extrajudicially executed. The testimony of the survivor is presented in Table 5.2.

3. Peru case III (n = 5): The remains of 15 individuals were recovered from clandestine graves located at a military base in the highlands of Peru. In this series, five individuals exhibited multiple blunt force injuries consistent with beatings. These individuals are yet to be unidentified and are alleged to be part of the more than 500 people who were arrested and detained at the base between 1983 and 1989 (Uceda 2004).

In total, skeletal evidence of torture has been documented in eight medicolegal death investigations within Peru. Of the eight cases described here, three cases have supporting witness testimony about the beatings that occurred. Skeletal evidence demonstrated that all eight cases shared specific and diffuse traumatic injuries in the thoracic cage or

Table 5.2 Testimony from a Survivor and Witness X of Torture in Peru

A survivor and witness of various acts of torture replies to questions during an interview about his detainment. This testimony was part of a report compiled by EPAF conducting a medicolegal investigation into the identification and COD of exhumed skeletal remains (EPAF, 2006.).

Q. And Witness, how was it? Was he lying down?
A. Yes.

Q. He was hit then?
A. Yes. From the back.

Q. Was he facing down?
A. Yes.

Q. Was he hit on the back?
A. Yes, on the back. They pulled his arms and then they hit him with the rifle butts … They also stomped him on the back.

Q. They stepped on him only, they do not stand on top of him, they do not stand on his back?
A. Yes, they stand on his back.

Q. They stand on his back?
A. Yes. They stop him breathing.

Q. I understand, two people are hitting him but how many of them step on his back?
A. Only one. He stepped on him, stomping, stopping him from breathing.

Q. In any instance, they stepped on him while lying facing up? Was he also facing up?
A. Yes, too.

Q. And when they were facing up what they did do to them?
A. They hit him with fists on the chest, kicked him on the chest; they made him sit as well, they kicked him.

spine, characterized by linear fractures on the ribs or the sternum located on the anterior, lateral, and posterior aspects. The witnesses stated that inhumane and cruel treatment was inflicted; the victims were stomped, kicked, and hit before being killed. Table 5.2 provides an excerpt of witness testimony from a documented case in one of the Peruvian series (case II) and accurately represents the mechanism of injuries in all of the cases presented (interview with witness X; EPAF 2006).

Skeletal Evidence

The fracture patterns for the 19 individuals from Kosovo and Peru are presented (Table 5.3). In 18 of the cases, the individuals exhibited skeletal trauma consistent with injuries resulting from BFT and stigmata consistent with torture or ill-treatment (i.e., beatings). In 13 of these cases, the cause of death was determined to be single or multiple gunfire injuries. In the remaining five cases, the cause of death was unascertained. The prevalent manner of death in all of the described cases from both Peru and Kosovo were homicide, specifically extrajudicial execution. The victims in all of these cases were found in circumstances of concealment, further indicating that they were victims of foul play. Additionally, of the victims that were later identified, all had been reported as missing persons.

Among blunt force injuries, the following regions were affected (n = number of individuals): cranial vault (n = 1), teeth (n = 1), sternum (n = 4), ribs (n = 16), and lumbar

Table 5.3 Summary of Cause of Death and Fracture Patterns in Cases of Known and Suspected Torture (n = 19)

Case Number	Cause of Death	Blunt Force Wounds
Kosovo 01	Unascertained	Multiple tooth fractures
Kosovo 02	Multiple GSW to chest and pelvis	Multiple rib fractures
Kosovo 03	GSW to the head	Multiple rib fractures
Kosovo 04	Multiple GSW to the head	Multiple rib fractures
Kosovo 05	GSW to the head	Isolated rib fracture; BFT to the head, hairline fracture on right temporal bone
Kosovo 06	Unascertained	Multiple rib and sternal fractures
Kosovo 07	Unascertained	Multiple rib fractures
Kosovo 08	Multiple GSW to the head and chest	Multiple rib fractures
Kosovo 09	Unascertained	Heavily scavenged; no injuries recorded
Kosovo 10	Multiple GSW	Multiple ribs and sternal fractures
Kosovo 11	Multiple GSW	Multiple rib fractures
Peru case I-01	Unascertained	Multiple rib fractures
Peru case II-02	Multiple GSW	Multiple rib fractures
Peru case II-03	Multiple GSW	Multiple rib fractures
Peru case III-04	Multiple GSW	Isolated rib fracture
Peru case III-05	Multiple GSW	Multiple rib fractures
Peru case III-06	GSW to the head	Fracture of transverse process 5th lumbar
Peru case III-07	Unascertained	Multiple rib and sternal fractures
Peru case III-08	Multiple GSW	Isolated rib fracture

Note: GSW = Gunshot wound.

vertebra (n = 1). The ribs are the most commonly fractured type of bone. In four cases, more than one region was affected resulting in the following fracture combinations: rib and skull (n = 1), rib and sternum (n = 3). The two most prevalent types of injuries observed include anteroposterior compression of the chest characterized by fractures adjacent to the costochondral cartilage and isolated and paired fractures in other various regions of the chest, likely resulting from direct impact. These injury patterns are consistent with the witness testimony that describes how the alleged trauma was inflicted (Figures 5.1–5.7). The Chamber accepted the physical evidence of skeletal trauma that corroborated witness testimony of the events that took place (*The Prosecutor v. Limaj et al.* IT-03-66, November 30, 2005, Summary Judgment, para. 322):

> … a newspaper report of 15 June 1998 stating [the victim] had been killed with five bullets to the chest. … relatives [of the victim] who viewed the body [reported that the] arm had been broken and there were signs of wounds to his stomach. There were also bruises and cuts on

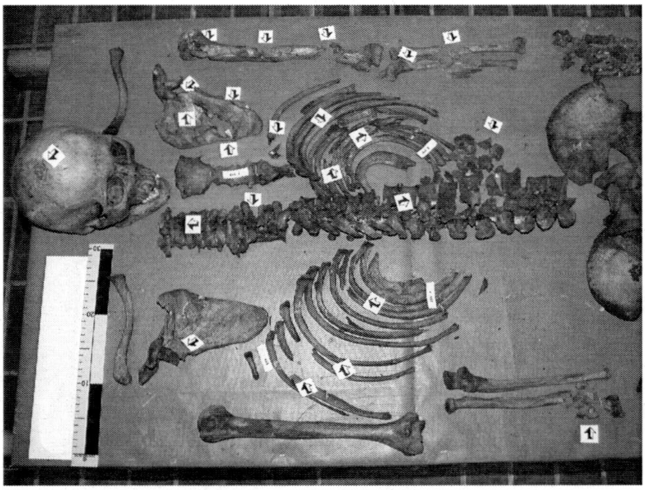

Figure 5.1 Skeleton in anatomical order. Arrows point to multiple gunshot wounds (Alain Wittmann, EPAF).

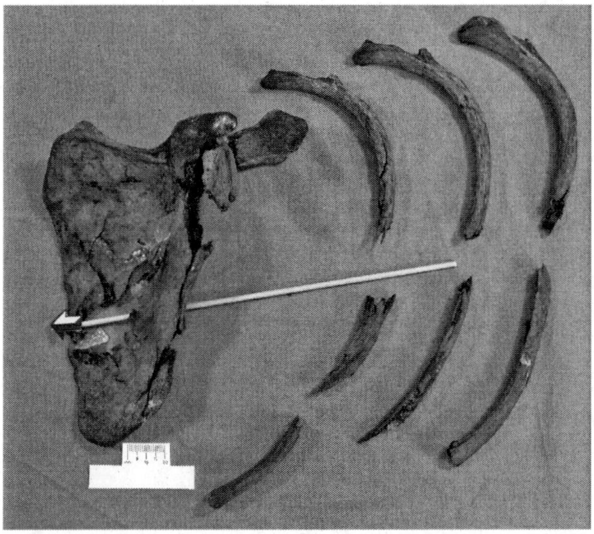

Figure 5.2 Gunshot wound to the left scapula and three left rib bodies. Rib fractures resulted from gunshot injury (Alain Wittmann).

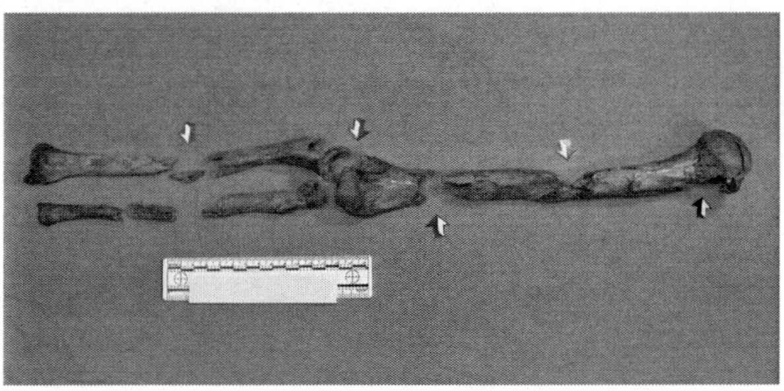

Figure 5.3 Multiple gunshot injuries in the form of complete and comminuted fractures and perforating defects to the left proximal, medial, and distal humerus; proximal ulna; and medial radius and ulna (Alain Wittmann).

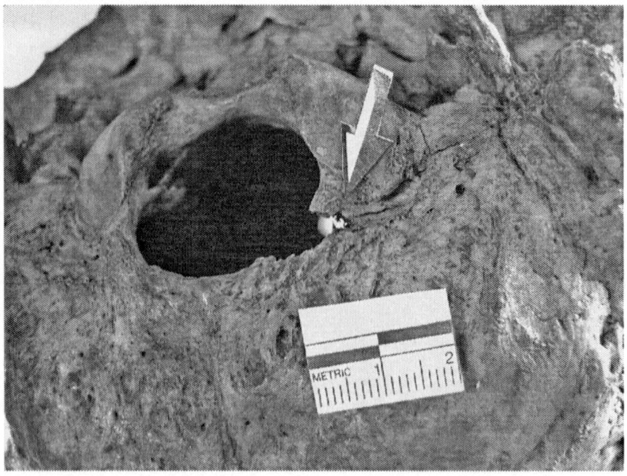

Figure 5.4 Small defect along the posterior aspect of the left occipital condyle with several small radiating fractures, gunfire entrance wound (Alain Wittmann).

his hands. Forensic examination of the body by José Pablo Baraybar confirms that the cause of death was multiple gunshot wounds to the head and trunk. It also reveals that there were gunshot wounds to his upper limbs.

Fractures of the Cranium and Teeth

One individual exhibited a hairline fracture on the right temporal bone. A second individual in the Kosovo series showed multiple linear longitudinal fractures extending in a

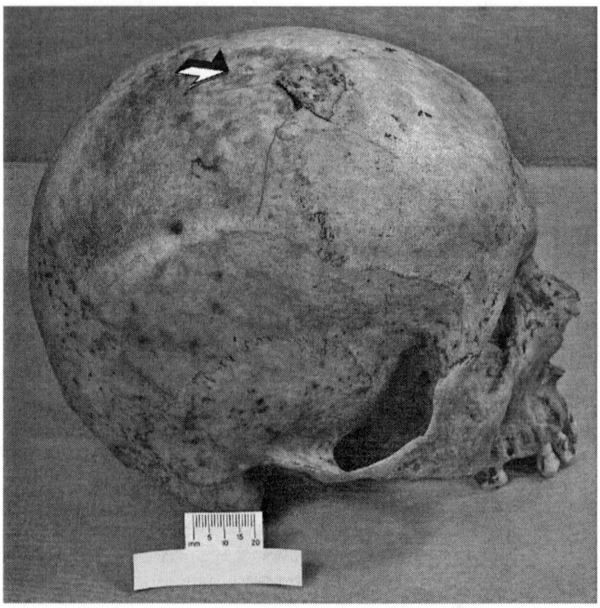

Figure 5.5 Gunfire injury from left to right, upward. Bullet penetrated the occipital bone (refer to Figure 5.4) and struck the frontal bone but did not exit the skull. A gunfire exit wound is present on the superior, right frontal bone, along the coronal suture, depicting an irregular-shaped defect with small radiating fractures (Alain Wittmann).

Figure 5.6 (See color insert following page 38) Close-up view of the cranial defect (see figure 5.5). Note the small area of bone completely fractured from the lateral margin (Alain Wittmann).

buccolingual direction across the axis of the crown in multiple teeth in both arcades. Only the crowns were fractured. The condition illustrated in Figures 5.8–5.11 appears similar to the condition known as *incomplete tooth fracture* (ITF) or *cracked tooth syndrome* (CTS), which refers to "a fracture plane of unknown depth and direction passing through tooth structure that, if not already involving, may progress to communicate with the pulp and/or periodontal ligament" (Ellis 2001, 428). Although multiple factors tend to contribute to ITF, dental restorations, the shape of the cusps, and load of force are most important factors (Patel and Burke 1995; Salis et al. 1987). Masticatory accidents, such as biting on a hard, rigid object with unusually extreme force can have a similar result (Lynch and McConnell 2002). Cracks in the enamel may be centrally or peripherally located and may result in

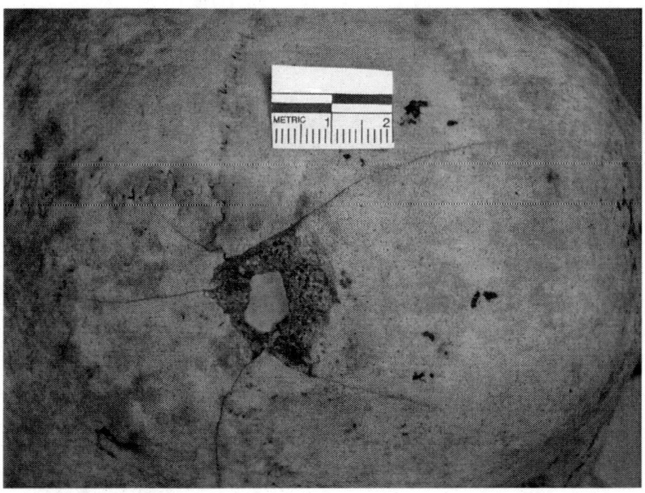

Figure 5.7 (See color insert following page 38) A circular-like bone plug was lifted away revealing a circular defect, exposing the diplöe and "external" beveling (Alain Wittmann). (Same defect as pictured in Figure 5.6.)

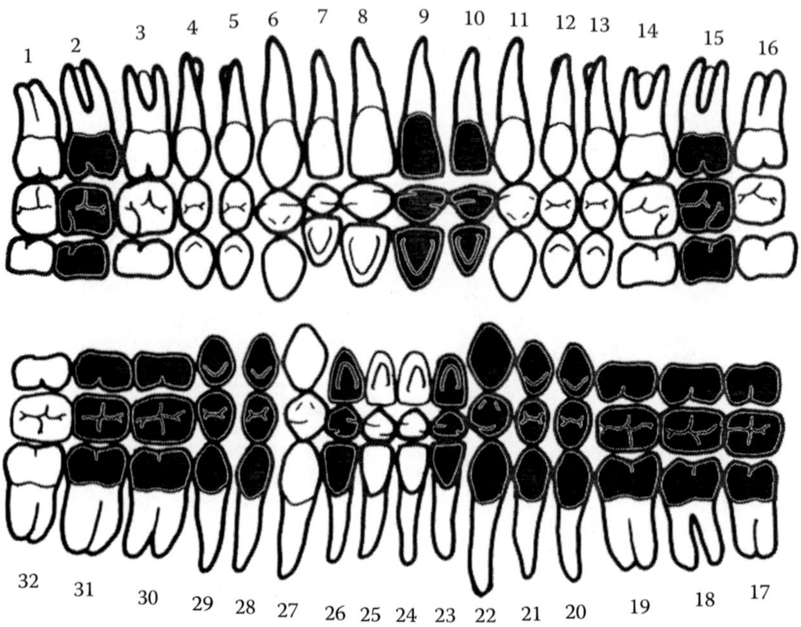

Figure 5.8 Schematic diagram illustrating tooth fractures, *cracked tooth syndrome*. Shaded areas represent fractured teeth (Erin Kimmerle, modified schematic from Buikstra and Ubelaker, 1994).

cusp fractures (Lynch and McConnell 2002). Considering the difference between anterior and posterior tooth loads, it is expected that posterior teeth will be more prone to fracture than anterior teeth because of the closeness of the former to the muscles generating normal amounts of force (Homewood 1998). Most commonly, maxillary first molars are the most affected teeth while maxillary canines and premolars are more resistant to impact (Roh and Lee 2006). In the Kosovan case, because the distribution of fractures encompassed posterior and anterior teeth of both arcades as well as opposing teeth, it is likely that the

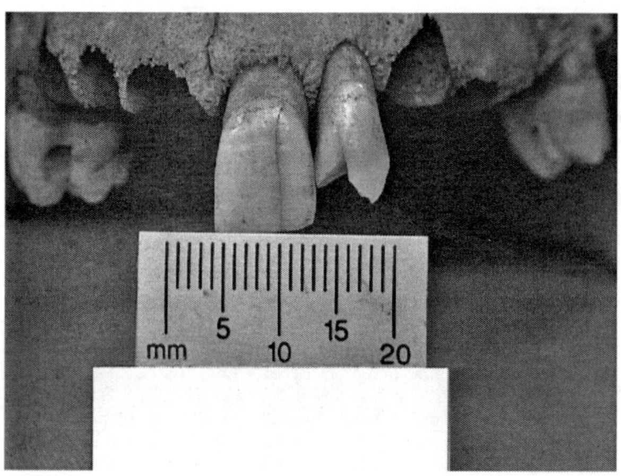

Figure 5.9 Longitudinal fracture lines of the upper central and lateral incisors, left side, Kosovo series (Alain Wittmann).

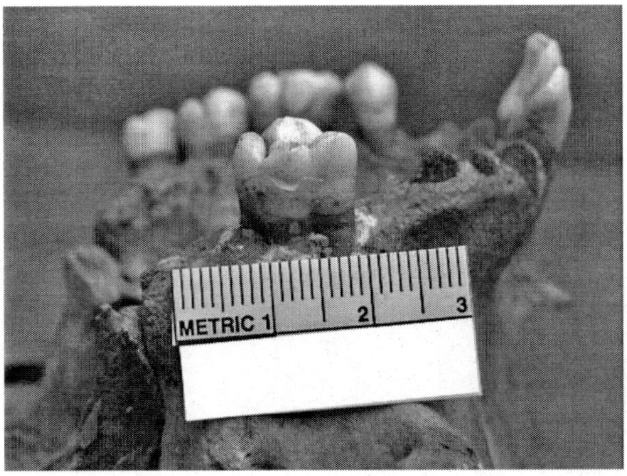

Figure 5.10 Multiple fractures of the second superior molar, left side, Kosovo series (Alain Wittmann).

fractures were caused while the teeth were biting into a hard object placed in the mouth and the lower jaw was thrust upward by a blow.

Fractures of the Sternum

Sternal fractures may be single or multiple, complete or incomplete. Typically, they are transverse and cut across the sternal body between the second and third costochondral notches (Figure 5.12) (Breederveld et al. 1988; Brooks et al. 1993; Cooper et al. 1982; Hills et al. 1993). When multiple fractures occur, they tend to be located more inferiorly, between the sternal notches 3 and 4, as well as sternal notches 4 and 5, respectively (Figures 5.13 to 5.14). In both instances, they occur as a result of a direct impact below the fracture line in the area of higher mobility of the sternum (Fowler 1957). When two or more fractures occur, the area of impact may actually be located between the two fracture lines. Fractures of the sternal body may also be associated to rib fractures, though not always. The ribs affected are often those at which level the fracture was identified and may be either unilateral or bilateral.

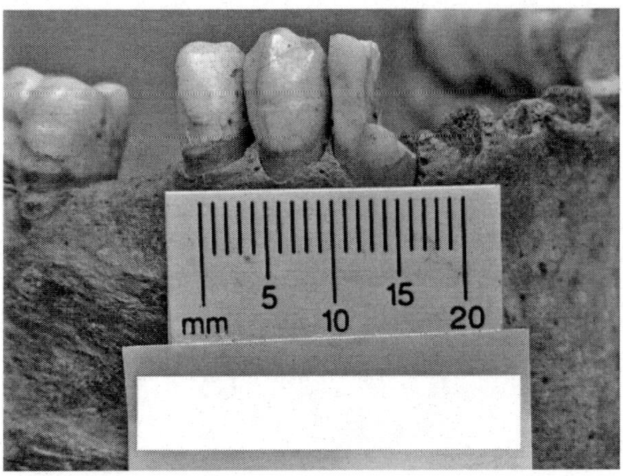

Figure 5.11 Longitudinal fracture lines of the anterior mandibular teeth, Kosovo series (Alain Wittmann).

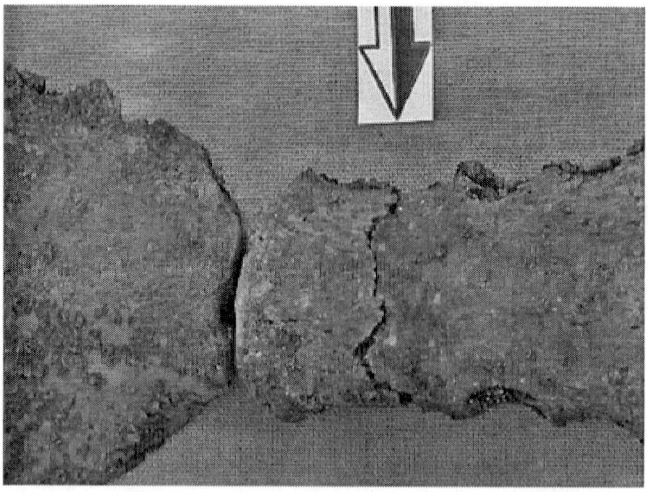

Figure 5.12 Transverse fracture of the proximal sternal body, Peru case III (Juan Carlos Tello, EPAF).

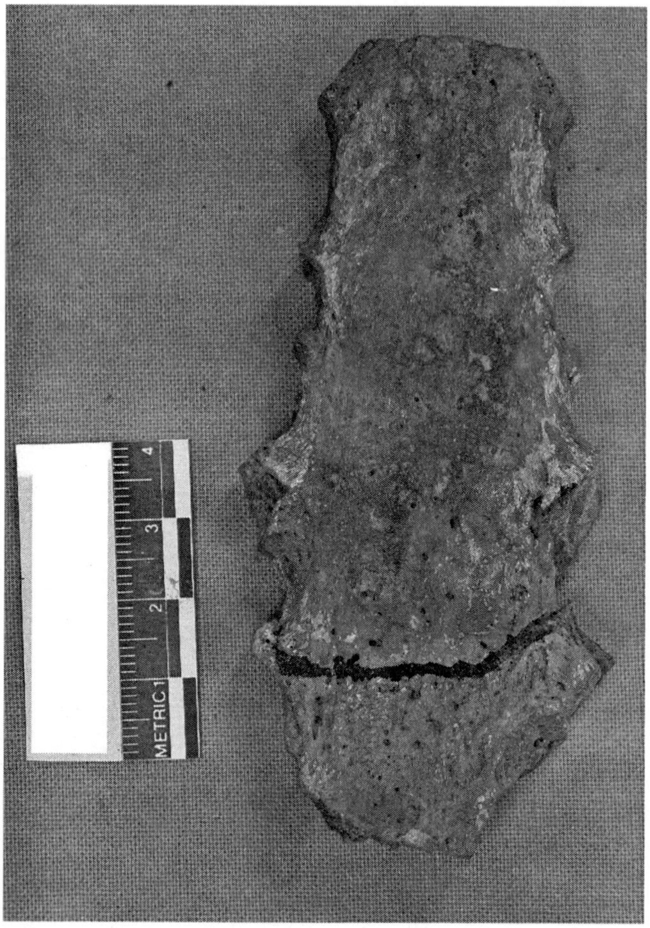

Figure 5.13a Transverse fracture of the distal sternal body, anterior view, Kosovo series (Alain Wittmann).

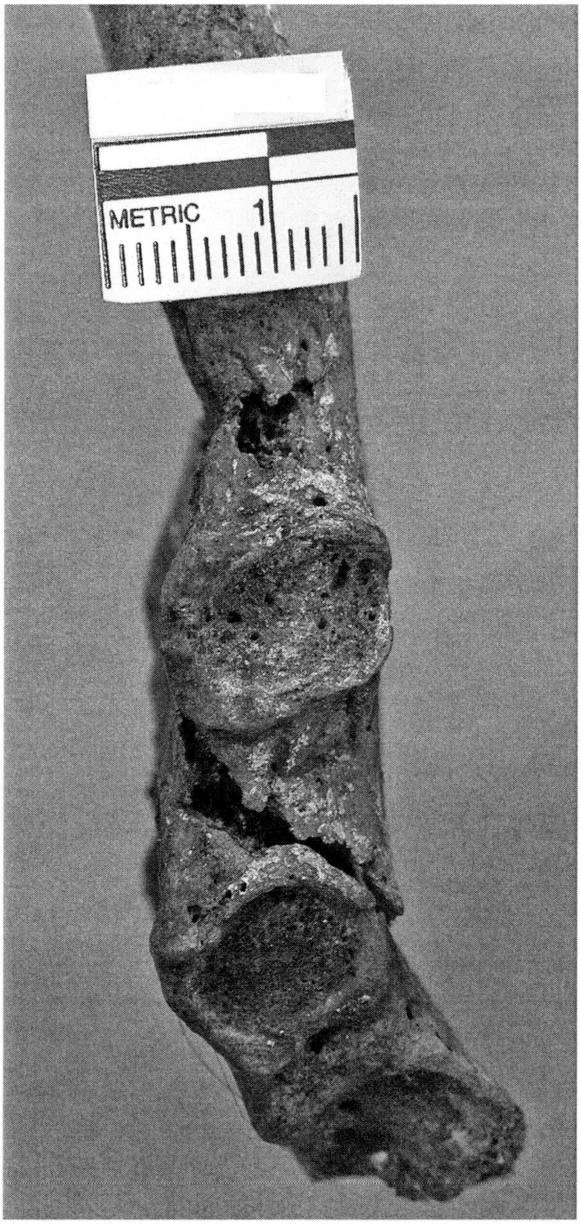

Figure 5.13b Transverse fracture of the sternal body, lateral view, Kosovo series (Alain Wittmann).

Fractures of the Ribs

Blunt force injury to the chest typically results in rib fractures (Figures 5.15–5.23). The attacker's foot, fist, or other blunt objects are the "weapons" used when a victims is punched, kicked, stomped, or beaten. Reportedly, rib fractures tend to be painful and, depending on the number of ribs affected, the age, and weight of the victim, may increase morbidity and mortality risks for victims (Bulger et al. 2000; Brukner and Khan 1996; Kleinman and Schlesinger 1997; Barness et al. 2003; Flagel et al. 2005; Holcomb et al. 2003; Karmakar

Figure 5.14 Transverse fracture of the sternal body, posterior view (same case as in Figure 5.13) Kosovo series (Alain Wittmann).

and Ho 2003; Liman et al. 2003; Sirmali et al. 2003). It has been argued that tolerance to blunt anterior loading of the chest is more dependent on age than on load distribution (Kent and Patrie 2005), implying that the age of the victim is paramount to the lethality of the injury. Frequent complications of blunt chest trauma include pneumothorax and hemothorax* (Simon et al. 1998), either at the time of injury or up to several days following the injury (Tekinbas et al. 2003). Long-term sequelae of blunt chest trauma may include persistent dyspnea and cardiac, neurological, or esophageal complications (Yeo 2001). It is important to point out the associated medical conditions of rib fractures and the potential health consequences of not obtaining treatment as many victims of chronic abuse or maltreatment show evidence of rib fractures in various stages of healing (Figures 5.24–5.26). Consequently, from the time of injury until death (in many cases this may be days or

* Pneumothorax occurs when air is forced into the thoracic cavity without means of escape, increasing the intrapleural pressure, often resulting in the collapse of one lung. Hemothorax occurs when blood accumulates in the pleural cavity (the space between the lungs and the wall of the chest) due to the rupture of veins or arteries associated with penetrating chest injuries. Some of the symptoms common to these conditions are air hunger, shortness of breath (dyspnea), respiratory distress, and chest pain (Tekinbas et al. 2003).

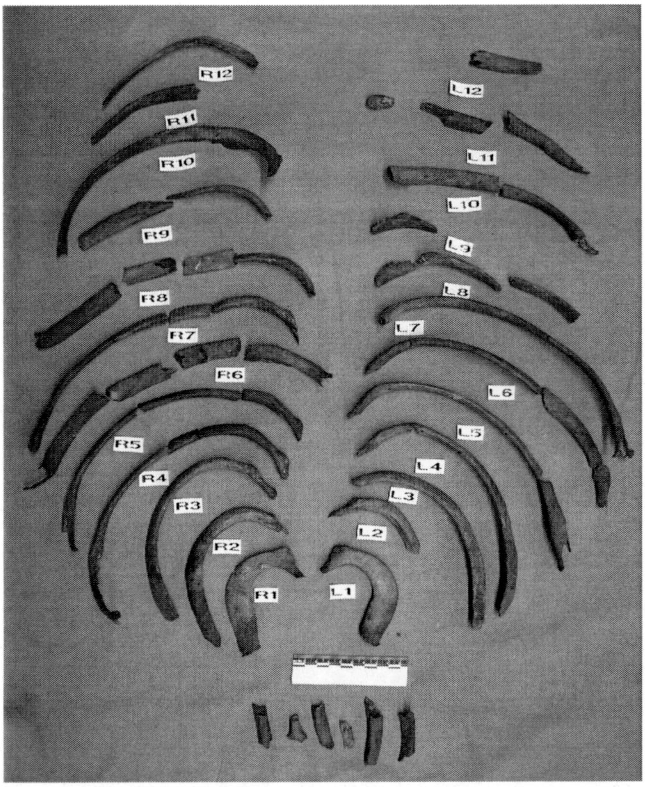

Figure 5.15a Multiple bilateral rib fractures, Kosovo series (Juan Carlos Tello, EPAF).

Figure 5.15b Multiple rib fractures, right side, Peru series (Juan Carlos Tello, EPAF).

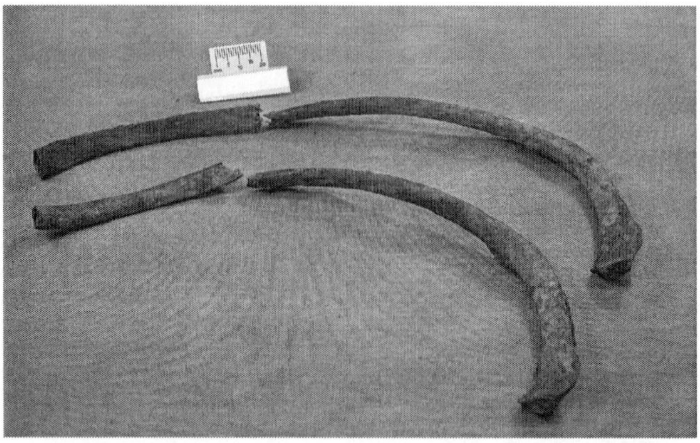

Figure 5.16 Overview of fractures on the 8th and 9th right ribs (Kosovo series). Blunt force trauma to the sternal body and anterior ribs along the rib head and sternal 1/3 shaft, as a result of stomping (Alain Wittmann).

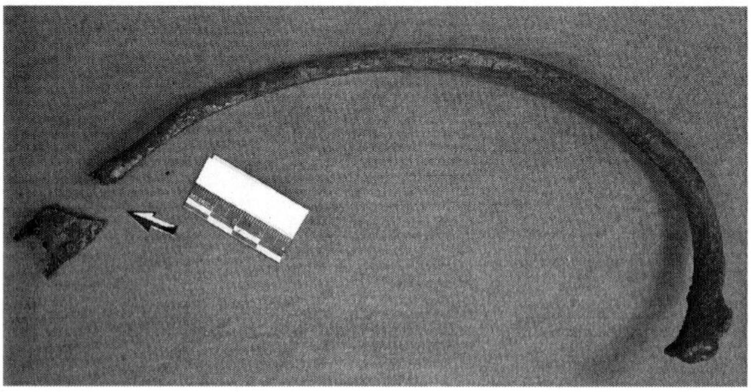

Figure 5.17 Fracture of the right 8th rib, adjacent to costochondral, Kosovo series (Alain Wittmann).

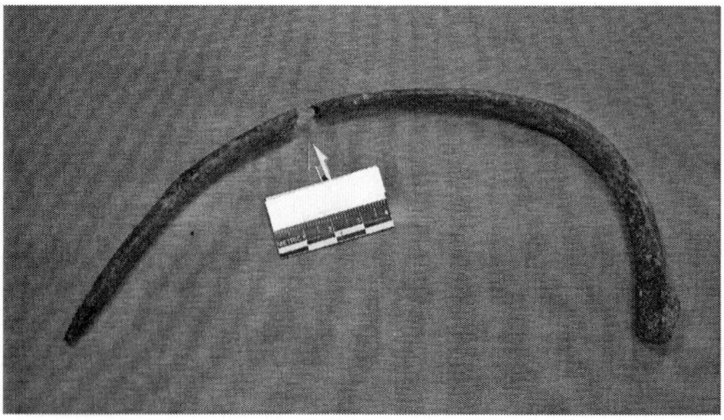

Figure 5.18 Overview of the right 9th rib, Kosovo series (Alain Wittmann).

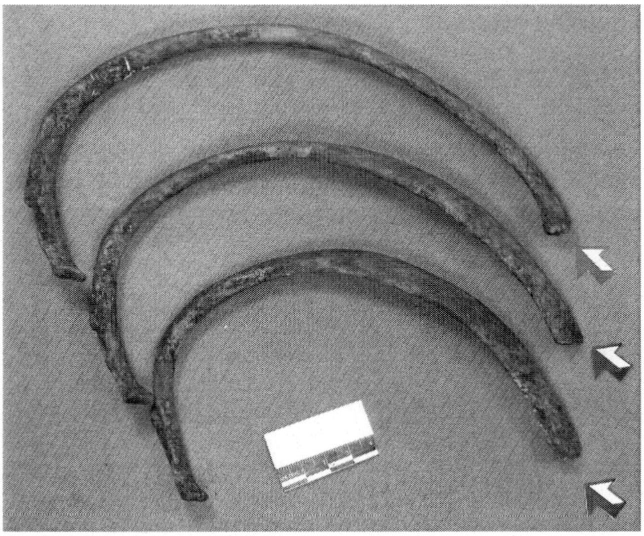

Figure 5.19 Overview of the left 3rd, 4th, and 5th ribs. Fractures adjacent to costochondral, Kosovo series (Alain Wittmann).

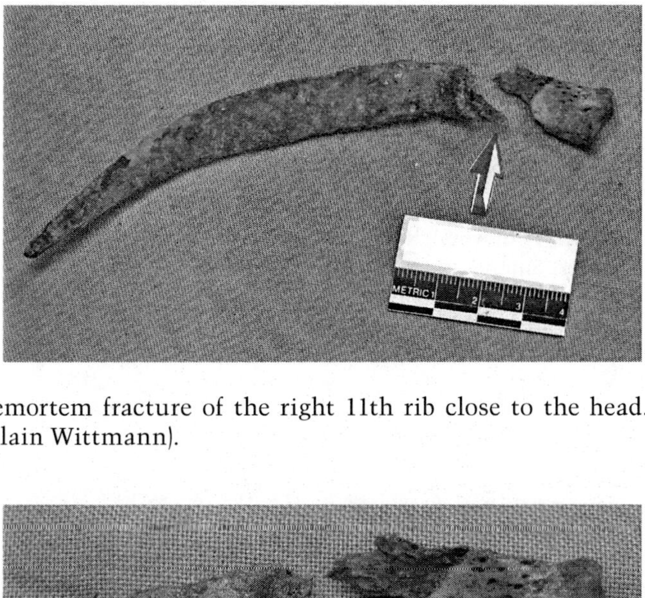

Figure 5.20 Antemortem fracture of the right 11th rib close to the head. Observe reactive bone formation (Alain Wittmann).

Figure 5.21 Close-up view of Figure 5.20. Antemortem fracture of the right 11th rib adjacent to rib head. Observe reactive bone formation (Alain Wittmann).

Figure 5.22 Overview of the right ribs #7 and 8 showing fractures close to costochondral joint (Alain Wittmann).

Figure 5.23 Right rib #6; transverse antemortem fracture, 20 mm lateral to costochondral joint with separation of fragments, smooth edges, reactive bone formation and areas of bone resorption (Alain Wittmann).

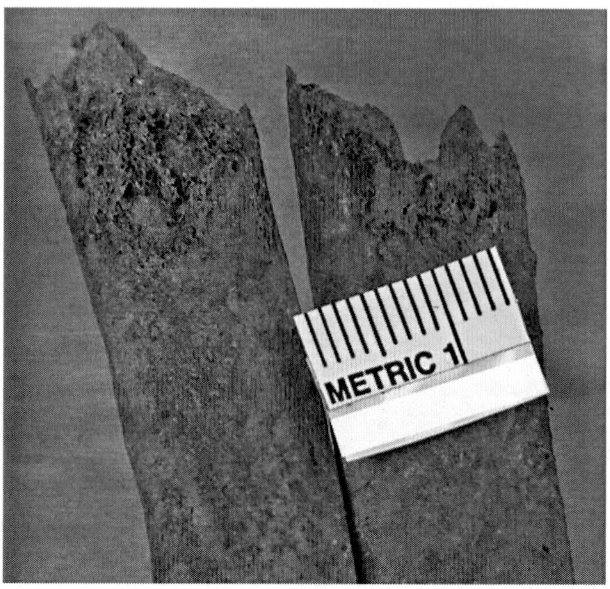

Figure 5.24 Sternal rib antemortem fracture with reactive bone formation (Alain Wittmann).

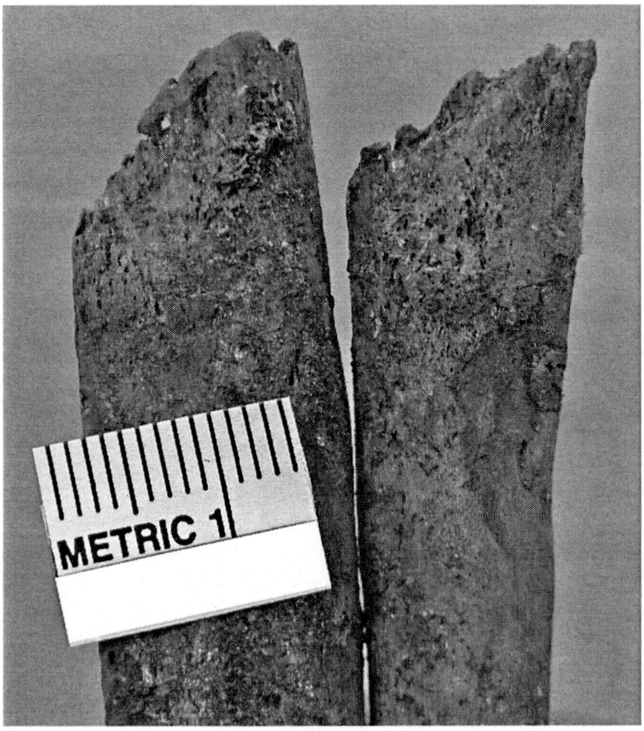

Figure 5.25 Sternal rib antemortem fracture with reactive bone formation (Alain Wittmann).

Figure 5.26 Second example of antemortem sternal rib fracture with reactive bone formation indicative of fracture occurring antemortem (Alain Wittmann).

months), victims suffer ill health effects that may contribute to death, if medical treatment is required but not received.

Rib fractures may occur in all aspects of the thorax and tend to be either transverse, oblique, or buckle (Love and Symes 2004). There is no single or predictable pattern of fracturing as it depends on the point of impact. Although most anterior fractures tend to be oblique, adjacent ribs sometimes exhibit transverse patterns. In general terms, there is a higher concentration of fractures in the anterior area, decreasing in frequency to the lateral aspect, and further decreasing in prevalence to the posterior area of the chest. The number of fractures per rib observed in the series presented here varied between one and three. When multiple fractures were observed on a single rib, they tended to occur in adjacent ribs as well.

Table 5.3 lists the consistently observed skeletal characteristics of BFT in documented torture cases, as described in this chapter. General findings include the following:

1. Anterior fractures occur lateral to the costochondral joint at the approximate level of the midclavicular line and between the latter and the axillary lines.
2. Lateral fractures occur at the level of the greater curvature of the rib, roughly between the axillary and scapular lines.
3. Posterior fractures occur between the scapular line and the midline.
4. Rib fractures may or may not occur in association with sternal fractures.
5. Numerous factures in various stages of healing are present.
6. Fractures affecting only the outer table of the rib, depressed fractures (V-shaped fractures) were caused by the direct impact of an edged object against the rib.
7. Linear, complete or incomplete fractures of the costal body, with failure of bone in tension along the outer wall. Breakaway spurs of bone along the internal wall may or may not be present and are caused by anterior, or anterolateral compression of the chest. Typically, this occurs in an anteroposterior direction below rib 3.
8. Linear, incomplete fractures of the costal body, with failure of bone in tension along the inner wall. These fractures tend to be associated to incomplete costochondral fractures with bone failure on the outer table, suggesting a compressive force between them. Typically one rib tends to be affected, whereas neighboring ribs may show only one costochondral fracture.
9. Oblique fractures, complete or incomplete, in the neck area with separation of the head from the neck, typically on ribs 10–12.

The fracture pattern described for the neck region typically observed for ribs 10–12 may be explained by the fact that these ribs do not possess an intra-articular ligament stabilizing the costocentral joint and the intervertebral disk, as discussed by Christensen and Dietz (1980).

Fractures of the Lumbar Spine

Isolated fractures of the transverse processes of lumbar vertebra are a rare finding except when directly impacted. In RTAs, they are uncommon, unless an object strikes the victim through abdominal trauma (Brynin and Gardiner 2001; Miller et al. 2000) or when the victim is struck by an automobile. Of the cases presented in this chapter, one individual exhibited a fracture to a lumbar vertebra. This case was from the Peruvian samples, Peru case III (Figures 5.27–5.29).

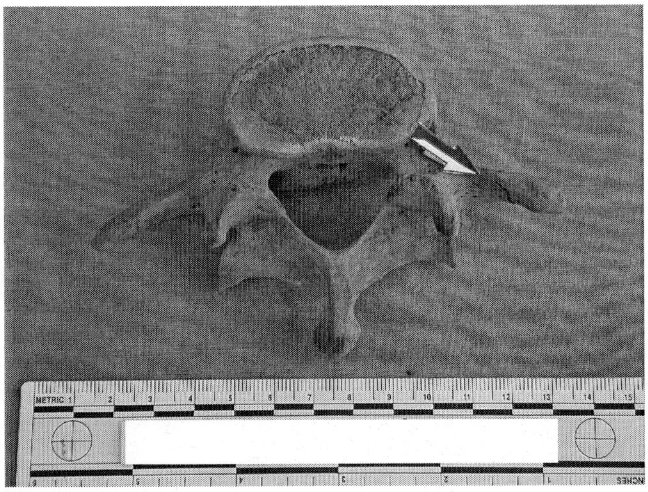

Figure 5.27 Superior view of the L5 showing fracture of right transverse process (Alain Wittmann, EPAF).

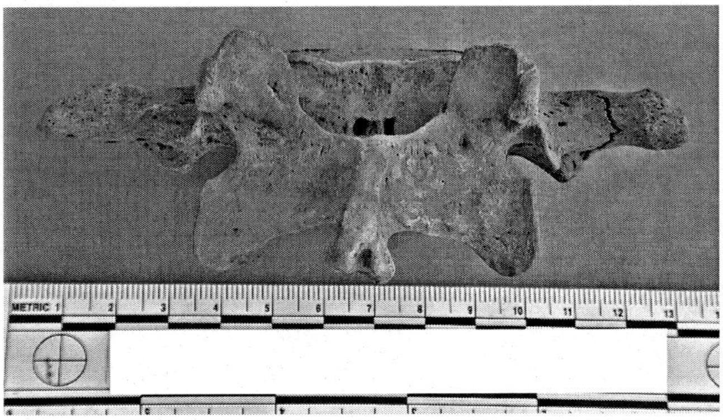

Figure 5.28 Close up posterior view of the L5 (See Figure 5.27) showing fracture of right transverse process (Juan Carlos Tello, EPAF).

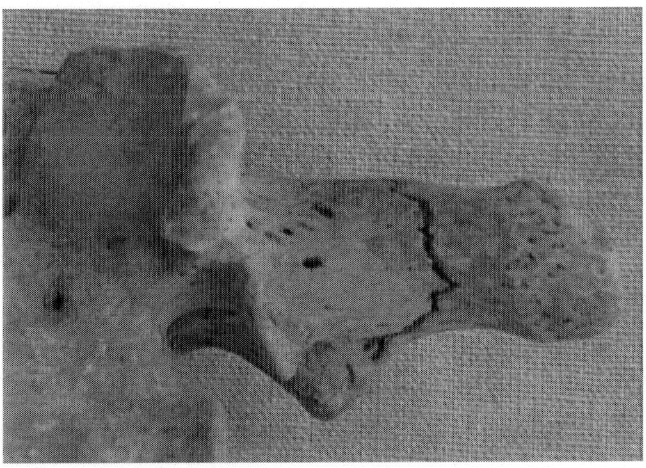

Figure 5.29 Close-up view of a fracture of the right transverse process (Juan Carlos Tello, EPAF).

Differential Diagnosis of BFT Resulting from Torture, Accidents, and Nonaccidental Mechanisms

RTAs are perhaps the foremost cause of thoracic injuries, including rib fractures. The ability to distinguish accidental from inflicted trauma is paramount to recognizing possible signs of torture in skeletal remains.* This is all the more critical in cases in which attempts to conceal a homicide are disguised as accidents.

Injuries resulting from RTAs primarily consist of chest injuries caused by the seatbelt or airbag to the driver or passenger, impacts of the steering wheel against the driver, or injuries characteristic of pedestrians struck by a moving vehicle. The patterns of injuries consist of rib fractures along the path of the wheel or seat belt, including specific aspects of the *manubrium sternii* (Arajarvi et al. 1987; Newman 1984) and bilateral fractures of the first ribs resulting from inflation of the airbag at collision (Stoneham 1995). In contrast, the particular location or distribution of wounds to the thorax in cases of assault are not patterned.

Additionally, deceleration injuries cause thoracic injuries by direct and indirect mechanisms (Richter et al. 1996; Tomczak and Buikstra, 1999; Rice et al. 2002). In a car crash, injury is caused as the body is thrust forward placing the spine in hyperflexion and compressive stress—an indirect mechanism (Fowler 1957; Helal 1964) or from impact of the steering wheel (a direct mechanism). The latter is an important factor in the differential diagnosis of probable accidental versus nonaccidental trauma. Fractures of the sternal body, regardless of their association to adjacent rib fractures (i.e., ribs #2–6) are most likely caused by direct trauma to the chest. In contrast, fractures of the manubrium (when associated to unilateral or bilateral rib fractures, occur on the first and second ribs, or clavicle) are an indication of deceleration injuries resulting from indirect force as in RTAs in which the mechanism of injury is flexion–compression of the chest. Consequently, there appears to be a difference in the location of sternal fractures depending on the mechanism of injury. The sternal body tends to break following a direct impact at or near the area of impact due to its capacity for movement. In contrast, the manubrium is firmly anchored by the clavicles and first ribs. Therefore, manubrial fractures primarily due to mechanisms of hyperflexion–compression rather than a direct impact, are indicative of an RTA. In contrast, crushing injuries due to falls or jumps are also responsible for rib fractures. The extent of damage is primarily dependent on the height of the fall. Jumpers, however, after landing on their feet, tend to break the impact with the dominant side in which thoracic trauma is involved (Teh et al. 2003).

Differential Diagnosis: A Practical Example

On November 3, 1991, a Peruvian military task force also known by the name of "Grupo Colina" burst into a party in a house of a poor neighborhood (Barrios Altos) in Lima, killing 15 people and maiming 4 others (CVR 2003). That same night, elsewhere in Lima, the body of a young army recruit was found dead on the sidewalk adjacent to a highway. The next day, the media published the list of dead from the killings of Barrios Altos, and the name of this recruit was among the victims (referred to as individual A). Shortly after the autopsy, the family was allowed to very briefly see the body of their son and was then

* Falls and accidents at the workplace are the most common form of thoracic injuries resulting from accidents, whereas nonaccidental trauma is primarily caused by assault (Sirmali et al. 2003; Atanasijevic et al. 2005).

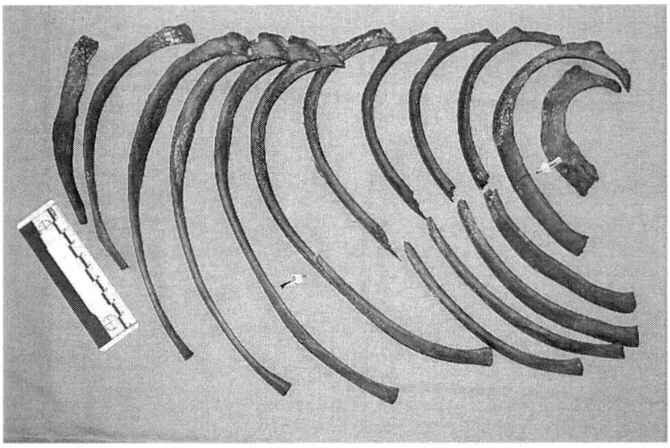

Figure 5.30 Patterned rib fractures apparent on ribs #2–11, indicated by arrows. Individual A, Peru series (Alain Wittmann, EPAF).

forced to bury him under tight military control. A few years later, when the political situation improved, the family requested an exhumation and second autopsy to determine whether or not their son had been tortured and then killed.

The original autopsy was very cursory and was plagued with inconsistencies. Likewise, information about the scene of the crime was almost nonexistent. For example, there was no information about how the body, allegedly run over by a car, was found on the sidewalk. During the second autopsy, it was noted that individual A represented the skeletonized remains of a young adult male with three injury patterns to the right side of the head, thorax, and fibula (EPAF 2006):

1. Fractures of the right anterior portion of the rib cage involving ribs #2–7. When observed in association, they compose a line running laterally and inferiorly (Figure 5.30). The second rib was not fractured but shows a 1 mm deep linear imprint of the external table (Figure 5.31).

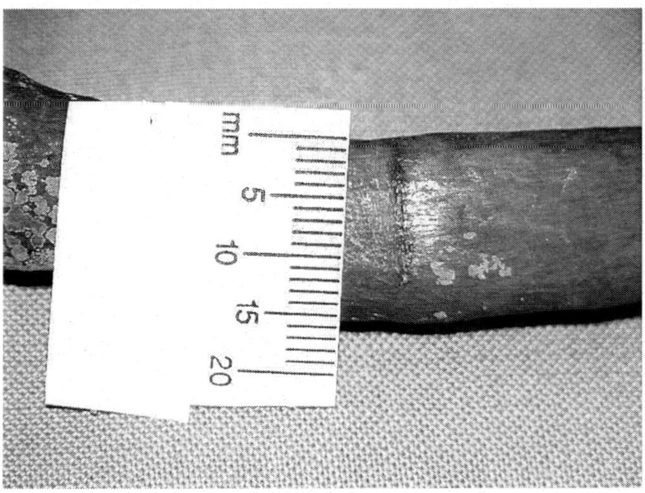

Figure 5.31 Close-up view of second rib showing linear imprint (Alain Wittmann, EPAF).

2. A complete linear fracture of the manubrium without associated fractures to the clavicles and/or first ribs (Figure 5.32).
3. A linear incomplete and undisplaced fracture of the spinous process of the thoracic vertebrae and of the head of the first right rib (Figure 5.33).
4. A complex of radiating fractures stemming from a large defect on the right parieto-temporal area, indicating a high-energy load had been applied. Another important observation was a fracture running across the right side of the maxilla and mandible (Figures 5.34–5.36).

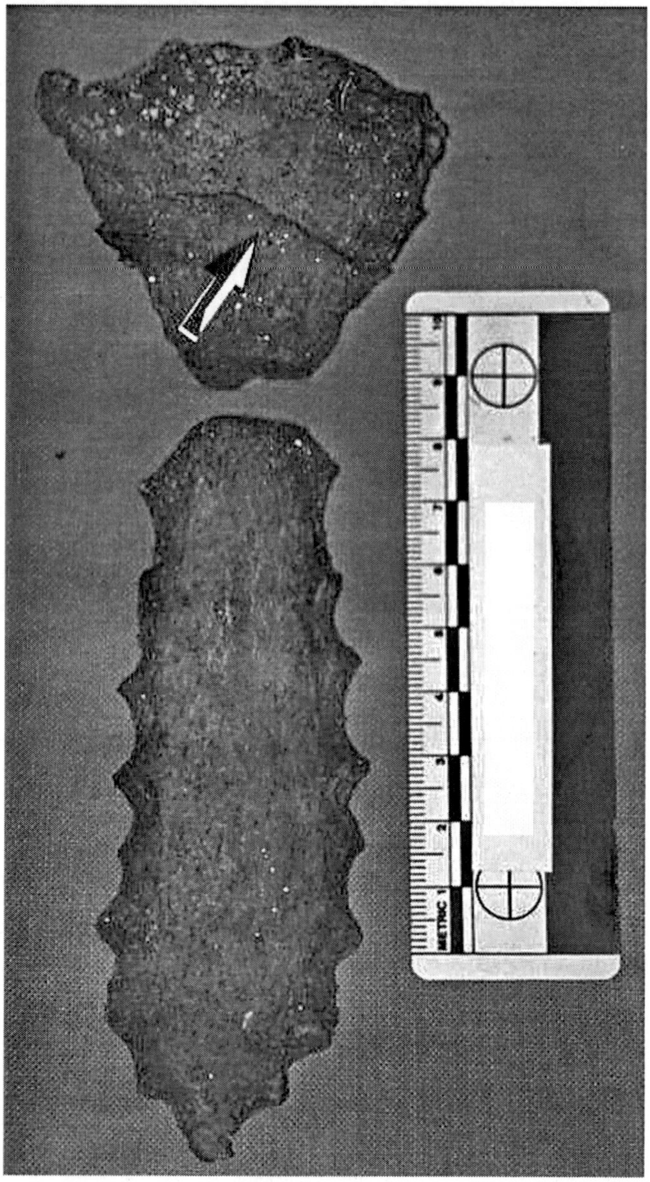

Figure 5.32 Fracture of the *manubrium sternii*; individual A, Peru series (Alain Wittmann, EPAF).

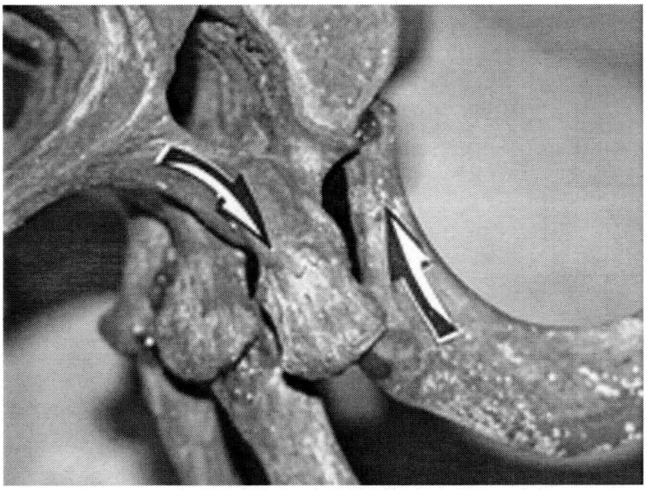

Figure 5.33 Fracture of the transverse process of T1 and first rib, right side. Individual A, Peru series (Alain Wittmann).

Taking into consideration the distribution of radiating fractures on the cranial vault and face, it was inferred that there were at least two points of impact: one localized anterolaterally in the insertion of the *temporalis muscle* with anterior projection toward the sphenofrontal area; and the other located anteriorly on the right side of the chin which caused the facial fractures of the mandible and the maxilla.

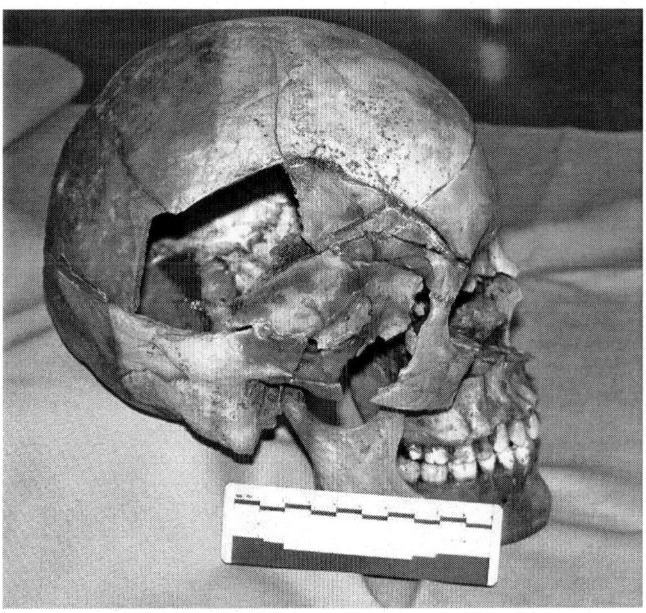

Figure 5.34 Lateral view of the skull and mandible (right side) showing massive trauma on the temporoparietal area (Alain Wittmann).

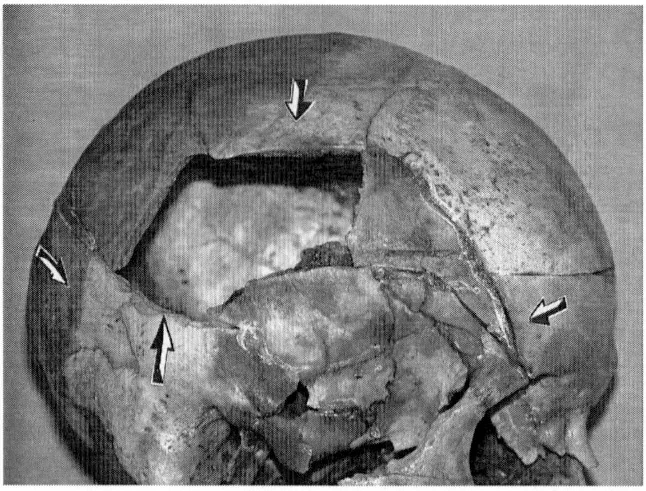

Figure 5.35 Close-up view of blunt force trauma (BFT) pictured in Figure 7.34 (Alain Wittmann, EPAF).

According to the original autopsy report, "abrasions located on the front, left eyelid, malar, and left temporal area were recorded … [as well as a] Contuse injury on the right frontal area of 15.0 × 18.0 mm and abrasion of the right side of the chin." This description of superficial wounds corroborates the finding of multiple impacts on the head based

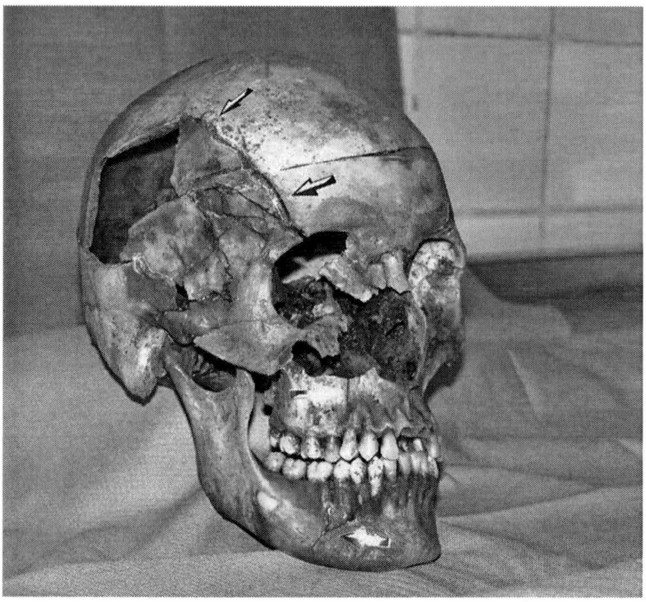

Figure 5.36 Anterolateral view of the skull pictured in Figures 7.34 and 35. Observe fracture on the right side of the face and mandible (Alain Wittmann).

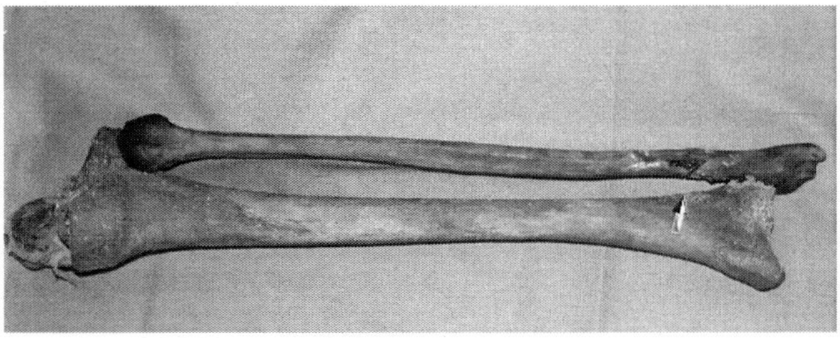

Figure 5.37 Fracture of the right fibula (Alain Wittmann).

on skeletal evidence. Additionally, there were skeletal fractures located in the following regions: a comminuted fracture, 60 mm above the styloid process on the right fibula with a butterfly fracture on the anteromedial aspect, with associated radiating fractures around the diaphysis, consistent with a compressive force applied anteriorly (Figure 5.37).

The torture cases (Tables 5.3 to 5.5) share similar patterns of sternal injuries, whereas individual A exhibits a different pattern with massive cranial trauma, unilateral rib fractures, and a sternal fracture located in the manubrium rather than the sternal body (Figure 5.38). Although the first group of cases suggest probable scenarios of beatings (torture), individual A fluctuates between possibility and exclusion, because the combination of injuries is located unilaterally throughout the body and exhibit injuries to different planes (right lateral and anterior planes) of body, including a fast-loading injury to the head. Therefore, the most probable mechanism of injuries for individual A is an RTA, in which case the victim was a pedestrian hit by a car. This does exclude the possibility that certain injuries attributable to beatings or torture could have occurred separately. However, the findings of the original autopsy report and investigation appear to be supported.

Table 5.4 Characteristics of Blunt Force Trauma from Documented Torture Cases

Variable	Anatomical Structures Affected
Location of Injuries	Chest/thorax
Skeletal Regions Most Affected	Sternum, ribs, lumbar spine
Type of Injury	Skeletal fractures consistent with blunt force mechanisms
Location of Injury per Region	
Ribs	Fractures tend to be adjacent to costochondral joint, axillary or paravertebral line; the latter especially in ribs 10–12
Sternum	Single or multiple fractures, displaced or undisplaced fracture of the sternal body
Lumbar vertebrae	Complete or incomplete fractures, typically a unilateral fracture of transverse process
Number of Fractures per Region	
Ribs	One to three fractures per rib; multiple fractures generally associated to multiple blows
Sternum	One to two fractures; one fracture likely to occur above the point of impact; two fractures generally result from a broader impact

Table 5.5 Differential Diagnosis of Blunt Force Trauma Resulting from Torture and Other Mechanisms of Injury

	Fractures				
Case	Sternum	Rib	Other	COD	Witness Testimony[a]
Kosovo 04	Single fx, notch #2–3	None	None	GSW	Yes
Kosovo 06	Two fx, notches #3–4 and 4–5	Bilateral ribs (#3–5), adjacent to costochondral joint.	Fractures exhibit bone proliferation, remodeling	Unascertained	Yes
Peru case III-07	Single fx, notch #2–3	Right ribs (#2–6), adjacent and posterior to costochondral joint. Left ribs not observable	None	Unascertained	Yes
Individual A	Single fx across manubrium; no fracture to sternal body	Right ribs (#3–7), between paravertebral and axillary lines; second right rib exhibits linear imprint	Massive blunt trauma on right side of head and face; displaced fx of right transverse process of T1 and head of right rib1	Unascertained	No

Note: GSW = gunshot wound.

[a] Supporting witness testimony corroborated physical evidence that ill-treatment, beatings, or torture occurred.

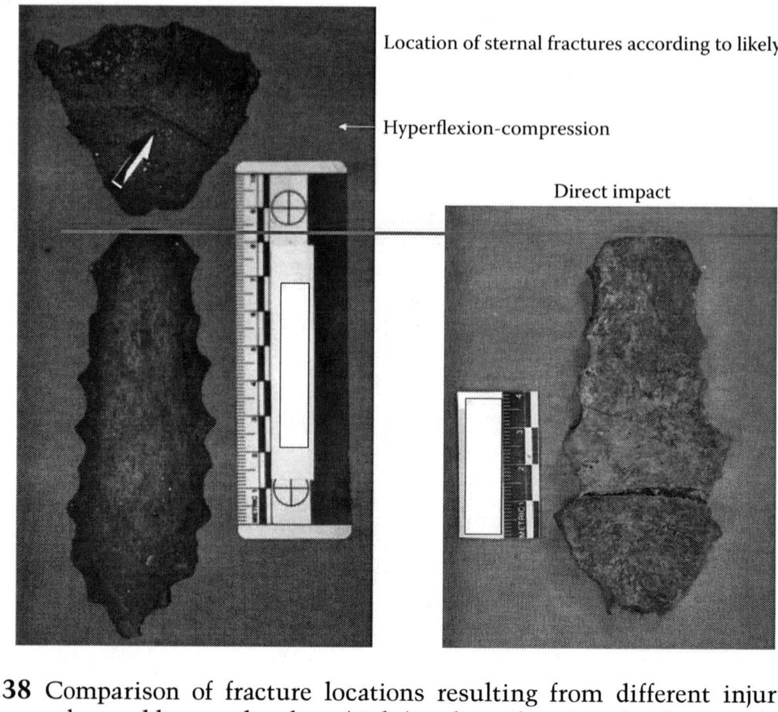

Figure 5.38 Comparison of fracture locations resulting from different injury mechanisms, direct force such as a blow to the chest (right) and acceleration–deceleration injuries resulting from compression due to a seatbelt in a road traffic accident (RTA) (left) (Alain Wittmann).

Summary Guidelines for Best Practice

The breath of information presented in this chapter assists us in formulating an epidemiological approach to the differential diagnosis of torture in human remains. From the data and examples of documented cases presented, it is shown that the rib cage (in part because of its size and accessibility by an attacker) exhibit fracture patterns from beatings that can be differentiated from accidental BFT. Constructing a differential diagnosis between accidental and nonaccidental mechanisms of trauma is important for a clear mechanism of injury and death, and provides evidence of context which is critical for demonstrating torture judicially. To make this diagnosis, examples have been provided, differentiating direct from indirect mechanisms for fractures of the manubrium and the body of the sternum. In addition, isolated fractures of transverse processes of the lumbar vertebrae tend to be associated to specific mechanisms resulting from direct impact. Finally, it must be stressed that the context in which the remains are found is a crucial element in considering the possibility of being confronted with a scenario of torture.

Case Study 5.1: Torture Sequels to the Skeleton

Hans Petter Hougen
Professor of Forensic Medicine
University of Copenhagen, Denmark

A large variety of torture methods have been described, both psychological and physical. The psychological and several of the physical forms of torture leave no traces on the body, but irrespective of the torture methods, mental sequels are very frequent. Immediate trauma due to torture is mainly detected on the skin and in the soft tissue. According to the torture methods, there can be bruises, abrasions, burns, and lacerations but also distortions, ruptured ligaments and various fractures. Sharp force injuries are less frequent but may also occur.

Beating and kicking of the head and body are almost invariably elements of physical torture, no matter in which country it has taken place. Studies of reports from torture victims have revealed that about 10% report fractures, most frequently, of the ribs, followed by legs and pelvis, hands and wrists, columnar spine, jaw, skull, and arms. The sequels are thickening of the bones (callus formation), positional abnormalities due to dislocated healing or insufficient fusion of fracture ends and pseudo-joint formation, besides after-effects of osteomyelitis secondary to either lacerations or fractures. Fracture sequels to the hyoid bone are strongly indicative of manual or ligature strangulation.

Amputation as part of torture seems to be extremely rare, but punitive amputations have frequently been recorded in several Islamic countries. Most of these cases have been amputations of the right hand, but cross-limb amputations (right hand and left foot) have also been reported in modern times. The United Nations, in Resolution 1948/22, explicitly states that amputations are incompatible with the Universal Declaration of Human Rights. Most unfortunately, local doctors have assisted in punitive amputations, and this is a clear violation of the World Medical Association's Declaration of Tokyo (1975), which forbids doctors to participate in torture or any form of cruel or inhuman treatment as punishment.

Shooting, although not a frequent torture method, may be a part of human rights violations. Gunshot wounds to the head usually are fatal and are outside the scope of this theme (refer to Chapters 7 and 8). However, fractures of arms and legs due to gunshot wounds have been reported in torture cases. These fractures are often splintered, especially if high-velocity weapons have been used. Healing of these fractures is often difficult and sequels such as periostitis and osteomyelitis are frequent. Projectile fragments may sometimes be detected in the affected bones.

As mentioned, sharp force is not a frequently reported torture method. However, the use of knives, bayonets, machetes, axes, swords, and even saws have been reported as torture instruments. Therefore, sharp force injuries to the skeleton could result in torture sequels; rounded edges of the marks show that they are old, and the victim has thus survived the torture session leaving the marks. Axes and heavy swords cause injuries that often have both sharp force and blunt force injury components. This is especially prevalent in the skull, where impression fractures, often with loose fragments, surround the sharp-edged wounds. However, if an axe or a sword hits the head at a sharp angle, a part of the skull can be chopped off, leaving no or minimal blunt force injuries. Machetes are not usually sharp, and the blunt force component of the injuries is therefore dominant (refer also to Chapter 6). Saw marks in the skeleton are often irregular and may have a patterned but irregular appearance indicating the general size and distance between the teeth of the saw (Figure 5.39).

Figure 5.39 Femur cut with a saw; the perimortem injury from a documented torture case (Hans Petter Hougen).

One form of torture, the *falanga*, may leave marks indicative of that particular torture method. Falanga has mainly been used in the Middle East but has been reported from Western Europe to East Asia. It consists of beating the foot soles of a victim who is lying down, with heavy sticks, metal tubes, or other hard instruments. The beating causes edema and hemorrhages in the muscles and the foot soles. Due to the firmly bound aponeurosis of the foot soles, muscles, nerves, and bones are exposed to high pressure and reduced blood flow. This leads to necrosis of the muscles, but the blood flow can be so impaired that the small bones—metatarsals and proximal phalanges—suffer and are partially necrotized. Secondary to this damage, fractures may occur, and reactive changes such as exostoses have also been reported.

Although torture sequels to the skeleton are not frequent, they have been reported. Specific trauma, such as atypical fractures of the feet (especially the metatarsals) are strongly indicative of falanga torture and fractures of the hyoid bone that may indicate strangulation. The physical evidence of injuries on the skeleton may not be direct evidence of torture *per se* but, used in combination with other forms of evidence, such as witness testimony, provide compelling and clear evidence of torture.

Case Study 5.2: Multiple Healed Rib Fractures—Timing of Injuries in Regard to Death

Tania Delabarde
Institut Français d'Etudes Andines
Whymper 442 y Coruña
Quito, Ecuador

Rib fractures are the most common thoracic injury, well studied and documented in clinical and forensic practice (Bulger et al. 2000; Holcomb et al. 2003; Galloway 1999). Approximately 25,000 cases of blunt chest trauma are observed each year in France (Debesse and Riquet 1994) and the leading causes of those injuries are motor vehicle, accidents at work, and falls from heights. Recently, rib fractures have also been used to document torture and ill-treatment. The lack of soft tissues makes the reconstruction of traumatic thoracic events and the understanding of bone biomechanics indispensable. Ribcage fracture patterns are complex; a single blow may cause multiple fractures at various locations, and the interpretation of injuries is complicated by the morphology and orientation of the ribs (Love and Symes 2004). Another important consideration in the analysis of skeletal trauma is the timing of injuries. This case study focuses on multiple rib fracture events sustained by one elderly individual who went missing during the conflict in Kosovo in 1999. This paper discusses the nature of the injuries regarding their timing and their relation to the manner of death.

Materials and Methods

In July 1999, shortly after the end of the conflict in Kosovo, local villagers cutting wood near the Macedonian border found the body of an unknown female. They decided to bury her in a grave near the place of discovery. Information regarding the whereabouts of the body, located in the middle of a dense forest, came about in 2005 only, and the Office on Missing Persons and Forensics (OMPF) performed an exhumation. The skeletonized remains of a woman dressed in traditional Albanian clothes were found in a shallow grave 1 m below the surface. The body was lying on its back with the lower extremities slightly flexed in order to fit in the grave. Four pairs of surgical gloves were also found associated with the remains. This feature is important considering that the burial location, in the middle of a forest, is far away from any human settlement and medical facilities.

The remains belong to an elderly female (70–85 years old) almost edentulous, with a general gracile morphology and a living stature of 161.01 ± 3.3 cm (Ross and Konigsberg 2002). The thoracic and lumbar spine show extensive lipping consistent with degenerative osteoarthropathy. Bones were very light and a section of the femoral shaft showed cortical thinning consistent with osteoporosis. According to witness testimony, the state of decomposition was really advanced when local villagers found and buried her; however, no evidence of scavenging was observed.

Multiple fractures in different stages of healing involving the left and right side of the rib cage and right humerus were found. Each fracture was described and classified into a stage according to three characteristics (type of fracture, morphology of edges, and bone proliferation). All the observations were made macroscopically and due to technical limitations, microradiography or microscopic analysis of thin sections was not performed. Four different stages (0 to 3) ranging from no osteogenic proliferation to bone remodeling were determined. A brief description of each stage is presented in Table 5.6.

Table 5.6 Description of Different Stages of Healing

Stage	Description
Stage 0	Perimortem fractures without any macroscopic evidence of bone proliferation.
Stage 1	Slight bone proliferation is visible around the injury; edges of fracture are sharp. Some injuries only show bone proliferation without a visible fracture line.
Stage 2	Open fracture with important bone proliferation; blunt fracture edges.
Stage 3	Healed fracture with callus formation and/or total bone remodeling.

Results

A total of 29 rib fractures, 11 on the left side and 18 on the right side of the rib cage were observed (Figures 5.40–5.46); refer to Table 5.7. In addition, one healed fracture of the proximal right humerus and two perimortem fractures of the sternal body were also recorded. The number of fractures varies between one and four per rib. Twenty-five fractures were clearly antemortem and in different stages of healing. Four did not show any bone proliferation. Three additional fractures were located in the humerus and sternum.

Discussion

The woman sustained a total of 32 fractures, from which 27 were clearly antemortem and 5 perimortem. With the exception of the right humerus and the sternal body, all the fractures are located on different planes of the ribs. Fractures occur on the anterior and right lateral aspect of the rib cage at three main locations: near the midsternal line (stages 0 and 1), between the scapular and axillary lines (stage 2), and between the paravertebral and scapular lines (stage 3). The relation between the stages of healing and the location of injuries seems to reflect the sequence of traumatic events. Based on the distribution of fractures and healing stages, a three-event chronology is proposed.

The first event is represented by fractures located between the paravertebral and scapular lines showing visible callus formation and well-remodeled bone, indicating an old injury. Only the right side of the rib cage is affected (right ribs #5–10) as well as the right proximal humerus. Considering this it is suggested that this event was synchronic and may have been caused by a road traffic accident (RTA) sometime in her past. Fracture patterns caused by RTAs generally involve one side of the rib cage and one of the arms (Newman and Jones 1984).

The second event is characterized by fractures at stage 2 located between the scapular and axillary lines, represented by transverse open fractures with bone activity and

Figure 5.40 Left rib #6; transverse fracture (Alain Wittmann).

Figure 5.41 Right rib #6; open fracture, blunt edges on the internal wall (stage 1), bone proliferation (stage 2) (Alain Wittmann).

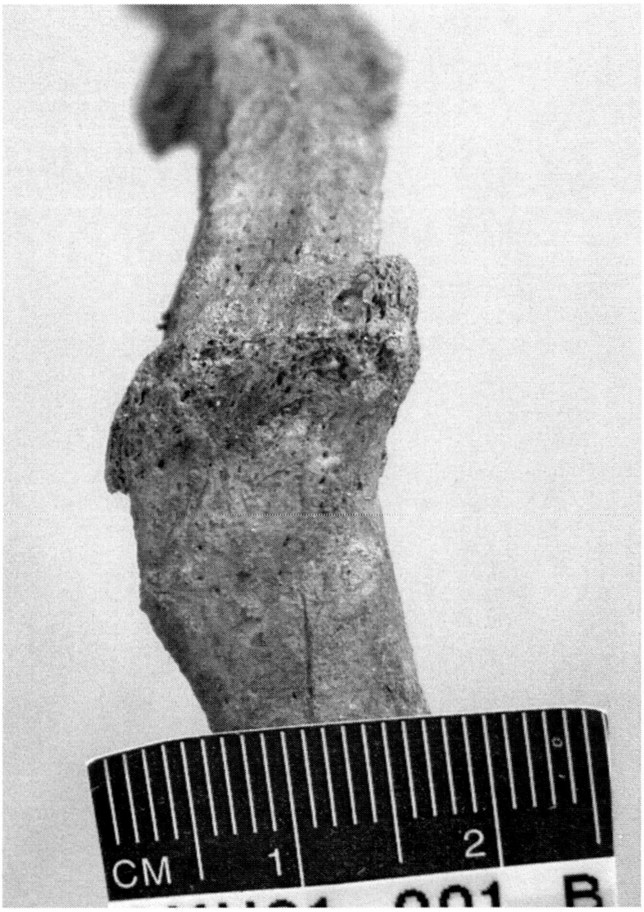

Figure 5.42a Right rib #8; healed fracture located at the level of the scapular line showing callus formation (stage 3) (Alain Wittmann).

sometimes discrete callus formation (right ribs #4, 6–8). Again, only the right side of the rib cage is concerned, but the location of injuries and stage of healing are different. Considering that this second traumatic event may have affected ribs already injured and in the healing process, fragility as well as extensive osteoporosis are factors that should be taken into account. Fracture due to severe coughing is well known in elderly patients who suffer from osteoporosis (Bulger et al. 2000). However, the characteristics of the fractures presented here tends to suggest induced force (i.e., BFT) rather than pathological fractures.

The last event is represented by bilateral fractures adjacent to the costochondral articulation (stages 0 and 1) and two fractures of the sternal body. Considering that all these fractures show a little bone proliferation or none at all (stages 0 and 1, respectively), we can conclude that they may be associated. This type of fracture complex has been described elsewhere in this chapter as being consistent with anteroposterior compression of the chest. It is important to stress that bone proliferation in the anterior chest is associated to bones that do seem to have been injured directly (i.e., proliferation of bone around the costochondral articulation without obvious fractures). The latter supports the hypothesis that the last event may have been caused by diffuse anteroposterior compression of the

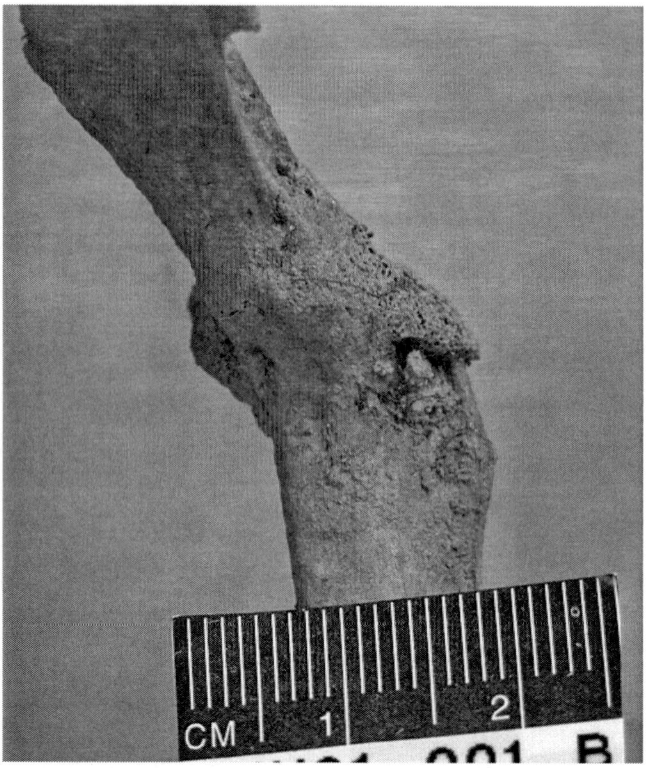

Figure 5.42b Anterior view showing callus formation (Alain Wittmann).

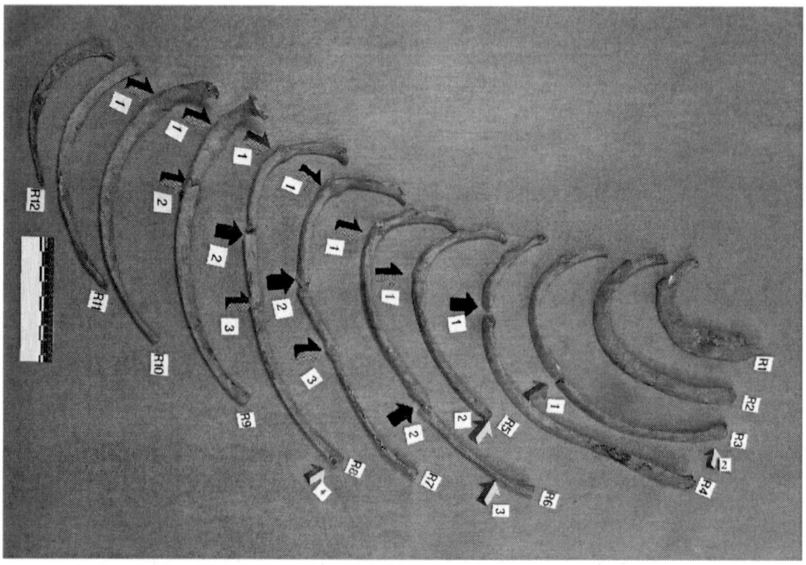

Figure 5.43 General view of the right ribs with three fractures at different stages of healing (Alain Wittmann).

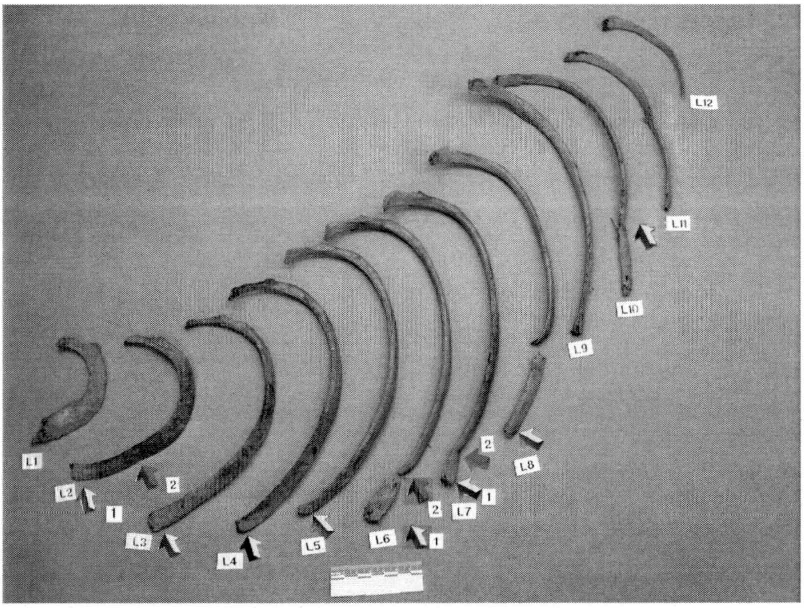

Figure 5.43 Corresponding left ribs with fractures (Alain Wittmann).

chest, sometime before her death. We understand that the lack of histological analysis of the broken ribs somewhat limits our interpretations and that the second and third event may have been part of the same continuum with different healing rates, depending on the type and location of bone. It is clear, however, that based on this study we can conclude that whereas the first traumatic event occurred before her death and most likely was accidental in nature, the last two are consistent with applied force, most likely, diffuse anteroposterior compression of the chest causing multiple fractures and leading eventually to her death. The age of the individual, as well as the high number of recent fractures (69% of fractures belong to stages 0 to 2) is an important factor in the reconstruction of the possible cause of death. As mentioned by Bulger and coworkers (2000), "Elderly patients who sustain blunt chest trauma with rib fractures have twice the mortality and thoracic morbidity of younger patients with similar injuries. For each additional rib fracture in the elderly, mortality

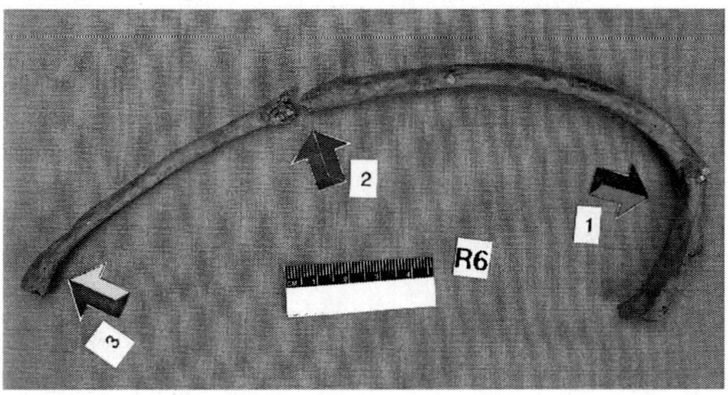

Figure 5.44 Right rib #6 showing three different fractures at different stages of healing (Alain Wittmann).

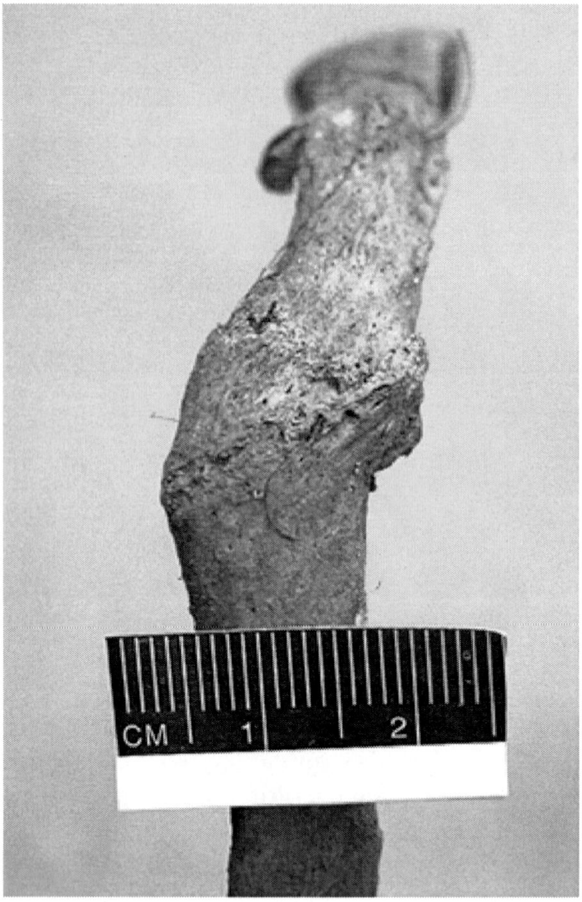

Figure 5.45 Right rib #6; fracture line with callus formation (Alain Wittmann).

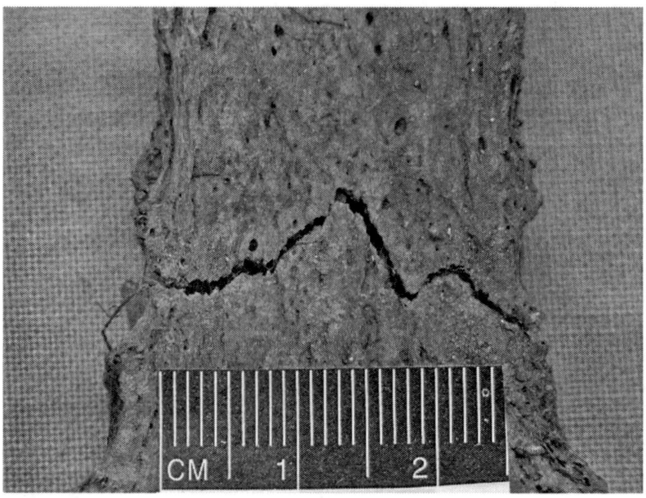

Figure 5.46 Sternal body showing a complete transverse fracture with sharp edges and no bone proliferation (Alain Wittmann).

Table 5.7 Description of Injuries

Location of Injury	Fracture Number and Type	Stage of Healing
Right rib #3	1. Complete transverse fracture, near rib head	0
	2. Transverse rib fracture to body	1
Right rib #4	1. Complete transverse fracture separating the body into two parts, 65 mm from the head	2
Right rib #5	1. Healed fracture with callus, 80 mm from the head	3
	2. Complete transverse fracture with sharp edges and recent bony formation, on the external wall, at 116 mm from the previous fracture	1
Right rib #6:	1. Complete healed fracture with callus formation, 80 mm from the head (Figure 5.46)	3
	2. Complete transverse fracture separating body into two fragments, 100 mm from midclavicular line (Figure 5.47)	2
	3. Transverse fracture on the internal wall, with sharp edges and recent bone proliferation, 10 mm from the costochondral joint (Figure 5.41)	1
Right rib #7	1. Healed fracture with callus formation, 45 mm from head between the vertebral and the scapular line	3
	2. Complete transverse fracture with important bone proliferation, 65 mm from the previous injury	2
	3. Healed fracture with callus, 115 mm from costochondral joint at the level of the posterior axillary line	3
Right rib #8	1. Healed fracture, 60 mm from the head (Figures 5.42 and 5.43)	3
	2. Open transverse fracture with blunt edges separating the body into two fragments, 60 mm from the previous injury	2
	3. Healed fracture with callus, 112 mm from the costochondral joint	3
	4. Evidence of bone proliferation but no fracture line visible	1
Right rib #9	1. Healed fracture, 55 mm from the head	3
	2. Healed fracture, 45 mm from the previous injury	3
Right rib #10	1. Healed fracture, 55 mm from the head between the vertebral and scapular line	3
Left rib #2	1. Transverse fracture line	0
	2. Costochondral joint broken and fragments missing	1
Left rib #3	1. Costochondral joint missing and fracture edges sharp	1
Left rib #4	1. Complete fracture around costochondral joint	1
Left rib #5	1. Complete fracture around costochondral joint	1
Left rib #6	1. Complete transverse fracture, 35 mm from the costochondral joint	0
	2. Transverse fracture line with sharp edges associated to bone proliferation, 15 mm from the costochondral joint (Figure 5.40)	1
Left rib #7	1. Oblique fracture on the external wall with sharp edges but no evidence of bone proliferation	0
	2. Bone proliferation without any visible fracture line	1
Left rib #8	1. Bone proliferation around the broken costochondral joint with plastic deformation of the internal wall	1
Left rib #10	1. Transverse fracture separating the rib body, 55 mm from the costochondral joint	1

(Continued)

Table 5.7 Description of Injuries (Continued)

Location of Injury	Fracture Number and Type	Stage of Healing
Sternum	1. Bone proliferation on both walls of the sternal body without any visible fracture line	0
	2. Complete transverse fracture with sharp edges separating the sternal body into two parts (Figure 5.48)	0
	3. Incomplete oblique fracture of the anterior part of the sternal body running from left to right with plastic deformation of the anterior wall	0
Right humerus (complete)	1. Healed transverse fracture at the level of the surgical neck	3

increases by 19% and the risk of pneumonia by 27%." Rib cage injuries have already been recorded for alleged cases of torture and/or ill-treatment. Evidence of reactive bone formation around or adjacent to the fracture edges and their remodeling indicates survival for several days after the injuries were inflicted.

Epilogue

The elderly lady was eventually identified through DNA testing in 2006. According to statements from relatives, in April 1999, she and her family, while escaping from the village of Vushtri (Northern part of Kosovo), were attacked by the Serbian army; as the lady was too old to walk fast, they decided to put her in a bus going to Mitrovica on the northern end of the province. The lady was never seen after that and her body was found three months later in a forest near the Macedonian border (the southern end of the province). According to some reports, the area where the body was found was controlled by the Serbian army between March and May 1999, and many killings of civilians took place there (*The Prosecutor v. Milosevic et al.*, IT-99-37-PT). In addition, some discrepancies remain unexplained by witnesses who found the remains (presence of surgical gloves, the circumstances of the discovery, etc.). Considering the age and health condition of the victim, it is unlikely that she could have survived alone in the woods for several weeks and considering the circumstances of her disappearance, as well as the sequence and characteristics of traumatic events, it is suggestive of a possible case of abduction and torture.*

* First, I would like to thank José Pablo Baraybar who reviewed and greatly improved the text with his suggestions. I also want to thank Alain Wittmann for taking the pictures of the case, as well as all of my colleagues in the Office on Missing Persons and Forensics who helped me with this complex case. Finally, I thank both authors of this book for their invitation to contribute.

Case study 5.3: Dating of Fractures in Human Dry Bone Tissue—The Berisha Case

George J.R. Maat
Department of Pathology, Netherlands Forensic Institute, The Hague
Barge's Anthropologica, Leiden University Medical Center, the Netherlands

As a consequence of the official end of the Serbian–Albanian hostilities in Kosovo (1998–1999), a series of investigations into crimes against humanity was started under the supervision of the International Criminal Tribunal for the former Yugoslavia (ICTY) of the United Nations. Although the following evaluation refers to one of those investigations in 2003, from a point of view of forensic anthropological methodology, the case has a potentially wider bearing in the sense that the applied investigation method could be useful for many other cases. At the time, a special mission was deployed to investigate possible cases of intentionally inflicted bone fractures prior to execution. The executions had taken place in the vicinity of Berisha. With respect to the preparation of evidence material for the related trial, it was of prime importance to estimate the passage of time after injury until the death of the victims. The existence of healing fractures in the related human remains had originally been noticed and recorded in 2001 by the forensic anthropologists of the OSCE (Organization for the Security and Cooperation in Europe) during their routine identification work in the Orahovac morgue near Prizren.

Materials and Methods

The skeletal remains were kept in boxes in the Orahovac morgue. The assemblage represented ten individuals. It consisted of eight excavated skeletons and two so-called surface finds. Many of the bones appeared to be broken. Nevertheless, the texture of the brittle dry bone tissue itself was well preserved. The human remains were of unknown identity. Forensic anthropological analysis by the anthropologists of the OSCE revealed that, within the group of deceased, at least nine individuals were male. Their ages ranged from 25 to 45 years.

Bones suspected to show healing fractures were anatomically gross-inspected in the Orahovac morgue. Subsequently, they were x-rayed at the Radiology Unit of the Deutches KFOR Feldlazarett in Prizren. Finally they were examined for histological changes at the unit Barge's Anthropologica, Department of Anatomy of the Leiden University Medical Center in the Netherlands. Prior to the preparation of ground sections, the specimens were vacuum-embedded in Epon to strengthen the brittle bone tissue (Burke and Geiselman 1971). Unstained and nondecalcified dry bone tissue section preparation was done according to Maat and coworkers (2001). After mounting of the ground sections onto glass microscope slides, the sections were studied by means of bright light and polarized light microscopy.

To create a useful core timetable of natural healing for the dating of fractures, a substantial amount of data from many authors was compiled into a single table (Table 5.8). Data were extracted and harmonized from Bennet (1966), Heppenstall (1980), Williams et al. (1989), Robbins et al. (1991), Buckwalter et al. (1996), Kleinman et al. (1996), O'Connor and Cohen (1998), Schiller and Teitelbaum (1999), Vigorita (1999), Islam et al. (2000), Klotzbach et al. (2003), Ortner (2003), and Prosser et al. (2005). In the resulting table, all soft and hard tissue changes and their radiological appearances are summarized (Table 5.8). When used, timing should be substantially reduced in case of children. Because the present case study focuses on diagnoses extracted from dry bones, in the table all changes relevant to dry

Table 5.8 Healing Phases and Histological Timetable for Natural Fracture Healing Without Surgical Intervention in Adults

Healing Phase	Time[a]	Features
Hemorrhage and torn periosteum	Immediate	Hematoma in fracture cleft > coagulation > loose fibrin mesh
	24–48 h after injury	Breakdown of blood > sterile inflammation reaction > edema, vascular congestion, mast cells, leukocyte infiltration
Cell debris phagocytosis	In 2–5 days	Macrophages appear (hemosiderophages)
		Absence of osteocytes near fracture cleft. Empty lacunae
		Fibroblast invasion at margin of blood clot > granulation tissue callus (weak procallus)
Newly formed cartilage and osteoid	After 3–5 days	Appearance of chondro and osteoblasts (fibrocartilaginous soft callus) > osteoid (bone matrix)
Loss of fracture line definition	After 4–7 days	**First Howship's lacunae**
		Beveling and smoothing of fracture ends (radiology!)
Well-developed new bone spicules and cartilage	After 7 days	**New bone spicules dispersed through soft tissue callus**
		Start of endosteal and periosteal osteogenesis separable from cortex (*radiology*)
Start of osteoid mineralization	After 10–12 days	Osteoid mineralization
Woven bone	After 12–20 days	**Aggregation of spicules into woven bone from periphery to center of fracture cleft** (*radiology*, opaqueness)
		Fusiform temporary union (not hard, but clinical stable union)
Osseous procallus (primary callus)	After 15 days	**Clearly visible external callus** (*radiology*)
	After 14–21 days	**Start of remodeling of woven bone into longitudinally orientated lamellar bone**
		Fields of calcified cartilage (*radiology*, opaqueness)
		Cortical cutting and closing cones > growth of longit. osteon extensions to fracture cleft
Bridging	After 3–4 weeks	**Union by bridging of cortical bone** (*radiology*)
		Maximum size of callus
Periosteal reaction incorporation	After 6 weeks	**Periosteal reaction becomes firmly incorporated in cortex** (*radiology*)
Osseous hard callus (secondary callus)	After 2–3 months	**Firm bony union** (*radiology*)
		Start of contour smoothening (*radiology*)
Perfect reconstruction	After 1–2 years	Adequate immobilization > **perfect reconstruction** (*radiology*)
Pseudoarthrosis	After 6–9 months	Inadequate immobilization > **(false-) pseudoarthrosis** of dense fibrous tissue (radiology!)

Note: **Bold type** shows features detectable by means of dry bone tissue histology of nondecalcified ground sections; *radiology* in parentheses indicates features detectable by radiological means.

[a] Timing may be substantially reduced in case of children.

bone tissue histology are printed in bold type. If changes are visible by radiological means, then the remark *radiology* is added in *italics*, within parentheses.

Results

Fresh Fractures

Except for one surface find without pathologic changes, all skeletons showed a great variety of "fresh" fractures. Many of these fractures had dark, discolored, and sharp fracture edges. Some had light-colored and clean fracture edges, exhibiting very recently exposed internal bone tissue. Perforating holes in the calvarium with multiple radiating linear fractures together with contralateral defects with beveled edges were seen in five skeletons (Figure 5.47). Injuries anatomically positioned in a direct line, often of comminuted nature, were recorded for multiple long bones in four of the skeletons. Seven skeletons had similar in-line injuries of the axial skeleton involving scapulas, vertebras, ribs, and sacrum. Radiologically, no increased density was seen along the sharp edges of the dark-discolored and light-colored fractures (Figure 5.48). Histologically, the edges were characterized by broken-off raveled lamellar bone fibers (Figure 5.49).

Healed Fractures

Fractures macroscopically displaying reactive bone tissue at rest were seen in three skeletons. Two of these, a 25- to 40-year-old male and a 30- to 40-year-old male, had only one smoothened and bridged fracture, respectively, a focal impression fracture of the right half of the frontal bone, and a fracture of the left scapula with ossifications of the acromioclavicular ligaments (Figure 5.50). The third skeleton exhibited a smoothened nonbridged fracture, i.e., a spondylolysis of the fifth lumbar vertebra (a vertebral arch separated from its vertebral body). The latter skeleton had two additional rib fractures with active reactive bone tissue near the fracture clefts. Those two will be dealt with in the following paragraph.

Healing Fractures

Three skeletons, including the last case of the previous paragraph, showed collectively 16 fractures with reactive bone tissue deposition at the fracture sites. They regarded fractures of a right tibia shaft, the body of a sternum, seven right ribs, and five left ribs. The related x-rays and microscopy observations have been summarized in Table 5.9. It should be mentioned here that the application of polarized light microscopy was very helpful in viewing the orientation of bone fibers, especially to assess whether the woven bone in callus formations had remodeled into longitudinally orientated lamellar bone. Examples of a range of key features indicating distinct timing steps in the histological healing process are shown in Figures 5.51–5.57. These features are as follows:

- Beveling and smoothening of the fracture ends together with the presence of empty osteocyte lacunae at the proximity of the fracture edges (Figure 5.51)
- Presence of Howship's lacunae due to bone tissue digestion by osteoclasts (Figure 5.52)
- Radiological loss of fracture line definition (Figure 5.53)

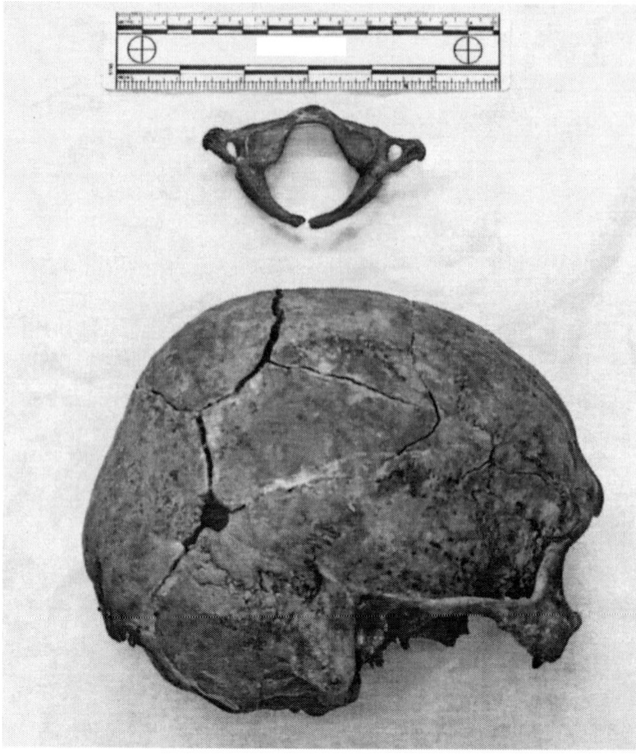

Figure 5.47 Skull with bullet hole and radiating linear fractures. Separate item: spina bifida of the atlas of the same individual (anomaly) (George Maat).

- Endosteal and periosteal osteogenesis, i.e., callus development separable from the compact cortex (Figure 5.54)
- Deposition of an endosteal callus made of woven bone without particular orientation of its bone tissue fibers (Figure 5.54)

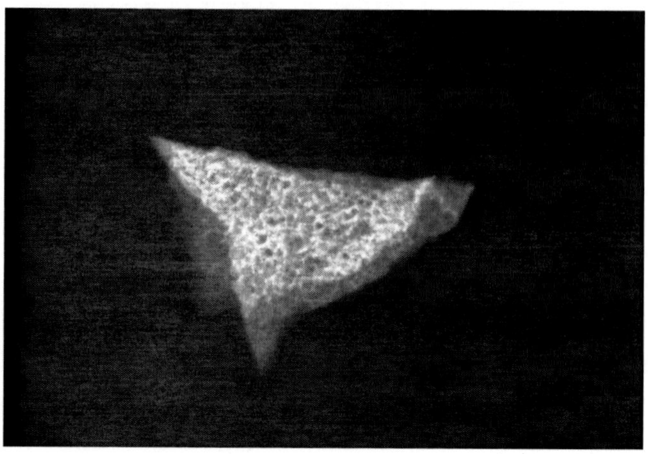

Figure 5.48 Fragment of parietal bone. Note the sharp edges lacking increased density. X-ray (George Maat).

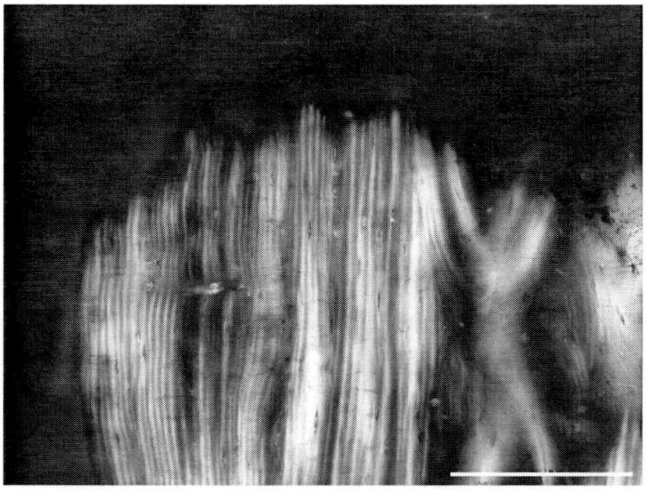

Figure 5.49 Micrograph of a fragment of parietal bone. Same specimen as shown in Figure 5.48. Note the broken off, raveled, lamellar bone fibers at the fracture edge. Polarized light. Objective 20× (George Maat).

- Increase of radiological density at the fracture ends due to endosteal and periosteal callus development (Figure 5.55)
- Remodeling of woven bone tissue into longitudinally oriented lamellar bone (Figure 5.56)
- Appearance of cortical cutting cones, during life occupied with osteoclasts, and related closing cones, during life occupied with osteoblasts, "drilling" their way to the fracture cleft (Figure 5.57)

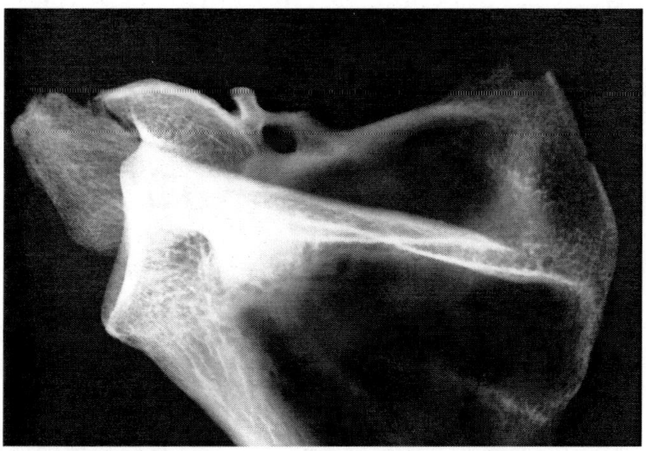

Figure 5.50 Left scapula with healed acromioclavicular displacement and ossification of the acromioclavicular ligaments. X-ray (George Maat).

Table 5.9 Observations on Healing Fractures and Assessment of Passed Healing Time

Case	Sex[a] (M/F)	Age[a] (years)	Gross Anatomy	X-Ray Observation	Microscopy	Passed Healing Time
NN 987	M	30–40	Sternum: (ant.) start periosteal callus	Increased density along fracture	Internal callus of woven bone, first transition woven to lamellar	About 3 weeks
			L-ribs: 5,6,7: start periosteal callus	Internal and external callus	Beveling, callus of woven bone, first cortical cutting cones	About 3 weeks
			R-ribs: 7,8,9: start periosteal callus	Internal and external callus	Beveling, callus of woven bone	About 3 weeks
NN 990	M	35–45	L-ribs: 7,8 ("greenstick" fracture)	Internal and external callus	Callus of woven bone, no cortical cutting cones	About 2 weeks
NN 991	M	30–40	R-tibia (shaft): start periosteal callus	Periosteal callus, rounded edges	First transition woven to lamellar, beveling callus of woven bone, first cortical cutting cones	About 3 weeks
			R-ribs: 6,9 (incomplete fracture)	Internal callus	First transition woven to lamellar, callus of woven bone, no cortical cutting cones	2–3 weeks
			R-ribs: 7,8 (incomplete fracture)	Internal callus	First transition woven to lamellar, callus of woven bone, no cortical cutting cones	2–3 weeks

Note: M/F = male/female, R/L = right/left, ant. = anterior, L5 = 5th lumbar vertebra, n.a. = not applicable.

[a] According to report of the forensic anthropologists of the Organization for Security and Cooperation in Europe (OSCE).

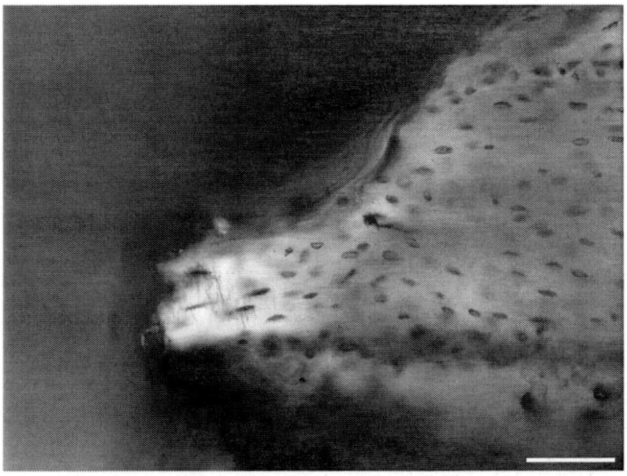

Figure 5.51 Fractured end of a left rib with beveling and smoothening of the cortex. Note the empty lacunae. Polarized light. Objective 20× (George Maat).

Figure 5.52 Distal fracture end of a right tibia with Howship's lacunae at the periosteal surface. Polarized light. Objective 20× (George Maat).

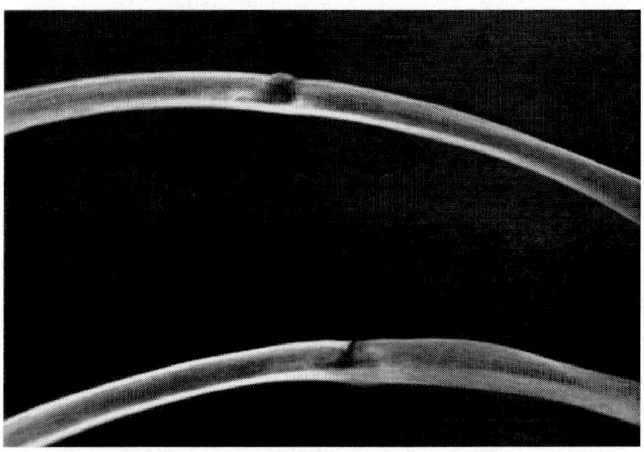

Figure 5.53 Left rib. Radiological loss of fracture line definition (George Maat).

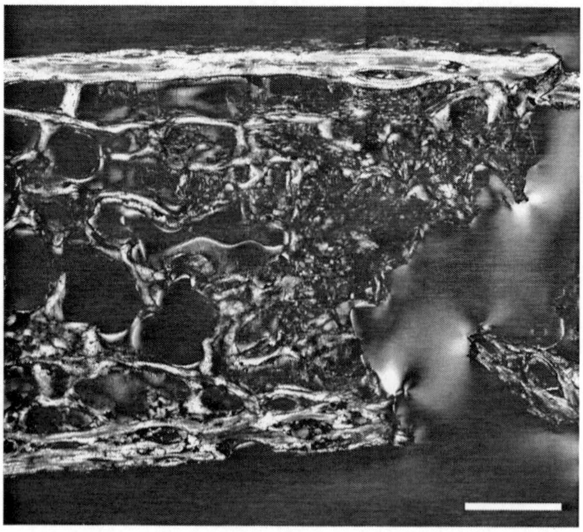

Figure 5.54 Sternum. Endosteal and periosteal osteogenesis separable from the cortex. The fracture cleft with its internal callus shows a random orientation of woven bone spicules. The upper end is the anterior face of the sternum. The lower end is the posterior face of the sternum. Polarized light. Objective 2×. Figure was mounted from six separate exposures (George Maat).

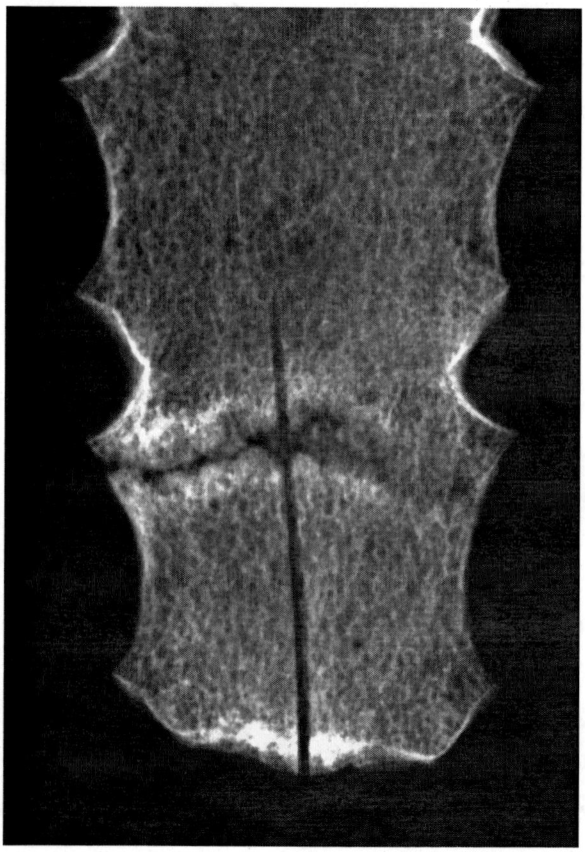

Figure 5.55 Sternum. Same specimen as in Figure 5.54. Radiological increased density due to internal and external callus development at the fracture ends (George Maat).

Figure 5.56 Right rib. Internal callus with first replacement of woven bone tissue by longitudinally orientated lamellar bone fibers parallel to the cortex. Due to the polarization of the light beam, both the longitudinally arranged fibers in the cortex and in the internal callus are enhanced. Polarized light. Objective 2× (George Maat).

Discussion

In principle, assessment of the passed time of healing after injury should be possible by systematically recording key features indicating distinct timing steps in the healing process. There is a vast amount of literature on the histopathology and radiology of the healing process of fractures itself. But a compilation of all published matter on the timing of the natural healing process, as seen without surgical intervention in adults, was not yet available. For understandable (medical) reasons, research has primarily focused on aspects complicating and delaying the natural healing process, e.g., by malnutrition, hormonal

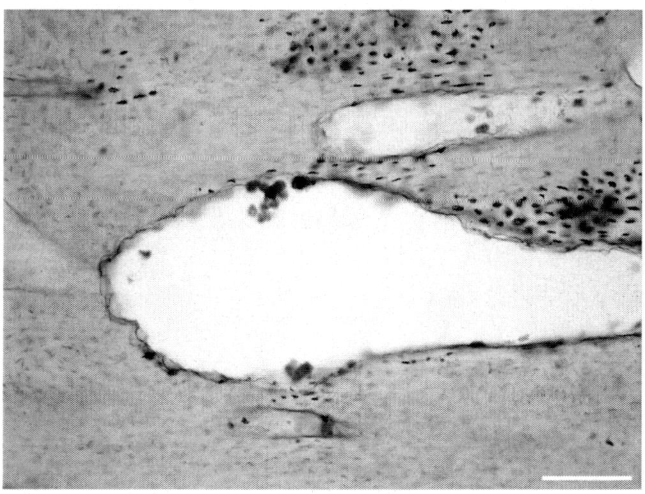

Figure 5.57 Right tibia. Cortical cutting cone with Howship's lacunae oriented toward the fracture cleft. Part of the related closing cone is seen at the right. Bright light. Objective 10× (George Maat).

imbalances, biomechanical friction, etc. Although all natural healing changes in life happen in a certain time interval (with a start, peak activity, and end phase), in forensic practice it is mostly only of interest to substantiate the minimum period of time that at least must have passed since the injury was inflicted, to explain the found changes in the specimen. The underlying premise for such reasoning is that nature is not able to produce similar changes in a shorter time span.

Fresh Fractures (Peri- and Postmortem Fractures)

Perimortem fractures are fractures which happen short before, during, or short after the moment of death. In our case, many of the so-called fresh fractures with dark discolored but sharp fracture edges showed anatomical changes consistent with mechanical traumata known from bullet impacts. A detailed account of such type of changes can for instance be found in Saukko and Knight (2004). The radiological and histological status of these fracture edges were in agreement with the assumption that most had indeed been inflicted perimortem, because in contrast to light-colored clean postmortem fracture edges caused by recent excavation activity, perimortem fracture edges become dark discolored due to the influence of soil and groundwater. Obviously, both types, peri- and postmortem fractures, show no healing. In the light of their characteristics, it was the perimortem fractures that most probably related to the direct cause of death of the men.

Healed Fractures (Antemortem Fractures)

In the case of the two males with just one fracture, as well as in the case of the man with spondylolysis, it was apparent from the smoothening (with and without bridging of the fractures) that the fractures had healed many years before death. When investigated microscopically, such fractures show resting bone tissue with regular remodeling from bone replacement by ageing. Obviously, the cause of these "old" healed antemortem fractures had nothing to do with events related to the deaths of the men.

Healing Fractures (Antemortem Fractures)

In case of the three skeletons with reactive bone tissue deposition at the fracture sites, the reactive tissue was characterized by tissue unrest. By cross-checking the features found on the x-rays and in the microscopic slides (refer to Table 5.9 and Figures 5.51–5.57) with data listed in the given timetable (Table 5.8), a minimum period of healing that had passed after the original injury could be assessed. In the case of these three males, this indicated that after the original injury a minimum period of 2–3 weeks had elapsed before they died.*

* I would like to acknowledge, for their cooperation and assistance, J.P. Baraybar and H. Sandhu (ICTY, The Hague), W. Poborsky (Radiology Unit, Deutches Feldlazarett, Pristina), E. Smyth, M. Toonen, A. de Rijk (UNICTY, Pristina), and M.J. Aarents (histology technician LUMC).

Case Study 5.4: Torture and Extrajudicial Execution in the Peruvian Highlands—Forensic Investigation in a Military Base

José Pablo Baraybar, Carmen Rosa Cardoza, and Vanessa Parodi
Peruvian Forensic Anthropology Team (EPAF)

In Peru, during the 1980s more than 60,000 people died, of which some 13,000 remain missing (Truth, Justice and Reconciliation Commission, CVR 2003) (EPAF 2006). These people died in a context of political violence and were in their majority poor and illiterate Quechua Indians. The preliminary results of an exhumation carried out in a military base in the Peruvian Highlands are presented. The base occupies an area of about seven hectares, of which only a small area was investigated and from where 15 complete sets of human remains were recovered. Additionally, traces of what seems to be an oven to cremate some of the remains were also found. To date, the case is under investigation by the Peruvian Judiciary. It has been determined that between 1981 and 1989, approximately 500 people entered this military base as detainees and were never seen again. According to the same sources, these people would have been tortured and executed, and the remains of some 300 would have been exhumed and burned in purposely made ovens sometime after their death (Uceda 2004). This military base was known as a place of detention where people arrived by land and air (helicopter) from different provinces of the South-Central Andes, making the reconstruction of the detention circuit of the victims difficult. Based on survivors' testimonies, it has been determined that while in detention prisoners were forced to exchange pieces of clothing to conceal their real identity.

Demographic Profile, Injury Patterns, and Cause of Death

The remains of 15 individuals between 16 and 45 years of age at death, including 13 males and 2 females were examined. The prevailing mechanism of injury in 14 cases was gunshot trauma, whereas the combination of perimortem blunt force and gunshot trauma occurred in 4 cases (Table 5.10). Injury patterns, namely, gunshot wounds to the head support the hypothesis that the detainees were executed. Table 5.11 shows the locations and

Table 5.10 Demographic and Cause of Death Patterns

Case #	Sex	Age	Cause of Death
1	Male	25–35	Gunshot wound to the head
2	Male	25–35	Gunshot wound to the head
3	Female	16–21	Gunshot wound to the head
4	Female	23–30	Gunshot wound to the head
5	Male	16–20	Gunshot wound to the head
6	Male	23–30	Gunshot wound to the head
7	Male	35–45	Gunshot wound to the mandible
8	Male	20–30	Gunshot wound to the head
9	Male	16–19	Gunshot wound to the head
10	Male	16–19	Gunshot wound to the head
11	Male	28–40	Gunshot wound to the head
12	Male	18–22	Gunshot wound to the head
13	Male	16–23	Indeterminate
14	Male	28–42	Gunshot wound to the head
15	Male	18–25	Gunshot wound to the head

Table 5.11 Number and Location of Injuries

Case #	Anatomical Area	Injury	Location and Details
1	Head	GSW	Frontal to left parietal, front to back, below to above
	Head	GSW	Left parietal-temporal to right parietal; keyhole
	Head	GSW	Occipital to left orbit, back to front
2	Head	GSW	Occipital to right parietal-frontal, back to front, left to right, below to above
	Head	GSW	Right auditory meatus to left parietal, left to right, front to back, below to above
	Head	GSW	Right orbit to right parietal, front to back
3	Head	GSW	Left zygomatic, auditory meatus to right frontal, left to right, back to front, below to above
4	Head	GSW	Left sphenoid-temporal to occipital, front to back, left to right
	Forearm	GSW	Right radius and ulna
5	Head	GSW	Occipital to frontal, back to front
6	Head	GSW	Occipital to left eye orbit, back to front, right to left, below to above
	Head	GSW	Right temporal to left parietal, right to left, front to back
7	Head	GSW	Mandible to cervical vertebrae 2 and 3, right to left, front to back, above to below
	Head	GSW	Mandible to cervical vertebrae 4 and 5, right to left, front to back, above to below
	Scapula	GSW	Left scapula, front to back
	Ribs	BFT	Right ribs 5 and 6, compression anteroposterior
8	Head	GSW	Frontal to left temporal, front to back, right to left
	Head	GSW	Right parietal to lambda, front to back right to left
9	Head	GSW	Right temporal to left temporal, right to left
	Head	GSW	Right parietal to left parietal, right to left
10	Head	GSW	Right auditory meatus to left parietal, front to back, right to left, below to above
	Head	GSW	Right temporal to left sphenoid, right to left
	Scapula	GSW	Left scapula, back to front, below to above
11	Head	GSW	Left parietal to right parietal, left to right, front to back,
	Scapula	GSW	Left scapula, back to front
12	Head	GSW	Occipital to right parietal, back to front, front to back, left to right
	Spine	BFT	Transverse process of lumbar vertebra 5
13	Sternum	BFT	Fracture of body, compression anteroposterior
	Ribs	BFT	Ribs 2,3,4,5,6, compression anteroposterior
14	Head	GSW	Occipital to right frontal, back to front, left to right, below to above
	Head	GSW	Asterion to left frontal, right to left, back to front, below to above
	Rib	BFT	Third left rib, compression anteroposterior
15	Head	GSW	Occipital to frontal, back to front, below to above
	Head	GSW	Left parietal to frontal, back to front, below to above, left to right
	Teeth	BFT	Linear fracture on most teeth

Note: GSW = gunshot wound, BFT = blunt force trauma.

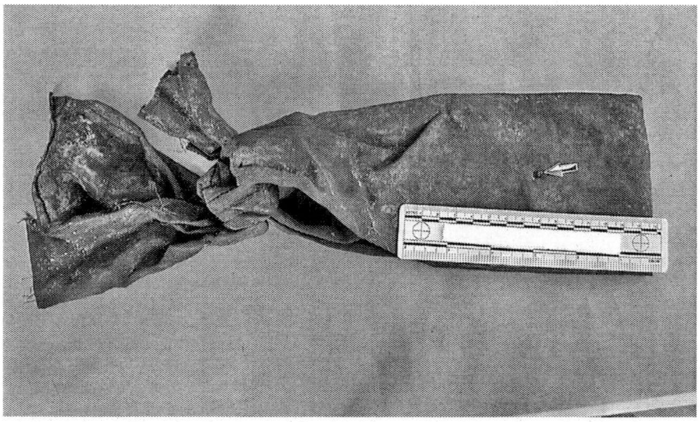

Figure 5.58 Overview of a blindfold associated to the body (Juan Carlos Tello, EPAF).

numbers of lesions in each body. Three victims were found with improvised blindfolds made with scraps of clothing or actual garments. In one case, the blindfold was used to match entrance and exit defects because two shots fired close to one another could have exited in either of the two defects (Figures 5.58–5.60). After positioning the blindfold on the skull, it was determined that the person had been shot through the ascertained exit of one of the two entrances (Figures 5.61–5.65).

One of the cases in which cause of death could not be ascertained shows a number of injuries consistent with BFT to the anterior chest, including a fracture of the sternum and of right ribs 2–6, without evidence of bone proliferation. Three other cases, however, shared similar injuries, and a fourth one showed linear fractures of the teeth probably caused when the mouth was closed with a hard object inside (i.e., the muzzle of a gun); in all four cases, death was attributed to gunshot wounds (GSW) to the head and chest. This type of blunt force injury is generally associated to torture and ill-treatment, and is consistent with anteroposterior compression of the chest. Jesús Sosa, a member of the Peruvian Army and a task force officer, who allegedly participated in the killings at the base, told

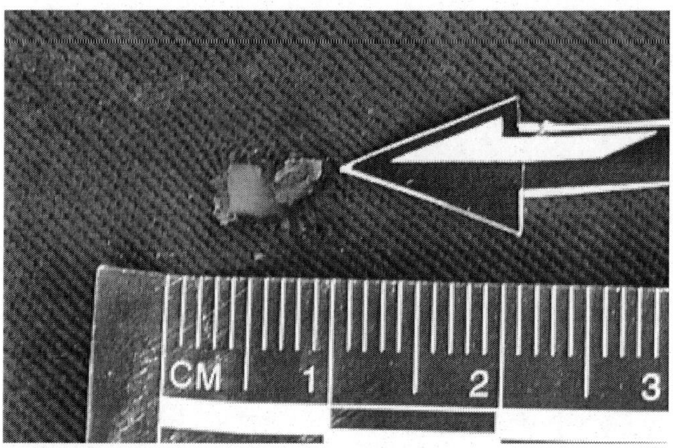

Figure 5.59 Detail of an entrance wound in the blindfold (Juan Carlos Tello, EPAF).

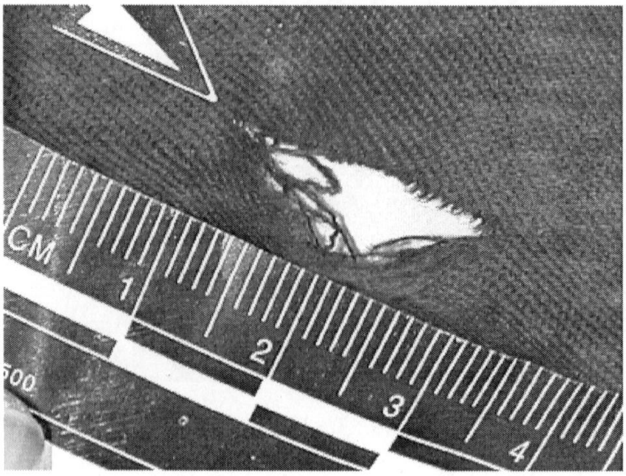

Figure 5.60 Detail of an exit wound in the blindfold (Juan Carlos Tello, EPAF).

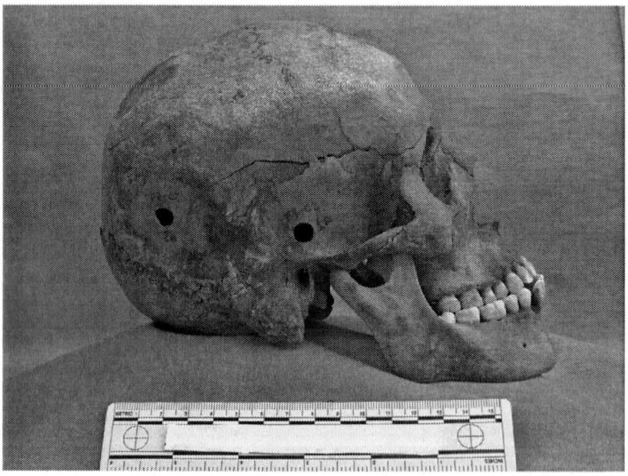

Figure 5.61 Lateral (right) view of the skull showing two entrance wounds (Juan Carlos Tello, EPAF).

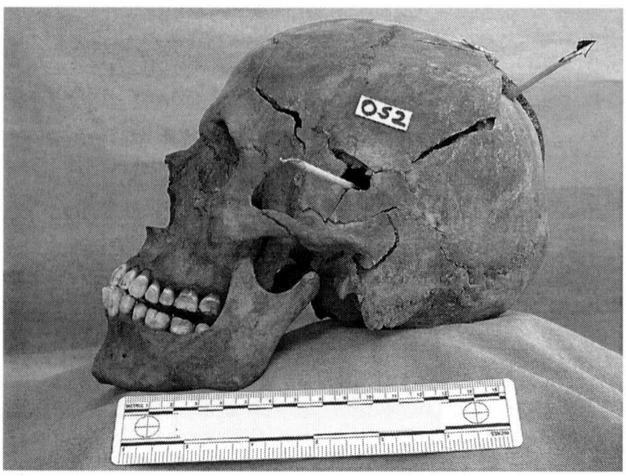

Figure 5.62 Lateral (left) view of the skull showing one exit wound (Juan Carlos Tello, EPAF).

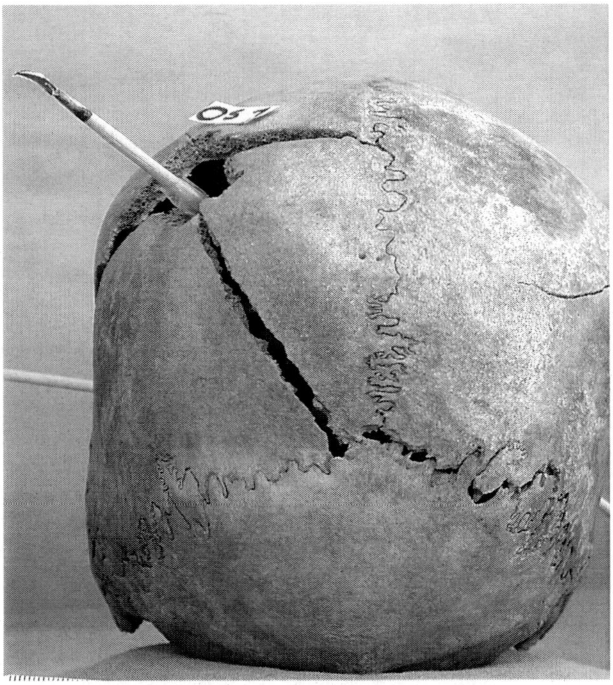

Figure 5.63 Posterior view of the skull showing a second, posterior exit wound (Juan Carlos Tello, EPAF).

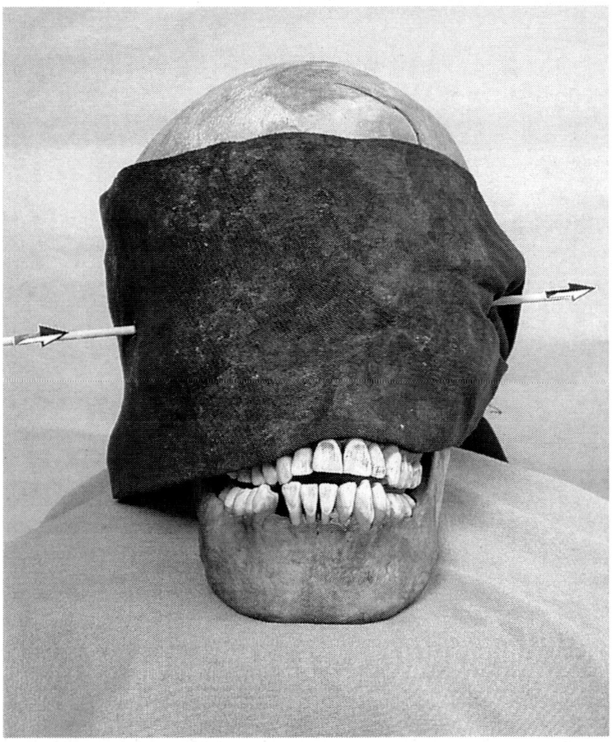

Figure 5.64 Anterior view of the skull with a blindfold. Trajectory of the bullet-penetrated skull (Juan Carlos Tello, EPAF).

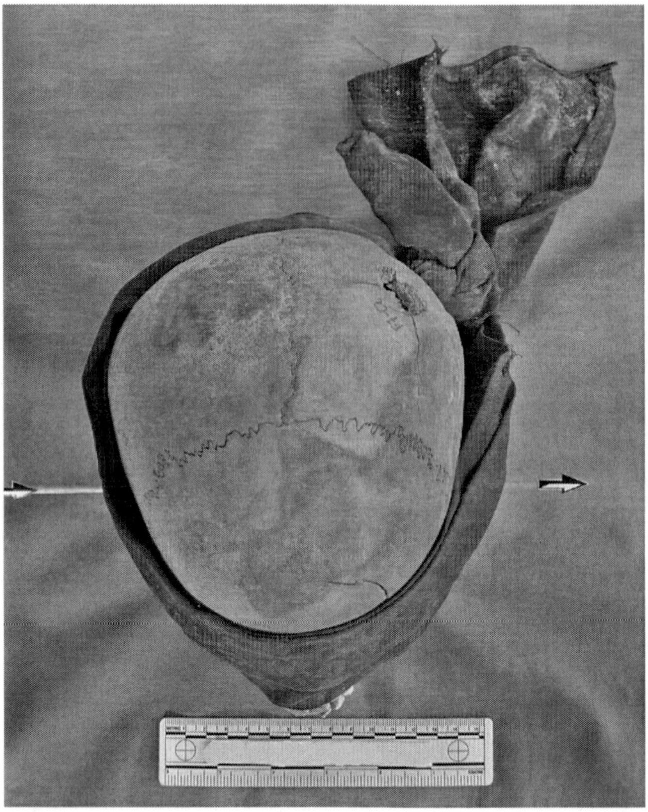

Figure 5.65 Superior view of the skull with a blindfold showing the second exit wound that was not associated to the defects on the blindfold (Juan Carlos Tello, EPAF).

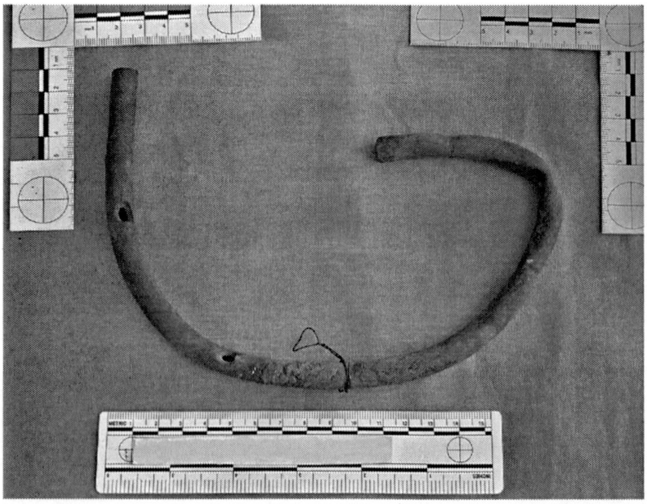

Figure 5.66 Intra-abdominal catheter found associated to one of the bodies (Juan Carlos Tello, EPAF).

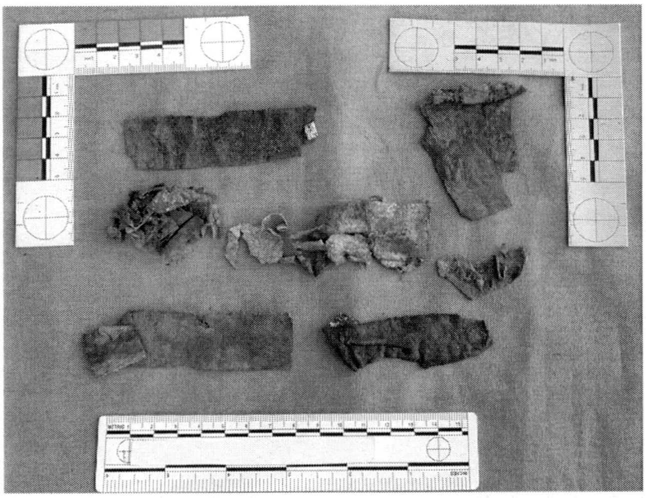

Figure 5.67 Pieces of surgical tape used to probably secure the catheter to the body (Juan Carlos Tello, EPAF).

Uceda (2004, 95) that in one instance "he had a terrorist who refused to confess, with a superhuman resistance; he never spoke, in spite of the fact that Sosa had hanged him, drowned him, and beat him to the point of breaking his bones."

Finally, one individual was found without clothes (most likely this individual had been buried naked), wrapped in a blanket and with the remains of a catheter and bandages. It was determined that the catheter is the type used after intra-abdominal surgery suggesting that the individual was taken out of the hospital shortly after such type of medical intervention (Figures 5.66 and 5.67). He was shot twice in the head.

Conclusion

The preliminary findings of the analysis of the human remains found in a military base strongly suggest the existence of extrajudicial executions carried out on those detained and later disposed of therein. As discussed, the pattern of blunt force trauma affects roughly one-third of the individuals and combines different mechanisms of injuries (i.e., BFT and GSW), suggesting that some people were subjected to ill-treatment/torture during their detainment at the base. The presence of an individual possibly taken from a medical facility shortly after intra-abdominal surgery further characterizes violations against International Humanitarian Law.*

* We would like to thank Juan Carlos Tello for taking the pictures of this case, Tanya Molina for assisting us with the analysis of the remains, and APRODEH (Asociación Pro-Derechos Humanos) for appointing us as experts.

Sharp Force Trauma

6

For us, genocide was the gas chamber—what happened in Germany.
We were not able to realize that with the machete you can create a genocide.

Boutros Boutros-Ghali*

Contents

Mechanisms of Sharp Force Wounds....................265
Identifying Sharp Injuries....................267
Cut Marks....................268
Peeling or Shaved Defects....................270
Point Insertions or Notched Defects....................272
Slot Fractures....................274
Chop Marks and Scoop Defects....................276
The Man in the Burning Car: A Practical Example of Cut Marks....................284
Sharp-Blunt Injury Associated with Chopping Weapons....................291
Hatchet Trauma from Colombia: A Practical Example....................291
Summary Guidelines for Best Practice....................295
Case Study 6.1: Disappearance, Torture and Murder of Nine Individuals in a Community of Nebaj, Guatemala *By S. Chacón, F.A. Peccerelli, L. Paiz Diez, C. Rivera Fernández and C. Jacinto*....................300
Case Study 6.2: Probable Machete Trauma from the Cambodian Killing Fields *By G.E. Berg*....................314

As a rule, the type of trauma inflicted in a specific context is dependent on the availability and access of weapons and the extent to which utilitarian tools are used as weapons. In Rwanda, machetes† and pangas are some of the most common agricultural tools, as expected for a tropical country where weeding and cutting shrubs are daily farming activities. These types of utilitarian objects were used to commit genocide in Rwanda, during the summer of 1994, when more than an estimated 800,000 people were murdered. The victims were primarily Tutsis and moderate Hutus, who were murdered by Hutu militia groups such as the *Interahamwe* and the *Gendarmerie Nationale* (Melvern 2004). The case of *The Prosecutor v. Clement Kayishema and Obed Ruzindana* (ICTR-95-1-T, Judgment, 21 May 1999) resulted in convictions of genocide for the former governor and businessman. Central to this case was establishing who the victims were (i.e., Tutsis, targeted because of their ethnicity) and the causes of death. In regard to the massacre site at the Home St. Jean Catholic Church in Kibuye, listed in the indictment, forensic anthropology and pathology

* Boutros Boutros-Ghali was the sixth UN Secretary-General. Quote in Sayegh (2006).

† The Lippincot Company, provider of machetes and pangas in Central Africa, recorded a peak sale during the year prior to the genocide, which in retrospect suggests an intention by those who bought them for the conflict, according to Prunier (1995).

witnesses testified to excavations of mass graves and the postmortem analysis of more than 600 individuals (*The Prosecutor v. Clement Kayishema and Obed Ruzindana* ICTR-95-1-T, Judgment, 21 May 1999, para. 326):

> Dr. Haglund's written report confirms that many people, men, women, and children, were killed at the Complex. Of the 493 dead examined by Dr. Haglund, only one gunshot injury was found. He estimated that 36% of people in the grave had died from force trauma, whereas 33% of the people died from an undetermined cause. Dr. Haglund selected an individual as an example who he identified as a fifty-year-old man. The man's fibula had been completely severed by some sharp object, which "would have severed the achilles"* tendon rendering this individual partially crippled. On the neck region, "all the soft tissue from the right side of the neck towards the back would have been cut through" and "a sharp cut mark in the tibia body, and in the inferior border of the scapular shoulder blade, another trauma caused by a blow of a sharp object." Dr. Haglund concluded that the fifty-year-old man was trying to protect himself by presenting different body aspects to the armed assailant. Dr. Peerwani found stab wounds indicating the use of sharp force instruments and confirmed that many of the victims were young children and the old.

This case highlights a number of critical issues; the high number of victims, patterns of widespread and systematic abuse, the use of individual injuries in court as examples that represent and reflect widespread abuse, and the value of an epidemiological approach, given the context, scope, and purpose of such investigations. Specifically, sharp force trauma (SFT) in this case demonstrates what is important about documenting trauma for judicial use:

- The number of injuries per individual
- The cause and manner of death
- Number of people killed and proportion that sustained specific injuries
- Nature of injuries that are fatal
- Prevalence of body regions targeted in the attack
- Demographic patterns of the victims
- Possible evidence of torture

In addition to causing fatal injuries, SFT may result from dismemberment when perpetrators attempt to conceal a crime (Spitz 1993; Houck 1998; Reichs 1998; Symes et al. 1998; Symes et al. 2001;). Postmortem modification such as excavation damage or carnivore tooth marks may mimic SFT, further complicating the interpretation of injuries. In our experience, we have seen efforts by perpetrators to conceal war crimes, such as hiding bodies or moving graves, but we have not seen the intentional dismemberment of bodies in massive cases of international humanitarian laws (IHL). In the creation of secondary graves, bodies may become dismembered from the use of heavy equipment (i.e., a backhoe), but this differs from the intentional act of dismembering bodies with the use of a saw or chopping instrument. Typically, such cases result in a high number of victims; therefore, the creation of more *body parts* is not usually the chosen method of disposal by those who seek to hide their actions. There are, however, documented cases where dismemberment was used as a form of torture. In case studies presented by Hougen (refer to chapter 5),

* The quotation marks within this quote refer to testimony from the trial transcripts, November 27, 1997, pp. 29–33.

Chacón and coworkers, and Berg (at the end of this chapter), multiple examples of dismemberment as a means of torture or as a result of the method of execution are illustrated—including a case where a saw was used to amputate a limb as a means of torture, a case of multiple victims in Guatemala who were tortured and murdered with machetes, and sharp force injuries resulting from extrajudicial executions in the form of beheadings from Cambodia.

The following chapter discusses mechanisms of sharp force injuries to bone, describes common wound and fracture characteristics useful for identification, and provides best practice recommendations for classification of sharp injuries that are commonly encountered in human rights (HHRR) cases. Chopping weapons such as machetes are common in such cases and create not only sharp force wounds, but also blunt crushing injuries (sharp–blunt trauma). The characteristics of sharp–blunt trauma are indicative of the class of weapon (i.e., a chopping tool), not to be interpreted as multiple and separate mechanisms. The discussion presented here includes examples from Colombia, Guatemala, the Balkans, and Cambodia; therefore, the injuries discussed are those encountered in HHRR cases or armed conflict. In other words, the full range of possible sharp injuries (i.e., nonmetal cutting instruments, postmortem dismemberment, or sawing) is extensive and goes beyond the scope of this chapter. The identification of SFT presented here is based on anthroposcopic analysis. Microscopic analysis of sharp injuries is a growing area of casework and experimental research but has not been routinely applied as part of the postmortem protocol in the context of the cases described here.* Overall, observed wound variation by bone type and weapon class is illustrated, including cut marks resulting from knives in cases from the Balkans (ICTY, 1991–1995) and chopping wounds resulting from machetes, hatchets, and axes from Guatemala (FAFG, 1980–1984) and Colombia (1990–present).

Mechanisms of Sharp Force Wounds

Sharp force trauma (SFT), as its name indicates, refers to an injury by an object that is pointed or edged. By definition, "a cut (or incised wound), results whenever a sharp-edged object is drawn over the skin with sufficient pressure to produce an injury that is longer than it is deep" (Spitz 1993, 252). In contrast, a stab wound is a penetrating wound that is deeper than it is wide, in soft tissues (Spitz 1993, 252). Depending on the weight and the pressure applied through contact with a given surface, sharp weapons may incise, cut, chop, dent, or crush bone. Therefore, the term *sharp force* is a bit misleading as they generally perform one of several mechanizing forces, such as, puncturing, cutting, chopping, sawing, or crushing.

The classification of SFT in bone, as with all injury mechanisms, is based on fracture and defect morphology. Variation in skeletal wounds result from the physical properties of various weapons and the biomechanical properties of the particular bones affected. The purpose of this chapter is to outline a simple and concise set of variables that may be applicable when a large number of cases are involved, with multiple injuries (a hallmark of HHRR violations), and typically weapons are not be available for comparison.

* One important aspect in the identification of SFT is the ability to reliably differentiate perimortem trauma from postmortem modification, which often appears similar to SFT; for more discussion on the timing of fractures, refer to chapter 2.

The objective in such cases is to establish broad categories that combine mechanisms and gross morphology that demonstrate the pattern and extent of injuries. This approach is descriptive and based on the morphology of defects or fracture patterns. The primary goal of postmortem examination is to interpret the mechanisms of force and manner of injuries from skeletal morphology to gain a clear understanding of injuries that contribute to death or were intended to inflict harm. It is also necessary to provide a differential diagnosis to separate injuries from postmortem modification and burial damage.

Generally, sharp objects can be divided into broad categories based on their size and weight, such as short or long and light or heavy. For example, *short-light* objects include all types of knives and bayonets that can be easily operated with one hand and where the primary function is to cut or saw, depending on the characteristics of the blade (i.e., straight or serrated). Short-light objects are not intended for use as high-force vectors; rather, they are instruments that if used offensively consist of short strokes or jabs. For this group of weapons, the force comes primarily from the weight of the attacker's body, rather than long sweeping strokes that build momentum released through the weapon (such as an axe).

Knives fall into the category of short-light weapons and are typically characterized by a pointed tip and a V-shaped blade (Reichs 1998). The blade may have a straight or serrated edge. Wound morphology will generally reflect these attributes, although the angle at which the blade strikes the bone, the number and association of impacts, the composition of bone affected, and the amount and composition of soft tissues, and clothing that the blade strikes prior to bone will also influence wound morphology. For example, if a knife is forced into someone's chest, it is possible that either one or two ribs will be affected, depending on the angle and depth of penetration of the blade into the body. In such a case, one rib may show a V-shaped cut mark, whereas the adjacent rib may show an imprint of the opposite (blunt) edge of the knife (Smith et al. 2003; Rao and Hart 1983). However, if the knife penetrates only one rib by the tip of the blade, a small defect mimicking the cross section of the tip (probably a small triangular-shaped defect) will be observed. The ratio of width to depth in bladed instruments such as knives will generally be proportional to the size of the blade; therefore, the longer the blade, the wider and deeper the groove. In this proportion, however, width will always be greater than depth due to lateral movement of the blade in a cutting stroke (Walker and Long 1977).

Long-heavy weapons such as machetes, pangas, swords, and axes are employed using either one or two hands, depending in part on the weight of the weapon. This class of weapons has also been termed *chopping weapons* (Spitz 1993). Hatchets and cleavers fall into an intermediate category between the short-light and chopping weapons; however, the skeletal defects and fractures that result are most consistent with chopping weapons. According to Humphrey and Hutchinson (2001), rather than perforating bone, cleavers tend to leave *kerf floors* (the grooves resulting from a sharp edge). Machetes and axes are objects that when swung will greatly increase the amount of force with which they strike the object. The design of these tools reflects this intended purpose through the size, weight, and shape of the blade. Wounds sustained from this class of weapons usually exhibit bone fragmentation around the edges of the defect.

Although the difference between *cutting* and *chopping* is primarily related to the force imparted by the instrument, sawing requires a serrated edge and a repetitive motion force back and forth. Chopping generally involves more force and greater weight from the weapon, as well as a complete interruption in the continuity of the bone, and often the separation of multiple bone fragments, or *chattering* (Kerley 1973). The proportion between width and depth in chopping wounds in bone is much more proportional (i.e., a ratio closer to 1) because the penetration of a heavy object limits the amount of lateral movement of the blade and the force is applied during a shorter area (Walker and Long 1977).

Spitz wrote (1993, 287), "Due to its rigidity, bone maintains the dimensions and shape of a stab wound far better than skin or other soft tissues." However, the degree to which sharp force injuries are patterned in bone depends largely on the type of bone affected. For example, ribs "possess a significant grain in its structure, similar to wood. This means that the bone has a tendency to split preferentially along the grain when penetrated" (Smith et al. 2003, 150).

Characteristics that may be used to identify specific weapons based on microscopic analysis of cut marks have been offered by various researchers (Quatrehomme et al. 1998; Reichs 1998; Bartelink et al. 2001; Humphrey and Hutchinson 2001; Tucker et al. 2001; Alunni-Perret et al. 2005). In the context of massive atrocities or HHRR violations, the type of object or general class of weapon is typically estimated, rather than matching particular knives or machetes to wounds. In addition to the large number of victims and context for postmortem analysis, there is a high amount of wounding variation, guided largely by the biomechanical properties of various skeletal features that may blur fine distinctions (de Gruchy and Rogers 2002). Therefore, focus should be on the class of weapon, rather than a particular weapon. The class of sharp object weapons may be differentiated with confidence, i.e., cut marks, defects with flaking around the edges, fragmentation or comminuted fractures around the border of wounds, peeling, incised defects, scoop marks or chopping defects, and exit defects (Wenham 1989; de Gruchy and Rogers 2002; Bauer and Patzelt 2002).

Identifying Sharp Injuries

The identification of SFT is based on the systematic collection of data from wound morphology, including the number, type, and distribution of defects (Stewart 1979; Sauer and Simson 1984; Frayer and Bridgens 1985; Maples and Browning 1986; Merbs 1989; Smith et al. 2003). Experimental research and case studies have been presented for SFT to bone, covering many aspects of wounding patterns and identification (Rao and Hart 1983; Spitz 1993, Reichs 1998; Symes et al. 1998; Houck 1998; Symes et al. 2001; Prieto 2007; Quatrehomme 2007). The association of injuries to one another, the superimposition of defects or cut marks, and their orientation provide essential information for estimating the class of weapon, such as what was the position of the victim relative to the assailant and relative timing of the defect (Reichs 1998). Sharp force wounds are often clustered, so estimating the minimum number of cut marks or blows may require special attention but is important for reconstructing the events surrounding the injury. For example, large chopping defects result in the fragmentation of bone around the margins. Based on these fracture patterns, the direction of force or orientation of victim may be understood, i.e., was the person's head in a moveable position or firm against the floor during the attack (Walsh-Haney 1999).

Table 6.1 Variables for Documenting Sharp Force Trauma

- Shape of cut mark, whether linear or irregular
- Cross section of cut mark—V, semi-V, or U shape
- Characteristics of walls of the defect, smooth or serrated
- Characteristics of "floor" of the defect, smooth or serrated
- Depth of the feature, particularly whether consistent throughout the cut mark
- Presence of hilt (more common in knife wounds)
- Presence and shape of defect
- Presence of associated fractures with defect
- Presence of crushing associated with cut mark or defect

The extent of sharp injuries is a primary result of the area of the body affected and the resistance of the underlying bone to the impacting force. For example, although a knife may penetrate the tables of the skull protected only by the scalp, the same knife may only cause a puncture defect into a femoral shaft that is well protected by many layers of muscle.

Likewise, a machete injury to the head may slice off a piece of skull while the same injury may partially or completely separate an extremity. A knife is typically small and used in such a manner that the applied force is limited in scope and generally insufficient to destroy a significant area or sever limbs. In contrast, a larger, heavier, sharp object such as an axe may impart enough force when swung to amputate a limb.

Spitz (1993, 287) points out an important aspect of knife wounds; upon penetration and extraction of the weapon, the blade moves upward, downward, or in a twisting motion. This motion results in injury from the impact and injury as the blade is moved or pulled from bone (a type of exit defect). Spitz (1993, 287) further points out that the back of the blade may leave an indented mark in bone that reflects the size of the blade. Often, an attack involving sharp weapons typically involves two people who are moving or struggling in close proximity (assuming the victim is not bound). Therefore, in such cases, the dimensions of the skeletal wound are likely to be larger or irregular compared to the size of blade, particularly in soft tissue.

Reichs (1998) further provides a useful list of criteria for the systematic collection of data and accurate interpretation of SFT. Adopted and modified from Reichs (1998), Table 6.1 lists a number of characteristics useful for documenting SFT. The following discussion of cut marks, slice or peeling defects, scoop and chop defects, point insertions, and exit defects (adapted from Seetah 2006 and Emanovsky et al. 2002) further provides a simple classification system useful for documenting and ultimately identifying sharp force injuries in bone.

Cut Marks

Cut marks (Figures 6.1–6.5) are shallow linear striations that interrupt the continuity of the surface of a bone and generally have a V-shaped cross section and are caused by a sharp or bladed instrument (this discussion does not cover cut marks created by nonmetal objects). The orientation of the "V" will vary depending on the direction/angle of the impact against

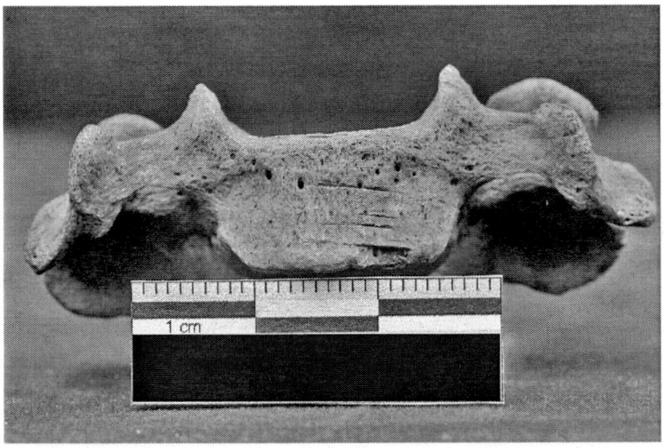

Figure 6.1a Anterior view of cervical vertebra showing parallel cut marks on the body, consistent with the use of bladed instrument, possibly a knife (Carlos Jacinto, FAFG).

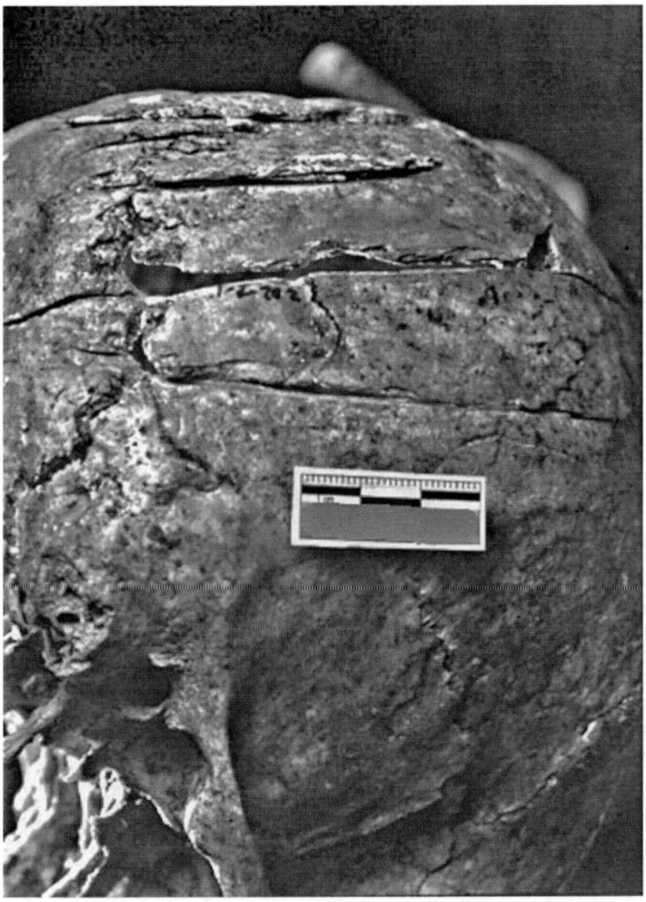

Figure 6.1b Multiple defects present on posterior cranial vault, resulting from a machete (Carlos Jacinto, FAFG).

Figure 6.2 Linear cut marks on the posterior aspect of a rib likely caused by the stroke of the blade during a stab wound of the chest (Carlos Jacinto, FAFG).

the bone. Therefore, perpendicular impacts tend to cause an almost horizontal V-shaped defect (Walker and Long 1977).

Peeling or Shaved Defects

Peeling or shaved defects result when the blade strikes the bone at an angle and, as a result, a sleeve or bone fragment is lifted or *peeled* from the surface, or when the bone is twisted due to torsion (Turner and Turner 1992). The fragment is not completely removed. Where a deeper penetration of the blade at a similar angle completely removes the sleeve of bone, the injury is classified as a *scoop* defect (refer to the following text). The width and depth of the shaved defect will vary, depending on the penetration and size of the blade. Ribs are commonly affected in this way. The blade penetrates the rib cage perpendicular to its

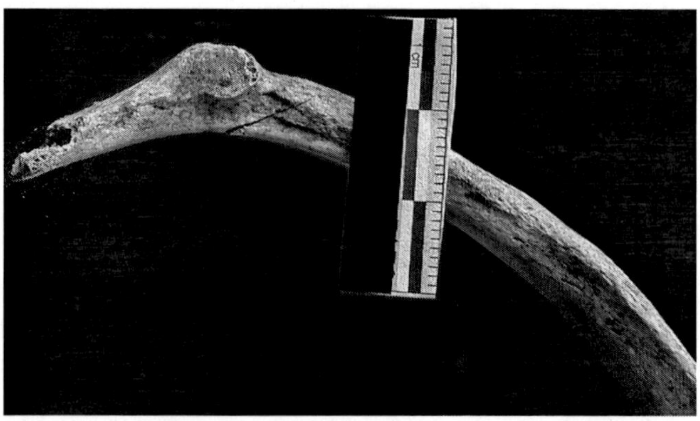

Figure 6.3 Cut mark in the inferior margin of a right rib, close to the tubercle; the location of the injury suggests a stab wound struck angular to the rib, consistent with a bladed weapon such as a knife (Carlos Jacinto, FAFG).

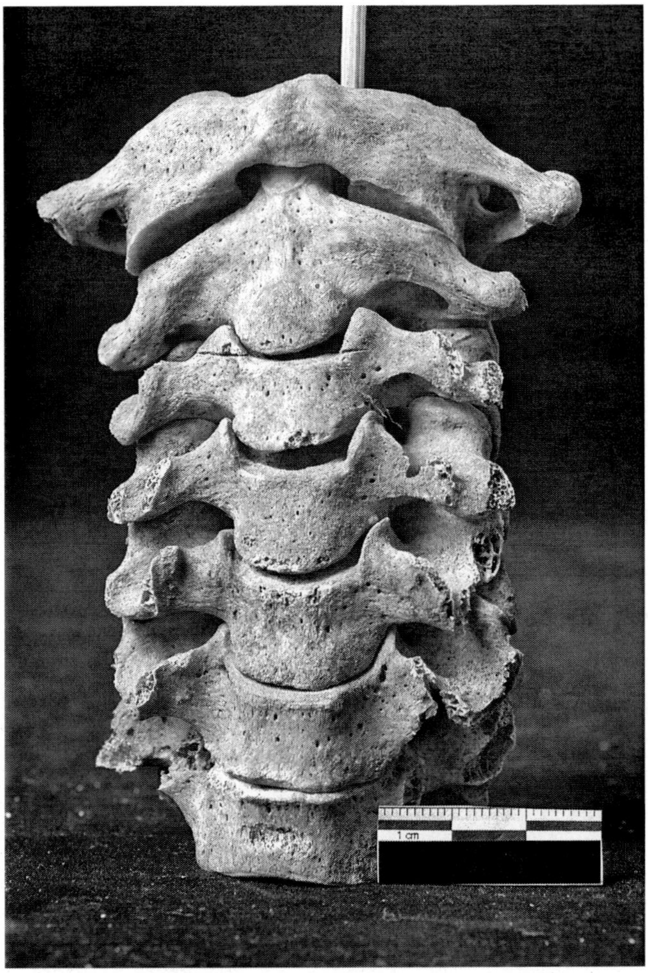

Figure 6.4 Cut mark on the anterosuperior aspect of the body of the third cervical vertebra, consistent with a bladed weapon such as a knife. The location of the cut mark is suggestive of cutting the throat. This body was found in a mass grave inside an army garrison (Carlos Jacinto, FAFG).

Figure 6.5 Close-up view of the cut mark on the third cervical vertebra; same bone as pictured in Figure 6.4 (Carlos Jacinto, FAFG).

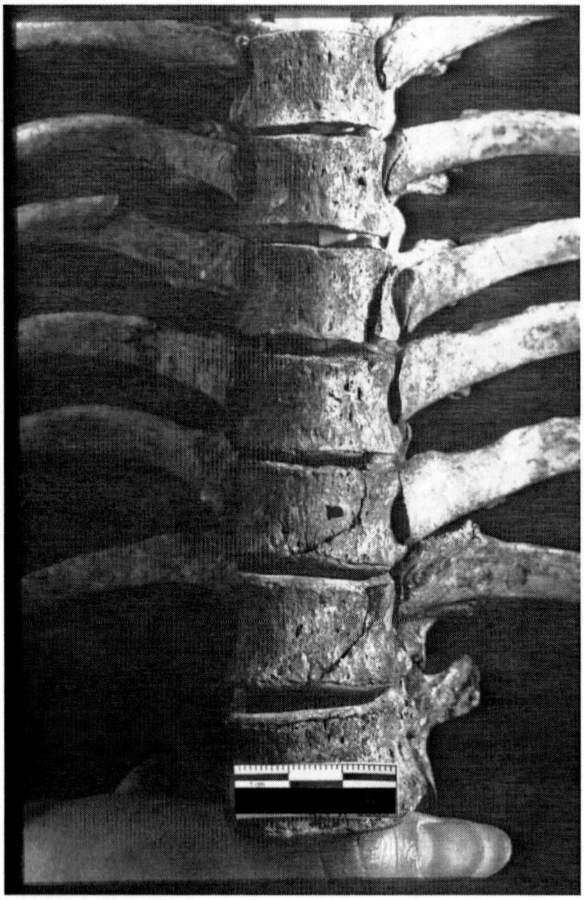

Figure 6.6 Anterior view of the thoracic cage showing cut marks, notch, and peeling defects. Considering the position of the spine in the thorax, the injuries were inflicted by a penetrating blade that incised the bone. A vertebral body (third from top) shows a notched injury caused by penetration of the blade tip and exit defect as the blade levered against the bone casing. A right rib (third left from top) shows an angled penetration of the blade through the rib body with a peeling defect. The injuries are consistent with a bladed weapon of sufficient length to cross through the thorax, such as a large knife (Carlos Jacinto, FAFG).

axis and strikes parallel to the rib body, thereby combing the rib (Emanovsky et al. 2002) (Figure 6.6).

Point Insertions or Notched Defects

Point insertions or notched defects are penetrating injuries in which only the tip of the instrument is drawn perpendicular to the grain or surface of the bone (i.e., a stab wound). They are generally deep and show an elongated, triangular, or V-shaped cross section. The shape and depth of the defect varies based on the shape and size of the penetrating blade and the biomechanical properties of the tissues affected; for example, the compact bone tends to show smaller point insertions than trabecular bone (Figure 6.7).

Figure 6.7a Elongated defect with a straight edge on left sphenoid. The superior end of the defect shows a V shape, whereas the posterior border is straight but shows an indentation in its middle part. The anterior border is irregular and somewhat curved. The defect is consistent with penetrating injury caused by a bladed instrument. Lateral rotation of the instrument may be responsible for the indentation seen on the posterior wall and the wide V shape on the superior part of the defect (ICTY).

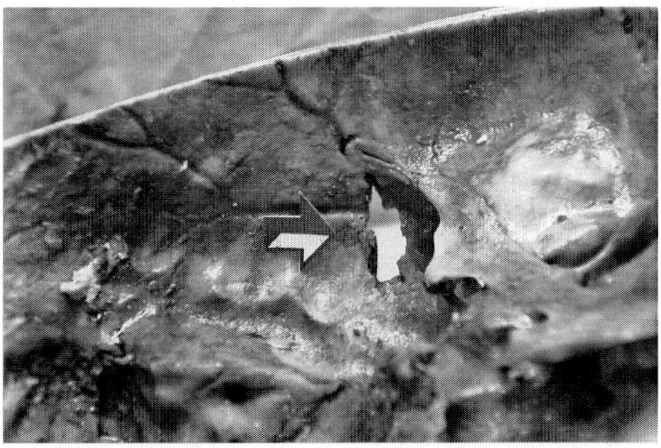

Figure 6.7b Endocranial view of notched defect (ICTY).

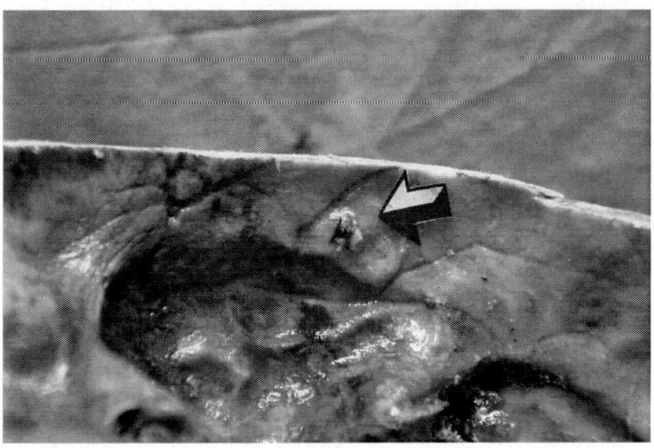

Figure 6.7c Endocranial view of the right parietal in which the tip of the weapon penetrated the bone (ICTY).

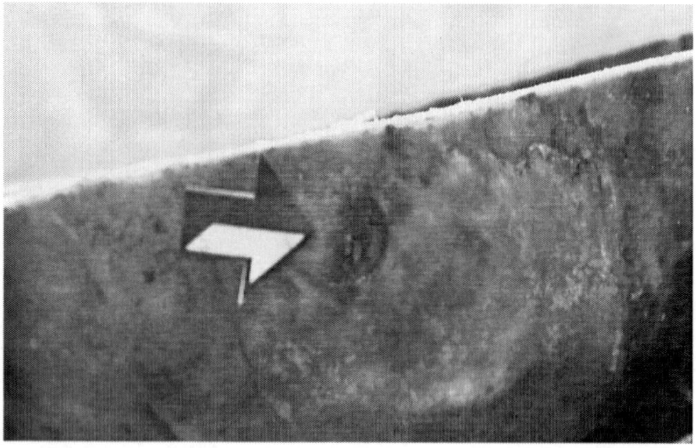

Figure 6.7d External view of the same defect (Figure 6.7c) showing how the tip of the weapon penetrated through and through (ICTY).

Slot Fractures

When impacting the skull, chopping wounds tend to fragment bone or penetrate the cranium, resulting in multiple fractures as the blade is removed from the bone. This type of injury has been called a *slot fracture* (Figures 6.8–6.9) and is characterized by a wide groove with one straight edge and an associated curved or concentric fracture that results from a rotational movement of the blade as it is removed from the skull (Weber and Czarnetzki 2001).

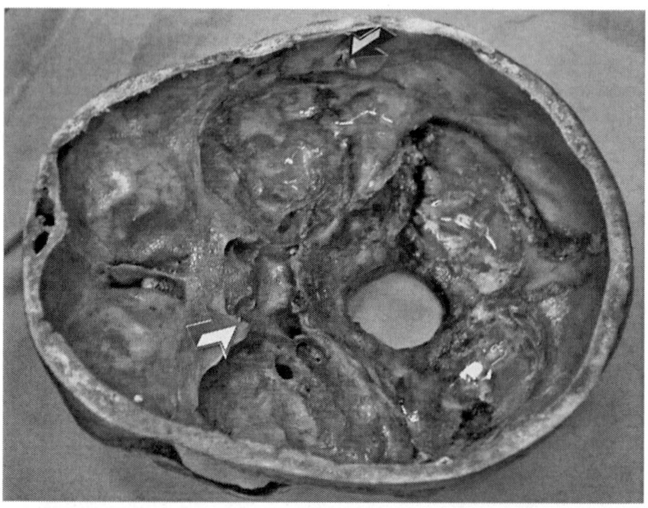

Figure 6.7e Endocranial view of the base of the skull showing the trajectory of the blade with the penetration of the tip on the right parietal (a large kitchen knife was used). In this case, the length of the blade is approximately the same width as the skull, and the characteristics of the injuries suggest a large knife. The individual may have been restrained with the right side of the head against a hard surface while the knife was put through, resulting in a notched defect on the left entry site. (Printed with permission from International Criminal Tribunal for the Former Yugoslavia [ICTY].)

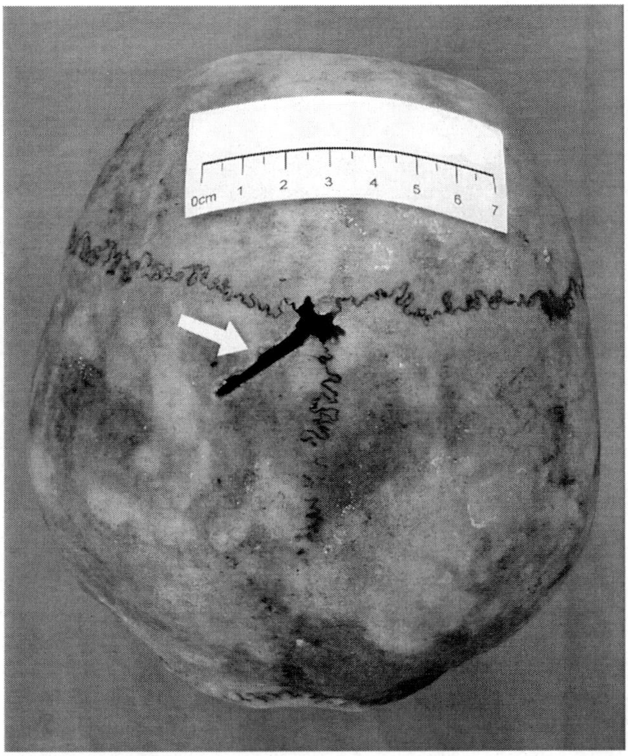

Figure 6.8 Slot fracture of the left parietal between coronal and sagittal sutures, with an irregular edge (anterior aspect) due to the location of the edge of the fracture on sutures. The shape of the defect mimics the cross section of the weapon that caused it, in this case, a short-bladed weapon, possibly a bayonet or knife. (Printed with permission from International Criminal Tribunal for the former Yugoslavia [ICTY].)

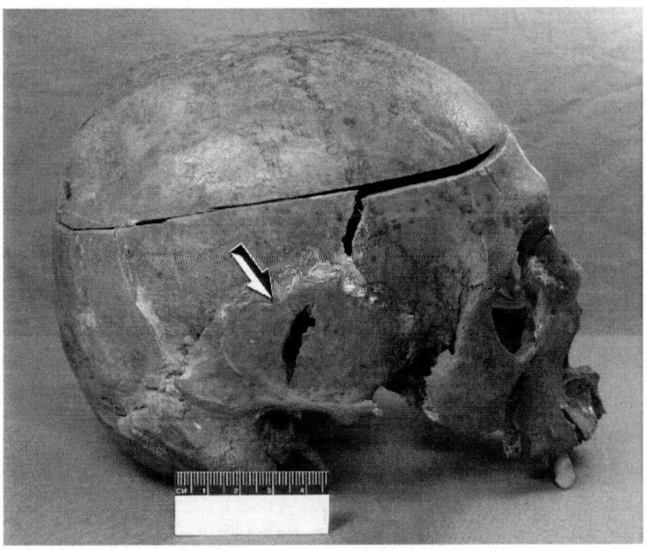

Figure 6.9a Left lateral view of an adult skull. Elongated defect on the right temporal bone, triangular in shape. This injury is consistent with a bladed weapon penetrating the skull, possibly a knife (Alain Wittmann).

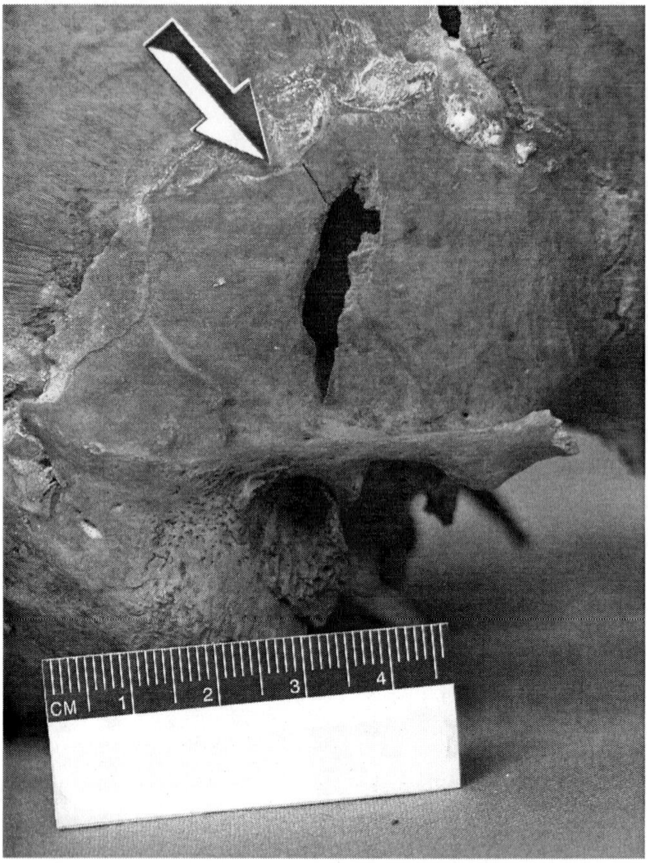

Figure 6.9b Close-up view of sharp force injury shown in Figure 6.9a (Alain Wittmann).

Chop Marks and Scoop Defects

Chopping instruments cause sharp and blunt injuries (as discussed in detail later in the chapter). Generally, they can be morphologically categorized by fractures and defects that result when the weapon strikes bone and those that result as the blade is removed from the bone.

Generally, chop marks are caused by a long- or thick-bladed instrument with at least one cutting edge such as a machete, an axe, or a cleaver; when impacting long bones, they tend to disrupt the continuity of the bone by severing the parts. In striking the bone, it tends to cause *chattering* (Kerley 1973) by microfracturing the edges of the bone it impacts (Figure 6.10). Depending on the size and weight of the weapon, one blow, or a few, may be enough to sever a long bone. Figures 6.11–6.20 illustrate numerous examples of these types of defects, some resulting in combination, from various chopping weapons.

Scoop marks generally characterize wounds caused by direct blows to long bones where the blade penetrates the compact bone and creates a fragment or wedge on removal

Figure 6.10 Right leg, knee region, anterior view. Multiple wounds with chattering on the distal end of femur, proximal fibula, and tibia impact (Carlos Jacinto, FAFG).

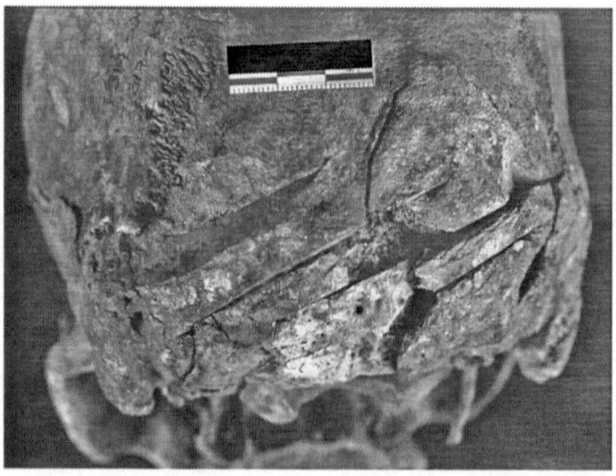

Figure 6.11 Posterior aspect of the skull showing chop and scoop marks, consistent with a long-bladed weapon such as a machete (Carlos Jacinto, FAFG).

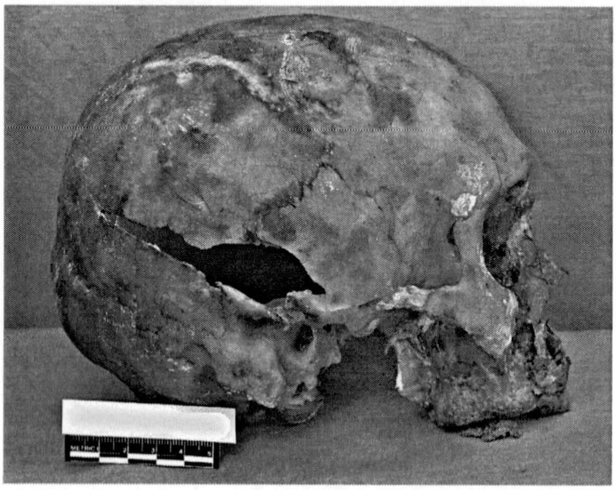

Figure 6.12a Large, irregular defect on the right temporoparietal area showing a straight edge along the inferior margin (Alain Wittmann).

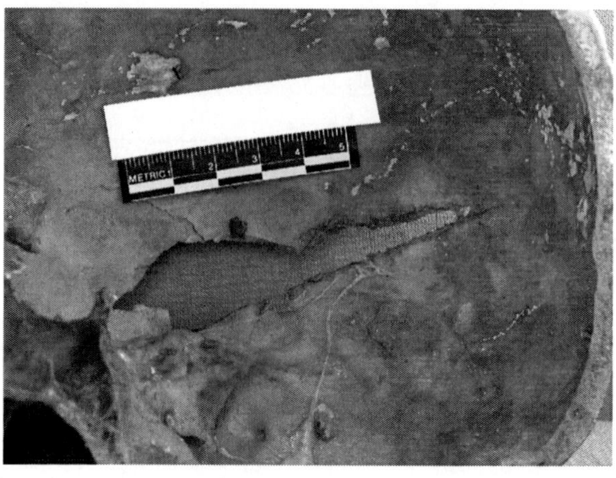

Figure 6.12b Endocranial view of the defect shown in Figure 6.12a, consistent with impact from a long-bladed weapon such as a machete. The irregular and wider superior aspect of the defect may have been caused by levering the blade upon removal (Alain Wittmann).

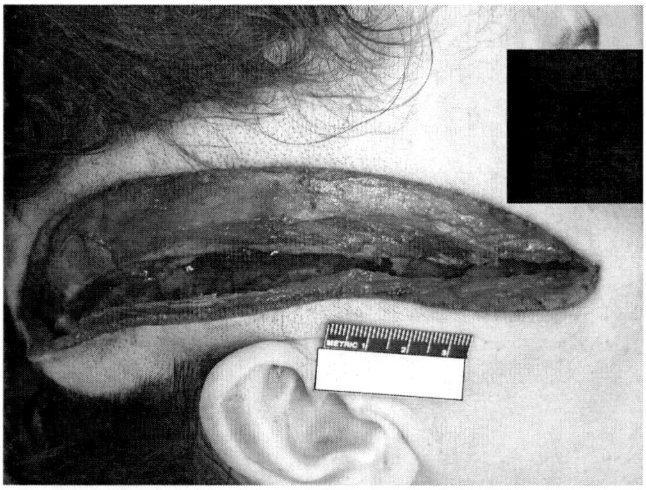

Figure 6.13a Sharp force trauma to the right temporal by a heavy bladed weapon (in this case an axe) above the right ear as seen on a cadaver. The impact was oblique to the head and penetrated into the bone. Note the somewhat pointed anterior end of the injury indicating the exit defect from the blade. The blow was therefore applied from above to below and left to right (Alain Wittmann).

of the blade. The resultant wound is generally a small, concave defect with multiple facets, where small "flakes" of bone are removed. Scoop marks are generally associated with long-bladed weapons such as swords, machetes, or pangas and require enough force to penetrate through the bone and remove a piece of it without compromising the overall integrity of the bone (exit defects). In other words, complete fractures are typically present in this category of defects, depending on the specific bone or region impacted.

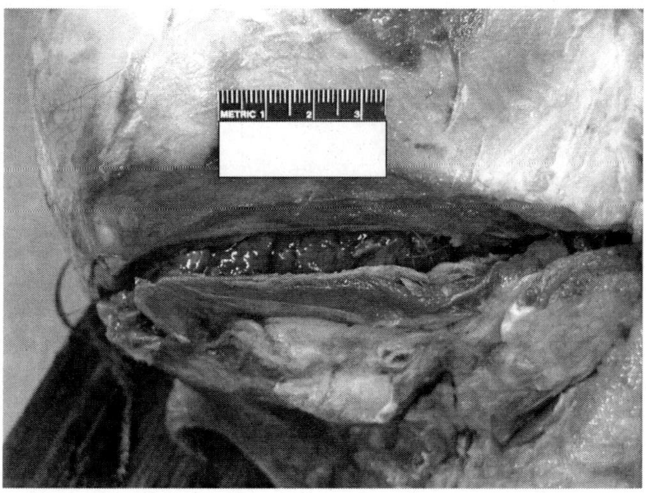

Figure 6.13b Detail of the same case (see Figure 6.13a) after reflection of soft tissues. The displacement of the edges of the chop is caused by rotational forces to remove the blade (Alain Wittmann).

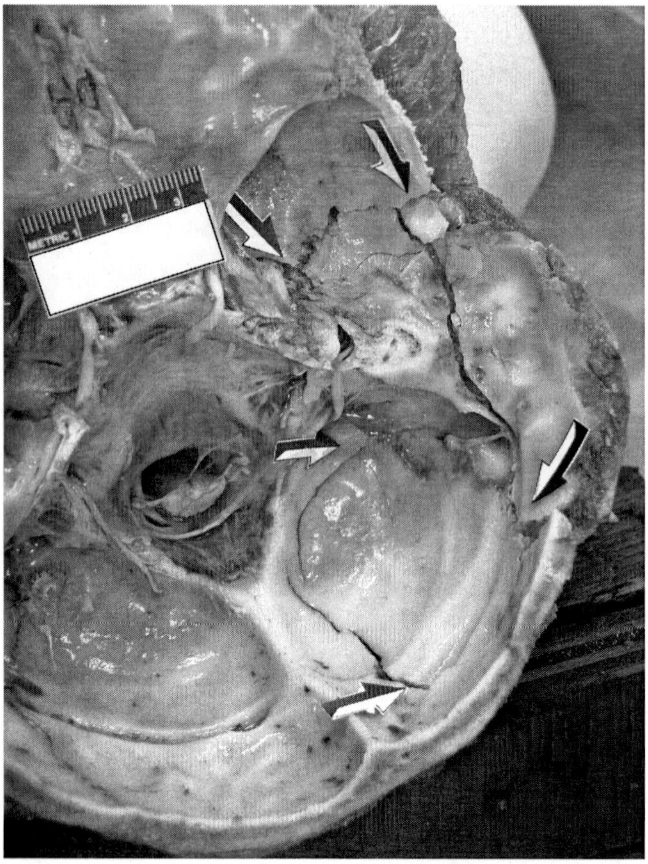

Figure 6.13c Endocranial view of the same case (see Figure 6.13a) observed from a posterior angle. Notice the fracture extending between the right middle and posterior fossae associated to the exit defect of the blade. The force exerted to the skull is equivalent to bending in which the bone fails first in tension in the inner table. An accessory fracture is also located on the occipital squama along the midline, possibly caused by a fall on the back of the head (Alain Wittmann).

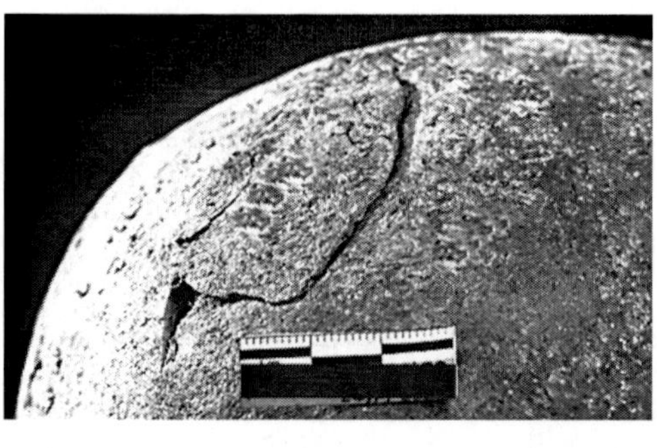

Figure 6.14a (See color insert following page 38) "Slot fracture" on the right parietal bone. The linear chop mark that runs along the sagital suture is associated to a concentric fracture, which almost joins both ends of the chop mark, and is caused by fragmentation of the bone as the blade penetrates and exits, causing internal compression and making the bone fail in tension externally. The injury is consistent with a long-bladed weapon such as a machete (Carlos Jacinto, FAFG).

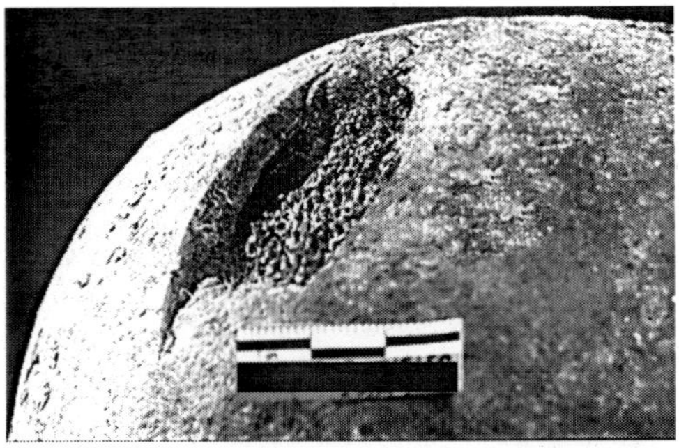

Figure 6.14b (See color insert following page 38) Close-up view after the bone fragment (plug) was removed (Carlos Jacinto, FAFG).

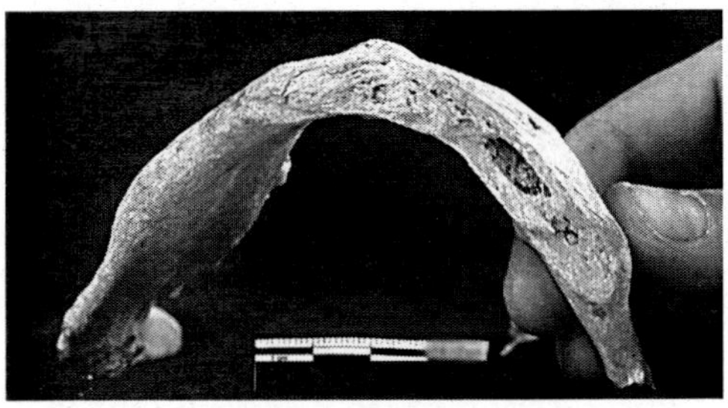

Figure 6.15a Inferior surface of an adult mandible. Chop marks and complete fracture along the inferior aspect of the mandible, exposing the dental sockets. Injuries are consistent with a long-bladed weapon such as a machete (Carlos Jacinto, FAFG).

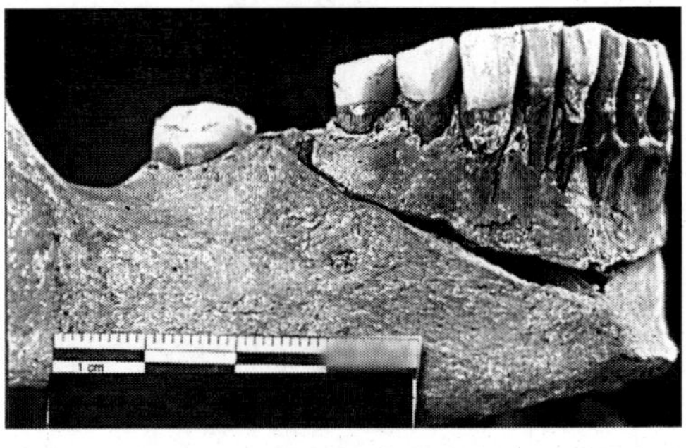

Figure 6.15b Chop mark above the mental eminence with oblique fracturing running superiorly toward the alveolar margin (Carlos Jacinto, FAFG).

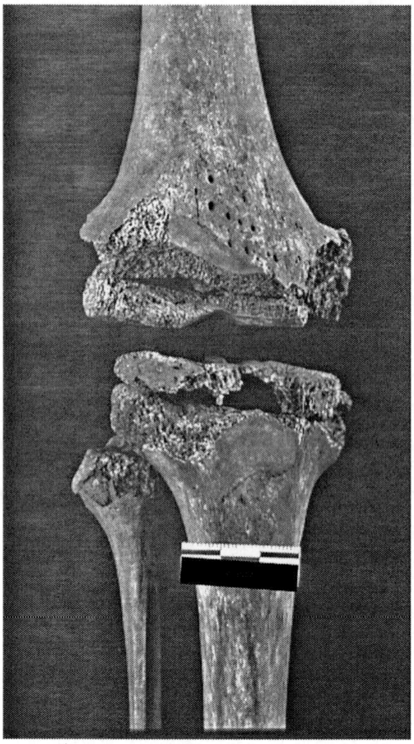

Figure 6.16 Anterior aspect of the right knee shows a minimum of two chop marks that deeply penetrated deep into the bone, causing near complete fracturing of both the distal femur and proximal tibia. The injuries are consistent with a long-bladed weapon such as a machete. The patella was not recovered. Both injuries were inflicted from front to back (Carlos Jacinto, FAFG).

Figure 6.17 Anterior view of the right distal femur, which shows multiple chop marks that expose and fragment the trabecular bone. An isolated cut mark extending in the same direction as the other injuries is also visible. The wounds resulted from a heavy bladed instrument such as an axe or a machete used repeatedly over the same area (Carlos Jacinto, FAFG).

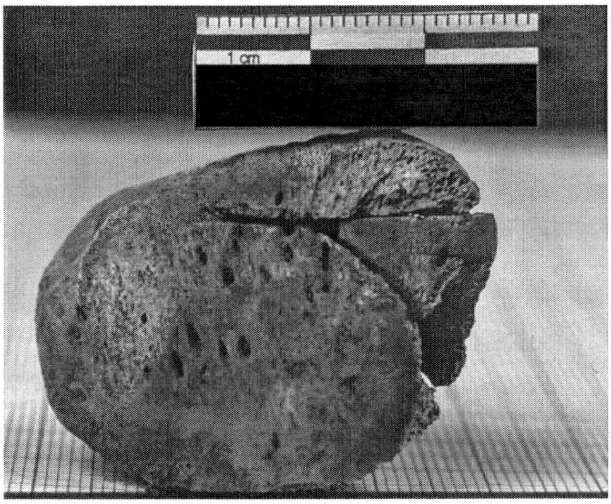

Figure 6.18 Anterior aspect of the right patella showing multiple chop marks, one of which (the top one) penetrates deep into the bone. The direction of the strokes was left to right, consistent with a long-bladed instrument such as a machete (Carlos Jacinto, FAFG).

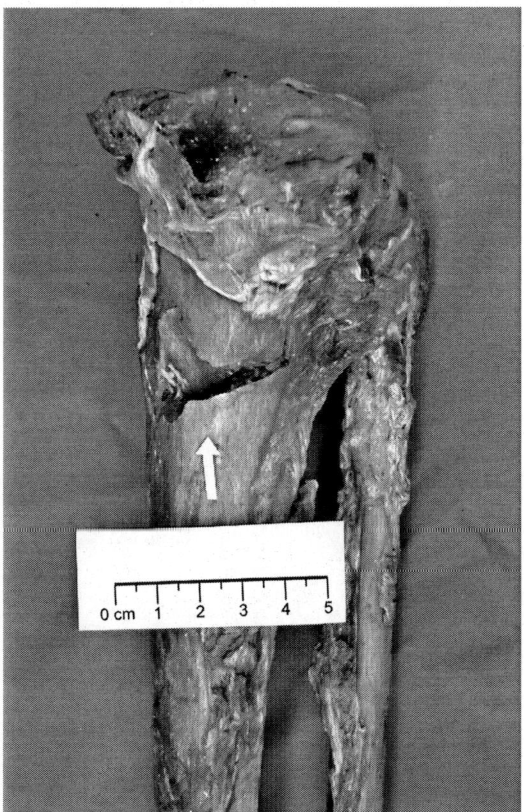

Figure 6.19 Chop mark on the medial aspect of the left tibial shaft with a protrusion of bone sleeve as a consequence of withdrawing of the blade, injury consistent with a heavy, long-bladed weapon. (Printed with permission from International Criminal Tribunal for the former Yugoslavia [ICTY]).

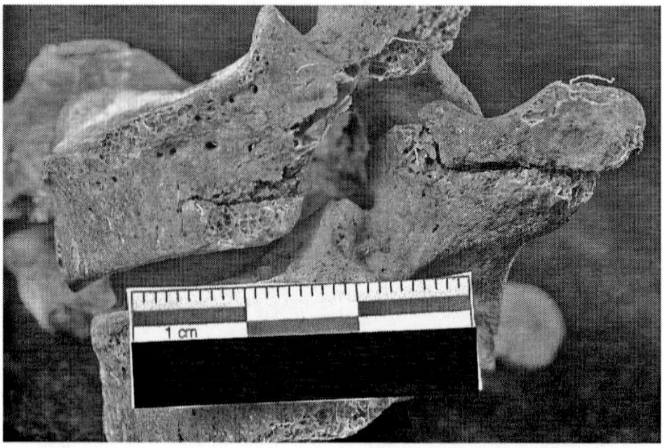

Figure 6.20 Chop mark across the spinous process and body of the first thoracic and seventh cervical vertebrae, respectively. Consistent with a long-bladed weapon such as a machete (Carlos Jacinto, FAFG).

The Man in the Burning Car: A Practical Example of Cut Marks

The following example illustrates how cut marks may be identified on burned bone and interpreted to estimate the cause and manner of death. Later in the chapter, a contrasting example discusses the identification of sharp and blunt injuries to the skull resulting from a hatchet. Identifying knife wounds or cut marks is possible, even when the remains have been burned (Mayne 1997, McKinley 2000, de Gruchy and Rogers 2002, Pope et al. 2004, Brinkley 2007). In January 2003, authorities were alerted of the discovery of a car burning on a dirt road in the Kosovo countryside. At the time of discovery, the police called the military for assistance and put the fire out with extinguishers (Figure 6.21). It became

Figure 6.21a Overview of burned car (Alain Wittmann).

Figure 6.21b Melted aluminum parts (Alain Wittmann).

apparent then that there was a body in the car on the passenger's seat. The high temperature attained by the fire (> 700°C) melted most of the aluminum structures of the car.

The body was burned beyond recognition, and showed the typical pugilistic position. In addition, most of the top of the head was missing. Once at the mortuary, through the autopsy it was determined that it was the body of a male; the internal organs were moderately preserved, but no other evidence of possible traumatic injuries was observable. Examination of the palate and upper airways did not show evidence of soot, indicating that the person was dead prior to the time of the fire (Di Maio and Dana 2007). Although all available elements strongly suggested a homicide, the autopsy could not establish the cause of death. Subsequently, the bones were examined for injury and possible contributing factors to the death of the individual.

Because the skull was missing a substantial number of fragments, the contents of the car, and crime scene were sifted to recover missing elements. This proved to be useful, and the skull was almost completely recovered and successfully reconstructed. It became apparent that most damage to the skull had been caused by fire, i.e., severe fragmentation of the neurocranium due to an increase in temperature and gas (Figures 6.22 and 6.23) (Bohnert et al. 1998). A fluoroscope examination of the skull did not show any metal particles that may suggest a gunshot wound. The skeleton was cleaned as much as possible, although due to time constraints complete maceration was not performed.

Through this examination, a number of injuries caused by a sharp instrument were observed, and it was likely they were related to the cause of death. Three distinct injuries were located on the left side of the chest, left shoulder, and lumbar spine. The left scapula exhibited a linear defect (~19 mm) on the distal one-third of the dorsal aspect of the blade, ~10 mm from the lateral margin and orientated perpendicular to the axis of the bone (Figure 6.24). The defect (Figure 6.25) showed separation of the edges with manifest posterior protrusion of the inferior edge and a short linear fracture extending inferiorly (perpendicular to the axis of the defect). Anteriorly, the defect appeared irregular with jagged edges (Figure 6.26), and two linear fractures were present, extending above

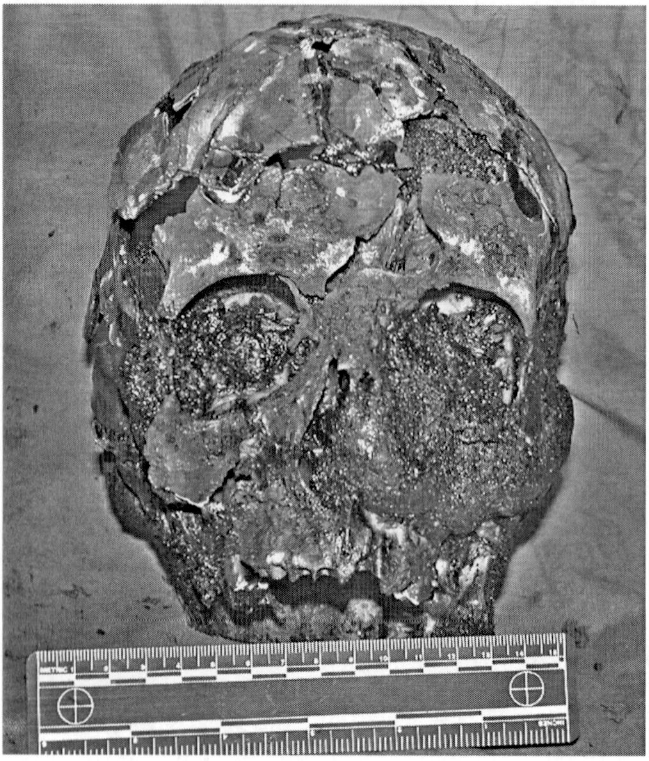

Figure 6.22 Anterior view of a reconstructed skull (Alain Wittmann).

the defect parallel to the lateral margin and inferiorly from the middle part of the defect (Figure 6.27). From the dorsal view, the reverse pattern was noted along the superior edge, which protruded anteriorly. These wounds and fracture patterns were consistent with the penetration of a sharp-bladed object, such as a knife, extending through the blade, along an almost parallel trajectory from back to front and downwards. The protrusion of the

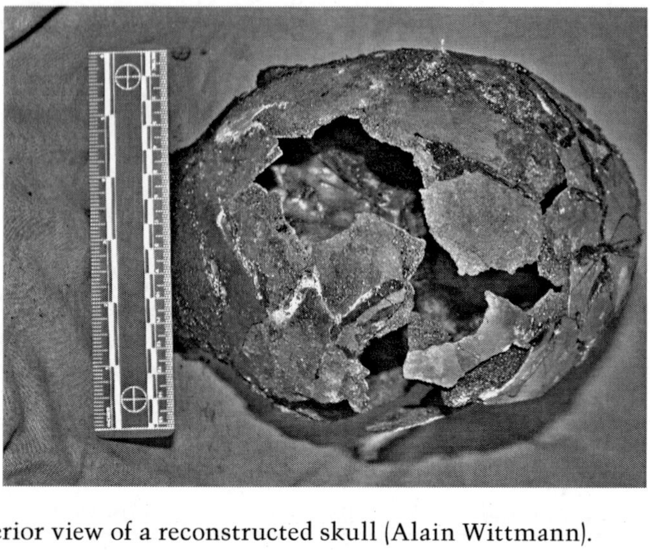

Figure 6.23 Superior view of a reconstructed skull (Alain Wittmann).

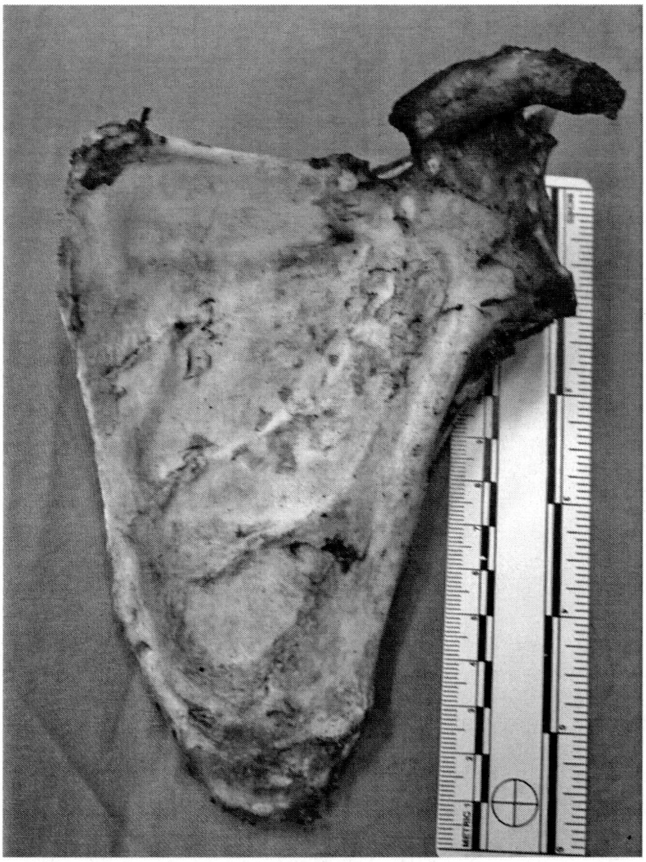

Figure 6.24 Anterior view of the left scapula with a sharp force defect on blade (Alain Wittmann).

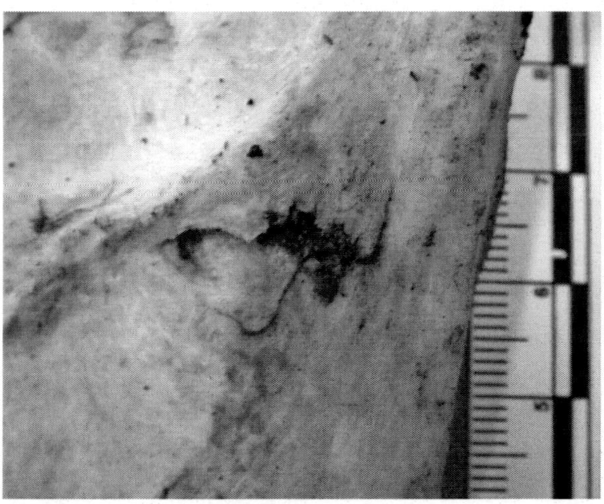

Figure 6.25 Close-up image of defect pictured in Figure 6.24 (Alain Wittmann).

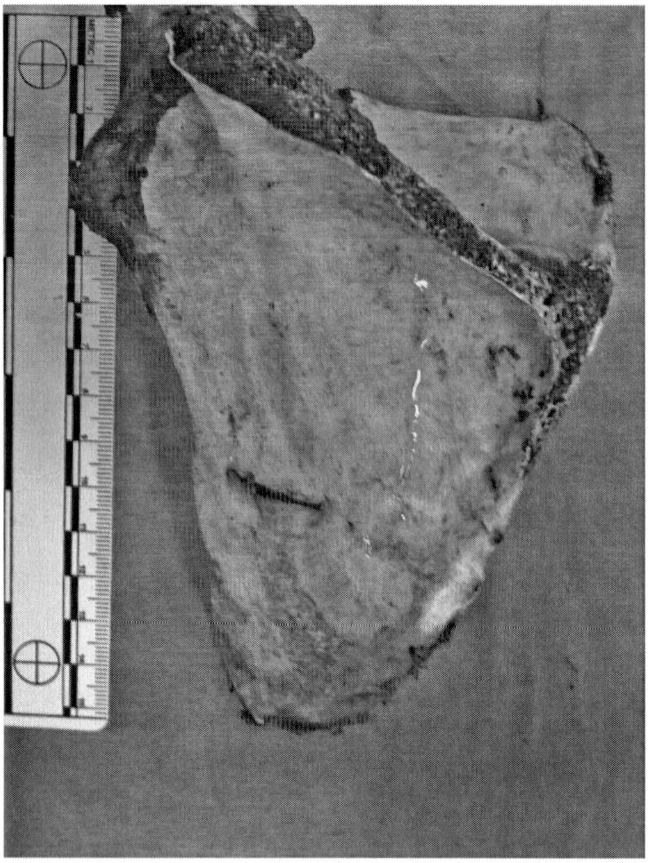

Figure 6.26 Posterior view of the left scapula with a visible defect (Alain Wittmann).

edges and the associated fractures were caused by the penetration of the blade and the leveling of the blade as it withdrew from the bone.

The second left rib (Figure 6.28) had an irregular-shaped defect (~10 mm in length) on the middle one-third of the body, adjacent to the superior border (Figure 6.29). The defect

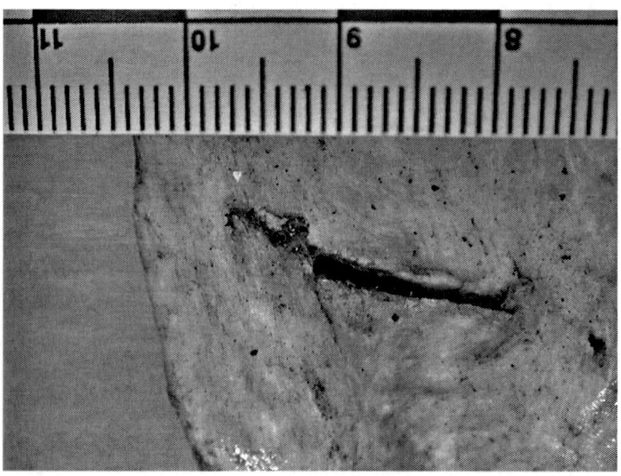

Figure 6.27 Close-up image of defect pictured in Figure 6.26 (Alain Wittmann).

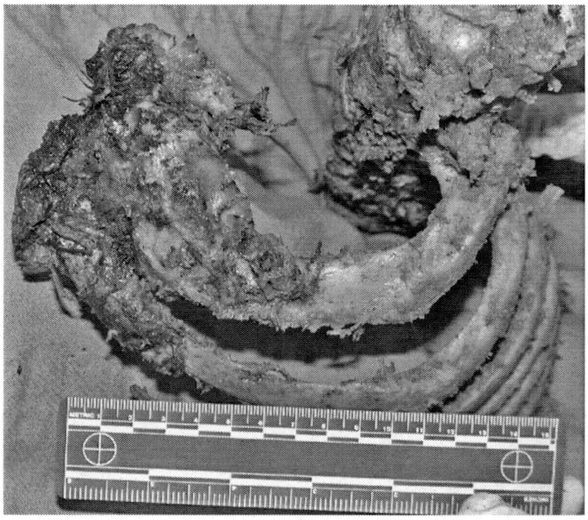

Figure 6.28 Superior view of the first and second left ribs (Alain Wittmann).

caused the rib to split along its grain by a pointed and sharp instrument, which upon penetration also fractured the superior edge of the defect and caused it to protrude posteriorly. The instrument (i.e., a knife) penetrated the rib at an acute angle, possibly from front to back and downward.

The left humerus exhibited a linear defect (~35 mm × 3 mm deep) on the anterior aspect of the metaphysis extending obliquely to the axis of the bone onto the humeral head. It is consistent with an angled entrance, as seen in previous injuries. The inferior border protrudes inferiorly, caused by the extraction of the blade from the bone. A closer examination of the defect shows a U rather than a V shape of the kerf floor and a discrete fracture extending inferiorly from the lateral end of the inferior edge (Figure 6.30). The injury is consistent with a bladed object that was applied with enough force to cut through soft tissues and become embedded in bone. The length of the defect, much larger than the previous injuries, resulted from the blade rather than the tip of the instrument striking the bone. It was not clear at autopsy whether this injury was caused by the same weapon

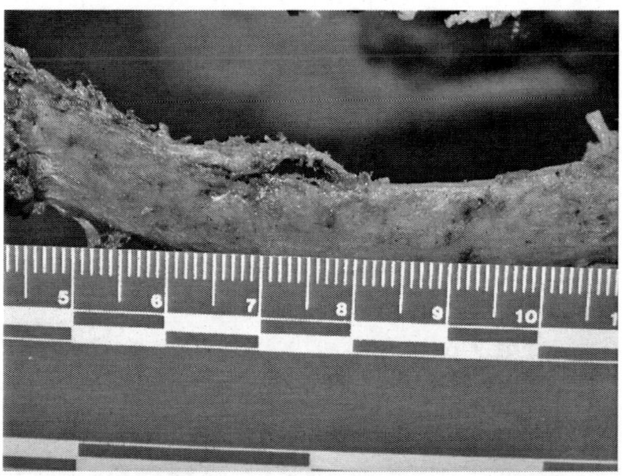

Figure 6.29 Detail of the second rib showing peeling cut mark (Alain Wittmann).

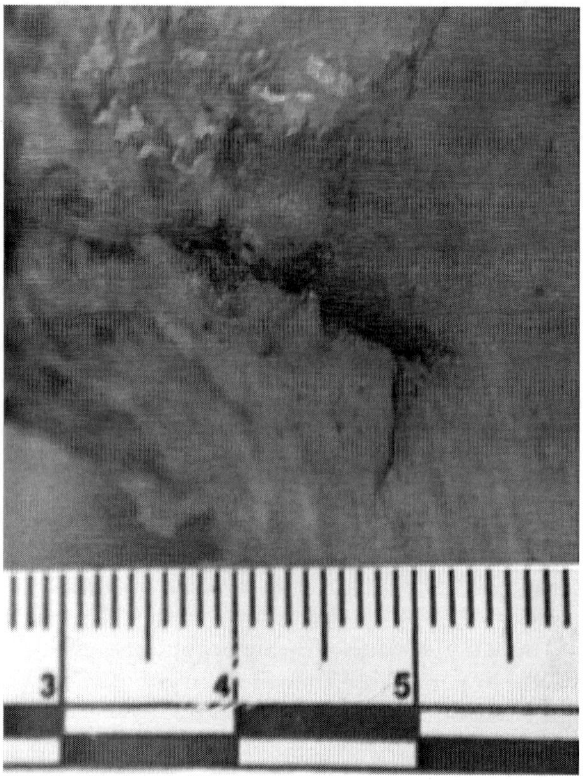

Figure 6.30 Proximal aspect of the left humerus with a sharp force defect (Alain Wittmann).

as were the previously described knife injuries, as a heavier and larger bladed object (i.e., machete or larger knife) could not be excluded.

Finally, the second lumbar vertebra exhibited a triangular-shaped defect on the anterior portion of the body adjacent to the inferior border (Figure 6.31). The defect measured 10 × 2 × 1 mm (length × base width × depth). The defect is consistent with a penetration wound from the pointed end of a bladed artifact (i.e., a knife) in which case, the shape of

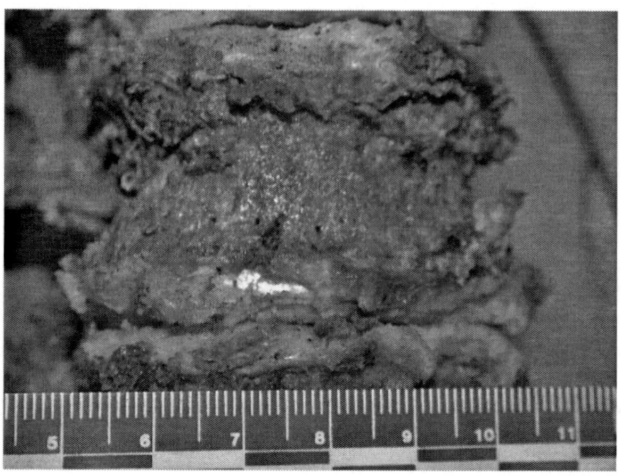

Figure 6.31 Anterior view of L2 with a notched defect (Alain Wittmann).

the defect mimics the cross section of the blade. Considering the location of the injury, the full length of the blade must have penetrated the abdomen to reach the anterior spine.

The death of this individual was attributed to multiple stab wounds, based on skeletal evidence. It was later discovered that the perpetrator had stabbed the victim many times, then put the body into the car, and set it on fire. The injury to the humerus was reportedly caused by the same instrument as were the other wounds, a *large kitchen knife*. Importantly, this example illustrates how the identification of cut marks, even after extensive burning, may provide physical evidence to support the most likely cause and manner of death.

Sharp-Blunt Injury Associated with Chopping Weapons

Blunt force injury in combination with SFT results in cases involving large or heavy tools used as weapons, such as a hatchet, machete, or axe. Chop marks, when inflicted to compact bone (with or without the underlying cancellous layer affected) typically leave a smooth surface along the point of impact. The opposing surface, however, will be invariably fragmented, and often completely separate, due to the force of the blow. A chop mark generally covers a larger area than cut marks. If the blow strikes cancellous bone (i.e., in the vertebrae), straight, complete fragments with angular surfaces are typically observed. In such injuries, linear fractures may also extend from the defect due to force of the blow, as well as the rotational damage when attempting to withdraw the weapon from the bone (exit defect). Consequently, blunt force injuries (i.e., large areas of crushed tissue) are often observed associated with cut tissue (refer to the following example of trauma resulting from a hatchet for an example with multiple sharp-blunt injuries).

In a comparative study of single-blade knives and a cleaver (chopping weapon), both types of instruments produced sharp-blunt injuries, and it was demonstrated that microscopic analysis could be used for weapon classification (Alunni-Perret et al. 2005; refer also to Wenham 1989 who reported similar findings). The general wound characteristics were described (Alunni-Perret et al. 2005) as follows: (1) knife wound edges are more even than a hatchet wound, (2) knife wounds are thinner and more linear, whereas hatchet defects are square in shape, and (3) knives result in unilateral flaking of the margins due to the blade striking bone at an angle and disrupting the outer cortex along one side (chattering).

Hatchet Trauma from Colombia: A Practical Example

A case of multiple sharp-blunt injuries to a skull from Colombia was provided by Jorge Pachón. Figure 6.32 illustrates the sharp and blunt force trauma caused to a cranium that received multiple blows from a hatchet. Two clusters of blows were recorded. The order of blows in the anterior cluster is indicated by the intersecting patterns of fracture lines (Figure 6.33). The defect to the left frontal area illustrates a crushing injury resulting in the displacement of a spall of bone with associated beveling. The spalls are caused by bone failure in tension along the inner table due to compressive forces following the penetration of the weapon externally (Figure 6.34). The triangular-shaped defect forms two borders at a 90° angle. The bevel of the fracture (left side) is external, indicating that it may have been caused when the weapon was pulled out of the head, resulting in the bone's fracturing externally (again on the side of tension) (Figure 6.35). The edges of the defect exhibit chipping caused by pulling the hatchet from the head following the blow (Figures 6.36

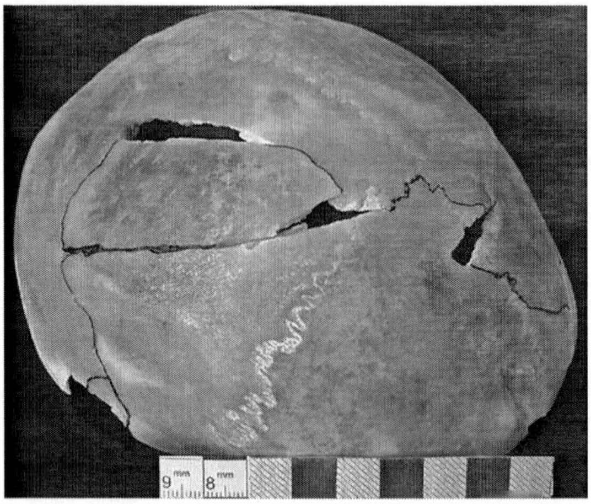

Figure 6.32 (See color insert following page 38) Right superior view of an adult skull. Three distinct injuries are visible: defect #1 (on the frontal bone adjacent to the metopic suture), defect #2 (in the center), and defect #3 (top slightly to the left, positioned most posteriorly) (Jorge Pachón).

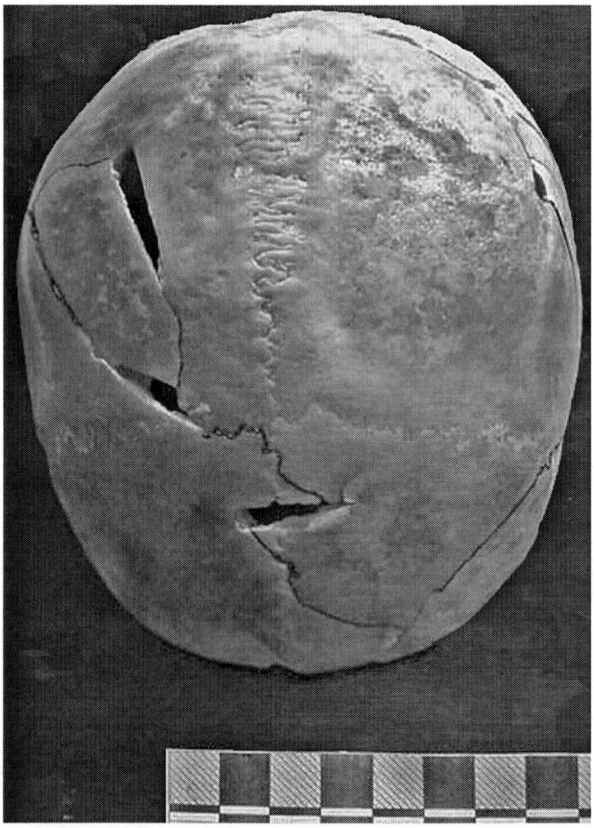

Figure 6.33 Superior view. Based on intersecting fracture lines, the first injury inflicted was #1, followed by #2 and #3. In addition, injury #3, postdates the injuries that occurred on the back of the head. Observe the fracture on the right side of the photograph running across the frontal. The fracture originated by the blow causing injury #1 is arrested by the preexisting fracture (Jorge Pachón).

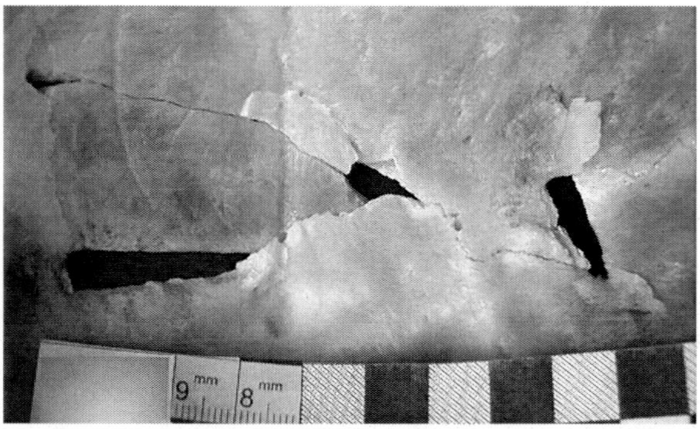

Figure 6.34 Endocranial view. Left frontotemporal area. Detail of defects #1–3 showing bone spalls detached from two of the defects. With the absence of the bone spall, internal beveling is visible. Bone spalls result from the failure in tension on the inner table due to compressive forces following the penetration of the weapon externally (Jorge Pachón).

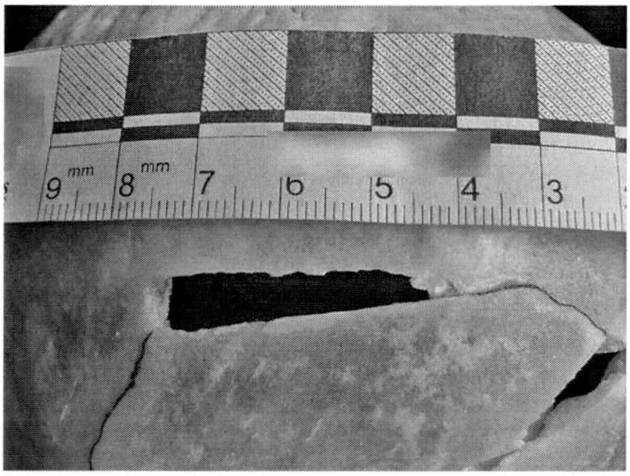

Figure 6.35 Ectocranial view. Left frontal area. Defect #1. Triangle-shaped defect with two net borders forming a 90° angle on the left side and tapering at the right end. The superior border is slightly more irregular. Two radiating fractures originate from the injury. The bevel of the fracture (left side) is external, indicating that it may have been caused when pulling the weapon out of the head and making it fail in tension externally (Jorge Pachón).

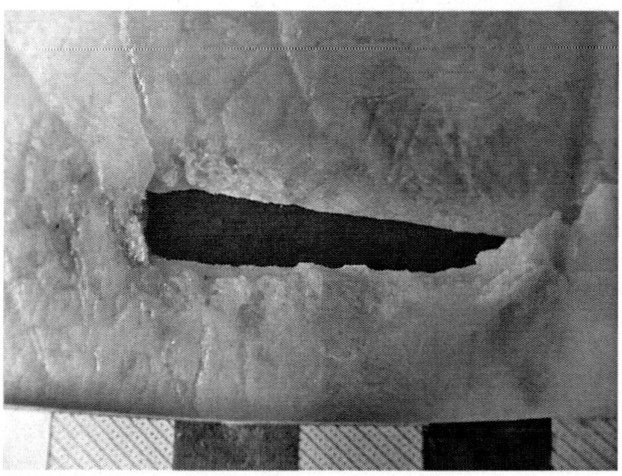

Figure 6.36 Endocranial view, detail of defect #3 (Jorge Pachón).

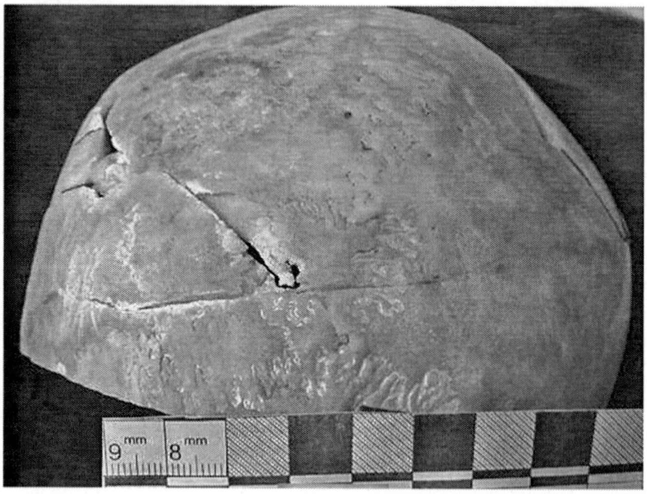

Figure 6.37 Posterior view of intersecting defects (Jorge Pachón).

and 6.37). In addition to spalls of bone, defects resulted from compressive forces applied externally, and the bone failed in tension internally. Figure 6.38 illustrates blunt-sharp trauma to the posterior skull. Reconstruction of the injury through the use of the paper outline of a hatchet reflects the same class of weapon used throughout the skull (Figures 6.39–6.43). In total, there were eight injuries (Figure 6.44). It is important to note that only the superior edge of the hatchet was used when impacting the head. Therefore, it is possible that the hatchet was used by the perpetrator with only one hand. Based on intercepting fracture lines, structural relationships can be established within and among the two groups of injuries:

Figure 6.38 Endocranial view, left side of the occipital and parietal bones. Detail of three partially penetrating defects. Unlike defect #3, these did not completely penetrate the skull and were caused primarily by blunt force trauma. Observe the defect to the left with a "slot" fracture, whereas the other two are primarily characterized by detached fragments of bone and resulted from its failing in tension internally as compressive force was applied externally (Jorge Pachón).

Figure 6.39 Reconstruction of the injury using a paper outline of the same class of weapon that caused the trauma (hatchet defect #3) (Jorge Pachón).

1. The group of injuries to the back of the head was likely inflicted first, whereas the injury to the front of the skull occurred subsequently.
2. Among the wounds to the frontal region, the sequence is approximated from front to back.

Radiographic images of the skull illustrate the points of impact from the hatchet edge and the associated displaced fractures (Figures 6.45 and 6.46).

Summary Guidelines for Best Practice

SFT has been a primary cause of injuries and death in many armed conflicts throughout Central and South America, as well as in genocide and the massive violations to HHRR in Africa. Moreover, attempts to dispose large numbers of bodies or move graves to hide their location may result in post-mortem damage that mimics cutmarks or other defects consistent with SFT. Therefore the ability to accurately identify and diagnosis SFT is critical for

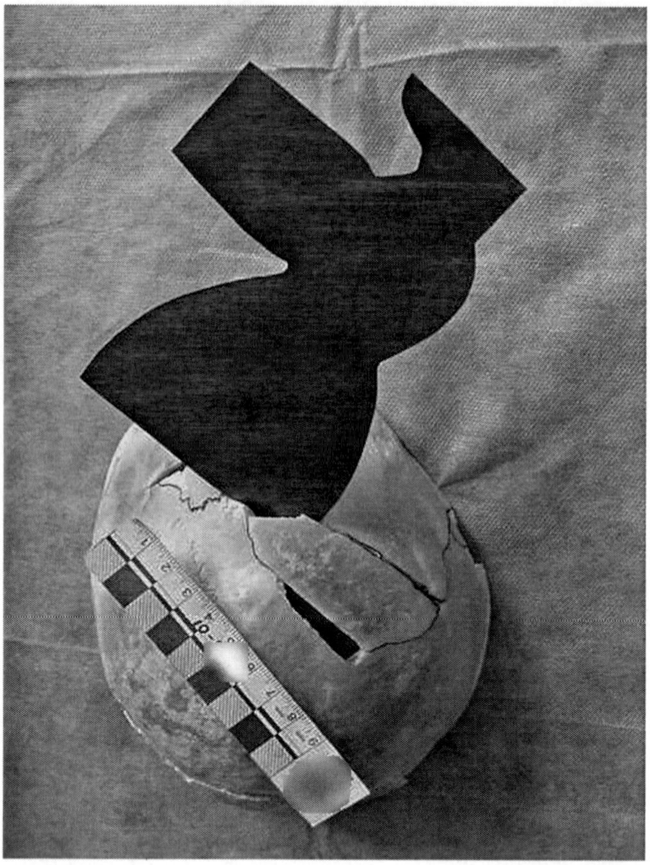

Figure 6.40 Reconstruction of the injury using a paper outline of the same class of weapon that caused the trauma (hatchet). The angle of impact and part of the weapon used (one of the edges) would cased the irregular defect (defect #2) (Jorge Pachón).

many investigations into violations of IHL and IHRL, whether it is to estimate the cause and manner of death or to reconstruct the circumstances surrounding the fatal incident. By nature, SFT injuries are inflicted in close proximity to the victim and may be accompanied by other forms of assault associated with a struggle, such as BFT or defensive wounds on the victim. In cases of torture or extrajudicial execution, victims may be bound or restricted in such a manner as to prohibit the victim to either fight back or simply place his/her arms in front of the face. Though not commonly, documented cases of SFT used for torture, have been also been reported in the forensic literature.

In many situations where SFT is the primary weapon used (i.e. Rwanda or Guatemala), the heavy long-bladed weapons result in *sharp-blunt injuries*. This concept specifically describes the defects and fracture patterns, associated with a single mechanism of injury and is well established among forensic HHRR investigators. In these contexts, the actual weapons used to commit the murders are not typically available for comparison. Forensics in such cases is not focused on the identification of the perpetrator or establishing the

Figure 6.41 Reconstruction of the injury using a paper outline of the same class of weapon that caused the trauma (hatchet) (defect #1) (Jorge Pachón).

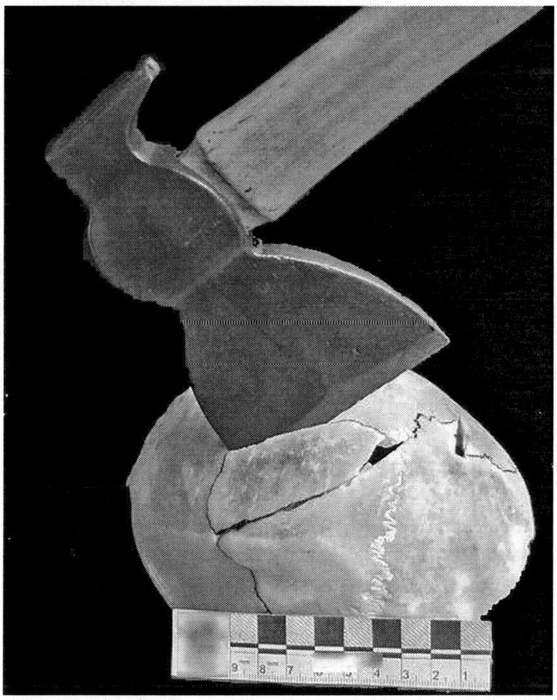

Figure 6.42 Reconstruction of the injury for defect #3 using an actual hatchet that is the same class of weapon that caused the injury (Jorge Pachón).

Figure 6.43 Reconstruction of the injury using for defect #1 using an actual hatchet (Jorge Pachón).

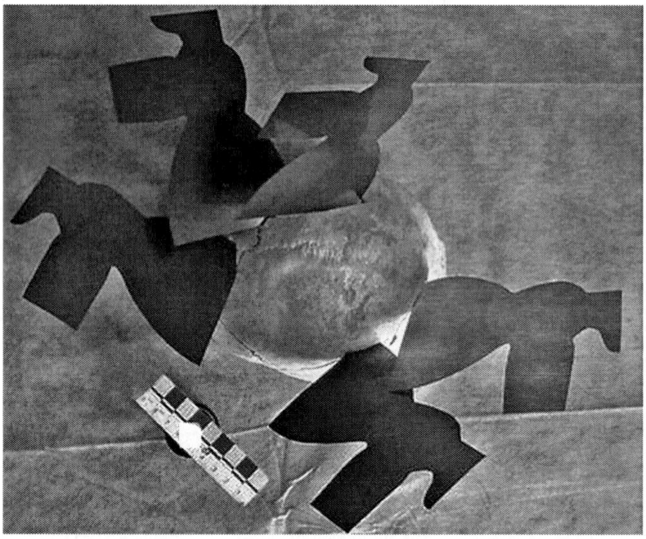

Figure 6.44 Reconstruction of the injury using a paper outline of the same class of weapon that caused the trauma (hatchet). Eight injuries were recorded. It is important to note that only the superior edge of the hatchet was used in impacting the head. It is very possible that the hatchet was used with only one hand. Based on fracture interception a structural relationship, the sequence of two groups of injuries (anterior and posterior) can be established. Further, injury order can be estimated for the anterior group and between the two groups: the group of injuries on the back of the head was inflicted first and the group on the frontal bone occurred subsequently. Within the second group of injuries, the three defects were inflicted from front to back (Jorge Pachón).

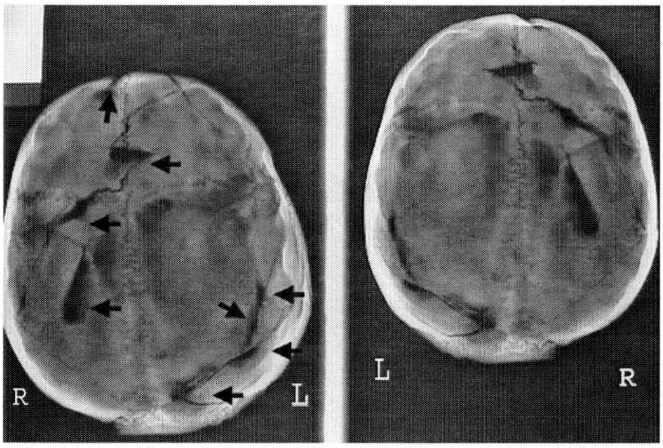

Figure 6.45 X-ray of cranial vault showing hatchet impact defects and associated displaced fractures. The left side shows the internal view and the right, the external view (Jorge Pachón).

presence of the accused to the crime scene. Rather, the issues for forensic scientists are to establish the cause and manner of death by estimating the timing of the injury, whether the injuries were fatal if untreated, and whether the action was to inflict harm or death based on the injury.

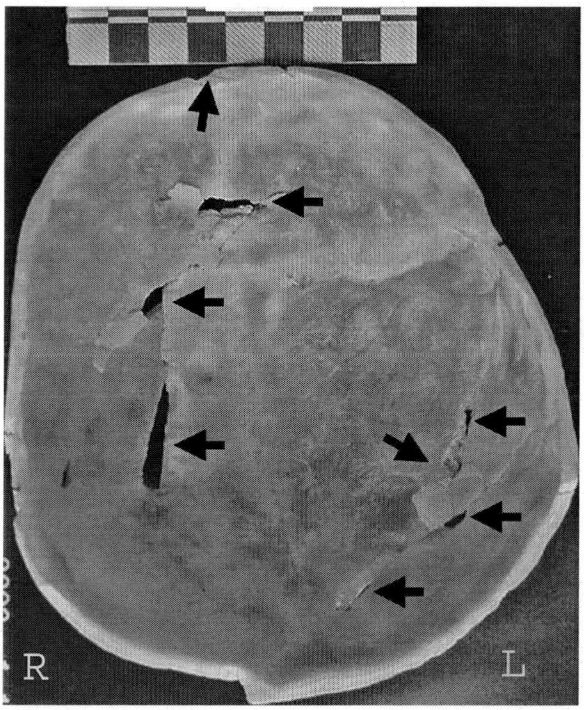

Figure 6.46 Ectocranial view of a cranial vault; black arrows point to the eight impacts (Jorge Pachón).

Case Study 6.1: Disappearance, Torture, and Murder of Nine Individuals in a Community of Nebaj, Guatemala

Shirley Carola Chacón, Fredy Armando Peccerelli, Leonel Paiz Diez, Claudia Rivera Fernández*

Fundación de Antropología Forense de Guatemala (FAFG)

The Guatemalan Historical Clarification Commission (CEH) registered 32 massacres and the partial or total destruction of 90 villages in the Ixil area. The majority of the rural populations were displaced from their territories. Most of the massacres occurred between 1980 and 1982. Among these, the following case from Nebaj, Quiché, represents the violence suffered by the Ixil community.

The investigations followed by the CEH revealed the presence of several clandestine cemeteries in the Nebaj area. The case had been reported twice with different dates. The first version reports that in February 1982 the remains of five individuals exhibiting signs of torture were found in the village. The second report states that in 1985, after a fight between the army and guerrillas, fifteen members of the community were captured, persecuted, and murdered. The bodies recovered were allegedly dismembered and mutilated.

According to witness testimonies collected by the FAFG after the confrontation, the following events took place. Soldiers had been looking for the people presumed to be the victims, which led to the capture of eight men on July 10 and another ten men on August 18, 1982. The men were captured while carrying out their daily labors in the fields. Some neighbors informed the relatives that they saw members of the army kidnapping these men and taking them to the garrison. The families were not given any information on the whereabouts of the men. About a month later on September 15, 1982, a man from the community, while walking toward his house, observed dogs digging in a cornfield. When the man looked closer, he saw that the area was covered with human remains. He talked to the owner of the field and to relatives of the abducted victims; all of whom went to the field and recognized the bodies.

Following this discovery, some relatives and neighbors opened a second grave, near the first and buried the body parts and bodies that were found on the surface to avoid more scavenging by dogs. They marked the graves with wooden crosses in case they would want to move them later. In November 2003, the Prosecutor of Nebaj requested that the FAFG exhume the two graves in the area.

Field Results

Following information given by the relatives, the two graves were located. Both graves were marked by wooden crosses. During the forensic archaeology phase, a trench 2 m in length was excavated to locate the first grave. Approximately 0.50 m deep, a piece of synthetic clothing was found (Figures 6.47 and 6.48). This grave was consistent with a primary direct mass burial. There were four skeletons in anatomical position and one body part, consisting of the distal diaphysis of the humerus, radius, ulna, and hand. The original grave measured 1.90 m in length by 1.40 m in width by 0.78 m in depth.

Three trenches were dug to locate the second grave. This grave was consistent with a secondary direct mass burial. The remains of 5 incomplete skeletons in anatomical position

* And Carlos Jacinto, Photographer.

Figure 6.47 Overview of grave 1 (FAFG).

Figure 6.48 Overview of grave 2 (FAFG).

Figure 6.49 Detail of rope around the neck of an individual in grave 2 (FAFG).

and 17 body parts were recovered. The body parts consisted of six left and five right superior extremities, as well as two left and four right inferior extremities. The original measurement of the grave was 2.27 meters in length by 0.80 in width by 0.95 in depth, with a north-eastern orientation. During the excavation, four ropes were found around the necks and both wrists of two different skeletons (Figures 6.49 and 6.50). In total, a minimum number of 9 incomplete and articulated skeletons and 18 body parts were found.

Lab Results

The human remains were processed for analysis in the FAFG laboratory. A minimum number (MNI) of individuals was estimated, all of them males aged between 14 and 56 years. Perimortem trauma was evident in most of the bones caused by sharp-blunt force trauma. The body parts were mutilated around the time of death; most of the injuries were located near joint articulations in the elbows and knees, some of which had completely separated the extremities. Some defensive injuries were also evident in the bones of the hands.

Figure 6.50 Detail of rope around the wrist of an individual in grave 1 (FAFG).

Table 6.2 Frequency of Injuries by Body Part

- Right scapula, posterior portion of acromion process (n = 1)
- Right humerus: from medial shaft to distal epiphysis (n = 4)
- Left humerus: from medial shaft to distal epiphysis (n = 7)
- Right ulna: from proximal epiphysis to medial shaft (n = 2)
- Left ulna: from proximal epiphysis to medial shaft (n = 1)
- Right radius: from proximal epiphysis to medial shaft (n = 1)
- Left radius: from proximal epiphysis to medial shaft (n = 1)
- Right hand (MTC #3, 4, and 5): shaft (n = 1)
- Right femur: from distal shaft to distal epiphysis (n = 5)
- Left femur: from medial shaft to distal epiphysis (n = 2)
- Right patella: anterior and posterior surface (n = 4)
- Left patella: anterior and posterior surface (n = 2)
- Right tibia: from proximal epiphysis to proximal shaft (n = 2)
- Left tibia: from proximal epiphysis to medial shaft (n = 2)

During analysis, an inventory of body parts was used to associate the remains with the articulated bodies. Three different criteria were used to make the association: osteometric, macroscopic comparison, and corresponding perimortem injuries. All the body parts were associated to a specific body without altering the MNI. Of the individuals, all were males, of whom there were adults and subadult.

In addition to the sharp-blunt trauma found in the upper and lower limbs of the nine individuals, blunt force trauma was present in the thorax of one skeleton that also exhibited cut marks (Table 6.3). The frequency of injuries is listed in Table 6.2 (note that the number refers to the number of individuals/cases):

Perimortem trauma observed in bone was matched with cut marks in clothing (Figure 6.51). It was possible to generally associate the upper and lower limbs for 7 of the bodies. Table 6.4 lists these correlations. Another important finding was the presence of tooth marks in the thoracic vertebrae, right clavicle, ribs, scapula, and humerus, which was consistent with scavenging. This taphonomic information is relevant to the witness testimonies, which mentioned that some human bones were scattered on the surface and that had subsequently lead them to dig looking for another grave.

As the results show, seven of the nine bodies had multiple sharp-blunt trauma in upper and lower limbs. Two types of mutilation were observed, the direct result of sharp-blunt trauma and the subsequent fractures of cut marks due to the dismemberment. According to he CEH, in Guatemala that kind of torture (i.e., cutting, amputations) was a common practice by the army during the internal armed conflict (Figures 6.52–6.62). As the archaeological findings and testimonies, show the nine individuals were tortured receiving dismemberment when they were alive.

Through the analysis in the morgue the cause of death was established, in four cases secondary hypovolemic shock resulting from the sharp-blunt and thoracic trauma. In the other five cases, death was attributed to secondary hypovolemic shock as a result of direct dismemberment of the upper and lower limbs. The CEH concluded that agents of the Guatemalan government were in charge of counterinsurgent operations between 1981 and 1983, and during this time genocide policies were followed against the main four ethnic Mayan groups, including the Ixiles.

Table 6.3 Sharp-Blunt Traumata

Body No.	Sharp-Blunt Trauma Bone (n)	Total (n)	Site of Trauma
FAFG-I-1 (subadult)	19 Right humerus 11 Right ulna 06 Right radius 09 Left humerus 09 Left ulna 08 Left radius 15 Right femur 09 Right patella 01 Right tibia	88	Left ribs #8, 10, and 11
FAFG-I-2 (adult)	17 Left humerus 11 Left femur 08 Left patella	36	Right ribs #3 and 4; left ribs #6, 7, and 9; sternum; proximal phalanges #3 and 4 of left hand
FAFG-I-3 (adult)	04 Left humerus 06 Right humerus 13 Left femur 01 Right patella	24	Right ribs #2, 3, 5, 7, 8, and 9; left ribs #1, 2, 3, 4, 5, 6, 7, 8, and 9; scapulas
FAFG-I-4 (adult)	03 Right humerus 02 Left humerus 02 Left femur 04 Left patella 05 Left tibia	16	Lumbar vertebrae #1 and 2; right ribs #3 and 4; left ribs #2, 3, 4, 5, 7, and 8
FAFG-II-1 (adult)	07 Right femur 05 Right patella	12	Right ribs #1, 3, 5, and 9; left ribs #8 and 9
FAFG-II-2 (adult)	17 Left humerus 04 Right femur 04 Right patella	25	Left ribs #4, 5, 6, and left radius
FAFG-II-3 (adult)	11 Right humerus 05 Left humerus 01 Right ulna 05 Right femur 04 Right tibia	26	Right zygomatic; right ribs #3 and 6; left ribs #4, 6, and 7; right scapula and right fibula
FAFG-II-4 (adult)	03 Right MTC #2 04 Right MTC #3 01 Right MTC #4 07 Left tibia	15	Right ribs #3, 5, 6, 7, 8, 9, 11, and 12; left ribs #4, 5, 6, 9, and right scapula
FAFG-II-5 (adult)	03 Left scapula 27 Left humerus	30	Right ribs #3, 4, 5, 6, and 7; left ribs #4, 5, and 6; right scapula; left ulna (secondary fracture associated to sharp-blunt trauma in left humerus) and right radius

Note: n = Number of traumata.

Figure 6.51 Clothing exhibiting cut marks (Carlos Jacinto, FAFG).

Table 6.4 Cuts in Clothing

Case	Cut Marks in Clothing	Bones
FAFG-I-1	Shirt, sweater, and trousers	Humerus, ulna, radius, femur, patella, and left tibia
FAFG-I-4	Trousers	Femur, patella, and left tibia
FAFG-II-1	Trousers	Femur and right patella
FAFG-II-2	Shirt and sweater	Left humerus
FAFG-II-3	Shirt and sweater	Humerus and right ulna
FAFG-II-4	Trousers	Left tibia
FAFG-II-5	Shirt and sweater	Left scapula

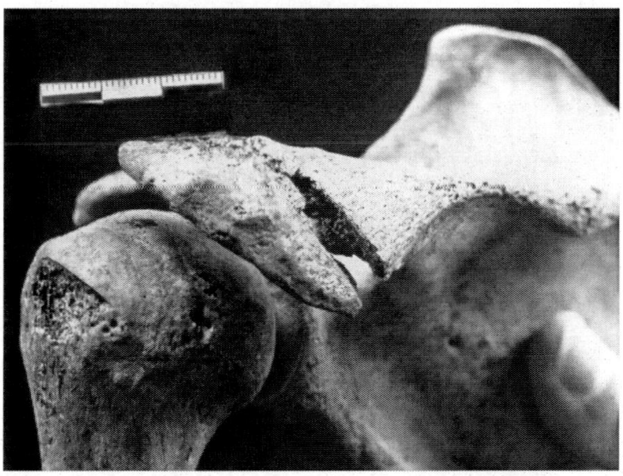

Figure 6.52 Lateral view of the left shoulder showing scoop mark on the humeral head and chop mark through acromium, both caused by a machete (Carlos Jacinto, FAFG).

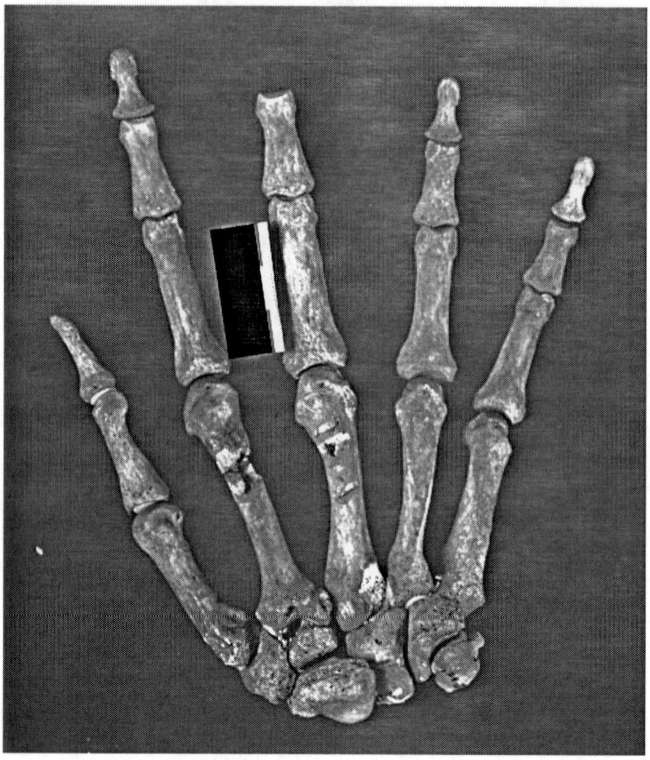

Figure 6.53 Dorsal aspect of right hand showing multiple chop and scoop marks on the second and third metacarpals. The injuries are probably defense wounds caused by a long-bladed weapon such as a machete (Carlos Jacinto, FAFG).

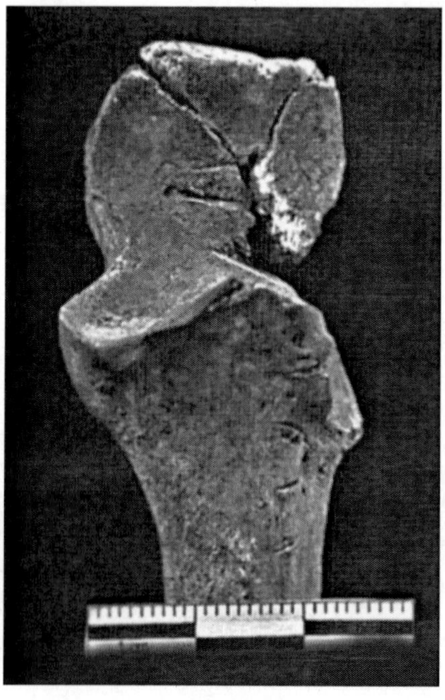

Figure 6.54 Anterior view of left ulna showing chop and cut marks through the olecranon process (Carlos Jacinto, FAFG).

Figure 6.55 (See color insert following page 38) Medial aspect of left distal humerus showing a "wood carving" appearance due to multiple chop and scoop marks from different angles. Although the defects could be confused with those caused by a short-bladed weapon, in this case the injuries were caused by a machete (Carlos Jacinto, FAFG).

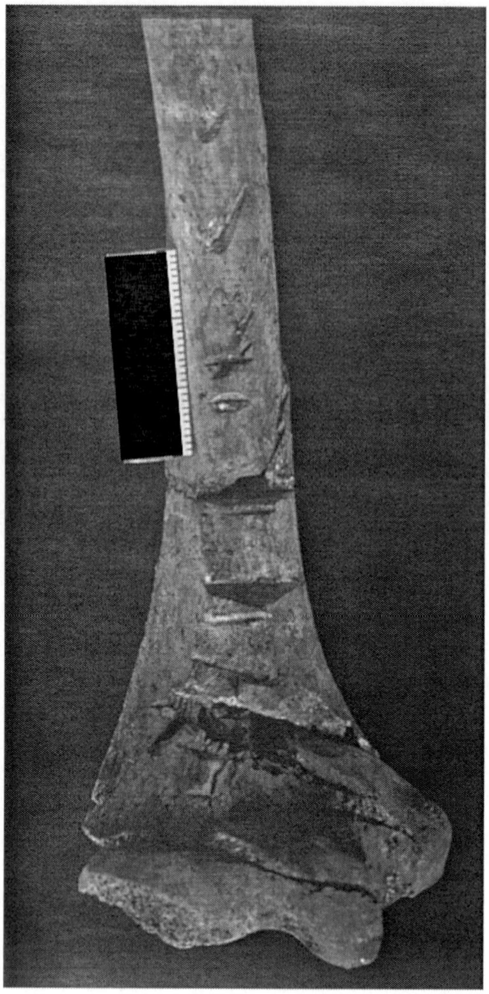

Figure 6.56a Anterior view of the right distal humeral diaphysis showing multiple cut, chop, and scoop marks (visible on the distal one-third of the shaft). A minimum of at least 17 injuries. As it can be observed, the differences in each feature are caused by the force applied to the bone and the angle of impact of the instrument. All injuries are consistent with a long-bladed instrument such as a machete striking the arm at different angles and with different force (Carlos Jacinto, FAFG).

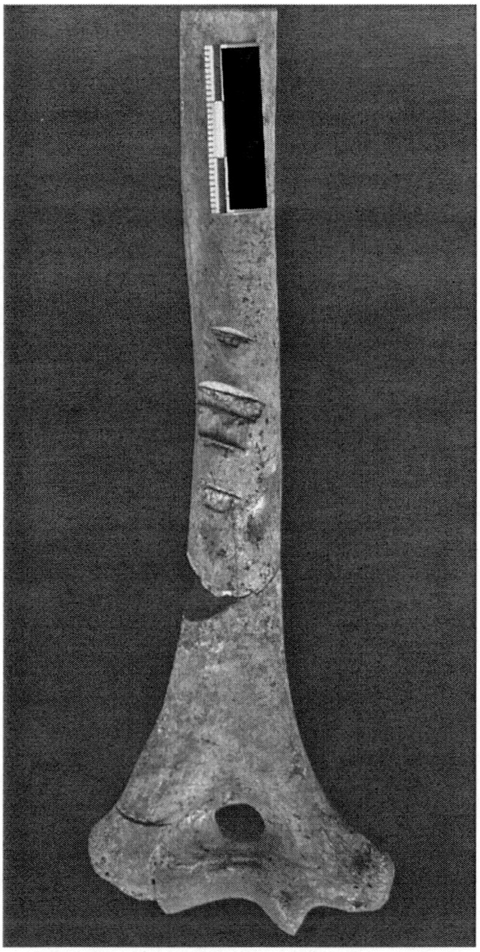

Figure 6.56b Left humerus, posterior surface. The shaft shows similar characteristics as the example illustrated previously (Figure 6.56a). At least six injuries are visible; from top to bottom, scoop marks (1–4), chop mark (5), and cut mark (6). Observe the chop mark (5) and the associated fracture of the shaft. The blade removed from the bone, caused the shaft to break (Carlos Jacinto, FAFG).

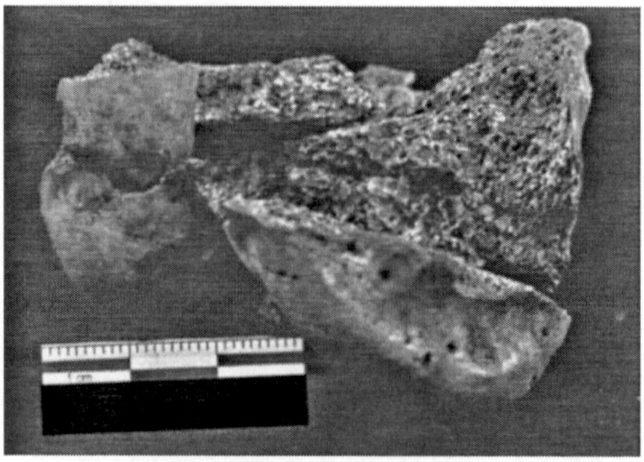

Figure 6.57 Lateral aspect of the right distal femoral shaft showing several chop marks that completely severed the shaft (Carlos Jacinto, FAFG).

Figure 6.58 Anterior aspect of the right knee shows a minimum of five chop marks. One wound is deep enough to cause a complete fracture of the distal femur. The injuries are consistent with a long-bladed weapon such as a machete (Carlos Jacinto, FAFG).

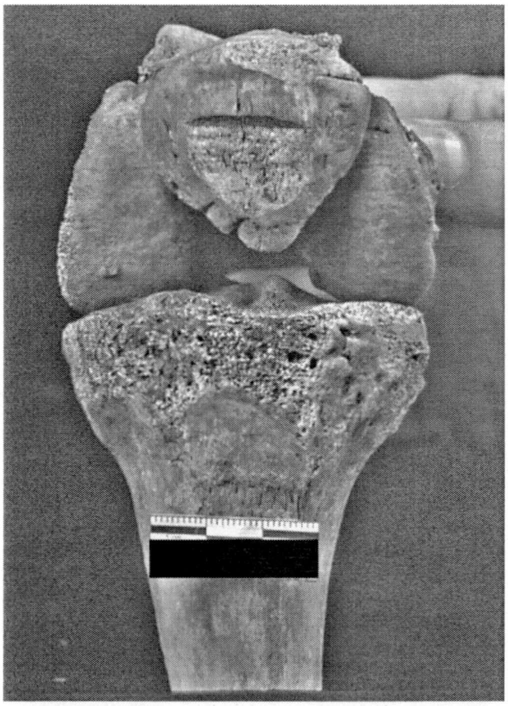

Figure 6.59 Overview of the left knee showing multiple chop wounds on the lateral condyle of a femur and patella (Carlos Jacinto, FAFG).

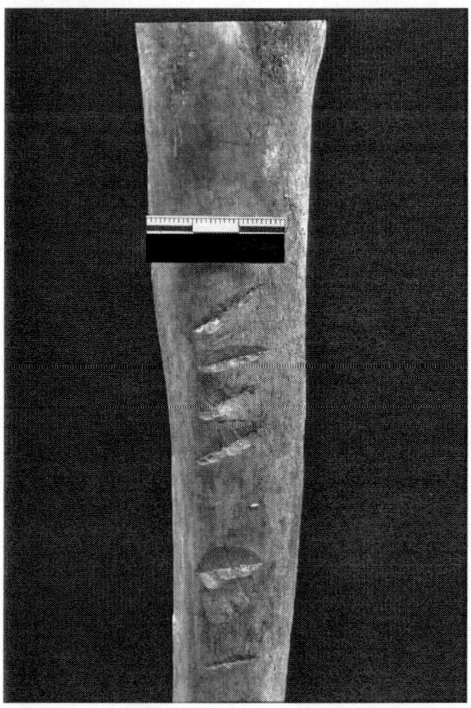

Figure 6.60 Anterior view of the humeral shaft showing at least six scoop marks and one cut mark. Most of the scoop marks show a very wide "V" shape with a central apex, a straight wall, and a striated or wavy wall (Carlos Jacinto, FAFG).

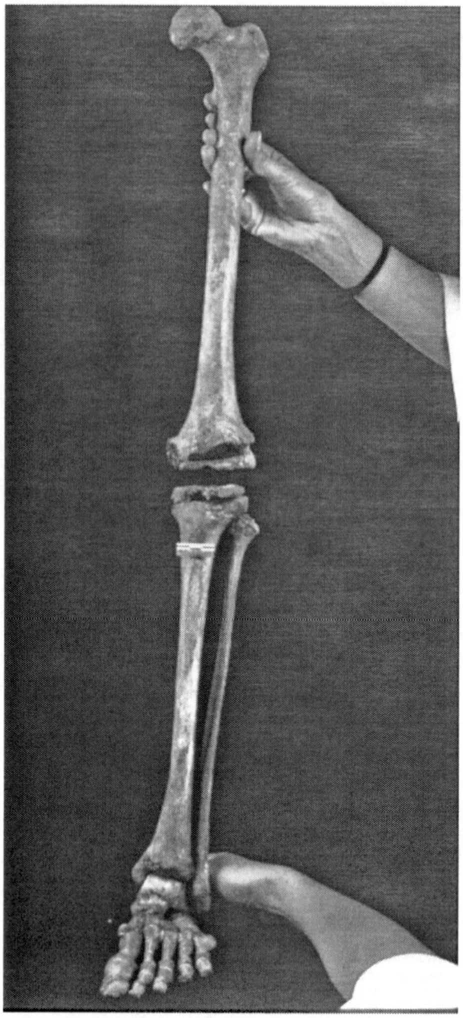

Figure 6.61 Anterior view of an articulated left leg showing multiple chop wounds on the knee region severing the femoral condyles and tibia plateau; refer to Figure 6.60 (Carlos Jacinto, FAFG).

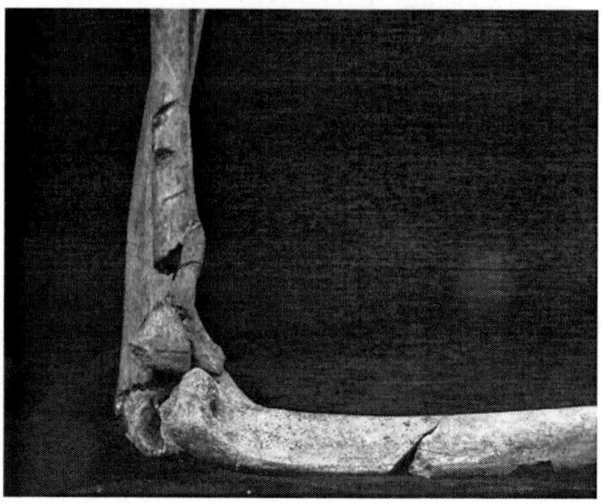

Figure 6.62 Articulated left forearm showing multiple chop and cut marks on the radius and a butterfly fracture of the humeral shaft (Carlos Jacinto, FAFG).

Conclusion

- Two graves were found in a community of the Nebaj area; one showed the pattern of a primary direct collective burial, and one exhibited the pattern of a secondary direct collective burial. Nine male bodies and eighteen body parts were found.
- Four ligatures were found associated with the bodies, showing that the victims were immobilized.
- Teeth marks were observed in thoracic bones, consistent with carnivores.
- Eighteen body parts were associated to nine bodies, through a comparison with three different criteria: macroscopic, morphometric, and perimortem trauma. In seven bodies, cut marks coincided with the cuts in clothing and skeletal injuries. All these aspects helped to reincorporate the body parts to the bodies.
- Nine bodies had sharp-blunt trauma in the upper and lower limbs and blunt trauma in the thorax; one body had a cut mark as a consequence of sharp-blunt trauma.
- It is concluded that the victims were subjected to torture by their captors immediately before their deaths, based on the anatomical location, pattern, amount, and sequence of the sharp-blunt trauma in the upper and lower limbs.
- The pattern of torture to the elbows and knees clearly showed that the intention was to immobilize the victims.
- The subadult had 88 sharp-blunt injuries, distributed in the same pattern on the upper and right lower limbs, and was the person who received the most impacts among the nine victims.
- The testimonies given by relatives and neighbors were compared with the information obtained through the archaeological and laboratory analyses. Comparison of these lines of evidence demonstrated consistency in the location and existence of two graves, the number of individuals, carnivorous tooth marks in some bones, location, and trauma. From this evidence, a reconstruction of the way in which the nine individuals were tortured and killed is possible and lends support to the testimony by witnesses.
- The investigations carried out by the FAFG contribute physical evidence to clarify the testimonies by relatives, neighbors, and victims, and gives support to the results obtained by the CEH. Evidence found in many cases such as this demonstrates violation of human rights during the internal armed conflict in Guatemala.

Case Study 6.2: Probable Machete Trauma from the Cambodian Killing Fields

Gregory E. Berg
Joint POW/MIA Accounting Command
Central Identification Laboratory (JPAC-CIL)

From 1975 to 1979, the Khmer Rouge regime is believed to be directly and indirectly responsible for the deaths of approximately 1.5 million Cambodians (Chandler 1999). The methods of killing ranged from starvation and disease to torture and execution. Many murdered individuals were buried in mass graves throughout the country. These mass graves frequently are colocated with prisons along major roadways, urban areas, or provincial towns. One of the most notorious prisons is located in the capital city of Phnom Penh, known as S-21 or Tuol Sleng, and was used as a place for the interrogation and torture of thousands of individuals. Detailed accounts of the incarcerated, including their names, birthplaces, and family members, were recorded by prison officials. Similarly, the particulars of their torture, confessions, and eventual disposal were also recorded. Many of these records were found at the facility after the fall of the Khmer Rouge regime.

Prisoners died at Tuol Sleng due to sickness, starvation, or simply succumbed to their wounds. For those who survived the lengthy torture process (often weeks or months), they were taken by truck to a killing field outside the city. The particular killing field employed by the S-21 prison officials for execution now is known as Choeung Ek; it was used to execute and bury several thousand individuals. Approximately half of those buried at Choeung Ek were disinterred between 1979 and 1980, after the Khmer Rouge were forced from power. Photographs from the excavations give some indication of the executions—some individuals were executed wearing clothing, blindfolded, and restrained, and others were not. Unfortunately, the photographs show the nature of the excavations—the remains were typically piled haphazardly along the gravesides in disarticulated stacks. At some point, the human remains were cleaned and possibly analyzed, although the details of this work are not available. Finally, the deceased were placed into a stupa (charnel house) at the site, which was constructed in 1988. The entire killing field was opened to the public as a national memorial site in 1989.

The 30+ m tall stupa contains multiple tiers, each of which holds stacks of human remains. Each tier is approximately 3 × 3 m, and the distance between them is approximately 1.25 m. The remains are stored by type, or by similar types, e.g., crania, femora, tibiae. The crania typically are stored on the bottom six to eight shelves, and long bones are stored on the upper shelving sets. The storage location of the vertebrae, ribs, innominates, and the smaller bones of the body is unknown.

The stupa is an open-air facility, although the remains are protected from rain by the surrounding glass and concrete structure. When the remains are examined, various taphonomic processes are patently visible on their exterior surfaces. Cracking, exfoliation, and sun bleaching are the most common types of damage noted. Postmortem breakage due to poor excavation and storage are also apparent. Although these processes can obfuscate, obliterate, or mimic trauma, various types of traumata have been documented in this collection (e.g., Ta'ala et al. 2006). Sharp force trauma, likely due to machetes or other heavy-bladed knives, was found on multiple mandibles from this collection.

The identified trauma pattern was not the original reason for the research at Cheoung Ek; as such, time constraints, physical access, and selection criteria (nearly complete mandibles, minimal damage) limited the number of mandibles available for analysis to only n = 343. Due to the disarticulated nature of the remains, all age and sex estimation should be considered tentative. No individuals less than approximately 12 years of age were present in this particular assemblage. Thirteen of the represented individuals were probably male and for the remainder of the sample, sex was indeterminate. All were adults, likely between 20–45+ years of age. Of the examined mandibles, 22 (6.4%) showed a pattern of perimortem sharp force trauma to the ascending rami and mandibular bodies. The overall frequency of the pattern is undoubtedly underestimated due to the selection criteria (partial mandibles were not selected for analysis by the local curator).

The trauma was visible as fracturing of the mandible, principally affecting the ascending rami and the lingual aspects of the mandibular bodies. Occurrence favored the right ramus (60% right side), and in no cases were both rami affected. All examined fracture margins were sharp and clean (a nonjagged appearance), indicating that they occurred while the bone was in green or fresh state (Galloway 1999). The exposed internal bone surfaces had similar coloration to the external surfaces, and sediment was embedded in these spaces, further indicating the fractures occurred before burial.

The typical case is a partial mandible in which a portion of the posterior ascending ramus was missing (Figure 6.63). Cut marks are found associated with the proximal aspect

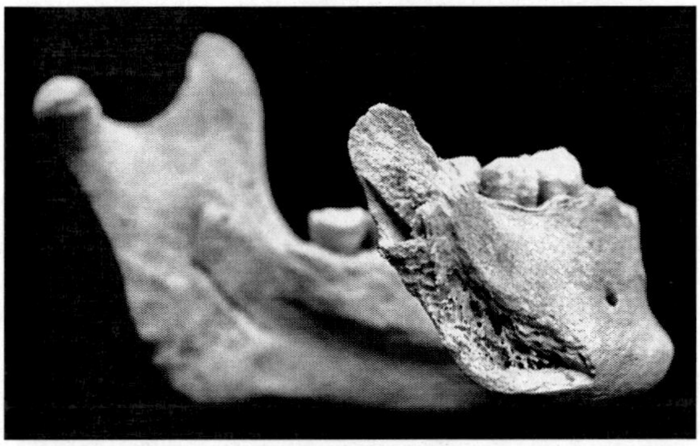

(a)

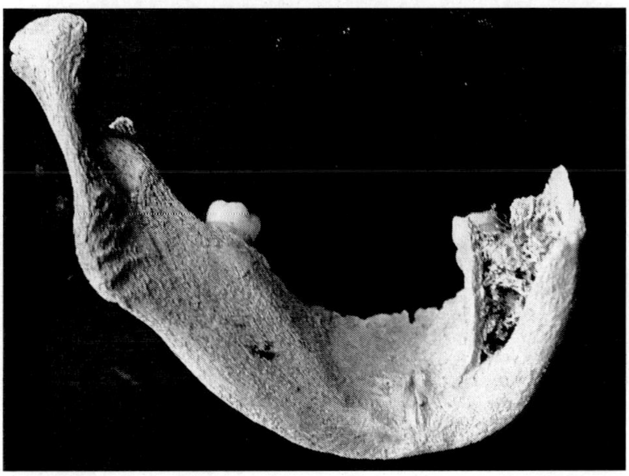

(b)

Figure 6.63 Four different mandibles with sharp force trauma (likely a machete) from the Cambodian killing fields. Note the presence of a "peeled" lingual surface (Figures a and b). The removal of an entire ramus frequently is observed in this pattern of trauma (Gregory E. Berg).

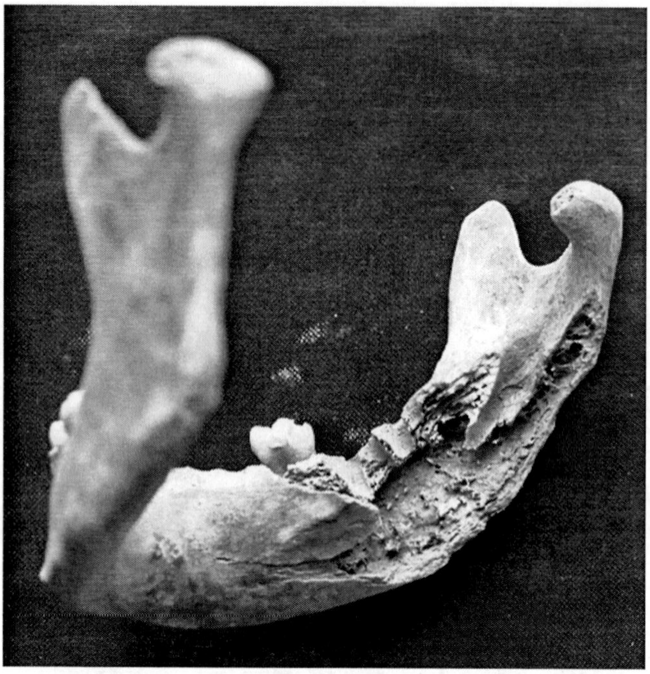

(c)

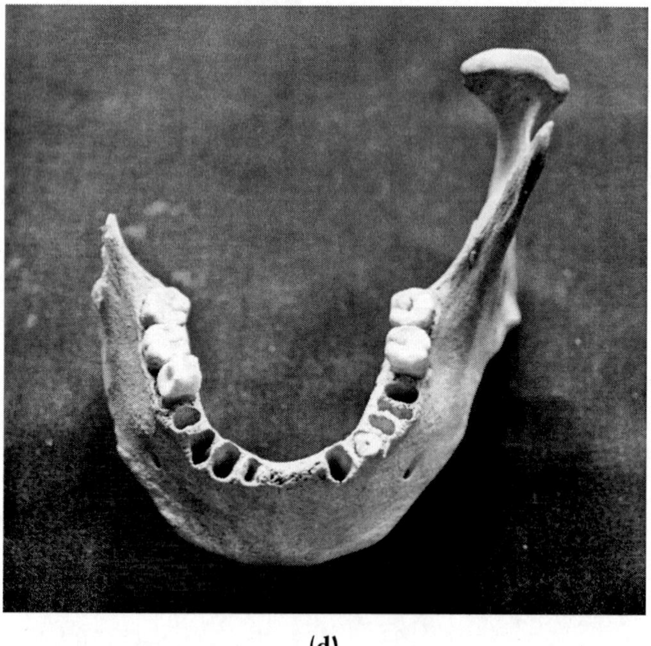

(d)

Figure 6.63 (Continued).

of the affected area. The gonial angle was the most frequently missing portion of bone; often fractures radiated from the affected region toward the midline on the lingual aspect of the mandibular body (Figure 6.64). These radiating fractures varied in length and complexity, although all terminated before reaching the mental spines. In multiple instances, a "peeled" appearance was present on the lingual aspect of the mandibular body. The peeling

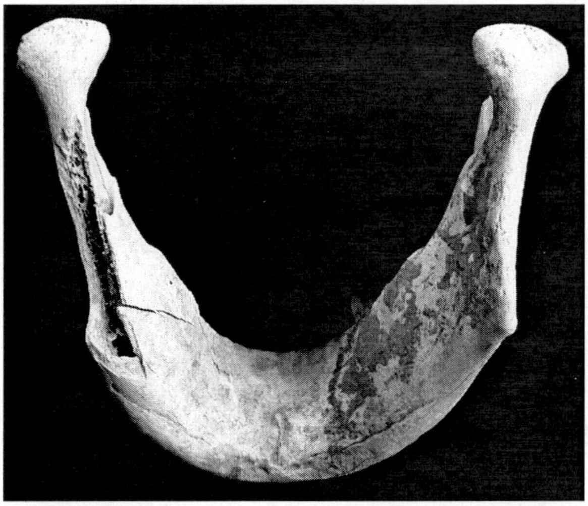

(a)

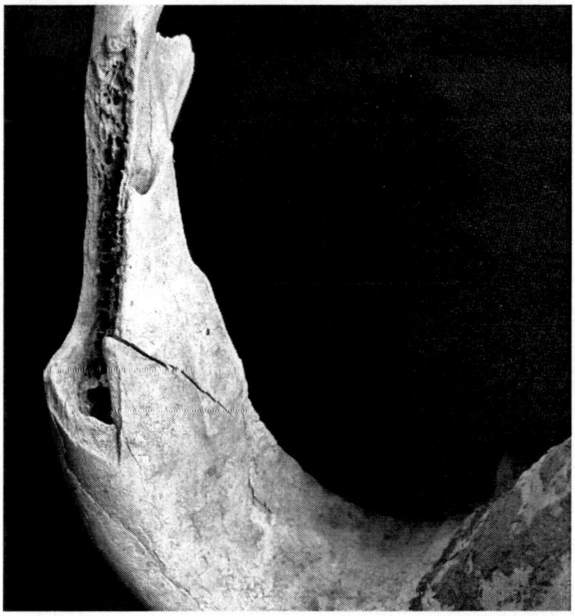

(b)

Figure 6.64 Sharp force trauma evident on the left mandibular ascending ramus of an individual from the Choeng Ek killing field near Phenom Penh, Cambodia. Note the removal of the left gonial angle coupled with fractures radiating toward the lingual mandibular midline (Gregory E. Berg).

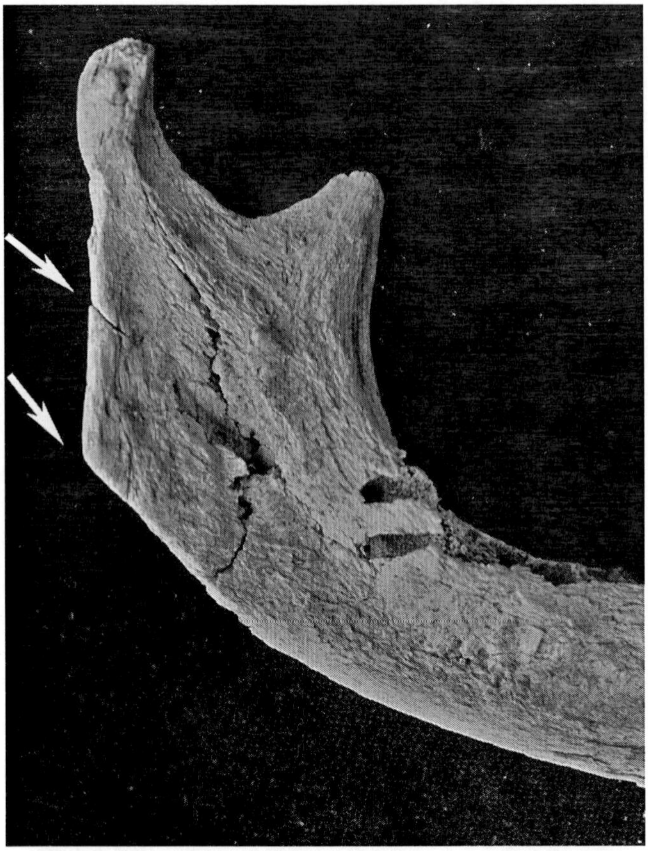

Figure 6.65 One of two cases with multiple blows to the ascending rami found in this population. One cut left a small incision near the midpoint of the ascending ramus. The second cut removed the gonial angle from the bone. Both are accented by white arrows (Gregory E. Berg).

removed the lingual surface of the mandibular body, exposing the tooth sockets, although leaving the buccal surface intact. The peeled areas were usually triangular in shape (apex toward the mandibular midline), and fractures radiated from the apex of the peeled area toward the mental spines. A completely missing ascending ramus often accompanied this trauma manifestation. In several cases, multiple cut marks along the ascending ramus were found. Figure 6.65 presents a clear case of multiple blows to the same mandible.

The described peeling damage is believed to be due to the method in which the weapon was removed from the bone. If insufficient force was applied to the weapon to completely decapitate the individual or if the individual was positioned in a head-down position with the mandible near the chest, the weapon could lodge in the stronger structures of the bone (i.e., the ascending ramus). To free the weapon, a sharp twist would likely be applied (other methods undoubtedly exist, but this action appears to be the most probable explanation for the observed pattern of trauma). The rotational forces applied would free the blade and, at the same time, peel the surface on which the force was applied. In all but one instance, this surface was the lingual aspect of the mandibular body.

If this trauma is viewed as an isolated instance, its mechanism of production would be unclear. Instead, if the pattern of trauma in these isolated elements is considered within the context or cultural circumstances, the mechanism of injury is more apparent—an execution method. Based on the extensive damage and evidence of sharp force injury, the likely weapon is the common machete, which was frequently used for beheadings (Chandler 1999; Ta'ala et al. 2006; Nath 1998). Although the machete is the most likely weapon used, other similarly heavy-bladed instruments (e.g., large knives, a broad-bladed axe) cannot be ruled out.

Gunfire Injuries

7

Shortly before the end of 1989, Charles Taylor invaded Liberia with 100 poorly trained soldiers equipped only with small arms: AK-47 assault rifles, a few machine guns, and some hand grenades ... By the time ceasefire ended in July of 1999, the death toll was greater than 50,000 people; another 100,000 were deliberately injured and mutilated.

Arya and Cukier*

Contents

The Pathophysiology of Gunfire Injury to Bone 322
Estimating the Class of Weapon and Ammunition 325
Differentiating Entry from Exit Defects on Bone 329
Perpendicular Circular Defects 331
Gutter Defects 338
Keyhole Defects 340
Eccentric or Irregular Defects 342
Atypical Wounds from Tandem or Double Tap Shots 346
Atypical Wounds from Embedded Projectiles 352
Exit Wounds 353
Establishing Bullet Trajectory 355
Range of Fire 367
Contact and Close-Range Wounds 371
Intermediate and Distant Range of Fire 371
Estimating Contact or Close Range 372
Estimating Intermediate Range 373
Estimating Intermediate Targets or Distant Range 373
Shotgun Injuries 377
Estimating the Number of Injuries 381
Sequencing Multiple Gunfire Injuries 382
Summary Guidelines for Best Practice 384
Case Study 7.1: Firearm Basics *By C.J. Waters* 385

Forensic investigations into war crimes and human rights (HHRR) abuses ultimately include analysis of firearm injuries and ballistics evidence regardless of the specific context. The particular firearms used vary greatly, from modern military-issued rifles to collectable firearms dating back to World War II. Diagnosing firearm injuries from skeletal wounds can at times be straightforward and at other times, less clear. There is a great amount of variation in skeletal morphology with regard to fracture patterns and defect typology. A multitude of intrinsic (i.e., the elastic modulus of the specific bone impacted), extrinsic

* 2005, 10.

(i.e., the weapon, ammunition, distance of fire, presence of an intermediate target), and epidemiological variables (i.e., context, location, positioning) affect wound morphology and account for the high degree of variation.

Typically, the identification of skeletal defects and fracture patterns has been used to interpret the direction and distance of fire, bullet trajectory, the number of injuries, and the class of weapon. Given the range of firearms and the modifying variables that influence the wounds they create (e.g., the distance of fire or size of ammunition), correctly interpreting skeletal evidence requires a basic understanding of firearms and wound ballistics. For example, the P90 personal defense weapon (PDW) from Fabrique Nationale (Belgium) is a submachine gun that fires ammunition (5.7 × 28 mm) otherwise used in rifles. A new pistol, also developed by Fabrique Nationale—the Five Seven—fires the same ammunition as the P90. Consequently, interpreting the class of weapon based on defect typology and fracture patterns observed skeletally at autopsy may prove challenging. Therefore, it is important to discern facts based on skeletal data and the interpretations drawn from these data, based on the common misconceptions about firearm injuries (Lindsey 1980; Fackler 1987, 1988).

As discussed throughout this book, the context, the location of the fatal environment, the intentions of the perpetrators, and the specific weapons used contribute to trauma variation and thereby may influence interpretations of the data. For example, one may not expect to find shotguns used in modern warfare. However, the use of shotguns in the massive violations of HHRR has been recorded. National security forces routinely used the Ithaca shotgun in Argentina during the "Dirty War (1976–1983)." In other contexts, paramilitary groups have also widely used shotguns or hunting rifles against civilians. Understanding the context and participants in a given situation opens the possibility for evidence (such as the pellets fired from shotguns) that might otherwise not be expected.

The main objective of this chapter is to illustrate the variation of skeletal wounding patterns resulting from gunfire injuries. The pathophysiology of skeletal wounds resulting from gunfire is briefly discussed and an outline for estimating the number of injuries, direction of fire, and sequence of shots is presented. In many armed conflicts, a multitude of different weapons are used, including handguns, hunting and assault rifles, and shotguns. Commonly, physical evidence demonstrates cases in which multiple weapons were used in a single case or multiple mechanisms of injury (e.g., gunfire and blasting injuries). The physical characteristics used to estimate the class of weapons and ammunitions are addressed. Cases of "double taps," in which two entry wounds overlap one another, and instances of atypical wound morphology are illustrated. Case Study 7.1 by C. J. Waters at the end of the chapter provides an overview of firearms and ammunition. For more information on assault rifles or gun basics, refer to Ryan et al. (1997), Di Maio (1999), Popenker and Williams (2004), and Santucci and Chang (2004). Chapter 8 of this book further discusses wound variation from gunfire injuries, illustrating numerous examples by anatomical region, and presents two case studies from Panama and Peru.

The Pathophysiology of Gunfire Injury to Bone

Elucidating the complex relationship between skeletal tissue and gunfire projectiles is a matter of understanding *wound ballistics*—the interaction between the material properties of bone and the mechanical variables of projectiles. Given the high amount of variation in

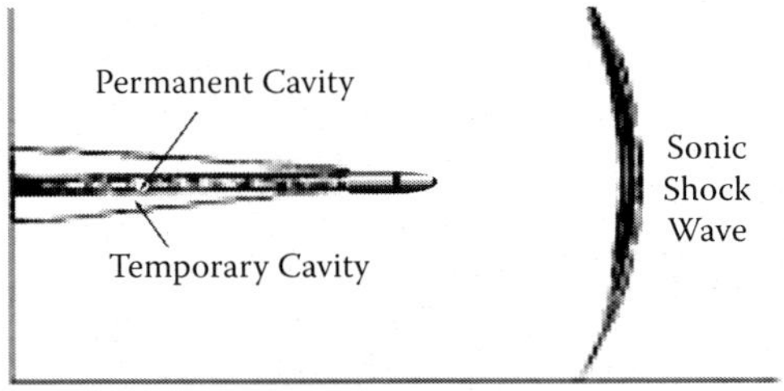

Figure 7.1 Diagram showing permanent and temporary cavity and shock wave. (Reprinted from *Emergency War Surgery*, 2nd United States revision, *NATO Handbook*. Washington, D.C., 1988.)

firearms and ammunition, as well as all the variables that interact in combination uniquely in each case, there is considerable debate among ballistics experts on the mechanisms resulting in fracture patterns and wounding potential; however, this is beyond the parameters of this discussion.

The unique challenge presented at autopsy is the task of reconstructing the events that occurred, starting with the analysis of skeletal fragments. The observations possible at autopsy differ from experimental research or clinical war medicine. The discussion presented here is based on the cases illustrated, and the analysis relies largely on the works of Huelke and coworkers (1968a, 1968b), MacPherson (1994), Sellier and Kneubuehl (1994), Fackler (1996), and Di Maio (1999). Although these authors vary in their opinions on some points, this discussion is based on findings for skeletal tissues without the added insight from soft-tissue injury. Readers should also refer to the following sources for more information on the pathophysiology of gunfire injuries and wounding properties: Cooper and coworkers (1990), Bellemy (1992), Coupland and coworkers (1992), Knudsen and Theilade (1993), Karger (1995), and Karger and coworkers (1995), Boyer and coworkers (1996), and Bartlett and coworkers (2000).

When a projectile enters the body, it crushes tissues creating a *permanent cavity* (Figure 7.1) and transfers energy that stretches soft tissues, forming a *temporary cavity* (Fackler 1987; Vellema and Scholtz 2005). The crushed tissue or permanent cavity is proportional to the size and shape of the projectile penetrating the tissue, whether intact or deformed (Fackler 1987; Jenkins and Dougherty 2005). The shape of the bullet and degree to which it tumbles following penetration may further increase the injured area (MacPherson 1994). Therefore, both fragmented and deformed bullets and the subsequent fractured bone fragments, or *secondary projectiles*, further increase the permanent cavity to the impacted areas (Vellema and Scholtz 2005). Fackler (1987, 2) wrote, "The wound produced by a particular penetrating projectile is characterized by the amount and location of tissue crush and stretch." The primary mechanism of wounding is the crushing of tissues, and the secondary mechanisms (i.e., intrinsic and extrinsic factors) are those that modify this effect (Table 7.1). Bone fragments and metal edges from the bullet or jacket may also cut tissues (MacPherson 1994). Fackler (1996, 195) wrote:

> Basic physics verifies that a projectile's potential to disrupt tissue is determined by both its mass and its velocity. Wounding potential is also determined to a great extent by a bullet's physical characteristics. Projectile construction and shape determine a bullet's tendency to deform, fragment, or change its orientation (by becoming unstable and "yawing" or turning

Table 7.1 Variable Classification for Factors in Skeletal Wounding Morphology Related to Gunfire Wounds

Intrinsic Factors	Extrinsic Factors	Epidemiological Modifiers
• Anatomical region affected and surrounding soft tissues	• Caliber, velocity, and weight of ammunition	• Political/cultural context
• Skeletal architecture and composition	• Weapon class	• Location of fatal environment
• Elastic modulus	• Distance of shot	• Intention of perpetrators
• Bone density, hardness, and stiffness	• Presence of intermediate target	• Availability/access to weapons
• Age, weight, and health of the victim (e.g., osteoporosis)	• Location of shooter relative to target and the position of the victim	

> sideways relative to the line of flight) … For example, an expanding soft-point or hollow-point bullet causes more tissue disruption than a similar but nonexpanding one, as demonstrated by comparison ….

Besides crushing tissue through direct impact, temporary cavity formation may be an agent responsible for fracturing of adjacent bony structures not directly impacted by the bullet or bullet fragments. Fackler explains temporary cavitation thus: "the penetrating projectile strikes tissue, which then accelerates radially away (like a splash) from where the projectile struck obeying Newton's laws of motion" (Fackler 1996, 197). The implication is that temporary cavitation will be more effective in disrupting (i.e., breaking) nonelastic material such as bone or the liver as compared to muscle or the lung (Fackler 1996, 197).

Bone responds to the compressive force of a projectile and reacts depending on the architecture of the area impacted. Skeletal defects and fractures occur primarily from the creation of a permanent cavity. However, it has been demonstrated experimentally that skeletal fractures may occur as a result of a temporary cavity in areas not in direct contact with the projectile. Some authors claim that this finding is rare in practice; it remains a source of debate among ballistics experts (Fackler 1988; Fackler 1996; Vellema and Scholtz 2005).

Fackler further makes the point (1996, 199):

> Fractures from cavitation are rare in the human being … When a bone is broken by cavitation, the fracture is a simple one. A gunshot fracture with multiple bone fragments separated by several centimeters and usually mixed with fragments of the projectile is a clear sign that the bone was struck by the bullet and not damaged by the temporary cavitation.

It is shown in this book, however, that this is more common than expected. The elastic modulus and architecture of various bones (i.e., compact versus trabecular bone, the amount of marrow present within, and cartilage surrounding the bone) influence wound characteristics. Therefore, tissue type is an important factor in the variation observed in skeletal wound morphology and fracture patterning, just as ballistic variables influence the amount and direction of abnormal stress applied through the injury.

Bones are firm structures filled with and surrounded by soft tissues or liquids; i.e., cartilage is more elastic than the bone itself. When force is applied to this medium, a hydraulic burst effect takes place. According to Sellier and Kneubneuhl (1994), unlike soft tissues in which shock waves are formed within the temporary cavity, pressure is applied in all directions, which fractures bone (The mineral components of bone dissipate energy through fracture lines). In areas containing cancellous bone, the motion of fluid within those spaces creates a temporary cavity that unlike soft tissue will not revert to the smaller, permanent wound track (Huelke et al. 1968a,b). Sellier and Kneubuehl (1994, 237 and 238) wrote:

> In the broadest sense, we can consider a bone as a hollow organ filled with a liquid and surrounded by a (very) solid wall. We can assume, therefore, that similar phenomena occur as they do to the penetration of the head, the heart, or the (filled) bladder, when the projectile is fast enough to fulfill some of the preliminary conditions. Damage to the bone is caused by the temporary cavity produced in the marrow by the projectile. Unlike in smooth tissue where the temporary cavity collapses quickly, in the case of a bone, the splinters produced by the projectile (secondary projectile) damage the surrounding tissue so that the size of the permanent cavity (shooting channel) matches that of the temporary cavity.

It has been demonstrated that the threshold velocity for a projectile to penetrate bone is 60 m/s (Huelke et al. 1968). Huelke and coworkers (1968) demonstrated that the type of bone and specific bone density significantly show differences in the loss of energy by as much as 40% between normal and osteoporotic bones. Consequently, these factors may explain some of the variation in the extent and patterning of fractures observed at autopsy.

Estimating the Class of Weapon and Ammunition

Once fragmented skeletal tissue is reconstructed, interpretations based on the morphology of skeletal defects and fractures, such as the direction of fire, bullet trajectory, number of wounds, shot sequence, projectile characteristics, and the class of weapon, may be made with varying levels of confidence depending on these factors and the intrinsic variables of the specific bone tissues affected. Interpreting wound characteristics to assign the class of firearm is largely dependent on factors attributed to *external* and *terminal ballistics*. More specifically, estimating ammunition caliber or weapon class has been based on the size of skeletal defects and the extent of fracturing. Ammunition size and velocity may overlap traditional handgun/rifle classifications. For example, a .22 short used in a handgun and a .22 long used in a rifle will have the same diameter but vary velocity due to the length of the barrel and cartridge case. Moreover, the highest velocity range for pistols (i.e., .44 Magnum, 1800 J) exceeds that of low-velocity rifles, such as the .222 Remington with 1200 J (Sellier and Kneubuehl 1994). Consequently, there is a lot of variation among guns and ammunition. Whereas these examples exist in the outer boundaries of such classifications, it is important to consider the wide range of modifiers that affect wounding patterns when interpreting skeletal injuries.

External ballistics explains the behavior of the bullet once it is fired and the variables affecting that behavior. In flight, the bullet is affected by gravity, a downward deceleration force, and air resistance that creates drag on the projectile as it travels. The rifling in the barrel of the gun is designed to minimize the effect of these forces on the projectile. Once a projectile leaves the barrel, its flight will be affected by *wobbling*, *yawing*, and *nutation*. *Wobbling* refers to the rotation of the bullet around its center. *Yawing* refers to the rotation of the nose of the projectile away from the line of flight. *Nutation* is the small circular movement of the tip of the projectile. Pressure differences inside and outside the barrel and the shape of the bullet influence these factors. However, these forces have a minimal effect on the bullet as it travels through the air (Fackler et al. 1986; Fackler 1987). Yawing becomes more significant once the bullet penetrates tissue. The deeper it travels through tissue (i.e., the abdomen, as compared to the skull or limb), the more the bullet tumbles or yaws. Yawing is defined as follows (Hollerman et al. 1990, 686):

> … the angle between the long axis of the bullet and its path of flight. If the bullet is traveling with its pointed end forward and its long axis parallel to the longitudinal axis of flight (0° yaw), it crushes a tube of tissue no greater than its approximate diameter. When the bullet yaws to 90°, the entire long axis of the bullet strikes tissue, and the amount crushed may be three times greater than at 0° yaw.

Fackler (1989) demonstrated that ammunition tends to yaw after average tissue penetration of 14 cm. More recently, Kneubuehl and Thali (2003) have shown that on impacting long bones at 10 m, high-velocity rounds (7.62 × 51 mm and 7.62 × 39 mm) penetrate bone through and through, tend to yaw on exit, and continue flight in a sideways pattern. In another study, Dakak and associates (2003) found that projectiles (7.62 × 39 mm) leaving the chest of anesthetized pigs shot at 100 m still possessed a terminal velocity of about 200 m/s. The latter implies that after striking a human intermediate target, a bullet can still cause penetrating injuries to bone. In these cases and, depending on the angle at which the bullet strikes the target, defects will mimic the cross section of the bullet. Eccentric defects tend to have full internal beveling and may or may not be associated with radiating fractures. These defects are more commonly found in the flat bones of the face and cranial vault, ilium, and scapula.

Terminal ballistics influence the behavior of the bullet at impact and the subsequent wounding. For example, if a bullet impacts sideways, more kinetic energy will be released upon impact because the cross-sectional area of the bullet will be larger. Impacting the body sideways does not generally result from yaw (Fackler and Malinowski 1985; Fackler et al. 1986; Fackler 1987) but from the bullet having hit an intermediate target, upon which it may tilt 180°, entering the body sideways (Fackler 1987). Refer to the following section on wound typology for examples observed skeletally.

Bullets will deform or yaw following penetration into tissues at predictable distances within the body cavities. Therefore, depending on the type of ammunition, one may expect greater damage at the entry point or deeper within tissues. According to Fackler (1987, 7),

> The maximum disruption produced by the sphere is always near the entrance hole, since projectile velocity is highest there. A pointed nondeforming bullet causes its maximum disruption not at the point of highest velocity, but where yaw increases the bullet's surface area striking the tissue, causing increased tissue disruption.

In part, the variation observed in defect size and the extent of fracturing in various structures (i.e., the head versus abdomen) results from the angle at which the bullet strikes bone. In other words, the extent of damage to internal structures is largely influenced by the depth of penetration and the degree to which the bullet deforms, mushrooms, fragments, or yaws through a particular body cavity. Figures 7.2 and 7.3 illustrate how various high-velocity rifle bullets yaw and tumble through soft tissues based on the elastic modulus of affected tissues. It should be pointed out that bullets designed to mushroom or deform

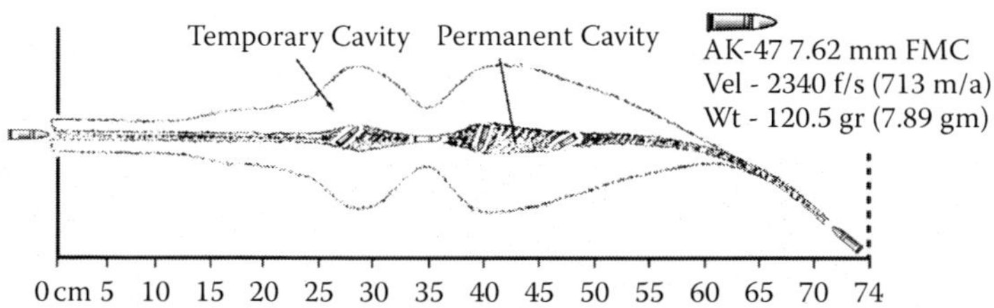

Figure 7.2 Diagram showing temporary and permanent cavity of the 7.62 × 39 mm projectile when fired in ordnance gelatin. (From *NATO Handbook*. Washington, D.C., 1988.)

on impact are strictly prohibited in war (Hague Convention of 1899, Declaration III*). Regardless, hollow-point bullets are extremely common, increase the wounding area, and tend to fragment.

A common classification for ammunition is based on *velocity;* although the exact meaning of the term is debated, this text follows Fackler's (1996) recommendations for distinguishing classes of force based on standard practices where *high velocity* generally refers to rifle ammunition and *medium velocity,* to handguns and submachine guns (a distinction based on 2,000–3,000 ft/s). Fackler wrote (1996, 200), "The British draw their line between low and high velocity at 1,100 ft/s (335 m/s), which is the speed of sound in air. Various American researchers draw the line at 2,000, 2,500, or 3,000 ft/s (610,762 and 914 m/s, respectively)." Therefore, the distinction between high and medium velocity rounds is based on this definition unless otherwise specified. Various skeletal characteristics have been commonly used to identify the class of weapon (i.e., handgun, rifle, or shotgun) and the velocity of the projectile (i.e., low, medium, or high). It is our opinion that major differences in skeletal wounds do occur between handguns and rifles, but more specifically between medium and high velocity rounds. Figures 7.4–7.8 illustrate variation in handgun wound and fracture patterns. Overall, the extent of damage is minimal and wounds are clearly recognizable. In contrast, Figures 7.9 and 7.10 illustrate examples of fracture patterns associated with rifle injuries. Note that the wounds and fractures are slightly larger. Refer also to chapter 8 for more examples on trauma variation resulting

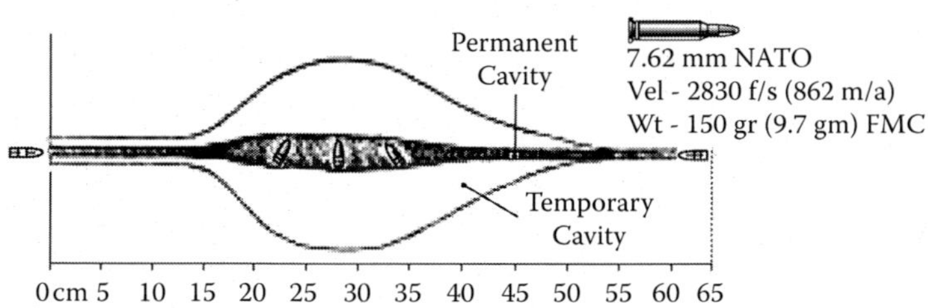

Figure 7.3 Diagram showing temporary and permanent cavity of the NATO 7.62 mm projectile when fired in ordnance gelatin. (From *NATO Handbook*. Washington, D.C., 1988.)

* "The Contracting Parties agree to abstain from the use of bullets which expand or flatten easily in the human body, such as bullets with a hard envelope which does not entirely cover the core, or is pierced with incisions." The Avalon Project at Yale Law School Laws of War: Declaration on the Use of Bullets Which Expand or Flatten Easily in the Human Body; July 29, 1899. http://www.yale.edu/lawweb/avalon/lawofwar/dec99-03.htm.

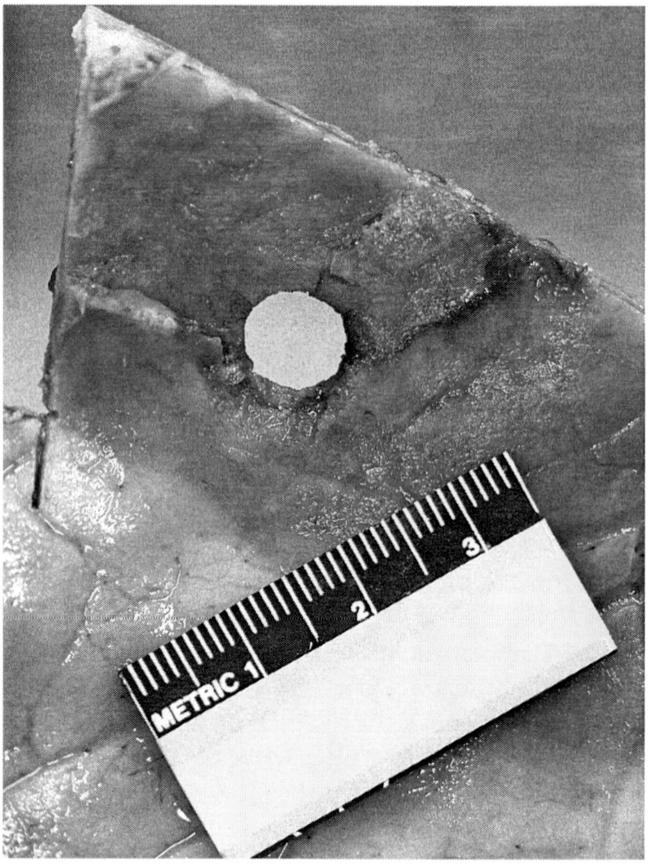

Figure 7.4 Endocranial view of an entrance wound showing circumferential beveling (Alain Wittmann).

from rifle injuries. The differences can be observed in bone without the presence of soft tissues. However, the exact distance between the muzzle and target in injuries other than contact wounds cannot be calculated based on such fracture patterns.

The muzzle speed of pellets leaving the barrel of a shotgun, in contrast to other firearm ammunition, is generally considered *medium velocity.* Generally, the shorter the range of fire, the greater the amount of energy released on contact. In other words, at close range, shotguns are far more damaging than at longer distances (Figures 7.11 and 7.12). As pellets spread out during flight, they create individual wound tracks (Figure 7.13). Overall, pellets may penetrate bone but typically do not perforate the head or body. Shotgun pellets are easily differentiated from bullets but may be confused with ball bearings from a grenade or sector mine as already discussed in chapter 3 on blast injury.

The general caliber of the bullet may be estimated based on the diameter of the entrance defect in some cases. More typically, defect size is used to eliminate possible ammunition classes (Di Maio 1999); for example, a wound measuring 7.5 mm in diameter is not likely caused by a .22 mm bullet. The caliber may be estimated in cases in which the projectile strikes perpendicular to the bone on impact and the entrance wound is circular. Ross (1996) calculated the diameter of the entrance wound in bone caused by weapons of

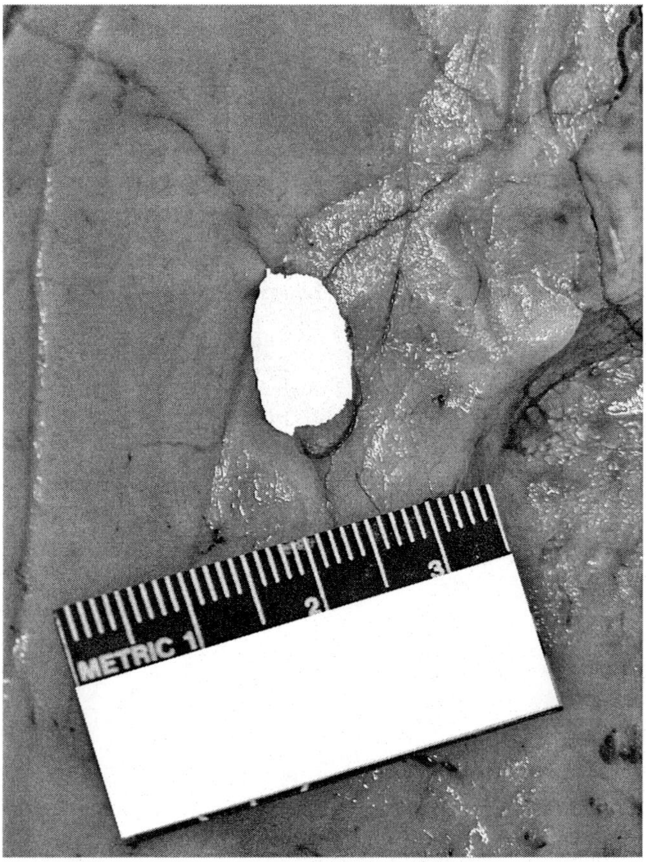

Figure 7.5 Endocranial view of an exit wound showing no internal beveling. Defect is oval in shape, reflecting the cross section of a 9 mm bullet (Alain Wittmann).

different calibers and found that there are statistically significant differences between certain calibers such as .22 and .38. The same applies for high-velocity rounds. In our experience, the diameters of entrance defects caused by standard former Eastern Block–issued ammunition, 7.62 × 39 mm, ranges between 7 and 8 mm. Some caution should be used when interpreting ammunition size from the diameter of a defect, as its size may vary from what the name suggests, e.g., a .38 caliber bullet is actually .357 in. in diameter. Additionally, lead bullets, special ammunition designed to deform upon impact (e.g., hollow points) and bullets modified to fragment or deform upon contact may have a larger diameter than the cross section of the bullet (Di Maio 1999; Berryman et al. 1995).

Differentiating Entry from Exit Defects on Bone

Penetrating wounds enter the body. Entrance wounds are classified based on their shape: *circular, keyhole, gutter, tangential, eccentric, irregular, sideways, tandem,* or *double tap* (Table 7.2). The variation in fracture patterns and defect typology may be used to differentiate entrance from exit wounds, count the number of wounds and injuries, and sequence

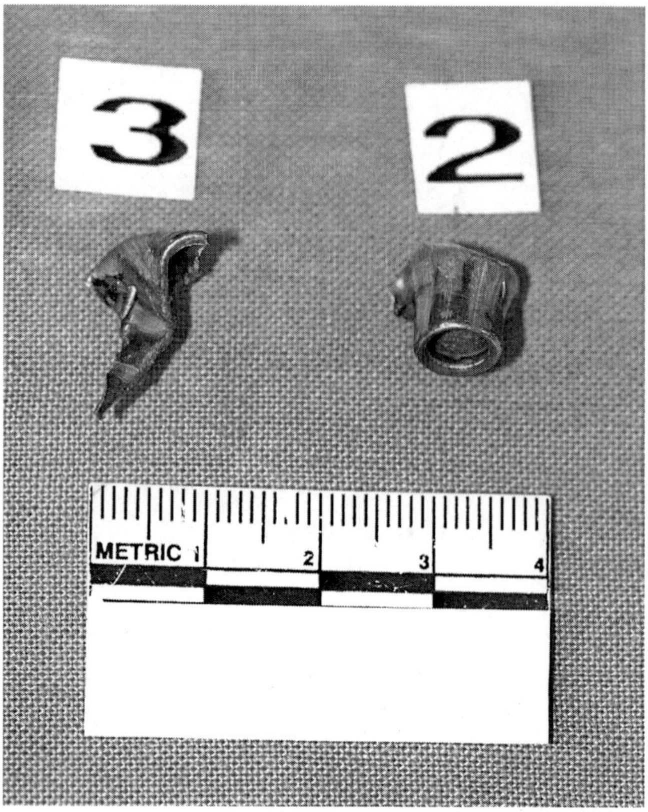

Figure 7.6 Two fragments of FMJ handgun ammunition. Shredded jacket (left) and base with shredded jacket and core (right) (Alain Wittmann).

multiple injuries. Several factors influence defect morphology, including the shape of the projectile (i.e., whether it is intact, deformed, or fragmented), the angle between the projectile and bone upon entry (i.e., the trajectory), the distance of fire, the presence of an intermediate target, velocity, and the biomechanical properties of anatomical tissues affected.

Skeletal wounds resulting from projectile trauma are highly variable, given the list of modifiers. However, they generally reflect the shape and size of the bullet, if the impact occurs perpendicularly, in which case the wound will be circular, reflecting the cross section of the bullet or oblong, reflecting the profile of the bullet. Numerous researchers discuss the patterned nature of projectile trauma (Berryman et al. 1995; Ross 1996). Further, more than one bullet can enter a single entry wound, as in tandem or double tap shots (refer to the section on atypical wounds later in this chapter) (Randall and Newby (1989) Quatrehomme, and Işcan [1997a, 1997b]).

Entrance wounds tend to be associated with radiating fractures that emanate away from the point of impact, across the bone, and toward the area where the bullet *perforates* (exits) the head or body. Considering that bullets release varying amounts of energy through bone, fractures do not tend to cut across contoured areas of bone buttresses, sutures, or preexisting fractures. Therefore, bullets striking preexisting defects may be smaller in size or exhibit radiating fractures redirected around anatomical features (Berryman et al. 1995).

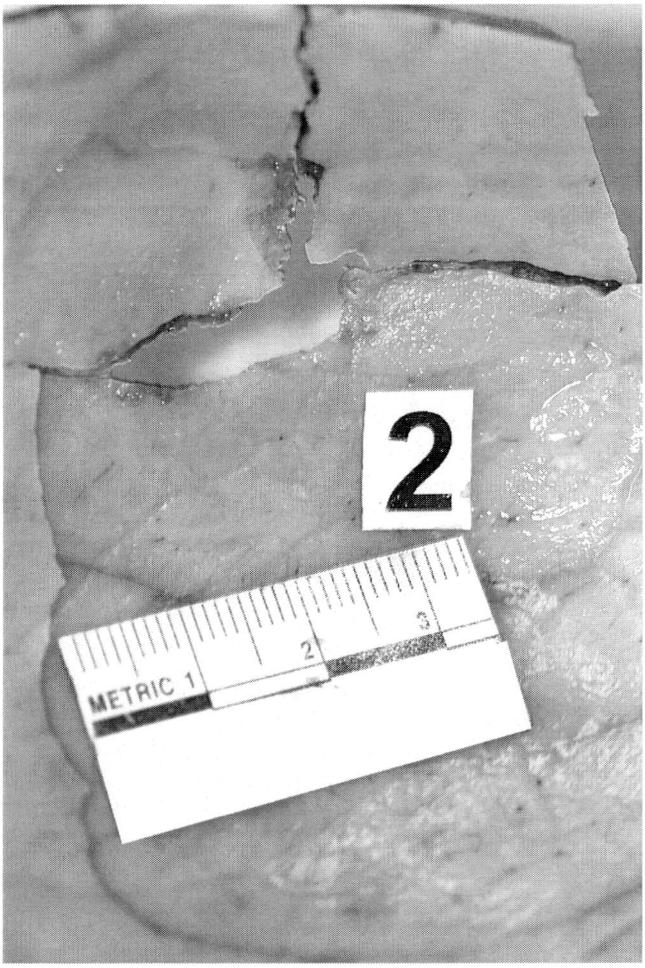

Figure 7.7a Endocranial view of an exit wound showing no internal beveling. Observe the shape of the defect mimicking the cross section of a 7.62 × 39 mm projectile (Alain Wittmann).

Linear fractures in the form of radiating and concentric fractures are typically associated with entrance wounds within close range and from medium- or high-velocity ammunition. Linear fractures emanating from entrance wounds may reach around the skull or bone before the bullet exits the cranial vault (Berryman and Symes 1998). Further, cranial hoop fractures may result in association with gunfire trauma. Linear fractures and even more extensive comminuted fracturing may also be present at the exit site, resulting from the heaving stress of intracranial pressure that lifts the already fractured fragments between radiating fractures (Berryman and Symes 1998).

Perpendicular Circular Defects

When the path of the bullet is perpendicular to the surface it impacts, the entrance wound tends to be circular in shape, generally reflecting the diameter of the projectile (Figures 7.14–7.17). As the projectile compresses bone, it produces a plug that shears the diplöe, producing beveling on the opposite side of the bone, the side of tension. For example,

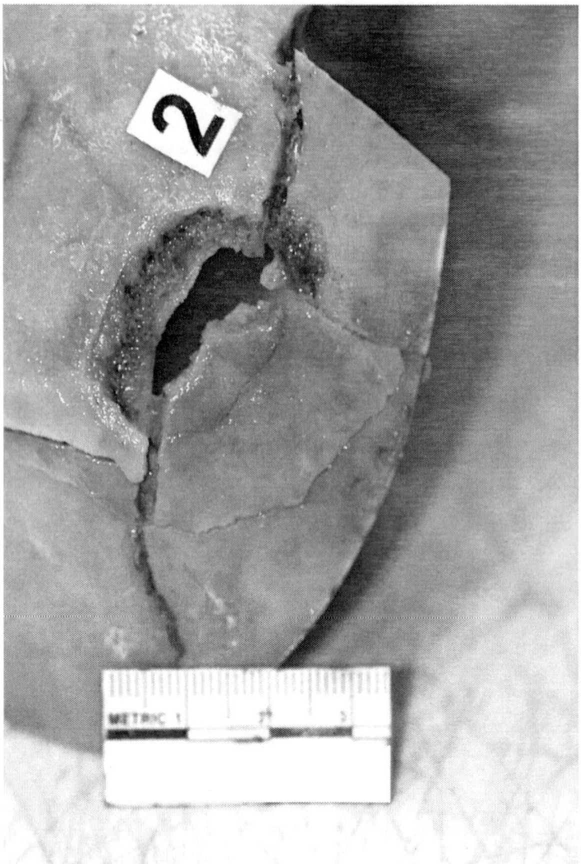

Figure 7.7b Ectocranial view of the same defect showing external beveling and radiating and concentric fractures (Alain Wittmann).

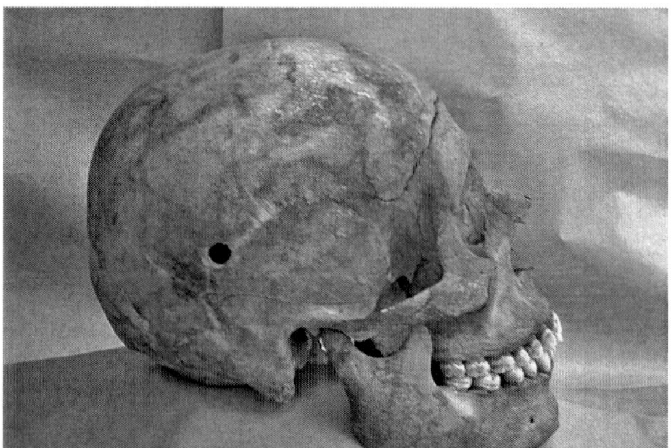

Figure 7.8 Circular defect on right parietal adjacent to a squamousal suture. Observe the discrete delamination of the edges around the defect and the lack of fractures, consistent with entrance wound from a handgun (Juan Carlos Tello, EPAF).

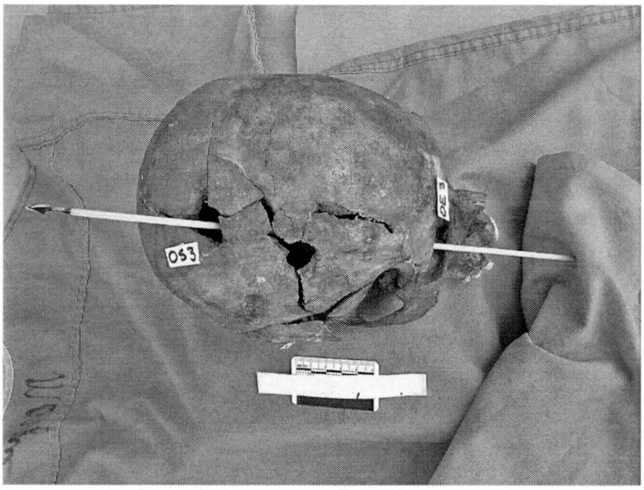

Figure 7.9 Gunshot wound through the right orbit with an exit through an irregular-shaped defect located on the right parietal bone with an almost straight trajectory from the entrance. The trajectory is described as front to back and slightly upward. Observe radiating and concentric fractures associated to the exit wound. A second circular exit defect from a shot through the base of the head is also visible on the right side of the frontal bone along the coronal suture (Juan Carlos Tello, EPAF).

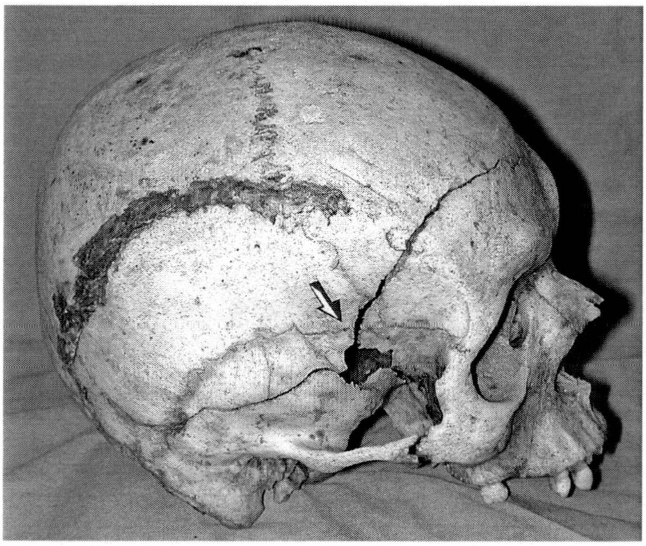

Figure 7.10 Irregular defect on the right sphenoid from which two radiating fractures originate running anteriorly and laterally through the frontal bone and posteriorly through the temporal squama. The defect is consistent with an entrance wound. As the wing of the sphenoid is a thin layer of bone; no beveling is generally encountered and defects are generally irregular in shape (Alain Wittmann).

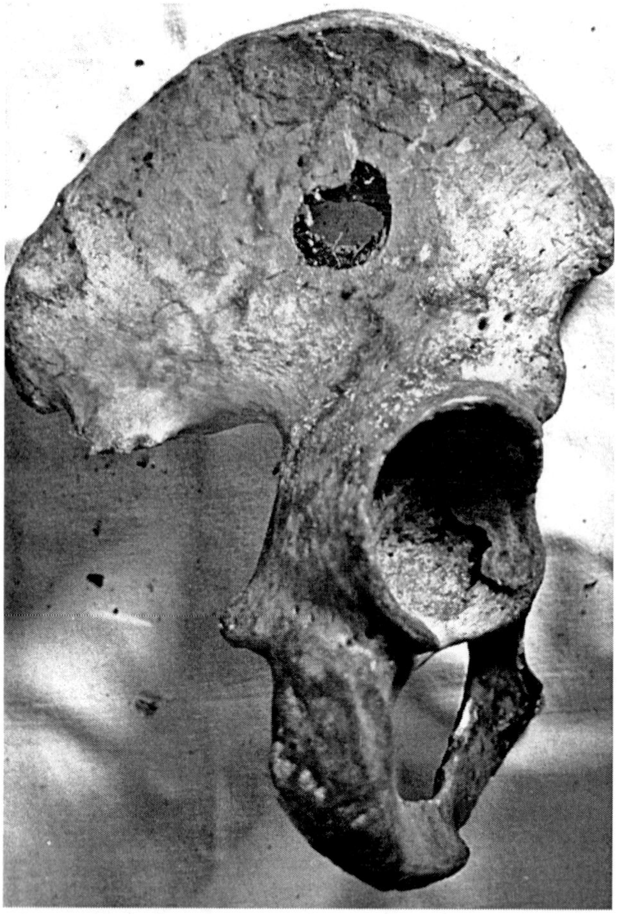

Figure 7.11 Shotgun injury to the posterior right ilium. Large circular defect with embedded wadding, indicating close range (Ann Ross).

Figure 7.12 Anterior surface, right ilium, with a shotgun injury and embedded casing, indicating a close range. (Printed with permission from International Criminal Tribunal for the former Yugoslavia [ICTY].)

Figure 7.13 Posterior view of the skull with multiple penetrating lead pellets causing small circular defects. Note the clustering of pellets and the radiating fracture associated with a row of pellets on the right parietal, indicating the direction of fire (Ann Ross).

entrance wounds to the skull will have internal beveling on the inner table of the bone. If the same bullet exits the skull, external beveling will occur on the outer table of the bone as it perforates the structure (Bhoopat 1995; Quatrehomme and Işcan 1998).

Circular entrance wounds to various regions of the cranium have shown *circumferential delamination*,* or flaking of the outer table, which ranges from 0.5 to 2.0 mm (Figure 7.18; refer also to Figure 7.8). Noncircumferential or incomplete delamination caused by angled impacts may also occur, occupying only a fraction of the circumference of the defect. When delamination is incomplete, its position indicates the direction

Table 7.2 Skeletal Defect Typology Associated with Gunfire Injuries

Entry Wounds	Exit Wounds
Circular—simple	Circular—simple
Circular—comminuted	Circular—comminuted
Keyhole	Eccentric or irregular (sideways)
Gutter (tangential)	Partial
Eccentric or irregular (sideways)	Bullet embedded in bone
Tandem	
Double tap	

* Di Maio (1999, 114–115) terms this finding, "external beveling." Considering whether or not the diplöe is affected, the defect may result from different mechanisms. Therefore, we differentiate between external beveling associated with entrance wounds from delamination.

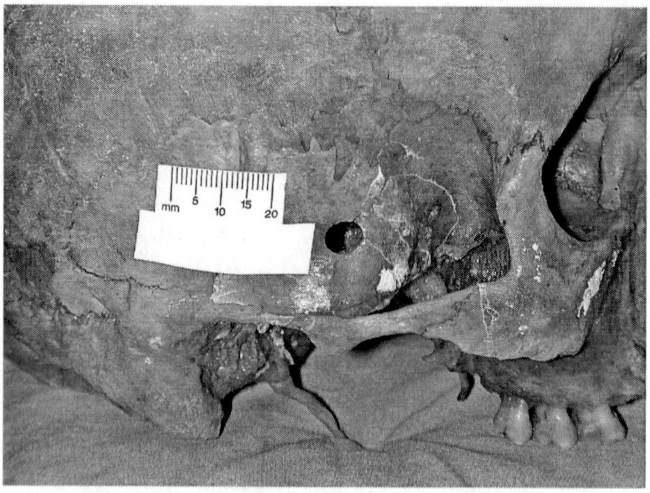

Figure 7.14 Circular defect on the right temporal squama, consistent with an entrance wound from a handgun (Alain Wittmann).

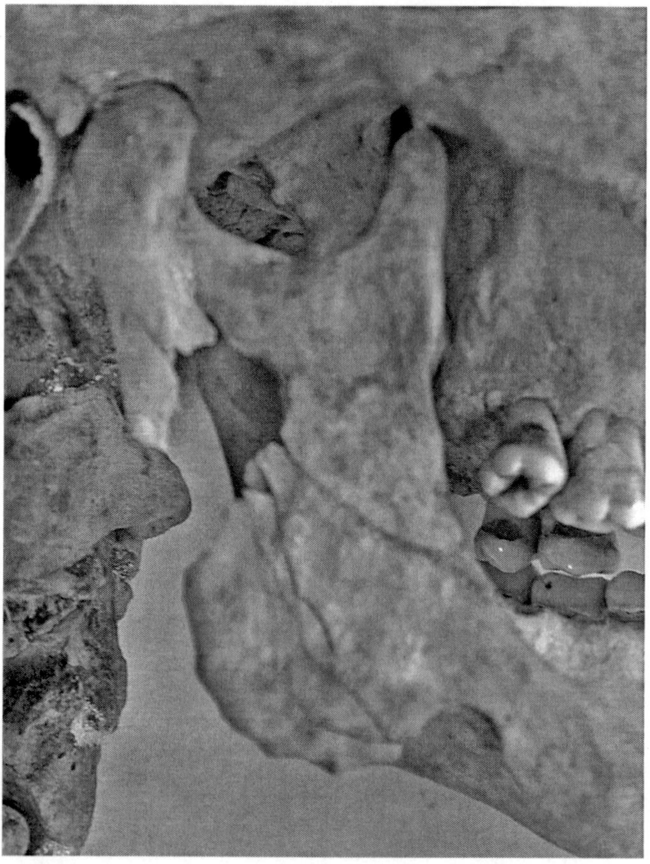

Figure 7.15 Two gunshot wounds through the right ascending ramus and mandibular body. The injuries were caused by 9 mm ammunition. According to the fracture interception, the bottom injury occurred prior to the injury on the posterior border of the ascending ramus (Juan Carlos Tello, EPAF).

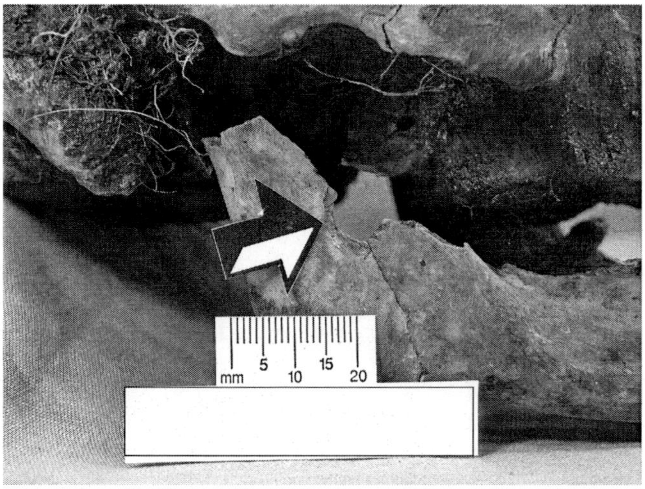

Figure 7.16 Semicircular defect on the ascending ramus of the mandible, consistent with a gunshot wound (Alain Wittmann).

followed by the projectile. Circumferential delamination is not deep enough to expose the diplöe and is not produced by the same mechanism as beveling. There does not appear to be a direct relationship between the caliber of ammunition and the presence of this feature (Figure 7.19). Circumferential delamination has been observed in skulls that sustained shots from both medium- and high-velocity weapons such as 9 mm and 7.62 × 39 mm ammunition (Di Maio 1999). Likewise, delamination may occur in both contact and intermediate range shots, although more frequent in contact/near-contact cases (Coe 1982; Di Maio 1999). Most importantly, it only appears to occur with full metal jacket (FMJ) ammunition. Figure 7.20 illustrates a skull with multiple gunshot injuries, from various views, depicting the types of defects and fracture patterns associated with a 9 mm FMJ ammunition.

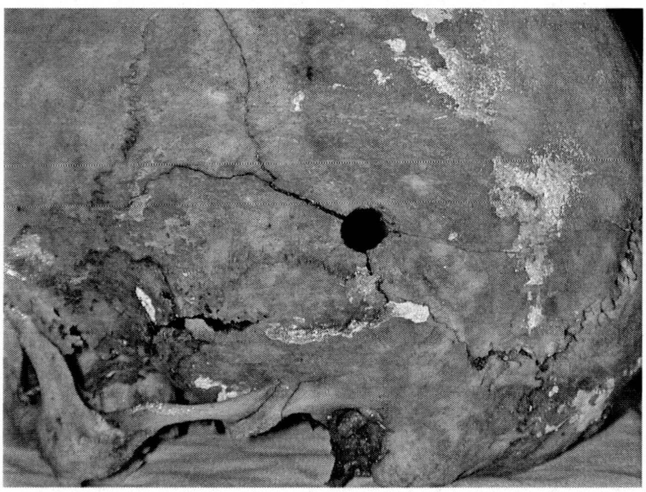

Figure 7.17 Circular defect on the left temporal bone, consistent with an entrance wound caused by a handgun. (Printed with permission from International Criminal Tribunal for the former Yugoslavia [ICTY].)

Figure 7.18 Close-up of an entrance defect in the glabella region of the frontal bone. Observe the circumferential delamination probably caused by a contact wound from a 9 mm pistol (Juan Carlos Tello, EPAF).

Gutter Defects

Gutter defects occur when the bullet penetrates along a path tangential to the surface of the bone (Figures 7.21). In these cases, the bullet is traveling tip forward and penetrates the bone, generally following a straight line. Bullets that produce a gutter wound and penetrate the cranial vault exhibit internal beveling at the point of entry and discrete delamination or external beveling at the point of exit. The anatomy of the bone affected tends to dictate the size and characteristics of the defect, such as beveling or fracture patterns. However, the general shape of the defect consistently reflects the profile of the bullet. Bullets may also

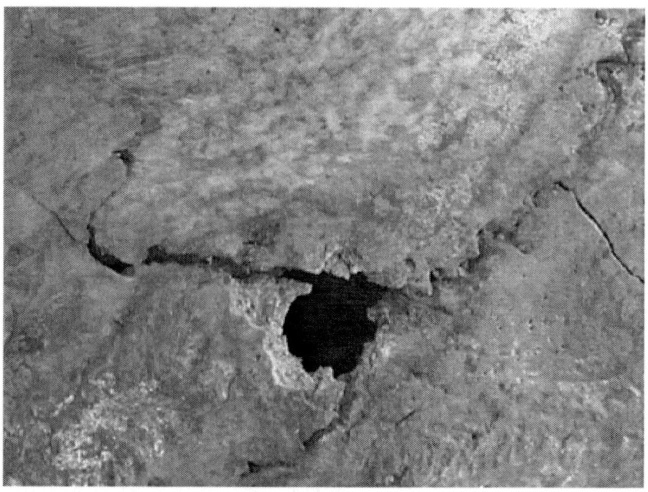

Figure 7.19 Detail of an entrance wound on the left parietal. As the bullet entered through a suture, there is an eccentric pattern of delamination of the edges (Juan Carlos Tello, EPAF).

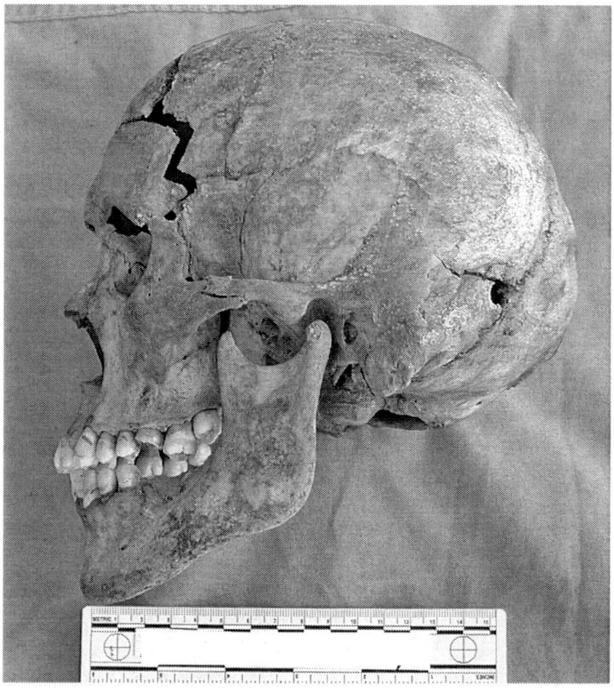

Figure 7.20a Small circular defect located on the left occipital bone between the lambdoid and parietomastoid sutures. Associated to the defect is a short radiating fracture extending anteriorly along the left parietal. Wound is consistent with the entrance of handgun projectile (Juan Carlos Tello, EPAF).

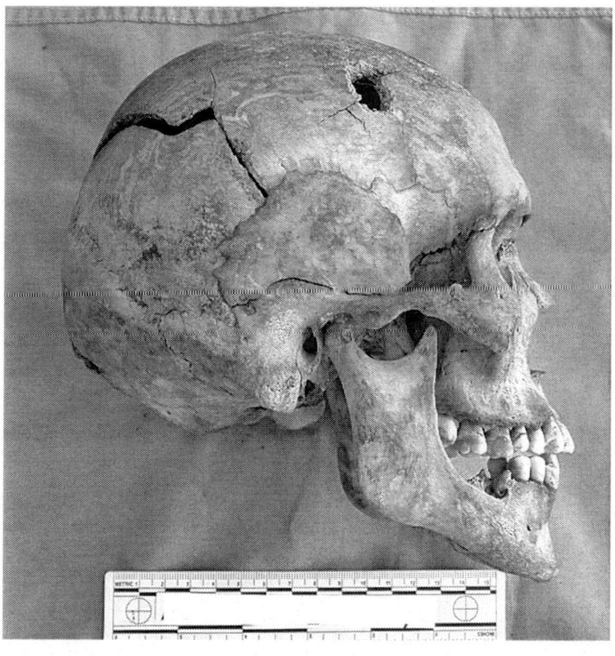

Figure 7.20b Right lateral view of the skull with an exit wound associated to Figure 7.20a (Juan Carlos Tello, EPAF).

Figure 7.20c Superior view of the skull showing a large irregular defect with a full external beveling and three radiating fractures, one of which was arrested by the coronal suture. This exit wound is from a second shot that entered through the posterior occipital bone (Juan Carlos Tello, EPAF).

become embedded in bone, creating gutter-shaped defects. This has been more commonly observed in the pelvis and vertebrae.

Keyhole Defects

As the bullet tumbles during flight, it may not enter the body at a perpendicular angle. Variation in the angle at which the bullet strikes the body often results in more skeletal damage and irregularly shaped entrance wounds (Messmer et al. 2003). *Keyhole defects* are a type of gutter wound that by definition show both internal and external beveling at the entrance site (Figure 7.22). Figure 7.23 illustrates a tangential entrance wound. Typically in keyhole defects, the entrance component appears as the rounded aspect of a keyhole with beveling present on the inner table. The geometric shape of the defect results from the bullet perforating the bone and producing external beveling. A keyhole defect results from a bullet that impacts the bone at a shallow angle, against the curvature of the skull, and thereby "punches" through the entrance defect. Di Maio (1999, 109) wrote:

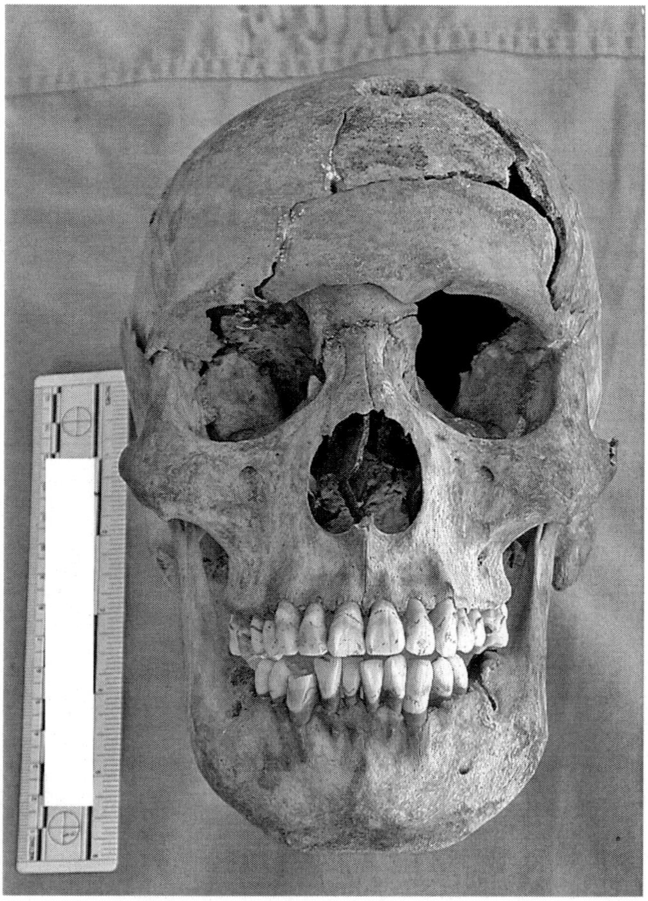

Figure 7.20d Anterior view of the skull with radiating fractures extending from the exit wound pictured in Figure 7.20c. Note the radiating and concentric fractures arrested by a preexisting fracture line running from the middle aspect of the right orbit toward the left frontosphenoid region (Juan Carlos Tello, EPAF).

> For both solid surfaces and water there is a critical angle of impact (incidence) below which a bullet striking the surface will ricochet rather than penetrate. The critical angle is determined by the nature of the surface, the construction of the bullet, and the velocity of the bullet. Thus, round nose bullets are more likely to ricochet than flat-nosed, full metal-jacketed than lead, and low-velocity more than high-velocity.

The shape of keyhole entry wounds is highly variable, as evident in the range of examples illustrated in this chapter. We have frequently observed keyhole-shaped wounds in skulls that sustained injuries from the FMJ ammunition used in both handguns and rifles. However, higher-velocity rounds generally caused more complex keyhole defects and extensive fracturing upon impact. The projectile may also fragment, or the layers of copper and lead may separate from the core of the bullet, leaving one fragment to penetrate the bone and the remaining aspect of the projectile to continue its trajectory, potentially even perforating the head or body. However, bullet fragmentation is not necessary for a keyhole defect to result (Thali et al. 2002a, 2002b). In some cases, the bullet continues its path

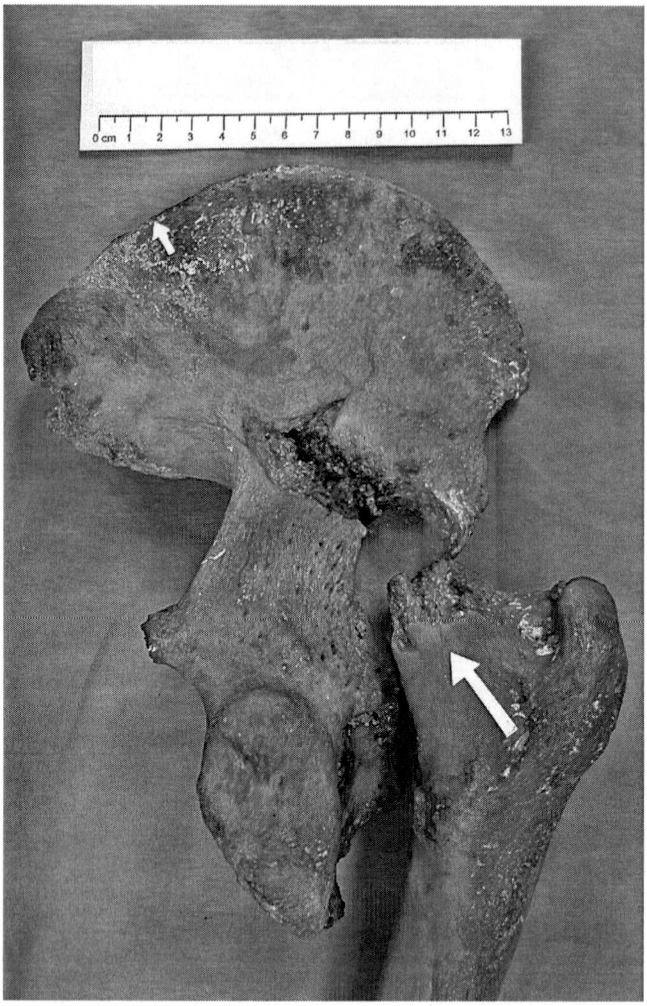

Figure 7.21 (See color insert following page 38) Posterior right ilium and femur. Gutter entrance wound extending through bones. This was a complete, through-and-through gunfire injury right to left. Note the bullet impacted the iliac crest upon exiting. (Printed with permission from International Criminal Tribunal for the former Yugoslavia [ICTY].)

parallel to the surface of the bone, creating an exit wound (Di Maio 1999; Thali et al. 2002a, 2002b). The trajectory of the injury is indicated by the position of the internally and externally beveled components (Dixon 1984).

Eccentric or Irregular Defects

To understand the context in which bullets are likely to strike an object (or person) and pass through it to strike a second target, one should consider the environments in which this has been observed, for example, in the context of extrajudicial executions where a high amount of firepower was used against individuals crowded together in densely packed spaces. Bullets may have ricocheted off the walls or floor and passed through multiple bodies stacked on one another, as in the massacres associated with the Kravica warehouse (*The Prosecutor v. Krstić*, IT-98-33).

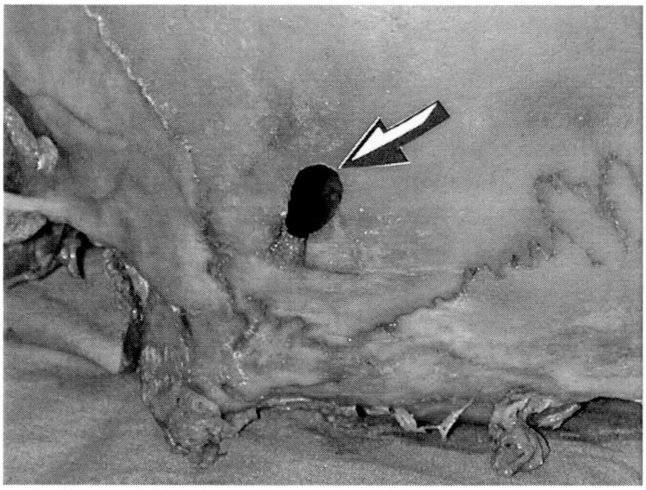

Figure 7.22 Left lateral view of the skull. Keyhole-shaped defect near the squamosal suture. The inferior aspect of the defect shows a spall of bone exposing the diplöe with a discrete circumferential fracture extending almost perpendicular to the defect. The arrow indicates an approximate trajectory of the injury. (Printed with permission from International Criminal Tribunal for the former Yugoslavia [ICTY].)

Eccentric entrance defects refer primarily to lateral or "sideway" entrance of the projectile, in which case the shape of the defect will mimic the cross section of the bullet (Figures 7.24 and 7.25). Note that this type of defect differs from gutter wounds, where the bullet travels tip forward and grazes the bone or strikes tangentially. Irregular wounds result from the bullet striking the bone at an angle. As discussed earlier, the bullet yaws very slightly in flight upon exiting the barrel. More commonly, a projectile may hit an intermediate target, losing stability but continuing flight while tumbling. We have seen many cases in which penetrating wounds to the head were irregular, caused by

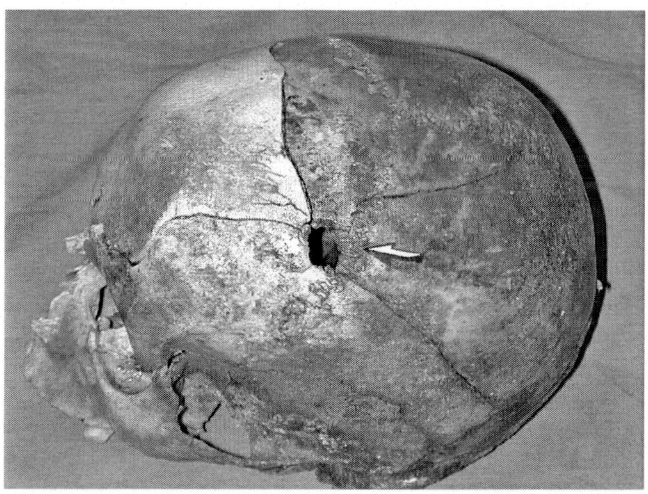

Figure 7.23 Left anterior, lateral view of the cranium. Keyhole entrance wound with large radiating fractures. (Printed with permission from International Criminal Tribunal for the former Yugoslavia [ICTY].)

Figure 7.24 Left lateral view of the parietal bone. Eccentric-shaped entrance wound with two radiating fractures extending laterally from the defect, indicating that the projectile struck the bone sideways. The projectile first struck the bone along the inferior component of the defect in a slightly upward motion. (Printed with permission from International Criminal Tribunal for the former Yugoslavia [ICTY].)

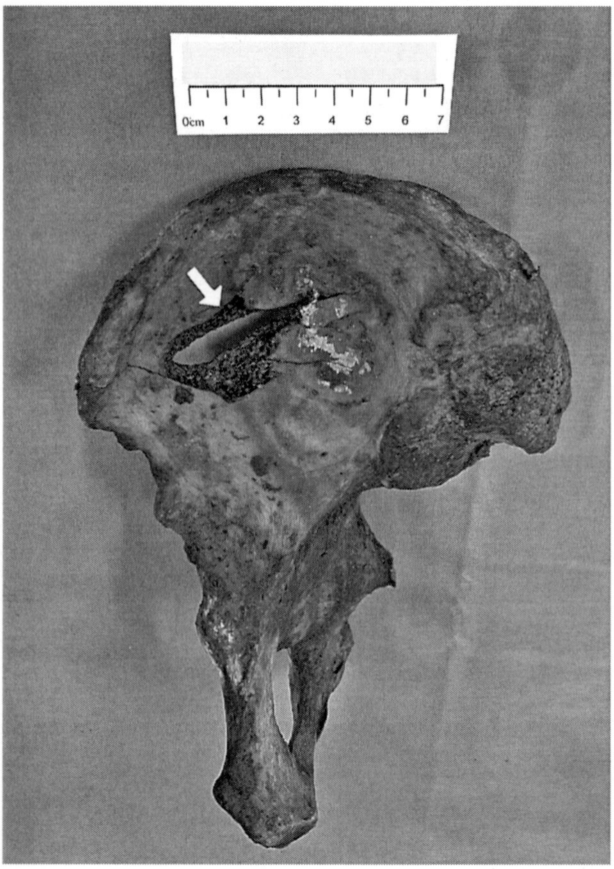

Figure 7.25 Right ilium, anterior surface. Exit wound with beveling, oblong in shape, indicative of a bullet entering the bone sideways. (Printed with permission from International Criminal Tribunal for the former Yugoslavia [ICTY].)

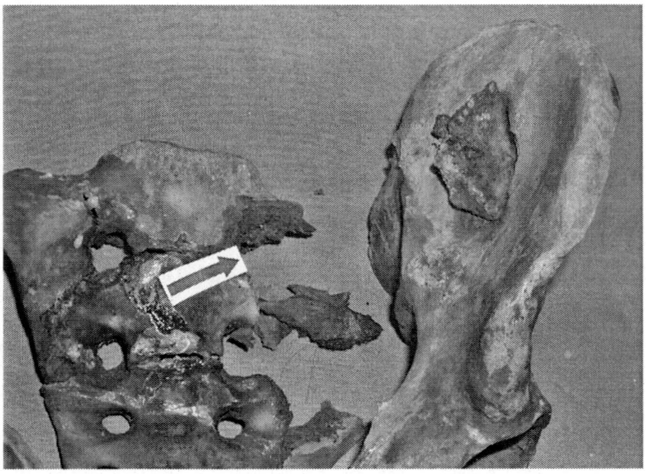

Figure 7.26a (See color insert following page 38) Rearticulated sacrum and left *Os coxae.* A 7.36 × 39 mm bullet struck the sacrum posteriorly and fragmented the sacral, which acted as a secondary projectile. Both the bullet and the sacral bone fragment penetrated the ilium and became embedded in the bone. (Printed with permission from International Criminal Tribunal for the former Yugoslavia [ICTY].)

high-velocity ammunition such as 7.62 × 39 mm, striking the bone at various angles. This ammunition is designed to resist fragmentation. Therefore, it may strike an intermediate target and retain enough velocity to continue its flight.

Messmer and coworkers (2003) point out that bone fragments may become internally displaced and act as secondary projectiles causing further tissue damage. This commonly occurs in the skull, where small bone fragments are displaced internally and damage brain tissue. We have also seen this occur in postcranial elements, including the sacrum and ilium. Not only have bone fragments created soft-tissue damage, but they have also embedded in other bones, creating crushing injuries to those skeletal structures. Figure 7.26

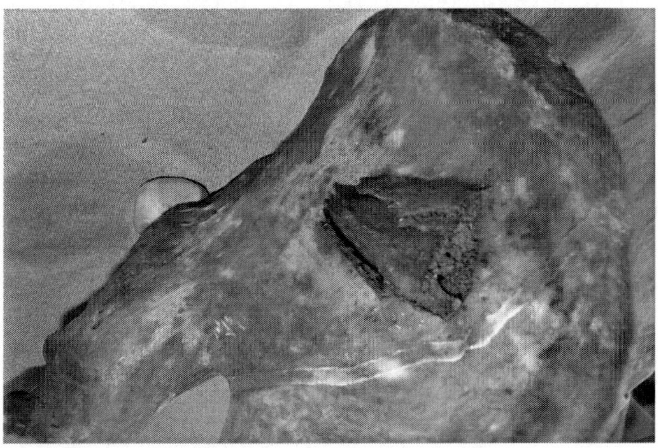

Figure 7.26b (See color insert following page 38) Posterior view of the left ilium. The sacral ala is shown to have perforated the ilium. (Printed with permission from International Criminal Tribunal for the former Yugoslavia [ICTY].)

illustrates a rearticulated sacrum and left pelvis. A 7.36 × 39 mm bullet struck the sacrum from back to front and fragmented the sacrum. The sacral ala completely fractured, and as a secondary projectile both the bullet and the sacral fragment penetrated the ilium and perforated the iliac fossa, becoming embedded in the pelvis.

A high-velocity round, depending on the specific type of ammunition, such as a 7.62 × 39 mm, may perforate the skull or a limb and strike a secondary target. The experiments of Dakak and associates (2003) concluded that the same projectile has a velocity of 200 m/s after leaving the thorax of a pig shot from a 100 m distance. This would be the same velocity as that of a .22 caliber pistol. However, the main difference is that the bullet, upon perforating the head, will tumble and most likely impact the secondary target sideways. Therefore, although the subsequent wounds are only penetrating, the extent of the injury upon entrance may be more substantial and eccentric in shape.

Atypical Wounds from Tandem or Double Tap Shots

Tandem refers to multiple bullets firing through the barrel "piggyback" or in "tandem" due to a malfunction of the weapon in which the projectile fails to leave the barrel and is subsequently pushed through it by the next shot. Such entry wounds will be still discernable as such, although they may have an irregular shape (Messmer et al. 2003). In a case presented by Jentzen and colleagues (1995), three bullets passed through the barrel in tandem, entering the victim in the same, single entrance wound, which was a small circular defect. The weapon was a .22 caliber rifle. The three bullets took different paths upon penetrating the skull and were recovered from different regions inside the crania; therefore, none of the bullets perforated the skull. Several researchers have described similar cases of tandem shots that occurred from low-quality handguns or rifles, low-velocity weapons (Jentzen et al. 1995), or malfunctioning weapons (Timperman and Cnops 1975; Mollan and Beavis 1978; Di Maio 1999).

The term *double tap* refers to a tactical shooting technique commonly employed by special forces and similar types of units by which the trigger is pulled in a quick succession allowing two shots to be fired in the same target zone. According to Kellog (2000), the shots should cluster within 1–2 in. of each another. As with tandem shots, double tap shots rarely occur in forensic cases, yet they are the hallmark of extrajudicial executions because it is a way to give "an insurance shot" to the intended target (Kellog 2000). This technique is executed with a semiautomatic weapon, most likely a pistol. In our careers, we have seen two such cases.

The entrance morphology of a double tap may be an 8-shaped defect, in which two coalescing, rounded defects are formed devoid of the lateral and medial arches. The ectocranial surface may show delamination around the edges, whereas the endocranial surface exhibits internal beveling. Although the shots enter through roughly the same area, they take separate wound tracks and do not exit at the same location.

Figures 7.27–7.32 show the cranial remains of a young adult, a male, who was the victim of an extrajudicial execution in Peru. Upon preliminary analysis of the skull, it may appear that there are entrance wounds located on the posterior skull (i.e., two defects on the occipital and one defect on the left parietal). One of the shots appears to have hit the mandible whereas the others may have exited through a large diamond-shaped defect located on the left frontal bone. The damage observed to this skull is consistent with trauma inflicted from a handgun. However, close review of these defects reveals different

Figure 7.27 Posterior view of the adult crania. Two oval-shaped defects are present on the occipital and left parietal bones, consistent with entrance wounds (Alain Wittmann).

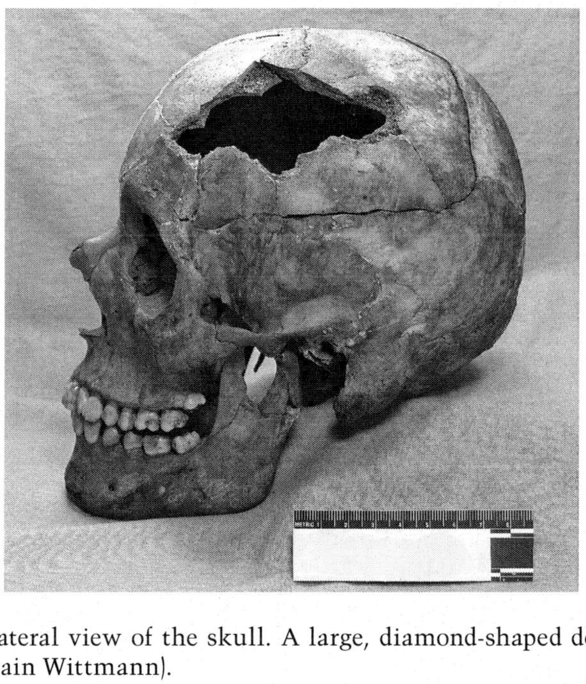

Figure 7.28a Left, lateral view of the skull. A large, diamond-shaped defect is present with external beveling (Alain Wittmann).

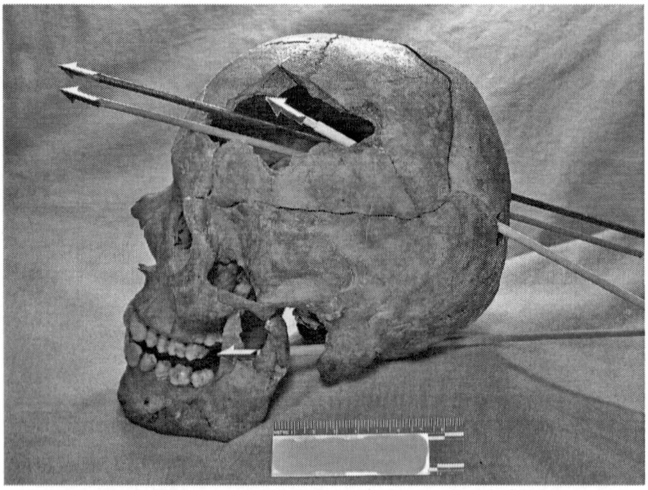

Figure 7.28b The individual sustained a fourth shot through the base of the cranium that exited through the mandible. The probes show the trajectory of the shots, three of which exited through the diamond-shaped defect (Alain Wittmann, EPAF).

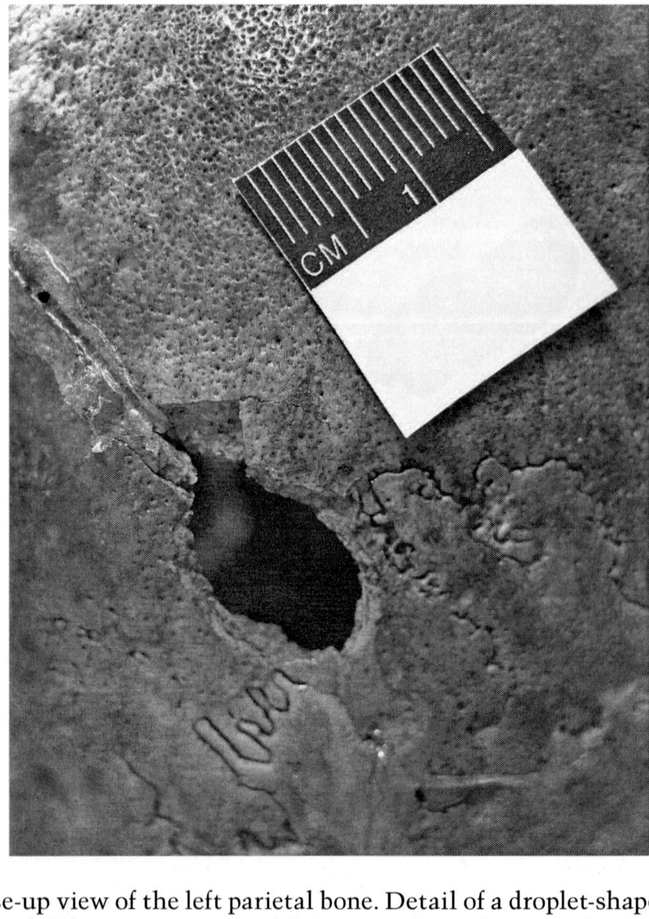

Figure 7.29 Close-up view of the left parietal bone. Detail of a droplet-shaped entrance wound with circumferential delamination around the outer edges. The irregular shape is partly due to the location of the wound on a suture (Alain Wittmann, EPAF).

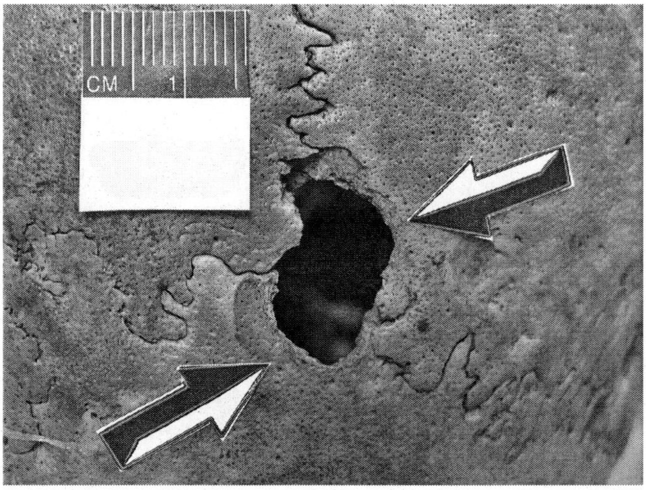

Figure 7.30 Close-up view of the posterior skull, lambda region. A defect roughly in the shape of the number 8 is present on the right lambdoid suture. The inferior and superior right edges of the defect are curved, with two overlapping circular defects likely, consistent with "double tap" (Alain Wittmann, EPAF).

wound trajectories. The entrance wound to the left parietal is in the shape of a "droplet" and shows circumferential delamination around the outer edges. Its shape is partially dictated by the fact that it crosses a suture. The associated exit wound is located through the right apex of the diamond-shaped defect on the left frontal bone. The defect on the occipital bone, 18 × 10 mm, has an irregular shape, also in part caused by the sutures it crosses. Close examination also reveals a number of other features. The *spall* of the outer table was not yet removed along the inferior edge of the defect, and delamination on the upper edge was caused by the removal of a similar bone spall, or flake. The inferior and superior right edges of the defect are curved, reflecting two rounded defects that coalesce one another.

Figure 7.31 (See color insert following page 38) Close-up of the left lateral skull, illustrating the detail of the diamond-shaped exit wound (Alain Wittmann, EPAF).

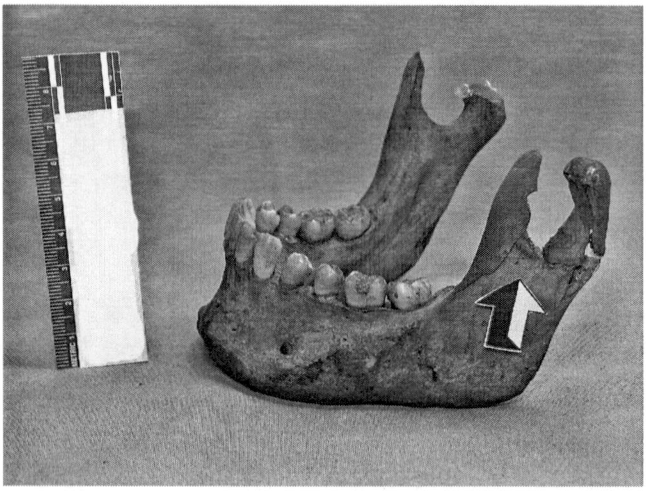

Figure 7.32 Left lateral view of mandible, illustrating an exit wound between the coronoid process and mandibular condyle. The shot originated from the left side of the cranial base (refer to Figure 7.48) (Alain Wittmann, EPAF).

Internally, there is beveling around the entire margin of the defect. When observing the diamond-shaped exit defect on the frontal bone, it is apparent that there are three distinct areas of external beveling, one of which shows a round shape reflective of the cross section of a bullet. This defect is the exit or perforating wound associated with the entrance defect on the parietal, as already discussed. The inferior and left apexes of the diamond do not show any specific patterned defect, but clearly exhibit external beveling. Therefore, it is most likely that the inferior and left apexes of the diamond correspond to the two shots that penetrated the occipital. For comparison, Figure 7.33 illustrates an adult male cranium that received two entry gunshot wounds to the left posterior temporal–occipital

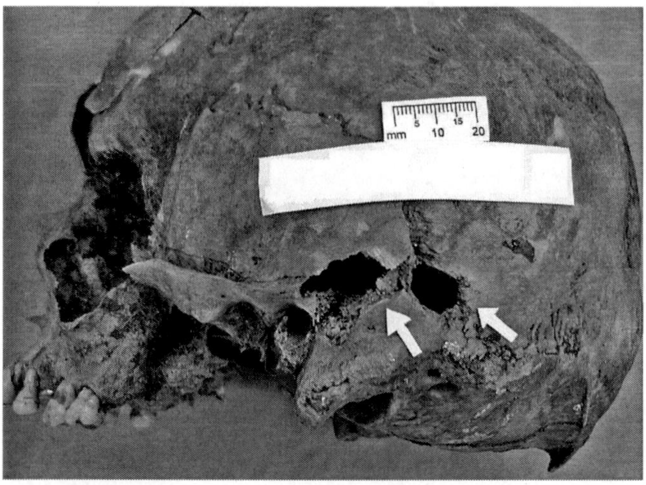

Figure 7.33a Left lateral aspect of the cranium, posterior temporal bone. Two entrance wounds are located on the left supramastoid area (double tap), likely from a handgun (Printed with permission from International Criminal Tribunal for the former Yugoslavia [ICTY].)

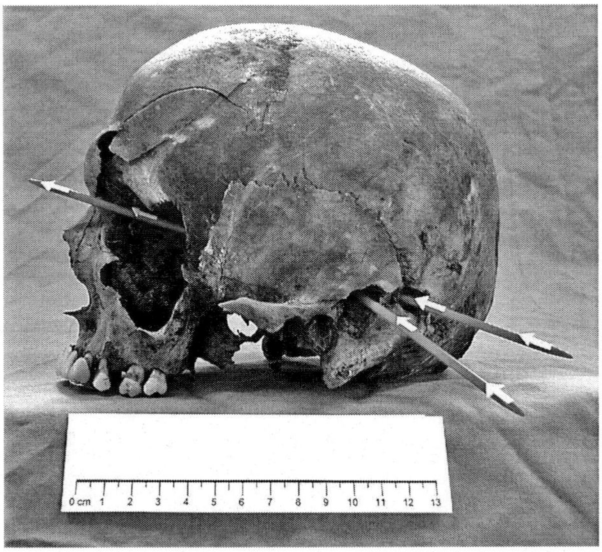

Figure 7.33b Close-up view illustrating trajectory. (Printed with permission from International Criminal Tribunal for the former Yugoslavia [ICTY].)

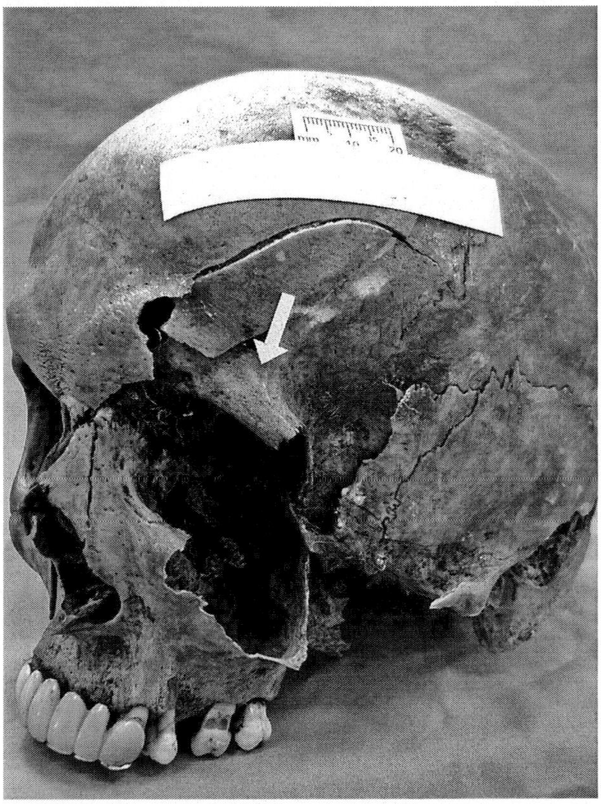

Figure 7.33c Detail of an exit wound on the left orbit. In addition, the area over the injury suffered postmortem fractures and modification. (Printed with permission from International Criminal Tribunal for the former Yugoslavia [ICTY].)

region. These two shots were probably fired with a handgun, most likely a semiautomatic pistol firing 9 mm FMJ ammunition. The shots were fired together, execution style. Note that there are two different exit tracks.

Atypical Wounds from Embedded Projectiles

A number of different wound shapes and injury mechanisms have been discussed to illustrate morphological variation. In addition to perforating bone, projectiles may become embedded in the bone, particularly in areas that are thick and composed of a dense amount of trabeculae such as the metaphyses of long bones or vertebrae (Figures 7.34–7.38), although bullets embedded in bone have been observed by the authors in nearly every type of bone, including the skull, long bones, scapula, vertebrae, sacrum, pelvis, and tarsals. Bullets or shotgun pellets may penetrate bone but lack sufficient velocity to perforate the bone, thus becoming lodged. Some reasons are that they hit intermediate targets before striking the victim (as already discussed) or have low velocity due to the ammunition or distance of fire. The orientation of the projectile and angle at which it strikes the target may provide additional evidence of the presence of an intermediate target in some cases.

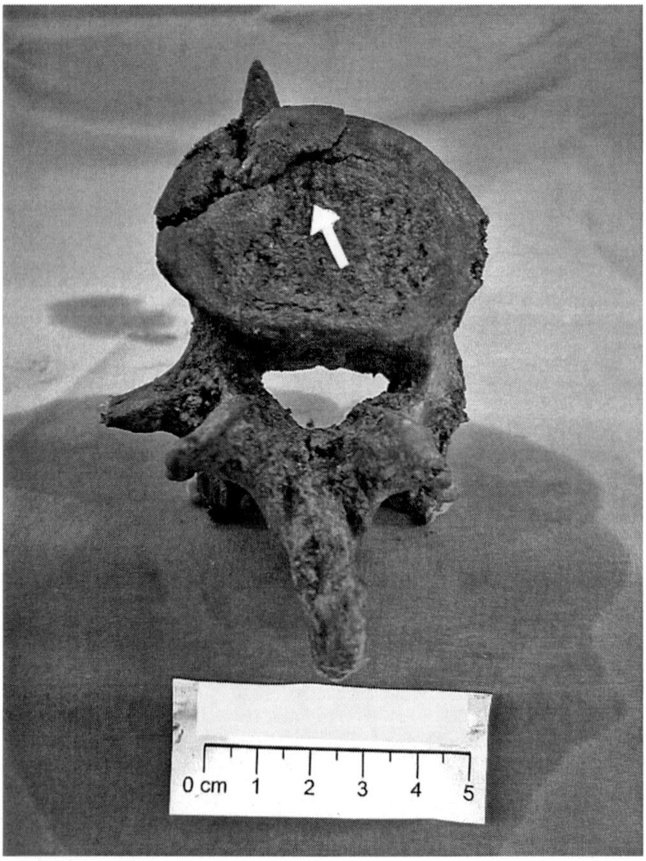

Figure 7.34a Inferior view of the lumbar vertebra showing an embedded 7.62 × 39 mm bullet. (Printed with permission from International Criminal Tribunal for the former Yugoslavia [ICTY].)

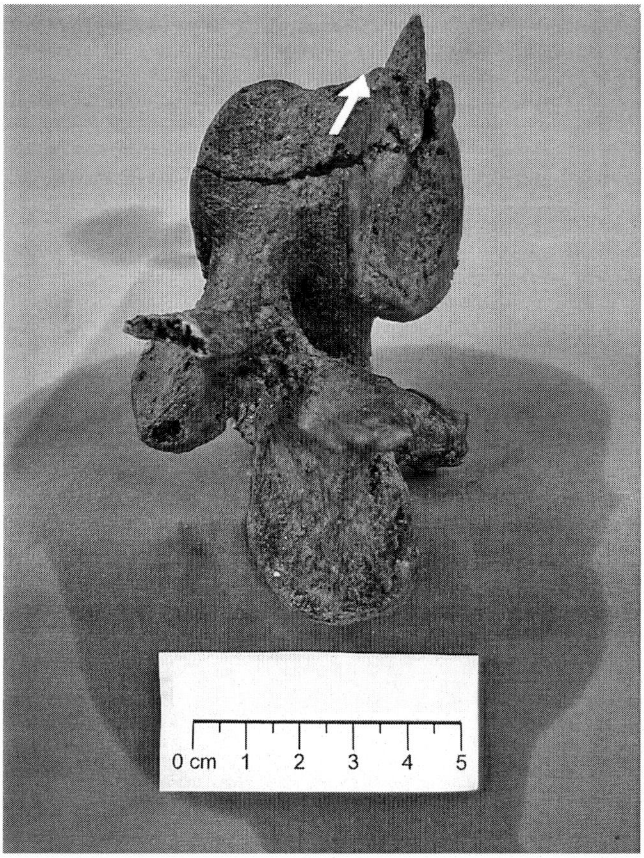

Figure 7.34b Lateral view. The projectile entered the vertebral bone anteriorly, or front to back. There are no fractures or defects on the posterior aspect. Therefore, the bullet had to have perforated the bone, base forward. This is expected for this region, as the bullet would tumble as it penetrated through the soft tissues of the abdomen prior to impacting the vertebra. (Printed with permission from International Criminal Tribunal for the former Yugoslavia [ICTY].)

Radiographs of skeletal remains may exhibit embedded pellets in bone. It is of paramount importance to determine by examination whether these pellets were retained as part of a healed antemortem event (i.e., a previous injury) or were related to the perimortem trauma or is a contributing factor in the victim's death (Di Maio 1999). Establishing the timing of the injury is necessary to resolve this question. Radiography can be useful in such cases and may elucidate metal fragments completely encased by bone or barely visible externally.

Exit Wounds

Perforating or through-and-through shots exit the head or body. Exit wounds are either regular or irregular in shape (Figures 7.39–7.57) and show variation by anatomical region. Their shape reflects the degree to which the bullet yaws as it passes through tissue, the biomechanical properties of the bone affected, and the shape of the projectile (Dixon 1984; Berryman et al. 1995; Di Maio 1999; Vellema and Scholtz 2005). Generally, exit wounds

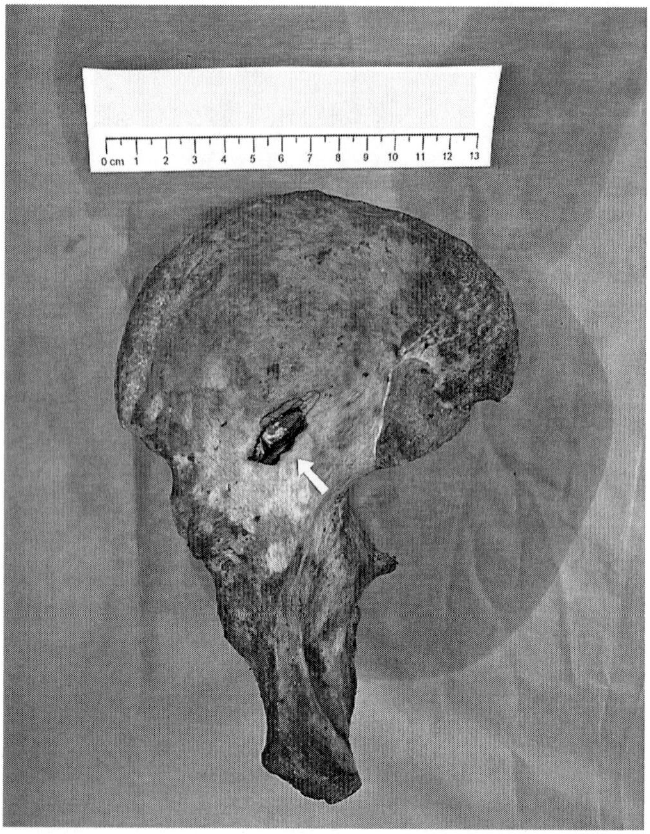

Figure 7.35a Anterior view of the right iliac fossa with an irregular-shaped defect. Embedded in the defect is a sideways positioned, 7.62 × 39 mm bullet. (Printed with permission from International Criminal Tribunal for the former Yugoslavia [ICTY].)

in bone exhibit more fracturing than the entrance site, although this varies based on anatomical structure and other extrinsic factors.

Exit wounds in the skull typically exhibit external beveling on the outer table and are associated with radiating and concentric fractures. Bullets that enter the body at a perpendicular angle with the tip forward will begin to yaw at predictable distances, depending on the caliber and construction of the ammunition. In the skull and limbs, the exit wounds are much larger because they occur at the point of the maximum diameter of the permanent cavity, as the bullet tumbles (Vellema and Scholtz 2005). In areas of the body where the bullet travels further through tissue before striking bone, such as in the abdomen or thorax, the exit wound will often be smaller in size (Fackler 1987), although in such cases the bullet may exit tip or base forward or become embedded in bone such as the anterior vertebrae or pelvis. Gunfire exit wounds through thin bones such as the face or eye orbits may be difficult to estimate because the anatomical properties of such regions result in a high amount of fracturing and an absence of beveling (i.e., *blowout* fractures). Consequently, skeletal reconstructions in those regions may be challenging. Additionally, bullets may remain inside the crania or only partially exit.

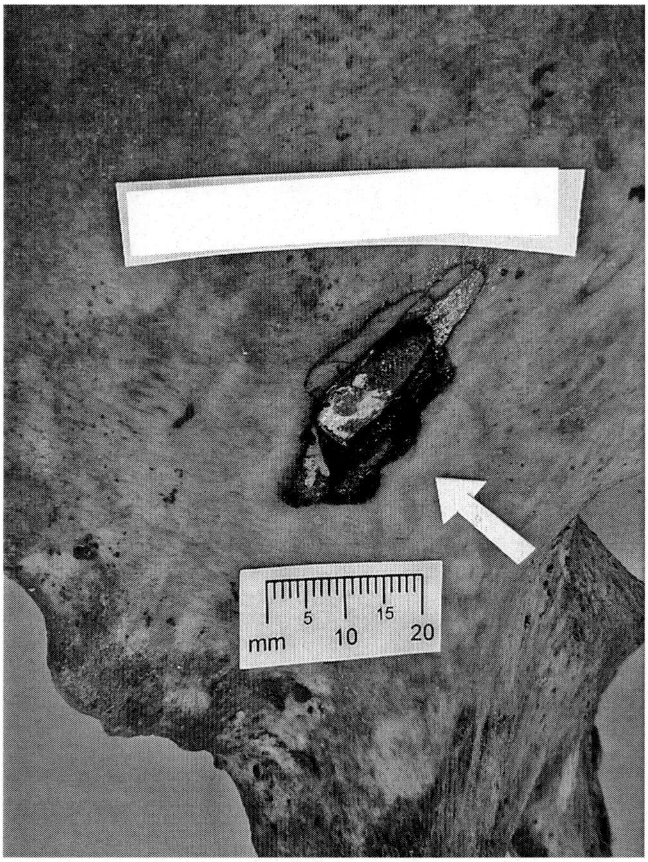

Figure 7.35b Close-up view of the wound. (Printed with permission from International Criminal Tribunal for the former Yugoslavia [ICTY].)

Establishing Bullet Trajectory

How is bullet trajectory interpreted from skeletal wounds?

- Defects are classified as entrance or exit wounds (Figure 7.58). The shape of the entrance wound, the edges of the fractured area, and the presence of beveling indicate the direction of fire.
- The linear fractures that radiate from the entrance point to the direction of the force (Figure 7.59).
- Multiple regions may exhibit wounds that associate with one another. In other words, do the entrance and exit wounds associate with a single injury, or are there multiple injuries present? Not all bullets create an exit wound, nor do all gunfire injuries strike bone.
- The wounds are examined to establish the presence of internal injuries that indicate the bullet hit bone and was redirected or ricocheted. One should also consider that there is an open end of possibilities about the position of the victim when shot and the physical relationship of the shooter to the victim.

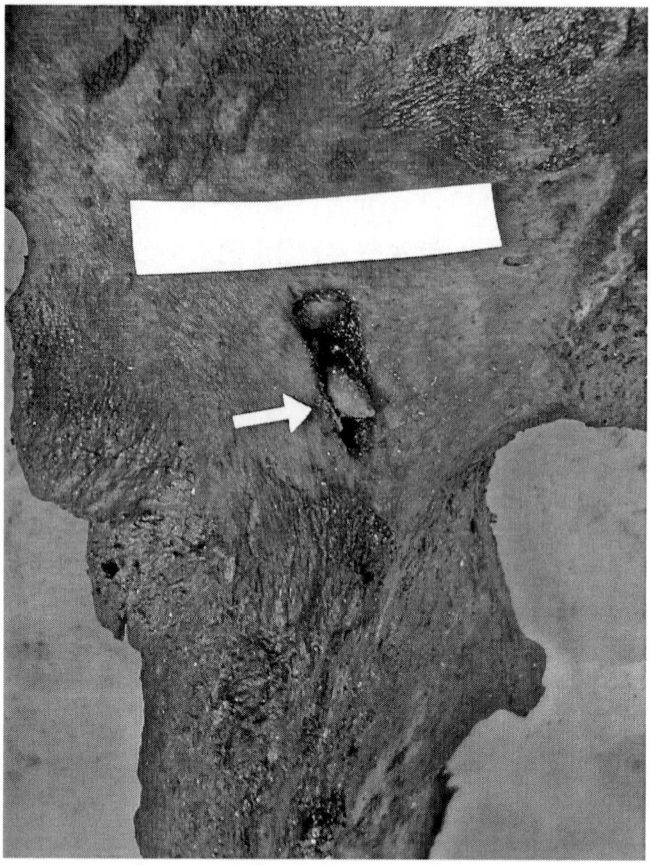

Figure 7.36 Left ilium, posterior view. Bullet embedded in bone, 7.62 × 39 mm. The tip of the defect is protruding through the bone; the shot was fired from front to back. (Printed with permission from International Criminal Tribunal for the former Yugoslavia [ICTY].)

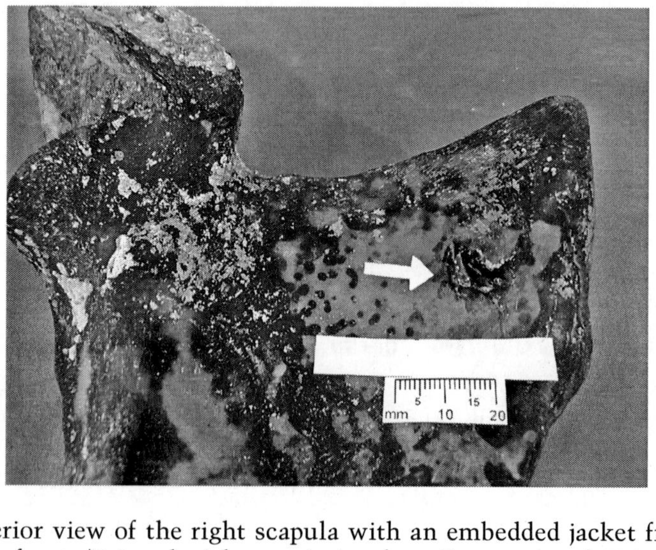

Figure 7.37 Anterior view of the right scapula with an embedded jacket fragment; the shot fired from back to front. (Printed with permission from International Criminal Tribunal for the former Yugoslavia [ICTY].)

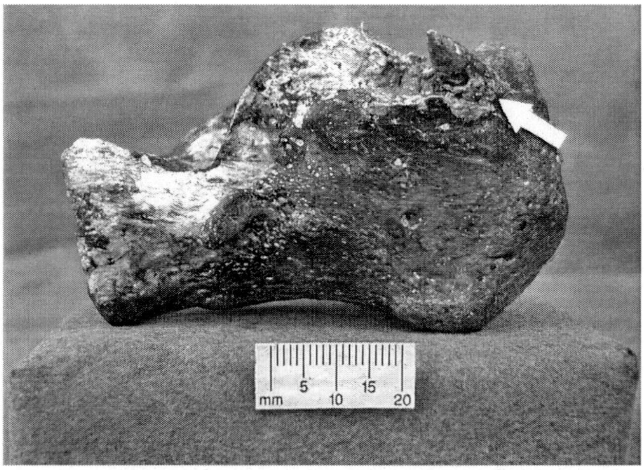

Figure 7.38a Left lateral view of the calcaneus showing an embedded 7.62 × 39 mm projectile. The bullet entered the bone from left to right. The tip of the projectile is facing laterally, indicating that the bullet struck the bone base forward and probably entered the foot after striking an intermediate object, such as the shoe or the floor. (Printed with permission from International Criminal Tribunal for the former Yugoslavia [ICTY].)

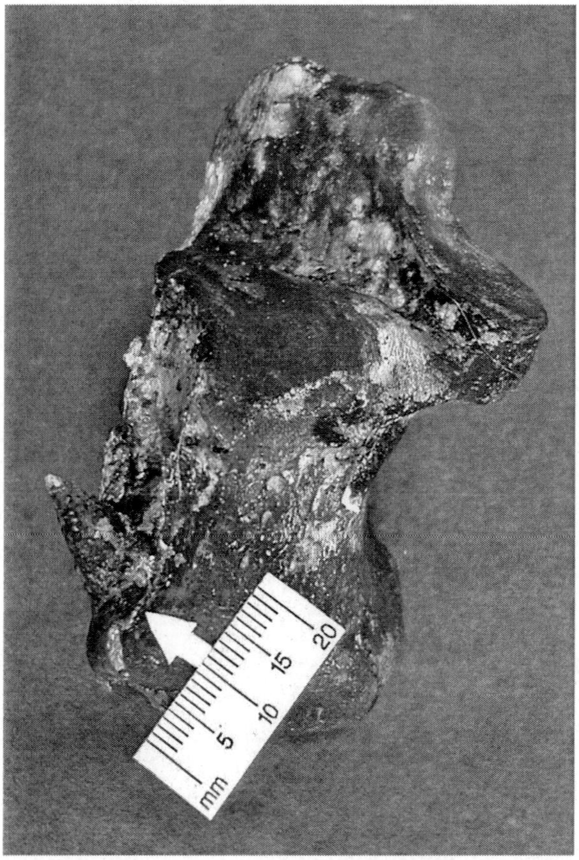

Figure 7.38b Superior view of the calcaneus shown in Figure 7.38a. (Printed with permission from International Criminal Tribunal for the former Yugoslavia [ICTY].)

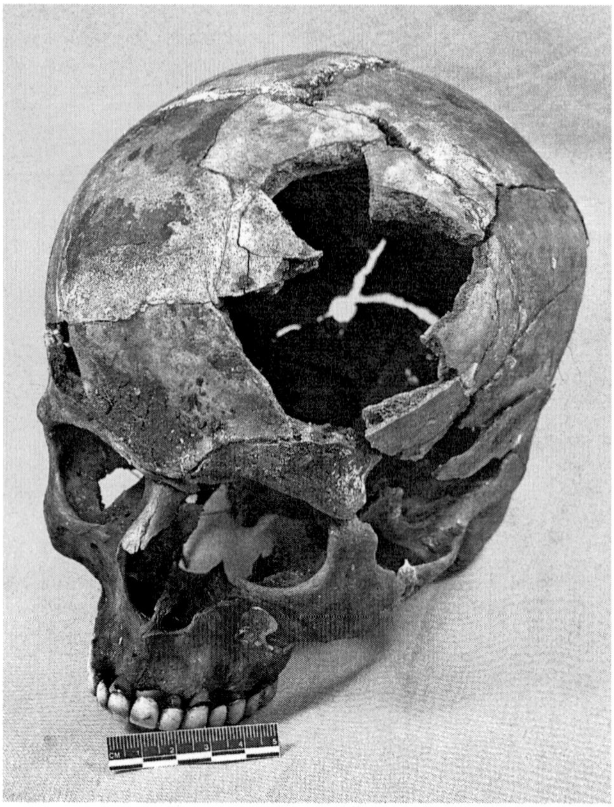

Figure 7.39 Left anterior view of the adult cranium. Massive exit wound on the left frontal bone associated with multiple radiating and concentric fractures. Note that through the defect a small circular entrance wound is observable on the posterior vault (Alain Wittmann).

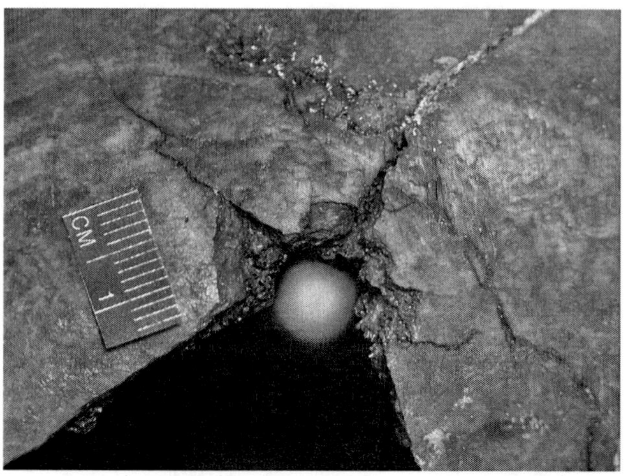

Figure 7.40 (See color insert following page 38) Close-up view of an exit defect on an adult cranial vault. The defect is circular in shape. A large triangular section of the bone is absent, having completely fractured from radiating and concentric fractures. The smaller circular entrance defect is visible in the background through the wound (Alain Wittmann).

Figure 7.41 (See color insert following page 38) Close-up view of the GSW to the cranial vault. Oval-shaped exit wound, with external beveling and small radiating fractures. Injury is oval in shape, consistent with the cross section of a 9 mm bullet. Note that a small circular entrance defect is present in the background through the wound (Juan Carlos Tello, EPAF).

Establishing trajectory means associating wounds together as a single injury; it is essential for establishing the number of injuries when multiple wounds are present. It is also useful to know the class of weapon used and characteristics of firing such a weapon. For example, Di Maio (1999, 13) points out, "Weapons fired in the full-automatic mode are very difficult to control. In most instances, while the first shot may be on target, subsequent rounds fly high and to the right." As always, the context is important in interpreting the trajectory of fire and the circumstances surrounding the incident.

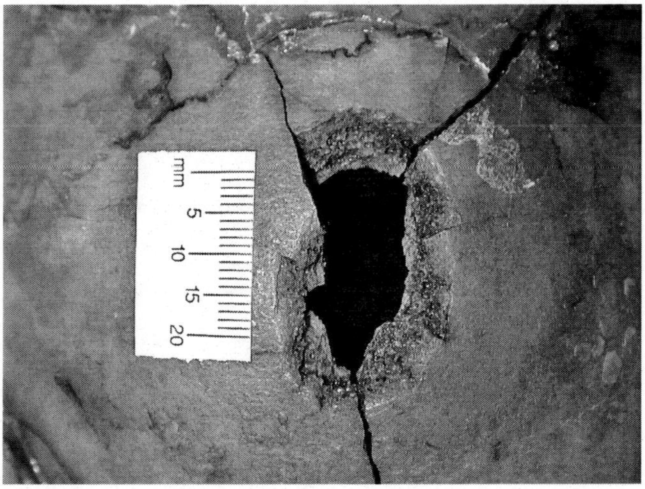

Figure 7.42 Close-up view of the GSW to the cranial vault. Large defect present with external beveling and large radiating fractures (Alain Wittmann).

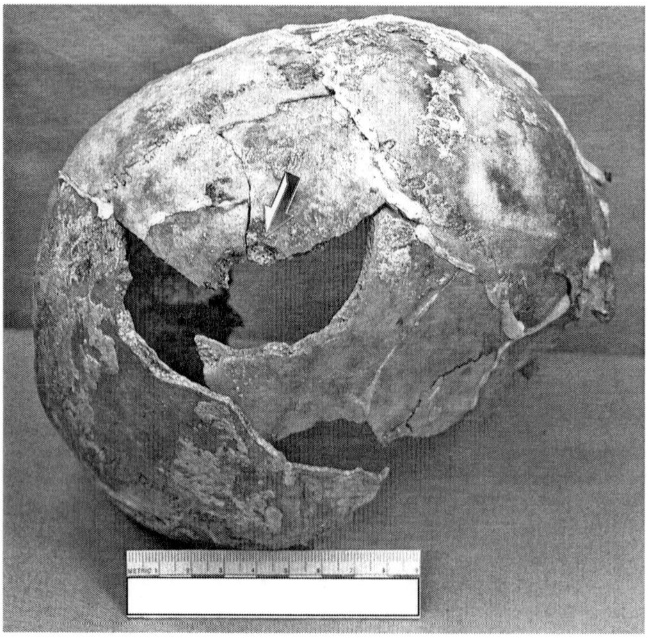

Figure 7.43 Right posterior/superior view of the cranial vault. Cranium was severely fragmented and recovery was incomplete. An exit defect is present on the right parietal (Alain Wittmann).

Di Maio (1999) describes rare patterns of bullets ricocheting upon striking bone, whereby their flight path is altered. Such cases were observed in the upper thigh, as the bullet struck the femur (Di Maio 1999, 115) and in the skull (Di Maio 1999, 264–265). Two similar cases are illustrated here. Figures 7.60 and 7.61 depict two cases with multiple views, in which bullets ricocheted inside the skulls, changed flight trajectory, and still retained enough velocity to perforate the skulls.

Figure 7.44 Adult cranial vault. Two exit wounds. Based on fracture interception, the defect on the lower left occurred prior to the shot that caused the second defect, pictured in the upper right (Juan Carlos Tello, EPAF).

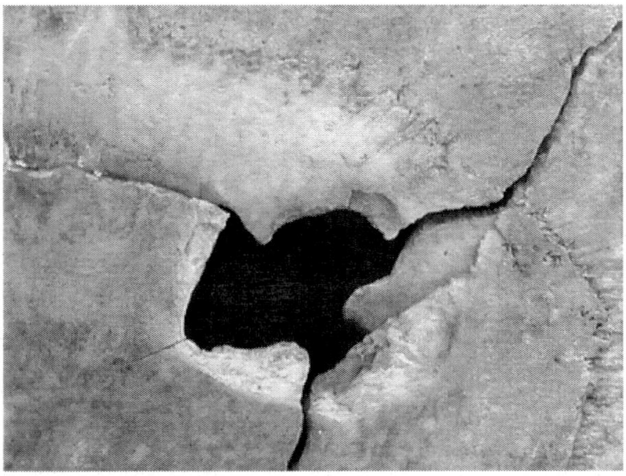

Figure 7.45 Adult cranial vault. Irregular-shaped exit defect on the temporal bone with incomplete beveling (Juan Carlos Tello, EPAF).

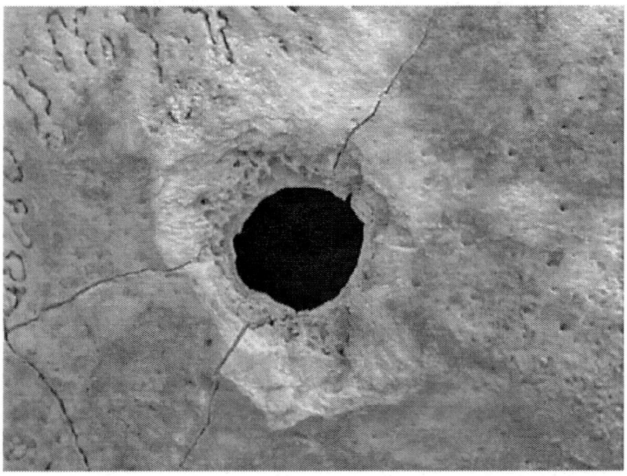

Figure 7.46 Adult cranial vault. Circular exit defect with external beveling; shot fired from a handgun (Juan Carlos Tello, EPAF).

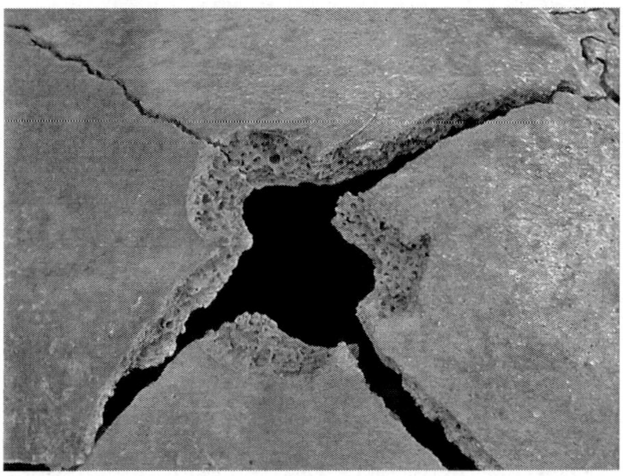

Figure 7.47 Adult cranial vault. Exit defect with external beveling and radiating fractures, resulting from a handgun (Juan Carlos Tello, EPAF).

Figure 7.48 (See color insert following page 38) Adult cranial vault. Exit defect caused by a handgun. Note the circular entrance wound visible through the defect, in the background (Juan Carlos Tello, EPAF).

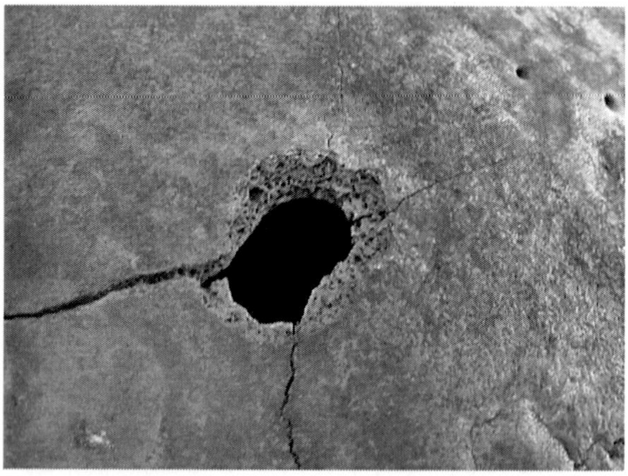

Figure 7.49 Adult cranial vault. Exit defect showing a shape that mimics the cross section of a handgun bullet, most likely a 9 mm (Juan Carlos Tello, EPAF).

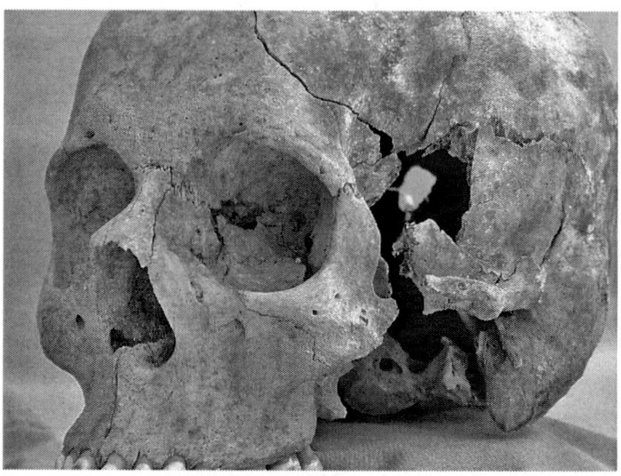

Figure 7.50 (See color insert following page 38) Left frontal view of skull. Irregular-shaped exit wound to the left sphenoid/temporal region. Through the defect, the oval entrance wound is visible. The bullet penetrated the cranial vault sideways upon impact. The size of the defect is consistent with a 9 mm bullet (Juan Carlos Tello, EPAF).

Figure 7.51 Close-up view of the left frontal bone. Irregular-shaped exit wound superior to left orbit caused by a gunshot, from a handgun (i.e., 9 mm). The shot originated from the right aspect of the occipital bone (Juan Carlos Tello, EPAF).

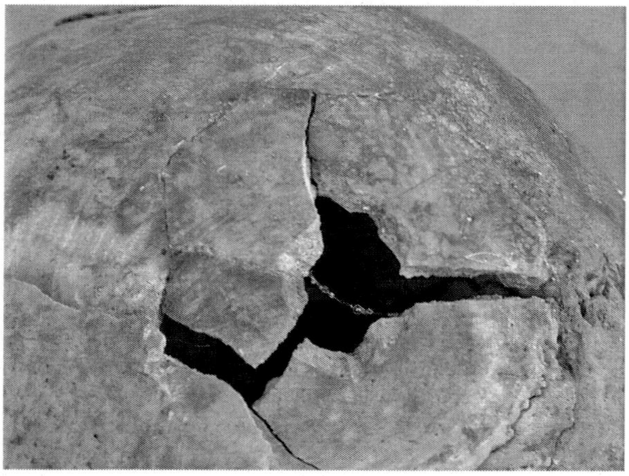

Figure 7.52 Adult cranial vault. Exit wound shown with external beveling and radiating and concentric fractures, caused by a handgun, most likely with 9 mm ammunition (Juan Carlos Tello, EPAF).

Figure 7.53 Exit wound on the left parietal caused by a handgun (i.e., 9 mm) (Juan Carlos Tello, EPAF).

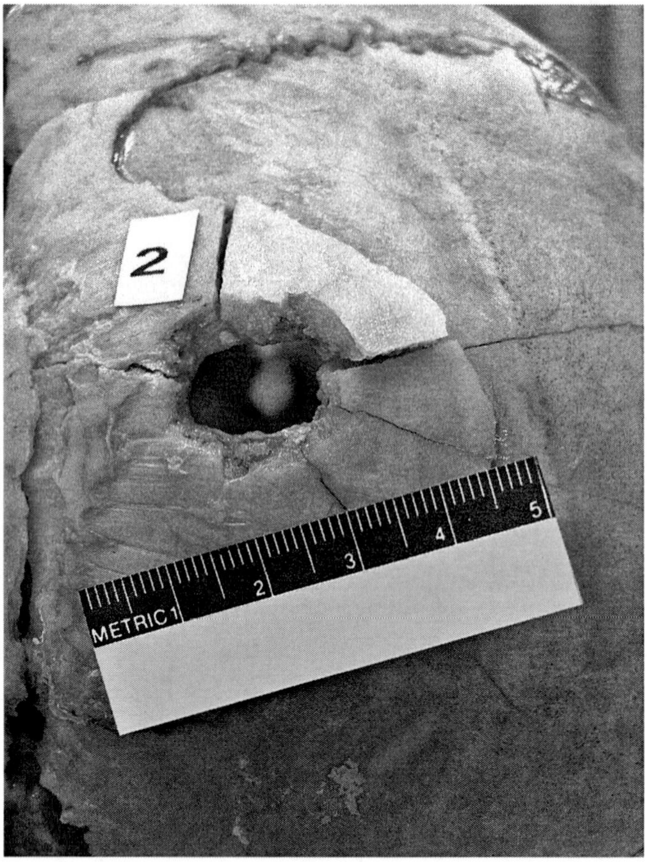

Figure 7.54 Exit wound on the left parietal from a suicide victim using a CZ 9 mm handgun (Alain Wittmann).

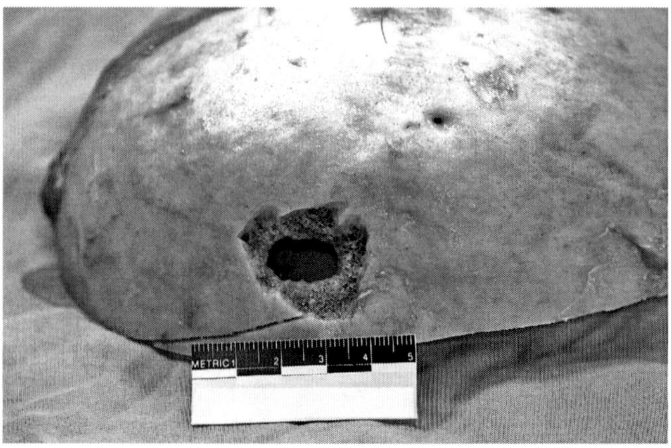

Figure 7.55 Exit wound on the right parietal from a suicidal shot using a 9 mm handgun (Alain Wittmann).

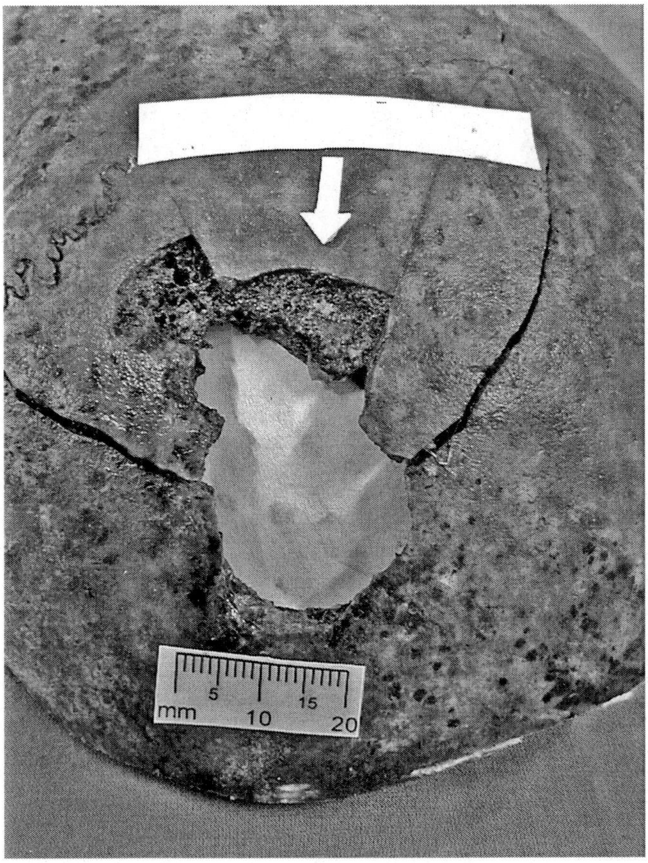

Figure 7.56 Close-up view of the cranial vault. A large oval defect with external beveling is present along the superior border. (Printed with permission from International Criminal Tribunal for the former Yugoslavia [ICTY].)

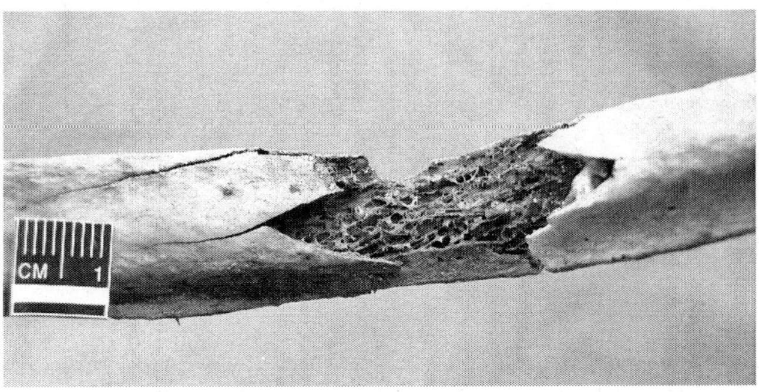

Figure 7.57 Internal surface of the anterior rib. Beveling is present, indicating the shot originated from front to back (Alain Wittmann).

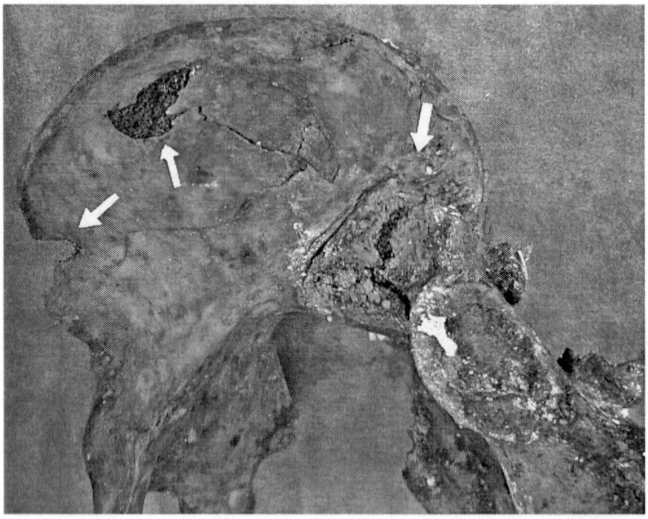

Figure 7.58a Right *Os coxae* and sacrum showing multiple defects caused by gunshot wounds, from left to right: (1) A semicircular defect is present between the iliac spines. This defect suggests that the bullet grazed the bone from right to left. (2) An oval defect along the superior border of the iliac fossa, consistent with the external table of an entrance wound. The shape of the defect and its position indicate that the bullet penetrated sideways. This irregular defect shows fracturing of the internal table (beveling) and associated fractures. (3) Incomplete fracture lines of the sacral ala. (Printed with permission from International Criminal Tribunal for the former Yugoslavia [ICTY].)

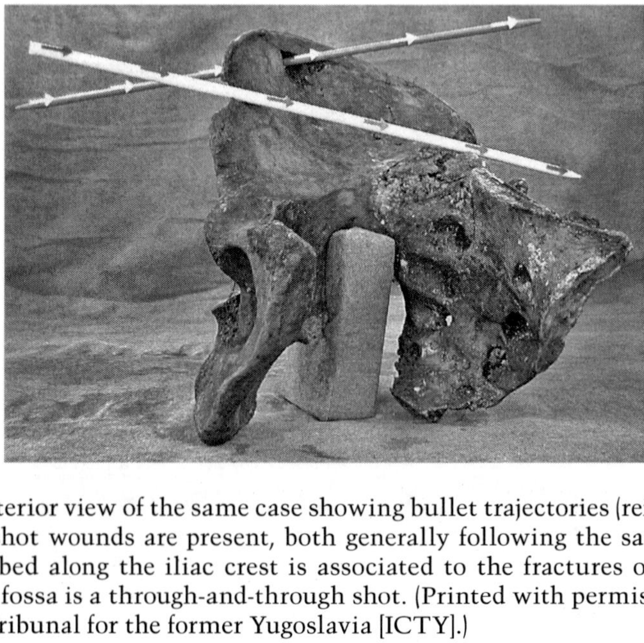

Figure 7.58b Anterior view of the same case showing bullet trajectories (refer to Figure 7.58a). At least two gunshot wounds are present, both generally following the same trajectory. The first injury described along the iliac crest is associated to the fractures of the sacrum. The injury to the iliac fossa is a through-and-through shot. (Printed with permission from International Criminal Tribunal for the former Yugoslavia [ICTY].)

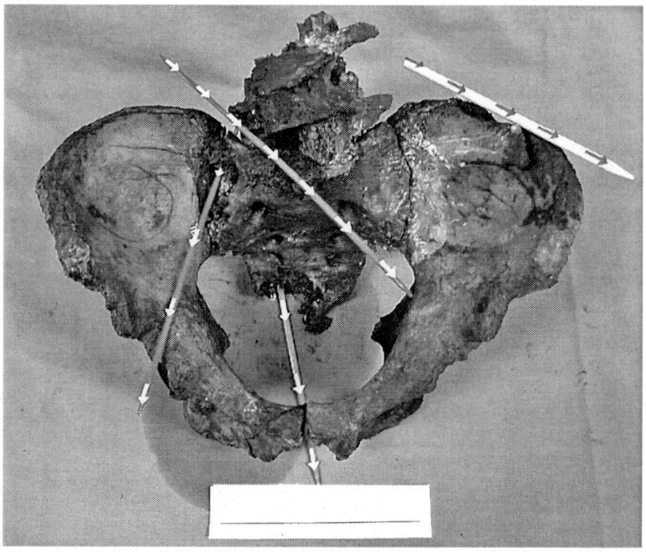

Figure 7.59 Superior view of the articulated pelvic girdle and L5 showing multiple, through-and-through gunshot wounds, all fired from back to front. The probes with arrows indicate the bullet trajectories. (Printed with permission from International Criminal Tribunal for the former Yugoslavia [ICTY].)

Range of Fire

The range of fire in gunfire injuries is typically classified as contact, close contact or intermediate, and distant. Characteristics for each category based on soft tissues distinguish these general ranges by the presence of soot, gunpowder, abrasion rings, and other residual materials (Spitz 1993). Estimating the range of fire based on skin characteristics is easier

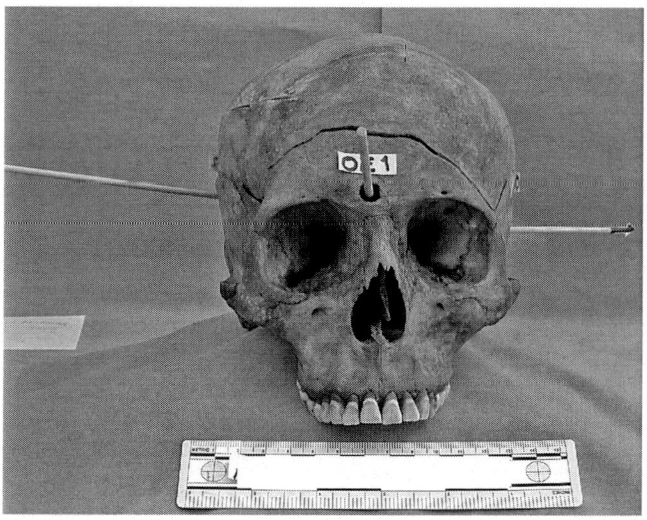

Figure 7.60a Superior view, adult cranium. The individual sustained two gunshot injuries, one from the front through the glabella and the other laterally through the right parietal (Juan Carlos Tello, EPAF).

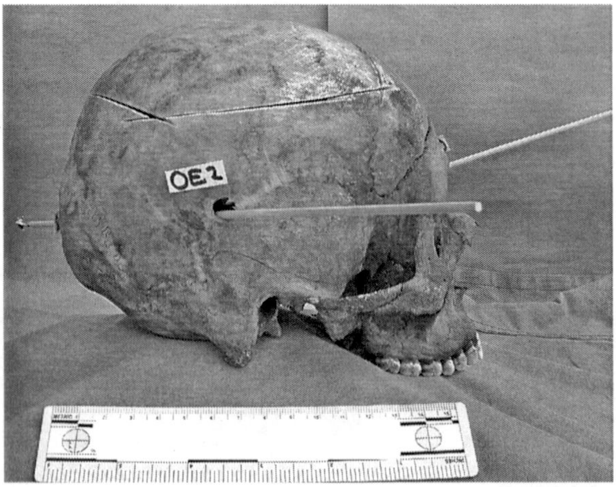

Figure 7.60b Right lateral view (refer to Figure 7.60a). Second gunshot entrance wound. Note the circumferential delamination around both defects (Juan Carlos Tello, EPAF).

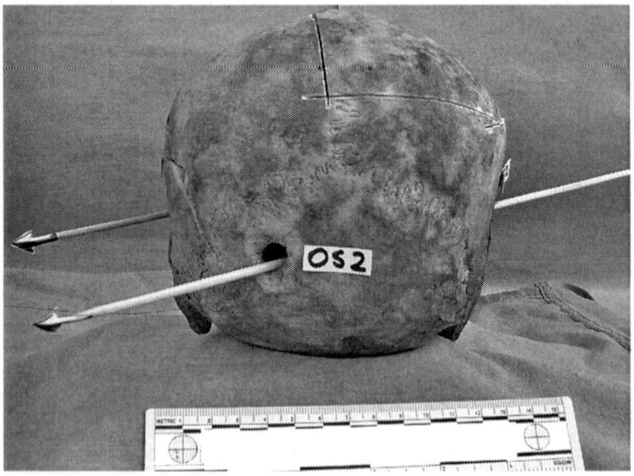

Figure 7.60c Posterior view (refer to Figure 7.60b). The exit wound associated with the second shot (entrance wound through the right parietal) is located on the left side of the occipital bone. Note the external beveling along the left aspect of the defect and the two small radiating fractures extending laterally to the left, indicating the direction of fire (Juan Carlos Tello, EPAF).

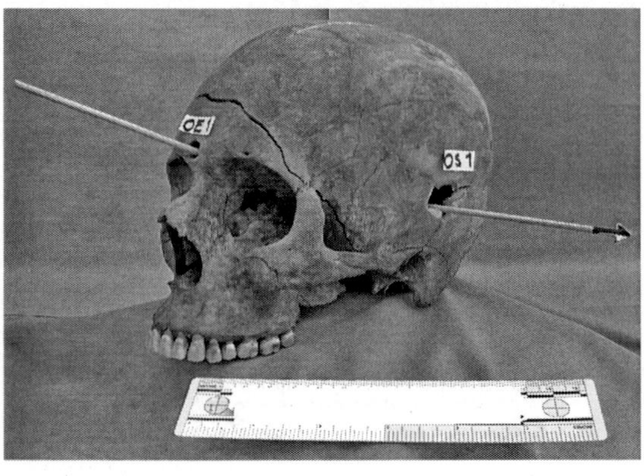

Figure 7.60d Left lateral view (refer to Figure 7.60a). Exit defect on the left temporal associated with the entrance wound to the frontal bone (Juan Carlos Tello, EPAF).

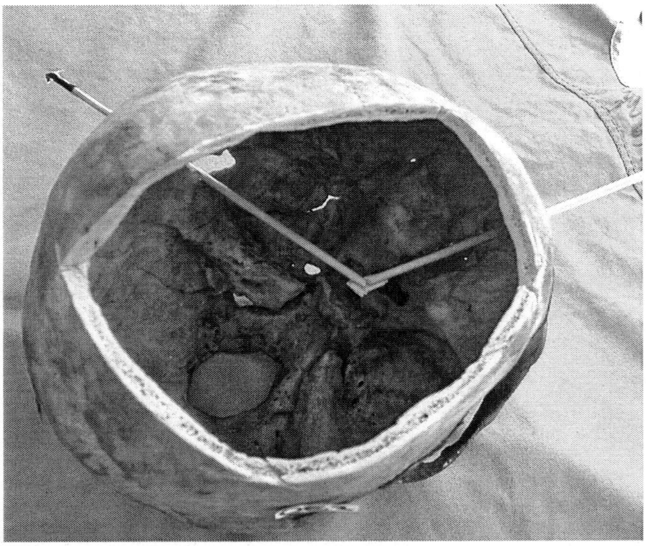

Figure 7.60e Endocranial view of the base of the skull (refer to Figure 7.60a). The injury through the frontal bone impacted the right aspect of the sella turcica and the anterior coronoid process of the sphenoid and deviated towards the left causing an exit through the left temporal. The defect in the sphenoid (covered in this image by the probe illustrating the trajectory) and the shape and location of beveling on the exit defects link these two wounds together and establish the trajectory (Juan Carlos Tello, EPAF).

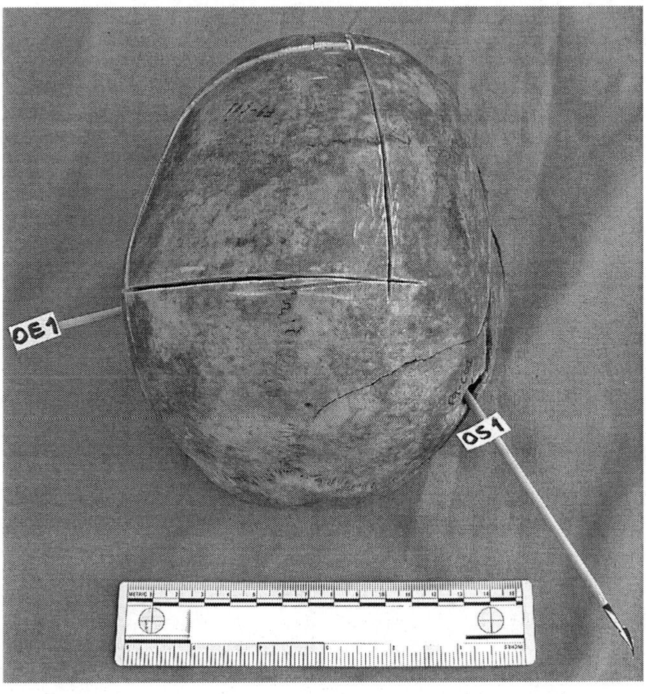

Figure 7.61a Superior view of the adult cranium. Single gunshot wound (GSW) to the left parietal perforated the cranium and exited through the right parietal. Note the apparent change in trajectory (Juan Carlos Tello, EPAF).

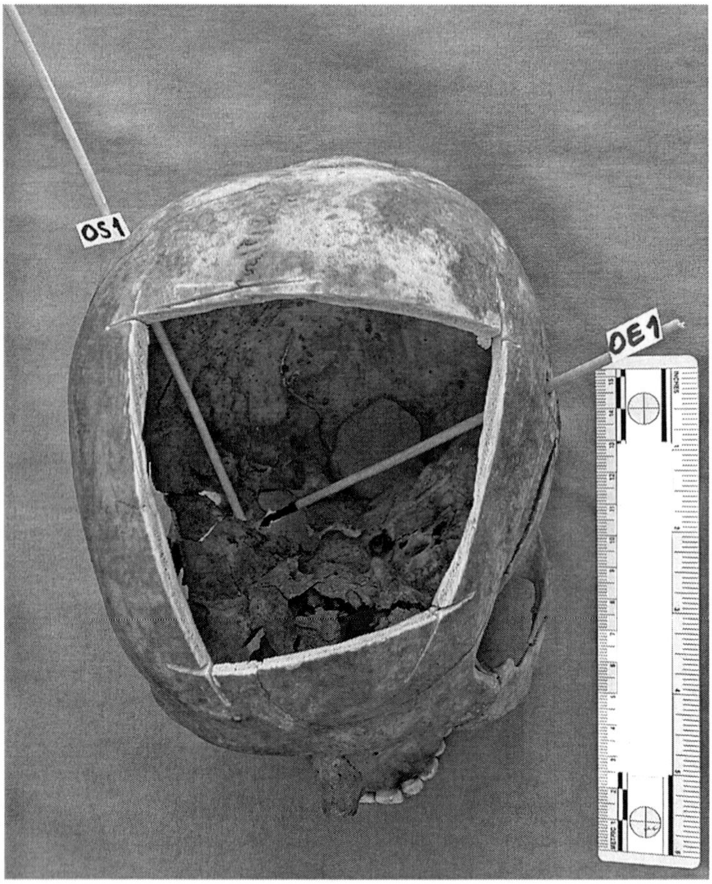

Figure 7.61b Endocranial view of the base of the skull. The projectile impacted the right sphenoid and temporal region, causing massive fracturing of the bone, deviated laterally, and exited (Juan Carlos Tello, EPAF).

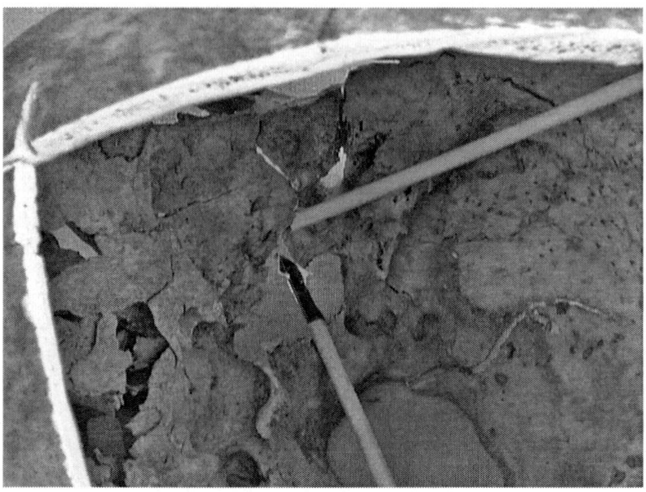

Figure 7.61c Close-up view. The individual may have been lying with the head (right side) against a solid surface such as the floor or ground (Juan Carlos Tello, EPAF).

because soft tissue exhibits features not evident on bone, such as an abrasion ring from the muzzle of a gun when fired on contact or gunpowder tattooing present in contact and near-contact shots (Di Maio 1999). So, can the range of fire be estimated from bone and what effect does range have on producing different wound characteristics? Typically, we can make broad generalizations about the distance of the shot based on skeletal morphology, differentiating contact or near-contact wounds from intermediate or distant fire, but precise distances are not calculated.

Contact and Close-Range Wounds

There are substantial morphological differences between contact wounds to the head from ammunition of different velocities. Contact wounds from low- or medium- velocity (i.e., 9 mm) ammunition will cause extensive fracturing but will not exhibit the major outward displacement of the fragments giving the impression of an "explosive injury." In contrast, contact wounds to the head from high-velocity rounds tend to obscure the exit defect due to intracranial pressure resulting in extensive fracturing. Large portions of the skull may be pushed outward giving the impression of an explosive injury. In contact wounds, the gas of the muzzle will follow the bullet into the wound cavity, causing a "blastlike injury" to this region (Di Maio 1999).

In general terms, close-range injuries to the head with high-velocity cartridges such as 7.62 × 39 mm will cause massive exit defects, sometimes more than ten times larger than the entrance wound. Contact wounds to the head are also characterized by soot deposits (Figure 7.62) on bone and circumferential delamination of the outer table (in cases of FMJ ammunition). Although there has not been a thorough study of the preservation of soot deposits on bone, it has been observed that soot may remain visible in dry burial conditions for many years after the incident. Figure 7.63 depicts a close-up gunfire entrance wound to the occipital bone of a victim of an extrajudicial execution, buried in soil for 23 years. The entrance wound is round, and there is circumferential delamination around the defect (indicative of FMJ). Note the black residue and soot deposit on the bone around the entrance wound. The bullet recovered was from a handgun (FMJ 9 mm). Based on the presence of soot, it is reasonable to conclude that the distance of the shot was contact or near contact (Di Maio 1999; Thali et al. 2002b).

Intermediate and Distant Range of Fire

Although the specific distance of fire, beyond contact and near contact, is indeterminate based solely on skeletal remains, there are certain characteristics that enable discrimination between handguns and rifles fired from a distance. In these examples, it is not so much a question of the type of weapon as the type of ammunition. For example, with regard to assault rifles, the approximate muzzle velocity of 700 m/s (high velocity) or more may be differentiated from handgun ammunition with an average muzzle velocity of 350 m/s (medium velocity).

From the examples presented, gunshot wounds to the head tend to fall into general patterns characterized by the extent of inflicted damage. The construction of the ammunition and the distance between the muzzle and target modify these patterns. The patterns of injury reflect the amount of destruction to the cranial vault and face, including the separation and loss of bony fragments in those areas. The trends described here apply to the first injury inflicted because, generally, subsequent shots to the head result in less fracturing.

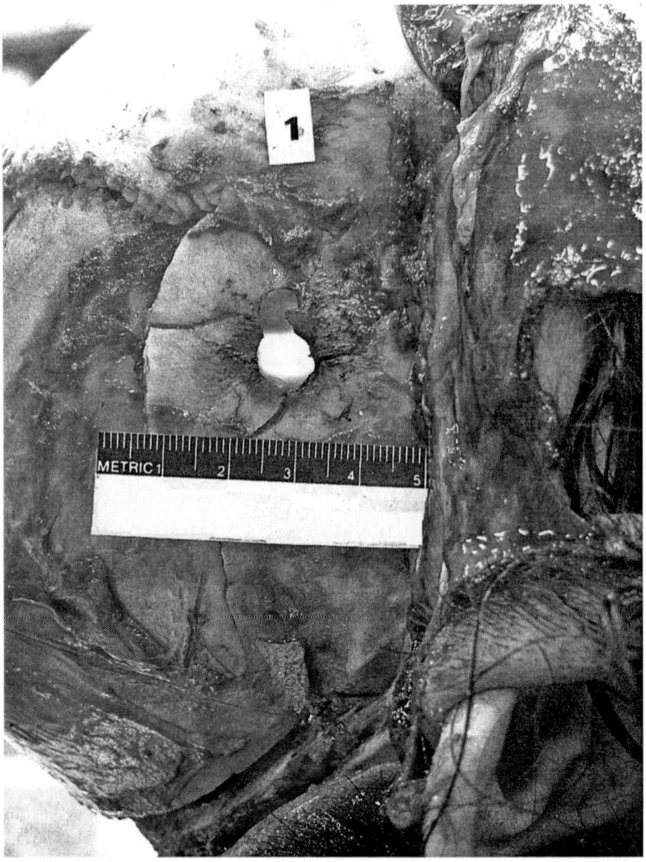

Figure 7.62 Contact wound of a suicide victim on the right temporal with a CZ 9 mm handgun illustrating soot deposit on the bone (Alain Wittmann).

The patterns described as follows illustrate the variation observed in cranial trauma from gunfire and demonstrate general trends:

Estimating Contact or Close Range

- High-velocity rounds: Extensive amount of destruction caused by high-velocity rounds fired at contact or close range (less than 5 cm between the muzzle and target). The full reconstruction of skeletal elements is compromised. Typically, more than half of the skull exhibits fracturing. Entrance and exit wounds may be difficult to discern (Figures 7.64–7.66).
- Medium-velocity rounds: The integrity of the cranial vault is maintained although complete or long radiating fractures extend across the vault with distinguishable entrance and exit defects visible. Displacement of bone fragments created by concentric fractures along already existing radiating fractures are common. Soot may be evident on bone at the site of entrance in contact/near-contact wounds (Figures 7.67–7.69).

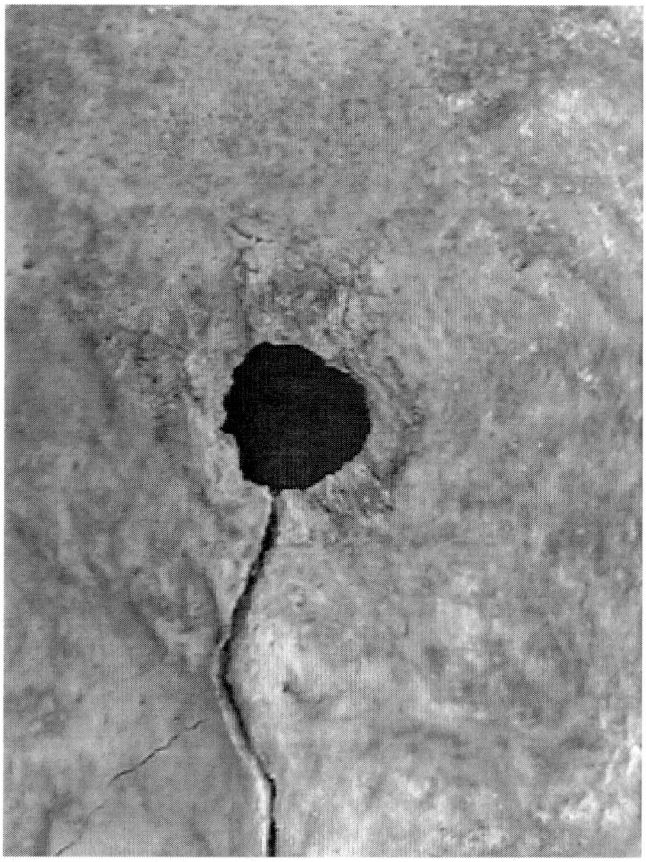

Figure 7.63 Posterior view, occipital bone of an adult. Circular defect, entrance wound. Soot present around the outer rim of the defect after 23 years of burial. Victim of an extrajudicial execution (Juan Carlos Tello, EPAF).

Estimating Intermediate Range

- High-velocity rounds impacting the skull at intermediate range tend to show small entrance (i.e., the cross section of the bullet) defects with large exit wounds and extensive fracturing (more than four times larger than the entrance defect). Fracturing is extensive including areas such as buttresses, yet the integrity of the skull is still maintained.
- Medium-velocity rounds at intermediate range tend to penetrate the skull without exit. The entrance is readily distinguishable and typically represents the cross section of the bullet. Fracturing is restricted to the areas of entrance. Incomplete exits are also common (Figures 7.70–7.72).

Estimating Intermediate Targets or Distant Range

- High-velocity rounds impacting intermediate targets may result in eccentric entrance wounds (i.e., the projectile enters sideways or base first).

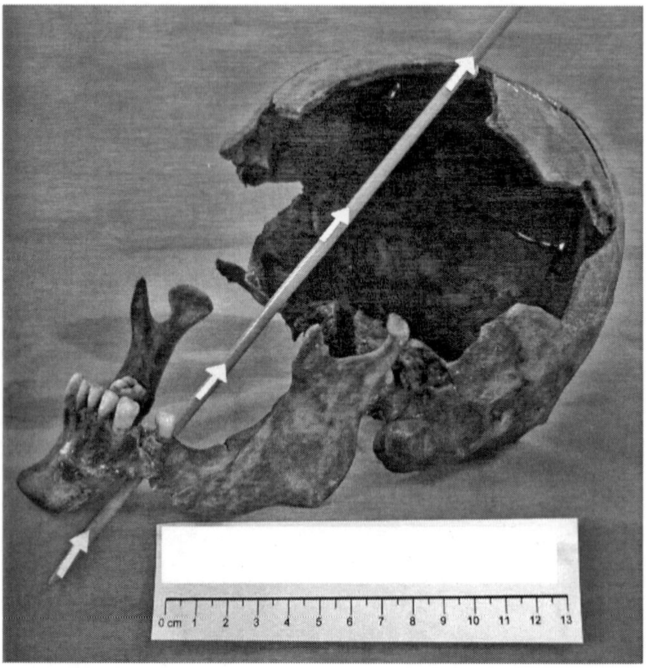

Figure 7.64 Left lateral/anterior view of the skull. Through-and-through shot penetrating the inferior margin of the mandible and causing fractures in at least two places. The projectile proceeds through the face penetrating the neurocranium and exits between both parietals along the midline. Observe the extent of damage and the amount of bone fragmentation, consistent with a high-velocity round fired at contact/near-contact range. (Printed with permission from International Criminal Tribunal for the former Yugoslavia [ICTY].)

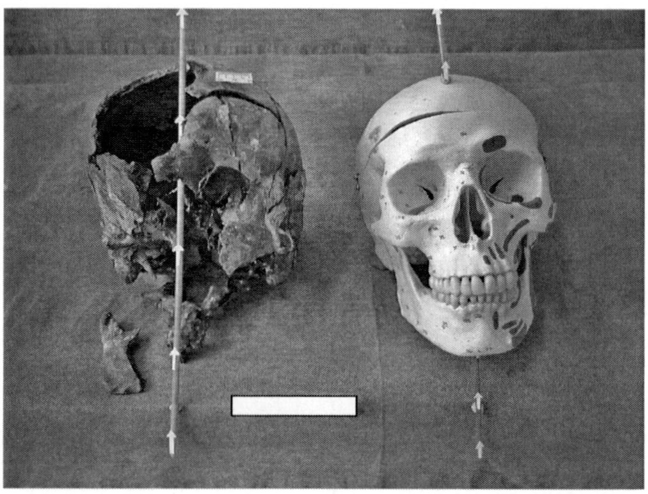

Figure 7.65 Anterior view of the skull with a single gunshot wound (GSW) (left) and plastic model for comparison (right). The trajectory of the bullet is demonstrated, arrows indicating direction of the shot (Alain Wittmann).

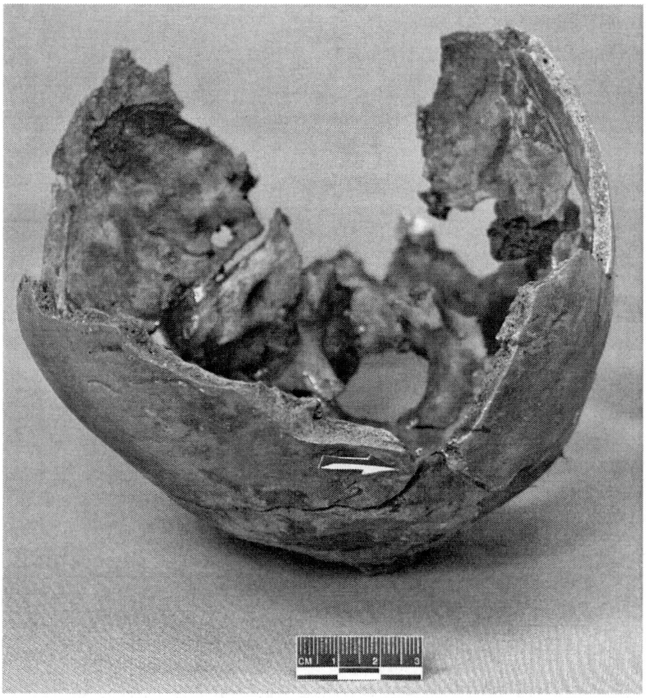

Figure 7.66 Posterior view of the skull with a rounded entrance defect on occipital bone. The defect is associated to multiple radiating fractures and to the loss of almost 50% of the neurocranium. The injury is consistent with a high-velocity round fired at contact/near-contact range (Alain Wittmann).

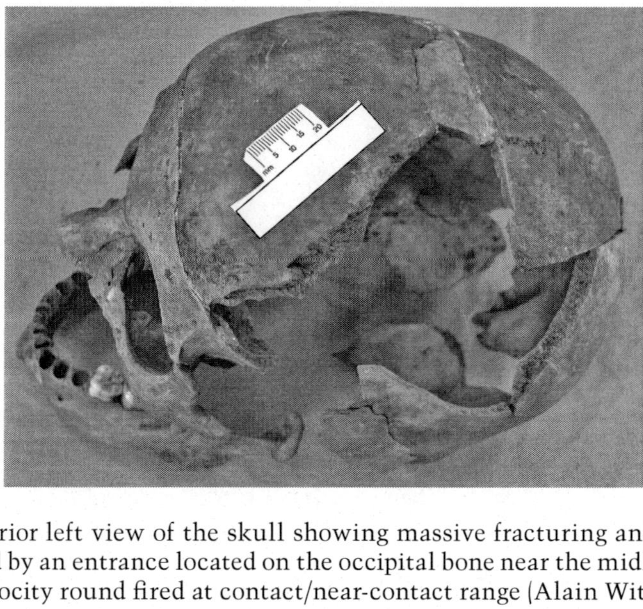

Figure 7.67 Superior left view of the skull showing massive fracturing and a large, irregular exit wound caused by an entrance located on the occipital bone near the midline. Injury consistent with high-velocity round fired at contact/near-contact range (Alain Wittmann).

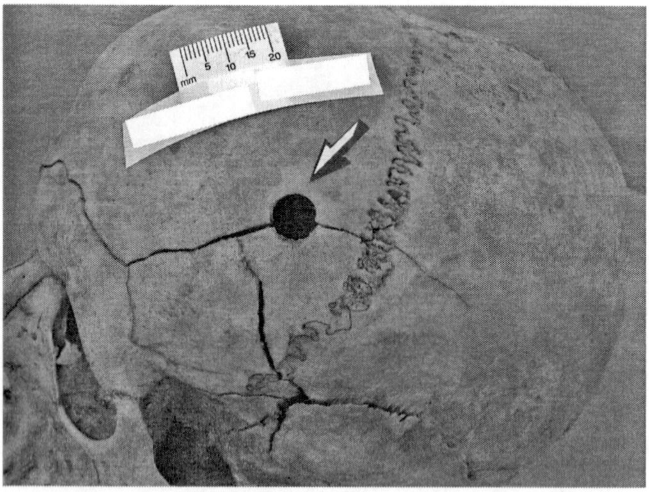

Figure 7.68 Superior left view of the skull showing a through-and-through gunshot wound (GSW). Circular entrance wound pictured on the frontal bone along the coronal suture. Radiating fractures are originating from both sides of the defect, but the general integrity of the skull is maintained (Alain Wittmann).

- Wounds resulting from shots fired from a distance impact with less force than closer shots, and bullets may penetrate thicker structures with minimal damage. The injuries tend to penetrate but not perforate the skull.
- Medium-velocity rounds tend to create minimal damage at the entrance and may not fully penetrate the structure, or may also become embedded in the bone (Figure 7.73).

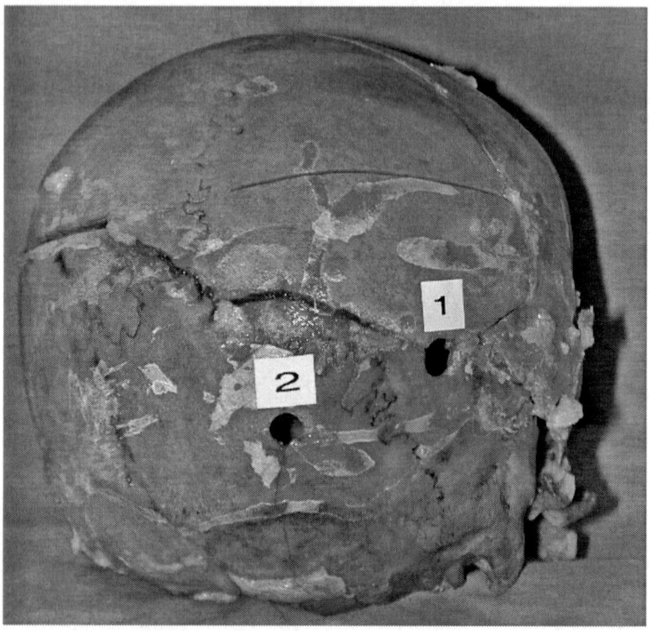

Figure 7.69a Posterior view of the skull with two gunshot wounds. The shots are labeled in the order they were inflicted. The first shot is associated with the long radiating fracture running laterally and anteriorly (ICTY).

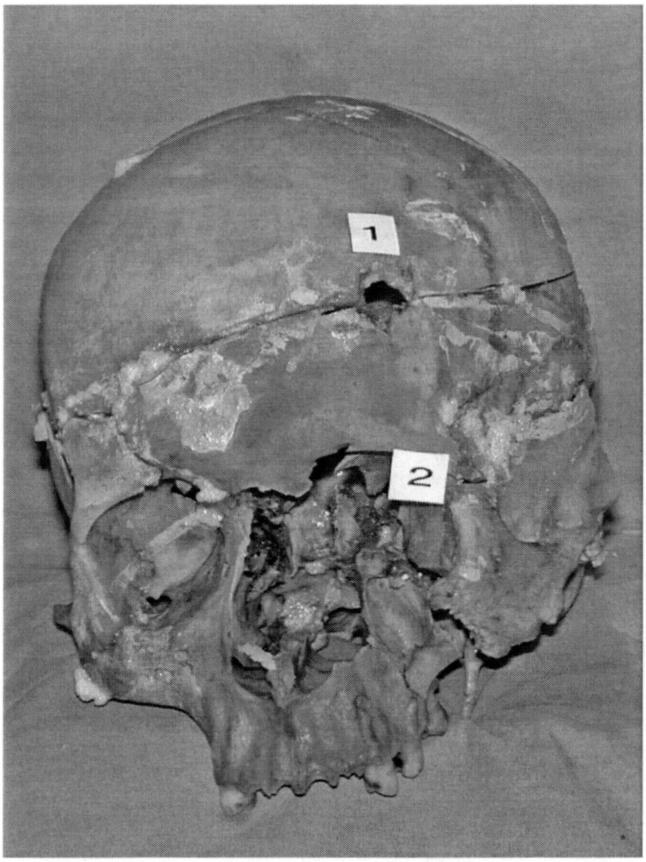

Figure 7.69b Anterior view. Two exit wounds through the frontal bone and left orbit. Observe the general integrity of the skull. Destruction is limited to the exit defects and associated radiating fractures. (Printed with permission from International Criminal Tribunal for the former Yugoslavia [ICTY].)

Shotgun Injuries

In cases of shotgun injuries, the distance of fire is evident from the size and severity of the defects and the spread or diameter of pellet injuries. Techniques for estimating the range and the accuracy of these methods have been extensively discussed in the literature (Nag and Sinha 1992; Horvath et al. 1993; and Rowe 2005). Contact shotgun wounds in bone are very evident and tend to mimic high-velocity rounds fired at the same range. The gases are expelled from the muzzle and the pellets are expelled in a tight pattern, resulting in a larger wound than a typical bullet entrance. The pellets may be followed by the plastic cap and *wadding*. The wadding or cap may even be present embedded in tissue (refer again to Figure 7.19). Intermediate and distant shots are distinguished by the spread of pellets, which generally increases with the distance. The dispersion of pellets during flight is a function of both distance and the size/weight of the pellets (Cakir et al. 2003). Estimation of the range of fire based on the pellet distribution is at times unreliable due to the "billiard ball effect" (Messmer and Fierro 1986). The billiard ball effect occurs as the pellets

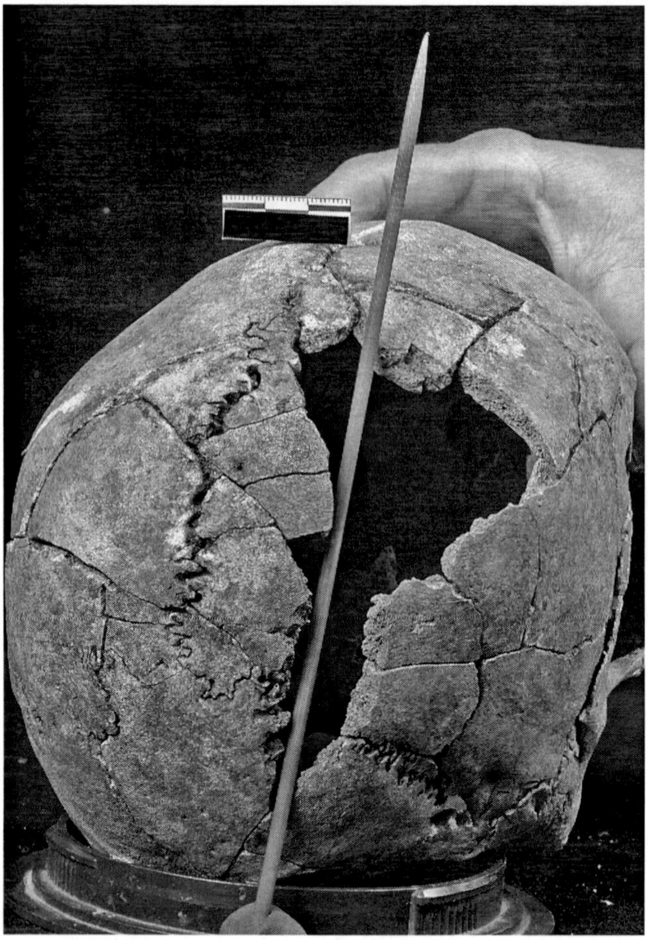

Figure 7.70a Eccentric shaped entrance wound. The bullet penetrates the skull at a tangential angle almost creating a long keyhole. The bullet exits the skull through a large, irregular defect that coalesces with the entrance. Observe multiple radiating and concentric fractures at entrance and exit (Carlos Jacinto, FAFG).

penetrate soft tissue. The first pellets to hit the body will be slowed by the resistance of the tissue. Subsequent pellets impact against the first pellets, creating a larger wound area of pellets than would be expected. Consequently, when only skeletal tissue remains, estimating the range of fire from bone should be approached cautiously or even avoided.

Pellets may penetrate bone but perforate or exit the body only in particular circumstances, such as contact wounds (Harruff 1995). In cases where pellets perforate bone, the resulting wound morphology is consistent with wounds caused by perforating bullets. Therefore, internal and external beveling will be common features in such injuries, and the diameter of the wounds will generally correspond to the size and shape of the pellets. The larger and heavier the pellet, the more resistant it is to perforate bone and therefore has a greater likelihood of deformation. When pellets do penetrate bone, the defects are likely to be circular in shape, reflecting the pattern or morphology of the projectile.

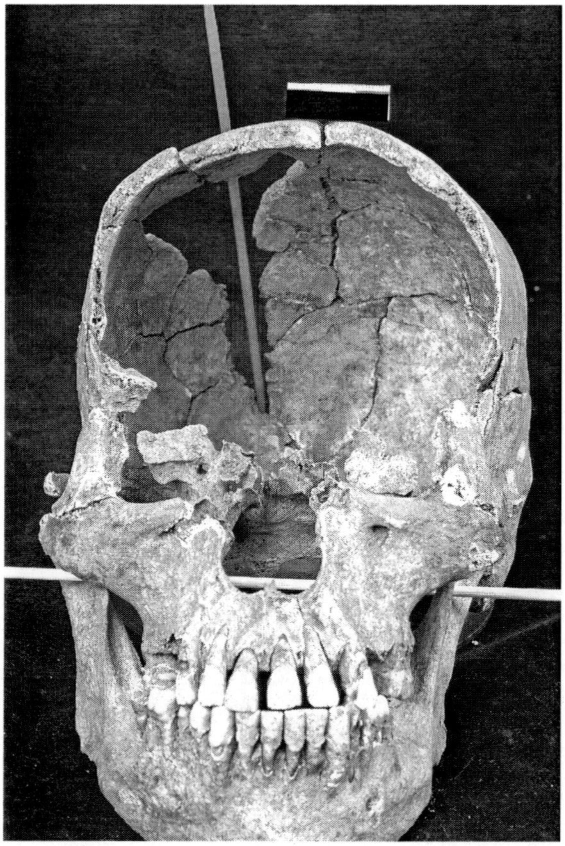

Figure 7.70b Anterior view of the same individual who sustained a second shot through the condyle and coronoid process of the mandible (Carlos Jacinto, FAFG).

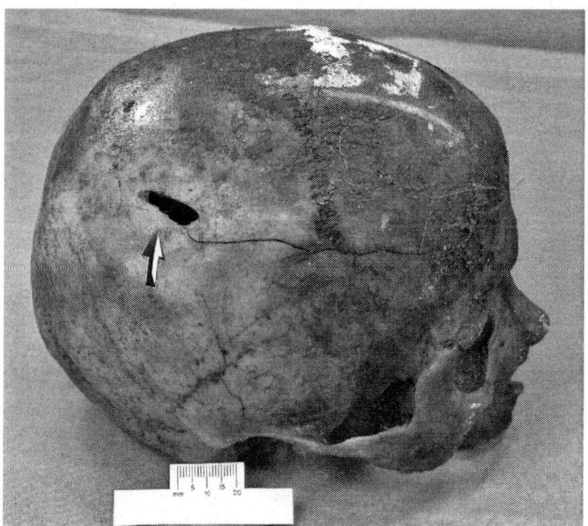

Figure 7.71a Adult skull showing a "triangle-shaped" defect on the right parietal and an associated isolated radiating fracture extending anteriorly (ICTY).

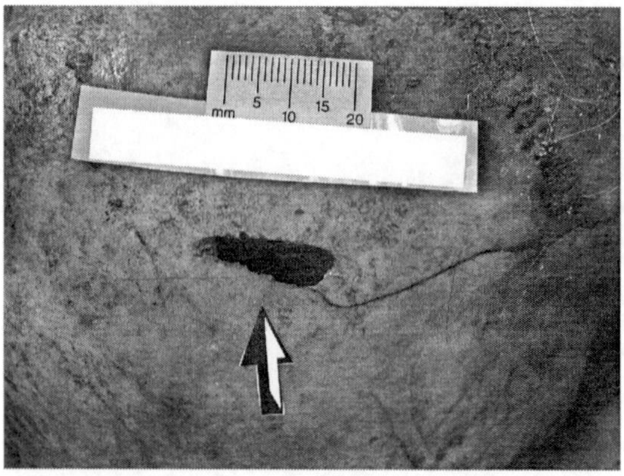

Figure 7.71b Close-up detail of the defect, consistent with the cross section of 7.62 × 39 mm bullet (ICTY).

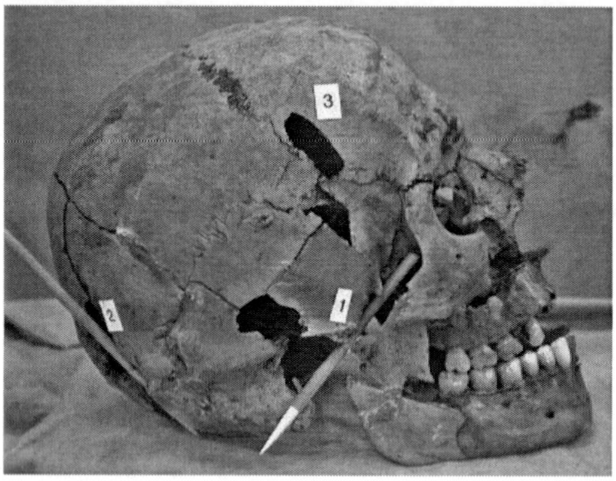

Figure 7.72 Multiple entrance wounds with different shapes on the left parietal (from left to right): (1) oval-shaped wound consistent with bullet striking the bone sideways, (2) circular, almost keyhole shaped indicating the bullet struck the bone tangentially from back to front, (3) keyhole shape defect, almost a gutter wound with external beveling indicating the bullet also struck tangentially from back to front, and (4) circular defect to occipital bone (ICTY).

Figure 7.73a Comparison of two mandibular fractures caused by different mechanisms, blunt force trauma (BFT) and a gunshot wound (GSW). The mandibular fracture resulting from BFT (a) to the face exhibits a discrete "butterfly" fracture along the inferior margin (Alain Wittmann).

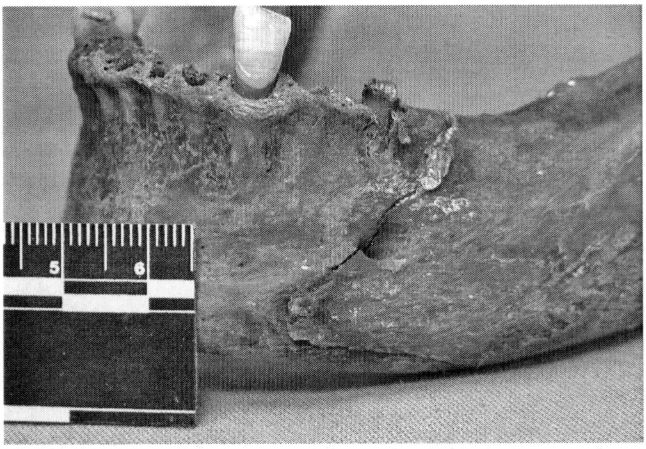

Figure 7.73b Indirect mandibular fracture caused by intraoral GSW. Breakaway spur is external indicating the force was applied internally (Alain Wittmann).

Estimating the Number of Injuries

Estimating the minimum number of injuries depends on the correct calculation and interpretation of each wound. An entry and exit wound on a skull may represent two distinct wounds but only one injury. In cases of multiple wounds, it is necessary to determine which associate together so that an accurate and minimum number of the injuries may be estimated. Essential to the estimation of wound number is first establishing what defects are wounds and how multiple regions may be affected in combination. For example, a shot to the head may also produce a wound in the forearm if the individual had his arm in front of his face at the time he was shot. (The body may be in any position when injured and the orientation of the shooter to the victim and the position of the weapon relative to the body of the victim at the time of the incident may vary.) Therefore, reconstructing events around the injury enables interpretations about the fracture patterns or defects. Such information is not always evident; therefore, the investigator must estimate the most likely scenario based on the facts of the case, rather than conjecture. Figure 7.74 shows the superior view of a skull with four visible and distinct defects numbered clockwise:

1. A rounded defect with external beveling on the anterior aspect, and no radiating fractures. The defect is consistent with a keyhole, from back to front and slightly right to left.
2. An oval defect with external beveling on the anterior half, also consistent with a keyhole defect, from back to front (there are traces of some metallic substance present, an artifact not to be confused with bullet wipe).
3. A large oblong-shaped defect with no external beveling but associated multiple radiating fractures. It is likely that this defect was caused by the lateral entrance of the projectile and was the first impact to the head. The endocranial view of all four defects show internal beveling. It is probable that these injuries were inflicted with a handgun.

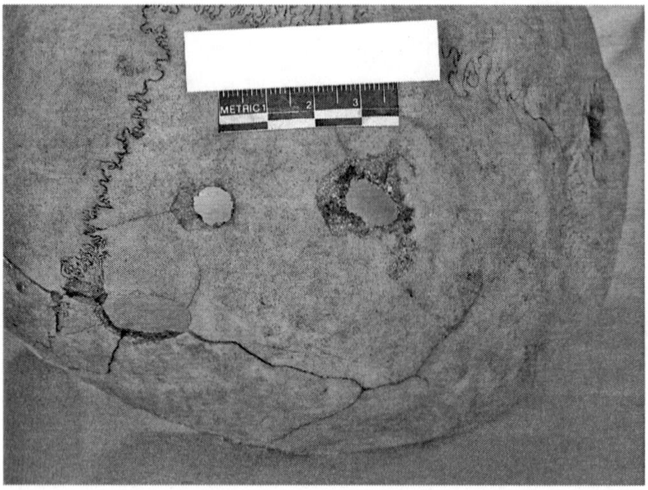

Figure 7.74a Multiple entrance wounds with different shapes on the left parietal (from left to right): (1) oval-shaped wound consistent with bullet striking the bone sideways, (2) almost keyhole-shaped wound indicating the bullet struck the bone tangentially from back to front, (3) keyhole-shaped defect, almost a gutter wound with external beveling indicating the bullet also struck tangentially from back to front, and (4) circular defect to occipital bone (ICTY).

Sequencing Multiple Gunfire Injuries

The intersection of multiple fracture lines is useful to sequence shots (as already discussed in Chapter 4). Figures 7.75 and 7.76 illustrate examples of multiple gunfire injuries with intersecting fractures, allowing for an estimation of the minimum number of injuries. Intersecting fractures are commonly found in the cranial vault, ilium, scapula, or long

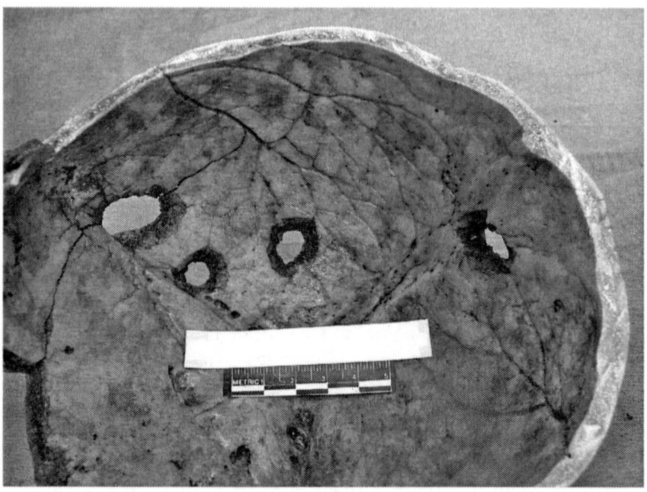

Figure 7.74b Endocranial view of the previous defects (refer to Figure 7.74a). Four gunshot entrance wounds are present. Note the extensive and complete internal beveling on the endocranial surface. There are a minimum of four injuries pictured here. Note the general absence of fracturing; injuries are likely caused by a handgun. (Printed with permission from International Criminal Tribunal for the former Yugoslavia [ICTY].)

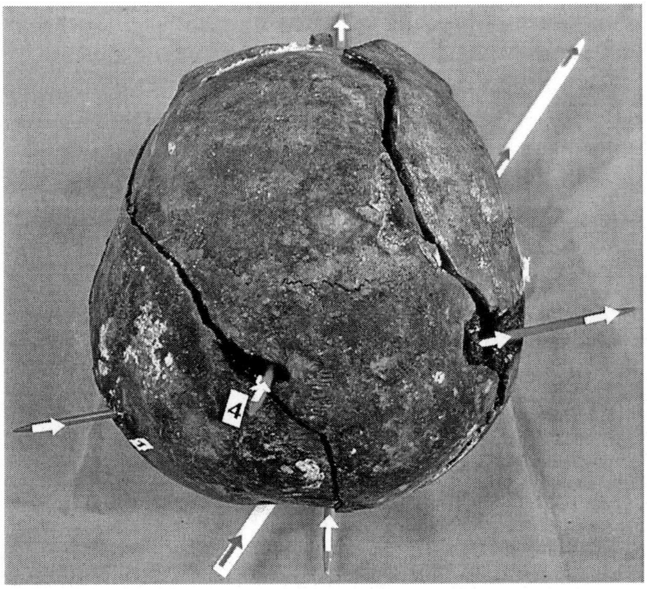

Figure 7.75 Superior view, adult crania. Multiple (n = 4) gunshot wounds through the skull, likely caused by a handgun. Probes indicate the bullet trajectories. (Printed with permission from International Criminal Tribunal for the former Yugoslavia [ICTY].)

bones. Experience shows that in the cranium, the first shot will cause most of the fracturing, whereas subsequent shots produce fewer or no fractures. Generally, through analysis of intersecting fracture lines, the order of multiple shots or injuries may be estimated. Although this technique was originally applied to blunt force trauma, by definition a low

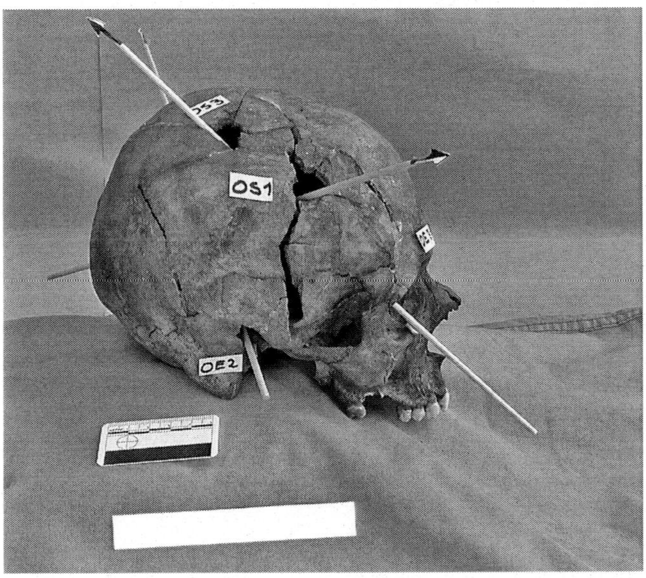

Figure 7.76 Multiple (n = 4) perforating gunshot wounds through the head, likely caused by a handgun. Probes indicate trajectories 2 right to left and 2 left to right (Carlos Jacinto, FAFG).

loading force, it can also be applied to gunfire injuries. Having said that, some high-velocity rounds occasionally break this rule by cutting across preexisting fracture lines. Intersecting fracture lines are further discussed in Chapter 8.

Wounds from different caliber ammunition present in the same individual may further indicate there were multiple shooters (Messmer et al. 2003). By establishing the order of shots based on fracture patterns, the sequence may be established. Other criteria, such as the patterns and shapes of defects will be useful for estimating the different number of projectiles and thereby inferring the number of shooters (which also may provide evidence of a crime or intent).

Summary Guidelines for Best Practice

The morphological features of skeletal trauma occurring from firearms result from the interaction between the material properties of the projectiles and the subsequent reaction of soft and skeletal tissues. Gunfire, unlike fragmented projectile or shrapnel injuries due to a blast, shows more predictable trends in defect morphology and fracture patterning because of consistency in the morphology and construction of ammunition. There is a wide range of factors that influence trauma morphology. This chapter summarized some of that variation and discussed patterns that may be useful for interpreting GSW. Of critical importance is the information revealed through skeletal GSW, which is more than sufficient to classify the mechanism of injury, the number of injuries, and direction of fire. Evidence such as the general range of fire, caliber of ammunition, class of weapon may be inferred from skeletal trauma, *albeit with caution,* depending on the case. Sequencing gunfire wounds is only possible when structural relationships among injuries (i.e., fracture lines) exist. Evidence may also show investigators whether there was more than one shooter, or indicate other information necessary to demonstrate criminal activity. The best practice recommendations when dealing with probable evidence of gunfire trauma is to reconstruct broken fragments to the extent possible, to ascertain it is in fact a gunshot wound, and to measure and describe each of the defects so associations may be drawn about related wounds to elucidate the number of injuries, the direction of fire, and whether the gunshot event is related to blunt force or other mechanisms of injury that may demonstrate a sequence of traumatic events leading up to the individual's death.

Case Study 7.1: Gunfire Basics

C. J. (Jack) Waters
Retired Police Sergeant
Forensic Investigation Unit
Tampa Police Department, Florida

There are numerous types of firearms, and most are beyond the scope of this book. Firearms are normally classified by the purpose for which they are designed and, within those categories, by the type of action they use to cause the propellant to push the projectile out of the barrel. They are also classified by design—to be used by one person or a crew. Crew-served weapons include heavy machine guns, cannons, automatic cannons, missiles, and rocket-propelled grenades (RPG). Individual weapons include handguns, rifles, submachine guns, and shotguns. Figures 7.77–7.96 illustrate common examples of firearms and ammunition, particularly as encountered in HHRR investigations, largely from cases presented throughout this book.

Cannons can use many different types of projectiles, but our primary interest in these weapons involve the type that explodes, either on contact or through a fuse that causes them to explode at a certain altitude or certain time upon firing. Exploding types of projectiles cause wounds by oddly shaped bits of metal from its casing or by round balls within the casing propelled in all directions upon explosion. RPGs, antipersonnel missiles, and other exploding ordnance also cause oddly shaped wounds from flying shrapnel (refer to chapter 3 for injuries resulting from blast injuries, penetrating projectiles, and guidelines for differential diagnosis of gunfire ammunition from fragmented shrapnel).

Rifles and shotguns are normally thought of as shoulder-fired weapons, as they are designed to be placed against the shoulder and held with both hands for firing. Handguns are so called because they are designed to be held in one or both hands and fired without being braced against the shoulder. The type of action classifies rifles, such as fully automatic, semiautomatic, bolt action, lever action, slide action (pump), single shot (breech loading), and muzzle loading. When a rifle described as *automatic* is fired, some of the energy from the shot is used to cycle the rifle's action to prepare the firearm for the next shot. This can be accomplished by capturing some of the gases produced by the combustion process from

Figure 7.77 Pistol recovered from a grave, CZ 7.65 mm. (Printed with permission from International Criminal Tribunal for the former Yugoslavia [ICTY].)

Figure 7.78 Example of an UZI. (Image courtesy of IWI Ltd, Israel and Modern Firearms at http:// world.guns.ru/main-e.htm.)

Figure 7.79 Pictured is a sample of the APS 94 Croatia assault rifle. This is similar to the Soviet Union's AK 47. Assault rifles with these characteristics have been made in many nations previously influenced by the Soviet Union (Modern Firearms at http://worldguns.ru/main-e.htm).

Figure 7.80 Semiautomatic shotgun, Browning "Auto 5" in 12 gauge. (Image courtesy of Max Popenker, Modern Firearms at http://world.guns.ru/main-e.htm.)

Figure 7.81 Rifle ammunition, bottleneck cartridge case, 5.56 × 45 mm NATO (standard military issue). (Image courtesy of Oleg Volk and Modern Firearms at http://world.guns.ru/main-e.htm.)

Figure 7.82 Handgun ammunition, a 9 × 19 mm pistol version with an expanding bullet, for civilian/police use. (Image courtesy of Oleg Volk and Modern Firearms at http://world.guns.ru/main-e.htm.)

Figure 7.83a Overview of a 7.62 × 39 mm expanded bullet with blunt tip, jacket torn, and lead sheet exposed. The steel core is also exposed (Alain Wittmann).

Figure 7.83b The three layers are shown separately (refer to Figure 7.83a). (Printed with permission from International Criminal Tribunal for the former Yugoslavia [ICTY].)

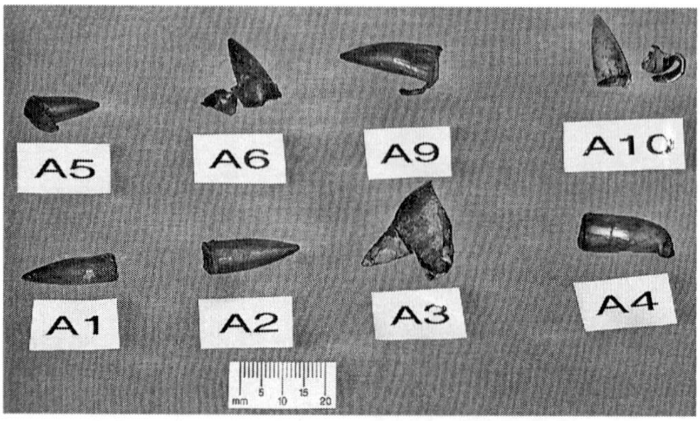

Figure 7.84 Eight 7.62 × 39 mm bullets recovered from the same individual (refer to Figure 7.83a). A6 and A3 are only jacket fragments. (Printed with permission from International Criminal Tribunal for the former Yugoslavia [ICTY].)

the barrel and using a gas cylinder and piston to cycle the action. Most automatic rifles and heavy and light machine guns use this system. The prominent cylinder on top of the AK-47 contains the gas system. Another and simpler type of action, called a *blowback action*, uses the recoil from the burning gases to cycle the action.

Fully automatic means that if the trigger is pulled and held down the weapon will be fired, the energy from that shot will cause the action to cycle, another shot will be fired, and so forth. In general, multiple shots will be fired as long as the trigger is held down. If the trigger is held long enough, the firearm will be emptied of its ammunition supply with one pull of the trigger. Semiautomatic means that when the trigger is pulled, one shot is fired, and the energy from that shot causes the action to cycle, preparing the firearm to fire another shot. However, the firearm will only fire one shot per pull of the trigger. The trigger must be released and pulled again to fire the second and all subsequent shots. With a bolt action, the shooter pulls the trigger to fire one shot. The shooter must then use the

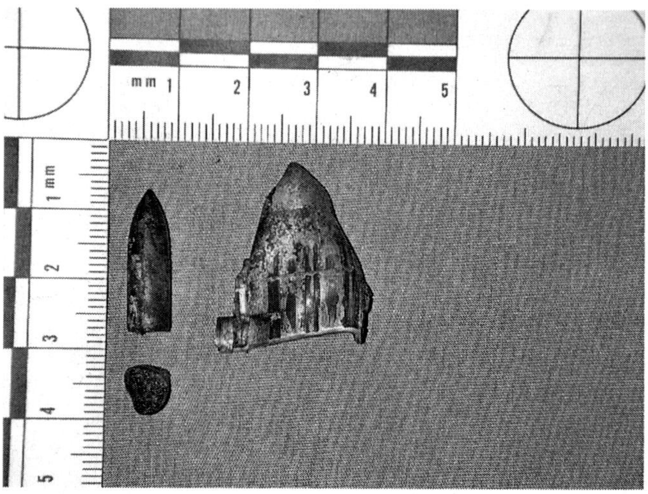

Figure 7.85 Overview of a bullet core with fragmented base and jacket, 7.62 × 39 mm. (Printed with permission from International Criminal Tribunal for the former Yugoslavia [ICTY].)

Figure 7.86 Comparison of two shell cases, rifle and handgun, respectively, 7.62 × 51 mm (NATO) and a 9 mm Parabellum. (Printed with permission from International Criminal Tribunal for the former Yugoslavia [ICTY].)

trigger hand to grasp a handle protruding from the right side of the receiver and move it up and rearward, then forward, and downward to extract and eject the fired cartridge, cock the weapon, and insert a new unfired cartridge into the firing chamber. Lever and slide actions are similar, except for the required movements. Breech loading or single-shot

Figure 7.87 Two 7.62 × 39 mm bullets. The bullet on the left lost the tip, typically made of lead. The bullet jacket on the right is torn open. (Printed with permission from International Criminal Tribunal for the former Yugoslavia [ICTY].)

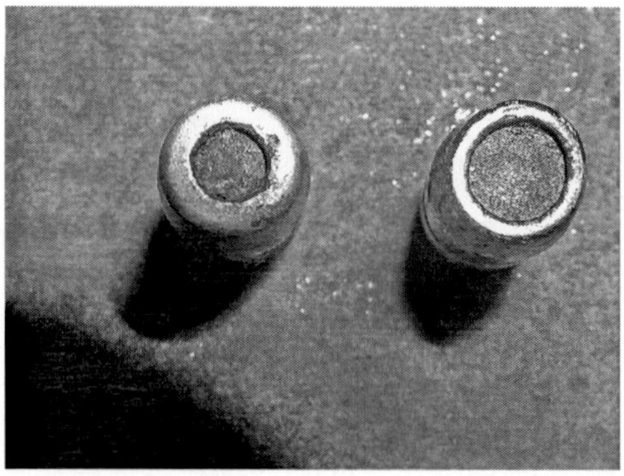

Figure 7.88 The bases of two bullets are shown. The base on the left is from an armor-piercing bullet with a steel core, and the base on the right is from a regular lead core bullet. (Printed with permission from International Criminal Tribunal for the former Yugoslavia [ICTY].)

Figure 7.89 A complete 7.62 × 39 mm bullet embedded in mummified tissue. (Printed with permission from International Criminal Tribunal for the former Yugoslavia [ICTY].)

Figure 7.90 Three 9 mm bullets found associated with a body. (Printed with permission from International Criminal Tribunal for the former Yugoslavia [ICTY].)

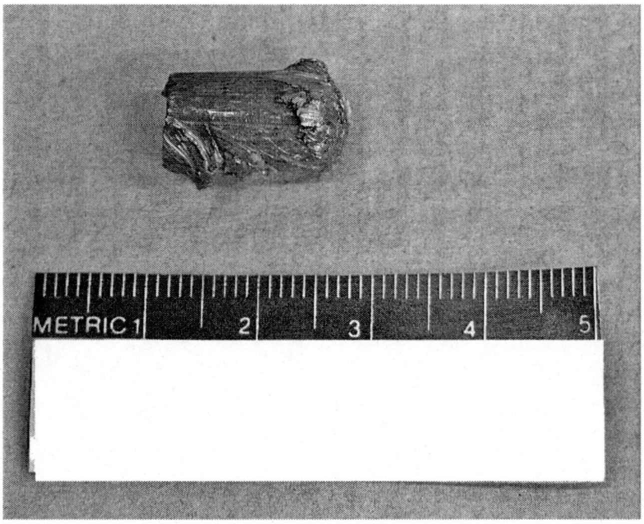

Figure 7.91 Lead cast bullet with rifling resulting from the passage through the muzzle of the gun. (Printed with permission from International Criminal Tribunal for the former Yugoslavia [ICTY].)

rifles are loaded by unlocking the breech, tilting the barrel downward, inserting a single cartridge into the firing chamber, and then tilting the barrel back into line with the stock and thereby locking it. After the weapon is fired, the same process is repeated to prepare it to fire again. Some breech loading rifles and shotguns have two barrels; rarely, some have three. Muzzle loading should be self-explanatory. Modern muzzle loading weapons are

Figure 7.92 Deformed FMJ handgun bullet. (Printed with permission from International Criminal Tribunal for the former Yugoslavia [ICTY].)

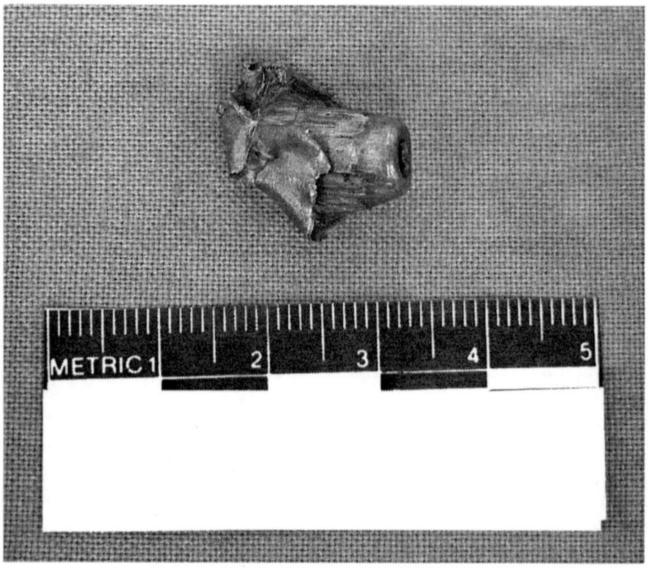

Figure 7.93 High-velocity (7.62 × 39 mm) bullet fragment with a shredded jacket. (Printed with permission from International Criminal Tribunal for the former Yugoslavia [ICTY].)

either replicas or hunting rifles. They always use rather soft lead projectiles, either ball- or conical-shaped.

Most fully automatic and semiautomatic rifles are supplied with ammunition via a box-type magazine. The magazine is a small box made of metal or plastic, with a spring-loaded platform called a *follower,* which pushes against the top of the magazine. Ammunition is loaded into the magazine against the spring tension. The magazine is then inserted into the

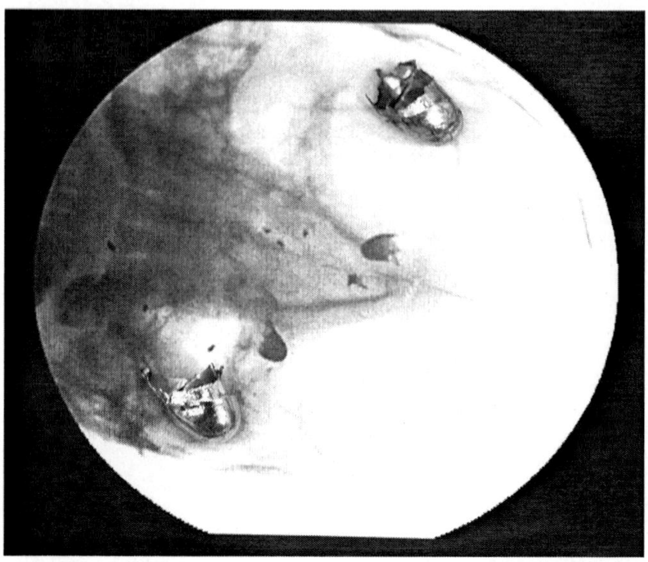

Figure 7.94 Fluoroscope image showing two metal jacket fragments removed from the skull of a homicide victim. The actual jacket fragments are shown next to the image. (Printed with permission from International Criminal Tribunal for the former Yugoslavia [ICTY].)

Figure 7.95a Lead mushroomed handgun bullet following impact. (Printed with permission from International Criminal Tribunal for the former Yugoslavia [ICTY].)

rifle's magazine well. To fire the weapon, the bolt is pulled to the rear by hand using some type of handle provided for the purpose, cocking the weapon. When the bolt is released, it slides forward, and the lower edge catches the rear of the top cartridge in the magazine and pushes it into the firing chamber of the firearm. The weapon is then ready to fire. Using a box magazine means that the shooter may carry spare magazines already loaded with

Figure 7.95b Inferior (base) view of the same bullet (refer to Figure 7.95a). (Printed with permission from International Criminal Tribunal for the former Yugoslavia [ICTY].)

Figure 7.96 Fired shotgun cartridge showing plastic cap and buckshot lead pellets recovered from a body. (Printed with permission from International Criminal Tribunal for the former Yugoslavia [ICTY].)

ammunition and has the ability to very quickly get the weapon back into action, after the magazine is emptied. Sometimes a magazine is called a clip. However, this is inaccurate as a clip is a steel cage that holds ammunition within by friction. It does not have a spring and built-in follower as the magazine does. Clips are used in some firearms, most notably the M1 Garand, the U.S. rifle of World War II fame. Other rifles have internal magazines with the ammunition loaded directly into the magazine from the top or side of the rifle. These rifles are normally loaded by hand, one round at a time. During World War I, stripper clips were invented, which are metal strips that hold five rounds, the capacity of most bolt action rifles of the time. Stripper clips allow the rifleman to open the bolt action, set it in place, and shove all five cartridges down into the breech at once. Some hunting and plinking rifles use a tubular-shaped magazine under the barrel.

Shotguns come in all of the same types of actions as rifles, with the possible exception of fully automatic (quite probably, now that I have written this, someone will start building a fully automatic shotgun).

Handguns also are available in different types of actions, including pistol (automatic, semiautomatic, and self-loader), revolver (single and double action), single shot, and muzzle loader. Although most pistols are mislabeled "automatic," in reality they are closer to the semiautomatic action described previously. There are a few fully automatic handguns, as they are difficult to control and are fairly rare.

In general, pistols can be identified because they are flat in shape and their ammunition supply is contained within a magazine. The magazine well is usually built into the handle, in modern pistols, although there have been pistols built with the magazine placed well forward of the handle. To fire the first shot, the pistol normally needs to be operated by hand. There will usually be a series of grooves to assist the shooter in grasping the slide of the pistol with a sweaty hand. The slide must be pulled to the rear, cocking the pistol, then released. As the slide moves forward, the lower edge of the bolt catches the top round in the magazine and slides it forward into the firing chamber. The pistol is now ready to fire by simply pulling the trigger. Most pistols are blowback-operated.

Another type of handgun is the revolver. Revolvers contain a cylindrical-shaped piece of steel that contains five or more firing chambers. Each firing chamber is loaded with a cartridge. The revolver operates by turning the cylinder until a cartridge is lined up with the rear of the barrel. The normally exposed hammer is cocked. When the shooter pulls the trigger, the hammer flies forward under the impetus of the main spring. The front of the hammer contains a firing pin. When it strikes the percussion cap, the cartridge fires. The expanding gases propel the projectile out of the cartridge and firing chamber, through the barrel of the revolver, and out.

Revolvers can be characterized by two types of actions: single action and double action. These terms refer to how the revolver is operated. In single action, the shooter must cock the hammer, which also rotates the cylinder, with the thumb of his shooting hand or off hand. This is accomplished by pulling the hammer to the rear until it catches and stays there. At this point, if the trigger is pulled, the revolver will fire. After firing, the shooter must again pull the hammer to the rear to prepare the weapon for the next shot. Double action means that the cocking of the hammer and rotating of the cylinder can be accomplished simply by pulling the trigger with the shooting hand. As the trigger is pulled, the cylinder rotates and the hammer moves to the rear. When the hammer reaches the release point, it automatically releases and fires the handgun. Double action is designed to allow the shooter to get the revolver into action quickly but is much less accurate than single action due to the long and heavy trigger pull. Handguns can also be single shot, top break, or muzzle loaded.

Another design in military weapons is the submachine gun. This is a weapon that is a combination of the rifle and pistol. It is larger than most pistols and is normally fired with two hands, or it may be shoulder fired. Submachine guns fire light recoil pistol ammunition and are capable of fully automatic fire. Some examples are the .45 caliber Thompson submachine gun made famous by the Ma Barker gang and the Federal Bureau of Investigation, the Sten gun of British World War II fame, and the MP34 (MachinenPistole, 1934) used by the German Wermacht in World War II. The Sten and MP34 both fire 9 mm pistol ammunition. Another famous and more modern weapon of this type is the Uzi developed by the Israeli defense force, which also fires 9 mm pistol ammunition.

Firearms are designed to be used for various purposes, such as the killing of people, hunting, serious marksmanship contests, or amateur marksmanship (plinking). Regardless of the purpose, all have been used to kill people, just as a baseball bat, a machete, or an ax although designed for specific purposes, make very efficient killing instruments at the same time (refer to numerous examples throughout this book).

Modern firearms use fixed cartridges. A cartridge consists of four different parts. The projectile, the case, the primer (percussion cap), and the propellant (gun powder). There are three different methods to describe the size of the various types of ammunition. These are caliber, gauge, and metric. Gauge is a holdover from the days of muzzle-loading cannon and large muskets, and refers to the weight of a projectile. A "twelve pounder" cannon fired a round iron ball that weighed 12 pounds. A 12 gauge shotgun describes a gun that fires a lead ball sized so that it would take 12 balls to make a pound. A 20 gauge shotgun fires a ball sized so that it would take 20 to make a pound. At various times through history, shotguns in 8-10-12-16-20, and 28 gauge sizes have been popular. In modern times, a 12 gauge shotgun has a bore diameter of .729 in. The only exception to this rule is the .410 shotgun, in which case the .410 is the actual size in thousandths of an inch.

Another measuring system used for guns and their ammunition is the metric system. Using this system, the bullet or bore diameter is expressed in millimeters. Sometimes, the length of the case is included as a second figure, and often there are multiple ways to describe the same cartridge. One of the most common military cartridges today is called the 9 mm parabellum, 9 mm Luger, or 9 × 19 mm. *Luger* refers to Georg Luger who invented the pistol that bears his name. *Parabellum* is a word that was coined by a German firearm manufacturer from a Latin phrase, *si vis pacem, para bellum,* which means "if you want peace, prepare for war." Parabellum was used to describe the original Luger cartridge, a 6.35 mm parabellum, and its later derivative, the 9 mm parabellum. The original Luger used the 6.35 mm parabellum (.30 Luger in the United States). When the German Army decided to adopt the Luger pistol as their standard sidearm, they demanded a larger, more powerful cartridge as the 6.35 mm was deemed too weak for military use. Thus, the 9 mm parabellum was developed. This is the standard pistol cartridge for the U.S. military, as well as of many other nations. There is also a 9 mm short, which in the United States is called the .380. World War II German Mausers were manufactured with dimensions of 7.92 × 57 mm; this caliber is variously referred to as 7.9 mm or 8 mm.

Traditionally in the United States, caliber has been measured in thousandths of an inch. In addition, occasionally the numbers will be expanded to include additional information. Somehow, during the settling of the American West, a bullet .357 in. in diameter came to be called .38 caliber. Therefore, one of the most common types of ammunition in the United States is the .38 special cartridge. Before the advent of pistols in police work, nearly every police jurisdiction in the nation carried the .38 special revolver. To compound the confusion, there is also a .38 S&W round which is also .357 in. in diameter. It was originally made by the Smith & Wesson gun manufacturing company but now is made by many other manufacturers as well. The difference between the .38 S&W and the .38 Special is that the cartridge case for the S&W is shorter. However, the .38 special was originally developed as a black powder cartridge, and its cartridge case is much larger than necessary for modern smokeless powder, so that only a tiny fraction of the case's volume is actually used for modern powder.

The standard military rifle cartridge for the United States during World War I and World War II was the 30.06 caliber. This is referred to as the "thirty ought six" by most shooters. After World War II, the 7.62 × 51 mm (.308) was developed. It was adopted as the official NATO round in 1950. The new NATO round had a slightly higher velocity than the 30.06, but other characteristics were similar. At the height of World War II, a German developed a short rifle capable of fully automatic or semiautomatic fire using a cut down version of the 7.92 mm Mauser rifle round. The new cartridge was called the 7.92 × 33 mm or 7.9 Kurz (short). The new rifle was named for propaganda purposes the Sturmgewehr, which literally means "storm rifle," as in *storm a bunker.* But it also refers to the weather phenomenon, *storm.* This term was translated into English as *assault rifle,* and that name, for similar cut down rifle/cartridge combinations, persists. Make no mistake; these are still high-powered rifle cartridges. Although they are commonly referred to in firearm writers' circles as *medium-velocity rounds,* they travel at much higher velocities than pistol ammunition.

Shortly after the end of World War II, a man named Kalashnikov invented the AK-47 assault rifle. His rifle was influenced by a number of previous developments from other nations, including the 7.9 Kurz. The new ammunition was described as 7.6 × 39 mm. He then designed a weapon that was a combination of a rifle and submachine gun. The AK-47 has become the most ubiquitous military weapon in the world today. It is rugged and simple. It is very forgiving of a lack of maintenance and care. In spite of the fact that the cartridge is considered less powerful than the rifle cartridges of earlier weapons, it is still most definitely a high-powered rifle cartridge and will do tremendous damage to the human body. This cartridge was the standard Soviet load from the 1950s to 1970s.

During the late 1950s, a man named Eugene Stoner was the chief engineer of a division of the Fairchild Aircraft company called ArmaLite. He developed a short rifle that used a cartridge called the .223 Remington, a smaller-diameter projectile than previous military rounds. Mr. Stoner's rifle was adopted by the U.S. military as a replacement for the .30 carbine to be used by air crew and other noninfantry military personnel, as people believed that they did not need the same firepower as the infantry. That weapon eventually proved to be superior to other weapons and was eventually adopted by the U.S. military as its standard firearm, the M16. Later, the cartridge was also adopted by NATO and was redesignated as the 5.56 × 45 mm (.223).

Through history, firearm projectiles have consisted of everything from similarly sized stones to scrap iron. For many years, lead was the bullet material of choice. Early firearms had smooth bores. By the late 1600s, manufacturers were learning to make rifled barrels. This meant that barrels were made with a number of grooves inside, arranged in a spiral, leading from the chamber to the muzzle end. The soft lead projectiles of the day would be caught between the grooves and the raised areas between the grooves, called *lands*. The spiral pattern of lands and grooves imparted a spin to the projectile as it passed down the barrel. The spinning action increased the range and accuracy of the firearms. The rifling also made the firearm slower to load from the muzzle, as in many cases the lead bullet had to be forced down the barrel, with the lands cutting the soft lead bullet as it went.

Later, a bullet was invented by a Frenchman named Minie. This bullet was of soft lead and was shaped a bit like a cone with a hollow base. It was smaller than the diameter of the bore and was loaded base down; when fired, the hollow base was forced to expand by the hot gases. While expanding, the base made contact with the lands and grooves, and thereby had spin imparted. The Minie was much faster to load than a lead ball. It was used extensively during the War between the States (i.e., American Civil War).

When fixed ammunition was invented, most bullets were still made of soft lead to allow the firing of many cartridges without excessive wear or damage to the firearm's barrel. Using soft lead in firearms also resulted in lead deposits being left behind in the barrel. The early cartridge cases were usually made of brass or a similar copper-based alloy. As a firearm becomes older, and the more it is used, the more the lead deposited on the barrel and other areas; this causes problems in the functioning and accuracy of the firearm. Gradually, other metals and alloys were used to help avoid this problem. Many bullets now have a thin copper or other metal jacket encasing a lead or steel core.

Cartridges also come in two main categories: rimless and rimmed. Revolvers and certain types of rifles use rimmed cartridges. At the base of the cartridge, there is a small flange around it, which protrudes from the side of the cartridge. In other words, the base of the cartridge is actually slightly larger in diameter than the rest of the cartridge case. So-called rimless cartridges actually have rims. However, it is formed by the cartridge case's being indented just ahead of or above the base of the cartridge. Pistols, submachine guns, and semiautomatic and automatic rifles use rimless cartridges.

At present, a firearm projectile can consist of any of a number of various metals and configurations. The 7.62 × 39 mm cartridge used in the AK-47 consists of a steel core surrounded by lead and coated on the outside by a copper jacket (FMJ). The cartridge case is also normally made of thin steel. The NATO 5.56 × 45 mm cartridge normally has a bullet consisting of a lead core surrounded by a copper jacket with a brass cartridge case. Ammunition is available for armor piercing purposes with a bullet consisting of a lead core with a tungsten carbide penetrator mounted in the center. All military ammunition may also be found in tracer form, meaning it is a normal bullet with a small pocket in the base designed to contain the chemical that makes it glow in the dark.

Shotgun ammunition usually consists of lead balls of various sizes. A shotgun "slug" is normally a soft lead projectile, weighing at least an ounce, and somewhat similar to a Minie bullet; that is, the front end is rounded and ball shaped, and the rear end is a hollow cavity. The "slug" usually has grooves cut or molded into the lead, made to look similar to rifling. The theory behind this is that as the "slug" passes through the air, the passing air will catch in the grooves and cause the "it" to spin. Testing has shown that this does not happen in practice. They are very destructive within a short range. They are notoriously inaccurate at anything more than approximately 100 m. Within 50 m or less, they will punch holes, very large holes, through a cinder block wall and a human standing behind the wall. Another type of shotgun catridge is the Brenneke. It consists of a dumbbell-shaped piece of steel, with thin lead coating on each of the expanded areas of the dumbbell. The "catridge" is loaded into the cartridge with one of the expanded parts to the front. When fired, the "it" flies down the barrel, the lead coating making contact with the sides of the barrel. In the past few years, rifled barrels were developed for shotguns. The first of these were called paradox barrels, because the whole idea of a shotgun was a smooth barrel and these barrels were rifled. Such barrels have given the shotgunner accuracy similar to that of the rifleman.

Other shotgun ammunition is referred to by numbers; for example, 00, 0, #1, and #4 buckshot are all considered deer or other big-game loads. Anything smaller than the #4 shot is usually considered a good duck or turkey load. The number #7½ and 8 shot are considered good loads for hunting quail, dove, and similar small birds. The number #9 shot is usually preferred for skeet and trapshooting contests. A 12 gauge 00 buckshot shell will contain 9 or 11 lead pellets or balls of .33 in. diameter. The #1 buckshot contains 16 pellets, each of .30 in. diameter. As the numbers on the shells go up, the size goes down, and the number of pellets increases. A 12 gauge #9 shot shell has over 500 pellets approximately .09 in. in diameter. Most shot is still made of lead. There are other types available, such as bismuth, steel, tungsten-iron, tungsten-nickel-iron, and even tungsten-polymer loads.

No matter how hard and smooth a piece of steel or other metal feels to the touch, it actually contains tiny imperfections. These imperfections can be made visible under the right microscope. When a lead or copper projectile passes down the barrel of a rifle or other firearm, the lands and grooves in the barrel leave microscopic marks on the projectile. These tiny impressions are called *striations*. Two bullets fired from the same gun can be matched one to the other. A ballistic expert can testify that the two bullets came from the same firearm and demonstrate this through photographs taken through a comparison microscope. Regrettably, unless the bullet is fired and recovered in a laboratory setting, the bullet is usually so damaged by whatever it strikes after leaving the barrel that a match by comparison is impossible. Sometimes a police officer, crime scene technician, or medical examiner will carelessly damage a bullet as it is recovered at a crime scene or from a murder victim's body.

When two articles strike each other, there is always an impression left by one on the other. This occurs when the firing pin of a firearm strikes the much softer primer or percussion cap of a cartridge and the rear of the cartridge is forced back against the bolt face of a firearm by the recoil of the cartridge firing. It also happens when the rear of the cartridge is forced sideways by the firearm's action as it ejects the cartridge from the chamber. These microscopic impressions and scratches are called striations. Again, a ballistics expert may be able to match a firearm to a cartridge case found at the scene of a shooting crime.

Therefore, it is important that police officers, crime scene technicians, forensic anthropologists, and pathologists carefully recover any spent bullets or cartridge cases found at the scene of a crime or within a dead body. As the position of victims, the locations of spent bullets, and the locations of fired cartridge cases can help investigators to reconstruct what happened, it is also important that any known facts of that nature be carefully recorded as the scene is cleared.

Variation in Gunfire Wounds by Skeletal Region

8

Other weapons and ammunition under development in recent years which could have an impact on patterns of battlefield wounding include: new shotguns capable of semiautomatic fire; small-caliber weapons firing flechettes (nail-like darts)... and rifle and handgun ammunition of various sorts including duplex ammunition (a cartridge containing two bullets which diverge in flight) and cartridges containing both a bullet and shotgun pellets.

Taipale et al.*

Contents

The Skull 402
The Thorax 406
Fractures to the Vertebra 406
Fractures to the Ribs and Sternum 408
Fractures to the Scapula and Proximal Humerus 411
Fractures to the Pelvis 416
The Limbs 422
Fractures of the Proximal Region of the Femur 422
Injuries to the Femoral Shaft 424
Fractures of the Distal Region of the Femur 430
Trauma to the Forearm and the Lower Leg 432
Fractures to the Hands and Feet 434
Summary Guidelines for Best Practice 435
Case Study 8.1: Tyranny and Torture in the Republic of Panama
By Ann H. Ross and Loreto Suarez S. 438
Case Study 8.2: The Pacific War: A Chilean Soldier Found in Cerro Zig Zag
By Elsa Tomasto Cagigo and Mellisa Lund, EPAF 441

The methodological framework presented throughout this book offers a systematic approach for collecting and interpreting data on skeletal wounds so that the accurate identification of skeletal trauma is possible. Understanding fracture patterns among various anatomical features assists in reconstructing the events that lead to the fragmentation of the bone in the first place. As discussed in Chapter 7, there are a multitude of variables and modifiers that affect trauma patterns in gunfire injuries: intrinsic, extrinsic, and epidemiological. Further, the occurrence of multiple or mass graves may result in incomplete recovery or partial reconstructions. The majority of cases presented here come from clandestine, multiple, or mass graves. Therefore, it is useful to look at the variation in skeletal morphology by anatomical region. In situations in which commingled remains or fragmented body parts are recovered, interpretations may have to be drawn from isolated bones or anatomical regions. In these

* Taipale et al. 2002: 69.

cases, it is critical that distinctions are made between the observable facts and interpretations drawn from the data to provide as much reliable information as possible. This chapter builds on the discussion of gunfire injuries from Chapter 7 and presents examples of some of the observed variation in cases from a variety of geographical locations, including Guatemala, the Balkans, Peru, and Colombia. To illustrate examples of skeletal trauma, morphological variation is organized by anatomical region. In the examples presented, the manner of death was homicide, and the context includes human rights (HHRR) violations, extrajudicial executions, and war crimes. There was no medical intervention after the incidents resulting in fatal injuries. The purpose of this chapter is not to provide a comprehensive classification system, nor is it an attempt to account for all possible variations or types of gunfire cases. Rather, the characteristics and trends presented here are meant to (1) illustrate a range of the variation in skeletal trauma that results from gunfire injuries and (2) describe general patterns that summarize the types of defects or fractures that result. In addition, two contributed case studies are presented. Throughout this chapter, "high velocity" generally refers to rifle ammunition and "medium velocity" typically refers to handguns and submachine guns (a distinction based on standard practice of approximately 2000–3000 ft/s; refer to Fackler [1996]), all of which are weapons commonly used in modern conflicts or HHRR abuses. Case Study 8.1 involves a case of extrajudicial homicide in Panama resulting from gunfire injury and torture (Ross and Suarez). Case Study 8.2 from Peru, demonstrates how skeletal evidence can piece together circumstances surrounding a death, particularly with regard to the timing of injuries and the manner of death (Tomasto and Lund). The lack of agreement regarding the classification of projectiles has prompted the authors to adopt the generally used system based on velocity, as described in Chapter 7. As the previous quote by Taipale et al. illustrates, gunfire injuries are complex and weaponry is rapidly evolving. Therefore, a systematic approach based on scientific methods is necessary for accurate analysis.

The Skull

Generally, basilar fracture lines tend to run either parallel to the occipital buttress or across the midline. The prevalence of fractures on one side or the other of the buttress is dependent on what side the shot penetrated bone. Betz and coworkers (1997) investigated fractures of the base of the skull in contact shots to the head (the majority of cases reported refer to contact injuries) as a function of bullet caliber and the impact of the bullet. They found that fractures of the base varied by location. Due to its thin bone density and lack of strength, the anterior fossae would fragment easier than the middle and posterior fossae (Figure 8.1). Importantly, any shot penetrating the base would likely fracture the anterior fossa irrespective of the class of weapon or ammunition caliber. When caliber is considered, bullets of 7.65 mm caliber and larger, tend to fracture the middle and posterior fossa upon penetrating the base of the skull, regardless of the exact point of impact. Among shots that did not penetrate the base, fractures to that area, also termed "indirect" fractures, would occur in ammunition 9 mm caliber and above (Betz et al. 1997). Fractures to the base of the skull are common with intracranial shots by handguns and/or low-velocity rifles (Betz et al. 1997; see brief description of velocities in Chapter 7). Fenton and coworkers (2005) proposed that bilateral fracturing of cranial structures occur in cases of intraoral or submandibular gunshot wounds (GSW) to the head. Experience shows that high-velocity rounds, traveling from intraoral or submandibular shots

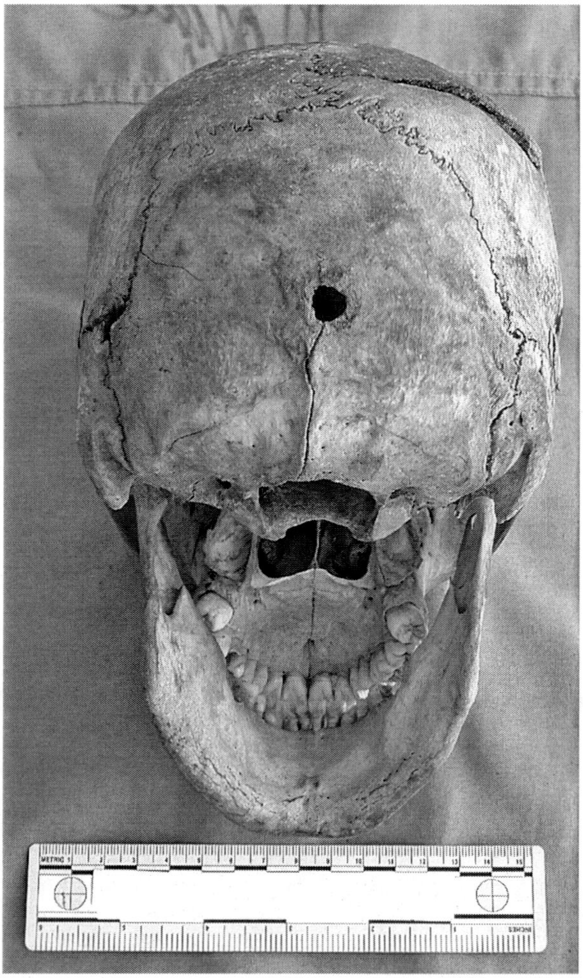

Figure 8.1 Posterior skull with a gunshot wound (GSW) to occipital bone, circular defect with small radiating fracture (Juan Carlos Tello, EPAF).

through the base of the head that impact perpendicular to the axis of the body, tend to cause fractures to the mandible, base of the skull, and the atlas and dens process of the axis. It has also been observed that fractures to the cranial base are common with shots penetrating the head at or about the line of the auditory meatus following a transverse trajectory. This pattern differs from shots fired through other aspects of the skull, or from a range of other trajectories, such as superior-inferior through the vertex or base of the skull and laterally through the meatal line of the temporal. Fractures to the mandible tend to be vertical and linear (Figure 8.2). There is an empirical correlation between the location of the fracture and the direction of the shot. Among injuries through the midline, fractures tend to be symmetrically located on both sides of the path of the bullet, whereas injuries located to either side of the midline tend to exhibit fractures unilaterally. Oblique fractures of the mandible may be isolated to only one side or may occur as part of complex fractures around the trigone area (e.g., this is where two fractures, each originating on one side of the mental eminence, converge into one fracture line

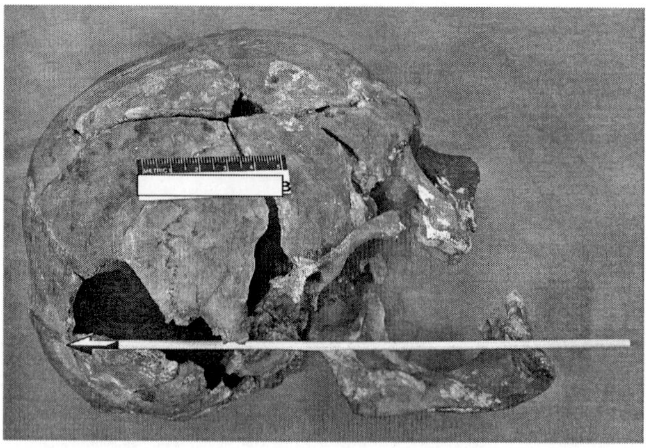

Figure 8.2a Lateral right view of the adult skull with a gunshot wound (GSW) from front to back through mandible and basilar skull (Alain Wittmann).

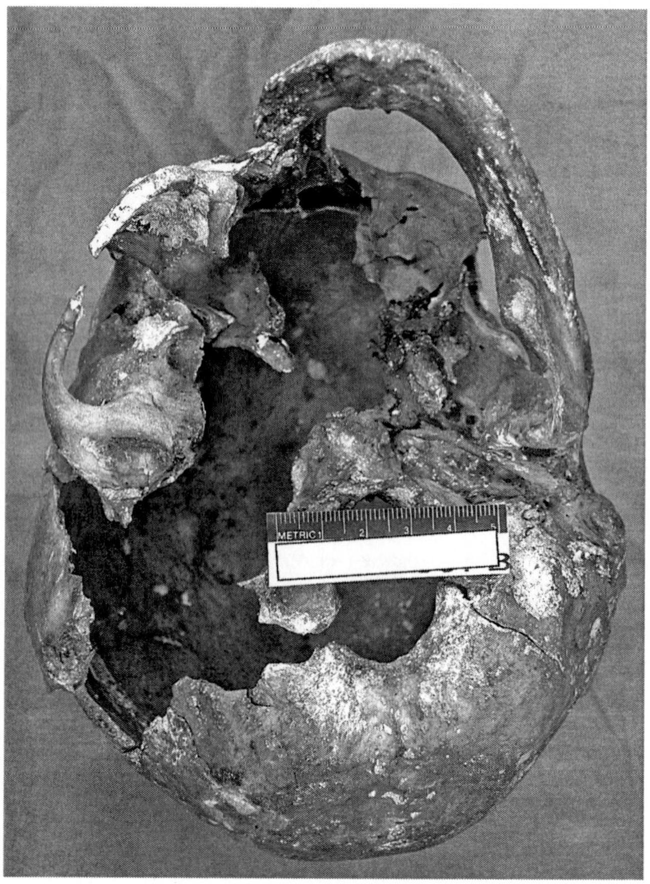

Figure 8.2b Posterior view of the cranium. Note the extensive fractures to the mandible and basilar occipital (Alain Wittmann).

Figure 8.3a Posterior view of the cervical spine (C2–C6) showing an irregular defect through the body of C2 (Alain Wittmann).

running vertically to the alveolar margin between both incisors). Blunt force injuries to the lower jaw can mimic fractures caused by gunshot trauma. Generally, these fractures are morphologically similar to *butterfly fractures* with the wings of the butterfly (or the base of the triangle) indicative of the direction of impact. Mandibular fractures caused by internal pressure from within the oral cavity, tend to mimic fractures caused by a bending force in which the bone fails in tension internally and exhibits a *breakaway spur* externally (refer also to Chapter 7, Figure 7.73b) (e.g., refer to Adi et al. 1990; Allan and Daly 1990; Chidzonga 1990; Warren 2007). Figure 8.3 illustrates fractures to the upper cervical vertebrae. The atlas (C1) tends to fracture along the midline through the arches, either anteriorly or posteriorly when the path of the projectile occurs along the midline. Also diastatic, linear fractures detaching each lateral mass through the anterior and posterior arches at each side of the midline are commonly observed. The axis (C2) exhibits similar features to C1, separating the body from each transverse process through the laminae. Separation of the dens process is also common and occurs when the path of the projectile transects through the vertebral body. For general information on GSW variation to the skull, refer to Thoresen (1984) and Thorn et al. (1986).

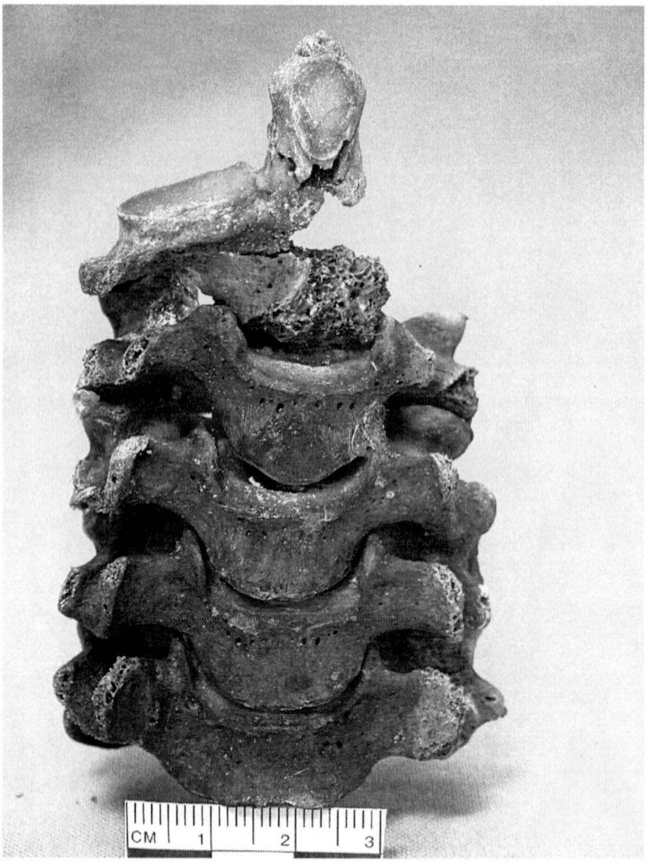

Figure 8.3b Anterior view. The trabecular bone of the body of C2 is exposed, suggesting the direction of fire is front to back (Alain Wittmann).

The Thorax

Fractures to the Vertebra

Injuries to the spine may be isolated or related to other injuries, commonly the head and pelvis, depending on which vertebrae are affected, the bullet trajectory, and type of ammunition (Figures 8.4–8.7). The architecture and thick trabecular bodies result in variable fracture patterns among the various aspects of the vertebrae. Two general types of defects are observed: (1) fractures affecting the vertebral bodies in the anteroposterior plane through the spine, and (2) fractures that affect other structures such as the laminae or spinous processes.

High-velocity or close-contact rounds that injure the spine in the anteroposterior plane tend to comminute the vertebral body upon impact. In addition, they may result in linear fractures across the bodies of neighboring vertebrae, above and below the point of impact. In cases in which the bullet penetrates in between two vertebrae at the level of the intervertebral disk, a gutter defect may be visible. The articulation of both vertebrae together may show a circular defect indicating the path of the projectile. As described for the skull, *beveling* may also be observed in such cases, indicating the direction of fire. In contrast,

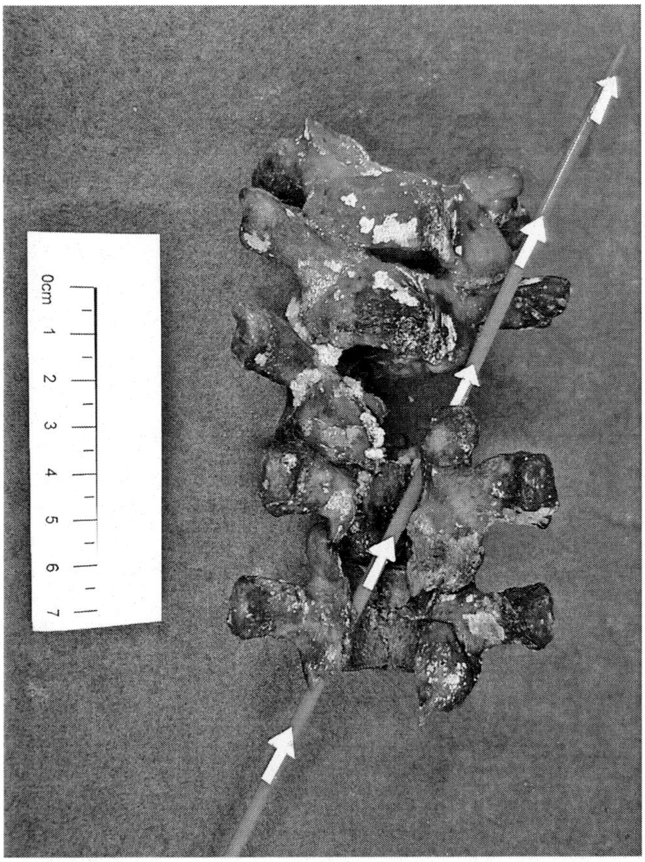

Figure 8.4 Cervical and thoracic spine (C7–T4) showing a gunshot injury that penetrates through the lamina-spinous process of T4 and continues through the neural canal in an upward direction, exiting through the right lamina of T2. Observe the destruction of the spinous processes and detachment from the left laminae of T3–4. (Printed with permission from International Criminal Tribunal for the former Yugoslavia [ICTY].)

low- and medium-velocity projectiles will not typically comminute vertebral bodies, but rather cause penetrating injuries and may remain embedded within the bone. The following features have been observed in cases of high-velocity ammunition, fired from intermediate or distant ranges:

- Comminution of vertebral body impacted, fractures may also be present on the adjacent vertebra to which it articulates. A linear fracture separating the arches from the body, generally at the level of the pedicle.
- A linear, complete fracture that separates the midline of the vertebral body into two halves, running above and below the point of impact.
- Random linear fractures of the spinous processes and/or the laminae. It may be that the arches and spinous processes of vertebrae divert the applied force through its structures in such a way that the fractures generally extend above and below the point of impact.

Comminuted fractures of vertebral bodies are almost exclusively the result of high-velocity rounds and occur only in the area of impact. Grazing wounds from an indeterminate range

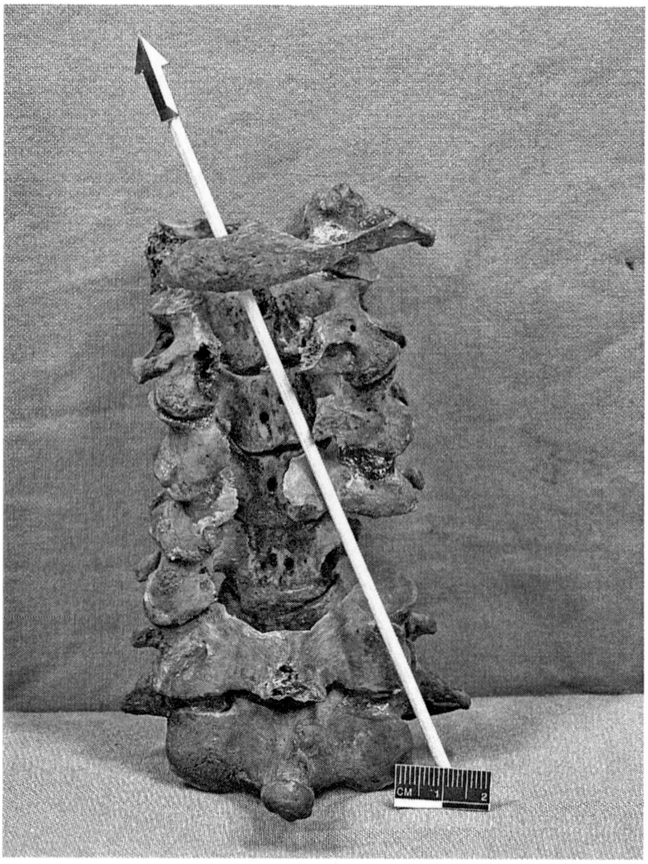

Figure 8.5a Variation in wound morphology is demonstrated for three different individuals, with gunshot injuries to vertebrae (A) Posterior view of cervical spine illustrates the trajectory of an injury through the lower neck, upward into the head. Note the destruction of the spinous processes from C5 to C2. The projectile trajectory was from right to left, as indicated by the destruction of the left mass of the atlas (Alain Wittmann).

can impact the center of the vertebral body, causing it to break into many pieces, and it may be impossible to reconstruct. Sellier and Kneubeuhl (1994) have argued that comminuted fractures of the vertebral bodies result from the "hydraulic burst effect" caused by the movement of fluids within the vertebral body. In these types of injuries, it is common to find that the spinous process is generally intact or exhibits minimal damage in comparison to the body; it may present a linear fracture or detachment of the body from the laminae. There is a clear distinction between the vertebral body and the spinous process in how each responds to applied force. Further, fractures to the cervical spine may be associated with rib fractures (Logan 1999).

Fractures to the Ribs and Sternum

Shots penetrating the thorax may or may not affect bone. However, gunfire injuries through the rib cage rarely occur in isolation but are often part of a system of entrance-exit-reentry set of events that may have originated elsewhere in the chest or upper limb (Figure 8.8).

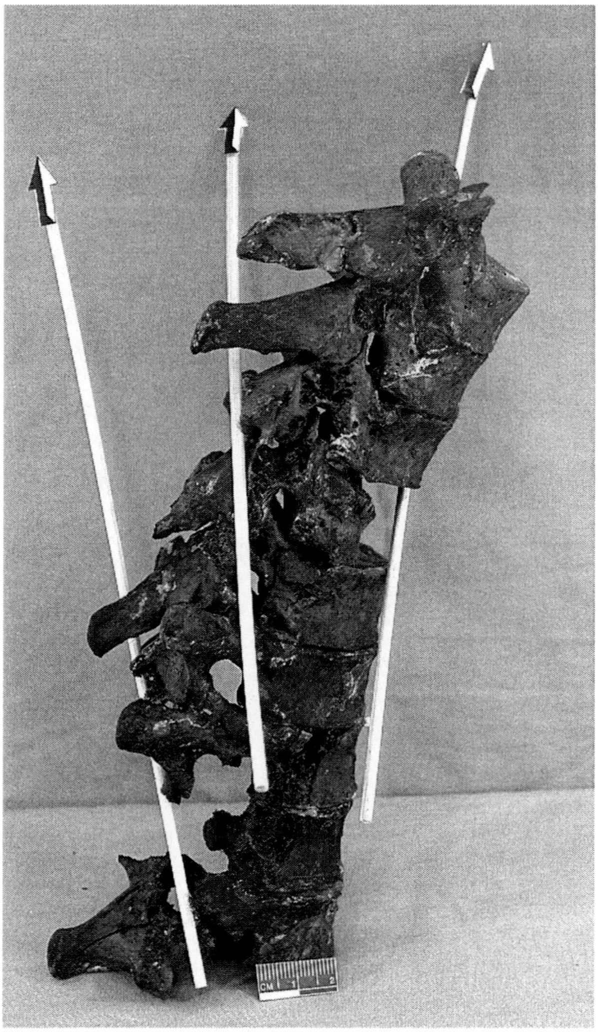

Figure 8.5b Articulated midthoracic spine showing the most probable trajectory of three bullets crossing the spine, from right to left, upward (Alain Wittmann).

The spine, clavicle, scapula, sternum, and one or more bilateral ribs may be involved. A projectile will typically do one of two things depending on the range of fire, velocity, and whether the projectile hit an intermediate target: (1) the bullet may perforate a rib without causing fractures to adjacent ribs, or (2) the bullet may cause multiple fractures to the ribs above and below the point of impact. Isolated defects in the ribs and sternum tend to exhibit similar fracture patterns as the skull (Figure 8.9). High-velocity rounds bearing sufficient force will perforate a rib in a similar fashion as the skull (i.e., if the bullet goes through the body and is not deformed, it is likely to make a rounded defect, reflecting the cross section of the projectile). Also, exit wounds tend to be larger than entrance defects, with comminuted fractures of the inner and outer tables of the rib, depending on the direction and distance of the shot. Radiating fractures, extending away from the point of impact may be present at either the entrance or the exit wound, or both wounds. If the projectile impacts only the superior or inferior rib edge, the wound generally consists of

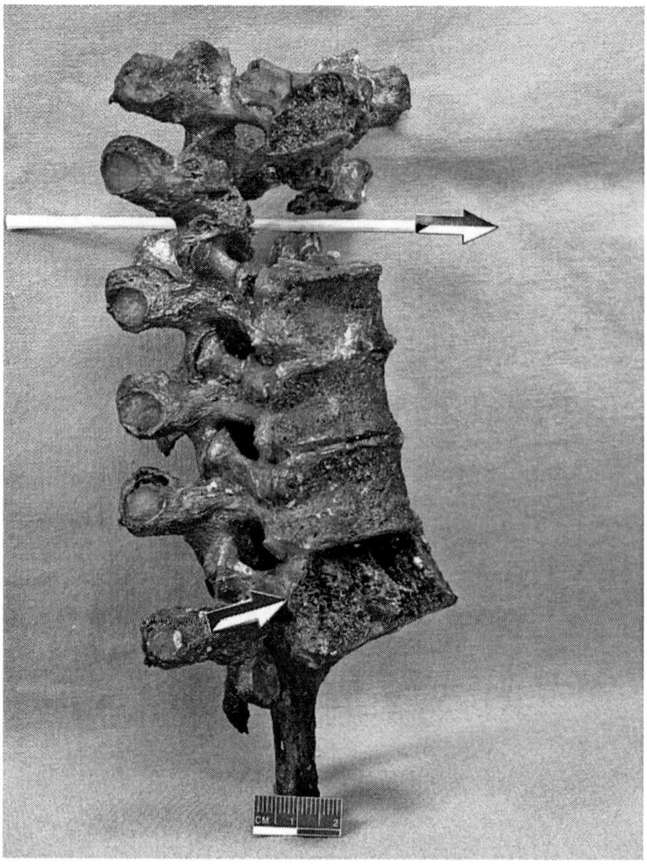

Figure 8.5c Right, lateral view of the thoracic spine. Through-and-through gunshot injury at the level of T2 from back to front. Arrow pointing to the body of T6 shows destruction of part of the body, possibly resulting from a second injury (Alain Wittmann).

a semicircular defect with similar characteristics as described previously. In such cases, it is common to encounter two radiating fractures occurring on the exit side, mimicking a *butterfly* fracture (Figure 8.10). Ribs are much thinner and have less spongy tissue between the two plates compared to the skull, therefore it is common to observe that although the entrance is a clear rounded defect, the exit may be smaller in size with a sleeve of bone (from one of the two plates) pushed outward but not completely separated from the defect. This type of feature is associated here with an entrance wound.

The specific location and the angle of impact among injuries to the ribs are informative about the position of the victim and illustrates whether other structures are affected. For example, comminuting fractures on ribs 4–8 along the rib angle most likely are associated to shots through the scapula, whereas injuries through or near the costochondral articulation of the first rib could also be associated to wounds of the sternum or clavicle. High-velocity rounds can cause substantial damage to certain areas of the body even when fired from long distances. For example, rib fractures were observed in an experiment carried out on anesthetized pigs shot through the chest mimicking a distance of 100 meters with an AK-47 (Dakak et al. 2003). Three of four cases showed rib fractures. The velocity of the

Figure 8.6a Thoracic vertebrae 8–11, anterior view. T9–T10 exhibit gunshot injury from front to back. Semicircular defect on T9. Fracture extends through T10 (Alain Wittmann).

bullets upon exiting the chest was an average of 200 m/s. In two other sets of shots carried out with obstacles placed in front of the chest (a G3 magazine with shell cases and a radio, respectively), the bullets entered the chest, fragmented, but did not exit. In these examples, no rib fractures were detected.

Shots through the sternum are not an uncommon type of injury in cases of extra-judicial executions. Generally, a shot through the sternum and the thoracic spine may sever the aorta and cause immediate death. Since the sternum is a two-plated bone like the skull, it is not difficult to identify the direction of penetrating shots.

Fractures to the Scapula and Proximal Humerus

Anatomically, the scapula is a complex structure that is comprised of a thick, irregular mass of trabecular bone (i.e., the acromion process and glenoid fossa) as well as the thin, flat compact bone of the body and spinous process. Consequently, the nature of the wound will depend on which aspect of the scapula is injured. Unlike the ribs, sternum, skull, and

Figure 8.6b Posterior view. Extensive fractures of the spinous processes above and below the defect (Alain Wittmann).

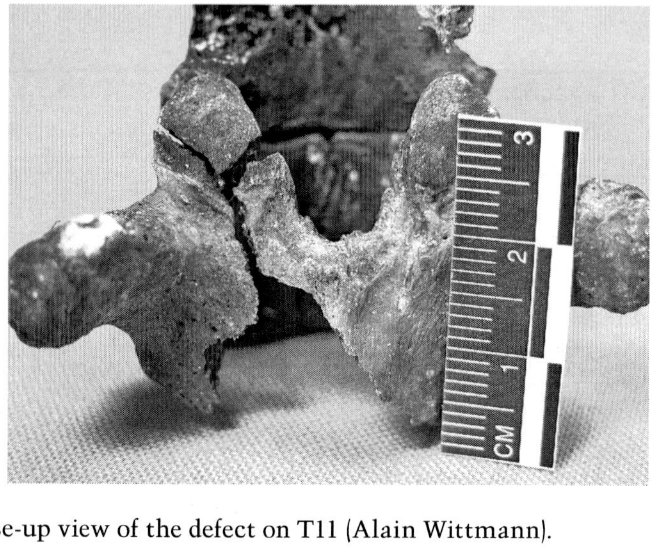

Figure 8.6c Close-up view of the defect on T11 (Alain Wittmann).

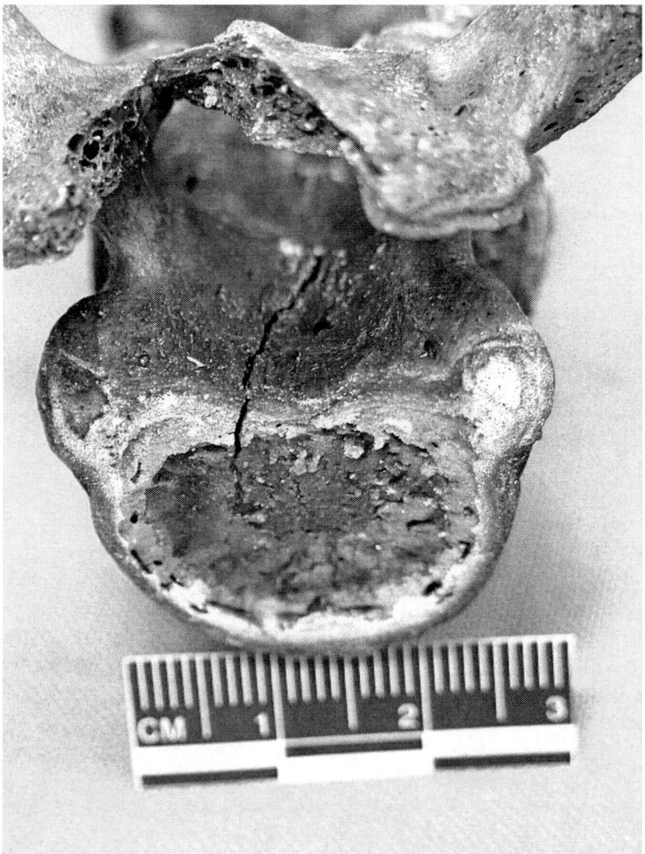

Figure 8.6d Inferior body of the T11. Close-up view of fracture (Alain Wittmann).

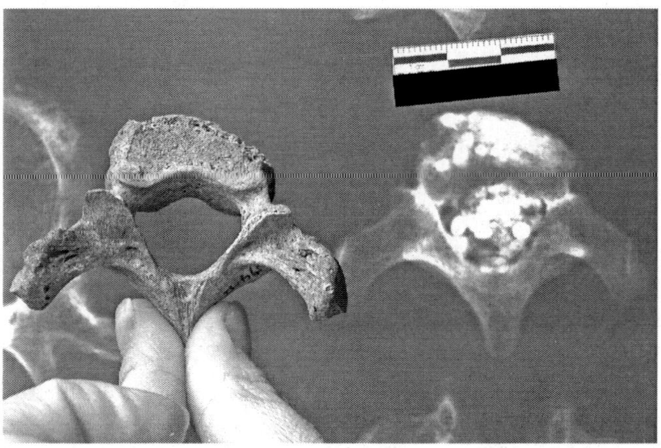

Figure 8.7 Thoracic vertebra (T1), superior surface shown next to fluoroscope image. Outer rim of vertebral body appears "eroded," similar to postmortem damage. The image reveals embedded pellets resulting from a shotgun injury taken prior to pm exam (Carlos Jacinto, FAFG).

Figure 8.8a Posterior view of the vertebra, T10–T12 and L1. Extensive fracturing of the spinous processes, vertebral bodies, and adjacent ribs (Alain Wittmann).

pelvis, the body of the scapula is comprised of a single sheet of bone, lacking spongy bone between plates. Thus, wound morphology varies:

- The scapular body does not typically exhibit beveling and tends to be friable. Defects may exhibit multiple radiating fractures. The shape of the wound tends to mimic the shape of the projectile and will be circular or irregular depending on the composition and completeness of the projectile, and the angle of impact (Figure 8.11).
- Projectile fragments may become embedded in the scapula, including the body (refer again to chapter 7, Figure 7.37).
- The lateral margin or border of the scapular body is a transitional area where bone is thicker and consists of trabeculae. Therefore, injuries along the border are more similar to wounds of the ribs and sternum than to the scapular body (Figure 8.12).

Figure 8.13 illustrates a case in which a single gunfire injury was sustained by an adult (from left to right), where the bullet entered the shoulder, penetrated and shattered the proximal humerus, penetrated the first and second intercostal space, through the midthoracic spine at the costovertebral articulation, and perforated the thorax. This example illustrates the capacity for a high-velocity round to strike through multiple bones and how multiple wounds in one skeleton, may be caused by a single bullet. In a second example (Figure 8.14),

Figure 8.8b Multiple rib fractures, both peri- and postmortem fractures. Two gunshot wound defects are visible on rib 7 and rib 9. Rib 7 shows a semicircular defect on upper margin with an associated fracture through the body below and to its left. Rib 9 shows the same type of defect but through the lower margin. Both shots were fired from the front (Alain Wittmann).

Figure 8.8c Semicircular defects in right rib 10, indicative of the gunshot entrance defect. Shot fired from front to back (Alain Wittmann).

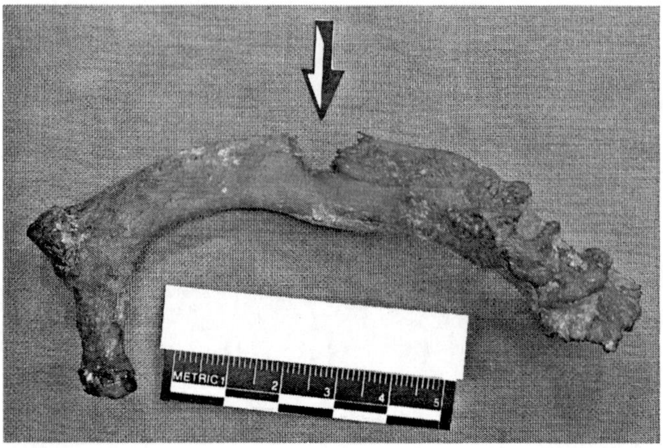

Figure 8.9 Superior view of left first rib showing semicircular defect caused by the penetrating gunshot wound (Alain Wittmann).

the left humerus and scapula of a juvenile sustained a penetrating shot to the shoulder. Note the extensive destruction and "crumbling" appearance of the humeral head.

Fractures to the Pelvis

Injuries through the pelvis tend to be complex and highly variable depending on what aspect is affected and may involve other structures such as the sacrum, lumbar spine, or proximal aspect of the femur.

Figure 8.15 presents an overview of an articulated pelvic girdle, lumbar spine, and right arm with a single GSW. A 7.62 × 39 mm bullet was found lodged in the posterior

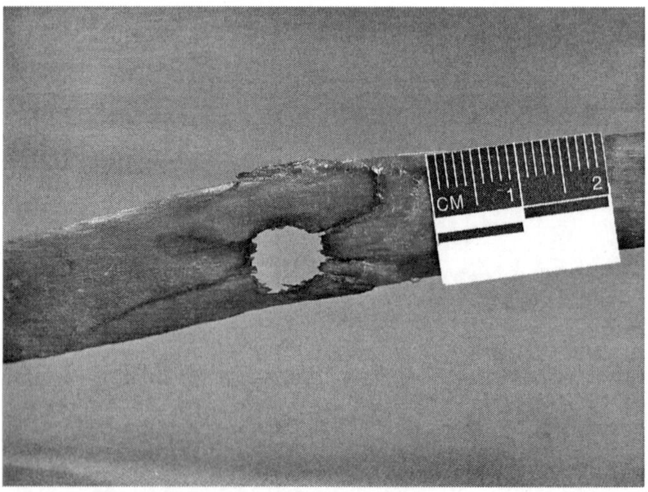

Figure 8.10a Circular defect on the anterior surface of rib body showing four radiating fractures. The somewhat ragged internal edges of the defect are *bone tags*, resulting from the crushing injury of a bullet. Wound is consistent with a gunshot entrance defect through the anterior wall of the rib (Alain Wittmann).

Figure 8.10b Internal view of the rib showing "internal beveling" and crushing of the bone creating small *bone tags* in the defect (Alain Wittmann).

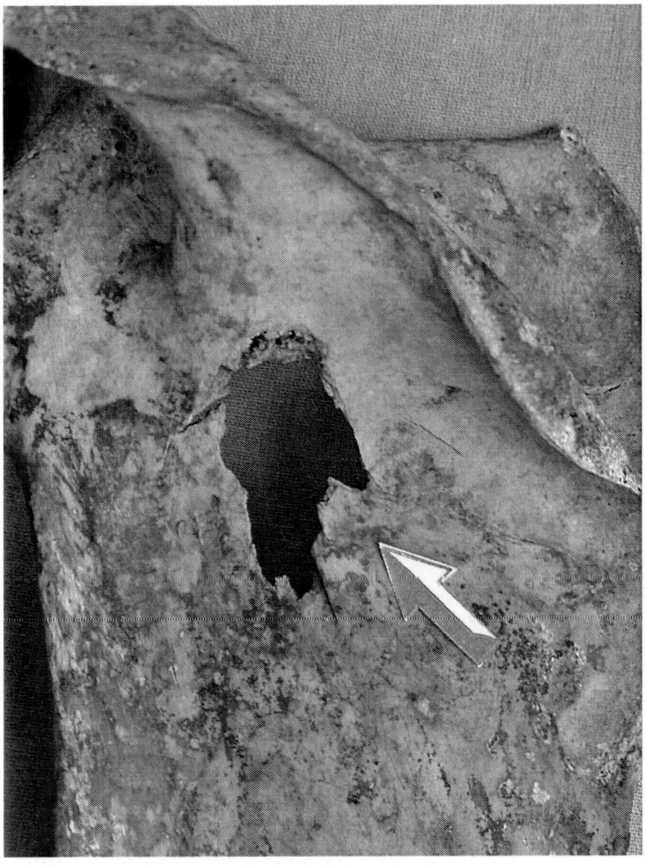

Figure 8.11 Posterior view, left scapula. Irregular defect through the body, inferior to the spinous process, with just enough trabecular bone impacted for discrete beveling to be present along the superior edge, whereas the inferior edge of the defect does not exhibit any beveling. The trajectory of the shot was from front to back. Ammunition associated to the body (but not specific to this injury) was from a handgun, i.e., 9 mm (Alain Wittmann).

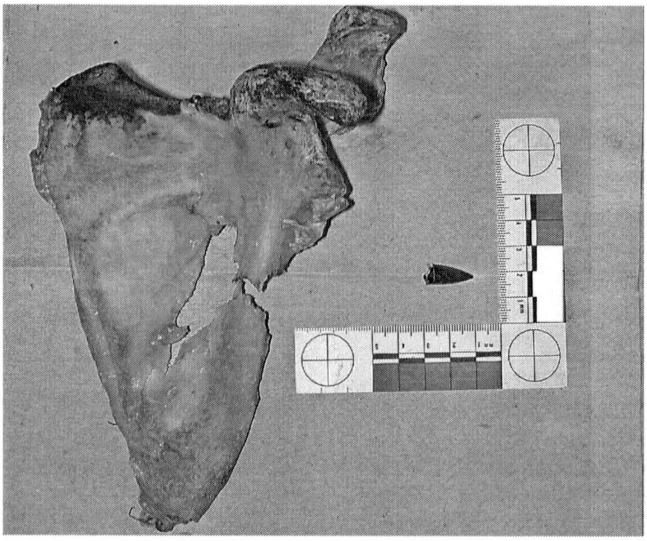

Figure 8.12a Anterior view of the left scapula with a gunshot injury along the lateral margin, front to back. A 7.62 × 39 mm bullet was recovered from the soft tissues of the back (ICTY).

aspect of the right hand. The bullet had crushed the central metacarpals. Extensive green staining from the copper chloride in the metal jacket of the bullet was found on the associated bones. The projectile penetrated through the posterior aspect of the left iliac crest, penetrated through the laminae of L5, impacted the right ilium (sideways, which caused an eccentric-shaped defect with concentric fractures), perforated the ilium, and proceeded to impact the right hand. Given the location and association of wounds, it is possible that

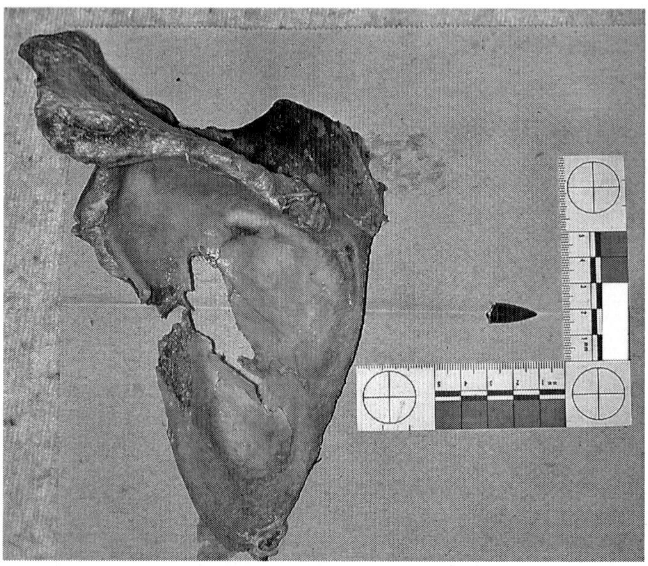

Figure 8.12b Posterior view of Figure 8.12. Extensive beveling around the exit defect. (Printed with permission from International Criminal Tribunal for the former Yugoslavia [ICTY].)

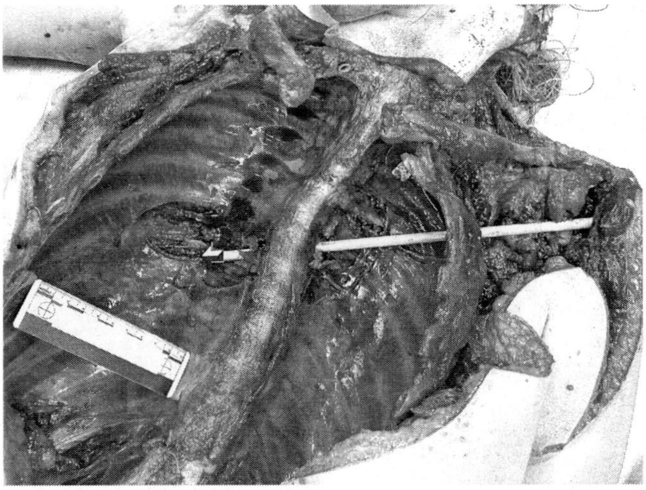

Figure 8.13a Single gunfire injury from left to right. The bullet entered the shoulder, striking the proximal humerus and resulted in massive fracturing. The bullet continued between the first and second intercostal space, penetrating through the midthoracic spine at the costovertebral articulation and exiting through the back. This case illustrates the capacity for a high-velocity round to strike through multiple bones, and how multiple wounds in one skeleton may be caused by a single bullet (Alain Wittmann).

the individual was bound or handcuffed at the time of the shooting, with the back of each hand in contact with one another and possibly against the hip.

The thickness of the iliac fossa varies in part based on the age and sex of the individual. In lateral penetrating GSWs, bullets may perforate both pelves. In such cases, each ilium may exhibit entrance and exit defects (Figures 8.16–8.18). The shapes of these defects are consistent with the variables observed for the cranial vault and other *flat* bones, such as the presence of beveling. Further, the shape of the beveling may indicate the trajectory

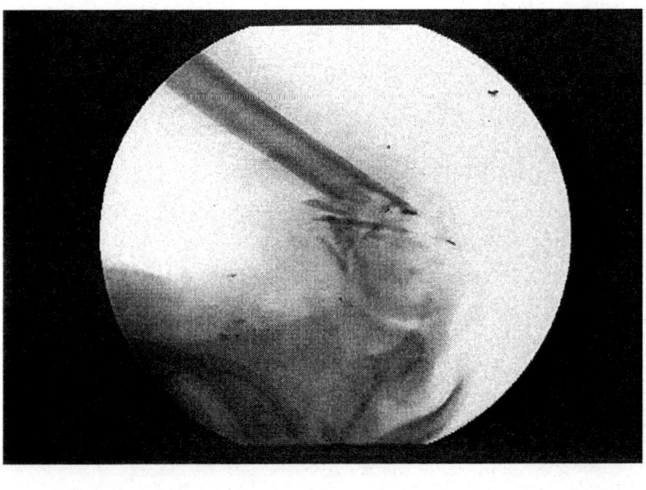

Figure 8.13b Fluoroscope image of the left shoulder of the victim seen in previous case (Alain Wittmann).

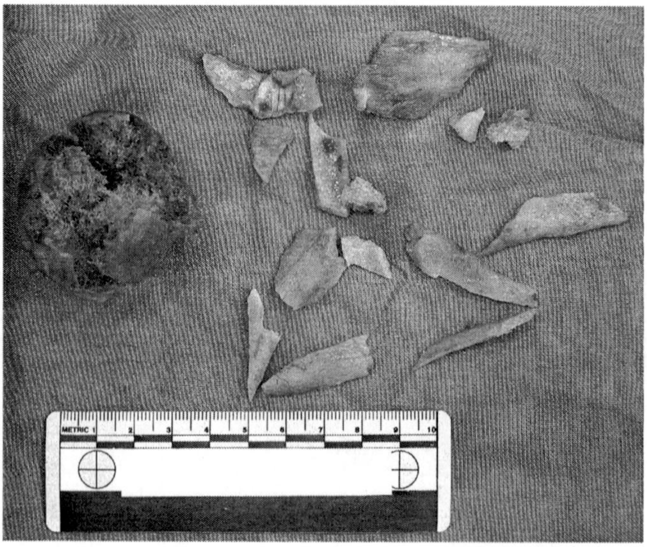

Figure 8.13c Comminution of the left humerus caused by high-velocity gunshot of previous case (Alain Wittmann).

of the shot. Depending on the velocity of the projectile at impact and the striking angle, defects will vary in shape. If the defect is irregular in shape, it may also be associated with extensive comminuting of the iliac fossa or radiating fractures. Injuries affecting the acetabulum rarely spare the femoral head, neck, or metaphysis. Figure 8.19 illustrates a through-and-through shot to the femur (which completely fractured the femoral neck, severing the head from the diaphysis), through the acetabulum of the pelvis.

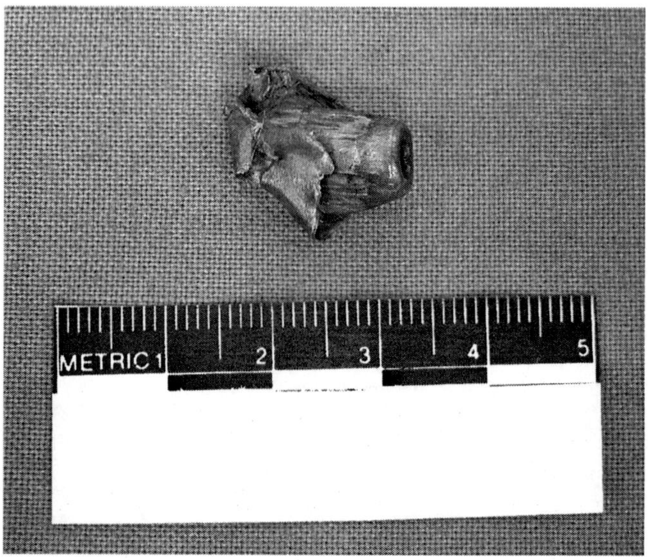

Figure 8.13d The 7.62 × 39 mm bullet recovered under the body at the scene. Note the shredding of the jacket and separation from the core (Alain Wittmann).

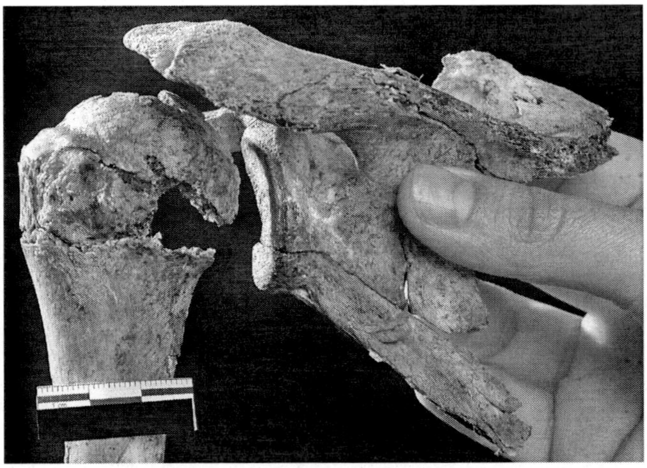

Figure 8.14a Posterior view of the juvenile, left humerus. Irregular-shaped entrance wound through the base of the humeral head, adjacent to the metaphysis. Shot fired from back to front (Carlos Jacinto, FAFG).

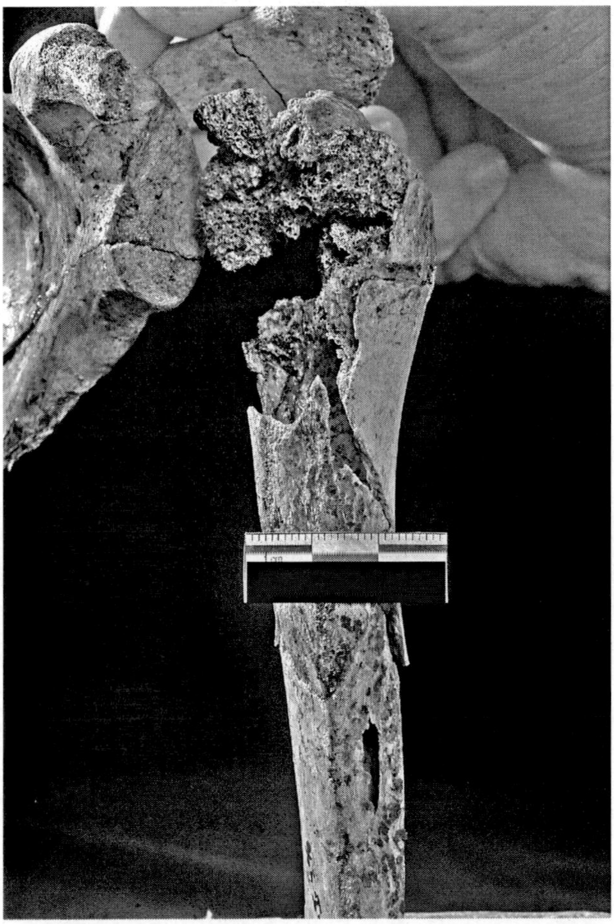

Figure 8.14b Anterior view of the humerus, gunshot exit wound. Note the extensive destruction and "crumbling" appearance of the humeral head (Carlos Jacinto, FAFG).

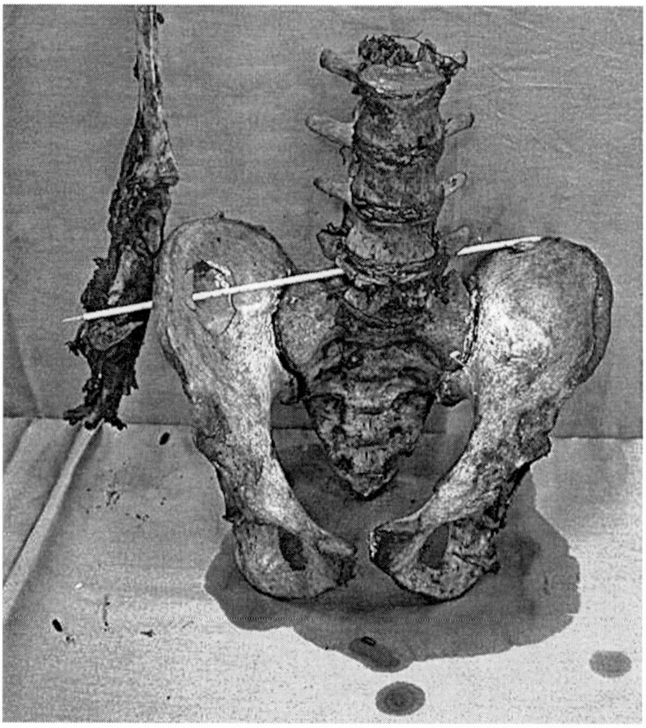

Figure 8.15 Multiple wounds to the pelvis, lumbar, and right metacarpals resulting from a single gunshot injury (Alain Wittmann).

The Limbs

Fractures of the Proximal Region of the Femur

Direct gunfire injuries to the femoral head often cause it to shatter, whereas grazing injuries that impact only the surface or peripheral areas of the femoral head create a gutter defect

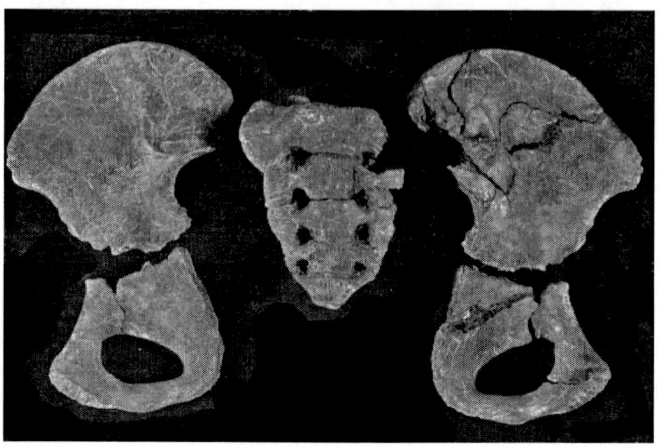

Figure 8.16a Juvenile pelvis. Bones unfused due to age. Gunshot wound through the left sacroiliac joint, severe fracturing of the left sacral ala and auricular area (Carlos Jacinto, FAFG).

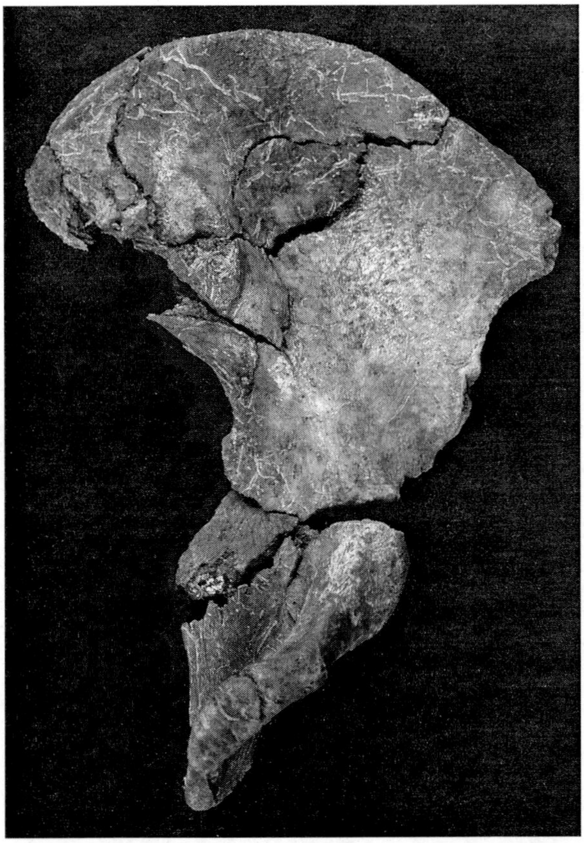

Figure 8.16b Close-up view of the injury to the left *Os coxae* (Carlos Jacinto, FAFG).

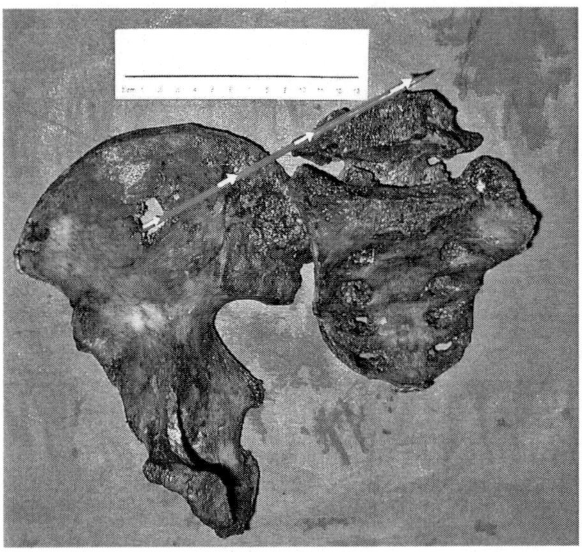

Figure 8.17 Right *Os coxae*, sacrum, and L5 showing a through-and-through gunshot wound entering the ilium, continuing in a superior direction, and impacting the body of L5. Complete comminution of the anterior half of the sacral body is apparent. (Printed with permission from International Criminal Tribunal for the former Yugoslavia [ICTY].)

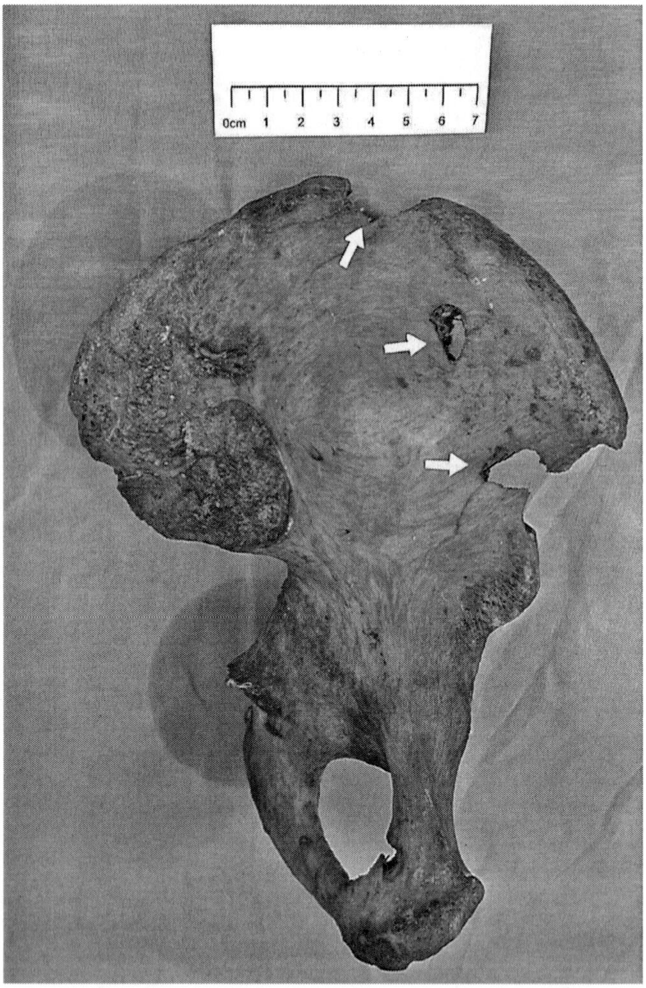

Figure 8.18a Anterior view of left *Os coxae* showing three distinct defects caused by multiple gunshot injuries. All three defects, pointed out by the arrows, are entrance wounds. Note that in the middle defect a sleeve of bone protrudes from the ilium. This defect is an entrance wound, where the bullet penetrated the ilium tangentially, lifting the plate of bone (ICTY).

with minimal linear fractures on the cortical surface (refer again to Figure 8.19). Injuries of the femoral head must be examined closely because they are generally associated to the pelvis as just described. Depending on the velocity of the projectile upon impact, it may remain lodged in the proximal area of the femur with minimal fractures. Through-and-through penetrating injuries of the proximal femur with comminution of the shaft tend to be associated with rupture of the femoral artery. This has been a useful finding when estimating the most probable cause of death because rupture of the femoral artery results in no survival if untreated (Baraybar and Gasior 2006).

Injuries to the Femoral Shaft

The biomechanical properties of gunfire injuries to the shafts of long bones tend to be similar when viewed morphologically at the macroscopic level (i.e., bones of the arms and

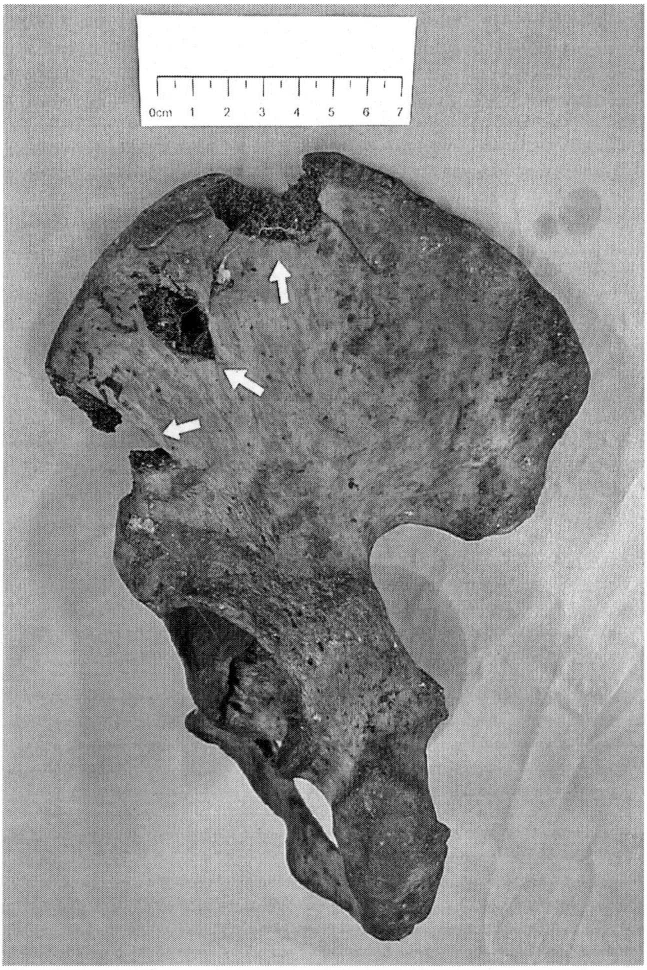

Figure 8.18b Posterior view of three distinct perforating gunshots, the presence of beveling indicate that the shots were from front to back. (Printed with permission from International Criminal Tribunal for the former Yugoslavia [ICTY].)

legs, clavicles, metacarpals, and metatarsals). Through-and-through shots may completely shatter the shafts of long bones, generating multiple radiating fractures, communition fractures, or spiral fractures extending around the shaft and extend toward the exit defect (Figure 8.20).

Figure 8.20 illustrates an adult right femur with multiple GSWs through the shaft. High-velocity rounds were recovered in the tissues of this individual, who also sustained injuries to other aspects of the body, although no bullets that associate directly with these wounds were recovered. Note the oblong-shaped defect and radiating fractures. Also, observe the delaminated edges of the defect, primarily above and along the right edge. This is consistent with a keyhole injury through the upper thigh, right to left and downwards. The bullet most likely fragmented upon impact when one fragment penetrated the bone. The thin fracture arrested by the large radiating fracture indicates that the former was caused when the projectile perforated the bone.

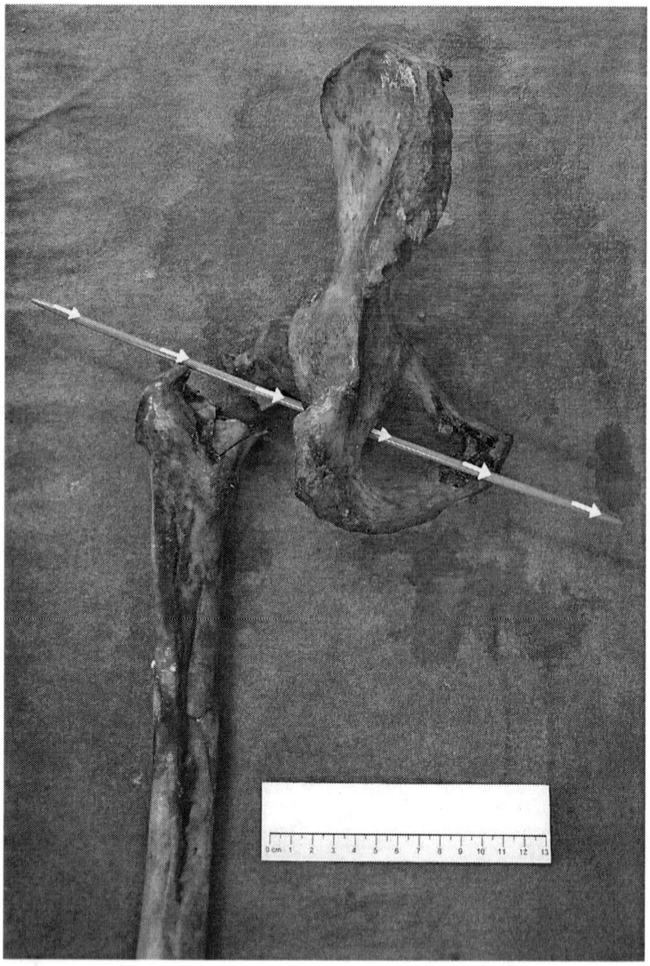

Figure 8.19 Left femur and *Os coxae*. Single, through-and-through gunshot injury to the femoral neck. Bullet separated the femoral head from the neck, penetrated through the acetabulum, and grazed the ventral surface of the pubic symphysis. Arrows indicate the direction of the shot from left to right. (Printed with permission from International Criminal Tribunal for the former Yugoslavia [ICTY].)

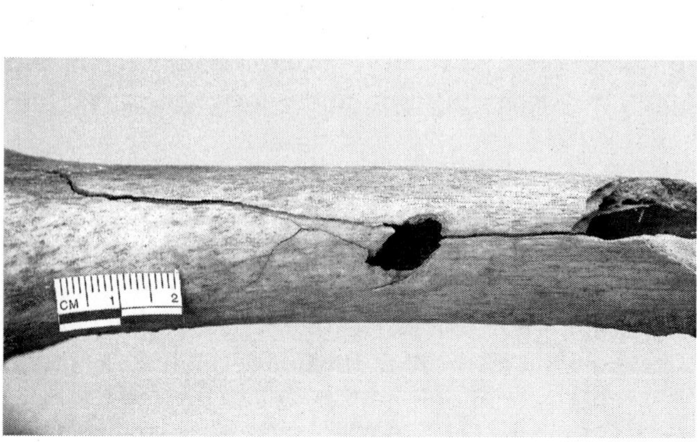

Figure 8.20a Anterior view of the right adult femur with a single gunshot wound (Alain Wittmann).

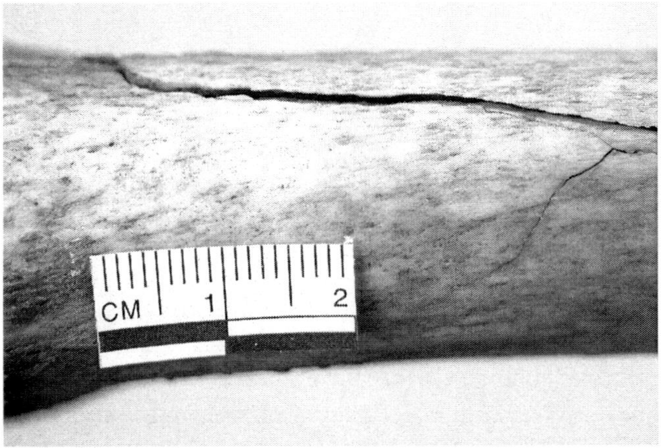

Figure 8.20b Large radiating fracture extending from the defect (Alain Wittmann).

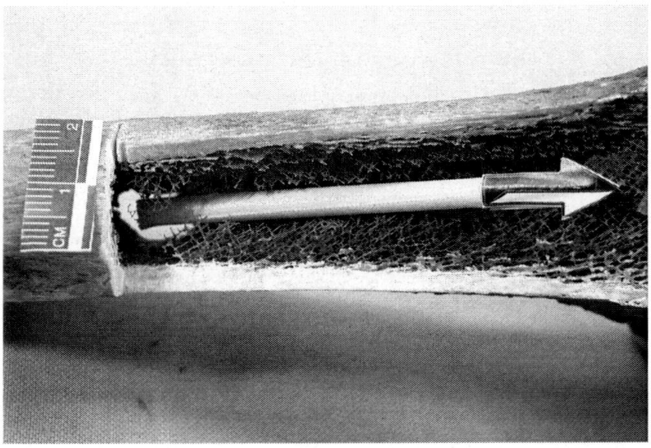

Figure 8.20c Posterior view of the femur. Probe demonstrates the bullet trajectory (Alain Wittmann).

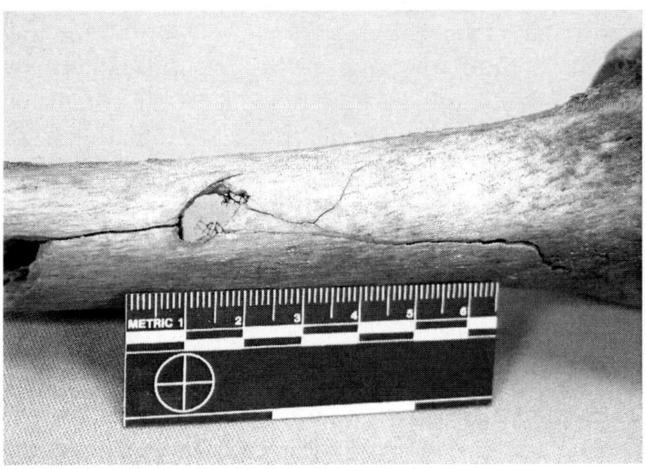

Figure 8.20d Medial aspect of the right femoral shaft with oblong-shaped defect, radiating fracture, and secondary fractures arrested by larger radiating fracture (Alain Wittmann).

The distribution and pattern of fractures associated to injuries of the femoral shaft include the following general observations: (1) linear fractures along the axis of the bone, (2) oblique fractures around the circumference of the shaft, or (3) a combination of both. Linear fractures are typically encountered in tangential or peripheral injuries to the shaft. Oblique fractures, commonly observed in through-and-through shots to the shaft, occur when the projectile impacts the bone at a perpendicular angle. The combination of these fractures may result in a "keyhole" type of defect along the surface of the long bone. In this scenario, fractures associated to the "exit" component of the defect tend to follow the circumference of the shaft toward those of the "entrance," creating a butterfly fracture. Such fractures may be redirected around anatomical structures that provide reinforcement to the structure of the bone, such as the greater or lesser trochanters, muscular insertions, or denser areas of bone. When the force is dispersed around anatomical structures, the fractures occur in an axial direction and may spiral around the circumference of the shaft, causing separation of the segments or comminuted fractures.

In an experimental study, Huelke et al. (1968a, 1968b) shot the anterior aspect of embalmed femoral shafts with steel balls of different diameters and at different velocities from a distance of 6 ft (1.8 m). Based on this experiment, they concluded that unlike the femoral metaphyses, cavitation (i.e., temporary cavity formation) was not an important factor in fracture patterns of the femoral shaft. They suggested that a shot entering the femur posteriorly through the *linea aspera* dissipated the force, resulting in fractures throughout the shaft. This effect was reported regardless of individual variation or pathological conditions of the femoral shaft. In other words, Huelke et al. (1968a, 1968b) found the same result, regardless of whether the individual was "normal," mildly osteoporotic, or osteoporotic. This finding explains why high-velocity rounds that impact perpendicular to the shaft show a pattern of spiral fractures arising from the point of impact. However, due to massive fracturing, the point of impact may be difficult to locate.

In contrast, injuries caused by lower-velocity ammunition or bullets that first impacted an intermediate target tend to cause penetrating injuries with radiating fractures originating from the point of impact, sometimes mimicking a *butterfly* or *double butterfly* fractures. A *double butterfly* fracture occurs from penetrating injuries of the femoral shaft, in which the projectile impacted perpendicular to the axis of the shaft and two to four radiating fractures extended away from the entrance defect, around the shaft, toward the exit (Figure 8.26). The number of radiating fractures is given in the terms *butterfly* or *double butterfly* fractures; both these types have been documented in clinical practice (Ryan et al. 1981, Smith and Wheatley 1984). In tangential shots, two radiating fractures may be associated to the "entrance" component of the defect, extending away from it and toward the opposite side and forming a butterfly effect at the entrance wound. These features have also been noted in cases of other tubular bones such as the humerus.

Gunfire shots directly impacting the middle aspect of the shaft may result in comminuted fractures, in which case a complete reconstruction of the wounds is possible. Radiating and concentric fractures may be present, but often the specific entrance and exit defects may not be evident (Figures 8.21 and 8.22). We have observed through-and-through injuries of the femoral shaft from high-velocity rounds with distant spiral fractures in the shaft not associated to the point of impact (refer to Case Study 3.1 on grenade injuries in chapter 3). Smith and Wheatley (1984) argued the presence of this type of fracture results from the victim's falling down, after being shot through the leg. More specifically, the spiral fracture was said to result from the muscles of the leg pulling on the bone, in torsion for support,

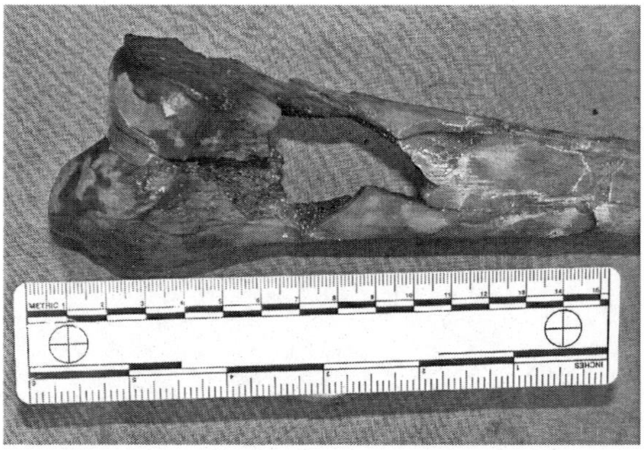

Figure 8.21 Anterior view of the distal portion of the femur showing a large, irregular defect associated to massive comminuted fractures of the shaft and a longitudinal fracture that separates the condyles. Upon reconstruction, some beveling indicates that the defect is consistent with an exit defect and posterior entrance (Alain Wittmann).

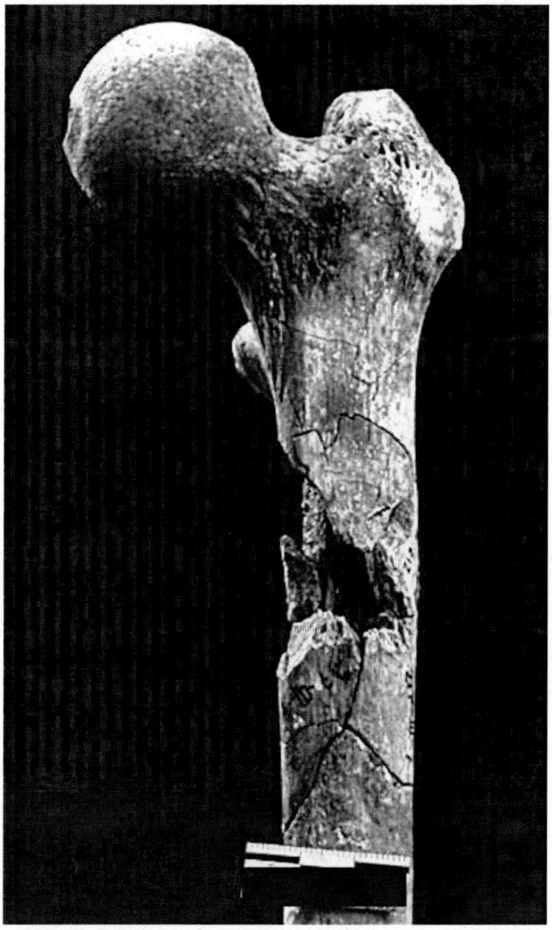

Figure 8.22 Anterior view of the left femur showing comminuting of the shaft caused by a gunshot. A discrete and unclear rounded defect is visible on the middle of the shaft suggesting the entrance of a bullet (Carlos Jacinto, FAFG).

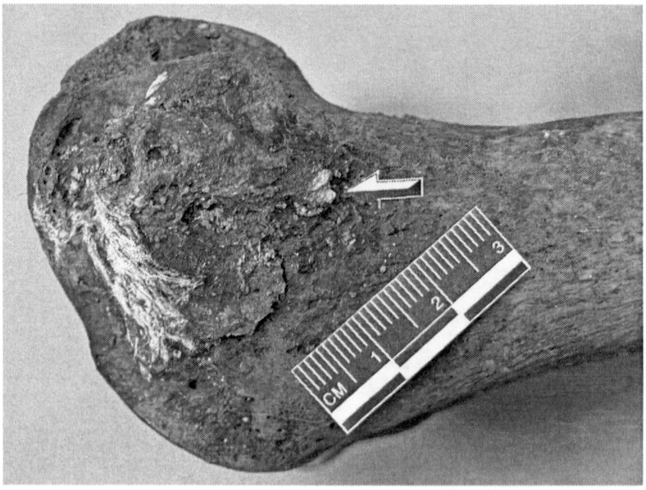

Figure 8.23a Distal portion of the femur showing an irregular defect on the lateral aspect of the medial condyle. A rounded defect was found in the intercondylar fossa. This is consistent with a gunshot wound through the intercondylar fossa from back to front, right to left, and downward (Alain Wittmann).

following comminuted fracturing of the shaft (Smith and Wheatley 1984); refer also to Tencer and Johnson (1994) and Tencer et al. (2002). It should be pointed out that, whether a subsequent fall or the direct gunfire injury is the primary cause of the fracture, most importantly, both injuries are related to the same event and must be interpreted as such.

Fractures of the Distal Region of the Femur

Injuries to the distal femur and medial and lateral condyles may exhibit through-and-through shots that penetrate, graze, or become embedded in the bone (Figure 8.23). In an

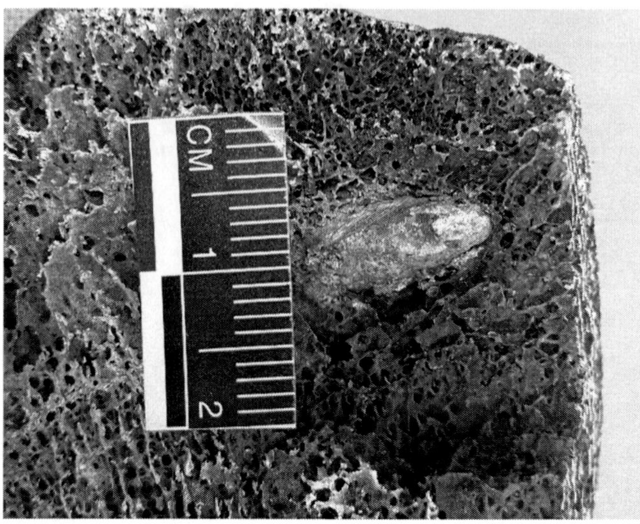

Figure 8.23b Outer fragmented bone removed, bullet embedded in trabeculae (Alain Wittmann).

Figure 8.23c Femoral fragment with bullet removed (Alain Wittmann).

experimental study by Huelke et al. (1968a, 1968b), bone consistency (rather than bone thickness) and the projectile's velocity at impact were the most important factors in wound variation and accounted for the greatest amount of damage inflicted to the bone. The diameter of the sphere also played an important role. Huelke et al. (1968a, 1968b) found that larger spheres shot at lower velocities and small spheres fired at high velocities both caused "explosive" type injuries. In some cases, the distal portion of the condyles were separated from the shaft.

Figure 8.23d Isolated bullet recovered from distal femur (Alain Wittmann).

Trauma to the Forearm and the Lower Leg

Injuries to the forearm or lower leg may affect only one bone or both in combination (Figures 8.24–8.27). In cases in which high-velocity rounds are used at short or intermediate distances, it has been observed that both penetrating and grazing injuries through one bone may cause transverse fractures across the shaft of the neighboring bone at the same level of the injury. In these regions, the bones are closely associated, held together tightly in a confined area and encased in muscle and fascia. The occurrence of fractures, outside the area directly impacted or crushed by the bullet (outside of experimental models) is debated, as already discussed (Leffers and Chandler 1985; Fackler 1996; Kneubuehl and Thali 2003).

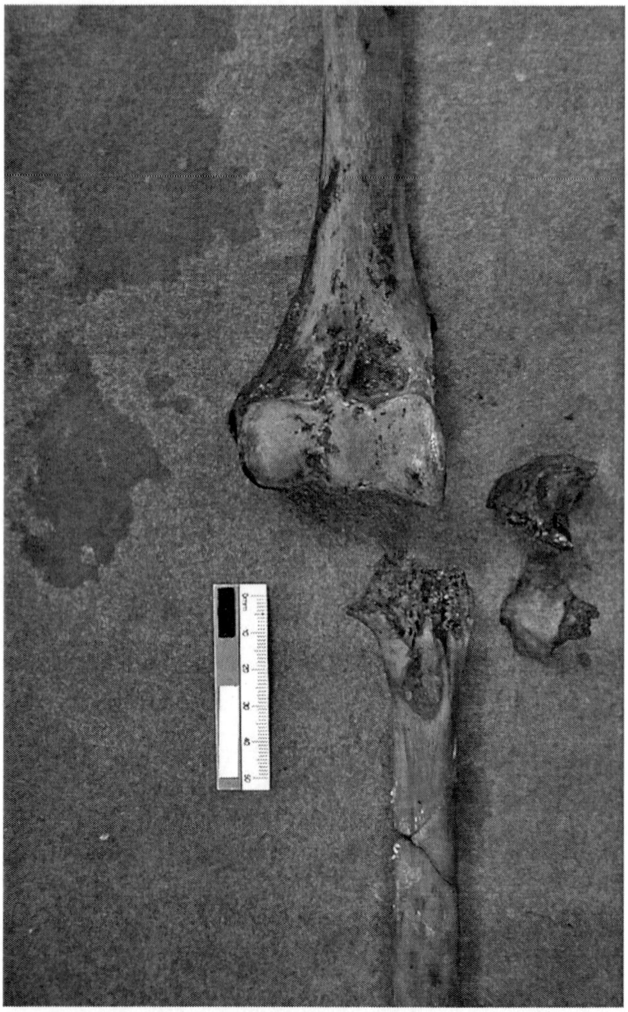

Figure 8.24 (See color insert following page 38) Gunshot wound through the right elbow with comminuted fractures of the proximal aspect of the ulna. (Printed with permission from International Criminal Tribunal for the former Yugoslavia [ICTY].)

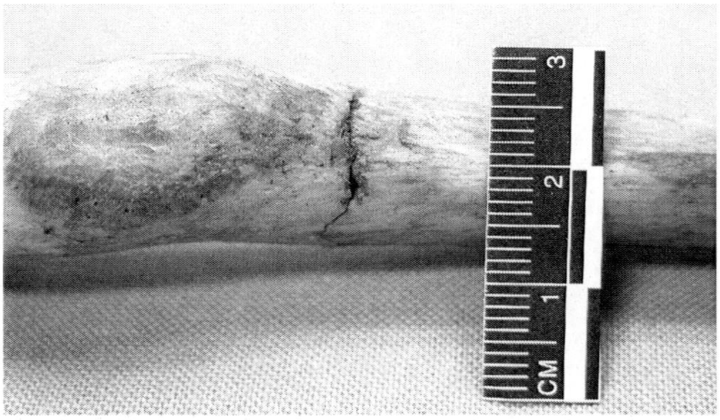

Figure 8.25a Anterior, medial view of the right radius. Transverse, complete fracture inferior to the radial tuberosity (Alain Wittmann).

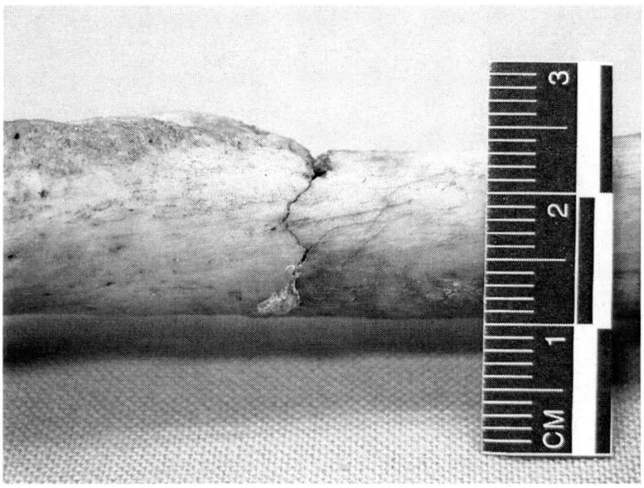

Figure 8.25b Posterior view of the radius. A distinct groove is present below the tuberosity. Fracture resulted from a gunshot injury, where the bullet impacted the ulna and grazed the radius. The radius, without the associated ulna, may suggest blunt force trauma (BFT), rather than a gunshot wound (GSW) due to the morphology of the defect (Alain Wittmann).

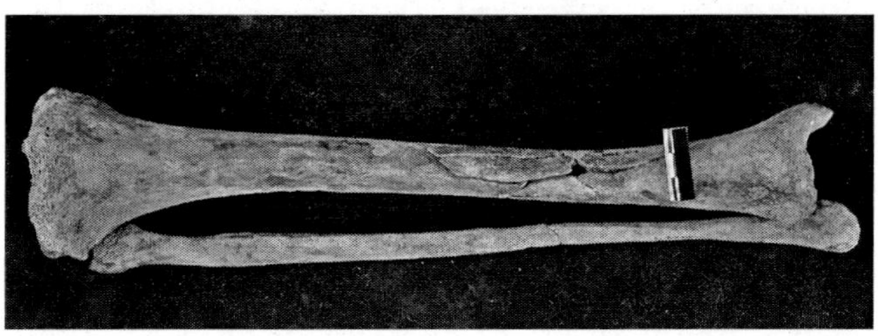

Figure 8.26 Anterior view of right tibia and fibula. The fibula also has a complete linear fracture though not directly impacted. A rounded defect associated to radiating fractures is visible on the anterior distal portion of the shaft, consistent with a gunshot wound through the tibia from left to right (Carlos Jacinto, FAFG).

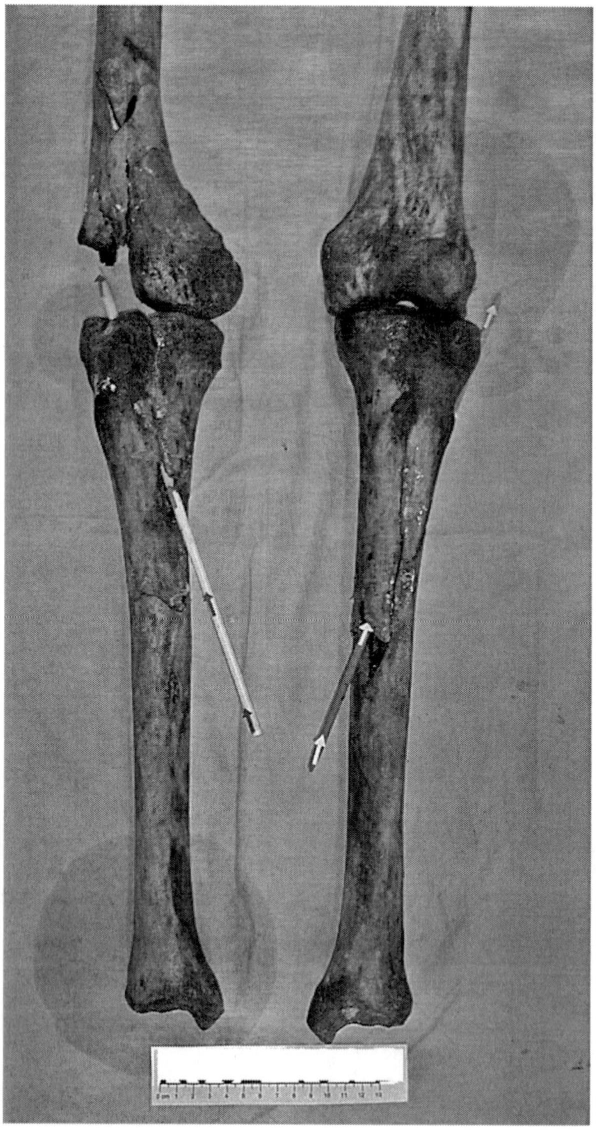

Figure 8.27 Two through-and-through gunshot wounds on the lower leg following a trajectory from down to up. The injury on the right leg penetrated below the knee and exited through the proximal articular surface of the tibia, shattering the lateral femoral condyle (right side). (Printed with permission from International Criminal Tribunal for the former Yugoslavia [ICTY].)

Fractures to the Hands and Feet

Injuries to hands and feet tend to be penetrating, although in some instances the projectile or a fragment may be retained in the bone (Figures 8.28 and 8.29). This is particularly true of bones of the feet, in which case, the bullet may be stopped by the floor. The larger tarsals or areas of trabecular bone tend to exhibit crushing injuries that have a *crumbling* appearance,

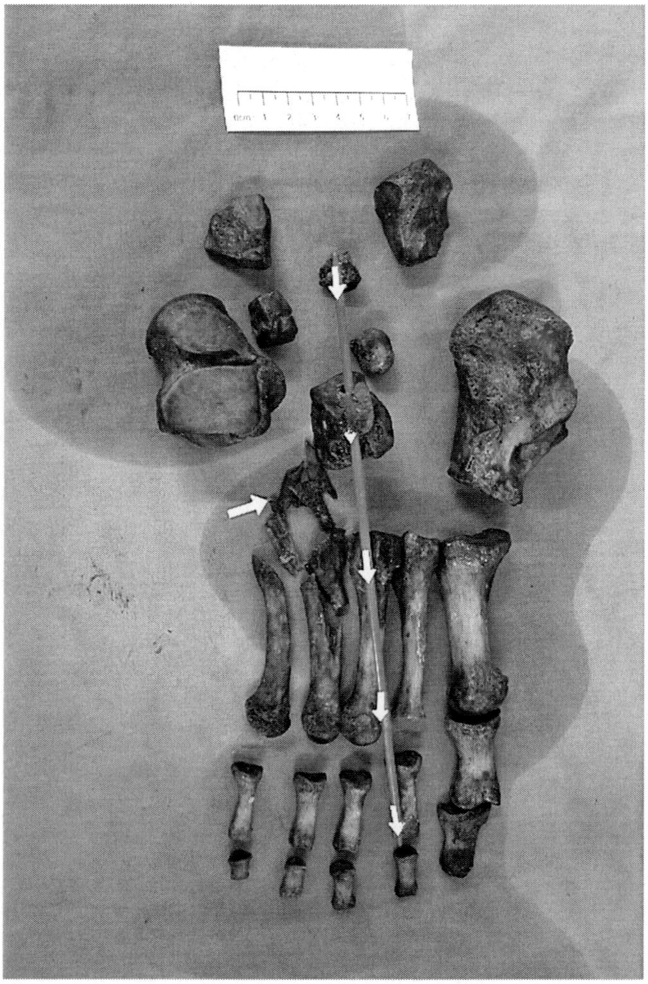

Figure 8.28 Superior view of the left foot showing a gunshot wound through fourth cuboid and proximal half of the fourth metatarsal. Note that the bones are shattered (Alain Wittmann).

rather than extensive comminuting fractures. In contrast, metacarpals and metatarsals tend to exhibit comminuting fractures of the shaft, which may affect multiple bones. Due to the size of hand and foot bones, the extent of damage may be extensive, further challenging interpretations.

Summary Guidelines for Best Practice

This chapter provided a simple overview of some of the common variations in GSWs to various parts of the skeleton. The examples presented here is not meant to be an exhaustive list; rather, they represent the common occurrences as observed through years of experience with such cases. Relying on data from skeletal tissue, without the added benefit of

Figure 8.29a Superior view of the articulated left calcaneus and talus showing a gutter wound through the two bones. Injury is consistent with a gunshot wound through the left foot, most likely from back to front (Alain Wittmann).

soft tissue, provides the opportunity to observe the entire skeleton without having to rely on radiographs. At the same time, it is clear that interpretations drawn from such data are limited to the estimation of some parameters such as the distance of fire or, in some cases, the type of ammunition. It is clear that in many recent armed conflicts and HHRR abuses, the types of weapons most commonly encountered are small arms such as handguns and rifles. Overall, there are identifiable patterns resulting from such weapons that provide critical information on the cause and manner of death. Such evidence is also shown to support witness testimony or other evidence of intentional murder or maltreatment. In cases where there are multiple mechanisms of injury, the series of events leading, and ultimately contributing, to death must be clearly interpreted as it provides evidence of what

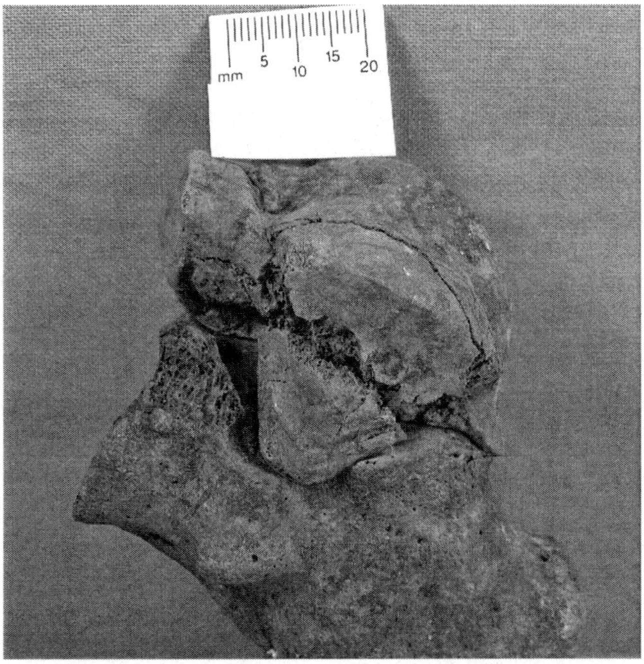

Figure 8.29b Lateral view of the calcaneus and talus showing "crumbling" appearance of talus from GSW (Alain Wittmann).

crimes (if any) may have been committed. The case studies presented in this chapter and throughout the book demonstrate the range of inflicted trauma and the common occurrence of torture and maltreatment before death. The wide range of variation in skeletal wounds also demonstrates how the context and other epidemiological factors are significant to interpreting evidence. As argued throughout this text, best practice guidelines begin with reconstruction of all broken bones, the association of wounds, and a methodological approach grounded in a framework to interpret injuries in a reliable and consistent manner based on observable skeletal and other supporting evidence.

Case Study 8.1: Tyranny and Torture in the Republic of Panama

Ann H. Ross
Department of Sociology and Anthropology, North Carolina State University, Raleigh, NC

Loreto Suarez S.
Former Director of Anthropology, Comisión De La Verdad, República de Panamá

The Republic of Panama has experienced a tumultuous first century of independence from Colombia, including the military dictatorships of Omar Torrijos (1968–1981), Manuel Noriega (1983–1989), and the U.S. invasion (*Operation Just Cause*) in 1989. In 2001, the Panamanian Truth Commission (Comisión de la Verdad) was formed in attempts to identify the "disappeared" during Torrijo's regime and offer some closure to the families of

Figure 8.30 T107, "El Pectorado," Marañon Cemetery, Coiba Island (Ross and Suarez).

the victims. During the previous investigations, the Truth Commission concluded that over 100 individuals were clearly certified as "disappeared" or executed for their political views, opposing the military regime. Informants' testimony, as well as written documents, strongly suggested that some of the "disappeared" ended up on the island of Coiba. The authors, under the auspices of the Truth Commission and with the cooperation of the National Police and the assistance of many others, undertook a large-scale excavation of the Marañon cemetery on Coiba, Republic of Panama, which is situated at the Central encampment of the Penal Colony. The Marañon cemetery has served as a final resting place for the inmate inhabitants of the Coiba prison colony from 1914 until 1992. The surrounding environment consists primarily of tropical rainforests with a rich red clay soil. The cemetery is oriented North to South and is clearly marked and demarcated by a barbed wire fence measuring 57.7 m at its longest by 21.9 m at its widest points. The individual represented in Figure 8.30 was nicknamed *El Pectorado*, for the large wooden cross lying on top of the chest cavity. The remains were determined to represent an adult male of indigenous ancestry (similar to the general population of Panama), most likely in his late thirties or forties. A reactive healing fracture was noted at the distal third of the left fibula along with a healed fracture to the right nasal and frontal process of the maxilla. A perimortem (probably GSW) comminuted fracture with no evidence of healing was observed approximately one-third of the distance from the acromial end on the left clavicle. Although clavicular fractures are relatively common, fractures of the outer third of the clavicle (class B) are relatively rare, involving only approximately 15% of clavicular fractures, and can result in complications (Figure 8.31).

The remains represented in Figure 8.32 were in a relatively good state of preservation suggesting probably the post-1980 period. A healed fracture complicated by infection with a large *cloaca* was evident on the distal shaft of the right humerus. Two large hypodermic bilaterally placed needles were evident within the rib cage, approximately at the level of the left and right ribs 2–7 (Figure 8.33). The placement of these devices is inconsistent with recognized medical interventions or procedures or the embalming process, which suggests they were used as a means of torture. For example, the medical procedure *thoracentesis*

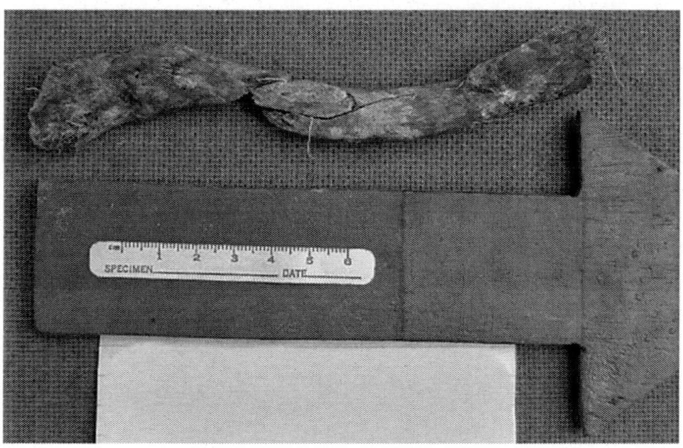

Figure 8.31 Perimortem comminuted fracture of the left clavicle, probably GSW (Ross and Suarez).

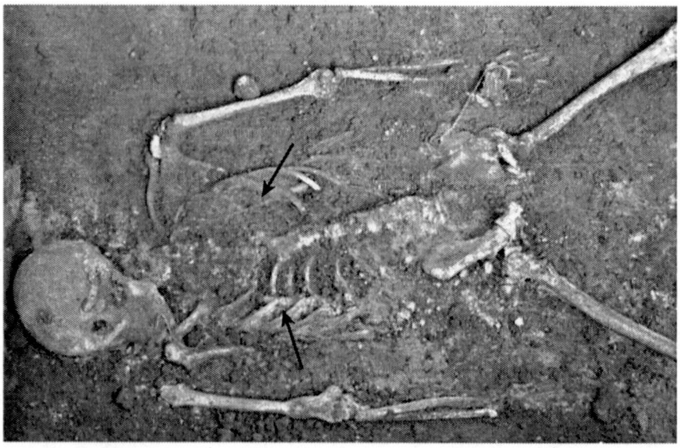

Figure 8.32 T112, Marañon cemetery, Coiba Island (Ross and Suarez).

(pleural cavity removal) requires a needle to be inserted at the second intercostal space at the level of the manubrium over the third rib, which is inconsistent with the pattern observed in these remains. Many of the individuals found in Marañon exhibited antemortem fractures throughout the skeleton in various stages of healing, which were obviously not "set," and had evidence of infection also suggesting they were not medically treated.

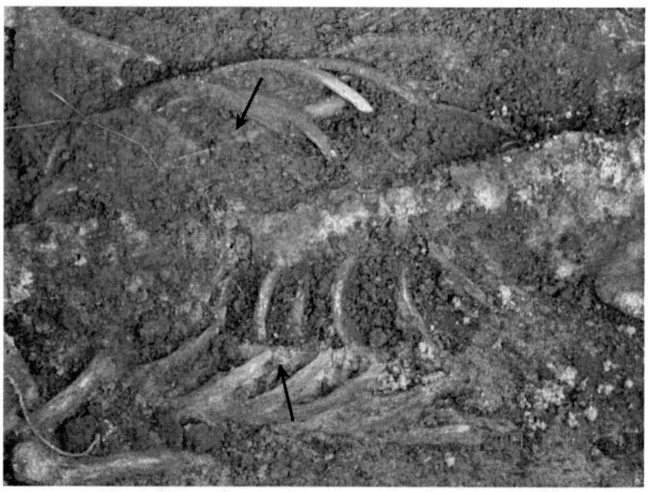

Figure 8.33 Evidence of torture using hypodermic needles (Ross and Suarez).

Case Study 8.2: The Pacific War: A Chilean Soldier Found in Cerro Zig Zag

Elsa Tomasto Cagigao
Curator of Human Remains National Museum of Archaeology, Anthropology and History of Peru, Professor, Catholic University of Peru

Mellisa Lund, EPAF
Assistant Curator of Human Remains National Museum of Archaeology, Anthropology and History of Peru, Peruvian Forensic Anthropology Team

In 1879, Peru and Chile fought a war, which culminated in the invasion of the Peruvian territory by Chilean troops in 1880 and the signing of a peace agreement in 1883 (Basadre 1968). In March of 1998, during the construction of a wall in the National Police School located in the outskirts of Cerro Zig Zag, south of Lima, the body of a Chilean soldier was found (Figure 8.34). It had been shallowly buried and carefully disposed of along with part of his possessions: a saber, a bag with pockets, each containing a box of bullets, a *poncho* beneath the body, and a bag under the head. He also had a notebook in which he described his trip from Chile to Peru and aspects of his last days of life. The body was dressed in a brown jacket, which was not the typical Chilean uniform but had buttons with the Chilean coat of arms, two trousers, a shirt and hide boots. A red scarf knotted on the chin was used to wrap the head, broken into multiple fragments, to keep it together (Figure 8.35). The body was partially mummified with remains of hair, beard, and moustache due to the dry conditions of the Peruvian coast. The available information indicates that this soldier died in the Battle of San Juan on January 13, 1881. In this battle, the Chilean troops attacked and broke the Peruvian lines defending Lima. Ten thousand soldiers from both sides died in the span of a morning (Basadre 1968; Ortiz 1996). Prior to examination, a full set of radiographs and a total body scan was carried out (Figures 8.36 and 8.37). The soldier, a Caucasian male 35 to 40 years of age at death, was about 1.66 m tall and showed a healed Bennett's fracture on his right hand suggesting he was right handed, as this kind of fracture occurs more frequently on the dominant hand (Angulo 1995; Galloway 1999). Radiographs showed a heavily fractured skull with an apparent injury on the left side of the frontal bone and some radio densities consistent with metal fragments. After reconstruction, the skull showed an oval defect with internal beveling on the left side of the frontal bone (Figure 8.38), between the frontal eminence and the temporal line, 27.4 mm from the supraorbital left arch and 46 mm from the coronal suture. The wound coalesces

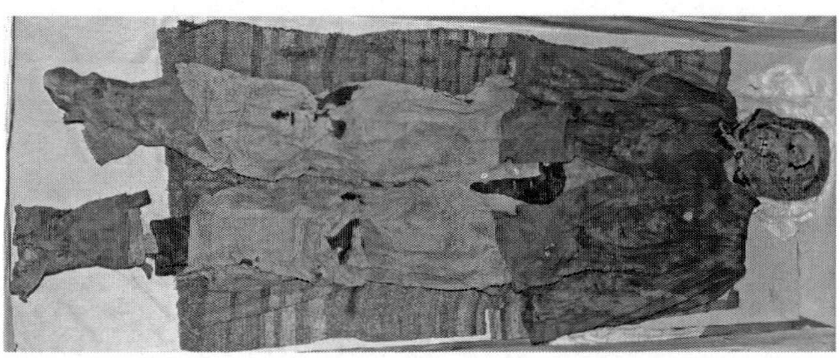

Figure 8.34 General view of a soldier's body with the Chilean uniform and *poncho* beneath the body (Alain Wittmann).

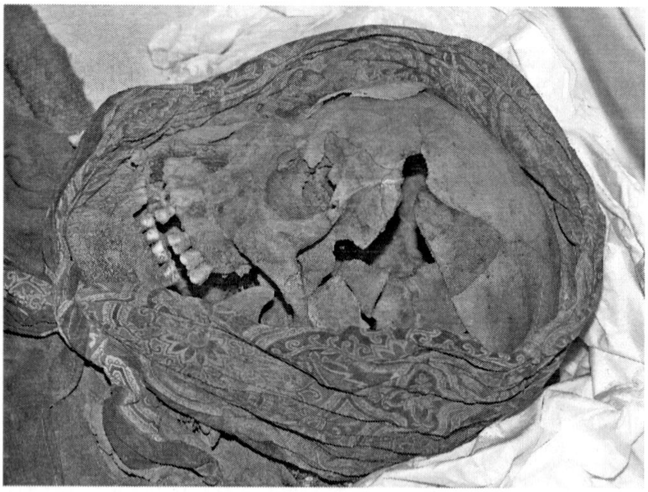

Figure 8.35 Close-up of the skull with a red scarf knotted at the chin. Note the good preservation of the soft tissue on the right side of the face (Alain Wittmann).

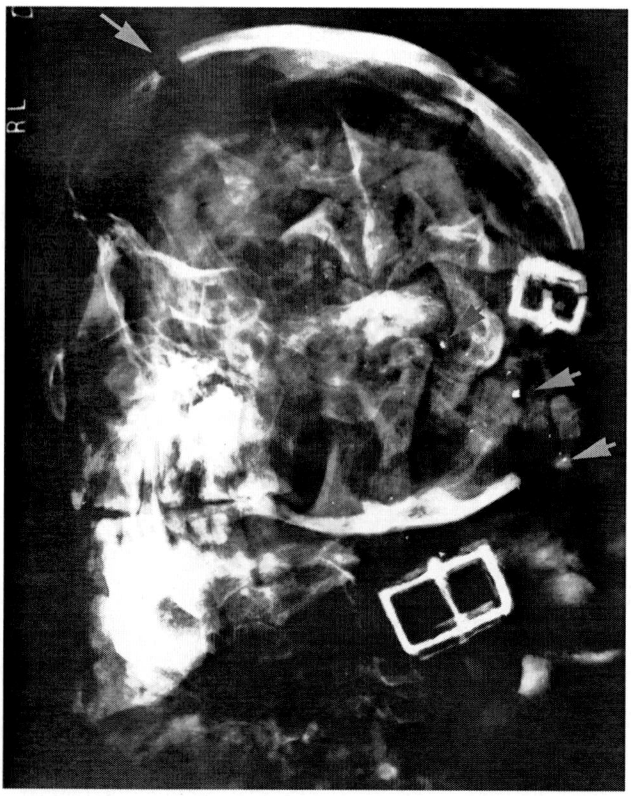

Figure 8.36 Radiograph taken before reconstructing the skull. Note the radio densities, possibly metal fragments (Tomasto and Lund).

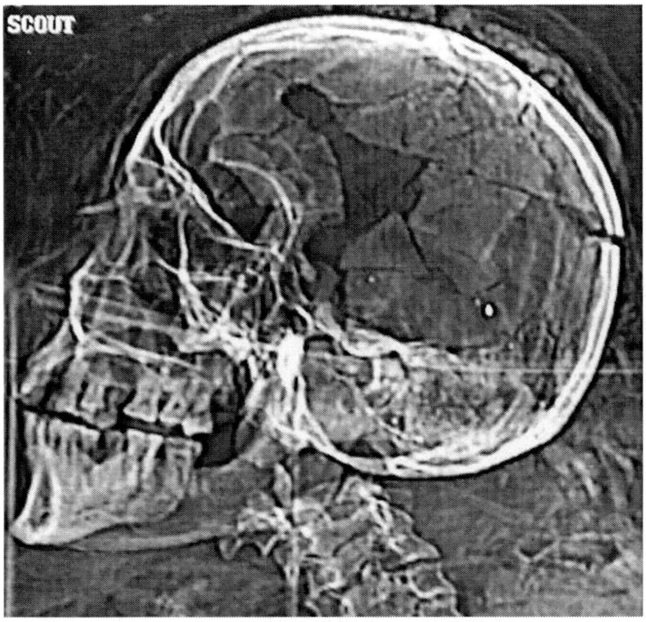

Figure 8.37 Scanning of the skull after the reconstruction. Note the radio densities, consistent with metal fragments (Alain Wittmann).

with a triangle-shaped defect (12.02 mm by 57.5 mm approximately) on the pterion region, the posterior border of which shows external beveling. The characteristics of this defect suggest a "keyhole" gunshot wound. Keyhole wounds are produced by tangential shots, in which the entrance and exit form a single structure (Byers 2002) (Figure 8.39). In the

Figure 8.38 Close-up view of the "keyhole" defect (Alain Wittmann).

Figure 8.39 Lateral view (left) showing an injury with radiating and concentric fractures and loss of bone fragments (Alain Wittmann).

present case, the entrance is on the left side of the frontal bone and is associated to multiple radiating fractures (Figure 8.40). One of these fractures contours the vault through the frontal bone below the bregma and proceeds posteriorly across the petromastoid area. A second fracture originating at the entrance proceeds inferiorly through the left side of the face (Figure 8.41). Regarding the exit, part of an external beveling is observed on the left parietal bone, next to the squamous suture and 45 mm from the superior temporal line, in the posterior edge of the triangle previously described. However, the fracture pattern of the temporal squama, and around the left lambdoid suture, suggests that there could have been another exit, possibly located about the left asterion (Figure 8.42).

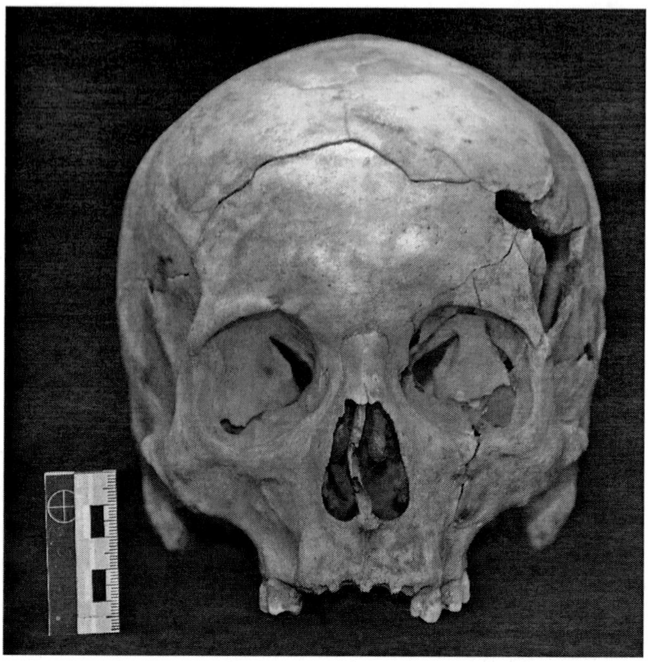

Figure 8.40 Frontal view of the skull showing keyhole and radiating fractures (Alain Wittmann).

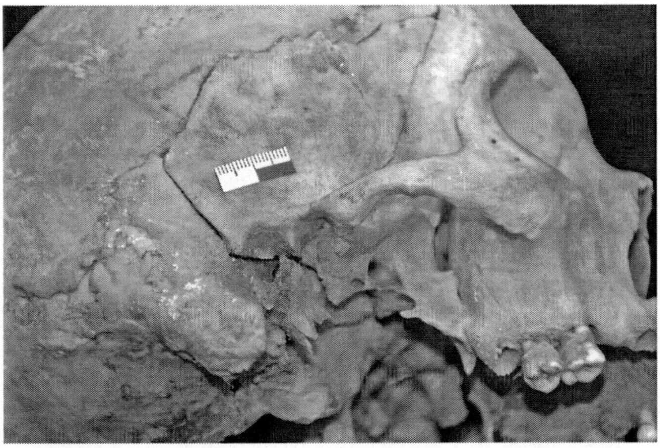

Figure 8.41 Fracture of the petromastoid area (Alain Wittmann).

Considering that we found a single entrance and two possible exits, the only possible explanation is that a single projectile split into two. Coe (1982) states that this situation is not impossible in tangential shots where a portion of the projectile is expelled, producing a keyhole defect, whereas the other fragment enters the skull cavity. In the present case, the existence of small radio dense areas inside the skull supports this explanation, suggesting that part of the projectile could have entered the cranial cavity, creating a second exit. The trajectory of the projectile, front to back, above to below, and right to left, is also consistent with only one entrance (Figure 8.43). When considering the trajectory, it is important to mention that according to the historical reconstruction of the events and the possible division the soldier belonged to, the individual was at the outpost trying to take a bastion where the enemy was in a superior location (Basadre 1968; Ortiz, n.d.). The degree of destruction of the skull is consistent with the use of a high-velocity weapon. In the Battle of San Juan, the Peruvian army mainly used Peabody Martini 0.45 caliber

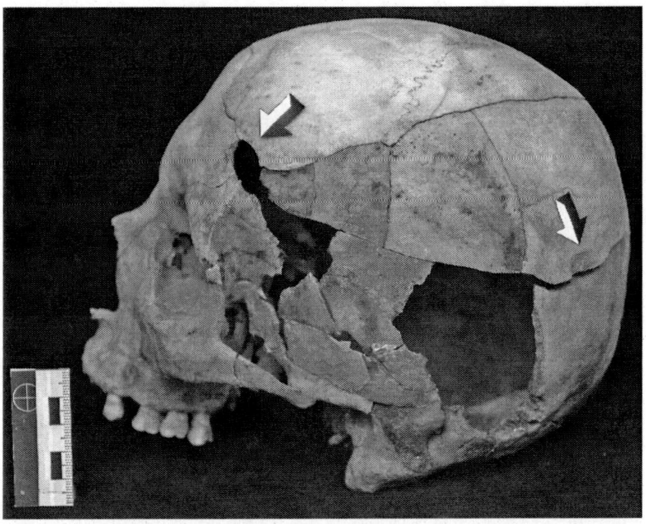

Figure 8.42 Lateral view. A possible second exit could be located in the area of the left asterion (Alain Wittmann).

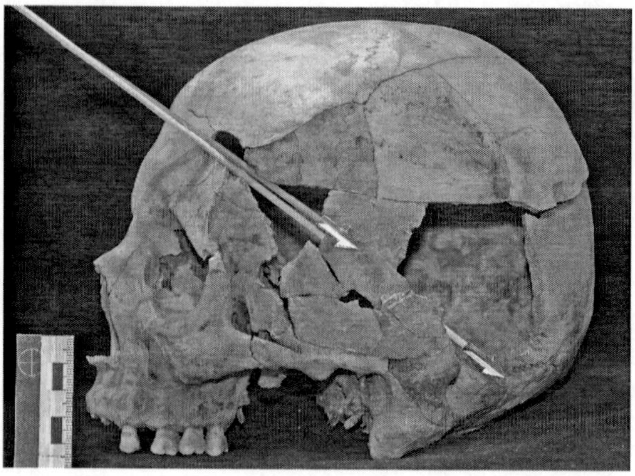

Figure 8.43 Projectile trajectory and two possible exits (Alain Wittmann).

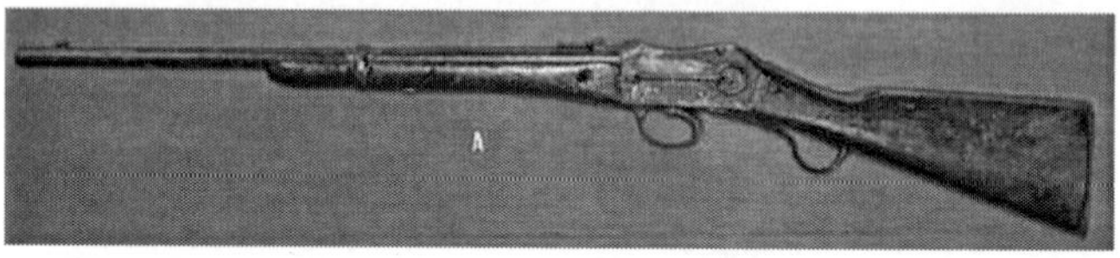

Figure 8.44 Peabody Martini rifle of 0.45 caliber used in the Pacific War (Alain Wittmann).

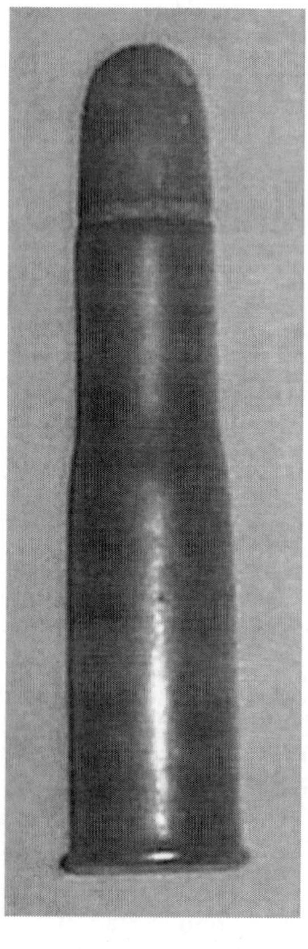

Figure 8.45 Peabody Martini bullet (Alain Wittmann).

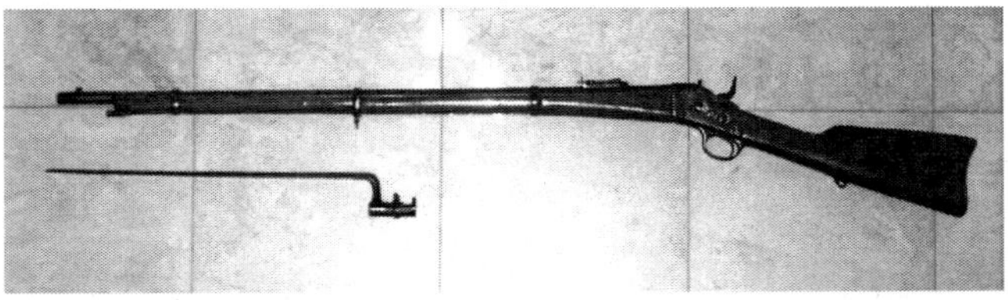

Figure 8.46 Remington rifle used in the Pacific War (Alain Wittmann).

rifles (Figures 8.44 and 8.45), and Remington 0.43 and 0.50 caliber (Figure 8.46), both of North American manufacture. Peabody Martini rifles have an initial velocity of 435 m/s and a kinetic energy of 184 kg/m. The side of the hill where the Soldier was found was defended by the IV Corps of the Peruvian army, under the command of General Cáceres (Basadre 1968; Ortiz 1996), armed with Peabody Martini rifles (Reynaldo Pizarro, personal communication). Most probably the soldier was injured with one of these weapons, considering all the characteristics described previously. Although the extent of the injury was life threatening and could cause immediate death, it would seem, as attested by certain findings, that the soldier survived for some hours and received some kind of medical attention. Soft-tissue samples from the lung showed evidence of pulmonary emphysema, consistent with a short survival of the victim (U. Garcia personal communication). On the other hand, an ultraviolet (UV) light examination of the clothing showed what seemed to be blood stains on the uniform. However, the scarf holding the head had most probably been placed after death as it did not show any staining (Thays 2006). Finally, the loss of some bone fragments of the left parietal could indicate an attempt to debride the wound by extracting intruding cranial fragments; this would also support the probability of treatment after the wound was inflicted. Although no cut marks were detected in the bones surrounding the wound, a small semicircular plug of bone chattered away from the external table of the left parietal was visible (Figures 8.47–8.48). We believe that this defect could have been produced

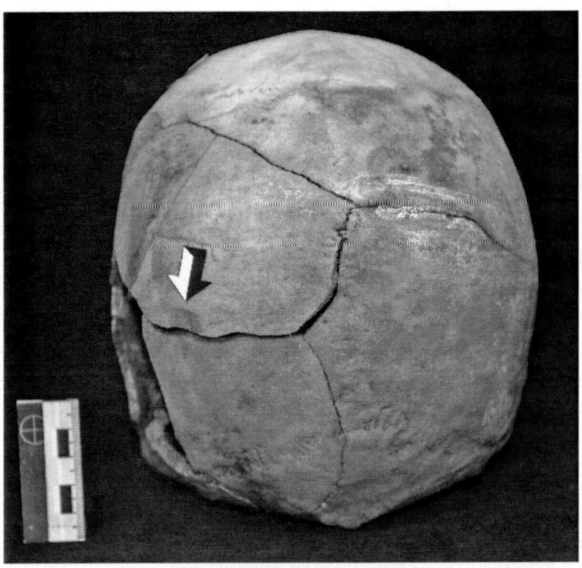

Figure 8.47 Small semicircular plug of bone chattered away from the external table of the left parietal (Alain Wittmann).

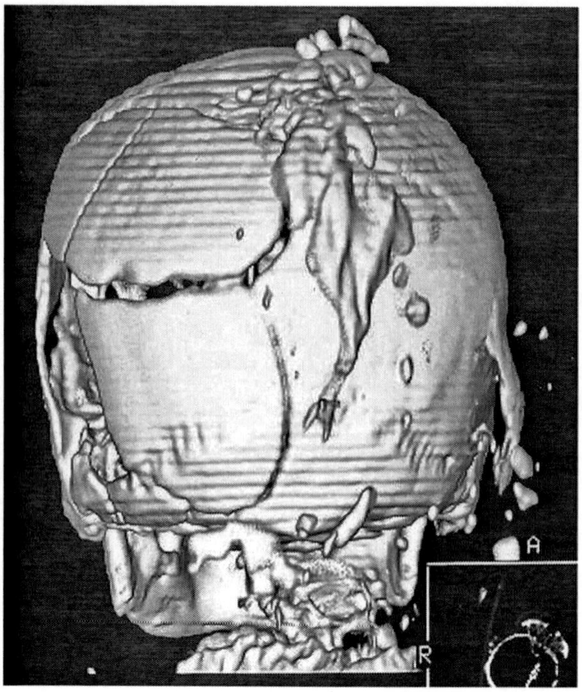

Figure 8.48 Scan of the skull showing the small semicircular plug (Alain Wittmann).

during the process of debriding the wound, in an attempt to extract a bone fragment still attached to the skull.*

* Acknowledgment: In this experiment, pigs were shot from a 3 m distance with an amount of gunpowder in the cartridges that would emulate the 100 m distance (Dakak et al. 2003). Member of the Navy Brigade Combatant of the Pacific War, a civil organization, whose objective is to recover military historical materials of Peru. The experiment was performed by Dr. Uriel García, Chief of the Pathology Section, Javier Prado Hospital, Lima, Peru. The study of the soldier was made by a multidisciplinary team working in the National Museum of Archaeology, Anthropology, and History of Peru. The discovery and field work was made by Dante Casareto and a team from the National Institute of Culture from Peru. The study and preservation of the uniform and associated metal objects was made under the direction of Carmen Thays and María Inés Velarde. Lizbeht Tepo helped with the reconstruction of the skull. We also want to specially thank José Pablo Baraybar, who helped us with the interpretation of the wound, Uriel García, who made the soft-tissue analysis and the CT scans, and Alain Wittmann, who kindly agreed to do all the photographs. Finally, we want to thank Jorge Ortiz and Reynaldo Pizarro who kindly assisted us with the historical reconstruction.

References

Aalund, O., Danielsen, L., and Sanhueza, R.O. 1990. Injuries due to deliberate violence in Chile. *Forensic Sci. Int.* 46(3): 189–202.

Aboutanos, M.B. and Baker, S.P. 1997. Wartime civilian injuries: epidemiology and intervention strategies. *J. Trauma Injury Infect. Crit. Care* 43(4): 719–726.

Adams, V.I. and Hirsch, C.S. 1993. Trauma and disease. In Spitz, W.U. and Fisher, R.S. (Eds.). *Medicolegal investigation of death: Guidelines for the application of pathology to crime investigation.* Springfield, IL: Charles C Thomas, pp. 175–198, 3rd ed.

Adi, M., Ogden, G.R., and Chisholm, D.M. 1990. An analysis of mandibular fractures in Dundee, Scotland (1977 to 1985). *Br. J. Oral Maxillofac Surg.* 28(3): 194–199.

Allan, B.P. and Daly, C.G. 1990. Fractures of the mandible. A 35-year retrospective study. *Int. J. Oral Maxillofac Surg.* 19(5): 268–271.

Altun, G. and Durmus-Altun, G. 2003. Confirmation of alleged falanga torture by bone scintigraphy-Case report. *Int. J. Legal Med.* 117(6): 365–366.

Altun, G., Akansu, B., Ugur Antun, B., Azmak, D., and Yilmaz, A. 2004. Deaths due to hunger strike: post-mortem findings. *Forensic Sci. Int.* 146: 35–38.

Alunni-Perret, V., Muller-Bolla, M., Laugier, J.P., Lupi-Pegurier, L., Bertrand, M.F., Staccini, P., Bolla, M., and Quatrehomme, G. 2005. Scanning electron microscopy analysis of experimental bone hacking trauma. *J. Forensic Sci.* 50(4): 796–801.

Ambade, V.N. and Godbole, H.V. 2006. Comparison of wound patterns in homicide by sharp and blunt force. *Forensic Sci. Int.* 156(2–3): 166–170.

Amnesty International. 1990. *El Salvador: Peace without justice.* London: Amnesty International.

Amnesty International. 2003. *Torture: A manual for action.* London: Amnesty International.

Anania, W.C., Rosen, R.C., and Giuffre, A.M. 1987. Gunshot wounds to the lower extremity: principles and treatment. *J. Foot Surg.* 26(3): 228–232.

Anderson, R. 2000. A study of the biomechanics of axonal injury [Ph.D. dissertation], University of Adelaide, South Australia.

Anglin, D., Hutson, H.R., Luftman, J., Qualls, S., and Moradzadeh, D. 1998. Intracranial hemorrhage associated with tangential gunshot wounds to the head. *Acad Emerg Med.* 5(7): 672–677.

Angulo, P. 1995. *Ortopedia y Traumatología. Patología del Aparato Locomotor. Tomo 2.* Lima, Peru: CONCYTEC.

Appleman, J.A. 1971. *Military tribunals and international crimes.* Westport, CN: Greenwood Press, 421 pp.

Arajarvi, E., Santavirta, S., and Tolonen, J. 1987. Abdominal injuries sustained in severe traffic accidents by seatbelt wearers. *J. Trauma Injury Infect. Crit. Care* 27(4): 393–397.

Arnold, B. 2002. Justifying genocide: Archaeology and the construction of difference. In Hinton, A.L. (Ed.). *Annihilating Difference: The Anthropology of Genocide.* California series in public anthropology 3, Berkeley, CA: University of California Press, pp. 95–116.

Arya, N. and Cukier, W.L. 2005. The international small arms situation: a public health approach. In Mahoney, P.F., Ryan, J.M., Brooks, A., and Schwab, C.W. (Eds.). *Ballistic Trauma.* 2nd ed. London: Springer-Verlag, pp. 3–30.

Asirdizer, M., Yavuz, M.S., Sari, H., Canturk, G., and Yorulmaz, C. 2004. Unusual torture methods and mass murders applied by a terror organization. *Am. J. Forensic Med. Pathol.* 25(4): 314–320.

Atanasijevic, T.C., Savic, S.N., Nikolic, S.D., and Djoki, V.M. 2005. Frequency and severity of injuries in correlation with the height of fall. *J. Forensic Sci.* 50(3): 608–612.

Aufderheide, A.C. and Rodriguez-Martin, C. 1998. *Cambridge encyclopedia of human paleopathology.* Cambridge, MA: Cambridge University Press.

Bandak, F.A., Zhang, A.X., Dimasi, F., Masiello, P., and Eppinger, R. 2001. SIMON: A simulated injury monitor: application to head injury assessment. Proceedings of the 2001 ESV Conference, Amsterdam, The Netherlands.

Bandak, F.A. and Chan, P.C. 1999. Influence of the subarachnoïd cerebrospinal fluid layer on the dynamic response of the brain: an experimental and computing study. Injury Biomechanical Research Program, Proceedings of the 27th Human Subject Biomechanical Workshop, San Diego, CA, pp. 115–139.

Baraybar, J.P. 2006. Summary findings on the forensic inspections carried out by the Office on Missing Persons and Forensics (OMPF) on the human remains found in three mass grave sites in Serbia after their transfer to Kosovo. Report submitted to the Office of the Prosecutor of the International Criminal Tribunal for the former Yugoslavia (ICTY). *The Prosecutor v. Milutinovic* et al. (Case No. IT-05–87).

Baraybar, J.P. and Gasior, M. 2006. Forensic anthropology and the determination of the most probable cause of death: an example from Bosnia and Herzegovina. *J. Forensic Sci.* 51(1): 103–108.

Barnes, E. 1994. *Developmental defects of the axial skeleton in paleopathology.* Colorado: University Press of Colorado, 392 pp.

Barrett, R., Kuzawa, C.W., McDade, T., and Armelagos, G.J. 1998. Emerging and re-emerging infectious disease: the third epidemiological transition. *Annu Rev. Anthropol* 27: 247–271.

Barsness, K.A., Cha, E.S., Bensard, D.D., Calkins, C.M., Partrick, D.A., Karrer, F.M., and Strain, J.D. 2003. The positive predictive value of rib fractures as an indicator of non accidental trauma in children. *J. Trauma Injury Infect. Crit. Care* 54(6): 1107–1110.

Bartelink, E.J., Wiersema, J.M., Demaree, and R.S. 2001. Quantitative analysis of sharp-force trauma: an application of scanning electron microscopy in forensic anthropology. *J. Forensic Sci.* 46(6): 1288–1293.

Bartlett, C.S., Helfet, D.L., Hausman, M.R., and Strauss. R. 2000. Ballistics and gunshot wounds: effects on musculoskeletal tissues. *J. Am. Acad Orthop. Surg.* 8(1): 21–36.

Basadre, J. 1968. *Historia de la República del Perú (1822–1933). Volumen VIII.* VIth Ed. Lima, Peru: Editorial Universitaria.

Bass, W.M. 1984. Is it possible to consume a body completely in a fire? In Rathburn, T. and Buikstra, J.E. (Eds.). *Human identification: Case studies in forensic anthropology.* Springfield, IL: Charles C Thomas, pp. 159–167.

Bass, W.M. and Jantz, R.L. 2004. Cremation weights in East Tennessee. *J. Forensic Sci.* 49(5): 529–533.

Bauel, M. and Patzelt, D. 2002. Intracranial stab injuries: case report and case study. *Forensic Sci. Int.* 129(2): 122–127.

Behrensmeyer, A.K. and Hill, A.P. 1980. *Fossils in the making: Vertebrate taphonomy and paleoecology.* Chicago, IL: University of Chicago Press, 345 pp.

Bellamy, R.F. 1992. The medical effects of conventional weapons. *World J. Surg.* 16(5): 888–892.

Bellamy, R.F. 2000. Why is marine combat mortality less than that of the army? *Mil. Med.* 165(5): 362–367.

Bennet, G.A. 1966. Bones. In: *Pathology.* Anderson, W.A.D., Ed., St. Louis, MO: C.V. Mosby Co. 5th ed. Vol. 2: 1300–1305.

Benomar, J. 1993. Confronting the past: Justice after transitions. *J. Dem.* 4(1): 3–14.

Ben-Ya'acov, Y., Amir, M., Arzy, R., and Kotler, M. 2005. Trauma in military and civilian settings. *Clin. Psychol Psychother* 12: 1–9.

Berryman, H. and Haun, S. 1996. Applying forensic techniques to interpret cranial fracture patterns in an archaeological specimen. *Int. J. Osteoarchaeol* 6: 2–9.

Berryman, H.E., Smith, O.C., and Symes, S.A. 1995. Diameter of cranial gunshot wounds as a function of bullet caliber. *J. Forensic Sci.* 40(5): 751–754.

Berryman, H.E. and Symes, S.A. 1998. Recognizing gunshot and blunt cranial trauma through fracture interpretation. In Reichs, K.J. (Ed.). *Forensic osteology II: Advances in the identification of human remains.* Springfield, IL: Charles C Thomas, pp. 487–496.

Best, G.F.A. 1994. *War and law since 1945.* Oxford: Clarendon Press.

Betz, P. and Liebhardt, E. 1994. Rib fractures in children—resuscitation or child abuse? *Int. J. Legal Med.* 106(4): 215–218.

Betz, P., Stiefelb, D., Hausmanna, R., and Eisenmenger, W. 1997. Fractures at the base of the skull in gunshots to the head. *Forensic Sci. Int.* 86(3): 155–161.

Beyer, J.C. (Ed.). 1962. *Wound ballistics.* Office of the Surgeon General Department of the Army, Washington, D.C. Electronic File: http://history.amedd.army.mil/booksdocs/wwii/wound blstcs/default.htm.

Bhoopat, T. 1995. A case of internal beveling with an exit gunshot wound to the skull. *Forensic Sci. Int.* 71(2): 97–101.

Binford, L. 1996. *The El Mozote massacre: Anthropology and human rights.* Tucson, AZ: University of Arizona Press, 263, pp.

Biocina, B., Sutlic, Z., Husedzinovic, I., Rudez, I., Ugljen, R., Letica, D., Slobodnjak, Z., Karadza, J., Brida, V., Vladovic-Relja, T., and Jelic, I. 1997. Penetrating cardiothoracic war wounds. *Eur. J. Cardio-Thorac Surg.* 11: 399–405.

Blau, S., Hill, A., Briggs, C.A., Cordner, and S.M. 2006. Missing persons-missing data: the need to collect antemortem dental records of missing persons. *J. Forensic Sci.* 51(2): 386–389.

Bohnert, M.T., Rost, T., and Pollak, S. 1998. The degree of destruction of human bodies in relation to the duration of the fire. *Forensic Sci. Int.* 95: 11–21.

Born, C.T. 2005. Blast trauma: the fourth weapon of mass destruction. *Scand J. Surg.* 94(4): 279–285.

Bosnar, A., Stemberga, V., Cuculic, D., Coklo, M., Cucic, T., and Dobi-Babic, R. 2005. Massacre over civilians during the war in Croatia. *Coll Antropologia* 29(2): 757–761.

Boutwell, J., Klare, M.E., and Reed, L.W. (Eds.). 1995. *Lethal commerce: The global trade in small arms and light weapons.* Cambridge, MA: Committee on International Security Studies American Academy of Arts and Sciences.

Bowen, T.E. and Bellamy, R.F. (Eds.). 2002. *Emergency war surgery.* Second United States Revision of the *Emergency war surgery NATO handbook.* Washington, D.C. In http://www.brooksidepress.org/Products/OperationalMedicine/DATA/operationalmed/Manuals/NATOEWS/ewstoc.htm.

Bowen, T.E. and Bellamy, R.F. (Eds.). 2004. *Emergency war surgery.* Third United States Revision of the *Emergency war surgery NATO handbook.* Washington, D.C.

Boyer, G.W., Cooper, G.J., and Rice, P. 1996. Small fragment wounds: biophysics and pathophysiology. *J. Trauma Injury Infect. Crit. Care* 40, Suppl.: S159–S164.

Bradtmiller, B. and Buikstra, J.E. 1984. Effects of burning on human bone microstructure: a preliminary study. *J. Forensic Sci.* 29: 535–540.

Breederveld, R.S., Patka, P., and van Mourik, J.C. 1988. Fractures of the sternum. *Netherlands J. Surg.* 40(5): 133–135.

Brickley, M.B. 2007. A case of disposal of a body through burning and recent advances in the study of burned human remains. In Brickley, M.B. and Ferllini, R. (Eds.). *Forensic anthropology: Case studies from Europe.* Springfield, IL: Charles C Thomas, pp. 69–85.

Brickley, M.B. 2005. Rib fractures in the archaeological record: a useful source of sociocultural information? *Int. J. Osteoarchaeol* 16(1): 61–75.

Brickley, M.B. and Ferllini, R. (Eds.). 2007. *Forensic anthropology: Case studies from Europe.* Springfield, IL: Charles C Thomas. 250 pp.

Briend, A. and Golden, M.H.N. 1993. Treatment of severe child malnutrition in refugee camps. *Eur. J. Clin. Nutr* 47(10): 750.

Brink, O., Vesterby, A., and Jensen, J. 1998. Pattern of injuries due to interpersonal violence. *Injury* 29(9): 705–709.

Brogdon, B.G., Vogel, H., and McDowell, J.D. (Eds.). 2003. *A radiologic atlas of abuse, torture, terrorism, and inflicted trauma*. Boca Raton, FL: CRC Press, 328 pp.

Brookes, J.G., Dunn, R.J., and Rogers, I.R. 1993. Sternal fractures: a retrospective analysis of 272 cases. *J. Trauma Injury Infect. Crit. Care* 35(1): 46–54.

Brothwell, D.R. 1981. *Digging up bones*. New York: Cornell University Press, 224 pp.

Brukner, P. and Khan, K. 1996. Stress fracture of the neck of the 7th and 8th ribs: a case report. *Clin. J. Sport Med.* 6(3): 204–206.

Brunborg, H. 2000. Contribution of statistical analysis to the investigations of the international criminal tribunals. *Stat J. UN Econ Comm Eur.* 18: 227–238.

Brunborg, H. and Tabeau, E. 2005. Demography of conflict and violence: an emerging field. *Eur. J. Popul* 21(2–3): 131–144.

Brynin, R. and Gardiner, L. 2001. Missed lumbar transverse process fractures in a high school football player. *J. Manipulative Physiol Ther* 24(2): 123–126.

Buchsbaum, H.J. and Caruso, P.A. 1969. Gunshot wound of the pregnant uterus: case report of fetal injury, deglutition of missile, and survival. *Obstet Gynecol* 33(5): 673–676.

Buckwalter, J.A., Einhorn, T.A., Bolander, M.E., and Cruess, R.L. 1996. Healing of musculoskeletal tissues. In Rockwood, C.A., Bucholz, R.W., Green, D.P., and Heckman, J.D. (Eds.). *Fractures in adults*, 4th ed., Vol. 1. Philadelphia, PA: Lippincott-Raven, pp. 267–283.

Budimlija, Z.M., Prinz, M.K., Zelson-Mundorff, A., Wiersema, J., Bartelink, E., MacKinnon, G., Nazzaruolo, B.L., Estacio, S.M., Hennessey, M.J., and Shaler, R.C. 2003. World Trade Center human identification Project: Experiences with individual body identification cases. *Croatian Med. J.* 44(3): 259–263.

Buikstra, J.E. and Beck, L.A. (Eds.) 2006. *Bioarchaeology: The contextual analysis of human remains*. Amsterdam, Netherlands: Elsevier, 606 pp.

Buikstra, J.E. and Ubelaker, D. (Eds.). 1994. Standards for data collection from human skeletal remains. Proceedings of a seminar at the Field Museum of Natural History. Arkansas Archaeological Survey Research Series No. 44, 218 pp.

Bulger, E.M., Arneson, M.A., Mock, C.N., and Jurkovich, J.G. 2000. Rib fractures in the elderly. *J. Trauma Injury Infect. Crit. Care* 48(6): 1040–1046; discussion: 1046–1047.

Bun Heng, M. and Key, P.J. 1995. Cambodian health in transition. *Br. Med. J.* 311(7002): 435–437.

Burke, C.N. and Geiselman, C.W. 1971. Exact anhydride epoxy percentages for electron microscopy embedding (Rpon). *J. Ultrastruct Res* 36: 119–126.

Burns, K. 1998. Forensic anthropology and human rights issues. In Reichs, K. (Ed.). *Forensic osteology: Advances in the identification of human remains*. 2nd ed. Springfield, IL: Charles C Thomas, pp. 63–85.

Butkovic-Soldo, S., Brkic, K., Puntaric, D., and Petrovicki, Z. 1995. Medical corps support to a brigade action during an offensive action including river crossing. *Mil Med.* 160: 408–411.

Byers, M., Ryan, J.M., and Mahoney, P.F. 2005. Part I. How guns work. In Mahoney, P.F., Ryan, J.M., Brooks, A., and Schwab, C.W. (Eds.). *Ballistic Trauma*. 2nd ed. London: Springer-Verlag, pp. 31–39.

Byers, S. 2005. *Forensic anthropology: A textbook*. 2nd ed. Boston, MA: Allyn and Bacon, 496 pp.

Byers, S. 2002. *Forensic anthropology: A textbook*. Boston, MA: Allyn and Bacon, 310 pp.

Bzik, K.D. and Bellamy, R.F. 1984. A note on combat casualty statistics. *Mil Med.* 149: 229–230.

Cakir, I., Cetin, G., Uner, H.B., and Albek, E. 2003. Shot range estimation based on pellet distribution in shots with a pump-action shotgun. *Forensic Sci. Int.* 132(3): 211–215.

Campobasso, C.P., Falamingo, R., and Vinci, F. 2003. Investigation of Italy's deadliest building collapse: forensic aspects of a mass disaster. *J. Forensic Sci.* 48(3): 635–639.

Catanese, C.A. and Gilmore, K. 2002. Fetal gunshot wound characteristics. *J. Forensic Sci.* 47(5): 1067–1069.

Cattaneo, C., Marinelli, E., Di Giancamillo, A., Di Giancamillo, M., Travetti, O., Vigano, L., Poppa, P., Porta, D., Gentilomo, A., and Grandi, M. 2006. Sensitivity of autopsy and radiological examination in detecting bone fractures in an animal model: implications for the assessment of fatal child physical abuse. *Forensic Sci. Int.* 164(2–3): 131–137.

CDC Primer. 2003. *Explosions and blast injuries: A primer for clinicians*. Department of Health and Human Services, Centers for Disease Control and Prevention: U.S. Government. Last Modification May 9. In http://www.bt.cdc.gov/masscasualties/explosions.asp.

Celiköz, B., Sengezer, M., Isik, S., Türegün, M., Deveci, M., Duman, H., Acikel, C., Nisanci, M., and Öztürk, S. 2005. Subacute reconstruction of lower leg and foot defects due to high velocity-high energy injuries caused by gunshots, missiles, and land mines. *Microsurgery* 25: 3–15.

Cernak, I., Savic, J., Ignjatovic, D., and Jevtic, M. 1999. Blast injuries form explosive munitions. *J. Trauma Injury Infect. Crit. Care* 47(1): 96–103.

Chambers, L.W., Rhee, P., Baker, B.C., Perciballi, J., Cubano, M., Compeggie, M., Nace, M., and Bohman, H.R. 2005. Initial experiences of U.S. Marine Corps forward resuscitative surgical system during Operation Iraqi Freedom. *Arch Surg.* 140(1): 26–32.

Champion, H.R., Bellamy, R.F., Roberts, P., and Leppaniemi, A. 2003. A profile of combat injury. *J. Trauma* 54: S13–S19.

Chandler, D. 1999. *Voices from S-21: Terror and history in Pol Pot's secret prison*. Berkeley, CA: The University of California Press, 238 pp.

Cheung, K.K. 1999. Identifying and documenting findings of physical child abuse and neglect. *J. Pediatr. Healthcare* 13: 142–143.

Chidzonga, M.M. 1990. Mandibular fractures, analysis of 541 cases. *Central Africa J. Med.* 36(4): 97–103.

Chinn, B.P., Doyle, D., Otte, D., and Schuller, E. 1999. Motorcyclists head injury: mechanisms identified from accident reconstruction and helmet damage replication. Proceedings of the 1999 IRCOBI Conference, pp. 53–71.

Chowdhury, R. and Mohan, M. 2004. Maxillofacial injuries in counter proxy war posture of the armed forces. *MJAFI* 60(4): 357–362.

Christensen, A.M. 2004. The influence of behavior on freefall injury patterns: possible implications for forensic anthropological investigations. *J. Forensic Sci.* 49(1): 5–10.

Christensen, E.E. and Dietz, G.W. 1980. Injuries of the first costoverebral articulation. *Radiology* 134: 41–43.

Clyne, A. 1955. The wounding and killing power of small arms fire in jungle operations. *J. R Army Med. Corps* 101: 33–38.

Coe, J.I. 1982. External beveling of entrance wounds by handguns. *Am. J. Forensic Med. Pathol.* 3(3): 215–219.

Comision de la Verdad, Reconciliación y Justicia (CVR). 2003. Informe Final. Lima. Perú. In www.cverdad.org.pe.

Cook, D.C. and Powell, M.L. 2006. The evolution of American paleopathology. In Buikstra, J.E. and Beck, L.A. (Eds.). *Bioarchaeology: The contextual analysis of human remains*. Amsterdam, Netherlands: Elsevier, pp. 281–322.

Cooper, G.J., Pearce, B.P., Stainer, M.C., and Maynard, R.L. 1982. The biomechanical response of the thorax to nonpenetrating impact with particular reference to cardiac injuries. *J. Trauma Injury Infect. Crit. Care* 22(12): 994–1008.

Cooper, G.J. and Ryan, J.M. 1990. Interaction of penetrating missiles with tissues: some common misapprehension and implications for wound management. *Br. J. Surg.* 77(6): 606–610.

Cooper, G.J., Maynard, R.L., Cross, N.L., and Hill, J.F. 1983 Casualties from terrorist bombings. *J. Trauma Injury Infect. Crit. Care* 23: 955–967.

Cordner, S. and McKelvie, H. 2002. Developing standards in international forensic work to identify missing persons. *IRRC* 848(84): 867–884.

Cory, C.Z., Jones, M.D., James, D.S., Leadbeatter, S., and Nokes, L.D. 2001. The potential and limitations of utilising head impact injury models to assess the likelihood of significant head injury in infants after a fall. *Forensic Sci. Int.* 123(2–3): 89–106.

Coupland, R.M. 2005. Ballistic trauma, armed violence, and international law. In Mahoney, P.F., Ryan, J.M., Brooks, A., and Schwab, C.W. (Eds.). *Ballistic trauma.* 2nd ed. London: Springer-Verlag, pp. 122–136.

Coupland, R.M. 2001. Armed violence. *Med. Global Survival* 7: 33–37.

Coupland, R.M.1997. Abhorrent weapons and "superfluous injury or unnecessary suffering": from field surgery to law. *Br. Med. J.* 315: 1450–1452.

Coupland, R.M.1994. Epidemiological approach to the surgical management of the casualties of war. *Br. Med. J.* 308: 1693–1697.

Coupland, R.M. 1993. Hand grenade injuries among civilians. *J. Am. Med. Assoc. (JAMA)* 270(5): 624–626.

Coupland, R.M., Hoikka, V., Sjoeklint, O.G., Cuenod, P., Cauderay, G.C., and Doswald-Beck, L. 1992. Assessment of bullet disruption in armed conflicts. *Lancet* 339(8784): 35–37.

Coupland, R.M. and Korver, A. 1991. Injuries from antipersonnel mines: the experience of the International Committee of the Red Cross. *Br. Med. J.* 303: 1509–1512.

Coupland, R.M. and Meddings, D.R. 1999. Mortality associated with the use of weapons in armed conflicts, wartime atrocities, and civilian mass shootings: Literature review. *Br. Med. J.* 319: 407–410.

Covey, D.C. 2002. Blast and fragment injuries of the musculoskeletal system. *J. Bone Jt. Surg.* 84: 1221–1234.

Crane, J. 2000. Violence associated with civil disturbance. In Mason J.K., Purdue B.N. (Eds.). *The pathology of trauma.* London: Edward Arnold, pp. 83–88.

Cukier, W. and Chapdelaine, A. 2002. Small arms, explosives, and incendiaries. In Levy, B.S. and Sidel, V.W. (Eds.). *Terrorism and Public Health: A balanced approach to strengthening systems and protecting people.* Oxford, England: Oxford University Press, 408 pp.

Cunha, E. 2006. Pathology as a factor of personal identity in forensic anthropology. In Schmitt, A., Cunha, E., and Pinheiro, J. (Eds.). *Forensic Anthropol. Med.* Totowa, NJ: Humana Press, pp. 333–358.

Curry, J.D. 1970. The mechanical properties of bone. *Clin. Orthop.* 73: 210–231.

Dakak, M., Uzar, A.I., Saglam, M., Ozer, T., Gurkok, S., Balkanli, K., Oner, K., and Sen, D. 2003. Increased damage from rifle wounds of the chest caused by bullets striking commonly carried military equipment. *J. Trauma Injury Infect. Crit. Care* 55(4): 622–625.

Danielsen, L., Aalund, O., Mazza, P.H., and Katz, E. 1989. Injuries due to deliberate violence in areas of Argentina. II. Lesions. Copenhagen Study Group. *Forensic Sci. Int.* 42(1-2): 165–175.

Davis, A.P. 1996. Targeting the vulnerable in emergency situation: who is vulnerable? (Mortality rates of children and adults during disasters). *Lancet* 348(9031): 868–871.

Davis, N.L., Kahana, T., and Hiss, J. 2004. Souvenir knife: a retained transcranial knife blade. *Am. J. Forensic Med. Pathol.* 25(3): 259–261.

de Gruchy, S. and Rogers, T.L. 2002. Identifying chop marks on cremated bone: a preliminary study. *J. Forensic Sci.* 47(5): 933–936.

de la Cruz, R.E. 2001. Excavando la verdad. *Revista Caretas* v. 1661. In http://www.caretas.com.pe/2001/1661/articulos/embajada.phtml.

Dean, C. 1992. Safe, but for the memory of guns (Children evacuated from war-torn Bosnia-Herzegovina adapt to their British environment). *Times Educational Supplement,* December 1992, 5.

Debesse, B. and Riquet, M. 1994. Traumatismes fermes du thorax. In Godeau, P., Herson, S., and Piette, J.C. (Eds.). *Traite de medicine troisieme ed.* France: Flammarion, pp. 999–1003.

Deck, C., Nicolle, S., and Willinger, R. 2004. Human head FE modelling: Improvement of skull geometry and brain constitutive laws. Proceedings of the International Research Council on Biokinetics of Impacts (IRCOBI), pp. 79–92.

Declaration of Tokyo. 1975. Guidelines for Medical Doctors concerning Torture and Other Cruel, Inhuman or Degrading Treatment or Punishment in relation to Detention and Imprisonment. Adopted by the 29th World Medical Assembly, Tokyo, Japan, October 1975. In http://www.cirp.org/library/ethics/tokyo/.

DePalma, R.G., Burris, D.G., Champoin, H.R., and Hodgson, M.J. 2005. Blast injuries. *New Engl J. Med.* 352(13): 1335–1342.

Dice, W. 1991. The role of military emergency physicians in an assault operation in Panama. *Ann Emergency Med.* 20: 1336–1340.

Di Maio, V.J.M. 1999. *Gunshot wounds: Practical aspects of firearms, ballistics, and forensic techniques.* 2nd ed. Boca Raton, FL: CRC Press, 402 pp.

Di Maio, V.J.M. and Dana, S.E. 2007. *Handbook of forensic pathology.* 2nd ed. Boca Raton, FL: CRC Press, 581 pp.

Dirkmaat, D.C. 2001. Recovery and interpretation of the fatal fire victim: the role of forensic anthropology. In Haglund W., Sorg M. (Eds.). *Advances in forensic taphonomy: Method, theory, and archeological Perspectives.* New York: CRC Press, pp. 452–469.

Dixon, D.S. 1984. Pattern of intersecting fractures and direction of fire. *J. Forensic Sci.* 29: 651–654.

Dolinak, D. and Matshes, E. 2002. *Medicolegal neuropathology.* Boca Raton, FL: CRC Press, 280 pp.

Donchin, Y., Rivkind, A., Bar-Ziv, J., Hiss, J., and Almog, J. 1994. Utility of postmortem computed tomography in trauma victims. *J. Trauma Injury Infect. Crit. Care* 37(4): 552–555.

Doretti, M. and Snow, C.C. 2003. Forensic anthropology and human rights. In Steadman D.W. (Ed). *Hard evidence: Case studies in forensic anthropology.* Upper Saddle River, NJ: Prentice Hall, pp. 290–310.

DuChesne, A., Unnewehr, M., Schmidt, P.F., Sotonyi, P., Brinkmann, B., Piffko, J., Fischer, G., and Bajanowski, T. 2003. Deformation characteristics of the human mandible in low impact experiments. *Int. J. Leg. Med.* 117: 257–262.

Edelenbosch, C. 1994. Human rights violations—A duty to prosecute? *Leiden J. Int. Law* 7(2): 5–22.

Ellis, S.G.S. 2001. Incomplete tooth fracture—proposal for a new definition. *Restorative Dentistry* 190(8): 424–428.

Emanovsky, P.D., Hefner, J.T., and Dirkmaat, D.C. 2002. Can sharp force trauma to bone be recognized after fire modification? An experiment using *Odocoileus virginianus* (White-Tailed Deer) ribs. In http://mai.mercyhurst.edu/PDFs/POSTER-FINAL-FINAL.pdf.

Equipo Peruano de Antropología Forense (EPAF). 2006. Informe del Proyecto Memoria de los Desaparecidos. Report to the International Committee of the Red Cross (ICRC). July. Lima, Peru.

Eriksson, M. and Wallensteen, P. 2004. Patterns of major armed conflicts 1990–2003. In *SIPRI Yearbook 2004 armaments, disarmament and international security.* Oxford: Oxford University Press, pp. 132–147.

Evans, F.G. 1973. *Mechanical properties of bone.* Springfield, IL: Charles C Thomas, 322 pp.

Fackler, M.L. 1996. Gunshot wound review. *Ann. Emergency Med.* 28: 194–203.

Fackler, M.L. 1989. Wounding patterns of military rifle bullets. *Int. Def. Rev.* 22: 59–64.

Fackler, M.L. 1988. Wound ballistics: a review of common misperceptions. *J. Am. Med. Assoc. (JAMA)* 259(18): 2730–2736.

Fackler, M.L. 1987. Bullet performance misconceptions. *Int. Defense Rev.* 3: 369–370.

Fackler, M.L., Malinowski, J.A., and Bellamy, R.F. 1986. Wounding mechanism of projectiles striking at more than 1.5 km/sec. *J. Trauma Injury Infect. Crit. Care* 26(3): 250–254.

Fackler, M.L. and Malinowski, J.A. 1985. The wound profile: a visual method for quantifying gunshot wound components. *J. Trauma Injury Infect. Crit. Care* 25(6): 522–529.

Farkash, U., Scope, A., Lynn, M., Kugel, C., Maor, R., Abargel, A., and Eldad, A. 2000. Preliminary experience with postmortem computed tomography in military penetrating trauma. *J. Trauma Injury Infect. Crit. Care* 48(2): 303–309.

Feik, S.A., Thomas, C.D.L., and Clement, J.G. 1997. Age-related changes in cortical porosity of the midshaft of the human femur. *J. Anat.* 191: 407–416.

Fenton, T.W., deJong, J.L., and Haut, R.C. 2003. Punched with a fist: the etiology of a fatal depressed cranial fracture. *J. Forensic Sci.* 48 (2): 277–281.

Fenton, T.W., Stefan, V.H., Wood, L.A., and Sauer, N.J. 2005. Symmetrical fracturing of the skull from midline contact gunshot wounds: reconstruction of individual death histories from skeletonized human remains. *J. Forensic Sci.* 50(2): 274–285.

Ferllini, R. 1999. The role of forensic anthropology in Human Rights issues. In Fairgrieve, S. (Ed.). *Forensic osteological analysis: A book of case studies.* Springfield, IL: Charles C Thomas, pp. 287–301.

Fitzpatrick, J. 1984. The role of radiology in Human Rights abuses. *Am. J. Forensic Med. Pathol.* 5(4): 321–325.

Fixott, R.H., Arendt, D., Chrz, B., Filippi, J., McGivney, J., and Warnick, A. 2001. Role of the dental team in mass fatality incidents. *Dental Clinicology N. Am.* 45(2): 271–292.

Flagel, B.T., Luchette, F.A., Reed, R.L., Esposito, T.J., Davis, K.A., Santaniello, J.M., and Gamelli, R.L. 2005. Half-a-dozen ribs: the breakpoint for mortality. *Surgery* 138(4): 717–723.

Fondebrider, L. 2002. Reflections on the scientific documentation of human rights violations. *IRRC* 84: 885–891.

Forrest, D.M. 1999. Examination for the late physical after effects of torture. *J. Clin. Forensic Med.* 6(1): 4–13.

Fowler, A.W. 1957. Flexion-compression injury of the sternum. *J. Bone Jt. Surg.—Br.* 3(39-B): 487.

Fraser, B.J. April 28, 2004. *When Peru's dead speak.* Globalvision News Network, World News Headline. Latin American Press. Electronic document, http://www.gvnews.net.

Frayer, D.W. and Bridgens, J.G. 1985. Stab wounds and personal identity determined from skeletal remains: a case from Kansas. *J. Forensic Sci.* 30(1): 232–238.

Frykberg, E.R. 2002. Medical management of disasters and mass casualties from terrorist bombings: how can we cope? *J. Trauma Injury Infect. Crit. Care* 53: 201–212.

Gaessner, S., Gurris, N., and Pross, C, (Eds.). 2001. At the side of torture survivors: treating a terrible assault on human dignity. *At the side of torture survivors.* Baltimore, MD: Johns Hopkins University Press, 272 pp.

Galloway, A. 1999. *Broken bones. Anthropological analysis of blunt force trauma.* Springfield, IL: Charles C Thomas, 371 pp.

Garfield, R.M. and Neugot, A.I. 1991. Epidemiologic analysis of war-fare, a historical review. *J. Am. Med. Assoc. (JAMA)* 266: 688–692.

Geiger, J. and Cook-Deegan, R. 1993. The role of physicians in conflicts and humanitarian crises: case studies from field missions of physicians for human rights. *J. Am. Med. Assoc. (JAMA)* 270(5): 616–620.

Geneva Conventions. 1977. Protocol Additional to the Geneva Conventions of 12 August 1949, and Relating to the Protection of Victims of International Armed. Conflicts (Protocol I–IV), Geneva. In http://www.unhchr.ch/html/intlinst.htm.

Geneva Conventions. 1949. Geneva Convention I for the Amelioration of the Condition of the Wounded and Sick in Armed. Forces in the Field of 12 August 1949. In http://www.unhchr.ch/html/intlinst.htm.

Geneva Conventions. 1949. Geneva Convention II for the Amelioration of the Condition of Wounded, Sick and Shipwrecked Members of Armed. Forces at Sea of 12 August 1949. In http://www.unhchr.ch/html/intlinst.htm.

Geneva Conventions. 1949. Geneva Convention III Relative to the Treatment of Prisoners of War of 12 August 1949. In http://www.unhchr.ch/html/intlinst.htm.

Geneva Conventions. 1949. Geneva Convention IV Relative to the Protection of Civilian Persons in Time of War of 12 August 1949. In http://www.unhchr.ch/html/intlinst.htm.

Gibbons, A. 1992. Scientists search for "the Disappeared" in Guatemala. *Science* 257(5069): 479.

Gillespie, A.K. 1999. *Twin towers: The life of New York City's World Trade Center.* New Brunswick, NJ: Rutgers University Press, 263 pp.

Giordano, G. 2003. *The Oklahoma city bombing.* New York: The Rosen Publishing Group, 64 pp.

Glass, R.T. 1998. The Oklahoma City bombing: the roles of the dental teams … and the lessons learned. *J. Oklahoma Dental Assoc.* 89(2): 20–36.

Glass, R.T. 2001. Forensic dentistry in the Oklahoma City disaster. *Gen. Dentistry* 49(6): 554–559.

Glencross, B. and Stuart-Macadam, P. 2000. Childhood trauma in the archaeological record. *Int. J. Osteoarchaeol.* 10(3): 198–209.

Gofrit, O.N., Leibovici, D., Shapira, C.S., Shemer, J., Stein, M., and Michaelson, M. 1997. The tri-modal death distribution of trauma victims: military experience from the Lebanon war. *Mil. Med.* 162: 24–26.

Goldson, E. 1996. The effect of war on children. *Child Abuse Neglect* 20(9): 809–820.

Goldstone, R. 1997. Assessing the work of the United Nations war crimes tribunal. *Stanford J. Int. Law* 33: 1–8.

Goodman, A.H. 1993. On the interpretation of health from skeletal remains. *Curr. Anthropol.* 34(3): 281–288.

Gorman, D. 1981a. *The body moveable. Volume I. The trunk and head.* Ampersand Press, London, 247 pp.

Gorman, D. 1981b. *The body moveable. Volume II. The upper limb.* Ampersand Press, London, 148 pp.

Gorman, D. 1981c. *The body moveable. Volume III. The lower limb.* Ampersand Press, London, 174 pp.

Gray, E. 1986. Human Rights convictions of former Argentine Military commanders. *Harvard Int. Law J.* 27: 688.

Greenfield, H.J. 1999. The origins of metallurgy: distinguishing stone from metal cut-marks on bones from archaeological sites. *J. Archaeol. Sci.* 26: 797–808.

Grodin, M.A. and Annas, G.J. 1996. Legacies of Nuremberg: medical ethics and human rights. *J. Am. Med. Assoc. (JAMA)* 276(20): 1682–1683.

Grossman, C. 1992. Disappearances in Honduras: the need for direct victim representation in human rights litigation. *Hastings Int. Comp Law Rev.* 15(3): 363–391.

Grossman, D. 1995. *On killing: the psychological cost of learning to kill in war in society.* Boston, MA: Little Brown Company, 400 pp.

Guidelines for the Conduct of United Nations Inquiries into Allegations of Massacres. 1997. Unpublished. Sales No. E.97.1.21. New York: Office of Legal Affairs, United Nations 108 pp.

Gurdjian, E.S. 1975. *Impact head injury: mechanistic, clinical, and preventative correlations.* Springfield, IL: Charles C Thomas, 370 pp.

Gurdjian, E.S. and Webster, A. 1958. *Head injury. Mechanisms, Diagnosis, and Management,* Boston, MA: Little Brown and Company.

Gurdjian, E.S., Webster, J.E., and Lissner, H.R. 1950. The mechanism of skull fracture. *Radiology* 54: 313–339.

Guy, R., Glover, M., and Cripps, N. 1998. The pathophysiology of primary blast injury and its implications for treatment. Part I: the thorax. *J. R. Nav. Med. Serv.* 84(2): 79–86.

Hadden, W.A., Rutherford, W.H., and Merrett, J.D. 1978. The injuries of terrorist bombing: a study of 1532 consecutive patients. *Br. J. Surg.* 65(8): 252–231.

Haden, K. and Berg, G. 2007. Ballistics-induced depressed skull fractures. Proceedings of the 59th Annual meeting of the American Academy of Forensic Sciences. [Abstract]. H27:337.

Haglund, W.D. 2001. Recent mass graves, an introduction. In Haglund, W.D. and Sorg, M.H. (Eds.). *Advances in forensic taphonomy: method, theory and archaeological perspectives.* Boca Raton, FL: CRC Press, pp. 234–262.

Haglund, W.D., Conner, M., and Scott, D.D. 2000. The archaeology of contemporary mass graves. *Hist Archaeol* 35(1): 57–69.

Haglund, W.D. and Sorg, M.H. (Eds.). 2001. *Advances in forensic taphonomy: Method, theory and archaeological perspectives.* Boca Raton, FL: CRC Press, 546 pp.

Hall, R.C.W., Hall, R.C.W., Chapman, M. 2005. Terrorism: Effects of Terrorist Attacks on the Elderly-Part I: Medical and Psychiatric Complications of Bombings and Biological, Chemical, and Nuclear attacks. *Clinical Geriatrics* 14: 26–35.

Handbook of the International Red Cross and Red Crescent Movement, 13th ed. 2004. International Committee of the Red Cross, 25-09-2001. In http://www.ifrc.org/publicat/catalog/autogen/3129.asp.
Harkess, J.W., Ramsey, W.C., and Ahmadi, B. 1984. Principles of fractures and dislocations. In Rockwood, C.A. and Green, D.P. (Eds.) *Fractures in adults*. Vol. I, Philadelphia, PA: JB Lippincott.
Harruff, R.C. 1995. Comparison of contact shotgun wounds of the head produced. by different gauge shotguns. *J. Forensic Sci.* 40(5): 801–804.
Hart, G.O. 2005. Fracture pattern interpretation in the skull: differentiating blunt force from ballistics trauma using concentric fractures. *J. Forensic Sci.* 50(6): 1276–1281.
Hayda, R., Harris, R.M., and Bass, D.C. 2004. Blast injury research: modeling injury effects of landmines, bullets and bombs. *Clin. Orthop. Relat. Res.* 422: 97–108.
Hayner, P.B. 1994. Fifteen truth commissions—1974–1994: a comparative study. *Hum. Rights Q*, 16: 597–655.
Haynes, G. 1983. A guide for differentiating mammalian *carnivore taxa* responsible for gnaw damage to herbivore limb bones. *Paleobiology* 9(2): 164–172.
Helal, B. 1964. Fracture of the manubrium sterni. *J. Bone Jt. Surg.—Br.* 4(46–B): 602.
Helling, T.S., Watkins, M., Evans, L.L., Nelson, P.W., Shook, J.W., and Van Way, C.W. 1999. Low falls: an underappreciated mechanism of injury. *J. Trauma Injury Infect. Crit. Care* 46(3): 453–456.
Henderson, P.L. and Biellik, R.J. 1983. Comparative nutrition and health services for victims of drought and hostilities in the Ogaden: Somalia and Ethiopia, 1980–1981. *Int. J. Health Serv.* 13(2): 289–306.
Heppenstall, R.B. 1980. Fracture healing. In Heppenstall, R.B. (Ed.). *Fracture treatment and healing*. Philadelphia, PA: Saunders, pp. 41–64.
Hill, J.F. 1979. Blast injury with particular reference to recent terrorist bombing incidents. *Ann. R. Coll. Surg. Engl.* 61(1): 4–11.
Hills, M.W., Delprado, A.M., and Deane, S.A. 1993. Sternal fractures: associated injuries and management. *J. Trauma Injury Infect. Crit. Care* 35(1): 55–60.
Hinsley, D.E., Rosell, P.A.E., Rowlands, T.K., and Clasper, J.C. 2005. Penetrating missile injuries during the initial phase of the 2003 Gulf Conflict-202 Field Hospital. *J. Bone Jt. Surg.—Br.* Vol. 87-B, Issue SUPP III, 258.
Hinton, A.L. (Ed.). 2002. *Annihilating difference: The anthropology of genocide*. California series in public anthropology 3, Berkeley, CA: University of California Press, 428 pp.
Hiss, J., Kahana, T., and Kugel, C. 1996. Beaten to death: Why do they die? *J. Trauma Injury Infect. Crit. Care* 40(1): 27–30.
Hiss, J. and Kahana, T. 2000. Modern war wounds. In Mason J.K. (Ed). *The pathology of trauma*. 3rd ed. London: Edward Arnold, pp. 89–97.
Hodalic, Z., Svagelj, M., Sebalj, I., and Sebalj, D. 1999. Surgical treatment of 1,211 patients at the Vinkovci General Hospital, Vinkovci, Croacia, during the 1991–1992 Serbian offensive in east Slovenia. *Mil Med.* 164: 803–808.
Holcomb, J.B., McMullin, N.R., Kozar, R.A., Lygas, M.H., and Moore, F.A. 2003. Morbidity from rib fractures increases after age 45. *J. Am. Coll. Surgeons* 196(4): 549–555.
Holdstock, D. 2004. Editorial—rights, wrongs and war. *Med. Conflict. Surv.* 19(3): 290–291.
Holdstock, D. 2002. Mortality and morbidity among soldiers and civilians. In Taipale, I., Mäkelä, P.H., Juva, K., Taipale, V., Tapanainen, H. Eds. *War or health? A reader*. London: Zed Books, pp. 183–97.
Hollerman, J.J., Fackler, M.L., Coldwell, D.M., and Ben-Menachem, Y. 1990. Gunshot wounds: 1. Bullets, ballistics, and mechanisms of injury. *AJR* 155: 685–690.
Homewood, C.I. 1998. Cracked tooth syndrome-incidence, clinical findings and treatment. *Aust. Dental J.* 43: 1–6.
Hopkins, J.E.T. 1962. *Casualty Survey—New Georgia and Burma Campaigns, in wound ballistics*. In Beyer, J.C. Ed. Office of the Surgeon General Department of the Army, Washington, D.C., pp. 281–436. Electronic File: http://history.amedd.army.mil/booksdocs/wwii/woundblstcs/chapter5.1.htm.

Horrocks, C. 2001. Blast injuries: biophysics, pathophysiology and management principles. *J. Army Med. Corps* 147: 28–40.

Horvath, F., Gardner, K., and Siegel, J. 1993. Range of fire estimates from shotgun pellet patterns: the effect of shell and barrel temperature. *J. Forensic Sci.* 38(3): 585–592.

Houck, M.M. 1998. Skeletal trauma and the individualization of knife marks in bones. In Reichs, K. (Ed.). *Forensic osteology: Advances in the identification of human remains.* 2nd ed. Springfield, IL: Charles C Thomas, pp. 410–424.

Hougen, H.P. 1988. Physical and psychological sequelae to torture: a controlled clinical study of exiled asylum applicants. *Forensic Sci. Int.* 39(1): 5–11.

Huang, J.Z., Yang, Z., Wang, Z., and Leng, H. 1996. Study on characteristics of blast-fragment combined injury in dogs. *J. Trauma Injury Infect. Crit. Care* 40 3(S): 63S–7S.

Huelke, D.F., Harger, J.H., Buege, L.T., Dingman, H.G., Harger, D.R. 1968a. An experimental study in bio-ballistics: femoral fractures caused by projectiles. *J. Biomech.* 1: 97–105.

Huelke, D.F., Harger, J.H., Buege, L.T., and Dingman, H.G. 1968b. An experimental study in bio-ballistics: femoral fractures caused by projectiles II. Shaft impacts. *J. Biomech.* 1: 313–321.

Hull, J.B. 1996. Management of gunshot fractures of the extremities. *J. Trauma Injury Infect. Crit. Care* 40(3S): 193S–197S.

Hull, J.B., Bowyer, G.W., Cooper, G.J., and Crane, J. 1994. Pattern of injury in those dying from traumatic amputation caused by bomb blast. *Br. J. Surg.* 81: 1132–1135.

Human Remains and Forensic Sciences Electronic Workshop. 2002. Human remains: Law, politics, and ethics 23–24.05.2002; and Human remains: Management of remains and of information on the dead 10–12.07.2002 (ICRC The Missing/10.2002/EN/3); In http://www.icrc.org/Web/eng/siteeng0.nsf/html/5CALR3/$File/ICRC_TheMissing_102002_EN3.pdf.

HRW (Human Rights Watch Report). 1998. Federal Republic of Yugoslavia: Humanitarian law violations in Kosovo. October 1998, Vol. 10, No. 9 (D), In http://www.hrw.org/reports98/kosovo/.

Human Security Report. 2005. Human Security Centre. The University of British Columbia. Oxford and New York: Oxford University Press.

Humphrey, J.H. and Hutchinson, D.L. 2001. Macroscopic characteristics of hacking trauma. *J. Forensic Sci.* 46(2): 228–233.

Hunter, J.R., Brickley, M.B., Bourgeois, J., Bouts, W., Bourguignon, L., Hubrecht, F., de Winne, J., Van Haaster, H., Hakbijl, T., De Jong, H., Smits, L., Van Wijngaarden, L.H., Luschen, M. 2001. Forensic archaeology, forensic anthropology and human rights in Europe. *Sci. Justice* 41(3): 173–178.

International Committee of the Red Cross (ICRC). 2004. The Handling of Human Remains and Information on the Dead in Situations Relating to Armed. Conflicts or Internal Violence and involving Missing Persons. Contribution to the 16th Meeting of the Standing Committee on Disaster Victim Identification, Lyon, France 5–7 May 2004 www.icrc.org/Web/eng/siteeng0.nsf/htmlall/52MJH51$File/Interpol_2004DVI_EN.pdf.

International Committee of the Red Cross (ICRC). 2003. The Missing and Their Families. Summary of the Conclusions Arising from Events held prior to the International Conference of Governmental and Non-Governmental Experts (19–21 February 2003). www.icrc.org/Web/eng/siteeng0.nsf/html/all/5JAHR8/$File/ICRC_TheMissing_012003_EN_10.pdf.

International Committee of the Red Cross (ICRC). 1987. Commentary on the Additional Protocols 8 June 1977 to the Geneva Conventions of 12 August 1949. In Geneva Conventions of 12 August 1949. Geneva: International Committee of the Red Cross.

Interpol Disaster Victim Identification Guide. 2005. Lyon, France: Interpol, first published 1984. Available at http://www.interpol.com/public/disastervictim/default.asp.

Islam, O., Soboleski, D., Symons, S., Davidson, L.K., Ashworth, M.A., and Babyn, P. 2000. Development and duration of radiographic signs of bone healing in children. *Am. J. Radiol.* 175: 75–78.

Istanbul Protocol: Manual on the Effective Investigation and Documentation of Torture and Other Cruel, Inhuman or Degrading Treatment or Punishment. 2004. Professional Training Series No. 8/Rev.1. United Nations Office of the High Commissioner for Human Rights (OHCHR). Geneva and New York.

Jenkins, D. and Dougherty, P. 2005. The effects of bullets. In Mahoney, P.F., Ryan, J.M., Brooks, A., and Schwab, C.W. (Eds.). *Ballistic trauma.* 2nd ed. London: Springer-Verlag, pp. 40–44.

Jentzen, J.M., Lutz, M., and Templin, R. 1995. Tandem bullet versus multiple gunshot wounds. *J. Forensic Sci.* 40(5): 893–895.

Jones, M.D., James, D.S., Cory, C.Z., Leadbeatter, S., and Nokes, L.D. 2003. Subdural haemorrhage sustained in a baby-rocker? A biomechanical approach to causation. *Forensic Sci. Int.* 131(1): 14–21.

Jordan, F.B. 1999. The role of the medical examiner in mass casualty situations with special reference to the Alfred P. Murrah Building bombing. *J. Okla. State Med. Assoc.* 92(4): 159–163.

Joyce, C. and Stover, E. 1991. *Witnesses from the grave: The stories bones tell.* Boston, MA: Little, Brown and Company, 352 pp.

Juhl, K. 2005. The contribution by (forensic) archaeologists to human rights investigations of mass graves. *AmS-NETT 5*, Stavanger, 77 pp.

Kahana, T., Ravioli, J.A., Urroz, C.L., and Hiss, J. 1997. Radiographic identification of fragmentary human remains from a mass disaster. *Am. J. Forensic Med. Pathol.* 18(1): 40–44.

Kamm, H. 1998. *Cambodia: Report from a stricken land.* New York: Arcade Publishing, 256 pp.

Kang, H.S., Willinger, R., Diaw, B., and Chinn, B. 1997. Validation of a 3D anatomic human head model and replication of head impact in motorcycle accident by finite element modelling, Proceedings of the 41st STAPP Car Crash Conference, pp. 329–338.

Kapur, G.B., Hutson, H., Davis, M.A., and Rice, P.L. 2005. The United States twenty-year experience with bombing incidents: implications for terrorism preparedness and medical response. *J. Trauma Injury Infect. Crit. Care* 59(6): 1436–1444.

Karger, B. 1995. Penetrating gunshots to the head and lack of immediate incapacitation I. Wound ballistics and mechanisms of incapacitation. *Int. J. Legal Med.* 108(2): 53–61.

Karger, B., Billeb, E., Koops, E., and Brinkmann, B. 2002. Autopsy features relevant for discrimination between suicidal and homicidal gunshot injuries. *Int. J. Legal Med.* 116(5): 273–278.

Karger, B., Zweihoff, R.F., and DuChesne, A. 1999. Injuries from hand grenades in civilian settings. *Int. J. Legal Med.* 112: 372–375.

Karlson, K.A. 1998. Rib stress fractures in elite rowers: a case series and proposed mechanism. *Am. J. Sports Med.* 26(4): 516–519.

Karmakar, M.K. and Ho, A.M. 2003. Acute pain management in patients with multiple fractured ribs. *J. Trauma Injury Infect. Crit. Care* 54: 615–625.

Katz, E., Ofek, B., Adler, J., Abramowitz, H.B., and Krausz, M.M. 1989. Primary blast injury after a bomb explosion in a civilian bus. *Ann. Surg.* 209(4): 484–488.

Kellogg, D. 2000. Guerrilla warfare: when taking care of your troops lead to war crimes. *J. Power Ethics: An Interdisciplinary Rev.* 1(1): 50–67.

Kent, R. and Patrie, J. 2005. Chest deflection tolerance to blunt anterior loading is sensitive to age but not load distribution. *Forensic Sci. Int.* 149(2–3): 121–128.

Kerley, E.R. 1973. *Forensic anthropology.* In Wecht, C.H. (Ed.). Legal Medicine Annual, pp. 161–198. New York: Appleton-Century-Crofts.

Kiernan, B. 1996. *The Pol Pot regime: Race, power, and genocide in Cambodia under the Khmer Rouge*, 1975–79. Chiang Mai, Thailand: Silkworm Books, 492 pp.

Kimmerle, E.H. 2004. Cause of death: The role of anthropology in the enforcement of human rights. Report submitted to the Human Rights Committee of the American Anthropological Association, 35 pp.

Kirschner, R. 1984. The use of drugs in torture and human rights abuses. *Am. J. Forensic Med. Pathol.* 5(4): 313–315.

Kirschner, R.H. and Hannibal, K.E. 1994. The application of the forensic sciences to human rights investigations. *Med. Law* 13(5–6): 451–460.

Kjaerulff, H., Jacobsen, J., Aalund, O., Albrektsen, S.B., Breiting, V.B., Danielsen, L., Helweg-Larsen, K., Staugaard, H., Thomsen, J.L. 1989. Injuries due to deliberate violence in areas of Denmark. III. Lesions. The Copenhagen study group. *Forensic Sci. Int.* 41(1–2): 169–180.

Kleinman, P.K., Marks, S.C., Jr., Nimkin, K., Rayder, S.M., and Kessler, S.C. 1996. Rib fractures in 31 abused infants: postmortem radiologic-histopathologic study. *Radiology.* 200(3): 807–810.

Kleinman, P.K., Marks, S.C., Spevak, M.R., and Richmond, J.M. 1992. Fractures of the rib head in abused infants. *Radiology* 185(1): 119–123.

Kleinman, P.K. and Schlesinger, A.E. 1997. Mechanical factors associated with posterior rib fractures: laboratory and case studies. *Pediatr. Radiol.* 27(1): 87–91.

Klotzbach, H., Delling, G., Richter, E., Sperhake, J.P., and Puschel, K. 2003. Post-mortem diagnosis and age estimation of infants' fractures. *Int. J. Legal Med.* 117(2): 82–89.

Kluger, Y. 2003. Bomb explosions in acts of terrorism—detonation, wound ballistics, triage, and medical concerns. *IMAJ.* 5: 235–240.

Kluger, Y., Nimrod, A., Biderman, P., Mayo, A., and Sorkin, P. 2006. The Quinary (Vth) injury pattern of blast. *J. Em. Manag.* 4:51–55.

Kneubuehl, B.P. and Thali, M.J. 2003. The evaluation of a synthetic long bone structure as a substitute for human tissue in gunshot experiments. *Forensic Sci. Int.* 138: 44–49.

Knight, B. 1991. Gunshot and explosion deaths. In Knight, B. *Forensic pathology* London. Edward Arnold, pp. 248–251.

Knudsen, P.J. and Theilade, P. 1993. Terminal ballistics of the 7.62 mm NATO Bullet. Autopsy Findings. *Int. J. Legal Med.* 106(2): 61–67.

Knudsen, P.J. and Heigaard Sørensen, T.O. 1997. The destabilizing effect of body armour on military rifle bullets. *Int. J. Legal Med.* 110(2): 82–87.

Koff, C. 2004. *The bone woman: A forensic anthropologist's search for truth in the graves in Rwanda, Bosnia, Croatia, and Kosovo.* New York: Random House, 256 pp.

Koff, C. 1996. Have trowel, will travel: scratching the surface layer. *Connect. Tiss.* 1: 8–11.

Komar, D. 2003. Lessons from Srebrenica: the contributions and limitations of physical anthropology in identifying victims of war crimes. *J. Forensic Sci.* 48(4): 713–716.

Kontio, R., Suuronen, R., Ponkkonen, H., Lindqvist, C., and Laine, P. 2005. Have the causes of maxillofacial fractures changed over the last 16 years in Finland? An epidemiological study of 725 fractures. *Dent. Traumatol.* 21(1): 14–9.

Koppl, R. 2005. How to improve forensic science. *Eur. J. Law Econ.* 20(3): 255–286.

Korzinek, K.1993. War injuries of the extremities. *Unfallchirurg* 96(5): 242–247.

Kravetz, D. 2004. The protection of civilians in war: the ICTY Galic Case. *Leiden J. Int. Law* 17: 521–536.

Krogman, W.M. and Iscan, M.Y. 1986. *The human skeleton in forensic medicine.* Springfield, IL: Charles C Thomas, 551 pp.

Kroman, A. 2004. Experimental study of fracture propagation in the human skull: A retesting of popular theories. *Proc. Am. Acad. Forensic Sci.* H79;314.

Lakstein, D. and Blumenfeld, A. 2005. Israeli Army casualties in the 2nd Palestinian uprising. *Mil. Med.* 170(5): 427–430.

Landmine Monitor Report 2000: Toward a mine-free world. Human Rights Watch. Webversion: http://www.icbl.org/lm/2000/.

Leaning, J. 2003. Medicine and international humanitarian law. *Br. Med. J.* 319: 393–394.

Lee, W.Y., Cameron, P.A., and Bailey, M.J. 2006. Road traffic injuries in the elderly. *Emerg. Med. J.* 23(1): 42–46.

Leffers, D. and Chandler, R.W. 1985. Tibial fractures associated with civilian gunshot injuries. *J. Trauma Injury Infect. Crit. Care* 25(11): 1059–1064.

Leibovici, D., Gofrit, O., Stein, M., Shapira, S.C., Noga, Y., Heruti, R., and Shemer, J. 1996. Blast injuries: bus versus open air bombings—A comparative study of injuries in survivors of open-air versus confined-space explosions. *J. Trauma Injury Infect. Crit. Care* 41(6): 1030–1035.

Leth, P.M. and Banner, J. 2005. Forensic medical examination of refugees who claim to have been tortured. *Am. J. Forensic Med. Pathol.* 26(2): 125–130.

Levy, B.S. and Sidel, V. (Eds.). 1997. *War and public health.* New York and Oxford: Oxford University Press, 432 pp.

Lie, B. and Skjeie, H. 1996. Torture-related injuries—a medical challenge. Diagnosis and treatment of Falanga victims. *Tidsskr nor Laegeforen.* 116(9): 1073–1075.

Liman, S.T., Kuzucu, A., Tastepe, A.I., Ulasan, G.N., and Topcu, S. 2003. Chest injury due to blunt trauma. *Eur. J. Cardiothorac. Surg.* 23: 374–378.

Lindsey, D. 1980. The idolatry of velocity, or lies, damn lies and ballistics. *J. Trauma Injury Infect. Crit. Care* 20(12): 1068–1069.

Logan, P.M. 1999. Is there an association between fractures of the cervical spine and first- and 2nd-rib fractures? *Can. Assoc. Radiol. J.* 50(1): 41–43.

Lollar, C. 1992. To witness and heal: what science can do to respond to human rights abuse. *Science* 255: 477.

Love, J.C. and Symes, S.A. 2004. Understanding rib fracture patterns: incomplete and buckle fractures. *J. Forensic Sci.* 49(6): 1153–1158.

Lovell, N.C. 1997. Trauma analysis in paleopathology. *Yearbook of Physical Anthropology* 104(S25): 139–170.

Lynch, C.D. and McConnell, R.J. 2002. The cracked tooth syndrome. *J. de l'Association dentaire canadienne* 68: 470–475.

Maat, G.J.R., van den Bos, R.P.M., and Aarents, M.J. 2001. Manual preparation of ground sections for the microscopy of natural bone tissue. Update and modification of Frost's "rapid manual method." *Int. J. Osteoarchaeol.* 11: 366–374.

Mabry, R.L., Holcomb, J.B., Baker, A.M., Cloonan, C.C., Uhorchak, J.M., Perkins, D.E., Canfield, A.J., and Hagmann, J.H. 2000. United States Army Rangers in Somalia: an analysis of combat casualties on an urban battlefield. *J. Trauma Injury Infect. Crit. Care* 49(3): 515–528.

MacPherson, D. 1994. *Bullet penetration: Modeling the dynamics and the incapacitation resulting from wound trauma.* El Segundo, California: Ballistics Publications, 303 pp.

Madea, B. and Staak, M. 1988. Determination of the sequence of gunshot wounds of the skull. *J. Forensic Sci. Soc* 28(5–6): 321–328.

Mahoney, P.F., Ryan, J.M., Brooks, A., and Schwab, C.W. (Eds.). 2005. *Ballistic trauma.* 2nd ed. London: Springer-Verlag, 304 pp.

Mann, R.W. and Hunt, D.R. 2005. *Photographic regional atlas of bone disease: A guide to pathologic and normal variation in the human skeleton.* Springfield, IL: Charles C Thomas, 297 pp.

Maples, W.R. and Browning, M. 1994. *Dead men do tell tales: The strange and fascinating cases of a forensic anthropologist.* New York: Doubleday, 280 pp.

Maples, W.R. and Browning, M. 1986. Trauma analysis by the forensic anthropologist. In Reichs, K. (Ed.). *Forensic osteology: Advances in the identification of human remains.* 2nd ed. Springfield, IL: Charles C Thomas, pp. 218–228.

Maples, W.R. and Browning, M. 1984. The identifying pathology. In Rathburn, T.A. and Buikstra, J.E. (Eds.). *Human identification: Case studies in forensic anthropology.* Springfield, IL: Charles C Thomas, pp. 363–370.

Marjoux, D., Baumgartner, D., Deck, C., and Willinger, R. 2006. Head injury prediction capability of HIC, HIP, SIMON and ULP criteria. Proceedings of the International Research Council on Biokinetics of Impacts (IRCOBI), pp. 120–130.

Marshall, T.K. 1978. The investigation of bombings. *Legal Med. Annu.* (6): 39–54.

Marshall, T.K. 1976. Death from explosive devices. *Med. Sci. Law* 16: 235–239.

Mason, J.K. and Purdue, B.N. (Eds.). 2000. *The pathology of trauma.* 3rd ed. London: Hodder Arnold, 528 pp.

Mayne, P.M. 1997. Fire modification of bone: A review of the literature. In Forensic taphonomy: The post-mortem fate of human remains. In Haglund, W.D. and Sorg, M.H. (Eds.). *Advances in forensic taphonomy: Method, theory, and archaeological perspectives.* Boca Raton, FL: CRC Press, pp. 435–450.

McKinley 2000. The analysis of cremate bone. In Cox, M. and Mays, S. (Eds.). *Archaeology and forensic science.* London: Greenwich Medical Media, pp. 403–421.

Meddings, D.R. 1997. Weapons injuries during and after periods of conflict: retrospective analysis. *Br. Med. J.* 315: 1417–1420.

Meddings, D.R. and O'Connor, S.M. 1999. Circumstances around weapon injury in Cambodia after departure of a peacekeeping force: prospective cohort study. *Br. Med. J.* 319: 412–415.

Mellor, S. 1992. The relationship between blast loading to death and injury from explosion. *World J. Surg.* 16: 893–898.

Mellor, S. and Cooper, G. 1989. Analysis of 828 servicemen killed or injured by explosion in Northern Ireland 1970–84: the Hostile Action Casualty System. *Br. J. Surg.* 76(10): 1006–1010.

Melsom, M.A., Farrar, M.D., and Volkers, R.C. 1975. Battle casualties. *Ann. R. Coll. Surgeons Engl.* 56(6): 289–303.

Melvern, L. 2004. *Conspiracy to murder: the Rwandan genocide and the international community.* London: Verso.

Merbs, C.F. 1989. Trauma. In Iscan, M.Y. and Kennedy, K.A.R. (Eds.). *Reconstruction of life from the skeleton.* New York: Alan R. Liss, pp. 161–189.

Messmer, J.M., Brogdon, B.G., and Vogel, H. 2003. Conventional weapons, including shotguns. In Brogdon, B.G., Vogel, H., and McDowell, J.D. *A radiologic atlas of abuse, torture, terrorism, and inflicted trauma.* Boca Raton, FL: CRC Press, pp. 161–178.

Messmer, J.M. and Fierro, M.F. 1986. Radiologic forensic investigation of fatal gunshot wounds. *RadioGraphics* 6(3): 457–473.

Meyers, J., Okoye, M., Kipple, D., Kimmerle, E.H., and Reinhard, K. 1999. Three dimensional (3–D) imaging in post-mortem examinations: elucidation and identification of cranial and facial fractures in victims of homicide utilizing 3–D computerized imaging reconstruction techniques. *Int. J. Legal Med.* 113: 33–37.

Michael, M., Meddings, D.R., Ramez, S., and Gutiĕrrez-Fisac, J.L. 1999. Incidence of weapon injuries not related to interfacional combat in Afghanistan in 1996: prospective cohort study. *Br. Med. J.* 319: 415–417.

Micozzi, M.S. 1991. *Postmortem changes in human and animal remains: A systematic approach.* Springfield, IL: Charles C Thomas, pp. 218–228.

Miller, C.D., Blyth, P., and Civil, I.D. 2000. Lumbar transverse process fractures—a sentinel marker of abdominal organ injuries. *Injury* 31(10): 773–776.

Missliwetz, J. and Wieser, I. 1989. Gunshot wounds of the head in soldiers wearing military helmets—general aspects and experiments and observations on the biomechanics and wound morphology. *Z. Rechtsmed.* 102(1): 41–54.

Mohanty, S., Mohanty, M.K., Panigrahi, M.K., and Das, S.K. 2005. Fatal head injury in homicidal victims. *Med. Sci. Law* 45(3): 244–248.

Moisander, P.A. and Edston, E. 2003. Torture and its sequel—a comparison between victims from six countries. *Forensic Sci. Int.* 137(2–3): 133–140.

Mollan, R.A.B. and Beavis, V. 1978. A curious gunshot injury. *Br. J. Accid. Surg.* 9(4): 327–328.

Moritz, A.R. 1954. *The pathology of trauma.* 2nd ed. Philadelphia, PA: Lea and Febringer, 414 pp.

Morley, D. 1994. Malnutrition in children. In Lankinen, K.S., Bergstroem, S., Mäkela, P.H., and Peltomaa, M. (Eds.). *Health and disease in developing countries.* London: MacMillan, pp. 297–304.

Morse, D. 1983. The skeletal pathology of trauma. In Morse, D., Duncan, J., and Stoutamire, J. (Eds.). *Handbook of forensic archaeology and anthropology.* Tallahassee: Florida State University Foundation, pp. 145–156.

Morse, D., Duncan, J., and Stoutamire, J., (Eds.). 1983. *Handbook of forensic archaeology and anthropology.* Tallahassee: Florida State University Foundation, 240 pp.

Murhad, T.A. 1998. The growing popularity of cremation versus inhumation: some forensic implications. In Reichs, K.J. (Ed.) *Forensic osteology: Advances in the identification of human remains.* 2nd ed. Springfield, IL: Charles C Thomas, pp. 86–105.

Murray, C.J.L., King, G., and Lopez, A.D. 2002. Armed conflict as a public health problem. *Br. Med. J.* 324: 346–349.

Nag, N.K. and Sinha, P. 1992. An investigation into pellet dispersion ballistics. *Forensic Sci. Int.* 55(2): 105–130.

Nahum, A.M. and Melvin, J. (Eds.) 1985. *The biomechanics of trauma.* Norfolk: Appleton-Century-Crofts.

Nath, V. 1998. *A Cambodian prison portrait: One year in the Khmer Rouge's S-21.* Bangkok: White Lotus, 136 pp.

Newman, R.J. 1984. Chest wall injuries and the seat belt syndrome. *Injury* 16(2): 110–113.

Newman, R.J. and Jones, I.S. 1984. A prospective study of 413 consecutive car occupants with chest injuries. *J. Trauma Injury Infect. Crit. Care* 24(2): 129–135.

Nye, P.J. 1996. The role of radiology in the Oklahoma City bombing. *Radiology* 200(2): 541–543.

O'Connor, J.F. and Cohen, J. 1998. *Dating fractures.* In Kleinman, P.K. (Ed.). *Diagnostic imaging of child abuse.* St. Louis: Mosby, pp. 168–177.

Oehmichen, M., Gehl, H.B., Meissner, C., and Petersen, D. 2003. Forensic pathological aspects of postmortem imaging of gunshot injury to the head. *Acta Neuropathologica* 105(6): 570–580.

Office on Missing Persons and Forensics (OMPF). 2004. Activity Report 2002–2004. Department of Justice, United Nations Mission in Kosovo. In http://www.unmikonline.org/justice/ompf/reports/OMPF_activ_rep_2002_04.pdf.

Okoye, M.I., Kimmerle, E.H., and Baraybar, J.P. 2006. Forensic investigations of human rights violations, abuse, mass graves, and war crimes. In *Forensic sciences,* Wright, C. (Ed.). Vol. 2: Lexis-Nexis Matthew Bender.

Oliver, W.R., Chancellor, A.S., Soltys, M., and Symon, J. 1995. Three-dimensional reconstruction of a bullet path: validation by computed radiography. *J. Forensic Sci.* 40(2): 321–324.

Olmo, D. 2006. Crimes against humanity. In Schmitt, A., Cunha, E., and Pinheiro, J. (Eds.). *Forensic anthropology and medicine.* Totowa, NJ: Humana Press, pp. 409–430.

Olson, R.A., Fonseca, R.J., Zeitler, D.L., and Osbon, D.B. 1982. Fractures of the mandible: a review of 580 cases. *J. Oral Maxillofac. Surg.* 40(1): 23–28.

Olumbe, A.K. and Yakub, A.K. 2002. Management, exhumation and identification of human remains: a viewpoint of the developing world. *IRRC* 84(848): 893–902.

Orentlicher, D.F. 1990. Bearing witness: the art and science of human rights fact-finding. *Harvard Human Rights J.* 3: 83–135.

Ormstad, K., Karlsson, T., Enkler, L., Law, B., and Rajs, J. 1986. Patterns in sharp force fatalities: a comprehensive forensic medical study. *J. Forensic Sci.* 31(2): 529–542.

Ortiz, J. 1996. *Apuntes sobre la Batalla de Miraflores* (15 de enero de 1881). Lima, Perú: Municipalidad de Surco.

Ortner, D. 2003. *Identification of pathological conditions in human skeletal remains.* 2nd ed. Amsterdam: Academic Press, 645 pp.

Ortner, D. and Putschar, W. 1981. *Identification of pathological conditions in human skeletal remains.* Washington, D.C. Smithsonian Institution Press, No. 28, 488 pp.

OSCE Report. 1999a. An analysis of the human rights findings of the OSCE Kosova verification mission, October 1998 to June 1999. Warsaw, Poland: OSCE (Office for Security and Cooperation in Europe) Office for Democratic Institutions and Human Rights, 433 pp.

OSCE Report. 1999b. A report on the human rights findings of the OSCE mission in Kosova, Part II, June to October 1999. Pristina, Kosova: OSCE (Office for Security and Cooperation in Europe) Mission in Kosova, 332 pp.

Oughterson, A.W., Hull, H.C., Sutherland, F.A., and Greiner, D.J. 1962. Study on wound ballistics—Bougainville Campaign. In Beyer, J.C. (Ed.). *Wound ballistics.* Office of the Surgeon General. Washington, DC.: Department of the Army, pp. 281–436. Electronic File: http://history.amedd.army.mil/booksdocs/wwii/woundblstcs/chapter5.1.htm.

Pachón, J. 2005. Detección de elementos constitutivos de proyectil de arma de fuego en restos oseos con microscopio electronico de barrido: Reporte de un caso. Paper presented at the III Congress of the Latin Am. Assoc. Forensic Anthropol-ALAF. Bogotá.

Patel, D.K. and Burke, F.J. 1995. Fractures of posterior teeth: a review and analysis of associated factors. *Prim Dent Care* 2(1): 6–10.

Peleg, K., Aharonson-Daniel, L., Stein, M., Kluger, Y., Simon, D., Noji, E.K., Israeli Trauma Group (ITG). 2004. Gunshot and explosion injuries: characteristics, outcomes, and implications for care of terror-related injuries in Israel. *Ann Surg.* 239(3): 311–318.

Perera, C. 2006. Review of initiatives adopted for effective documentation of torture in a developing country. *J. Clin. Forensic Med.* 13(6–8): 288–292.

Petersen, H.D. and Wandall, J.H. 1995. Evidence of physical torture in a series of children. *Forensic Sci. Int.* 75(1): 45–55.

Petricevic, A., Ilic, N., Radonic, V., Mimica, Z., Petricevic, M., Busic, Z., and Tanfara, S. 1998. Our experience with 2693 wounded treated at the Split University Hospital during the 1991–1995 period. *Int. Surg.* 83(2): 98–105.

Pike, J. (Ed.). 2005. U.S. military operations: Casualty breakdown. GlobalSecurity.org, Alexandria, VA. Electronic Document: http://www.globalsecurity.org/military/ops/casualties.htm.

Pollak, S. and Wieser, I. 1988. Teeth as an intermediate target—a cause for rapid disintegration of the full metal-jacketed bullets used by the military. *Wien Klin Wochenschr* 100(22): 729–733.

Pollanen, M.S. 2002. Torture by excision and ingestion of the ear helix. *J. Clin. Forensic Med.* 9(4): 183–184.

Pope, E.J. and Smith O'Brian, C. 2004. Identification of traumatic injury in burned cranial bone: an experimental approach. *J. Forensic Sci.* 49(3): 431–440.

Popenker, M. and Williams, A.G. 2004. *Assault rifle.* U.K.: Crowood Press, 224 pp.

Pounder, D.J. 1997. Shaken adult syndrome. *Am. J. Forensic Med. Pathol.* 18(4): 321–324.

Prieto, J.L. 2007. Stab wounds: The contribution of forensic anthropology: A case study. In Brickley, M.B. and Ferllini, R. (Eds.). *Forensic anthropology: Case studies from Europe.* Springfield, IL: Charles C Thomas, pp. 19–37.

Principles on the Effective Prevention and Investigation of Extra-Legal, Arbitrary and Summary Executions. Adopted by ECOSOC and the General Assembly. 1989. www.unhchr.ch/html/menu3/b/54.htm.

Prosser, I., Maguire, S., Harrison, S.K., Mann, M., Sibert, J.R., and Kemp, A.M. 2005. How old is this fracture? Radiologic dating of fractures in children: a systematic review. *Am. J. Radiol.* 184(4): 1282–1286.

Prunier, G. 1995. *The Rwanda crisis: history of a genocide.* New York: Columbia University Press, 389 pp.

Pryor, J.P. 2003. The 2001 World Trade Center disaster—summary and evaluation of experiences. *Int. J. Disaster Med.* 1(1): 56–68.

Puskas, C.M. and Rumney, D.T. 2003. Bilateral fractures of the coronoid processes: differential diagnosis of intra-oral gunshot trauma and scavenging using a sheep crania model. *J. Forensic Sci.* 48(6): 1219–1225.

Quatrehomme, G. 2007. A strange case of dismemberment. In Brickley, M.B. and Ferllini, R. (Eds.). *Forensic anthropology: case studies from Europe.* Springfield, IL: Charles C Thomas, pp. 99–119.

Quatrehomme, G., Bolla, M., Muller, M., Rocca, J.P., Grevin, G., Bailet, P., and Ollier, A. 1998. Experimental single controlled study of burned bones: contribution of scanning electron microscopy. *J. Forensic Sci.* 43(2): 417–422.

Quatrehomme, G. and İşcan, M.Y. 1998. Analysis of beveling in gunshot entrance wounds. *Forensic Sci. Int.* 93: 45–60.

Quatrehomme, G. and İşcan, M.Y. 1997a. Beveling in exit gunshot wounds in bone. *Forensic Sci. Int.* 89: 93–101.

Quatrehomme, G. and İşcan, M.Y. 1997b. Postmortem skeletal lesions. *Forensic Sci. Int.* 89(3): 155–165.

Rae, L.J. 1969. Radiology and its forensic applications. In Camps, F.E. (Ed.). *Recent advances in forensic pathology.* London: Churchill, pp. 149–160.

Rajs, J., Moberg, B., and Olsson, J.E. 1987. Explosive-related deaths in Sweden: a forensic-pathologic and criminalistics study. *Forensic Sci. Int.* 34: 1–15.

Randall, B. and Newby, P. 1989. Comparison of gunshot wounds and field-tipped arrow wounds using morphological criteria and chemical spot tests. *J. Forensic Sci.* 34(3): 579–586.

Rao, V.J. and Hart, R. 1983. Tool mark determination in cartilage of stabbing victim. *J. Forensic Sci.* 28(3): 794–799.

Raul, J.S., Baumgartner, D., Willinger, R., and Ludes, B. 2006. Finite element modelling of human head injuries caused by a fall. *Int. J. Legal Med.* 120(4): 212–218.

Raul, J.S., Deck, C., Meyer, F., Geraut, A., Willinger, R., and Ludes, B. 2005. A finite element model investigation of gunshot injury. *Int. J. Legal Med.* 17: 1–4.

Rautio, J. and Paavolainen, P. 1988. Afghan War wounded: experience with 200 cases. *J. Trauma Injury Infect. Crit. Care* 28(4): 523–525.

Reichs, K.J. 1998. *Forensic osteology: Advances in the identification of human remains.* 2nd ed. Springfield, IL: Charles C Thomas, pp. 204–236.

Reinhard, K.J. and Fink, T.M. 1994. Cremation in south-western North America: aspects of taphonomy that affect pathological analysis. *J. Archaeol. Sci.* 21(5): 597.

Reynolds, P. Activism, politics, and the punishment of children. 1998. In Van Bueren, G. (Ed.). *Childhood abused: Protecting children against torture, cruel and inhuman and degrading treatment and punishment.* Dartmouth, U.K.: Ashgate, pp. 43–56.

Reza, A., Mercy, J.A., and Krug, E. 2001. Epidemiology of violent deaths in the word. *Inj. Prev.* 7: 104–111.

Rhine, J.S. and Curran, B.K. 1990. Multiple gunshot wounds of the head: an anthropological view. *J. Foensic Sci.* 35(5): 1236–1245.

Rice, D., Bikkasani, N., Espada, R., Mattox, K., and Wall, M. 2002. Seat belt-related chondrosternal disruption with lung herniation. *Ann. Thorac. Surg.* 73(6): 1950–1951.

Richter, D., Hahn, M.P., Ostermann, P.A., Ekkernkamp, A., and Muhr, G. 1996. Vertical deceleration injuries: a comparative study of the injury patterns of 101 patients after accidental and intentional high falls. *Injury* 27(9): 655–659.

Roberts, C.A. and Manchester, K. 1995. *The archaeology of disease.* New York: Cornell University Press.

Robbins, S.L., Cotran, R.S., and Kumar, V. 1991. *Pathologic basis of disease.* Philadelphia, PA: Saunders Company, pp. 1227–1229.

Rodriquez-Martin, C. 2006. Identification and differential diagnosis of traumatic lesions of the skeleton. In Schmitt, A., Cunha, E., and Pinheiro, J. (Eds.). *Forensic anthropology and medicine.* Totowa, NJ: Humana Press, pp. 197–224.

Rogers, L.F. 1982. *Radiology of skeletal trauma.* New York: Churchill Livingstone, 2nd ed., 1521 pp.

Roh, B.D. and Lee, Y.E. 2006. Analysis of 154 cases of teeth with cracks. *Dental Traumatol.* 22(3): 118–123.

Romano, C.P.R., Nollkaemper, A., and Kleffner, J.K. (Eds.). 2004. *Internationalized criminal courts: Sierra Leone, East Timor, Kosovo, and Cambodia.* Oxford, U.K.: Oxford University Press, 552 pp.

Ropac, D. and Milas, J. 1999. Military casualties in Baranja and east Slavonia during the first 9 months of the war in Croatia. *Mil. Med.* 164(9): 643–647.

Ross, A.H. 1996. Caliber estimation from cranial entrance defect measurements. *J. Forensic Sci.* 41(4): 629–633.

Ross, A.H. and Konigsberg, L.W. 2002. New formulae for estimating stature in the Balkans. *J. Forensic Sci.* 47: 165–167.

Roth, S., Raul, J.S., Ludes, B., and Willinger, R. 2006. Finite element analysis of impact and shaking inflicted to a child. *Int. J. Legal Med.* (Epub ahead of print; 8 November).

Rowe, W.F. 2005. The distribution of shotgun pellets after ricochet from an intermediate target surface. *Forensic Sci. Int.* 155(2–3): 188–192.

Ruan, J.S., Khalil, T.B., and King, A.I. 1993. Finite element modelling of direct head impact. Proceedings of the 37th STAPP Car Crash Conference, SAE Paper 933114, 69–81.

Rukavina, A. 1998. War injuries in civilians treated in Pozega Hospital, Croatia. *J. R. Army Med. Corps* 144(3): 149–151.

Rules of Procedure and Evidence of the ICTY, http://www.un.org/icty/legaldoc-e/index.htm.

Runyon, R.P. 1985. *Fundamentals of statistics in the biological, medical, and health sciences.* Boston, MA: Duxbury Press, 393 pp.

Ryan, J.R., Hensel, R.T., Salciccioli, G.G., and Pedersen, H.E. 1981. Fractures of the femur secondary to low-velocity gunshot wounds. *J. Trauma Injury Infect. Crit. Care* 21(2): 160–162.

Ryan, J.M., Rich, N.M., Dale, R.F., Morgans, B.T., and Graham, J.C. (Eds.). 1997. *Ballistic trauma: clinical relevance in peace and war.* London: a Hodder Arnold Publication, 290 pp.

Salama, P., Laurence, B., and Nolan, M.L. 1999. Health and human rights in contemporary humanitarian crises: is Kosovo more important than Sierra Leone? *Br. Med. J.* 319: 1569–1571.

Salis, S.G., Hood, J.A., Kirk, E.E., and Stokes, A.N. 1987a. Impact-fracture energy of human premolar teeth. *J. Prosthet. Dentistry* 58(1): 43–48.

Salis, S.G., Hood, J.A., Stokes, A.N., and Kirk, E.E. 1987b. Patterns of indirect fracture in intact and restored human premolar teeth. *Dent. Traumatol.* 3(1): 10–14.

Salvolini, U. 2002. Traumatic injuries: imaging of facial injuries. *Eur. Radiol.* (12)6: 1253–1261.

Santucci, R.A. and Chang, Y. 2004. Ballistics for physicians: myths about wound ballistics and gunshot injuries. *J. Urol.* 171(4): 1408–1414.

Sauer, N.J. 1998. The timing of injuries and manner of death: distinguishing among antemortem, perimortem and postmortem trauma. In Reichs, K. (Ed.). *Forensic osteology: advances in the identification of human remains.* 2nd ed. Springfield, IL: Charles C Thomas, pp. 321–332.

Sauer, N.J. and Simson, L.R. 1984. Clarifying the role of forensic anthropologists in death investigations. *J. Forensic Sci.* 29(4): 1–6.

Saukko, P. and Knight, B. 2004. *Knight's forensic pathology.* London: a Hodder Arnold Publication, pp. 101–189, 201–295.

Savnik, A. Amris, K., Rogind, H., Prip, K., Danneskiold-Samsoe, B., Bojsen-Moller, F., Bartels, E.M., Bliddal, H., Boesen, J., and Egund, N. 2000. MRI of the plantar structures of the foot after falanga torture. *Eur. Radiol.* 10(10): 1655–1659.

Sayegh, J. (Ed.). 2006. *Africa Notes.* Ithaca, New York: Cornell University, p. 1–20.

Schiller, A.L. and Teitelbaum, S.L. 1999. Bones and joints. In Rubin, E. and Farber, J.L. (Eds.). *Pathology.* Philadelphia, PA: Lippincott-Raven, pp. 1354–1356.

Schmidt, G. 1979. Rib cage injuries indicating the direction and strength of impact. *Forensic Sci. Int.* 13: 103–110.

Schmitt, K.U., Niederer, P., and Walz, F. 2004. *Trauma biomechanics: Introduction to accidental injury,* Zurich: Springer, 188 pp.

Schmitt, A., Cunha, E., and Pinheiro, J. (Eds.). 2006. *Forensic anthropology and medicine.* Totowa, NJ: Humana Press, 464 pp.

Schmitt, S. 2001. Mass graves and the collection of forensic evidence: genocide, war crimes and crimes against humanity. In Haglund, W.D. and Sorg, M.H. (Eds.). *Forensic taphonomy: the postmortem fate of human remains.* Boca Raton, FL: CRC Press, pp. 277–292.

Scott, B. A., Fletcher, J. R., Pulliam, M. W., and Harris, R. D. (1986). The Beirut terrorist bombing. *Neurosurgery,* 18(1): 107–110

Scott, D.D. and Conner, M. 1997. Context delicti: archaeological context in forensic work. In Haglund, W.D. and Sorg, M.H. (Eds.). *Forensic taphonomy: The postmortem fate of human remains.* Boca Raton, FL: CRC Press, pp. 27–38.

Seetah Krish, N.D. The importance of cut placement and implement signatures to butchery interpretation. University of Cambridge. In http://www.alexandriaarchive.org/bonecommons/prize/Seetah_TextImages.pdf.

Sellier, K.G. and Kneubuehl, B.P. 1994. Wound ballistics: And the scientific background. Missouri: Elsevier, 502 pp.

Shah, A. 2006. Arms trade—a major cause of suffering: Small arms—they cause 90% of civilian casualties. *Global Issues.* Last updated January 21, 2006. Electronic document: http://www.globalissues.org/Geopolitics/ArmsTrade/SmallArms.asp.

Shepherd, J.P., Shapland, M., Pearce, N.X., and Scully, C. 1990. Pattern, severity and aetiology of injuries in victims of assault. *J. R. Social Med.* 83(2): 75–78.

Shipman, P., Foster, G., and Schoeninger, M. 1984. Burnt bones and teeth: an experimental study of color, morphology, crystal structure and shrinkage. *J. Archaeol. Sci.* 11: 307–325.

Shipman, P. 1981. *Life history of a fossil: an introduction to taphonomy and paleoecology.* Cambridge: Harvard University Press, 222 pp.

Simon, B.J., Chu, Q., Emhoff, T.A., Fiallo, V.M., and Lee, K.F. 1998. Delayed hemothorax after blunt thoracic trauma: an uncommon entity with significant morbidity. *J. Trauma Injury Infect. Crit. Care* 45: 673–676.

Singh, A.I. 2001. *Diversity, Human Rights, and peace—culture watch.* UN Chronicle. June–August 2001.

Sirmali, M., Turut, H., Topcu, S., Gulhan, E., Yazici, U., Kaya, S., and Tastepe, I. 2003. A comprehensive analysis of traumatic rib fractures: morbidity, mortality and management. *Eur. J. Cardiothorac. Surg.* 24(1): 133–138.

Situm, M., Milinovic, I. Poje, G., Bucan, Z., and Ozanic-Bulic, S. 2004. Lethal injuries among the members of the 4th Guardian Brigade of Croatian Army during the 1991–1995 War. *Mil. Med.* 169(4): 288–291.

Skinner, M.F. 1987. Planning the archaeological recovery of evidence from recent mass graves. *Forensic Sci. Int.* 34: 267–287.

Skinner, M.F., York, H.P., and Connor, M.A. 2001. Postburial disturbance of graves Bosnia-Herzegovina. In Haglund, W.D. and Sorg, M.H. (Eds.). *Advances in forensic taphonomy: Method, theory and archaeological perspectives.* Boca Raton, FL: CRC Press, pp. 293–308.

Skolnick, A. 1991. Medicine and war: Recognizing common vulnerability of friend and foe. *J. Am. Med. Assoc. (JAMA)* 265(7): 834–835.

Smith, D. 2002. *Report from Ground Zero: The story of the rescue efforts at the World Trade Center.* New York: Viking, 416 pp.

Smith, H.W. and Wheatley, K.K., Jr. 1984. Biomechanics of femur fractures secondary to gunshot wounds. *J. Trauma Injury Infect. Crit. Care* 24(11): 970–977.

Smith, O.C., Pope, E.J., and Symes, S.A. 2003. Look until you see: identification of trauma in skeletal material. In Wolfe Steadman, D. (Ed.). *Hard evidence: case studies in forensic anthropology.* Upper Saddle River, NJ: Prentice Hall, pp. 138–154.

Snow, C.C., Levine, L., Lukash, L., Tedeschi, L.G., Orrego, C., and Stover, E. 1984. The investigation of human remains of the "Disappeared" in Argentina. *Am. J. Phys. Anthropol.* 5(4): 297–299.

Snow, C.C. and Bihurriet, M.J. 1992. An Epidemiology of homicide: Ningun Nombre burials in the province of Buenos Aires from 1970 to 1984. In Jabine, T.B. and Claude, R.P. (Eds.). *Human rights and statistics: getting the record straight.* Philadelphia, PA: University of Pennslyvania Press, pp. 328–363.

Snow, C.C. 1982. Forensic anthropology. *Annu. Rev. Anthropol.* 11: 97–130.

Snyder, H.E. and Culbertson, J.W. 1962. Study of Fifth U.S. Army Hospital battle casualty deaths. In Beyer, J.C. (Ed.) *Wound ballistics.* Office of the Surgeon General, Department of the Army: Washington, D.C.: pp. 473–530.

Soldado desconocido? Unpublished paper of the National Museum of Archaeology, Anthropology and History of Peru. Lima, Peru.

Soldo, S. and Puntaric, D. 1998. Injuries in Croatian Army brigade soldiers inflicted in an offensive action during the 1991/1992 war in Croatia. *Mil. Med.* 163(6): 420–422.

Spalding, T.J.W., Stewart, M.P.M., Tulloch, D.N., and Stephens, K.M. 1992. Penetrating missile injuries in the Gulf War. *J. R. Army Med. Corps* 138(3): 129.

Spiegel, P.B. and Salama, P. 2000. War and mortality in Kosovo, 1998–99: an epidemiological testimony. *Lancet—London* 9222: 2204–2209.

Spitz, W.U. (Ed.). 1993a. *Spitz and Fisher's medicolegal investigation of death: Guidelines for the application of pathology to crime investigation.* 3rd ed. Springfield, IL: Charles C Thomas, 829 pp.

Spitz, W.U. 1993b. Sharp Force Injury. In Spitz WU (Ed.). 1993. *Spitz and Fisher's medicolegal investigation of death: Guidelines for the application of pathology to crime investigation.* 3rd ed. Springfield, IL: Charles C Thomas, pp. 252–310.

Spitz, W.U. 1993c. Injury by Gunfire. In Spitz, W.U. (Ed.). 1993. *Spitz and Fisher's medicolegal investigation of death: Guidelines for the application of pathology to crime investigation.* 3rd ed. Springfield, IL: Charles C Thomas, pp. 311–412.

Statute of the International Tribunal for the Former Yugoslavia. Adopted 25 May 1993 by Resolution 827, as amended 13 May 1998 by Resolution 1166, as amended 30 November 2000 by Resolution 1329. Available: http://www.icls.de/dokumente/icty_statut.pdf.

Stawicki, S.P., Grossman, M.D., and Hoey, B.A. 2002. Rib fractures in the elderly: a marker of injury severity. *J. Am. Geriatr. Soc.* 52(5): 805–808.

Steadman, D.W. (Ed.). 2003. *Hard evidence: case Studies in forensic anthropology.* Upper Saddle River, NJ: Prentice Hall, 310 pp.

Steadman, D.W., DiAntonia, L.L., Wilson, J.J., Sheridan, K.E., and Tammariello, S.P. 2006. The effects of chemical and heat maceration techniques on the recovery of nuclear and mitochondrial DNA from bone. *J. Forensic Sci.* 51(1): 11–17.

Steinbock, R.T. 1976. *Paleopathological diagnosis and interpretation.* Springfield, IL: Charles C Thomas, 423 pp.

Stewart, T.D. 1979. *Essentials forensic anthropology: especially as developed in the United States.* Springfield, IL: Charles C Thomas, 300 pp.

Stoneham, M.D. 1995. Bilateral first rib fractures associated with driver's air bag inflation: case report and implications for surgery. *Eur. J. Emergency Med.* 2(1): 60–62.

Stover, E. and Eisner, T. 1982. Commentary: Human rights abuses and the role of scientists *BioScience* 32(11): 871–875.

Stover, E. and Peress, G. 1998. *The graves: Srebrenica and Vukovar.* Zurich: Scalo Publishers, 336 pp.

Stover, E. and Shigekane, R. 2002. The missing in the aftermath of war: when do the needs of victims' families and international war crimes tribunals clash? *IRRC* 84: 845–866.

Strouse, P.J. and Owings, C.L. 1995. Fractures of the first rib in child abuse. *Radiology* 197(3): 763–765.

Summerfield, D. 1995. Raising the dead: war, reparation, and the politics of memory. *Br. Med. J.* 311(7003): 495–497.

Symes, S., Berryman, H.E., and Smith, O.C. 1998. Saw marks in bone: introduction and examination of residual kerf contour. In Reichs, K.J. (Ed.). *Forensic osteol II: Advances in the Identification of Human Remains.* Springfield, IL: Charles C Thomas, pp. 289–409.

Symes, S., Pope, E., Saul, F., Saul, J., Smith, O.C., and Zephro, L. 2001. Taphonomic context of sharp-force trauma in suspected cases of human mutilation and dismemberment. In Haglund, W. and Sorg, M. (Eds.). *Advances in forensic taphonomy: method, theory, and archeological perspectives.* New York: CRC Press, pp. 403–433.

Ta'ala, S.C., Berg, G.E., and Haden, K. 2006. Blunt force cranial trauma in the Cambodian killing fields. *J. Forensic Sci.* 51: 996–1001.

Taback, N. and Coupland, R. 2005. Towards collation and modeling of the global cost of Armed violence on civilians. *Med. Conf. Survival* 21(1): 19–27.

Taipale, I., Mäkelä, P.H., Juva, K., Taipale, V., and Tapanainen, H. (Eds.) 2002. *War or health? A reader.* London: Zed Books. 652 pp.

Tedeschi, L. 1984. Human Rights and the forensic scientist. *Am. J. Forensic Med. Pathol.* 5(4): 295–296.

Teh, J., Firth, M., Sharma, A., Wilson, A., Reznek, R., and Chan, O. 2003. Jumpers and fallers: a comparison of the distribution of skeletal injury. *Clin. Radiol.* 58(6): 482–486.

Tekinbas, C., Eroglu, A., Kurkcuoglu, I.C., Turkyilmaz, A., Yekeler, E., and Karaoglanoglu, N. 2003. Chest trauma: analysis of 592 cases. *Ulus Travma Acil Cerrahi Derg* 9(4): 275–280.

Tencer, A.F., Kaufman, R., Ryan, K., Grossman, D.C., Henley, B.M., Mann, F., Mock, C., Rivara, F., Wang, S., Augenstein, J., Hoyt, D., and Eastman, B. 2002. Femur fractures in relatively low speed frontal crashes: the possible role of muscle forces. *Accident Anal. Prev.* 34(1): 1–11.

Tencer, A.F. and Johnson, K.D. 1994. *Biomechanics in orthopedic trauma: bone fracture and fixation*. Canada: Informa Healthcare, 320 pp.

Tessier, P. 1972a. The classic reprint: experimental study of fractures of the upper jaw. I and II. Rene Le Fort, M.D. Lille, France.

Tessier, P. 1972b. The classic reprint: experimental study of fractures of the upper jaw. III. Rene Le Fort, M.D., Lille, France. *Plast. Reconstr. Surg.* 50(6): 600–607.

Testerman, G.M. 2006. Adverse outcomes in younger rib fracture patients. *South. Med. J.* 99(4): 335–359.

Tewes, D.P., Fischer, D.A., Quick, D.C., Zamberletti, F., and Powell, J. 1995. Lumbar transverse process fractures in professional football players. *Am. J. Sports Med.* 23(4): 507–509.

Thali, M.J. 2003. Image-guided virtual autopsy findings of gunshot victims performed with multi-slice computed tomography (MSCT) and magnetic resonance imaging (MRI) and subsequent correlation between radiology and autopsy findings. *Forensic Sci. Int.* 138(3): 8–16.

Thali, M.J., Kneubuehl, B.P., Vock, P., Allmen, G., and Dirnhofer, R. 2002a. High-speed documented experimental gunshot to a skull-brain model and radiologic virtual autopsy. *Am. J. Forensic Med. Pathol.* 23(3): 223–228.

Thali, M.J., Kneubuehl, B.P., Zollinger, U., and Dirnhofer, R. 2002b. A study of the morphology of gunshot entrance wounds, in connection with their dynamic creation, utilizing the "skin-skull-brain model." *Forensic Sci. Int.* 125(2–3): 190–194.

Thali, M.J., Kneubuehl, B.P., Zollinger, U., and Dirnhofer, R. 2003a. A high-speed study of the dynamic bullet-body interactions produced by grazing gunshots with full metal jacketed and lead projectiles. *Forensic Sci. Int.* 132(2): 93–98.

Thali, M.J., Yen, K., Schweitzer, W., Vock, P., and Ozdoba, C. 2003b. Into the decomposed body—Forensic digital autopsy using multi-slice computed tomography. *Forensic Sci. Int.* 134(3): 109.

The Hague Peace Conferences of 1899 and 1907. Declaration III. *Laws of War: Declaration on the Use of Bullets Which Expand or Flatten Easily in the Human Body.* First Peace Conference at The Hague, Signed July 29, 1899 and entered into force September 4, 1900. In The Avalon Project at Yale Law School Laws of War http://www.yale.edu/lawweb/avalon/lawofwar/dec99-03.htm.

The Prosecutor v. Dusko Tadic "Prijedor," Case No IT-94-1-T; Trial and Appeals Chamber Judgment, July 30, 2002. International Criminal Tribunal for the former Yugoslavia. In http://www.un.org/icty/tadic/trialc2/judgement/tad-sj970714e.pdf.

The Prosecutor v. Zlatko Aleksovski "Lasva Valley," Case No IT-95-14/1; International Criminal Tribunal for the former Yugoslavia. Trial and Appeals Chamber Judgment, May 30, 2001 International Criminal Tribunal for the former Yugoslavia. In http://www.un.org/icty/aleksovski/appeal/judgement/nob-aj010530e.pdf.

The Prosecutor v. Zdravko Tolimir, Radivoje Miletic, Milan Gvero, Vinko Pandurevic, Ljubisa Beara, Vujadin Popovic, Drago Nikolic, Milorad Trbic and Ljubomir Borovcanin, Case No IT-05-88-PT; Transcripts February 20–21, March 13–15, International Criminal Tribunal for the former Yugoslavia. In http://www.un.org/icty/transe88/070220ED.htm, http://www.un.org/icty/transe88/070221IT.htm, http://www.un.org/icty/transe88/070313ED.htm, http://www.un.org/icty/transe88/070314IT.htm, http://www.un.org/icty/transe88/070315IT.htm.

The Prosecutor v. Ranko Cesic "Brcko," Case No IT-95-10/1; Trial Chamber Judgment, March 11, 2004. International Criminal Tribunal for the former Yugoslavia. In http://www.un.org/icty/cesic/trialc/judgement/ces-tj040311e.pdf.

The Prosecutor v. Mile Mrksic, Miroslav Radic, Veselin Sljivancanin, Case No IT-95-13/1-PT; Second Modified Consolidated Amended Indictment, August 26, 2004. International Criminal Tribunal for the former Yugoslavia. In http://www.un.org/icty/indictment/english/mrk-ai040826e.htm.

The Prosecutor v. Goran Jelisic, Case No. IT-95-10; Trial and Appeals Chamber Judgments, December 14, 1999 and July 5, 2001. International Criminal Tribunal for the former Yugoslavia. In http://www.un.org/icty/jelisic/trialc1/judgement/index.htm.

The Prosecutor v. Zoran Kupreskic et al., Case No. IT-95-16-T; Appeals Chamber Judgment, July 5, 2001. International Criminal Tribunal for the former Yugoslavia. In http://www.un.org/icty/kupreskic/appeal/judgement/kup-aj011023e.pdf.

The Prosecutor v. Dario Kordic and Mario Čerkez, Case No. IT-95-14/2-T; Trial and Appeals Chamber Judgments, December 14, 1999 and July 5, 2001. International Criminal Tribunal for the former Yugoslavia. http://www.un.org/icty/kordic/trialc/judgement/kor-tj010226e.pdf.

The Prosecutor v. Radovan Karadzic, Case No. IT-95-5/18-I; Amended Indictment, May 31, 2000. International Criminal Tribunal for the former Yugoslavia. In http://www.un.org/icty/indictment/english/kar-ai000428e.htm.

The Prosecutor v. Ratko Mladic, Case No. IT-95-5/18-I; Amended Indictment, October 10, 2002. International Criminal Tribunal for the former Yugoslavia. In http://www.un.org/icty/indictment/english/mla-ai021010e.htm.

The Prosecutor v. Kayishema and Ruxindana, Case No ICTR-95-1; International Criminal Tribunal for Rwanda. In www.un.org/ictr.

The Prosecutor v. Miroslav Kvocka, Dragoljub Prcac, Milojica Kos, Mlado Radic and Zoran Zigic, Case No. IT-98-30/1; Appeals Chamber Judgment, February 28, 2005, International Criminal Tribunal for the former Yugoslavia. In http://www.un.org/icty/kvocka/appeal/judgement/kvo-aj050228e.pdf.

The Prosecutor v. Rutaganda Case No ICTR-96-3; International Criminal Tribunal for Rwanda. In www.un.org/ictr.

The Prosecutor v. Dragoljub Kunarac, Radomir Kovac, and Zoran Vukovic, Case No. IT-96-23/1-T; Judgement, 2001. International Criminal Tribunal for the former Yugoslavia. In http://www.un.org/icty/kunarac/appeal/judgement/index.htm.

The Prosecutor v. Milorad Krnojelac, Case No.IT-97-25-I; Appeals Chamber Judgment June 12, 2002, International Criminal Tribunal for the former Yugoslavia. In http://www.un.org/icty/krnojelac/trialc2/judgement/krn-tj020315e.pdf.

The Prosecutor v. Stanislav Galič, Case No. IT-98-29; Appeals Chamber Judgment. November 13, 2006. International Criminal Tribunal for the former Yugoslavia. In http://www.un.org/icty/galic/judgment/gal-acj061130e.pdf.

The Prosecutor v. Kvocka Mlado Radic, Zoran Zigic, and Dragnoljub Prcac, Case No. IT-98-30/1; Appeals Chamber Judgment. February 28, 2005. International Criminal Tribunal for the former Yugoslavia. In http://www.un.org/icty/kvocka/appeal/judgement/index.htm.

The Prosecutor v. Radislav Krstic, Case No. IT-98-33-T; Judgment. 2001. International Criminal Tribunal for the former Yugoslavia. In *http://www.un.org/icty/krstic/TrialC1/judgement/krs-tj010802e.pdf*, Appeals Chamber judgment of 19 April 2004, www.un.org/icty/Supplement/supp49-e/krstic.htm, Trial transcript, www.un.org/icty/transe33/000530it.htm, Trial Chamber judgment, www.un.org/icty/krstic/TrialC1/judgment/index.htm.

The Prosecutor v. Slobodan Milosevic, Milan Milutinovic, Nikola Sainovic, Dragoljub Ojdanic and Vlajko Stojiljkovic, Case No. IT-99-37-PT (Kosovo); 29 October 2001 and The Prosecutor v. Slobodan Milosevic, Case IT-02-54-T (Croatia), 28 July 2004. "Kosovo, Croatia and Bosnia." International Criminal Tribunal for the former Yugoslavia. In http://www.un.org/icty/indictment/english/mil-2ai011029e.htm and http://www.un.org/icty/indictment/english/mil-2ai020728e.htm.

The Prosecutor v. Radislav Brdjanin, Case No. IT-99-36-T and Stojan Zupljanin, Case No. IT-99-36-I; Appeals Chamber Judgement April 3, 2007. International Criminal Tribunal for the former Yugoslavia. In http://www.un.org/icty/brdjanin/trialc/judgement/brd-tj040901e.pdf.

The Prosecutor v. Pavle Strugar, Case No. IT-01-42-T; Trial Chamber Judgement. January 31, 2005. International Criminal Tribunal for the former Yugoslavia. In http://www.un.org/icty/strugar/trialc1/judgment/str-tj050131e.pdf.

The Prosecutor v. Zeljko Mejakic, Momcilo Gruban, Dusan Fustar, and Dusko Knezevic Case No IT-02-65; Consolidated Indictment, November 21, 2002 and Appeals Chamber Judgement, April 7, 2006. International Criminal Tribunal for the former Yugoslavia. In http://www.un.org/icty/indictment/english/mea-ci020705e.htm and http://www.un.org/icty/banovic65-1/trialc/judgment/ban-sj031028e.pdf.

The Prosecutor v. Vidoje Blagojevic, Dragan Obrenovic, Dragan Jokic and Momir Nikolic. Amended joint indictment, Case No. IT-02-60-PT; May 26, 2003. International Criminal Tribunal for the former Yugoslavia. In http://www.un.org/icty/indictment/english/nik-ai020527e.htm.

The Prosecutor v. Fatmir Limaj, Haradin Bala and Isak Musliu, Case No. IT-03-66-PT; Decision on Prosecution's Motion to Amend the Amended Indictment, ("Second Amended Indictment" attached to the "Prosecution's Motion to Amend the Amended Indictment" filed on 6 November 2003). 2004. International Criminal Tribunal for the former Yugoslavia. In http://www.un.org/icty/limaj/trialc/decision-e/040212.pdf.

The Prosecutor v. Milan Milutinovic, Nikola Sainovic, Dragoljub Ojdanic, Nebosjsa Pavkovic, Vladimir Lazarevic and Streten Lukic, Case No. IT-05-87; Transcript 6 March 2007. International Criminal Tribunal for the former Yugoslavia. In www.un.org/icty/transe87/070306IT.htm.

The Prosecutor v. Ante Gotovina, Ivan Cermak and Mladen Markac, Case No. IT-06-90-PT; Amended Joint. Indictment, March 6, 2007. International Criminal Tribunal for the former Yugoslavia. In http://www.un.org/icty/indictment/english/got-jind070306e.pdf.

Thompson, T. 2004. Recent advances in the study of burned bone and their implications for forensic anthropology. *Forensic Sci. Int.* 146: S203–S205.

Thomsen, J.L., Helweg-Larsen, K., and Rasmussen, O.V. 1984. Amnesty International and the forensic sciences. *Am. J. Forensic Med. Pathol.* 5(4): 305–311.

Thomsen, J.L. and Voigt, J. Forensic medicine and human rights. *Forensic Sci. Int.* 1988; 36: 147–151.

Thoresen, S. 1984. Fatal head injuries from firearms. An autopsy study of 270 cases. *Z. Rechtsmed.* 93(2): 65–69.

Thorn, J.J., Mogeltoft, M., and Hansen, P.K. 1986. Incidence and aetiological pattern of jaw fractures in Greenland. *Int. J. Oral Maxillofac. Surg.* 15(4): 372–379.

Thornton, B.S. 1999. The international criminal tribunal for Rwanda: a report from the field. *J. Int. Aff.* 52(2): 639.

Tidball-Binz, M. 2006. Forensic investigations into the Missing: Recommendations and operational best practices. In Schmitt, A., Cunha, E., and Pinheiro, J. (Eds.). *Forensic anthropology and medicine.* Totowa, NJ: Humana Press, pp. 383–408.

Timperman, J. and Cnops, L. 1975. Tandem bullet in the head in a case of suicide. *Med. Sci.* 15(4): 280–283.

Tomczak, P.D. and Buikstra, J.E. 1999. Analysis of blunt trauma injuries: vertical deceleration versus horizontal deceleration injuries. *J. Forensic Sci.* 44(2): 253–262.

Toole, M.J. and Waldman, R.J. 1993. The role of physicians in conflicts and humanitarian crises: case studies from field missions of physicians for Human Rights. *J. Am. Med. Assoc. (JAMA)* 270(5): 600–605.

Toole, M.J., Galson, S., and Brady, W. 1993. Are war and public health compatible? *Lancet* 341: 935–38.

Tsokos, M., Turk, E.E., Madea, B., Koops, E., Longauer, F., Szabo, M., Huckenbeck, W., Gabriel, P., and Barz, J. 2003. Pathological features of suicidal deaths caused by explosives. *Am. J. Forensic Med. Pathol.* 24(1): 55–63.

Tucker, B.K., Hutchinson, D.L., Gilliland, M.F., Charles, T.M., Daniel, H.J., and Wolfe, L.D. 2001. Microscopic characteristics of hacking trauma. *J. Forensic Sci.* 46(2): 234–240.

Tuller, H. and Djuric, M. 2006. Keeping the pieces together: comparison of mass grave excavation methodology. *Forensic Sci. Int.* 156: 192–200.

Turner, C.G. II, and Turner, J.A. 1992. *The first claim for cannibalism and violence in the prehistoric American Southwest.* American antiquity 57(4): 661–682.

Ubelaker, D.H. and Adams, B.J. 1995. Differentiation of perimortem and postmortem trauma using taphonomic indicators. *J. Forensic Sci.* 40(3): 509–512.

Uceda, R. 2004. *Muerte en el pentagonito. Los cementerios secretos del Ejercito Peruano.* Editorial Planeta. Bogota. Colombia.

UN Manual on the Effective Prevention and Investigation of Extra-Legal Arbitrary and Summary Executions. (1991) UN Publications No. E.91. IV. 1 includes:

-- Model Protocol for a Legal Investigation of Extra-legal, Arbitrary, and Summary Executions ("Minnesota Protocol"), www.icrc.org/themissi.nsf/b5a5eed1a93ca649c12569dd00505aca/448d147db779628ac1256b02005c3e62?OpenDocument.

-- Model Autopsy Protocol, www.icrc.org/themissi.nsf/b5a5eed1a93ca649c12569dd00505aca/ba3902ca62ce4044c1256b02005c999f?OpenDocument.

-- Model Protocol for Disinterment and Analysis of Skeletal Remains, www.icrc.org/themissi.nsf/b5a5eed1a93ca649c12569dd00505aca/4734c01eedc22795c1256b02005cc01c?OpenDocument.

UN Security Council Resolution 995 [8 November 1994], http://www.un.org/ictr/english/Resolutions/955e.htm.

UN Security Council Resolution 827 [25 May 1993], http://www.un.org/icty/legaldoc-e/basic/statut/S-RES-827_93.htm.

UN Security Council Resolution 39/46 [Adopted December,1984; Entered into force 1987], *Convention against Torture and Other Cruel, Inhumanor Degrading Treatment or Punishment.* http://www.unhchr.ch/html/menu3/b/h_cat39.htm.

UN Security Council Resolution 1244 [10 June 1999], http://www.nato.int/Kosovo/docu/u990610a.htm.

United Nations, *Declaration of Human Rights.* Adopted and proclaimed by General Assembly Resolution 217 A (III) of 10 December 1948. http://www.un.org/Overview/rights.html.

United Nations, International Criminal Court (ICC). Electronic Documents, http://www.un.org/law/icc/index.html.

United Nations, International Criminal Tribunal for the Former Yugoslavia. *ICTY at a Glance.* Electronic Document, http://www.un.org/icty/glance-e/index.htm. General case information, http://www.un.org/icty.

United Nations, International Criminal Tribunal for Rwanda. *ICTR The Tribunal at a Glance.* Electronic Document, http://69.94.11.53/default.htm.

United States v. Michael J. Fortier (D.C. No. 95-CR-111-VB). United States Court of Appeals Tenth Circuit, Case No. 99-6381, March 16, 2001. In http://www.kscourts.org/ca10/cases/2001/03/99-6381.htm.

United States v. Timothy James McVeigh (D.C. No. 96-CR-89-M). United States Court of Appeals Tenth Circuit, Case No. 01-1273, June 7, 2001. In http://fl1.findlaw.com/news.findlaw.com/cnn/docs/mcveigh/10thorderjud60701.pdf.

United States v. Terry Lynn Nichols (D.C. No. 96-CR-89-M). United States Court of Appeals Tenth Circuit, Case No. 98-1231, Feb. 26, 1999. In http://www.kscourts.org/ca10/cases/1999/02/98-1231.htm.

Unnewehr, M., Homann, C., Schmidt, P.F., Sotony, P., Fischer, G., Brinkmann, B., Bajanowski, T., DuChesne, A. 2003. Fracture properties of the human mandible. *Int. J. Legal Med.* 117(6): 326–330.

Vance, B.M. 1927. Fractures of the skull. *Arch. Surg.* 14: 1023–1091.

Van Herp, M., Parque, V., Rackley, E., and Ford, N. 2003. Mortality, violence and lack of access to health-care in the Democratic Republic of Congo. *Disasters* 27(2): 141–153.

Van Vark, G.N. 1970. *Some statistical procedures for the investigation of prehistoric human skeletal material.* Ph.D. dissertation, Rijksuniversiteit de Groningen, Groningen, The Netherlands.

Vellema, J. and Scholtz, H.J. 2005. Forensic aspects of ballistic injury. In Mahoney, P.F., Ryan, J.M., Brooks, A., and Schwab, C.W. (Eds.). *Ballistic trauma.* 2nd ed. London: Springer-Verlag, pp. 91–121.

Vigorita, V.J. 1999. Fracture healing. In Vigorita, V.J. (Ed.). *Orthopaedic pathology.* Philadelphia, PA: Lippincott Williams and Wilkins, pp. 85–96.

Villa, P. and Mahieu, E. 1991. Breakage patterns of human long bones. *J. Hum. Evol.* 21: 27–48.
Vock, R. 2001. Liver rupture caused by isolated blunt force impact: the result of a blow, a kick or a fall? *Int. J. Legal Med.* 114(4–5): 244–247.
Vogel, H. 2003a. Postural Torture. In Brogdon, B.G., Vogel, H., and McDowell, J.D. *A Radiologic atlas of abuse, torture, terrorism, and inflicted trauma.* Boca Raton, FL: CRC Press, pp. 133–135.
Vogel, H. 2003b. Explosives. In Brogdon, B.G., Vogel, H., and McDowell, J.D. *A radiologic atlas of abuse, torture, terrorism, and inflicted trauma.* Boca Raton, FL: CRC Press, pp. 139–143.
Vogel, H. and Brogdon, B.G. 2003a. Child Abuse. In Brogdon, B.G., Vogel, H., and McDowell, J.D. *A radiologic atlas of abuse, torture, terrorism, and inflicted trauma.* Boca Raton, FL: CRC Press, pp. 3–45.
Vogel, H. and Brogdon, B.G. 2003b. Beating. In Brogdon, B.G., Vogel, H., and McDowell, J.D. *A radiologic atlas of abuse, torture, terrorism, and inflicted trauma.* Boca Raton, FL: CRC Press, pp. 109–118.
Vollen, L. 2001. All that remains: identifying the victims of the Srebrenica massacre. *Cambridge Q Healthcare Ethics* 10: 336–340.
Walker, P.L. 2001. A bioarchaeological perspective on the history of violence. *Annu. Rev. Anthropol.* 30: 573–596.
Walker, P.L. and Long, J.C. 1977. An experimental study of the morphological characteristics of toolmarks. *Am. Antiq.* 42: 605–616.
Walker, P.L., Cook, D.C., and Lambert, P.M. 1997. Skeletal evidence for child abuse: a physical anthropological perspective. *J. Forensic Sci.* 42(2): 196–207.
Walsh-Haney, H.A. 1999. Sharp-force trauma analysis and the forensic anthropologist: techniques advocated by William, R. Maples, Ph.D. *J. Forensic Sci.* 44(4): 720–723.
Warren, M.W. 2007. Interpreting gunshot wounds in the Balkans: Evidence for genocide. In Brickley, M.B. and Ferllini, R. (Eds.). *Forensic anthropology: case studies from europe.* Springfield, IL: Charles C Thomas, pp. 151–164.
Weber, J. and Czarnetzki, A. 2001. Neurotraumatological aspects of head injuries resulting from sharp and blunt force in the early medieval period of southwestern Germany. *Am. J. Phys. Anthropol.* 114: 352–356.
Weinberg, J. and Simmonds, S. 1995. Public health, epidemiology and war. *Soc. Sci. Med.* 40(12): 1663–1639.
Wenham, S.J. 1989. Anatomical interpretations of Anglo-Saxon weapon injuries. In Hawkes, S.C. (Ed.) *Weapons and warfare in Anglo-Saxon England.* Oxford, pp. 123–139.
Welsh, J. and van Es, A. 2003. Forensic medicine and human rights. In Payne-James, J., Bussutil, A., and Smock, W. (Eds.). *Forensic medicine: clinical and pathological aspects.* London: Greenwich Medical Media, pp. 39–48.
Willey, P. and Snyder, L.M. 1989. Canid modification of human remains: implications for time-since-death estimations. *J. Forensic Sci.* 34(4): 894–901.
Williams, P.L., Warwick, R., Dyson, M., and Bannister, L.H. 1989. *Gray's anatomy. The response of bone to injury.* Edinburgh: Churchill Livingstone, pp. 313–315.
Willinger, R. and Baumgartner, D. 2003. Human head tolerance limits to specific injury mechanisms. *Int. J. Crashworthiness* 8(6): 605–617.
Wilson, R.A. 2005. Judging history: The historical record of the international criminal tribunal for the former Yugoslavia. *Hum Rights Q* 27: 908–942.
World Health Organization (WHO). 2004. Guidelines for essential trauma care/injuries and violence prevention department. World Health Organization and the International Association for the Surgery of Trauma and Surgical Intensive Care (IATSIC), International Society of Surgery/Société Internationale de Chirurgie. http://whqlibdoc.who.int/publications/2004/9241546409.pdf.

World Health Organization (WHO). 2002. The world health report (WHO), 2002. Reducing risks, promoting healthy life. World Health Organization Annual Report. In http://www.who.int/whr/2002/en/index.html.

Wright, J. and Kariya, A. 1997. Assault patients attending a Scottish accident and emergency department. *J. R. Soc. Med.* 90(6): 322–326.

Wrightman, J. and Gladish, S. Explosions and blast injuries. *Ann. Emerg. Med.* 37: 664–687.

Yang, K.H. and King, A.I. 2003. A limited review of finite element models of development for brain injury biomechanics research. *Int. J. Vehicle Des.* 31: 116–30.

Yeo, T.P. 2001. Long-term sequelae following blunt thoracic trauma. *Orthop. Nurse* 20: 35–47.

Yoganandan, N. and Pintar, F.A. 2004. Biomechanics of temporo-parietal skull fracture. *Clin. Biomech.* 19(3): 225–239.

Zaidi, S. and Smith Fawzi, M. 1995. Health of Baghdad's children. *Lancet* 346: 1485.

Zhang, L., Yang, K.H., Dwarampudi, R., Omori, K., Li, T., Chang, K., Hardy, W.N., Khalil, T.B., and King, A.I. 2001. Recent advances in brain injury research: a new human head model development and validation, SAE Paper 2001-22-0017.

Zhou, C., Kahlil, T.B., and Dragovic, L.J. 1996. Head injury assessment of a real world crash by finite element modelling. Proceedings of the AGARD Conference, New Mexico, November 1996.

Index

A

Aalund studies, 204
Abbreviated injury scale (AIS), 88
Aboutanos and Baker studies, 9–10, 95–96, 100
Abrasion rings, 367, 371
Accidents, 226–231, *227–232*, *see also* Road traffic accidents (RTA)
Adams, Ubelaker and, studies, 61
Adams and Hirsch studies, 11–12
Adi studies, 405
Age, rib injury lethality, 218, 241, 244
AIS, *see* Abbreviated injury scale (AIS)
AK-47 weapon
  cartridges, 397
  development, 396–397
  differential diagnosis, 115
  fundamentals, *386*
  rib fractures, 410
Allan and Daly studies, 405
Altun studies, 39
Alunni-Perret studies, 291
Ambade and Godbole studies, 204
American velocity, 327
Ammunition
  classification, 327
  estimation, 325–329, *327–355*
  fixed cartridges, 395
  fundamentals, 395–399
  magazines, 392–394
  pistols, 394
  shotgun, 398
  standard military rifle cartridges, 396
Amputation as punishment, 234, *see also* Dismemberment; Torture
Anderson studies, 88
Angle, embedded projectiles, 352
Anglin studies, 174
Angulo studies, 441
Annas, Grodin and, studies, 2
Antemortem fractures
  timing of, 55, *55–59*
  torture, 247, *249*, 254–255
Anthroposcopic examination, 30–31, *31*
Antipersonnel weapons, 10, 385
Arajarvi studies, 226
Argentina, 322
ArmaLite, 397
Arnold studies, 3
Asirdizer studies, 203
Assault rifles, 396
Atlas trauma, 403, 405
Atypical wounds
  blunt force trauma, *164–166*, 164–167
  gunfire entry wounds, 346–353
Aufderheide and Rodriguez-Martin studies, 38
Automatic rifles
  firing, 385, 388
  rimless cartridges, 397
Ax, 266, *see also* sharp force trauma (SFT)
Axis, 403, 405

B

Baker, Aboutanos and, studies, 9–10, 95–96, 100
Bala, Haradin, 206–207
Bandak and Chan studies, 87
Bandak studies, 87–88
Banner, Leth and, studies, 203
Baraybar and Gasior studies, 13, 63, 102, 424
Baraybar studies, 8, 14–19, 83, 102, 205, 212, 255–261
Barness studies, 217
Barnes studies, 32–33
Barrett studies, 5
Bartelink studies, 267
Bartlett studies, 323
Basadre studies, 441, 445, 447
Basilar fractures, 158
Bass and Jantz studies, 65
Bass studies, 65
Battered child syndrome
  diagnosis, 38–40
  timing of fractures, 55
Bauer and Patzelt studies, 267
Baumgartner, Willinger and, studies, 88
Beating foot soles, *see* Falanga
Beavis, Mollan and, studies, 346
Beheadings, 319, *see also* Cambodian killing fields
Behrensmeyer and Hill studies, 55
Bellamy, Bowen and, studies, 10
Bellamy studies, 10, 323
Bending joints, 50, 52–53
Bennet studies, 245
Benomar studies, 2
Ben-Ya'acov studies, 10
Berg, Haden and, studies, 174
Berg studies, 196–199, 265, 314–319
Berisha case, 245–254, *248–249*, *251–253*
Berryman and Haun studies, 46
Berryman and Symes studies, 38, 46, 53, 152, 159, 187–188, 199, 331
Berryman studies, 46, 65, 152, 329–330, 353
Best practice guidelines

blast injuries, 116
blunt force trauma, 176–177
differential diagnosis, 86
epidemiological approaches, 13
gunfire injuries, 384, 435–437
sharp force trauma, 295–296
torture, 233
Best studies, 2
Betz and Leibhardt studies, 39
Betz studies, 402
Beveling
Chilean soldier case study, 443–444
circular fractures, 335
gutter fractures, 338
keyhole defects, 340, 342
pelvis, 419–420
ribs, blunt force trauma, 186
scapula fractures, 414
shotgun injuries, 378
shrapnel, 106
tandem entrance wounds, 350
vertebrae trauma, 406
yawing, exit wounds, 354
BFT, *see* Blunt force trauma (BFT)
Bhoopat studies, 335
Biellik, Henderson and, studies, 35
BiH, *see* Bosnia-Herzegovina (BiH)
Bihurriet, Snow and, studies, 4
Billiard ball effect, 377–378
Binford studies, 2
Biocina studies, 102
Blast injuries
best practice guidelines, 116
blast injury case study, 124, *125–127*
causation mechanisms, 133–136, *134–137*
cause of death, 149
context, 102–107, *103–111*
differential diagnosis, *106–107*, 107–115, *110*, *112–116*
explosive ordnance devices, 97–99, *98–99*
fatal environment, 102–107, *103–111*
fundamentals, 54, 95–97
grenades, 113, 117–123, *117–123*
human bomb case study, 128, *128–133*, 130, 132
injury patterns, *137–148*, 137–149
intent, 102–107, *103–111*
pathophysiology, *100*, 100–101
prevalence, 96
skeletal and soft tissue injuries, 117–123, *117–123*
"Blastlike" injuries, 371
Blast wave force, 98
Blau studies, 2
Blewitt studies, 4
Blindfolds, 8, 257
Blowback action
firing automatic rifles, 388
pistols, 395
Blowout fractures
cranial fractures, 158
exit wounds, 354
Blunt force trauma (BFT)
atypical wounds, cranial vault, *164–166*, 164–167
best practice guidelines, 176–177
blunt force trauma, 187–188, *192–193*
blunt-sharp injuries, 296, 302–303
case studies, 181, 196, *197–198*, 199
classification of injuries, 49
cranial, 158–167, *159–163*
fractures, 158–164, *159–163*, 191–192, 194
freefall injuries, 181–194
fundamentals, 54, 151–152
gunfire injury, 174–176, *176–180*
gunshot trauma comparison, 405
Khmer Rouge execution method, 196, *197–198*, 199
low- to medium-velocity projectiles, 188–189
mandibular fractures, 167, *168–170*
number of injuries, 157, *158*
pathophysiology, 152–157, *153–157*
pelvis, 181–183, 194
postcranial variation, 170–173, *170–175*
ribs, 184, 186, 191–192, 194
right parietal bone, 189, 191, *193*
sequence of injuries, 157, *158*
sharp-blunt injuries, 296
skull, 186–187, *191–192*
torture, 226–231
vertebrae, 184, *185*
Body trauma, human bombs, 128, *128–133*, 130, 132
Bohnert studies, 285
Bolt action weapons, 385, 388
Bombs, 98, *see also* Blast injuries; Explosive ordnance devices (EOD)
Bones, *see also specific type*
chop marks, 291
consistency, 431
dating of fractures, 245–254
hydraulic burst effect, 325
pathophysiology, gunfire injuries, 322–325, *323–324*
shotgun injuries, 378
thickness, 431
variations, 6–7, 32–42, *32–45*
Born studies, 102
Bosnar studies, 2
Bosnia-Herzegovina (BiH), 40, 97
Boutwell studies, 10
Bowen and Bellemy studies, 10
Boyer studies, 323
Bradtmiller and Buikstra studies, 65
Breakaway spurs, 405
Breech loading weapons, 385, 389, 391
Breederveld studies, 215
Brenneke cartridge, 398
Brickley studies, 55
Bridgens, Frayer and, studies, 267
Brinkley studies, 3, 284
Brink studies, 203
British velocity classification, 327
Brogdon, Vogel and, studies, 204
Brogdon and Vogel studies, 39
Brogdon studies, 71, 203
Brooks studies, 215
Brothwell studies, 38
Browner studies, 46

Browning, Maples and, studies, 81, 267
Brukner and Khan studies, 217
Brunborg and Tabeau studies, 5
Brunborg studies, 5
Brynin and Gardiner studies, 224
Buchsbaum and Caruso studies, 38
Buckle fractures, 194, 224
Buckwalter studies, 245
Budimlija studies, 97
Buikstra, Bradtmiller and, studies, 65
Buikstra, Tomczak and, studies, 226
Buikstra and Ubelaker studies, 9, 31–32
Bulger studies, 217, 236, 239, 241
Bullets
  classification, 395–396
  Minie type, 397
  trajectory, 355, 359–360, *366–370*
Bunee, Patel and, studies, 213
Bun Heng and Key studies, 96
Burke and Geiselman studies, 245
Burning, 55, 65, *66–70*
Burns studies, 3
Butterfly fractures
  bending force, 53
  femoral shaft, 428
  fractures classification, 50
  rib trauma, 410
  skull trauma, 405
Byers studies, 46, 50, 53, 152, 188, 443

C

Cagigao studies, 441–448
Cakir studies, 377
Caliber
  ammunition classification, 395–396
  fundamentals, 328–329
  yawing, exit wounds, 354
Cambodian killing fields, 314–319, *315–318*, *see also* Choeung Ek trauma pattern
Campobasso studies, 3, 97
Cannons, 385
Cardoza studies, 255–261
Caretas studies, 15
Carnivores, evidence of, 54–55, 61, 205, 264, 300
Cartridges
  classifications, 397
  military rifle standard, 396
Caruso, Buchsbaum and, studies, 38
Case studies
  Berisha case, 245–254, *248–249, 251–253*
  blast injuries, 124, *125–127*
  blunt force trauma, 181, 196, *197–198,* 199
  body trauma, 128, *128–133,* 130, 132
  Cambodia killing fields, 314–319
  Chilean soldier, gunfire injuries, 441–448, *441–448*
  dating of fractures, 245–254, *248–249, 251–253*
  dry bone tissue, 245–254, *248–249, 251–253*
  firearm types, *385–394,* 385–399
  firefight in Lima, 14–19, *16*
  freefall injuries, 181
  gunfire injuries, *385–394,* 385–399, 438–448
  hostage rescue operation, 14–19
  human bombs, 128, *128–133,* 130, 132
  human dry bone tissue, 245–254, *248–249, 251–253*
  human head, FEM, 87–93, *89–92*
  Japanese Embassy, 14–19
  Khmer Rouge execution method, 196, *197–198,* 199
  MRTA casualties, 14–19
  multiple healed rib fractures, 236–244, *238–242*
  Nebaj, Guatemala victims, 300–313
  Peruvian military base, 255–261, *257–261*
  Republic of Panama, 438–440, *438–440*
  sequels, 234–235, *235*
  sharp force trauma, 300–319
  skeletal and soft tissue injuries, 117–123, *117–123*
  timing of injuries before death, 236–244, *238–242*
  torture and extrajudicial execution, 234–261, *257–261*
  torture sequels, 234–235, *235*
  wounded/killed ratio analysis, 14–19, *16*
Catanese and Gilmore studies, 38, 44
Categories, *see* Classifications
Catheter, 261
Cattaneo studies, 39, 73
Causation mechanisms, 133–136, *134–137*
Cause of death, *see also* Manner of death
  blast injuries, 149
  cut marks after burning, 291
  defined, 11
  framework for determination, 13
  torture, 255, 257, 261
  trauma analysis, 10–12
Cavitation
  femoral shaft, 428
  fractures from, 324
Celiköz studies, 10
Cerebro-spinal fluid (CSF), 88
Cernak studies, 97
Cerro Zig Zag, 441–448, *441–448*
C4 explosives, 130
Chacón studies, 6, 265, 300–313
Champion studies, 10
Chan, Bandak and, studies, 87
Chandler, Leffers and, studies, 432
Chandler studies, 196, 314, 319
Chang, Santucci and, studies, 322
Chapdelaine, Cukier and, studies, 99
Chattering (chopping)
  cutting comparison, 267
  knife wounds comparison, 291
  scoop defect comparison, 276
Cheung studies, 39
Chidzonga studies, 405
Children
  battered child syndrome, 38–40
  targeting, 6
  timing of fractures, 55, 245
Chilean soldier case study, 441–448, *441–448*
Chinn studies, 88
Choeung Ek trauma pattern, 196, *197–198,* 199, *see also* Cambodian killing fields

Chopping
to compact bone, 291
compared to cutting, 266–267, 291
fundamentals, 54
sharp weapons class identification, 267
Chopping weapons, *see also* Sharp force trauma (SFT)
defined, 266
sharp force trauma, 291–295
Chowdhury and Mohan studies, 98–99
Christensen and Dietz studies, 224
Christensen studies, 191, 194
Circular entrance wounds
classification, 329
gunfire, 331, 335, *336–341,* 337
scapula fractures, 414
Circumferential delamination
circular entrance wounds, 335
circular fractures, 335, 337
close-contact wounds, 371
tandem entrance wounds, 349
Classifications
ammunition, 395
cartridges, 397
fractures and mechanisms of injury, 44–54, *46–53*
manner of death, 11
sharp objects, 266
skeletal wounds, 31
weapon action, 385, 394
Cleavers
fundamentals, 266
single-blade knives comparison, 291
Clips, 394
Cloaca, 42, 439
Close-contact wounds
abrasion rings, 371
gunpowder tattooing, 371
vertebrae fractures, 406
Close-range wounds, 371, 372, *372–377*
Clothing
Albanian, elderly woman, 236
blindfolds from, 257
Chilean soldier case study, 441
cut marks in, 303
differential diagnosis, *80–84,* 80–85
identification, 83
live munitions in, 71
proximity of blast victim, 112–123
reconstruction of trauma, 26
Cnops, Timperman and, studies, 346
Coe studies, 337, 445
Cohen, O'Conner and, studies, 245
Coiba, Republic of Panama, 439
Colombia case study, 291–295, *292–299*
Combat death, *see* Conventional warfare (CWF)
Commingled remains, 10
Comminuted fractures, *see also* Butterfly fractures
classification, 46, 50
cranial fractures, 158
femoral shaft, 425, 428, 430
hands and feet, 435
rib fractures, 409
sharp weapons class identification, 267
vertebrae fractures, 407–408
Complete fractures, ribs, 224
Compression forces, 52–53
Concentric fractures, *see also* Linear fractures; Radiating fractures
classification, 46, 48
cranial fractures, 162
entrance wounds, 331
femoral shaft, 428
Conner, Scott and, studies, 3
Contact wounds
abrasion ring, 371
gunpowder tattooing, 371
range of fire, 371, *372–377*
shotgun injuries, 377
Context
blast injuries, 102–107, *103–111*
trauma analysis, 7–8
Conventional warfare (CWF), 11, 18
Cook and Powell studies, 5
Cook-Deegan, Geiger and, studies, 2
Cooper studies, 99, 215, 323
Cordner and McKelvie studies, 3–4
Cory studies, 87
Countre-coup fractures, 164
Coupland, Taback and, studies, 5, 7
Coupland and Korver studies, 96
Coupland and Meddings studies, 7, 14–15, 17, 95
Coupland studies, 2, 5–7, 10, 99, 323
Courtroom, images use, 75, 79
Covey studies, 96, 100–101, 107
Cowin studies, 46
Cracked tooth syndrome (CTS), 213, *see also* Tooth fractures
Crane studies, 134, 136, 138–139, 150
Cranial trauma
blunt force trauma, 158–167, 170–173
documented torture cases, 212–214, *214–215*
fractures, 158–164, 212–214
multiple gunfire injuries, 382
postcranial, 170–173, *170–175*
torture, 212–214, *214–215*
Craniofacial area, most affected region, 203
Crew-served weapons, 385
Croatia
cranial vault, atypical wounds, 164
Strugar indictment, 9
Vukovar Hospital incident, 6
Cross-limb amputations, 234
Crumbling appearance, 434
Crushed tissues, 323–324
Cruz Sanchez, Eduardo Nicolas, 15
CSF, *see* Cerebro-spinal fluid (CSF)
CTS, *see* Cracked tooth syndrome (CTS)
Cukier and Chapdelaine studies, 99
Curran, Rhine and, studies, 157
Curry studies, 152
Cut marks case study, *284–290,* 284–291, *see also* Sharp force trauma (SFT)
Cutting, compared to chopping, 266–267, 291

CWF, *see* Conventional warfare (CWF)
Czarnetzki, Weber and, studies, 274

D

Dakak studies, 346, 410
Daly, Allan and, studies, 405
Dana, Di Maio and, studies, 285
Danielsen studies, 204
Dating of fractures, 245–254, *248–249, 251–252*
Dean studies, 6
Death, *see also* Cause of death; Manner of death
  blast injuries, 149
  timing of injuries before, 236–244, *238–242*
  torture, 255, 257, 261
Debesse and Riquet studies, 236
Debriding wounds, 447–448
Deck studies, 89
Defect-free injury diagnosis, 70–71
Defects
  eccentric, 342–346, *344–345*
  gutter, 338, 340, *342*
  irregular, 342–346, *344–345*
  keyhole, 340–342, *343*
  notched, 272, *273–274*
  peeling, 270, *272*
  perpendicular circular, 331, 335, *336–341,* 337
  point insertion, 272, *273–274*
  scoop, 276, *277–284,* 279
  shaved, 270, *272*
Defensive wounds, 170–171, 173, 204
De Gruchy and Rogers studies, 65, 267, 284
Delabarde studies, 236–244
Delamination
  circular fractures, 335, 337
  femoral shaft, 425
  gutter fractures, 338
Demographic profile, 255, 257, 261
Dens process trauma, 403, 405
De Palma studies, 99
Depressed fractures
  compression injuries, 53
  cranial fractures, 158, 162, 164
Diastatic, linear fractures, 405
Dietz, Christensen and, studies, 224
Diez studies, 300–313
Differential diagnosis
  antemortem fractures, 55, *55–59*
  anthroposcopic examination, 30–31, *31*
  best practice guidelines, 86
  blast injuries, *106–107,* 107–115, *110, 112–116*
  case study, 87–93
  classifications, 44–54, *46–53*
  clothing importance, *80–84,* 80–85
  defect-free injury diagnosis, 70–71
  finite element models, human head, 87–93
  fundamentals, 21–22, *31,* 54–55
  human head, finite element model, 87–93
  microscopic examination, tissue, 54
  pathology, 32–42, *32–45*
  perimortem burning, 65, *66–70*
  perimortem fractures, 57–65, *60–64*
  photography, 85
  postmortem burning, 65, *66–70*
  postmortem fractures, 57–65, *60–64*
  radiography, 71–79, *72–79*
  reconstruction of fractures, 22, *23–26,* 25–30
  remains from multiple sites, 27–28, *27–30,* 30
  three-dimensional imaging, 71–79, *72–79*
  timing of fractures, 54–65
  tissue, microscopic examination, 54
  torture, 226–231
  variations, normal, 32–42, *32–45*
Di Maio and Dana studies, 285
Di Maio studies, 322–323, 328–329, 337, 340, 342, 346, 353, 359–360, 371
Direction of force, 48
Dirkmaat studies, 65
Dirty War (1976-1983), 322
Discrete delamination, 338
Disease as weapon, 34–42
Dismemberment
  destroying evidence, 55
  evidence of, 303
  punishment, 234
  torture use, 264–265
Disorganization, 55
Distal region fractures, *430,* 430–431
Distant range gunfire, 371, 373, 376–377, *380–381*
Dixon studies, 342, 353
Djuric, Tuller and, studies, 63
Documented torture cases
  cranial fractures, 212–214, *214–215*
  Kosovo/Kosova, 205–207, *208*
  lumbar spine fractures, 224, *225*
  Peru, 207–209, *209*
  rib fractures, *210,* 217–218, *219–223,* 224
  skeletal evidence, 209–210, *210–213,* 212
  sternum fractures, 215, *216–218*
  tooth fractures, 212–214, *214–215*
Dolinak and Matshes studies, 199
Donchin studies, 79
Doretti and Snow studies, 81, 83, 85
Double action revolvers, 395
Double butterfly fractures, 428, *see also* Butterfly fractures
Double tap entrance wounds
  classification, 329
  wound features, 322, 346–352, *347–351*
Dougherty, Jenkins and, studies, 323
Dubrovnik, Croatia, 9
DuChesne studies, 167
Dust tattooing, 139, *see also* Gunpowder tattooing; Soot

E

Eccentric entrance wounds
  classification, 329
  gunfire, 342–346, *344–345*
  intermediate range, 373
Edelenbosch studies, 2
Edston, Moisander and, studies, 203

Egeland, Jan, 6
Eisner, Stover and, studies, 4
Ellis studies, 213
El Mozote Massacre (El Salvador), 6
El Pectorado (individual), 439
Emanovsky studies, 268, 272
Embedded projectiles, 352–353, *352–357*
Entrance wounds
  AK-47 weapon, 411
  atypical wounds, 346–353
  caliber, 328–329
  close-contact wounds, 372
  double tap shots, 346–352, *347–351*
  eccentric defects, 342–346, *344–345*
  embedded projectiles, 352–353, *352–357*
  femoral shaft, 428
  fundamentals, 329–331
  gutter defects, 338, 340, *342*
  intermediate range, 373
  irregular defects, 342–346, *344–345*
  keyhole defects, 340–342, *343*
  perpendicular circular defects, 331, 335, *336–341,* 337
  rib fractures, 409
  tandem shots, 346–352, *347–351*
EOD, *see* Explosive ordnance devices (EOD)
EPAF, *see* Peruvian Forensic Anthropology Team (EPAF)
Epidemiological approach
  best practice guidelines, 13
  cause and manner of death, 10–12
  context, 7–8
  firefight in Lima case study, 14–19, *16*
  fundamentals, 1–2
  intent, 8
  international law and forensics, 2–5
  MRTA incident, 17–18
  scientific protocol, 8–9
  trauma analysis, *5,* 5–12
  weaponry, 9–10
Eriksson and Wallensteen studies, 4
Estimation
  number of injuries, 381, *382*
  weapon class, 325–329, *327–355*
Evans studies, 38, 44
Examples, *see also* Case studies
  cut marks, *284–290,* 284–291
  hatchet trauma, 291–295, *292–299*
Exit wounds
  AK-47 weapon, 411
  close-contact wounds, 372
  femoral shaft, 428
  gunfire injuries, 353–354, *358–365*
  intermediate range, 373
  rib fractures, 409
  sharp weapons class identification, 267
  shotgun injuries, 378
Expert testimony, 8–12
Explosive injuries
  close-contact wounds, 371
  distal region, femur, 431
Explosive ordnance devices (EOD)
  blast injuries, 97–99, *98–99*
  fundamentals, 385
External ballistics, 325–326
Extrajudicial executions
  close-contact wounds, 371
  Peru case studies, 167, 208, 255–261
  sternum injuries, 411
  tandem entrance wounds, 346, 349–350, 352
  timing of fractures and injuries, 54

F

Fackler and Malinowski studies, 326
Fackler studies, 49, 322–324, 326–327, 354, 402, 432
Fact of death establishment, 12
FAFG, *see* Guatemalan Forensic Anthropology Team (FAFG)
Falanga, 53, 235
Farkash studies, 71
Farming tools, 10, *see also* Machete and heavy-bladed instruments trauma
Fatal environment, blast injuries, 102–107, *103–111*
Fatal if untreated wounds, 13
Fatal wounds (FW), *16,* 17, *see also* Injuries; Wounds
Feet fractures
  falanga (applied force), 53, 235
  gunfire injuries, 434–435, *436–437*
Feik studies, 54
FEM, *see* Finite element modeling (FEM)
Femoral shaft, 424–430, *426–427, 429, 433*
Femur fractures
  distal region, *430,* 430–431
  proximal region, 422, 424, *426*
Fenton studies, 53, 402
Ferllini studies, 3
Fernández studies, 300–313
Fierro, Messmer and, studies, 377
Finegan studies, 181
Finite element modeling (FEM), 87–93
Fink, Reinhard and, studies, 65
Firearms, 10, *385–394,* 385–399
Firefight in Lima case study, 14–19, *16*
Firing pins, 398
Fitzpatrick studies, 71
Five Seven, 322
Fixed cartridges, 395
Fixott studies, 97
Flagel studies, 217
Flake, 279, 349
Flame burns, 140
Flash burns, 101, 140
Flat bones
  blunt force injury, 152
  cranial fractures, 162
  fractures classification, 50
  minimum number, injuries, 157
  pelvis fractures, 419
FMJ, *see* Full metal jacket (FMJ)
Focus, fractures classification, 48
Fondebrider studies, 3
Foot, *see* Feet fractures

Force, direction of, 48
Forearm trauma, 432, *432–433*
Fowler studies, 215, 226
Fractures
antemortem, 55, *55–59*
buckle, 224
classifications, 44–54, *46–53*
complete, 224
concentric, 428
cranial, 158–164, *159–163*
dating, 245–254, *248–249, 251–253*
diastatic, 405
distal region, *430*, 430–431
documented torture cases, 212–215, 217–218, 224
feet, 434–435, *436–437*
femur, 422, 424, 430–431
forearm, 432
freefall injuries, 191–192, 194
fresh, 247, *248–249*, 254
hands, 434–435, *435*
incomplete, 224
linear, 46, 224, 331, 405, 407
location classification, 49–50
lower leg, 432
lumbar spine, 224, *225*
mandibular, blunt force trauma, 167, *168–170*
oblique, 224, 403, 428
pattern interpretation, 71, 73
pelvis, 194, *195*, 416, 418–420, *422–426*
perimortem, 57–65, *60–64*
postmortem, 57–65, *60–64*
proximal humerus, 411, 414, 416, *417–421*
proximal region, 422, 424, *426*
radiating, 409–410
radiographic techniques, 71, 73
random linear, 407
reconstruction, 22, *23–26*, 25–30
ribs, 191–194, 217–218, 224, 408–411
scapula, 411, 414, 416, *417–421*
spiral, 425, 428
sternum, 215, *216–218*, 408–411, *414–417*
timing of, 54–65
tooth, 212–214, *214–215*
transverse, 224, 432
vertebra, 406–408, *407–413*
Frayer and Bridgens studies, 267
Freefall injuries, blunt force trauma
fractures, 191–192, 194
fundamentals, 187–188, *192–193*
low- to medium-velocity projectiles, 188–189
pelvis, 181–183, 194
ribs, 184, 186, 191–192, 194
right parietal bone, 189, 191, *193*
skull, 186–187, *191–192*
vertebrae, 184, *185*
Fresh fractures, 247, *248–249*, 254
Frykberg studies, 100
Fujimori, Alberto, 15
Full metal jacket (FMJ)
AK-47, 397
circular fractures, 337
close-contact wounds, 371
example, 175
keyhole defects, 341
Fully automatic weapons, 385, 388, 392
FW, *see* Fatal wounds (FW)

G

Galloway studies, 46, 152, 170, 236, 315, 441
GAMBIT, *see* General acceleration model for brain injury threshold (GAMBIT)
Gardiner, Brynin and, studies, 224
Garfield and Neugot studies, 35
Gasior, Baraybar and, studies, 13, 63, 102, 424
Gauge, 395
Geiger and Cook-Deegan studies, 2
Geiselman, Burke and, studies, 245
General acceleration model for brain injury threshold (GAMBIT), 88
Gibbons studies, 4
Gillespie studies, 97
Gilmore, Catanese and, studies, 38, 44
Giordano studies, 96
Glass studies, 97
Glencross and Stuart-Macadam studies, 54
Gloves, surgical, 236
Godbole, Ambade and, studies, 204
Goldson studies, 35
Goldstone studies, 2
Goodman studies, 32
Gorman studies, 7, 44–45, 52–53
Gray studies, 2
Grazing wounds, 407–408, 430
Greenfield studies, 63
Grenades
blast injuries, 117–123, *117–123*
differential diagnosis, 113
Grodin and Annas studies, 2
Grossman studies, 19
Group identification, clothing, 83
GSW, *see* Gunshot wounds (GSW)
Guatemalan Forensic Anthropology Team (FAFG), 159, 300–313
Gunfire injuries
ammunition estimation, 325–329, *327–355*
atypical wounds, 346–353
best practice guidelines, 384
bullet trajectory, 355, 359–360, *366–370*
case studies, *385–394*, 385–399
contact and close-range wounds, 371, 372, *372–377*
distant range, 371, 373, 376, *380–381*
double tap shots, 346–352, *347–351*
eccentric defects, 342–346, *344–345*
embedded projectiles, 352–353, *352–357*
entry wounds, 329–353
estimation, number of injuries, 381, *382*
exit wounds, 353–354, *358–365*
firearm types, *385–394*, 385–399

  fundamentals, 54, 321–322, 329–331, 367, 371
  gutter defects, 338, 340, *342*
  intermediate range, 371, 373, *377–380*
  irregular defects, 342–346, *344–345*
  keyhole defects, 340–342, *343*
  number of injuries estimation, 381, *382*
  pathophysiology to bone, 322–325, *323–324*
  perpendicular circular defects, 331, 335, *336–341,* 337
  range of fire, 367, 371–378
  sequencing multiple injuries, 382–384, *383*
  shotgun injuries, 377–378
  tandem shots, 346–352, *347–351*
  weapon class estimation, 325–329, *327–355*
Gunfire injuries, variation by skeletal region
  best practice guidelines, 435–437
  case studies, 438–448
  Chilean soldier case study, 441–448, *441–448*
  distal region fractures, *430,* 430–431
  femoral shaft, 424–430, *426–427, 429, 433*
  femur fractures, distal region, *430,* 430–431
  femur fractures, proximal region, 422, 424, *426*
  foot fractures, 434–435, *436–437*
  forearm trauma, 432, *432–433*
  fundamentals, 401–402
  hand fractures, 434–435, *435*
  limbs, 422–435
  lower leg trauma, 432, *434*
  pelvis fractures, 416, 418–420, *422–426*
  proximal humerus fractures, 411, 414, 416, *417–421*
  proximal region fractures, 422, 424, *426*
  Republic of Panama case study, 438–440, *438–440*
  rib fractures, 408–411, *414–417*
  scapula fractures, 411, 414, 416, *417–421*
  skull, 402–405, *403–406*
  soldier case study, 441–448, *441–448*
  sternum fractures, 408–411, *414–417*
  thorax, 406–420
  vertebrae fractures, 406–408, *407–413*
Gunpowder, 367, 371
Gunpowder tattooing, 371, *see also* Dust tattooing; Soot
Gunshot wounds (GSW), *see also* Gunfire injuries
  blunt force trauma, 189
  pelvis, 419
  skull trauma, 402
Gurdjian and Webster studies, 88–89
Gurdjian studies, 44–46, 48, 152, 158
Gutter entrance wounds
  classification, 329
  gunfire, 338, 340, *342*
  proximal region, femur, 422, 424
  sideway entrance comparison, 343

H

Hadden studies, 96
Haden and Berg studies, 174
Haden studies, 196–199
Haglund studies, 3, 264
Hall studies, 101–102
Hand fractures, 434–435, *435*
Handguns
  classifications, 394
  fundamentals, 385
  human rights abuses, 436
  skeletal wound differences, 327
  skull trauma, 402
Hannibal, Kirschner and, studies, 3–4, 6
Harkess studies, 44, 48, 53, 152
Harruff studies, 378
Hart, Rao and, studies, 266–267
Hart studies, 38, 46, 53
Hatchet trauma, *see also* Sharp force trauma (SFT)
  fundamentals, 266
  knife comparison, 291
  sharp force trauma, 291–295, *292–299*
Haun, Berryman and, studies, 46
Haung studies, 111
Hayda studies, 95
Hayner studies, 2
Haynes studies, 65
HE, *see* High-order explosives (HE)
Head injury criterion (HIC), 87, 88
Healed fractures, 247, *249,* 254, *see also* Timing of fractures and injuries
Healing fractures, 247–249, *250–253,* 254–255
Health consequences, armed conflict, 34–42
Heavy-bladed instruments, *see* Machete and heavy-bladed instruments trauma
Heavy equipment, 61, 63
Helal studies, 226
Henderson and Biellik studies, 35
Heppenstall studies, 245
HIC, *see* Head injury criterion (HIC)
High-order explosives (HE), 98, 100–101
High-velocity gunfire wounds
  ammunition classification, 327
  close-contact wounds, 371, 372
  distal region, femur, 431
  femoral shaft, 428
  intermediate range, 373
  keyhole defects, 341
  rib fractures, 409–410
  scapula fractures, 414
  skeletal wound differences, 327
  vertebrae fractures, 406–407
Hijacked airplanes (September 11, 2007), 97
Hill, Behrensmeyer and, studies, 55
Hills studies, 215
Hill studies, 102
Hinsley studies, 102
Hinton studies, 2
Hirsch, Adams and, studies, 11–12
Hiss and Kahana studies, 99, 101
Ho, Karmakar and, studies, 217–218
Hodalic studies, 102
Holcomb studies, 217, 236
Holdstock studies, 35
Hollerman studies, 326
Home St. Jean Catholic Church (Kibuye), 263
Homewood studies, 214
Hoop fractures, 46, 162
Horvath studies, 377

Hospitals, removal from, 6, 261
Hostage rescue operation, 14–19
Houck studies, 264, 267
Hougen studies, 203, 234–235, 264
Huelke studies, 323, 325, 428, 431
Hull studies, 101, 136–137
Human bomb case study, 128, *128–133,* 130, 132
Human dry bone tissues, fracture dating, 245–254, *248–249, 251–253*
Human head, FEM, 87–93
Humphrey and Hutchinson studies, 266–267
Hunger as weapon, 34–42
Hunt, Mann and, studies, 38
Hunter studies, 3
Hutchinson, Humphrey and, studies, 266–267
Hutus, 263
Hydraulic burst effect, 325, 408
Hypodermic needles, 439–440

I

ICC, *see* International Criminal Court (ICC)
ICRC, *see* International Committee of the Red Cross (ICRC)
ICTJ, *see* International Center for Transitional Justice (ICTJ)
ICTR, *see* International Criminal Tribunal for Rwanda (ICTR)
ICTY, *see* International Tribunal for the Prosecution of Persons Responsible for Serious Violations of International Humanitarian Law Committed in the Territory of the Former Yugoslavia since 1991 (ICTY)
Identification, sharp force trauma injuries
  chop marks, 276, *277–284,* 279
  cut marks, 268, *269–271,* 270
  fundamentals, 267–268, *268*
  notched defects, 272, *273–274*
  peeling defects, 270, *272*
  point insertion defects, 272, *273–274*
  scoop defects, 276, *277–284,* 279
  shaved defects, 270, *272*
  slot fractures, 274, *275–276*
IED, *see* Impoverished ordnance device (IED)
Ilium, 382
Impoverished ordnance device (IED), 99, *see also* Explosive ordnance devices (EOD)
Inbending, 158
Incomplete delamination, 335, 337
Incomplete fracture, ribs, 224
Incomplete tooth fracture (ITF), 213, *see also* Tooth fractures
Indirect deaths, 34–42
Indirect fractures, 402
Individual weapons, 385
Infarctions, 46
Initiation, cause of death, 11
Injuries, *see also* Wounds; specific type
  blasts, *137–148,* 137–149
  classifications, 44–54, *46–53*
  defect-free injury diagnosis, 70–71
  gunfire, blunt force trauma, 174–176, *176–180*
  number establishment, 157, *158*
  pathophysiology, 101
  patterns, *137–148,* 137–149, 255, 257, 261
  range of fire, 367, 371–378
  sequence establishment, 157, *158*
  sequencing multiple from gunfire, 382–384, *383*
Injuries, sharp force trauma identification
  chop marks, 276, *277–284,* 279
  cut marks, 268, *269–271,* 270
  notched defects, 272, *273–274*
  peeling defects, 270, *272*
  point insertion defects, 272, *273–274*
  scoop defects, 276, *277–284,* 279
  sharp, identification of, 267–279
  shaved defects, 270, *272*
  slot fractures, 274, *275–276*
Intent
  blast injuries, 102–107, *103–111*
  context, 7
  defensive wounds, 171, 204
  demography, 6
  trauma analysis, 8
Intermediate range, 371, 373, 377, *377–380*
International Center for Transitional Justice (ICTJ), 3
International Committee of the Red Cross (ICRC), xii
International Criminal Court (ICC), 3
International Criminal Tribunal for Rwanda (ICTR), 2, 4
International Criminal Tribunal for the Former Yugoslavia, *see* International Tribunal for the Prosecution of Persons Responsible for Serious Violations of International Humanitarian Law Committed in the Territory of the Former Yugoslavia since 1991 (ICTY)
International law and forensics, 2–5
International Tribunal for the Prosecution of Persons Responsible for Serious Violations of International Humanitarian Law Committed in the Territory of the Former Yugoslavia since 1991 (ICTY), 3–4, 12, 27, 95, 97, 245
Interpersonal violence, skeletal trauma, 203
Intersecting fractures, 382–383
Irregular bones, fractures classification, 50
Irregular entrance wounds
  classification, 329
  gunfire, 342–346, *344–345*
  scapula fractures, 414
İscan, Quatrehomme and, studies, 46, 330, 335
İscan studies, 39
Islam studies, 54, 245
Istanbul Protocol, xi, 8–9
ITF, *see* Incomplete tooth fracture (ITF)
Ithaca shotgun, 322

J

Jacinto studies, 300–313
Jantz, Bass and, studies, 65
Japanese Embassy case study, 14–19
Jenkins and Dougherty studies, 323
Jentzen studies, 346

Johnson, Tencer and, studies, 430
Jones, Newman and, studies, 237
Jones studies, 87
Jordan studies, 97
Joyce and Stover studies, 4
Juhl studies, 3

K

Kahana, Hiss and, studies, 99, 101
Kahana studies, 97
Kalashinkov, 396, *see also* AK-47 weapon
Kamm studies, 196
Kang studies, 87–88
Kapur studies, 97
Karger studies, 323
Kariya, Wright and, studies, 204
Karmakar and Ho studies, 217–218
Katz studies, 102
Kellogg studies, 346
Kent and Patrie studies, 218
Kerf floors, cleavers, 266
Kerley studies, 267, 276
Key, Bun Heng and, studies, 96
Keyhole entrance wounds
  Chilean soldier case study, 443, 445
  classification, 329
  femoral shaft, 425, 428
  gunfire, 340–342, *343*
Khan, Brukner and, studies, 217
Khmer Rouge execution method, 196, *197–198,* 199, *see also* Cambodian killing fields
Kiernan studies, 196
King, Yang and, studies, 87–88
Kirschner and Hannibal studies, 3–4, 6
Kirschner studies, 3
Kitchen knives, 291, *see also* Knives
Kjaerulff studies, 204
KLA, *see* Kosovo Liberation Army (UÇK, Ushtria Clirimatre e Kosovoës)
Kleinman and Schlesinger studies, 203, 217
Kleinman studies, 203, 245
Klotzbach studies, 245
Kluger studies, 95–98, 100–102
Kneubuehl, Sellier and, studies, 323, 325, 408
Kneubuehl and Thali studies, 326, 432
Knight, Saukko and, studies, 254
Knight studies, 71, 133
Knives, 266, 291, *see also* Machete and heavy-bladed instruments trauma; Sharp force trauma (SFT)
Knudsen and Theilade studies, 323
Koff studies, 3
Komar studies, 3
Konigsberg, Ross and, studies, 236
Kontio studies, 203
Koppl studies, 97
Korver, Coupland and, studies, 96
Korzinek studies, 102
Kosovo/Kosova, 205–207, *208,* 236–244, *238–242*
Kosovo Liberation Army (UÇK, Ushtria Clirimatre e Kosovoës), 27
Kravetz studies, 12
Kravica warehouse massacres, 102–103, 342
Krogman studies, 39
Kroman studies, 159
Krstic, Radislav, 8, 11
Kurz cartridge, 396

L

Lands, 397
Large, oblong defects, 381
LE, *see* Low-order explosives (LE)
Leading cause, skeletal trauma, 203
Leaning studies, 2
Lee, Roh and, studies, 214
Lee studies, 6
Leffers and Chandler studies, 432
Lefort studies, 45
Leg trauma, 432, *434*
Leibhardt, Betz and, studies, 39
Leibovici studies, 5–6
Leth and Banner studies, 203
Lever action weapons, 385, 389
Levy and Sidel studies, 35
Liberation Tigers of Tamil Eelam (LTTE), 128
Lie and Skjeie studies, 203
Ligatures, 8
Limaj, Fatmir, 206
Liman studies, 218
Limbs, accident victims, 204
Limbs, gunfire injuries
  distal region fractures, *430,* 430–431
  femoral shaft, 424–430, *426–427, 429, 433*
  femur fractures, 422, 424, *426, 430,* 430–431
  foot fractures, 434–435, *436–437*
  forearm trauma, 432, *432–433*
  hand fractures, 434–435, *435*
  lower leg trauma, 432, *434*
  proximal region fractures, 422, 424, *426*
Lindsey studies, 322
Linear fractures, *see also* Concentric fractures; Radiating fractures
  classification, 46
  entrance wounds, 331
  ribs, 224
  vertebrae fractures, 407
Logan studies, 408
Lollar studies, 3
Long, Walker and, studies, 266–267, 270
Long bones, 382–383
Long-heavy weapons, 266
Love and Symes studies, 224, 236
Lovell studies, 46, 49–50, 152, 158–159
Lower leg trauma, 432, *434*
Low-order explosives (LE), 98, 101
Low- to medium-velocity projectiles, 188–189
Low-velocity gunfire
  close-contact wounds, 371
  distal region, femur, 431
  femoral shaft, 428

skull trauma, 402
vertebrae fractures, 407
LTTE, *see* Liberation Tigers of Tamil Eelam (LTTE)
Ludes studies, 87–93
Luger, George, 396
Lumbar spine fractures, 224, *225*
Lund, Tomasto and, studies, 402
Lund studies, 441–448
Lynch and McConnell studies, 213–214

M

Maat, George, 205
Maat studies, 245–254
Machete and heavy-bladed instruments trauma, *see also* Knives; Sharp force trauma (SFT)
Cambodia killing fields case study, 314–319
fundamentals, 10, 266
Nebaj, Guatemala case study, 300–313
MacPherson studies, 323
Madea and Staak studies, 157
Magazines, 392–394
Mahieu, Villa and, studies, 61
Malinowski, Fackler and, studies, 326
Manchester, Roberts and, studies, 38
Mandibular trauma
blunt force trauma, 167, *168–170*
Cambodian killing fields, 314–319
gunfire, 403, 405
reconstruction, 25
Man in burning car, *284–290*, 284–291
Mann and Hunt studies, 38
Manner of death, *see also* Cause of death
classification, 11
cut marks after burning, 291
defined, 11
trauma analysis, 10–12
Maples and Browning studies, 81, 267
Maples studies, 58
Marañon cemetery, 439–440
Marjoux studies, 89
Marshall studies, 136, 138, 149
Mason and Purdue studies, 9
Mass disasters, 97
Masticatory accidents, 213, *see also* Tooth fractures
Matshes, Dolinak and, studies, 199
Mauser rifle round, 396
Maxillary canine teeth, 214
Maxillary first molars, 214
Mayne studies, 65, 284
McConnell, Lynch and, studies, 213–214
McKelvie, Cordner and, studies, 3–4
McKinley studies, 284
McVeigh, Timothy, 96
Meatal line, temporal, 403
Mechanisms of injuries, 44–54, *46–53*, 265–267
Meddings, Coupland and, studies, 7, 14–15, 17, 95
Meddings and O'Connor studies, 6, 8
Meddings studies, 7
Medium velocity gunfire wounds
ammunition classification, 327–328
assault rifles, 396
close-contact wounds, 371, 372
intermediate range, 373, 376
skeletal wound differences, 327
vertebrae fractures, 407
Melvern studies, 263
Melvin, Nahum and, studies, 44
Merbs studies, 267
Messmer and Fierro studies, 377
Messmer studies, 340, 345–346, 384
Metric classification, 395–396
Meyers studies, 75, 153
M16 firearm, 397
M1 Garand, 394
Michael studies, 7, 102
Micozzi studies, 55
Microscopic examination, differential diagnosis, 54
Milas, Ropac and, studies, 102
Military base case study, 255–261, *257–261*
Military rifle cartridges, 396
Miller studies, 224
Milosevic, Slobodan, 205
Minie type bullets, 397
Minimum number, injuries, 157, 177
Minnesota Protocol, xi, 8
Missile, 10
Missliwetrz and Wieser studies, 5–6
Mohan, Chowdhury and, studies, 98–99
Mohanty studies, 204
Moisander and Edston studies, 203
Mollan and Beavis studies, 346
Moritz studies, 9, 45, 152, 159
Morley studies, 35
Morse studies, 38
Mother of Satan, 130
Movimiento Revolucionario Tupac Amaru (MRTA), 14–19, 207
Multi-fragmented fractures, 46
Multiple healed rib fractures, 236–244, *238–242*
Multiple radiating fractures, 414, 425
Murad studies, 65
Murrah Federal Building (Oklahoma), 96
Murray studies, 35
Musliu, Isak, 206
Muzzle loading weapons, 385, 391–392, 394–395
My Lai massacre, 7

N

Nag and Sinha studies, 377
Nahum and Melvin studies, 44
Nath studies, 196, 319
National Highway Traffic Safety Administration (NHTSA), 87
Nebaj, Guatemala victims, 300–313
Netanyas Park Hotel Bombing, 102
Neugot, Garfield and, studies, 35
Newby, Randall and, studies, 330
Newman and Jones studies, 237

Newman studies, 88, 226
NHTSA, *see* National Highway Traffic Safety Administration (NHTSA)
Nicholas, Terry, 96
Nonaccidental mechanisms, 226–231, *227–232*
Noncircumferential delamination, 335, 337
Non-fatal wounds (NRW), *16,* 17, *see also* Injuries; Wounds
Noriega, Manuel, 438
NRW, *see* Non-fatal wounds (NRW)
Number of injuries, establishment, 157, *158*
Number of injuries estimation, 381, *382*
Nutation, 325–326
Nye studies, 97

O

Oblique fractures
  femoral shaft, 428
  gunfire, 403
  ribs, 224
Oblong defects, 381
O'Conner, Meddings and, studies, 6, 8
O'Connor and Cohen studies, 245
Oehmichen studies, 74
Office on Missing Persons and Forensics (OMPF), 85, 236
Ogura, Hidetaka, 15
Okoye studies, 3
Oliver studies, 74
Olmbe and Yakub studies, 9
OMPF, *see* Office on Missing Persons and Forensics (OMPF)
Oral cavity, gunfire, 405
Orentlicher studies, 9
Orientation, embedded projectiles, 352
Ormstad studies, 5
Ortiz studies, 441, 445, 447
Ortner and Putschar studies, 9, 31–32, 38, 45–46, 48, 53, 55, 71
Ortner studies, 31, 38, 46, 245
Outbending, 158–159
Oval defects, 381

P

Paavolainen, Rautio and, studies, 102
Pachón studies, 97, 124, 159
Pacific War, 441–448, *441–448*
Panama, *see* Republic of Panama case study
Panamanian Truth Commission, 438–439
Pangas, *see* Sharp force trauma (SFT)
Parabellum, 396
Paradox barrels, 398
Parietal bone, right, 189, 191, *193*
Parodi studies, 255–261
Parry fractures, 173
Patel and Burke studies, 213
Pathology, differential diagnosis, 32–42, *32–45*
Pathophysiology
  blast injuries, *100,* 100–101
  blunt force trauma, 152–157, *153–157*
  gunfire injuries, 322–325, *323–324*
Patrie, Kent and, studies, 218
Patterned injuries, 152–153, 155
Patzelt, Bauer and, studies, 267
PDW, *see* Personal defense weapon (PDW)
Peabody Martini weapon, 445, 447
Peccerelli studies, 300–313
Pec/Peja region, 27
Peeling
  Cambodian killing fields, 317–318
  sharp force trauma identification, 270, *272*
  timing of fractures, 63
Peerwani studies, 264
Peja/Pec region, 27
Peleg studies, 6–7, 31
Pellets, 328, 377
Pelvis injuries
  blunt force trauma, 194, *195*
  freefall injuries, 181–183, 194
  gunfire injuries, 416, 418–420, *422–426*
Penetrating entry wounds, 329
Perera studies, 203
Perforations, 330, 353
Perimortem fractures
  sharp-blunt force trauma, 302–303
  timing of, 57–65, *60–64*
  torture, 247, *248–249,* 254
Permanent cavity, 323
Perpendicular circular defects, 331, 335, *336–341,* 337
Personal defense weapon (PDW), 322
Peru, 167, 207–209, 255–261
Peruvian Forensic Anthropology Team (EPAF), 255–261
Petersen and Wandall studies, 203
Petricevic studies, 102
Phnom Penh, *see* Cambodian killing fields
Photography, 85
Pintar, Yoganandan and, studies, 88
Pistols, 394, 397
Pollak and Wieser studies, 40
Pollanen studies, 203
Pope, Elayne, 65
Popenker and Williams studies, 322
Pope studies, 284
Positional torture, 50, 52
Postcranial trauma
  reconstruction, 25
  variation, 170–173, *170–175*
Postmortem fractures
  excavation, 264
  timing of, 57–65, *60–64*
  torture, 247, *248–249,* 254
Pounder studies, 203
Powell, Cook and, studies, 5
Prediction interval (PI), 17
Premolars, 214
Prieto studies, 267
Primary burial sites, *see also* Secondary burial sites
  intent, 8
  Volljak/Volujak site, 30
Projectiles
  blast comparison, 111
  classification of injuries, 49

construction and shape, 323–324
embedded, 352–353, *352–357*
fundamentals, 54
gunfire comparison, 111
low- to medium-velocity, freefall injuries, 188–189
scapula fractures, 414
Prosser studies, 245
Protocari village, 102
Proximal humerus fractures, 411, 414, 416, *417–421*
Proximal region fractures, 422, 424, *426*
Pryor studies, 97
Pump weapons, 385
Puntavic, Soldo and, studies, 102
Puppe's rule, 157
Purdue, Mason and, studies, 9
Puskas and Rummey studies, 61
Putschar, Ortner and, studies, 9, 31–32, 38, 45–46, 48, 53, 55, 71

Q

Quatrehomme and İscan studies, 46, 330, 335
Quatrehomme studies, 267
Quechua Indians, 255

R

Radiating fractures, *see also* Concentric fractures; Linear fractures
Chilean soldier case study, 444
classification, 46
cranial fractures, 158
entrance wounds, 330–331
femoral shaft, 425, 428
rib fractures, 409
scapula fractures, 414
Radiography
Chilean soldier case study, 441
differential diagnosis, 71–79, *72–79*
embedded projectiles, 353
hatchet trauma, 295
Rae studies, 39
Rajs studies, 101
Randall and Newby studies, 330
Random linear fractures, 407
Range of fire
contact and close-range wounds, 371, 372, *372–377*
distant range, 371, 373, 376, *380–381*
fundamentals, 367, 371
intermediate range, 371, 373, *377–380*
MRTA incident, 19
shotgun injuries, 377–378
Rao and Hart studies, 266–267
Raul studies, 87–93
Rautio and Paavolanien studies, 102
Recoil, 388
Reconstruction of fractures
challenges, 323
differential diagnosis, 22, *23–26*, 25–30
Reichs studies, 264, 266–268
Reinhard and Fink studies, 65
Remains from multiple sites, 27–28, *27–30*, 30, *see also* Secondary burial sites
Remington weapon, 325, 447
Republic of Panama case study, 438–440, *438–440*
Residual materials, 367
Revolvers, 394–395, 397
Reynolds studies, 39
Reza studies, 7
Rhine and Curran studies, 157
Rib injuries
documented torture cases, *210*, 217–218, *219–223*, 224
freefall trauma, 184, 186, 191–192, 194
gunfire injuries, 408–411, *414–417*
peeling, 270, 272
scapula fractures comparison, 414
torture, *210*, 217–218, *219–223*, 224
Rice studies, 226
Richter studies, 226
Ricocheted bullets
bullet trajectory, 355–356
eccentric/irregular defects, 342
trajectory tracking, 113
Rifles, *see also specific type*
fundamentals, 385
human rights abuses, 436
rimmed cartridges, 397
skeletal wound differences, 327–328
Right parietal bone, 189, 191, *193*
Rimless cartridges, 397
Rimmed cartridges, 397
Riquet, Debesse and, studies, 236
Road traffic accidents (RTA)
blunt force trauma comparison, 202
timing of injuries, 237
torture comparison, 226–231, *227–232*
Robbins studies, 245
Roberts and Manchester studies, 38
Rocket propelled grenade (RPG), 385
Rodriguez-Martin, Aufderheide and, studies, 38
Rogers, de Gruchy and, studies, 65, 267, 284
Rogers studies, 44, 46, 152, 159
Roh and Lee studies, 214
Romano studies, 3
Ropac and Milas studies, 102
Ross and Konigsberg studies, 236
Ross and Suarez studies, 402
Ross studies, 46, 328, 330, 438–440
Roth studies, 87
Rounded defect, 381
Rowe studies, 377
RPG, *see* Rocket propelled grenade (RPG)
RTA, *see* Road traffic accidents (RTA)
Ruan studies, 87
Rukavina studies, 102
Rummey, Puskas and, studies, 61
Rwanda, 263, *see also* Sharp force trauma (SFT)
Ryan studies, 7, 322, 428

S

S-21, *see* Cambodian killing fields
Salama, Spiegel and, studies, 35
Salama studies, 6–7, 35
Salis studies, 40, 213
Salvolini studies, 74
Samarasekera studies, 97, 128–132
Santucci and Chang studies, 322
Saucedo, Cesar, 15
Sauer and Simson studies, 267
Sauer studies, 55, 58
Saukko and Knight studies, 254
Savnik studies, 203
Scapula fractures
  gunfire injuries, 411, 414, 416, *417–421*
  multiple gunfire injuries, 382
Scavenging, 54–55, 61, 205, 303
Schiller and Teitelbaum studies, 245
Schlesinger, Kleinman and, studies, 203, 217
Schmidt studies, 38
Schmitt studies, 3, 26, 81, 194
Scholtz, Vellema and, studies, 323–324, 353–354
Scientific protocol, 8–9
Scoop defects
  compared to peeling and shaved defects, 270
  sharp force trauma, 276, *277–284,* 279
  sharp weapons class identification, 267
Scott and Conner studies, 3
Scott studies, 99
SDH, *see* Subdural haematoma (SDH)
Secondary burial sites, *see also* Primary burial sites
  clothing importance, 83
  intent, 8
  remains from multiple sites, 27–28, *27–30,* 30
  skeletal reconstruction, 26
  timing of fractures, 54–55
  Volljak/Volujak site, 30
Secondary hypovolemic shock, 303
Secondary projectiles, 323
Second blows, 164
Second-generation courts, 3
Seetah studies, 268
Sellier and Kneubuehl studies, 323, 325, 408
Semiautomatic weapons
  classification, 385
  fundamentals, *386,* 388, 392
  rimless cartridges, 397
Seneviratne studies, 128–132
September 11, 2007, 97
Sequels of torture, 234–235, *235*
Sequence of injuries
  blunt force trauma, 157, *158*
  multiple, gunfire, 382–384, *383*
SFT, *see* Sharp force trauma (SFT)
Shah studies, 98
Sharp-blunt injuries, 296, 302–303
Sharp force, 234, 265
Sharp force trauma (SFT)
  best practice guidelines, 295–296
  Cambodian killing fields, 314–319, *315–318*
  case studies, 300–319
  chop marks, 276, *277–284,* 279
  chopping weapons, 291–295
  Colombia example, 291–295, *292–299*
  cut marks, 268, *269–271,* 270, *284–290,* 284–291
  defined, 265
  fundamentals, 54, 263–265, 267–268, *268*
  hatchet trauma, 291–295, *292–299*
  identification of injuries, 267–279, *268*
  machete (probable) trauma, 314–319, *315–318*
  man in burning car, *284–290,* 284–291
  mechanisms of wounds, 265–267
  Nebaj, Guatemala victims, 300–319
  notched defects, 272, *273–274*
  peeling defects, 270, *272*
  point insertion defects, 272, *273–274*
  scoop defects, 276, *277–284,* 279
  shaved defects, 270, *272*
  slot fractures, 274, *275–276*
Shearing force, 53
Shepherd studies, 203
Shigekane, Stover and, studies, 2
Shipman studies, 54–55, 65
Short-light objects, 266
Shotguns
  ammunition, 398
  fundamentals, 385, 394
  injuries, range of fire, 377–378
Shoulder-fired weapons, 385
Shrapnel
  beveling, 106
  classification of injuries, 49
  differential diagnosis, 111–113, 115
  fundamentals, 54, 98
  injury pathophysiology, 101
  3-7mm ball bearings, 132
Sidel, Levy and, studies, 35
Sideways entrance wounds, 329, *see also* Eccentric entrance wounds
Simmonds, Weinberg and, studies, 35
SIMON, *see* Simulated injury monitor (SIMON)
Simon studies, 218
Simple fractures, 46
Simson, Sauer and, studies, 267
Simulated injury monitor (SIMON), 88, 89
Single action revolvers, 395
Single-blade knives, 291
Single shot weapons
  action classification, 394
  classification, 385
  fundamentals, 389, 391, 395
Sinha, Nag and, studies, 377
Sirmali studies, 218
Situm studies, 102
Skeletal trauma
  blast injuries, 117–123, *117–123*
  classification, 31
  documented torture cases, 209–210, *210–213,* 212
  interpersonal violence, 203
  leading cause of, 203

normal variation comparison, 32–42, *32–45*
torture, 209–210, *210–213,* 212
Skinner studies, 3, 26
Skjeie, Lie and, studies, 203
Skolnick studies, 3
Skull trauma
exit wounds, 354
freefall injuries, 186–187, *191–192*
gunfire injuries, 402–405, *403–406*
high-velocity gunfire, 409
Slide action weapons, 385, 389
Small arms, 9–10, 436
Smith and Wheatley studies, 428, 430
Smith studies, 97, 266–267
Snow, Doretti and, studies, 81, 83, 85
Snow and Bihurriet studies, 4
Snow studies, 3, 9, 14–19
Snyder, Willey and, studies, 55, 65
Soft tissue
blast injuries, 117–123, *117–123*
eccentric/irregular entrance wounds, 345
radiography, 73
range of gunfire, 367
shotgun injuries, 377–378
Soldier case study, 441–448, *441–448*
Soldo and Puntavic studies, 102
Soot
close-contact wounds, 371, 372
range of gunfire, 367
Sosa, Jesús, 257, 261
Spalls, 291, 294, 349
Spiegel and Salama studies, 35
Spiral fractures, 425, 428
Spirer studies, 14–19
Spitz studies, 9, 31, 151, 164, 199, 264–268, 367
Srebrenča massacre, 102–103
Sri Lanka, *128,* 128–133, *130, 132*
Staak, Madea and, studies, 157
Starvation as weapon, 34–42
Stawicki studies, 7
Steinbock studies, 38
Sternum fractures
documented torture cases, 215, *216–218*
gunfire injuries, 408–411, *414–417*
scapula fractures comparison, 414
torture, 215, *216–218*
Stewart, T.D., 10
Stewart studies, 152, 164, 267
Stoneham studies, 226
Stoner, Eugene, 397
Storming a bunker, 396
Stover, Joyce and, studies, 4
Stover and Eisner studies, 4
Stover and Shigekane studies, 2
Streamlining, 101
Striations, 398–399
Strugar, Pavle, 9, 12
Stuart-Macadam, Glencross and, studies, 54
Suarez, Ross and, studies, 402
Suarez S. studies, 438–440
Subdural haematoma (SDH), 88, 89
Submachine guns, 385, 395, 397
Suicide, 11
Swords, *see* Sharp force trauma (SFT)
Symes, Berryman and, studies, 38, 46, 53, 152, 159, 187–188, 199, 331
Symes, Love and, studies, 224, 236
Symes studies, 65, 152, 264, 267

T

Ta'ala studies, 152, 196–199, 314, 319
Taback and Coupland studies, 5, 7
Tabeau, Brunborg and, studies, 5
Taipale studies, 35, 100, 402
Tandem entrance wounds
classification, 329
wound features, 346–352, *347–351*
Tangential entrance wounds
Chilean soldier case study, 443, 445
classification, 329
femoral shaft, 428
keyhole defects, 340
Target density, 19
TATP (homemade), 130
Taylor, Charles, 321
Tedeschi studies, 3
Teeth, *see* Tooth fractures; Tooth marks
Teh studies, 226
Teitelbaum, Schiller and, studies, 245
Tekinbas studies, 218
Temporary cavity, 323–325
Tencer and Johnson studies, 430
Tencer studies, 430
Terminal ballistics, 325, 326
Thali, Kneubuehl and, studies, 326, 432
Thali studies, 75, 79, 341–342, 371
Thays studies, 447
Theilade, Knudsen and, studies, 323
Third-generation courts, 3
Thompson studies, 65
Thomsen and Voight studies, 203
Thoracentesis, 439–440
Thorax, 406–420
Thoresen studies, 405
Thorn studies, 405
Three-dimensional imaging, 71–79, *72–79*
Through-and-through shots
distal region, femur, 430
exit wounds, 353
femoral shaft, 425, 428
femur, 420
proximal region, femur, 424
Tidball-Binz studies, 2, 11
Timing of fractures and injuries
antemortem fractures, 55, *55–59*
embedded projectiles, 353
fundamentals, 54–55
healed fractures, 247, *249,* 254
human dry bone tissue, 245–254, *248–249, 251–253*
materials and methods, 245, *246,* 247
perimortem burning, 65, *66–70*

perimortem fractures, 57–65, *60–64*
postmortem burning, 65, *66–70*
postmortem fractures, 57–65, *60–64*
torture, 236–244, *238–242*
Timperman and Cnops studies, 346
Tissue, microscopic examination, 54
TNT, 130
Tomasto and Lund studies, 402
Tomczak and Buikstra studies, 226
Toole studies, 35
Tooth fractures, 212–214, *214–215*
Tooth marks, 264, 303
Top break handguns, 395
Torrijos, Omar, 438
Torsion, 53, *see also* Bending joints
Torture
accidents, 226–231, *227–232*
antemortem fractures, 247, *249,* 254–255
bending joints, 50, 52–53
Berisha case, 245–254, *248–249, 251–253*
best practice guidelines, 233
blunt force trauma, 226–231
case studies, 234–261
cause of death, 255, 257, 261
cranial fractures, 212–214, *214–215*
defined, 202–204
demographic profile, 255, 257, 261
differential diagnosis, 226–231
dismemberment, 264–265
documented cases, 205–224
fresh fractures, 247, *248–249,* 254
fundamentals, 201–202
healed fractures, 247, *249,* 254
healing fractures, 247–249, *250–253,* 254–255
human dry bone tissues, fracture dating, 245–254, *248–249, 251–253*
injury patterns, 255, 257, 261
Kosovo/Kosova, 205–207, *208,* 236–244, *238–242*
lumbar spine fractures, 224, *225*
military base case study, 255–261, *257–261*
multiple healed rib fractures, 236–244, *238–242*
nonaccidental mechanisms, 226–231, *227–232*
perimortem fractures, 247, *248–249,* 254
Peru, 207–209, *209*
Peru military base case study, 255–261, *257–261*
positional, 50, 52
postmortem fractures, 247, *248–249,* 254
proof, establishment of, 202
rib fractures, *210,* 217–218, *219–223,* 224
road traffic accidents, 226–231, *227–232*
sequels of torture, 234–235, *235*
skeletal evidence, 209–210, *210–213,* 212
sternum fractures, 215, *216–218*
timing of injuries, 236–244, *238–242*
tooth fractures, 212–214, *214–215*
torture defined, 202–204
Trajectory of bullets
gunfire, 403
gunfire injuries, 355, 359–360, *366–370*
pelvis, 419–420
Transitional law, 3
Transverse fractures, 224, 432
Transverse trajectories, 403
Trauma, *see also specific type*
cause and manner of death, 10–12
context, 7–8
intent, 8
scientific protocol, 8–9
weaponry, 9–10
Trigone area, 403
Tsokos studies, 101
Tucker studies, 267
Tuller and Djuric studies, 63
Tuol Sleng, *see* Cambodian killing fields
Turner and Turner studies, 270
Tutsis, 263
Twisting, 53, *see also* Bending joints

U

Ubelaker, Buikstra and, studies, 9, 31–32
Ubelaker and Adams studies, 61
Uceda studies, 208, 255, 261
UÇK, Ushtria Clirimatre e Kosovoës, *see* Kosovo Liberation Army (UÇK, Ushtria Clirimatre e Kosovoës)
Université Louis Pasteur (ULP), 87–89
UN Manual on the Effective Investigation and Documentation of Torture and Other Cruel, Inhuman, or Degrading Treatment or Punishment (Istanbul Protocol), xi, 8–9
UN Manual on the Effective Prevention and Investigation of Extra-legal, Arbitrary and Summary Executions (Minnesota Protocol), xi, 8
Unnewehr studies, 167
Utilitarian tools, 10, *see also* Knives
UZI weapon, *386*

V

Vance studies, 159
Van Es, Welsh and, studies, 4
Van Herp studies, 35
Van Vark studies, 65
Variations, normal, 32–42, *32–45*
Vellema and Scholtz studies, 323–324, 353–354
Velocity classification, 327
Vertebrae injuries
freefall trauma, 184, *185*
gunfire injuries, 406–408, *407–413*
hydraulic burst effect, 325
Vigorita studies, 245
Villa and Mahieu studies, 61
Vock studies, 87
Vogel, Brogdon and, studies, 39
Vogel and Brogdon studies, 204
Vogel studies, 50, 52–53
Voight, Thomsen and, studies, 203
Volljak/Volujak site, 27–28, 30
Vukovar Hospital (Croatia), 6

W

Wadding, 377
Walker and Long studies, 266–267, 270
Walker studies, 5, 203
Wallensteen, Eriksson and, studies, 4
Walsh-Haney studies, 54, 267
Wandall, Petersen and, studies, 203
Ward studies, 88
Warren studies, 2, 405
Waters, C. J., 322
Waters studies, 385–399
Wayne State University (WSU), 87
Weapons
  class estimation, 325–329, *327–355*
  control, full-automatic mode, 359
  human securities manipulation as, 35–36
  trauma analysis, 9–10
Weber and Czarnetzki studies, 274
Webster, Gurdjian and, studies, 88–89
Weinberg and Simmonds studies, 35
Welsh and Van Es studies, 4
Wenham studies, 267, 291
Wheatley, Smith and, studies, 428, 430
Wieser, Missliwetrz and, studies, 5–6
Wieser, Pollak and, studies, 40
Willey and Snyder studies, 55, 65
Williams, Popenker and, studies, 322
Williams studies, 245
Willinger and Baumgartner studies, 88
Willinger studies, 87–93
Wilson studies, 2–3
W/K, *see* Wounded/killed ratio (W/K) analysis
Wobbling, 325
World Trade Center bombing, 96–97
Wound ballistics, 322
Wounded/killed ratio (W/K) analysis, 14–19
Wounds, *see also specific type of injury*
  atypical blunt force trauma, *164–166,* 164–167
  atypical gunfire entry wounds, 346–353
  close-range, 371, 372, *372–377*
  contact, 371, *372–377*
  double tap shots, 346–352, *347–351*
  eccentric defects, 342–346, *344–345*
  embedded projectiles, 352–353, *352–357*
  entry wounds, 329–353
  exit, 329–354, *358–365*
  gutter defects, 338, 340, *342*
  irregular defects, 342–346, *344–345*
  keyhole defects, 340–342, *343*
  mechanisms, sharp force trauma, 265–267
  perpendicular circular defects, 331, 335, *336–341,* 337
  tandem shots, 346–352, *347–351*
Wright and Kariya studies, 204
WSU, *see* Wayne State University (WSU)

Y

Yakub, Olmbe and, studies, 9
Yang and King studies, 87–88
Yawing, 323–326, 353–354
Yeo studies, 218
Yoganandan and Pintar studies, 88

Z

Zaidi studies, 35
Zhang studies, 87
Zhou studies, 87–88